Business Ethics

Business Ethics provides students with a comprehensive understanding of the relationships between organizations and stakeholders (customers, employees, society, stockholders, etc.) and the many ways in which ethics affects these relationships. Authors K. Praveen Parboteeah and John B. Cullen highlight how ethics is a fundamental part of any business strategy with a step-by-step approach, examining each aspect of businesses and their key stakeholders.

The text is illustrated with diagrams and real-world case studies throughout, making business ethics accessible and relevant to students. Features include:

- Learning Objectives
- Business Ethics Insights Boxes
- Key Terms
- Discussion Questions
- Internet Activities
- What Would You Do? Ethical Dilemma Boxes
- 30 Real-World Case Studies

A companion website features additional resources for both students and instructors expanding on the points within the text. *Business Ethics* demonstrates the power of social responsibility and ethical decisions in today's rapidly changing business environment.

www.routledge.com/cw/parboteeah

K. Praveen Parboteeah is Professor of Management in the Department of Management, University of Wisconsin–Whitewater. He received his PhD from Washington State University, holds an MBA from California State University–Chico and a BSc (Honors) in Management Studies from the University of Mauritius.

John B. Cullen is Professor of Management and Huber Chair of Entrepreneurship at Washington State University. He received his PhD from Columbia University.

Business Ethics

K. Praveen Parboteeah
University of Wisconsin–Whitewater

and

John B. Cullen
Washington State University

Routledge
Taylor & Francis Group

NEW YORK AND LONDON

To
Kyong, Alisha, and Davin
and
Jean and Jaye

First published 2013
by Routledge
711 Third Avenue, New York, NY 10017

Simultaneously published in the UK
by Routledge
2 Park Square, Milton Park, Abingdon, Oxon OX14 4RN

Routledge is an imprint of the Taylor & Francis Group, an informa business

Library of Congress Cataloging in Publication Data
Parboteeah, Praveen.
    Business ethics / K. Praveen Parboteeah and John B. Cullen.
    p. cm.
    Includes bibliographical references and index.
    1. Business ethics. I. Cullen, John B. (John Brooks), 1948– II. Title.
    HF5387.P3656 2012
    174'.4—dc23   2011053003

ISBN: 978-0-415-89368-8 (hbk)
ISBN: 978-0-415-89369-5 (pbk)
ISBN: 978-0-203-10762-1 (ebk)

Typeset in Perpetua and Bell Gothic
by Florence Production Ltd, Stoodleigh, Devon, UK

Printed and bound in the United States of America by Edwards Brothers, Inc.

Brief Contents

Contents

Preface

Despite several well-known ethical scandals in the 1980s, frequent ethical transgressions continue to characterize the business world. The latest crises involving global corporations suggest that business ethics continue to be extremely important today. No companies are immune from such forces. To cope adequately with such needs for ethical behavior, managers of global and domestic companies will need to be able to develop and implement successful strategies to encourage ethical behavior. *Business Ethics* provides students with the latest insights into managing companies to become more ethical and to build an ethical culture. *Business Ethics* provides students with the necessary theoretical background and subsequent practical applications to understand the complexities of business ethics in the workplace. The text uses a strategic stakeholder approach to emphasize these core issues. Furthermore, the text also recognizes key forces such as globalization of business, increased reliance on information technology, and increased pressure for environmental sustainability as key drivers of business ethics today.

The motivation to write this text came from the authors' frustrations with current text offerings. Most texts tend to be either too theoretical for students (thereby being too abstract) or too practical (thereby not offering the students the necessary framework to understand the ethical concepts). *Business Ethics* aims to provide students with the right balance of theory and practice for a deeper understanding of business ethics.

PEDAGOGICAL APPROACH

Business Ethics provides a thorough review and analysis of business ethics issues using several learning tools.

Strategic Stakeholder Management as the Theme: All chapters use a strategic stakeholder approach as a unifying theme. The text is thus the first text that adopts this approach. Most business ethics scholars and practitioners agree that successful ethical companies are the ones that can strategically balance the needs of their various stakeholders.

By adopting this approach, students will be able to see how the various aspects of business ethics are connected.

Theory-based and Application-based: All chapters have important applicable theories integrated with discussion of how such theories apply in practice. Unlike other texts that are either too theoretical or too practical, this text provides the appropriate blend of theory and practice to provide deeper insights into the concepts covered in the chapter. Furthermore, each chapter includes many opportunities for readers to apply the knowledge gained from reading, an internet activity, a "What Would You Do?" scenario, and an end-of-chapter case study. All three activities help students apply the concepts to real-life situations.

Integrating: Chapters build on each other in a logical way in contrast to many texts that have stand-alone chapters. The stakeholder approach presented in the text provides a good integrating mechanism and the last chapter brings it all together.

Current: The text includes many of the most recent examples pertaining to business ethics issues. Furthermore, discussion of most current trends was not limited to U.S.-only examples. The authors took great effort to ensure that the examples pertain to multinationals worldwide.

Global Perspective: Unlike most other texts, this text provides a global perspective on business ethics. Most chapters include material pertaining to ethics in global contexts. Included are cases about companies in a wide range of countries including Japan, U.K., China, and India.

KEY FEATURES

Chapter Case Studies, Internet Activities, and "What Would You Do?": Each chapter provides several opportunities to apply text material to real-life business ethics problems. Short cases provide the instructor with the ability to assign an activity that students can read and discuss within 30 minutes. The "What Would You Do?" feature provides students with scenarios to confront potential personal ethical dilemmas and how they would react to such decisions. Chapter case studies are longer cases that provide students with the opportunity to examine case material in much more depth. Internet activities acknowledge the growing importance of the internet as a learning tool and allow students to explore business ethics issues in that environment.

Extensive Examples: Throughout the text, many examples enhance the text material by showing actual business ethics situations. The text uses several different formats to illustrate the environment driving business ethics today:

* *Preview Business Ethics Insight* discusses how a multinational or other entity has dealt with ethical situations pertaining to the chapter.
* *Business Ethics Insight* pertains to specific examples of companies dealing with the general business ethics issues discussed in the text.
* *Strategic Business Ethics Insight* provides information regarding the strategic implications of the ethical issues discussed in the chapter.

- *Ethics Sustainability Insight* where we discuss the environmental or sustainability implications of the ethical issues discussed in the chapter.
- *Global Business Ethics Insight* provides information on the global nature and implications of the ethical issues in the chapter.

Learning Aids: The companion website has been designed to complement (and not repeat) the text. The website includes an extensive selection of regularly updated internet links to resources and information.

CONTENTS

This book includes four major sections. Each section contains chapters that provide information on essential topics of international business. The intent is to give you an overview of the complex and exciting world of business ethics.

In Part I, we present a general introduction to business ethics. Chapter 1 presents the readers with a general introduction to business ethics. As we saw earlier, a strategic business ethics approach means that a company is properly balancing the needs of its various stakeholders. As such, in Chapter 2, we will discuss the many core stakeholder issues such as the types of stakeholders, the characteristics of stakeholders, etc. We conclude that chapter with a tool to assess stakeholder needs. Furthermore, a background understanding of ethics is not complete without understanding the individual factors affecting ethics. As such, Chapter 3 explores the many facets of individual ethics. Recognizing that the ethical orientation of a company often subsumes the ethical orientations of individuals within the company, we discuss some of the most important determinants of individual ethics.

In Part II, we examine certain stakeholders. Specifically, we argue that there are four critical organizational stakeholders; namely, employees, customers, investors, and the media/special interest groups. These stakeholders are conveniently categorized as primary and secondary stakeholders. Because primary stakeholders are more likely to affect companies, Part II devotes three chapters to such stakeholders. In Chapter 4, we consider the role of employees as stakeholders and the many obligations companies have with respect to employees. In that chapter, we consider key aspects of the relationship between a company and its employees such as compensation practices and policies, discrimination, and sexual harassment. In Chapter 5, we consider another important stakeholder; namely, the customer. In this chapter, we consider the many responsibilities a company has with respect to its customers. We also consider customer rights and what companies do to respect such rights. Finally, we discuss some of the proactive approaches companies use today to keep this stakeholder group happy. Chapter 6 discusses the role of shareholders as stakeholders of a company. As we discussed earlier, shareholders are typically the owners of a public company. However, managers are the ones running the company. This poses special issues that reflect the unique relationships between shareholders and companies. We will also consider corporate governance issues as they relate to the mechanisms available to shareholders to control management. Corporate governance is a key aspect of how any company manages ethics. Finally, in Chapter 7, we examine a number of other stakeholders; namely, the government, the media, and non-governmental organizations. While these stakeholders may not always have direct impact on the organization like employees or customers, they are nevertheless very influential stakeholders. We will therefore consider the roles played by these three stakeholders and the influences they have on companies.

In Part III, we examine the environment that most companies are facing today. Each chapter is dedicated to important driving forces that are shaping business environments in most countries. Chapter 8 examines the role of information technologies and their impact on ethics. As the use of information technologies continues to explode, more companies are facing unexpected ethical issues. In Chapter 9, we discuss another important aspect of any company's setting; namely, the environment and environmental sustainability. In this chapter, we discuss the growing pressure companies are facing to become more environmentally sensitive. We consider the various approaches to managing the environment and best practices of the world's most environmental multinationals. Finally, Chapter 10 considers another critical aspect of the environment: the global environment. In this chapter, we consider why countries view business ethics issues differently. We also learn about the major international ethics issues with a special focus on corruption and bribery.

Finally, Part IV is dedicated to understanding how managers can build an ethical company. Chapter 11 considers the company's ethical culture and how the culture affects ethical behaviors. We will discuss the most popular way of characterizing ethical culture; namely, through ethical climates. Finally, Chapter 12 integrates the various chapters to present a strategic approach to managing business ethics; namely, through corporate social responsibility.

SUPPORT MATERIALS

Business Ethics: A Strategic Stakeholder Perspective offers a website for both students and instructors at www.routledge.com/cw/parboteeah. This site contains supplements to the text that give students and instructors many more options for learning and teaching the text content.

For Instructors

Web support is available with the following features:

- *Instructor's Manual.* Chapter-by-chapter outlines with teaching tips, web and in-class exercises, relevant YouTube videos and other video resources.
- *Test Bank.* A full test bank for each chapter including both multiple choice and true/false questions. These are available both as Word documents and in formats compatible with uploading to Blackboard or WebCT.

- *PowerPoint Slide Presentations.* Instructors have access to more than 40 slides that complement the main points of each chapter.
- *Weblinks.* Useful links to as instructional resources including all links in the Instructor's Manual.

For Students

Web support is available with the following features:

- *Practice Quizzes.* The website provides practice quizzes to students with instant feedback on their answers.
- *Flashcards.* Interactive flashcards allow students to test their knowledge of the book's key concepts.
- *Weblinks.* Informational links give students easy access to online resources.

Acknowledgments

Writing a book may seem a lonely activity. However, such an activity is not possible without the support of numerous individuals. We thank our families for giving us the time and quiet to accomplish this task:

- Kyong Pyun, Praveen's wife, was very helpful with another book project. She allowed uninterrupted time blocks of time to finish this new project. She again provided her expertise by completing the instructor's manual, teaching outline, and other supporting materials. We continue to be a great team. Alisha, Praveen's daughter, remained curious about Daddy's projects and provided the patience as Praveen focused on the project. Davin, Praveen's son, was not as curious and patient. But he keeps the title "Best Son in the World!"
- Jean Johnson, John's wife, and also an academic, provided council, support, and occasional goal-setting to keep John on schedule.

The inspiration for this text comes from Praveen's parents. They raised him with a strong work ethic while also emphasizing honesty and integrity. Praveen's foray and interest in business ethics is only natural. However, the text would not have been possible without the support and inspiration of many of Praveen's colleagues. John Cullen provided the inspiration by encouraging Praveen to work on the concept of ethical climates. Former chair of the Management Department Yezdi Godiwalla initially assigned Praveen his first business ethics course. This led to sustained interest in business ethics issues. Current chair, James Bronson, continues such teaching assignments. Praveen is also grateful to his colleagues Jerry Gosenpud and Lois Smith for intellectual discussions that helped refine his teaching. Praveen is also very grateful to Dean Christine Clements for supporting all business ethics endeavors, including a faculty workshop and many other activities.

This text would have been impossible without the support of a professional editorial team. In particular, we thank Routledge editor John Szilagyi, who encouraged us to write the text on business ethics. He helped us navigate the many challenges that we faced as we went along the process. Developmental editor Jill D'Urso kept us on track for a very tight writing schedule. She was also very patient with us. Our thanks go to several other professionals who contributed to this project, including the individuals who contributed cases in the book. We also appreciate the efforts of individuals involved in the marketing and production.

Finally, the authors would also like to thank the many reviewers from a wide array of universities and countries, including Wim Vandekerckhove of the University of Greenwich; Raymond Vegso of Canisius College; Thomas Beschorner of the University of St. Gallen; and Andra Gumbus of Sacred Heart University. You provided valuable feedback that was used in refining the text.

K. Praveen Parboteeah
John B. Cullen

About the Authors

K. Praveen Parboteeah is Professor of Management in the Department of Management, University of Wisconsin–Whitewater. He received his Ph.D. from Washington State University, holds an MBA from California State University–Chico and a BSc (Honors) in Management Studies from the University of Mauritius.

Parboteeah regularly teaches international management, business ethics, and strategic management at both undergraduate and graduate levels. He has received numerous teaching awards and is included in multiple editions of *Who's Who Among America's Teachers* and is a University of Wisconsin–Whitewater Master Teacher and Teaching Scholar. He also received a Certificate of Excellence for Teaching from the University of Wisconsin–Whitewater during the 2006–2007 academic year. He was also the recipient of the 2007–2008 University of Wisconsin–Whitewater Research Award.

Parboteeah's research interests include international management, ethics, and technology and innovation management. He has published over 30 articles in leading journals such as the *Academy of Management Journal, Organization Science, Decision Sciences, Journal of Business Ethics, Human Relations, Journal of International Business Studies, Journal of Business Research*, and *Management International Review*.

Parboteeah has been involved in many aspects of business ethics at the University of Wisconsin–Whitewater. He initiated a faculty workshop where faculty members met and discussed business ethics issues. He is also the faculty advisor-founder of the Business Ethics Student Association at the University of Wisconsin–Whitewater. He is among a handful of judges for Wisconsin's only business ethics award; namely, the Better Business Bureau Torch Award. He also lectures on the matter worldwide and is an honorary faculty member of the Center for Ethical Leadership at the Otto Beisheim School of Management at WHU, Germany.

Of Indian ancestry, Parboteeah grew up on the African island of Mauritius and speaks Creole, French, and English. He currently lives in Whitewater with his South Korean wife, Kyong, and children, Alisha and Davin.

John B. Cullen is Professor of Management and Huber Chair of Entrepreneurship at Washington State University. He received his Ph.D. from Columbia University.

Professor Cullen is the author or co-author of five books and over 70 journal articles, most of which appeared in major business journals such as *Administrative Science Quarterly, Journal of International Business Studies, Academy of Management Journal, Organization Science, Journal of Management, Organizational Studies, Journal of Vocational Behavior, American Journal of Sociology, Organizational Dynamics,* and the *Journal of World Business.* In the area of business ethics, he is known primarily for his groundbreaking work on ethical climates. Most recently, his work examines business ethics in the international context.

Professor Cullen is currently Senior Editor for the *Journal of World Business.* He is also a past president of the Western Academy of Management and a former Fulbright Scholar. He lives with his wife, Jean Johnson, with whom he has co-authored one child and numerous academic publications.

Part I

Introduction

Chapter 1

Introduction to Business Ethics

LEARNING OBJECTIVES

After reading this chapter you should be able to:

- Understand what business ethics is
- Appreciate the global nature of business ethics
- Be aware of the prevalence of unethical behavior around the world
- Appreciate the benefits of ethical companies
- Understand the types of business ethics issues
- Understand the stakeholder approach discussed in this book

PREVIEW BUSINESS ETHICS INSIGHT

Ethical Scandals Worldwide

Companies such as Enron and WorldCom are well known for their ethical scandals. Both companies engaged in fraud and used questionable accounting practices to inflate their financial records. Both companies had senior executives and top management involved in such unethical transactions. Consequently, both companies suffered, resulting in tremendous losses for a substantial number of people. Employees lost their jobs and years of retirement savings. Investors lost billions of U.S. dollars after their shares became worthless. Both companies also led to the demise of their accounting auditors. These auditors were blamed for turning a blind eye to these accounting improprieties and for not doing their job properly.

Although most people have heard about these well-publicized cases, other companies worldwide were also embroiled in similar scandals. Consider the following examples. Satyam used to be India's fourth largest information technology services exporter alongside other Indian IT giants such as WIPRO and Infosys. In January 2009, the news broke that the company had been engaged in one of India's biggest frauds. The chairman of the company and nine other top executives had manipulated the company's accounting records over the previous years to inflate revenues. Fake customers and invoices were created to generate fictitious revenue. Furthermore, these individuals forged board decisions in order to obtain unauthorized loans to buy property and land. The company's founder, Ramalinga Raju, admitted to overstating company profits resulting in the creation of a fake cash balance of over $1 billion. These activities also resulted in similar disastrous consequences for people. Investors lost significant amounts of money as shares of the company tumbled. However, the industry also feared losing lucrative customers such as GE and IBM. While the Indian IT sector was generally seen as clean, the Satyam incident could potentially result in the loss of trust and billions of dollars outsourcing loss.

Italy has also seen its share of fraud and deception. Parmalat, an Italian dairy group with operations in Europe, U.S., and Latin America was also found to have been involved in serious fraud. Mr. Tanzi, the former chief executive of the company, was recently found guilty of creating fake accounts, inflating revenues and thereby misleading investors and regulators. The company misled investors about its true financial health for years. Shockingly, Parmalat also revealed that a Bank of America account supposed to hold over 4 billion Euros was fictitious. This resulted in Europe's largest corporate bankruptcy and over 100,000 Italian shareholders, including many pensioners, lost their life's savings overnight. Mr. Tanzi was found guilty of the charges and given a ten-year sentence in 2009.

Based on Boland, Vincent. 2008. "Parmalat's Tanzi gets 10 years." *Financial Times*, 8; Boland, Vincent. 2009. "Parmalat assets seized." *Financial Times*, 16; Bray, Chad. 2009. "Judge throws out Parmalat lawsuits." *Wall Street Journal*, B3; Fontanella-Khan, James. 2009. "Satyam shares tumble over fresh charges." *Financial Times*, 24; Guha, Romit. 2009. "Wider fraud is seen at India's Satyam." *Wall Street Journal*, B1.

The Preview Business Ethics Insight above shows the prevalence of unethical behavior worldwide. While attention in the U.S. has been mostly focused on companies such as Enron, WorldCom, and Arthur Andersen, there are many examples of companies worldwide that have been involved in fraud and other deceptive and unethical behaviors. It is therefore imperative for any business student to have a solid foundation in understanding business ethics globally. As the public and the media grow more wary or suspicious of the motives of companies, large and small, it is becoming ever more critical for companies to become more ethical.

WHAT IS BUSINESS ETHICS?

To understand the meaning of business ethics, we must first understand the meaning of ethics. **Ethics** refer to society's perception of what is right or wrong. Consider, for example, that some people consider abortion as unethical as they believe abortion is wrong. Others believe that abortion pertains to a woman's ability to decide and is therefore right. This simple example shows the complexity involved in understanding ethics. As you see, ethics may not be viewed similarly by all. Furthermore, ethics do change over time.

When applied to the business context, **business ethics** refer to the principles and standards that guide business. For instance, consider the real situation of a corporation that was created to trade in blood. The entrepreneur who created the company saw a market for blood. The company purchased blood from African nations and sold to hospitals in the U.S. The blood was purchased at very low prices in Africa and sold at what would be considered exorbitant prices in the U.S. There was significant controversy around the entrepreneur and his actions. Many questions relating to business ethics were asked. Should that corporation be allowed to continue business? Is it ethical to trade in blood? Or is the company simply satisfying a market need and should thus be allowed to operate? Is it appropriate for the company to buy blood at very low prices and sell to U.S. hospitals at much higher prices? The views on these subjects varied. Some people felt that a market existed and that the entrepreneur was simply satisfying that need. Others could not understand how someone could actually trade in blood and charge very high prices for something acquired very cheaply.

As you can see from the above example, business ethics is a very complex subject and decisions are seldom black and white. Often, ethical dilemmas have shades of gray that require intense consideration before a resolution can be achieved. Similar to individual ethics, people may have different perceptions of what is considered ethical or not. For instance, some argue that the high level of compensation given to top executives is fair as it reflects the forces of demand and supply. Others see executive compensation as exaggerated given how much lower level workers may be paid.

This book will therefore prepare you to first understand the complexity inherent in business ethics dilemmas. It will also provide solutions to these dilemmas and situations. The framework in the book will allow you to systematically understand business ethics and to learn about tools and techniques that can help resolve these ethical dilemmas.

To help drive the concepts, this text has several boxed features. The **Preview Business Ethics Insight** discusses how a multinational or other entity has dealt with ethical situations pertaining to the chapter. The **Business Ethics Insight** pertains to specific examples of companies dealing with the general business ethics issues discussed in the text. In contrast, the **Strategic Business Ethics Insight** provides information regarding the strategic implications of the ethical issues discussed in the chapter. Furthermore, given the current emphasis on the environment and sustainability, each chapter also contains an **Ethics Sustainability Insight** where we discuss the environmental or sustainability implications of the ethical issues discussed in the chapter.

Finally, this book is the first to provide a global orientation toward understanding business ethics. While most other business ethics texts have considered ethics mostly

GLOBAL BUSINESS ETHICS INSIGHT

Siemens and Bribery

Siemens, based in Germany and operating for more than 160 years, is Europe's biggest engineering firm. It operates in the industry, energy, and healthcare industries and manufactures electronics electrical engineering products. In 2009, it had over 405,000 employees with revenues of about 77 billion Euros.

Despite Siemens' prominence in Europe and worldwide, it was recently embroiled in an embarrassing and widespread bribery scandal. For over a decade, Siemens would readily pay foreign officials to win contracts. Siemens would also engage in the routine practice of claiming the bribes as tax deductions for "useful expenditures." However, what surprised investigators was the candor with which these bribes were taking place. Siemens created three "cash desks" where employees could stop by with empty suitcases to be filled with cash. More surprisingly, these cash desks operated on an honor system and employees were allowed to take as much as 1 million Euros without filling out any documents. As reported, employees carried over $67 million between 2001 and 2004.

However, in 1999, Germany made bribery illegal. Siemens also listed its shares on the New York Stock Exchange in 2001. While these activities should have stopped bribery, because of a strong culture of permitting bribes, bribery continued. Siemens created special accounts that were not included in the corporate books. Managers could still get easy access to millions of dollars for bribery purposes and over $805 million were paid out to win contracts worldwide.

As the company was operating at a global level and it is listed on the New York Stock Exchange, Siemens had to abide by strict worldwide bribery laws. When investigators found about the extent of bribery, Siemens had to face legal action. As such, in 2008, Siemens agreed to pay $800 million to U.S. authorities and over $540 million in Germany. It pleaded guilty to the charges of bribery and corruption to turn a new leaf.

Today, bribery and corruption is a distant past for Siemens. When Peter Losch took over in 2007, he implemented drastic changes that have radically turned around the company. Unlike its main rivals such as GE or Philips, it even managed to show strong financial performance in 2009.

Based on *The Economist*. 2008. "Business: Bavarian baksheesh; The Siemens scandal." 389: 8611, 112; Schafer, Daniel. 2009. "Siemens strengthened in wake of damaging bribery scandal." *Financial Times*, 23; Schafer, Daniel. 2009. "Siemens ultimatum in bribery scandal." *Financial Times*, 18.

from a U.S. perspective, trade has never before crossed international borders so much and it is necessary to integrate this international dimension. This book therefore also includes **Global Business Ethics Insights** providing information on the global nature and implications of the ethical issues in the chapter. Why this global focus? Consider the Global Business Ethics Insight on page 6.

As the Global Business Ethics Insight shows, business ethics has a decidedly global flavor. Although Siemens is a German company, it is also listed on the New York Stock Exchange and is therefore liable under U.S. laws. Furthermore, any unethical behavior on its part could have repercussions for people beyond German borders. For instance, U.S. stockholders of Siemens shares could lose money. Employees in its foreign plants could lose their jobs because of poor ethical practices. This text therefore acknowledges the global nature of business ethics and adopts this perspective. Next we discuss the prevalence of unethical behavior worldwide.

How Prevalent are Unethical Behaviors Worldwide?

This text presupposes that unethical behavior is very frequent. But how prevalent is unethical behavior worldwide? Fortunately, there are many organizations undertaking business ethics surveys worldwide. Most societies want their companies to behave ethically and there is an understandable focus on assessing the degree of ethicality in societies.

One of the most well-known organizations promoting ethical behavior worldwide is Transparency International (TI; http://www.transparency.org). Created in

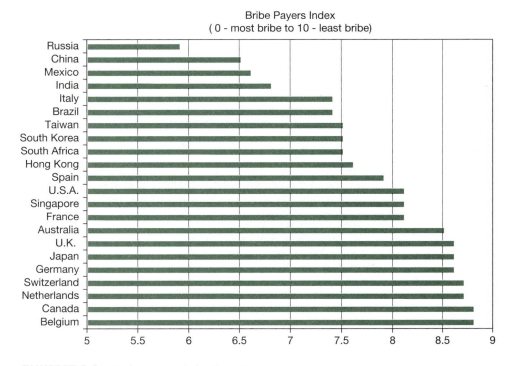

EXHIBIT 1.1—Bribery Levels by Country

1993, TI is actively engaged in eradicating corruption worldwide. It is now made up of a network of around 90 local chapters leading campaigns to lobby governments to put in practice anti-corruption efforts.

In its 2008 Bribe Payers Index (BPI), TI interviewed 2,742 top executives in over 26 countries. These executives were first asked which countries they had commercial relationships with. The **Bribe Payers Index** was measured by asking these executives the degree to which they expected companies in these countries to engage in bribery with their own companies. The countries were then rated on a score of 10 (least likelihood of companies to engage in bribery) to 0 (highest likelihood of bribery). Exhibit 1.1 shows the rankings of these countries.

As Exhibit 1.1 shows, bribery is much more prevalent in countries such as Russia, China, India, and Mexico. **Bribery** refers to the degree to which individuals have to be provided with some compensation (e.g., money, gift, etc.) to influence the individual. Such findings are not surprising given the acknowledged level of corruption in some of these countries. As we will see later in Chapter 10 on global ethics, there are differences between countries in culture that explain the higher levels of bribery. However, what is troubling is that even the top BPI performers tend to report weaker in other areas. For instance, TI breaks down bribery into categories such as using personal relationships to win contracts or engaging in bribery to low level public officials to speed up things abroad. Some of the findings for top BPI performers are as follows:

- Sixteen percent of Belgian companies and around 10% of Canadian companies report using familiar or personal relationships to win public contracts
- Seven percent of Dutch companies reported that they were engaged in bribery to low level officials to speed up things
- Five percent of respondents from Swiss companies engaged in bribery to high-ranking officials to obtain public contracts.

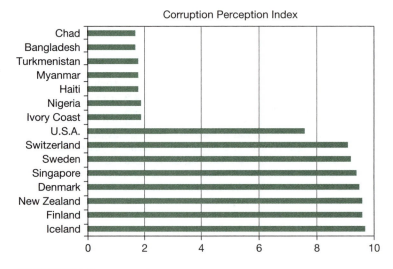

EXHIBIT 1.2 — Corruption Levels by Country

As the above shows, unethical behaviors are prevalent in all societies. Furthermore, TI broke down the results of the survey by sector. Results show that the incidence of bribery is much higher in industries such as public works and construction, oil and gas, mining, real estate, pharmaceuticals, and medical care. In contrast, industries such as fisheries, agriculture, information technology, and light manufacturing had the lowest likelihood of bribery.

The TI index shows that bribery is very prevalent worldwide. In fact, they also publish a perception of corruption in the public sector. Exhibit 1.2 shows the list of top ten and bottom ten countries. As Exhibit 1.2 shows, no country has a perfect score of ten suggesting that there is no corruption. Most societies have varying degrees of corruption.

Although Exhibit 1.2 paints a very bleak picture of ethics worldwide, not all organizations are focused on unethical behavior. Consider the Business Ethics Insight below.

BUSINESS ETHICS INSIGHT

United Nations Global Compact

The extent of unethical behaviors worldwide is so widespread that even the United Nations got involved in helping curb such unethical actions. In 2000, it created the United Nations Global Compact. However, rather than focus on unethical behavior, the Global Compact encourages companies to voluntarily abide by ten key principles. These principles include human rights (companies should respect international human rights and should not participate in human rights abuses), labor rights (companies should allow workers to unionize, companies should not force compulsory labor and should not employ child labor, companies should eliminate discrimination), environment (companies should support environmental causes and greater environmental responsibility, companies should encourage environmentally friendly technologies) and anti-corruption (businesses should work against corruption).

The Global Compact message of ethical behavior and social responsibility has been very successful. The Global Compact has over 6,500 signatories based in over 135 countries. In 2008 alone, the Compact welcomed 1,473 new business signatories—a significant increase over the previous year. Furthermore, the signatories come from both developed and emerging economies. The signatories also represent an even split between small and medium companies with less than 250 employees and large companies.

To be listed on the Global Compact list of signatories, companies must submit yearly reports on how they are abiding by and making progress on the ten principles. If companies do not submit the yearly reports, they can be delisted from the Global Compact.

Based on United Nations. 2010. United Nations Global Compact 2008. http://www.un.org.

As Exhibit 1.2 shows, unethical behavior is very prevalent worldwide. However, the most recent business ethics survey in the U.S. done by the Ethics Resource Center shows that unethical behavior also occurs in the U.S. The Ethics Resource Center was created in 1922 to advance high ethical standards. In 2009, it polled over 16,000 employees and received responses from around 2,852 employees of the private sector. Here are the main findings:

- Forty-nine percent of employees surveyed reported that they had seen misconduct at work. What types of misconduct were observed? See Exhibit 1.3 for the types of and frequency of misconduct
- Eight percent of employees surveyed reported that they perceived some form of pressure to cut corners
- Nine percent of employees revealed that they observed a weak learning culture in their companies
- Fifteen percent of employees who observed and reported misconduct perceived retaliation against them.

However, despite these findings, the Ethics Resource Center also notes that many of these numbers have improved over time. For instance, around 86% of employees reported not observing any red flag behavior related to accurate financial reporting (i.e., falsifying financial information, stealing assets, etc.). The center notes that U.S. companies have weathered the recession well with respect to unethical behaviors.

Another reputed organization that studies unethical behavior in the U.S. is the Association of Certified Fraud Examiners (ACFE). They release an annual "Report to the Nation" on incidences of occupational fraud and abuse. The ACFE defines **occupational fraud** as "the use of one's occupation for personal enrichment through

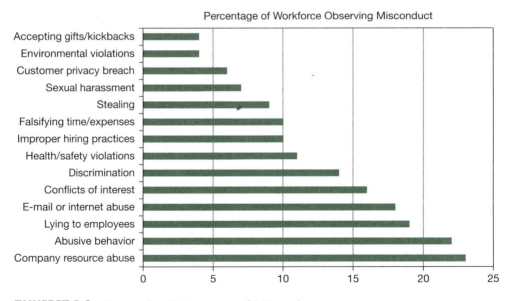

EXHIBIT 1.3—Types of and Frequency of Misconduct

the deliberate misuse or misapplication of the employing organization's resources or assets."[1] Examples of occupational fraud include such activities such as skimming (cash is stolen from the company before the cash is recorded), billing (submission of fictitious invoices to the company), expense reimbursement (submission of fictitious business expenses for reimbursement), and payroll (false claims for compensation).

In 2008, the ACFE based its survey on over 959 cases of occupational fraud. Major findings include:

- Participants report that their companies lose approximately 7% of revenues to occupational fraud, close to $994 billion losses
- Occupational fraud is costly for the average company. More than a quarter of frauds reported in the survey were over $1 million
- Occupational fraud tends to go undetected for long periods of time. The typical frauds in the study went undiscovered for over two years
- Smaller companies are especially susceptible to occupational fraud
- People committing occupational fraud were often first-time offenders with no prior criminal conviction
- Most cases were committed by members of top management or the accounting department
- Occupational frauds occur in a wide range of industries, with most cases occurring in banking and financial services, government and healthcare
- Most cases of occupational fraud were discovered as a result of tips rather than audits and controls.

Exhibit 1.4 shows the breakdown of types of occupational fraud.

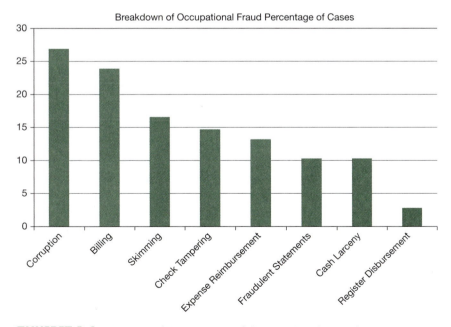

EXHIBIT 1.4 — Types and Percentage of Occupational Fraud

As the above reviews of the reported survey results from worldwide organizations reveal, unethical behavior is extremely prevalent in most societies. Even in countries that score highly on the Transparency International Bribe Payer Index, there are still incidences of such behaviors in these countries. Furthermore, the fact that the United Nations got involved implies that business ethics need to be taken seriously. This book therefore argues that it is critical for companies to be more ethical. To further build the case for the crucial need for companies to be ethical, we next discuss some of the benefits of being ethical.

WHAT ARE THE BENEFITS OF BEING ETHICAL?

As the previous section demonstrated, unethical behaviors occur with some regularity in corporations around the world. Such unwanted behaviors can take many shapes and forms. However, an important question is to ascertain why companies should be ethical. Any serious ethics program is costly both in terms of human and capital resources. It is therefore critical to demonstrate that being ethical has important benefits for any corporation. In this section, we examine the many benefits accruing to corporations for their ethical actions.

At a fundamental level, an organization can only exist if it has the ability to build and sustain competitive advantage to make profits. Without profits, a company will eventually cease to exist. A basic defense of business ethics should therefore pertain to financial performance. In other words, we need to determine whether ethical companies perform better financially than unethical companies. A recent review of the literature by van Beurden and Gossling[2] provides some answers to this important question. In this review, the authors examine a very large number of studies linking corporate social responsibility and many aspects of performance. As you will see in Chapter 12, **corporate social responsibility** represents a strategic approach to managing ethics in an organization.

Results reviewed in the study show that corporate social responsibility has many positive benefits for organizations. The authors show that having strong corporate social responsibility programs have positive effects on many performance aspects such as 1) firm financial performance, 2) firm market value, 3) stock market value, 4) stock market returns, and 5) perceived future financial performance. Perhaps, most importantly, the authors reviewed many different dimensions of business ethics such as adherence to global environmental standards, environmental purchasing, corporate reputation for social performance, strong environmental management, philanthropy, social programs, and voluntary disclosure regarding matters of social concerns. While there were few studies that showed that business ethics program do not have any benefits, the overwhelming majority of the studies reviewed show that having various aspects of a business ethics program has significant financial benefits for the organization. Does this relationship hold worldwide? Consider the following Global Business Ethics Insight for a brief review of studies in various countries.

As the reviews show, clearly business ethics have positive benefits for companies worldwide. However, it is important to also see the effects of unethical behavior.

GLOBAL BUSINESS ETHICS INSIGHT

Benefits of Business Ethics Worldwide

Do worldwide companies benefit financially from having business ethics programs? Fortunately, a number of studies have been done in various countries showing similar findings. For instance, Peinado-Vara uses two case studies to show that corporate actions such as philanthropy and other corporate business ethics program resulted in higher levels of accounting-based performance measurements in Latin America.[3] Kumar et al. (2002) studied the consequences of social behaviors on stock market value during apartheid and found that South African firms displaying social behaviors had higher stock market values.[4] In a more recent study, Choi and Jung find that South Korean companies that displayed ethical commitment (level of commitment to ethics) had higher stock valuation on the Korean stock market.[5] Donker, Poff, and Zahir also find that Canadian companies with strong ethical corporate values had higher levels of performance.[6] Finally, Saadaoui shows that socially responsible French funds performed better and were less risky than other funds. However, these results were not statistically significant.[7]

Based on Choi, Tae Hee and Jung, Jinchul. 2008. "Ethical commitment, financial perform-ance, and valuation: An empirical investigation of Korean companies." *Journal of Business Ethics*, 81, 447–463; Donker, Han, Poff, Deborah, and Zahir, Saif. 2008. "Corporate values, codes of ethics, and firm performance: A look at the Canadian context." *Journal of Business Ethics*, 82, 527–537.

In that context, Sims argues that company reputation is a key aspect that any company is eager to protect.[8] Reputation represents the belief people have about a company based on their experiences and knowledge of the company. Ethical scandals can seriously damage a company's reputation and its future. Furthermore, the process of rebuilding reputation can take years. It is therefore critical for any company to be ethical to enhance its reputation and to minimize the risk of damaging such reputation.

How do good ethics benefit a company? An examination of the processes suggests that good ethics benefit the organization through employees, customers, suppliers, and investors among others. However, the company itself has a lot to gain from being ethical. As we saw with the example of Siemens, unethical behavior can result in significant fines that can appreciably impair a company's ability to survive. Because of its size and clout, Siemens was able to weather over $800 million fine to the U.S. and over $540 million fine paid to the German authorities. Other companies such as Food Lion or Martha Stewart were not as fortunate and may suffer serious consequences after unethical behaviors occur. The legal woes and other associated fines may prove very unsettling for any organization involved in ethical scandals.

Beyond the benefits of minimizing the chances of fines and other legal woes, organizations can enjoy other benefits from being ethical. Vilanova, Lozano. and Arenas argue that a strategic approach to business ethics (i.e., corporate social responsibility) can also make a company more innovative.[9] They argue that implementing a corporate social responsibility program typically results in new corporate values, policies, and practices that are being constantly defined and re-defined. During that process, the company also starts focusing on new groups that may not have mattered to the company before. For instance, there is more concern to satisfy the needs of employees, customers, suppliers, etc. This new focus can also result in innovative practices that help the company become more competitive. Thus, business ethics can help a company become competitive.

Gilley, Robertson, and Mazur examine business ethics benefits through the commitment to have a code of ethics.[10] They argue that a properly developed code of ethics should incorporate the focus of key stakeholders such as the community, employees, etc. By incorporating such needs, the codes of ethics affect the corporate culture of the organization to reflect these new values. In turn, such values should deter unethical behavior and provide operational advantages through new partnerships with key stakeholders. Such processes can also result in competitive advantage ultimately benefiting the company.

In addition to direct benefits to companies, business ethics can have important benefits for employees. Sharma, Borna, and Stearns (2009) review the recent literature to discuss some of these benefits.[11] First, employees who identify with the ethics of his or her organization are more likely to be intrinsically motivated at work. It is more probable that employees identify with more ethical companies and are thus more likely to be motivated. Second, because of the compatibility of values, employees working in companies with stronger ethical values are also more likely to be committed to these organizations. Higher levels of commitment may result in additional benefits for the company. Third, research also shows that this high congruity in ethical values between the employee and the company should also result in higher job performance. Thus, more ethical companies tend to have employees with higher levels of motivation, commitment, and performance.

Beyond the above, Prottas provides more evidence of other benefits of being ethical.[12] The study shows that employees who perceived their managers as being more ethical had higher levels of job and life satisfaction. In other words, being more ethical had benefits beyond the work environment. However, most importantly, the research also shows that employees who perceived their managers as having higher levels of integrity were also less likely to be stressed, had better health and were less likely to be absent. Thus, perception of managerial ethics also had benefits for employees.

Companies also enjoy significant benefits as strong ethics program cultivate customer trust and satisfaction. Previous research has shown that consumers expect companies to be ethical. Furthermore, customers are prepared to punish those companies that are unethical. Specifically, Trudel and Cotte note the asymmetric way people react to positive and negative information.[13] They argue that consumers tend to react more to negative information than positive information. As such, it is critical for companies to properly manage their ethics to avoid any unethical behaviors. Companies such as

Exxon with the Exxon Valdez scandal and Nike with the sweatshop scandals have suffered significant consumer backlash as a result of these unethical behaviors. However, as was stated at the beginning of this chapter, being ethical carries significant costs. It is therefore critical to consider whether consumers are willing to reward companies for being ethical. Consider the Ethics Sustainability Insight on page 16.

The Ethics Sustainability Insight clearly shows that consumers are willing not only to reward more ethical companies but also to punish unethical companies. In fact, research reviewed by Bhattacharya, Korschun, and Sen also shows that consumers who perceived that a company is involved in corporate social responsibility are more inclined to positively evaluate such companies as well as to purchase the company's products.[14] Furthermore, companies can build trust through good ethics. Through good ethics, a company can provide evidence of its caring for various aspects of its environment. This display of caring is likely to result in higher levels of customer trust thereby enhancing the company's chances of building market share.

Worthington proposes that being ethical can have benefits for both suppliers and the organization.[15] One manifestation of responsible ethics is socially responsible purchasing. In such cases, large purchasing organizations provide opportunities to suppliers that are usually underrepresented in the typical supplier chains. Examples of underrepresented suppliers are smaller firms, ethnic minority firms, and women-owned firms. Through purchases with these suppliers, an organization can show its effort to build supplier diversity. While U.S. companies have been involved in such efforts, Worthington contends that companies in the U.K. and Europe are now also implementing initiatives to engage in responsible purchasing.

Worthington argues that many benefits accrue to companies involved in responsible purchasing.[16] The suppliers benefit through the additional sales opportunities. However, responsible purchasing through increased supplier diversity can also have many benefits for the participating companies. By interacting with an ethnic minority supplier, a company can get access to new ethnic minority market knowledge. Such markets are important to companies worldwide. Furthermore, by providing opportunities to smaller suppliers, a company can reduce its dependence on its more traditional suppliers. These actions can also result in enhanced reputation for the company as it engages with a larger group of stakeholders. Consider the Strategic Business Ethics Insight on page 17.

As the Strategic Business Ethics Insight shows, Johnson Controls has made supplier diversity a key aspect to help it achieve its strategic goals. Clearly, responsible manufacturing provides significant advantages to the company. Next we discuss a final benefit that companies enjoy as a result of their relationships with investors.

More ethical companies also benefit through increased interest from investors. As Petersen and Vredenburg suggest, business ethics and corporate social responsibility efforts signal that the company is taking into consideration the needs of its various stakeholders.[17] Such efforts signal the potential to add value to the company in the long term. Investors tend to look for such factors and are therefore more likely to invest in such companies. In fact, many investors see the link between corporate social responsibility and profits as we discussed earlier. In contrast, examples of companies such as Martha Stewart and others show that unethical behavior may result in damages

ETHICS SUSTAINABILITY INSIGHT

Are Consumers Willing to Pay More for More Ethical Products?

Do consumers care if a company is more ethical? Are they willing to pay higher prices if they feel that a company is being more ethical? If consumers reward ethical companies, how far do these companies have to go to gain such rewards? These are the questions Trudel and Cotte set out to test.[18] In several separate experiments, the researchers provided some insights into how one aspect of ethics, namely sustainability, affects consumers.

In the first experiment, coffee-drinking adult consumers were assigned to three groups. All three groups were told that they were helping a local grocery store evaluate a specific coffee brand. The first group was told that the coffee was sourced from fair trade organizations dedicated to better trading and working conditions for the coffee bean farmers. The second group was told that the coffee was being sourced from a company that had been criticized for unsustainable farming practices, unfair trade practices, and employing children. The third group was told that they were evaluating a typical coffee and were not provided any ethical or unethical information.

Results showed that consumers from the first group were willing to pay a premium of $1.40 over those from the second group. However, most importantly, the results showed that consumers who evaluated the more unethical coffee brand were more willing to punish the company by wanting to pay $2.40 less than the control group. In other words, consumers were willing to punish unethical companies at more than double the rate of rewarding ethical companies. Exhibit 1.5 shows the various price levels customers were willing to pay in the three groups.

In a second experiment, the authors wanted to determine how ethical a company has to be to get rewarded. In this experiment, participants were divided into five groups. They were all told that they had to evaluate cotton t-shirts that were manufactured according to varying degrees of environmental standards. Participants were informed about conventionally grown cotton and the resulting environmental damage due to widespread use of harmful insecticides. They were told that the t-shirt they were evaluating was made by a company that only used natural fertilizers and that the company was 100% organic (Group 1), 50% organic (Group 2), 25% organic (Group 3), control where no ethical information was provided (Group 4), and the unethical group where the company used harmful pesticides (Group 5).

Results were similar to the first experiment, where it was found that consumers were willing to pay more for the ethical situations (Groups 1, 2, and 3) than the unethical situations (Group 5). However, the results showed that consumers responded fairly similarly to the different levels of ethicalness. Once a level of ethicalness is achieved, the results show that consumers will not reward the company more for higher levels of ethics.

Based on Trudel, Remi and Cotte, June. 2009. "Does it pay to be good?" *MIT Sloan Management Review*, 50:2, 61–68.

STRATEGIC BUSINESS ETHICS INSIGHT

Supplier Diversity at Johnson Controls

Johnson Controls, based in Milwaukee, Wisconsin was founded in 1885 to manufacture electric room thermostats. Today it is a global leader in 1) manufacturing automotive interiors to make driving more comfortable and safer, 2) offering products and services that optimize energy use in buildings, and 3) manufacturing batteries and other power devices to power hybrid vehicles and other products.

Johnson Controls is recognized as one of the most ethical companies and has made supplier diversity one of its core strategic elements. Specifically, the company's mission is based on achieving economic, social, and environmental goals to benefit its various stakeholders. A core element of its social approach to business involves working with underrepresented suppliers to expand and strengthen their supply chain. As of 2009, Johnson Controls had over 420 diverse suppliers (up from 300) spending around $938 million. Furthermore, Johnson Controls is working to increase its diverse suppliers worldwide. It joined the Minority Supplier Development in the U.K. and China to find ways to increase business opportunities to minority suppliers in these countries.

Johnson Controls has enjoyed many of the earlier discussed benefits accruing to working with diverse suppliers. However, Johnson Controls has also won many significant contracts from the U.S. government as a direct result of its work with minority suppliers. Johnson Controls' reputation continues to grow as it wins many awards for its work. For instance, it was recognized as the Corporation of the Year by the U.S. Minority Supplier Development Council. Additionally, it is only one of 16 corporations worldwide to have been named member of the Billion Dollar Roundtable for spending more than $1 billion with women and other minority-owned suppliers.

Based on http://www.johnsoncontrols.com.

to the company. As investors hear about investigations or the potential for ethical scandals, they are more inclined to sell their shares, thereby hurting the company's market valuation.

A recent study by Brammer, Brooks, and Pavelin provides further evidence of the advantages to both companies and investors of being ethical.[19] In that study, the authors examine the effects of the announcement of the inclusion of a company in the Business Ethics Survey of America's 100 Best Corporate Citizens. They find that there is a positive reaction to a company being present in the Top 100 list. Specifically, more investors tend to purchase shares in these companies, driving up the market valuation. Furthermore, holders of stocks of these companies tend to earn abnormal returns for a period of time after the announcement.

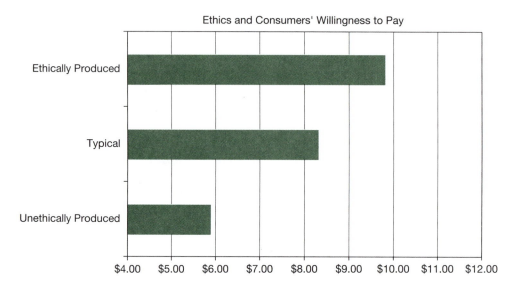

Ethics and Consumers' Willingness to Pay

EXHIBIT 1.5—Willingness to Pay Specific Prices

Clearly, being ethical presents many benefits to any organization. Such benefits range from stronger financial performance to more committed employees to more loyal customers. It is therefore in the best interest of any organization to behave ethically. Exhibit 1.6 summarizes the many benefits discussed in this section.

BENEFITS OF BEING ETHICAL

- Positive effects on many performance aspects such as firm financial performance, firm market value, stock market value and returns, and perceived future financial performance
- Minimization of loss of reputation and financial losses due to legal costs and fines
- Increased potential to achieve sustainable competitive advantage through the consideration of various stakeholders inherent in an ethical approach
- Many employee benefits such as higher organizational commitment, better identification with company values, and higher job satisfaction
- Higher customer trust and satisfaction
- Potential willingness for consumers to pay higher prices
- Potential to increase supplier diversity and benefit from these partnerships
- Increased interest from investors

EXHIBIT 1.6—Benefits of Business Ethics

However, beyond these benefits, many companies have realized that being ethical is the strategic approach to managing their businesses. In the face of constant criticisms from both the media and the public, most multinationals view a strong business ethics program as a way to manage their relationship with these groups.

Next we discuss the two major approaches to business ethics and finally the approach adopted in this text.

APPROACHES TO BUSINESS ETHICS

To understand the current approach to business ethics, it is necessary to examine the evolution of business ethics over the past decades. Being ethical was not always an important aspect of any corporation. In fact, in 1970, Milton Friedman, a Nobel Prize winner in economics, argued that the sole responsibility of any corporation is to make profits. Friedman argued that companies are not people but entities and therefore cannot have social responsibilities. Furthermore, he asserts that in a free enterprise economy, managers are employees of the owners of the business. Thus, managers should operate businesses in the best interests of the owners. This often means that managers should run the organization to make more money for shareholders. Additionally, Friedman posits that if a company is being socially responsible, then it is diverting money away from the owners of the company (i.e., shareholders). Shareholders are then double taxed, as their money is being taken away on top of all taxes that they already paid. Friedman thus argues that the company should only strive to achieve shareholder goals.

The best articulation of this approach to business is probably Boatright's (2002) **stockholder theory**.[20] According to Boatright, shareholders or owners have the right to control and earn residual earnings (or profits). However, Boatright's arguments are somewhat different than Friedman's. Specifically, Boatright argues that there are costs associated with any owners whether they are employees, customers, or shareholders. However, one of the most pertinent costs related to the role of shareholders is the cost of decision-making. Specifically, if a company was owned by different entities such as customers, employees, or shareholders, each of these groups could have conflicting interests regarding the goals of the company. However, Boatright suggests that the suppliers of equity capital or shareholders are the ones that have the least cost of decision-making because they are the ones with the least conflicting interests. Thus, the most efficient arrangement is ownership by suppliers of equity capital or shareholders and they have the right and control of profits. Boatright therefore argues that the best way to organize a company is through the stockholder model whereby managers are hired to achieve shareholders' goals.

As this chapter shows, the approach adopted in this book is that any company has to go beyond just shareholders. The many examples we have discussed show that any successful company has to take into consideration the needs of other groups such as employees, customers, suppliers, the community, etc. Any company that ignores the needs of these various groups does so at its own risk. Next we discuss the contrasting theory to stockholder theory.

GLOBAL BUSINESS ETHICS INSIGHT

Business Ethics Approaches Worldwide

Do other countries view business ethics similarly? In an interesting review of business ethics approaches, Liedekerke and Dubbink provide some insights into how business ethics have been viewed in Europe.[21] In the 1960s and 1970s, business ethics tended to be viewed suspiciously. In fact, the European view assumes that humans are greedy beyond redeem and that businesses can only be regulated by the state. As such, the corporate social responsibility movement was viewed with suspicion as it was seen as another way to convince society that businesses could actually be a positive force in society. Business ethics was seen as the proverbial oxymoron as critics wondered how businesses could be ethical or moral. Adding to this view was the traditional philosophy viewing ethics as a more theoretical and meta-physical concept as opposed to practice. Additionally, Europeans tended to see the market as imperfect and the profit motive as an abuse. Early perspectives of business ethics were thus seen with suspicion.

However, more recent reviews suggest that the ethical responsibilities of businesses have always been the dominant approach. While more U.S.-based companies operate in an individualist environment characterized by the free market, Europe has always seen societal responsibilities of companies as critical. Thus, Europe has had a more social view of businesses and the stakeholder approach is also very popular. However, it is only recently that Europeans have formally acknowledged this stakeholder approach.

Canto-Mila and Lozano discuss corporate social responsibility in the Spanish context.[22] They show that corporate social responsibility is a very important area for Spanish business. In fact, even the parliament has been involved in defining corporate social responsibility and providing the guidelines by which Spanish companies should operate.

Is this view also preferred in former socialist East European countries? Kooskora shows that post-socialist Estonia readily embraced a form of "cowboy" capitalism.[23] During that transition, Estonia experienced an economic boom and is benefiting from these experiences today. Estonia has enjoyed increased political and economic stability. However, while there is now some concern for corporate social responsibility, a recent survey of managers shows that Estonian managers still prefer economic success over business ethics. Nevertheless, the future will likely see a push as Estonia continues its efforts to be integrated into the European Union.

Based on Canto-Mila, Natalia and Lozano, Josep M. 2009. "The Spanish discourse on corporate social responsibility." *Journal of Business Ethics*, 87, 157–171; Kooskora, Mari. 2006. "Perceptions of business purpose and responsibility in the context of radical political and economic development: The case of Estonia." *Business Ethics: A European Review*, 15, 2, 183–199; Liedekerke, Lue van and Dubbink, Wim. 2008. "Twenty years of European business ethics—Past developments and future concerns." *Journal of Business Ethics*, 82, 273–280.

Edward Freeman (2010) presents the **stakeholder theory** of the modern corporation, basically arguing that companies need to go beyond satisfying the needs of shareholders only.[24] Freeman bases his theory on a few arguments. First, he asserts that although any company should operate in the interests of stockholders, the company also has to operate within the boundaries imposed by the legal system. Many new laws have been implemented over time worldwide and such laws suggest that companies need to take into consideration the needs of stakeholders governed by these laws. For instance, laws protecting employees imply that companies need to take into consideration the needs of employees. Such principles apply to most other stakeholders such as consumers, suppliers, and the community.

Second, Freeman defends his stakeholder theory based on economic arguments. He asserts that pure capitalism suggests that companies will operate according to the invisible hand argument, producing the greatest good for the greatest number. However, the invisible hand may not always function properly, especially in the presence of externalities and monopoly power. Consider, for example, air or water pollution. Often companies have no incentive to engage in cleanups, as these costs may only create marginal benefits for them. Thus, letting the company operate only in shareholders' interests may result in other stakeholders' needs being ignored (i.e., in this case, pollution can be detrimental to society). A second facet of the economic argument is in cases where a company has monopoly power. In these cases, it is very easy for any company to abuse its market power. Thus, in these cases, it is also critical to consider the needs of all stakeholders. Clearly, the current environment demands that stakeholder needs be satisfied. Is this view shared worldwide? Consider the Global Business Ethics Insight on page 20.

This Global Business Ethics Insight clearly shows that a stakeholder approach is the preferred way to approach business ethics worldwide. This is the approach adopted in this book. Next, we next discuss the many ethical issues any corporation faces. We also frame the various chapters of this book within this context.

WHAT BUSINESS ETHICS ISSUES DO COMPANIES FACE? PLAN OF THE BOOK

In the previous sections, you have already read about the many ethical issues facing any company. How can a systematic approach be used to determine the key ethical issues? In that context, it is important to understand that a company's actions have consequences for many different groups or individuals. For instance, in an earlier Global Business Ethics Insight (page 6), we saw how Siemens' bribery had damaging consequences for its employees (some were fired, others were hurt by the illegal activities), the societies in which it operates (illegally getting contracts by bribing individuals in these societies and affecting free market forces in these societies), investors (hurting their chances of future earnings), and for the company itself (hurting chances of survival given the fines imposed on the company). As such, these various groups are known as stakeholders. This stakeholder approach provides the framework around which the various parts of the book are organized.

In Part I, we present a general introduction to business ethics. Specifically, Part I includes chapters 1, 2, and 3. As we saw earlier, a strategic business ethics approach means that a company is properly balancing the needs of its various stakeholders. As such, in Chapter 2, we will discuss stakeholders in much more depth. A stakeholder approach provides a systematic framework to understand the key ethical issues facing any corporation. In that chapter, we will discuss the many core stakeholder issues such as the types of stakeholders, the characteristics of stakeholders, etc. We conclude that chapter with a tool to properly assess stakeholder needs.

A background understanding of ethics is not complete without understanding the individual factors affecting ethics. As such, Chapter 3 explores the many facets of individual ethics. Recognizing that the ethical orientation of a company often subsumes the ethical orientations of individuals within the company, we discuss some of the most important determinants of individual ethics. We also investigate some of the major ways individuals approach ethical decision-making. Finally, we also discuss various forms of moral development and the critical need for organizations to carefully recruit new employees.

In Part II, we examine specific stakeholders. In particular, we argue that there are four critical stakeholders that any organization has to deal with; namely, employees, customers, investors, and the media/special interest groups. In Chapter 4, we consider the role of employees as stakeholders and the many obligations companies have with respect to employees. In that chapter, we look at key aspects of the relationship between a company and its employees such as compensation practices and policies, discrimination, and sexual harassment. How critical are employees as stakeholders? To give you more insights into the employee as a stakeholder, consider the Business Ethics Insight on SAS on page 23.

As this Business Ethics Insight shows, considering employees as critical stakeholders is an important consideration for any company. In Chapter 5, we consider another important stakeholder; namely, the customer. In earlier parts of the chapter, we discuss the benefits that accrue to companies as they deal with their employees in an ethical fashion. Furthermore, in this current age of information technology, it is easy for unhappy customers to vent their frustration globally simply through a blog or uploaded video. It is now much harder to manage one's reputation reactively. As such, in Chapter 5, we consider the many responsibilities a company has with respect to its customers. We also consider customer rights and what companies do to respect such rights. Finally, we discuss some of the proactive approaches companies use today to keep this stakeholder group happy.

Chapter 6 discusses the role of shareholders as stakeholders of a company. As we discussed earlier, shareholders are typically the owners of a public company. However, managers are the ones running the company. This poses special issues that reflect the unique relationships between shareholders and companies. We consider corporate governance issues as they relate to the mechanisms available to shareholders to control management. Corporate governance is also a key aspect of how ethics are managed in any company.

BUSINESS ETHICS INSIGHT

Employees at SAS

SAS is the world's largest private software business maker. It has revenues of over $2.3 billion and around 7,000 employees (with around 4,200 based in its headquarters in North Carolina). As the amount of data grows, SAS's services are used to mine information from the limitless amount of data the company collects. In fact, 75% of *Fortune* 500 uses SAS services to make decisions such as where to locate stores or whether money laundering is occurring.

In its 2010 Best Companies to Work For, *Fortune* ranked SAS at number one. In fact, SAS has been on *Fortune*'s Best Companies to Work For since the list was created. What did SAS do to achieve this ranking? While SAS does not pay the most and does not provide stock options, it considers its employees as its main stakeholder. SAS provides numerous perks and benefits to its employees. Google actually considered SAS as its model when it was deciding on its campus perks.

Although it operates in a very cut-throat environment, employees face a work environment that values work–life balance. Employees' weeks are typically only 35 hours long and they can also set their own schedule. SAS's campus includes two subsidized day-care centers for its employees' children, three subsidized cafeterias, and numerous other services such as a UPS depot, dry cleaning, etc. The most prized perk is a centrally located health center that is free. Last year, around 90% of SAS employees and their families used the center. SAS also provides wellness centers as well as a 66,000 square-foot fitness center to cater for their employees' well-being.

Any employer would rightly balk at providing so many perks and benefits. However, SAS has enjoyed tremendous benefits by providing these perks. For instance, while the average employee turnover rate for the industry is 22%, SAS annual turnover is only 2%. Furthermore, the average tenure of employees at SAS is ten years, with a significant number having worked more than 25 years. Such long tenure and low turnover means that SAS does not have to continue investing in training of new recruits constantly.

The various perk centers have also benefited SAS. For example, while the healthcare center costs around $4.5 million to operate, SAS has shown benefits of $5 million in terms of less time spent waiting to get care. Employees are more likely to see care at SAS when they need such care. The health and wellness centers also provide important services to help employees stay focused on their health.

Besides the above benefits, SAS also enjoys bottom-line benefits that show the value of its approach. SAS has seen revenue grow for 33 straight years with double-digit profit margins. Furthermore, while 2010 has been a difficult year, SAS has not laid off any employees.

Based on Kaplan, David A. 2010. "#1 SAS—The Best Company to Work For." *Fortune*, February 8, 57–64.

In Chapter 7, we examine a number of other stakeholders; namely, the government, the media, and non-governmental organizations. While these stakeholders may not always have direct impact on the organization like employees or customers, they are nevertheless very influential stakeholders. We will therefore consider the roles played by these three stakeholders and the influences they have on companies. We will also consider how companies can proactively manage these groups. To give you examples of ethical issues emanating from each of the above stakeholder group, consider Exhibit 1.7.

Stakeholders and Ethical Issues

Employees
- Employee conflict of interest
- Honesty and integrity
- Discrimination, diversity, and sexual harassment
- Compensation and benefits
- Employee screening and privacy

Customers
- Fairness in pricing and marketing
- Advertising content and truth in advertising
- Customer privacy
- Dealing with customer complaints
- Product safety and quality

Shareholders
- Shareholder interests
- Transparency in accounting
- Transparency in shareholder communications
- Executive salaries and compensation
- Corporate governance

Suppliers
- Enforcing contracts
- Supplier diversity in terms of country, gender, and race
- Appropriation of supplier ideas

Government
- Respecting rules and regulations
- Practices in foreign nations with weak governments
- Lobbying

Community
- Corporate social responsibility
- Pollution and environmental degradation issues
- Donation to local community charities and organizations

EXHIBIT 1.7—Stakeholder Ethical Issues

Chapter 7 also devotes a significant part to the role of governments. How critical are governments in other societies? Consider the following Global Business Ethic Insight on the role of the government in China.

In Part III, we start examining the environment that most companies are facing today. Our decision to dedicate three chapters to understanding the environment is based on the fact that any company has to consider these issues as they implement their business ethics initiatives. Each chapter is dedicated to important driving forces that are shaping business environments in most countries.

GLOBAL BUSINESS ETHICS INSIGHT

Government and Business in China

How influential are governments in shaping the business environment? While governments are considered less influential in more laissez-faire countries such as the U.S. and the U.K., governments in other countries play a much more active role. Consider the case of China. The Chinese government routinely implements new regulations that have significant consequences for companies operating there.

Both Google and Microsoft have changed their operations to accommodate Chinese governmental demands. Specifically, when Google started operations, it agreed to censor search results that could be seen as detrimental to the Chinese government. However, Google may change its policy as recent claims of hacking have emerged. In contrast, Microsoft has agreed to abide by these censorship requests to take advantage of a soaring market.

The extent of Chinese influence goes beyond the software industry. For example, the Chinese government has recently decided to tighten land sale regulations to developers. Instead of asking for a minimum downpayment of 20% to 30% of the value of the land, the Chinese government is asking developers to put down 50%. In another example, the Chinese government recently implemented new regulations to control the companies that can sell high-technology products to Chinese governmental agencies. The new regulation requires that companies first get accreditation by demonstrating that the products have some form of local innovation. However, more than 30 industry groups from Asia, Europe, and North America have argued that these new rules will prevent these international companies from selling to the Chinese government.

Based on Chao, Loretta. 2009. "World news: China firms defend tech-purchase rules." *Wall Street Journal*, A10; Chao, Loretta. 2009. "World news: China's curbs on tech purchases draw Ire-I.S. government, dozens of global industry groups speak against push for state agencies to buy 'Indigenous innovation'." *Wall Street Journal*, A11; Shaw, Joy C. 2009. "China tightens land rules." *Wall Street Journal*, C8; Vascellaro, Jessica. 2010. "Google says it is committed to China as net soars." *Wall Street Journal*, B1.

Chapter 8 examines the role of information technologies and their impact on ethics. As the use of information technologies continues to explode, more companies are facing unexpected ethical issues. This chapter will therefore examine the many aspects of information technologies and the ease of collecting data and the consequent ethical issues associated with these new aspects.

Chapter 9 discusses another important aspect of any company's setting; namely, the environment and environmental sustainability. As discussions regarding climate change and the contributions of companies to carbon emissions continue, more companies are implementing environmental programs to be proactive. In this chapter, we discuss the growing pressure companies are facing to become more environmentally sensitive. We consider the various approaches to managing the environment and best practices of the world's most environmental multinationals. We conclude with the need for companies to actively integrate their environmental efforts in their business ethics programs.

Finally, Chapter 10 considers another critical aspect of the environment: the global environment. Although this book is among the first business ethics texts to adopt a global perspective on business ethics, we believe it is critical to have a chapter dedicated to global ethics. In this chapter, we consider why countries view business ethics issues differently. We also learn about the major international ethics issues with a special focus on corruption and bribery. Finally, we look at the many efforts and regulations that have been implemented worldwide to encourage multinationals to eliminate bribery and be more ethical.

Part IV is dedicated to understanding how an ethical company can be built. In Part IV, we first discuss some of the major factors contributing to unethical behavior by considering both the individual and the corporate culture. Both factors have been recognized as major determining factors regarding unethical behavior. We also discuss the steps a company needs to take to become more socially responsible.

Chapter 11 considers the ethical culture of any company and how that culture contributes to ethical behavior within the company. We discuss the most popular way of characterizing ethical culture; namely, through ethical climates. We review the three major forms of ethical climates and the consequences of these different types for any company. Lastly, we discuss how a company can encourage some forms of ethical climates.

Finally, Chapter 12 integrates the various chapters to present a strategic approach to managing business ethics. As mentioned earlier, this book adopts a strategic approach to business ethics. Why a strategic approach? To succeed in today's chaotic and constantly changing environment, companies have to devise strategies to outmaneuver competitors in order to enjoy a sustainable competitive advantage. A **strategic approach to business ethics** means that a company will integrate business ethics issues across all of its operations and activities. A less holistic approach to business ethics will not provide the strategic approaches compared to a more integrated business ethics approach. Consider, for instance, the Business Ethics Insight discussed earlier on Johnson Controls (page 17). Johnson Controls has adopted a very strategic approach to manage its business ethics activities. All decisions are guided by what is known as the triple bottom line: do the decisions contribute to economic, social, and environmental goals? With this strategic approach, Johnson Controls ensures that all activities and operations are guided by ethical principles.

Chapter 12 therefore discusses corporate social responsibility as a strategic approach to business ethics. We explore the various approaches to corporate social responsibility, and look at the key aspects of a corporate social responsibility program. In doing so, you learn how a company can strive to balance the needs of its various stakeholders.

CHAPTER SUMMARY

This chapter provides some introductory background business ethics information. We first defined business ethics and considered some examples of current ethical dilemmas. We then presented the case for business ethics. You read about the many benefits pertaining to any company for its ethical efforts. For instance, you learned that more ethical companies tend to perform better than less ethical ones on many measures, including financial performance. You also read about many other benefits that accrue to companies through their employees (more satisfied, happier, and more committed employees), customers (more trusting, more loyal, and willing to pay more for ethical products), and investors (more loyalty).

The chapter then provides some insights into the two main approaches to business ethics. You first read about the stockholder approach where the needs of stakeholders have strong influences on decisions. However, you also learned about the stakeholder approach where the stakeholder needs are balanced.

The final part of the chapter presents an overview of the chapters that you will be reading throughout the text. We frame these chapters within a strategic approach and argue that these chapters all converge in Chapter 12 on corporate social responsibility.

NOTES

1 ACFE, 2008. Available at http://www.acfe.com.

2 Beurden, P. van & Gossling, T. 2008. "The worth of values—A literature review on the relation between corporate social and financial performance." *Journal of Business Ethics*, 82, 407–424.

3 Peinado-Vara, E. 2006. "Corporate social responsibility in Latin America." *Journal of Corporate Citizenship*, Spring, 61–69.

4 Kumar, R., Lamb, W.N. & Wokutch, R.E. 2002. "The end of South African sanctions, institutional ownership, and the stock price performance of boycotted firms: evidence on the impact of social-ethical investing." *Business and Society*, 41, 2, 133–165.

5 Choi, T. H. & Jung, J. 2008. "Ethical commitment, financial performance, and valuation: An empirical investigation of Korean companies." *Journal of Business Ethics*, 81, 447–463.

6 Donker, H., Poff, D. & Zahir, S. 2008. "Corporate values, codes of ethics, and firm performance: A look at the Canadian context." *Journal of Business Ethics*, 82, 527–537.

7 Saadoui, K. 2009. "L'engagement éthique pénalise-t-il la performance?" *Revue Française de Gestion*, 196, 15–28.

8   Sims, R.R. 2009. "Toward a better understanding of organizational efforts to rebuild reputation following an ethical scandal." *Journal of Business Ethics*, 90, 453–472.

9   Vilanova, M., Lozano, J.M. & Arenas, D. 2009. "Exploring the nature of the relationship between CSR and competitiveness." *Journal of Business Ethics*, 87, 57–69.

10 Gilley, M.K., Robertson, C.J. & Mazur, T.C. 2010. "The bottom-line benefits of ethics code commitment." *Business Horizons*, 53, 31–37.

11 Sharma, D., Borna, S. & Stearns, J.M. 2009. "An investigation of the effects of corporate ethical values on employee commitment and performance: Examining the moderating role of perceived fairness." *Journal of Business Ethics*, 89, 251–260.

12 Prottas, D.J. 2008. "Perceived behavioral integrity: Relationships with employee attitudes, well-being, and absenteeism." *Journal of Business Ethics*, 81, 313–322.

13 Trudel, R. & Cotte, J. 2009. "Does it pay to be good?" *MIT Sloan Management Review*, 50, 2, 61–68.

14 Bhattacharya, C.B., Korschun, D. & Sen, S. 2009. "Strengthening stakeholder–company relationships through mutually beneficial corporate social responsibility initiatives." *Journal of Business Ethics,* 85, 257–272.

15 Worthington, I. 2009. "Corporate perceptions of the business case for supplier diversity: How socially responsible purchasing can 'pay'." *Journal of Business Ethics*, 90, 4.

16 Worthington, "Corporate perceptions."

17 Petersen, H.L. & Harrie Vredenburg, H. 2009. "Morals or economics? Institutional preferences for corporate social responsibility." *Journal of Business Ethics,* 90, 1, 1–14.

18 Trudel & Cotte, "Does it pay to be good?"

19 Brammer, S., Brooks, C. & Pavelin, S. 2009. "The stock performance of America's 100 best corporate citizens." *Quarterly Review of Economics and Finance*, 49, 1065–1080.

20 Boatright, J.R. 2002. "Ethics and corporate governance: justifying the role of shareholder." In N.E. Bowie (Ed.), *The Blackwell guide to business ethics*. Malden, MA: Blackwell, pp. 38–60.

21 Liedekerke, L. van & Dubbink, W. 2008. "Twenty years of European business ethics—past developments and future concerns." *Journal of Business Ethics*, 82, 273–280.

22 Canto-Mila, N. & Lozano, J.M. 2009. "The Spanish discourse on corporate social responsibility." *Journal of Business Ethics*, 87, 157–171.

23 Kooskora, M. 2006. "Perceptions of business purpose and responsibility in the context of radical political and economic development: The case of Estonia." *Business Ethics: A European Review*, 15, 2, 183–199.

24 Freeman, E. 2010. "Managing for stakeholders." In T.L. Beauchamp, N.E. Bowie & D.G. Arnold (Eds.), *Ethical theory and business*, Upper Saddle River, NJ: Prentice Hall, pp. 56–68.

KEY TERMS

Bribe Payers Index: the degree to which executives expect companies to engage in bribery with their own companies in specific countries.

Bribery: the degree to which individuals have to be provided with some compensation (e.g., money, gifts, etc.) to influence the individual.

Business ethics: refer to the principles and standards that guide business.

Business Ethics Insight: pertains to specific examples of companies dealing with the general business ethics issues discussed in the text.

Corporate social responsibility: a strategic approach to managing ethics in an organization.

Ethics: refer to society's perception of what is right or wrong.

Ethics Sustainability Insight: discussion of the environmental or sustainability implications of the ethical issues discussed in the chapter.

Global Business Ethics Insight: provides information on the global nature and implications of the ethical issues in the chapter.

Occupational fraud: use of one's occupation for personal enrichment through the deliberate misuse or misapplication of the employing organization's resources or assets.

Preview Business Ethics Insight: discusses how a multinational or other entity has dealt with ethical situations pertaining to the chapter.

Stakeholder theory: approach that assumes that companies need to go beyond satisfying the needs of shareholders only.

Stockholder theory: approach that assumes that shareholders or owners have the right to control and earn residual earnings (or profits).

Strategic approach to business ethics: a company will integrate business ethics issues across all of its operations and activities.

Strategic Business Ethics Insight: provides information regarding the strategic implications of the ethical issues discussed in the chapter.

DISCUSSION QUESTIONS

1. What is business ethics? Give some examples of business ethics dilemmas.
2. What do the various surveys of business ethics worldwide reveal? What are some of the common unethical behaviors?
3. Discuss specific findings of any of the business ethics surveys mentioned in this chapter. What are the implications of these findings?
4. What are some of the benefits companies enjoy for their ethics program? Be specific.
5. What are the benefits of good ethics for employees?
6. Why do investors prefer to invest in companies with good ethics?
7. How do customers react to companies with good ethics? Be specific.
8. Describe stockholder theory. What are the main arguments supporting stockholder theory?
9. What is stakeholder theory? Why is the stakeholder theory approach the way companies should manage their ethics?
10. Compare and contrast stakeholder and stockholder theory.

INTERNET ACTIVITY

1. Access the website of one of the organizations, assessing ethical behavior (e.g., Transparency International, United Nations Global Compact, etc.) mentioned in the text.
2. How does that organization define ethics? Which aspects of ethics are they most concerned with?
3. What are some of the major findings of recent surveys? Prepare a presentation and share with the class.
4. What lessons do you learn regarding ethics?

For more Internet Activities and resources, please visit the Companion Website at www.routledge.com/cw/parboteeah.

WHAT WOULD YOU DO?

Facebook and Cheating

You are currently taking an online section of the Business Ethics course as part of your undergraduate program. The course is now a permanent part of your school's business curriculum. Because the course is being taught online, you never meet your classmates in person. Rather, you have "befriended" many of the students on Facebook. Occasionally, you discuss the course on Facebook.

For this week's lessons, you will be assessed primarily through a quiz conducted in an online environment. The quiz will cover a third of the semester's chapters and you will have a fairly short period of time to answer a relatively large number of questions. Because the quiz is an open book, you therefore realize that you will need to read the chapters a few times to make sure to know where information is located in the text. Once you start taking the quiz, you won't have much time to look for relevant information in the text for the questions.

When you logged into your Facebook account this morning, you see that one of your classmates (who also happens to be a very close friend) has decided to post the questions he had to attempt on the quiz. While each student gets a random list of questions from a test bank, most students will still get a significant overlap among questions. Studying the posted questions could thus be helpful.

What would you do? Did you do anything wrong by simply looking at the questions? Would you report your close friend to the teacher?

BRIEF CASE: BUSINESS ETHICS INSIGHT

Anna Hazare and Corruption in India

Vishal is a typical New Delhi resident and owns a fried chicken stall on the streets of New Delhi. However, he faces a range of petty corruption as he operates his fried chicken stand. He has to bribe the senior police officers to stay open late while the more junior police officers routinely take free lunches. He also pays local officials to make sure that he does not have any problems with health and safety inspections. He gets stopped by the police almost every other week and is asked to pay so that he is not "bothered." He also has to pay the headmaster of the best local school to ensure that his son has access to the best local school. Altogether, Vishal spends almost a third of his restaurant earnings as bribe. Many of the emerging middle-class Indians seem to have similar experiences on a daily basis.

In the face of such growing frustration, it is not surprising to see that India is experiencing the emergence of an anti-corruption social activist Anna Hazare. Hazare, a retired army driver from the state of Maharashtra, has become the voice of people frustrated with corruption. He has held a number of hunger strikes to force the local government to enact laws to combat corruption. However, he is now campaigning at the national level and wants the Indian government to adopt a version of his own Jan Lokpal Bill, a bill that most see as very weak. In his own version, the bill would call for the creation of a powerful ombudsperson to investigate top officials for corruption.

In August 2011, Anna Hazare was arrested by the Indian government for refusing to accept police restrictions on his proposed anti-corruption protests. His arrest immediately sparked demonstrations across India. Thousands of middle-class individuals frustrated with corruption marched in cities around India to protest at his arrest. Furthermore, as hundreds gathered outside the jail where he was housed, the government quickly capitulated and gave him permission for a 15-day public protest. He triumphantly left the jail and has renewed demand that his version of the anti-corruption bill be passed. While some see his efforts as likely to bring changes to Indian corruption, others believe that business as usual will be back as the protests subside.

Based on Anonymous, 2011. "Indian activist leads Delhi protest." *Wall Street Journal*, August 19, online version; Associated Press. 2011. "Anna Hazare leaves jail to begin public hunger strike." *Guardian*, August 19, online version http://guardian.co.uk; Burke, J. 2011. "Corruption in India: 'All your life you pay for things that should be free'." *Guardian*, August 19, online version http://guardian.co.uk.

BRIEF CASE QUESTIONS

1. Research Transparency International website and find India's ranking on the Corruption Index. Is India's ranking consistent with the Business Ethics Insight? Why or why not?
2. Why is corruption so rampant in India? Who should be blamed for such corruption?
3. How effective is social activism like Anna Hazare's actions? Do you share optimism that things will change in India? Or do you believe that "business will be back to usual"?
4. What roles do multinationals have to play to combat corruption in societies like India? What can multinationals do to combat such corruption?
5. What can be done at the societal level to combat corruption?

LONG CASE: BUSINESS ETHICS

ACCELERATING INTO TROUBLE: AN ANALYSIS OF TOYOTA MOTOR COMPANY AND ITS RECENT RECALLS*

1. Overview

Newly appointed President and CEO Akio Toyoda, grandson of Toyota Motor Company's founder, would unknowingly soon be faced with the biggest crisis in the company's history a few short months after taking the reins. It started with a single, horrifying car crash in southern California in August 2009.[1] And after two separate vehicle recalls attributed to hundreds of consumer claims of Sudden Unintended Acceleration covering 10 million vehicles, the company was forced to announce it was suspending the sale of eight of its best-selling vehicles, a move that would ultimately cost the company and its dealers a minimum of $54 million a day in lost sales revenue at its peak.[2] How did a company that became the world's largest automaker on the back of a rock-solid reputation for quality and dependability find itself at the center of one of the biggest product recalls in company history?[3] And what does this mean for Toyota's brand image in the United States, its largest and most profitable market?

2. A Brief History of Toyota Motor Company

2.1 Toyota Motor Company Background

The Toyota Motor Co. Ltd was first established in 1937 as a spin-off from Toyoda Automatic Loom Works, one of the world's leading manufacturers of weaving machinery.[4] Toyota Motor Sales Co., Ltd was later established in 1950, and the first Toyota cars arrived in the United States in 1957 which would lead to the founding of Toyota Motor Sales, U.S.A., Inc. on October 31 in the same year. Toyota began manufacturing operations in the U.S. by 1972 and expanded to include vehicle production in 1986.[5]

Toyota Motors is a publicly traded company on the New York Stock Exchange (NYSE), the Tokyo Stock Exchange and the London Stock Exchange under the symbol TM. The company's principal competitors within the industry are Ford Motor Company, General Motors Corporation, and Honda Motor Co., Ltd. and as of 2010, Toyota held over 16% of the U.S. market share.[6] With more than 1,500 Toyota, Lexus, and Scion dealers in the U.S. alone and a worldwide employment of over 320,000, Toyota sells vehicles in 170 countries and is currently regarded as the world's largest automobile manufacturer by both sales and production.[7]

2.2 Continued Success

Over the past 25 years, Toyota has had a steady increase in both sales and market share within the automotive industry. By the end of the 1980s, Toyota had garnered the reputation of being a powerful and exceptionally well-run car company.[8] After a decade of consistent growth, the company stood atop the Japanese automobile industry and ranked number three worldwide.[9]

By the beginning of the 1990s, Toyota commanded an overwhelming 43% of the Japanese car market, and in the United States it sold more than one million cars and trucks for the first time in its history.[10] Toyota also spearheaded the Japanese automobile industry's venture into the luxury car market, leading the way with its Lexus LS400 luxury sedan, which by the mid-1990s was outselling market veterans BMW, Mercedes-Benz, and Jaguar.[11]

In 2000, Toyota introduced its first Hybrid model, the Prius, continuing the company's success into the new millennium. Toyota has gone on to develop multiple hybrid options and extend their availability to seven of their models. Currently, 10% of total sales in the U.S. are hybrids and Toyota has sold nearly 75% of all the hybrids in America so far. Worldwide, Toyota has sold over 2 million hybrid cars.[12]

2.3 Corporate Philosophy

Toyota is driven by a corporate purpose that combines "harmonious growth" and "enhancement of profitability," and this purpose is clearly understood and internalized by its senior management and employees.[13] At Toyota, employees are continuously trained in the "Toyota Production System," or TPS. The main objectives of the TPS are to phase out overburden and inconsistency and to eliminate waste. The most significant effects on process value delivery are achieved by designing a process capable of delivering the required results smoothly by designing out inconsistency.[14]

Unyielding attention for product quality and cost awareness has become an almost religious way of life for everyone in the organization. TPS enables Toyota to construct automobiles at low cost and develop new products faster than any of their competitors. Not only have Toyota's rivals such as Chrysler, Daimler, Ford, Honda, and General Motors developed TPS-like systems, organizations such as hospitals and postal services also have adopted its underlying rules, tools, and practices to become more efficient.[15]

2.4 Corporate Social Responsibility

While Toyota's reputation has taken a beating in terms of safety, it continues to boast a record of quality corporate citizenship in other areas. In 2009, Ethisphere ranked Toyota as one of the "World's Most Ethical Companies" based on criteria that included Corporate Citizenship/Responsibility, Legal/Regulatory Reputation and Track Record, and Industry Leadership to name a few.[16] Since 1991, Toyota has contributed more than $464 million to philanthropic programs in the U.S. and supports numerous programs focused on environmental, educational, and safety issues in an effort to "strengthen diverse communities throughout the U.S."[17] In 2008, Toyota launched *TogetherGreen*, a $20 million, five-year alliance with Audubon, an environmental conservation organization, to fund conservation projects, train environmental leaders, and offer volunteer opportunities to significantly benefit the environment.[18]

For the past 20 years, the Toyota U.S.A. Foundation has funded K-12 educational programs that focus on the areas of math and science. Currently, the company provides $2 million a year in support of various programs and partners with some of America's leading organizations and institutions through grants and scholarships. Toyota also created a driving safety program located in California called *Toyota Driving Expectations,* a free program for teens and their parents. The goal of Toyota Driving Expectations is to proactively take America's driving youth through a safe driving experience.[19]

3. The Issue of Sudden Unintended Acceleration

3.1 A Sticky Situation

The issue of Sudden Unintended Acceleration (SUA), or sticky accelerators, is no new phenomenon. Beginning in 1986, the issue of SUA was examined in depth by the National Highway Traffic Safety Administration (NHTSA) due to an "above average" number of incident reports.[20] According to a 1989 NHTSA report, SUA was defined as "the unintended, unexpected, uncontrolled acceleration of a vehicle from a stationary position, low initial speed or at cruising speed, often accompanied by an apparent loss of braking effectiveness."[21] Despite the research invested in this topic over time, it still remains unclear whether problems are caused by driver error, mechanical or electrical problems with automobiles, or some combination of these factors.[22]

3.2 A Trip Down Memory Lane

Since 2007, issues with brakes, acceleration, floor mats and gas pedals have led to probes by U.S. agencies landing the world's largest carmaker in trouble.[23] However, the issue of unintended acceleration is not a problem unique to Toyota. If any company can relate to Toyota's recall woes, it's Audi. During the 1980s, the German automaker suffered similar allegations of unintended acceleration when supposed faulty gas pedals on its popular Audi 5000 series sedan were linked to six deaths and 700 crashes.[24] And although the problem was eventually ruled a case of driver error—people were applying the accelerator instead of the brake—Audi had to issue a major recall.[25] A 1986 *60 Minutes* investigation aired a short time after the announcement of the recall, showing an Audi 5000 sedan accelerating out of control to an audience of millions.[26] The investigation was later debunked when it was discovered that the car had been modified by the television producers, but the damage was done.[27] Audi sales dropped 80% over the next five years.[28] It wasn't until 2000 that it reached its peak sales mark from 1985.[29]

In the years following the Audi experience, incidents of unintended acceleration continued to be reported to the NHTSA from all makes of vehicles. The frequency of such incidents was seen by NHTSA as "unremarkable," given the millions of cars involved.[30] They were viewed through the lens of the 1989 NHTSA study which had concluded that all incidents of unintended acceleration were the result of driver error. Unintended acceleration thus attracted little attention until August 28, 2009, when the U.S. public once again became aware of the phenomenon.[31]

3.3 Back to the Future

On that day, Mark Saylor, an off-duty California Highway Patrol officer, left his Lexus at the Bob Baker Lexus Dealership in El Cajon, California. The dealership loaned him a 2009 Lexus ES350 to use until his car had been serviced. Hours later, he was driving the Lexus along California Highway 125 when it accelerated on its own to 120 miles per hour.[32] As the car sped down the highway, Saylor's brother in law, Chris Lastrella, called 911. He was heard saying:

> "We're in a Lexus . . . and we're going north on 125 and our accelerator is stuck . . . we're in trouble . . . there's no brakes . . . we're approaching the intersection . . . hold on . . . hold on and pray . . . pray."[33]

The Lexus slammed into a Ford Explorer at the intersection of Highway 125 and Mission Gorge Rd., went over a curb and through a fence before it flipped and caught fire, killing Saylor along with his wife Cleofe, 45, and daughter, Mahala, 13, and Chris Lastrella. The incident was widely covered and publicized by media outlets and the recording of the phone call eventually became one of many 911 calls recorded of people whose vehicles were speeding out of control. The combination of the dramatic 911 call, the horrifying accident that ensued, and the implausibility of "driver error" by a highway patrol officer created a national buzz.[34]

As a result, 23 years after the Audi *60 Minutes* episode, an eerily similar program was seen by millions of viewers on an installment of ABC World News. On February 22, 2010, David Gilbert, an automotive technology professor of Southern Illinois University, assisted by ABC correspondent Brian Ross, demonstrated how, under certain conditions, a Toyota vehicle can accelerate rapidly and not record any error on the computer monitoring system of the car.[35]

This report was aired a few weeks after the announcement of two recalls in response to numerous claims of SUA that accounted for over 8 million vehicles at the time and the night before the beginning of highly anticipated Congressional hearings in which the Toyota leadership was called to testify.[36] The following day, Professor Gilbert offered a preliminary report of his findings in testimony to the U.S. House of Representatives in these hearings.[37] Much like its German predecessor, Toyota eventually found that the ABC report was flawed and had in fact exacerbated the problem. And again, like Audi, the damage had already been done. Whatever the given cause of SUA may be, one lesson from both the Audi and the Toyota experiences is that a single highly publicized incident could be devastating to a brand.

4. Chronology of the Toyota SUA Case: August 2009–August 2010

August 28, 2009: Off-duty California Highway Patrol officer Mark Saylor was traveling on Highway 125 in Santee, California (northeast of San Diego), with three family members, when the 2009 Lexus ES350 he was driving suddenly accelerated out of control, hits another car, tumbled down an embankment, and caught fire. While the car was careening down the highway at speeds estimated to exceed 100 mph, one of the occupants called 911 and reported that the car had "no brakes." All four people were killed in the ensuing crash.[38]

September 14, 2009: Preliminary reports from Toyota and local authorities indicated that the Lexus, which had been on loan from Bob Baker Lexus of San Diego, where Saylor's personal Lexus vehicle was being serviced, may have had the wrong floor mats installed, interfering with the gas pedal.[39]

September 29, 2009: Toyota announced it was recalling the floor mats on 4.2 million Toyota and Lexus vehicles. The company advised owners to remove their floor mats and place them in the trunk and directed dealers to use zip ties to secure the floor mats in their vehicles so they could not interfere with the gas pedal.[40]

October 1, 2009: Toyota reported a September sales decrease of 16.1% from last September on a daily selling rate basis. However, the third quarter showed a 28% increase over the second quarter. "Improving economic conditions and the CARS program led to a significant increase for the industry in the third quarter over the first half-year," said Don Esmond, senior vice president of automotive operations for TMS. "Moving into the fourth quarter, we expect continued momentum will close the year on a bright note."[41]

October 2, 2009: Newly installed Toyota CEO Akio Toyoda publicly apologized to the Saylor family members killed in the accident, to every customer affected by the recall, and for the recent drop in sales during a briefing at the Japanese Press Club. "Toyota," he stated, is "grasping for salvation." He went on to state that Toyota was "wholly unprepared for the current economic free-fall," and that the company is now a single step away from "capitulation to irrelevance or death."[42]

October 18, 2009: The *Los Angeles Times* published the first of several stories concerning claims of unintended acceleration in Toyota vehicles. A Toyota spokesperson admitted there is no safety override programmed into its computer to disable the throttle pedal when the brake pedal is pressed, but said Toyota is considering adding one, as well as modifying the pedals themselves to keep them from getting caught on the floor mats. The story also revealed the Lexus' push-button starter must be depressed for at least three seconds to shut down the engine when the vehicle is in drive.[43]

October 25, 2009: The results of an investigation by local authorities and the NHTSA revealed a set of rubber floor mats designed for the Lexus RX 400 SUV had been placed over the top of the ES 350's stock carpeted floor mats and that the accelerator pedal had become jammed against them, causing the car to accelerate out of control.[44] NHTSA also pointed out the gas pedal on the car was solidly mounted to its stalk, whereas other vehicles use hinged pedals.[45]

October 30, 2009: Toyota began sending letters to U.S. owners notifying them of an unspecified upcoming recall to fix the unintended acceleration issue. In the letters Toyota said "no defect exists."[46]

November 2, 2009: NHTSA took the highly unusual step of publicly rebuking Toyota, calling a company press release reiterating the statements made in the October 30 letter to owners "inaccurate" and "misleading," noting that the floor mat recall was an "interim" measure and that it "does not correct the underlying defect."[47]

November 4, 2009: Toyota issued another press release denying media reports that a problem exists with its drive-by-wire electronic throttle system.[48]

November 8, 2009: The *Los Angeles Times* claims reports in an article that Toyota had ignored over 1,200 complaints of unintended acceleration over the past eight years because NHTSA had thrown out those reports that claimed the brakes were not capable of stopping the car under an unintended acceleration scenario. In the story a Toyota spokesman confirms the brakes are not capable of stopping a vehicle accelerating at wide open throttle.[49]

November 16, 2009: Japanese media reports claimed Toyota had made a deal with NHTSA over a recall. Toyota denied any agreement had been reached, but the company admitted it had already set aside $5.6 billion to deal with the issue.[50]

November 25, 2009: Toyota dealers were instructed to remove the gas pedal and shorten it so it cannot interfere with the floor mats. As an "extra measure of confidence," the company also directed dealers to update the onboard computers on the Toyota Camry and Avalon, and Lexus ES 350, IS 250, and IS 350 with a new program that overrides the electronic gas pedal when the brake pedal is pressed.[51]

December 5, 2009: Following an op-ed piece in the *Los Angeles Times*,[52] Toyota wrote a letter to the paper reiterating its stance that the floor mats were the root cause of most unintended acceleration claims that would be published December 9.[53]

December 26, 2009: A Toyota Avalon crashed into a lake in Southlake, Texas after accelerating out of control. All four occupants died. Floor mats were ruled out as a cause because they were found in the trunk of the car.[54]

January 11, 2010: Toyota announced its brake override software fix will be made global by 2011.[55]

January 21, 2010: Toyota recalled another 2.3 million Toyota-brand vehicles because of a problem with the gas pedal. Toyota described it as "a rare set of conditions which may cause the accelerator pedal to become harder to depress, slower to return or, in the worst case, stuck in a partially depressed position." The company said the new recall is unrelated to the floor mat recall.[56]

January 26, 2010: Toyota announced it is immediately halting the sale of all models affected by the January 21 pedal recall, and that it will shut down assembly lines for those models at five North American plants for one week beginning February 1 "to assess and coordinate activities."[57] Toyota does not explain why it waited five days to stop sales after announcing the recall.[58]

January 27, 2010: U.S. Transportation Secretary Ray LaHood told Chicago radio station WGN the government asked Toyota to stop selling the recalled vehicles. Toyota confirms LaHood's statement. Other media reports claimed Toyota had quietly informed its dealers and factories the problem was a result of pedals made by the supplier CTS Corporation of Elkhart, Indiana. Lexus and Scion models, it turns out, used pedals made by Japanese supplier Denso, hence their exemption from the recall. The problem was said to occur after 38,000 miles, though the cause was still under investigation.[59]

The *Wall Street Journal* estimated that Toyota dealers could lose as much as $1.5 million in profit every week of the sales freeze.[60] Toyota shares dropped more than 10% over the day and a half after the freeze was announced and CTS' shares dropped 2.4%. Toyota notified NHTSA late in the day that it would expand its November 25 recall to cover an additional 1.1 million vehicles. The recall now included the Toyota Venza and more model years of the Toyota Highlander, as well as the Pontiac Vibe.[61]

February 1, 2010: Toyota announced it had developed a plan to fix the accelerator pedals and that parts were being shipped to dealers so they can carry out the repairs.[62]

February 5, 2010: Toyota President and CEO Akio Toyoda apologized for the car recalls at a news conference at the World Economic Forum and promised to beef up quality control.[63] "I apologize from the bottom of my heart for all the concern that we have given to so many customers," said Toyoda.[64]

February 9, 2010: An editorial written by President and CEO Akio Toyoda entitled "Toyota's Plan to Repair Public Image" was published in the *Washington Post*.[65] Toyota announced it would recall about 437,000 Prius and other hybrid vehicles worldwide to fix brake problems after more than 100 complaints were received from the NHTSA from Prius owners. The announcement raised the number of vehicles recalled by Toyota to more than 8.5 million.[66]

February 23, 2010: Jim Lentz, the top U.S. executive for Toyota, testified before a House committee on Energy and Commerce stating the company is still investigating whether electronics of the gas pedal system may be at fault.[67]

February 24, 2010: Toyota President Akio Toyoda apologized during a congressional hearing for the Committee on Oversight and Government Reform. He pledged Toyota's full cooperation with U.S. government officials investigating safety problems.[68]

March 2, 2010: Toyota Motor North America, Inc. announced that former U.S. Secretary of Transportation Rodney E. Slater would lead an independent North American Quality Advisory Panel to advise the company's North American affiliates on quality and safety issues.[69] Toyota also announced plans to launch the company's most far-reaching sales program in its history. Starting on March 2 and lasting through April 5, 2010, the national marketing program would include financing, leasing, and customer loyalty offers.[70]

April 5, 2010: The U.S. government accused Toyota of hiding "dangerous defects" and sought a record $16.4 million fine, dwarfing the previous record of $1 million levied against General Motors in 2004 for a unsatisfactory response to a windshield wiper recall.[71]

April 8, 2010: Toyota announced it will not contest the pending fine presented by the U.S. government and agreed to pay.[72] The company also announced it had established a new SMART (Swift Market Analysis Response Team) business process to quickly and aggressively investigate customer reports of unintended acceleration in Toyota, Lexus, and Scion vehicles in the United States.[73]

April 20, 2010: The Deepwater Horizon oil rig exploded in the Gulf of Mexico, shifting national media and consumer attention away from Toyota.[74]

May 18, 2010: Toyota paid a $16.4 million fine to settle allegations by U.S. regulators that the company was too slow to recall vehicles with defective gas pedals.[75]

August 4, 2010: Toyota announced it had returned to a profit of $2.2 billion in the April-to-June quarter because of strong sales in emerging markets and aggressive cost-cutting.[76]

5. Repercussions

5.1 Media Response

When reporting of the August car crash in California showed a potential link with Toyota, the media became heavily involved. Much of the news coverage was critical of Toyota. One study found that 106 of 108 observed media mentions of Toyota during the August 2009–February 2010 period were negative in attitude toward the company.[77]

A large portion of the coverage concerning the recall was spearheaded by the *Los Angeles Times* and proposed many questions as to the safety concerns of Toyota. A series of stories were published before the acceleration issues were widely known, and while the company was blaming mechanical problems, starting with defective floor mats, and driver error, the *Times'* reporting raised the possibility that safety issues went deeper than that.[78] What began as a simple series of stories quickly became syndicated in many publications nationwide, such as the *Wall Street Journal*, reaching an unprecedented audience. The *Los Angeles Times'* work was eventually named a finalist for the Pulitzer Prize in national reporting, drawing even more attention to Toyota's issues.[79]

The main underlying issue throughout the media coverage in general was that many believed Toyota was withholding information concerning the accelerator glitches.[80] This was accompanied with the belief that Toyota had compromised safety and quality in their engineering in efforts to displace General Motors as the number one car manufacturer in the world.[81] Another key talking point for media outlets focused on the lack of a definite cause for the incidents and the consistently changing stance from Toyota in regards to the issue.[82]

5.2 Consumer Response

While Toyota owners remained predominantly supportive of their vehicles, they were negatively impacted.[83] One major concern arose when buyers purchased models that would soon be recalled and halted for production during the same day.[84] Toyota dealers claimed to have no knowledge of the looming recalls, but this did little to diminish the disdain of these purchasers. This resulted in questioning whether they should get their money back after buying a car that was deemed defective by the company itself.[85]

One of the most harmful examples of consumer backlash was found to be directly related to the amount of media coverage over SUA. As media coverage concerning unintended acceleration increased, so did the number of complaints from Toyota owners. Specifically in the months of February and March, when the coverage reached its highest point, the number of complaints had tripled from its average amount. At its peak, the number of complaints reached over 1,500 in the month of February.[86]

5.3 Economic Impact

In the wake of the recall announcements, Toyota felt an immediate economic impact. The first of these was the decision on January 26 to temporarily halt production at six assembly plants in North America and suspend sales of eight of its most popular models, including the Camry, the best-selling car in the United States.[87] Although recalls are somewhat a routine matter for carmakers, taking cars off the market is not. The decision to stop sales and production in America took a substantial toll on Toyota. These eight models accounted for about 60% of sales in 2009 and 60% of the carmaker's U.S. inventory.[88]

The timing was also a concern because the last week of the month is a peak time for car sales.[89] U.S. Toyota dealers were projected to lose as much as $2.47 billion in combined monthly revenue from the halt in sales of both new and used versions of those models with each of the individual dealers in the U.S. potentially losing out on $1.75 million to $2 million a month in revenue.[90]

The economic news also cast a cloud of uncertainty over the company shareholders and caused the stock price to plummet.[91] Toyota's U.S. market share fell by 16% to its lowest level since January 2006, and its monthly sales dropped below 100,000 vehicles for the first time in more than a decade. Fears of an extended sales slump pushed Toyota's shares down 3.7% in a flat market in Tokyo, compounding a slide that had sent the stock down 17% since its recall was announced.[92]

To compound Toyota's internal financial troubles, this crisis created an opportunity for other carmakers to claim a portion of Toyota's slipping market share. As Toyota sales spun into reverse, Ford and Hyundai Motor Co. emerged as the big winners, each posting 24% sales gains.[93] In one telling benchmark, the Ford brand outsold Toyota, Scion, and Lexus on a combined basis. GM's volume-leading Chevrolet brand also topped Toyota on its own.[94] The tremendous gains of these companies was also attributed to generous rebates specifically to current Toyota owners, such as discounts and no-interest financing.[95]

The decision to halt production to fix the recalls then led to the suspended production of two plants in Kentucky and Texas on February 16 due to lagging sales following the recall announcements.[96] The temporary shutdowns were aimed at adjusting production levels to prevent overstocked lots and massive losses for dealerships.[97]

5.4 Government Criticism and Investigations

The events that took place during the recalls also led to sharp criticism and a number of investigations from U.S. government agencies. U.S. Transportation Secretary Ray LaHood announced two major investigations to "resolve the issue of sudden acceleration" within Toyota and across the entire automotive industry.[98] LaHood first called upon the National Assembly of Sciences' National Research Council to examine the subjects of unintended acceleration and electronic vehicle controls over the course of 15 months during which it would cover all manufacturers.

Secretary LaHood then asked the U.S. Department of Transportation Inspector General to review whether NHTSA's Office of Defect Investigation had the necessary resources and systems to identify and address safety defects as it moves forward. Finally, Secretary LaHood asked the U.S. Department of Transportation Inspector General to assess whether the NHTSA Office of Defect Investigation conducted an adequate review of complaints of alleged unintended acceleration reported to NHTSA from 2002 to the present.[99] This was the most comprehensive collective action ever taken toward investigating Sudden Unintended Acceleration.

Along with numerous investigations being initiated by the NHTSA for accelerator complaints, the most visible and perhaps harmful criticism of the company occurred with the U.S. Congressional Hearings, in which the leadership in Toyota was called to testify. President and CEO of Toyota Motor Sales, U.S.A., Inc. Jim Lentz testified before the House Energy committee on February 23 and Toyota Motor President Akio Toyoda testified before the House Oversight committee on February 24 in an effort to resolve the numerous unresolved unintended acceleration reports and to verify the root of the problem. In the two days of congressional hearings, the company sought to assure that an electronic glitch was not the culprit and that its recent recalls due to gas pedals potentially sticking to floor mats had solved the problem.[100]

While Akio Toyoda testified that electronics weren't to blame, Jim Lentz said he wasn't sure the current recalls had entirely solved the problem. This not only discredited any and all statements from both individuals, but also made many stakeholders question the communication within the company. This resulted in a crucial blow to Toyota's recovery efforts, and according to Rep. Bart Gordon of Tennessee, "raised more questions than answers."[101] A survey taken after the hearings revealed that 47% of respondents felt worse about Toyota's image after the hearings.[102] Shortly after the hearings, stories began surfacing that Toyota was now related to 52 deaths in regards to unintended acceleration.[103] The NHTSA also took a rare step in publicly criticizing the company's slow response in addressing and fixing the issue and eventually fined them a record $16.4 million on April 5, dwarfing the previous record of $1 million levied against General Motors in 2004 for an unsatisfactory response to a windshield wiper recall.[104]

6. Internal Discord

The discrepancies between Jim Lentz and Akio Toyoda in their Congressional testimonies were just a small example of the major role a lack internal communications played in turning this issue into a full-blown crisis. From the beginning, Toyota was inconsistent in what it was communicating through its response. But in order to best understand the extent in which internal communications suffered, one must look at the foundation of the company's managerial approach as a whole.

6.1 The Toyota Way

Toyota's business philosophy and values are summed up in a set of 14 principles dubbed *The Toyota Way*. This system consists of multiple principles in two key areas, with the first being continuous improvement, and the second being respect for people. Continuous improvement, according to the system, is built upon establishing a long-term vision, working on challenges, seeking continual innovation, and going to the source, or issue, of the problem.

Similarly, respect for people is built on taking responsibility, building mutual trust, and maximizing both individual and team performance.[105] This approach not only helped Toyota become one of the world's top car manufacturers, but also one of the world's top companies in general. Soon after the recalls, however, the company that appeared to put customers first had its reputation shattered by an e-mail that surfaced on April 8, 2010.[106]

6.2 A Crisis Made in Japan

Written in mid-January, just days before the company was plunged into its most damaging vehicle recall ever, the e-mail referred directly to company efforts to cover-up mechanical problems with accelerator pedals. Before January, Toyota had only acknowledged publicly that accelerator pedals could become stuck by becoming entangled in loose floormats. But the internal e-mails, which were quickly in the hands of U.S. investigators along with over 70,000 additional documents, revealed a tussle within Toyota's corporate leadership over whether or not to inform the public over more fundamental flaws in the pedal mechanism—problems that had not at the time been fully understood by Toyota's engineers and to which there was no clear "fix" available.[107]

Irv Miller, who has since retired but was then Toyota's vice president for public affairs, sent the e-mail in response to comments by his Japanese colleague, Katsuhiko Koganei—a senior executive who had been dispatched from Toyota's Japanese headquarters to coordinate with his U.S. colleagues. Mr. Koganei argued in a previous e-mail that the company "should not mention about the mechanical failures of the pedal," because the cause of the fault had not yet been identified and that a statement by Toyota would unsettle motorists.[108] "We are not protecting our customers by keeping this quiet," replied Mr. Miller, who went on to say, "WE HAVE a tendency for MECHANICAL failure in accelerator pedals of a certain manufacturer on certain models."[109] In response to the surfaced e-mail, Toyota quickly issued the following statement through the virtual newsroom on its website:

> While Toyota does not comment on internal company communications and cannot comment on Mr. Miller's email, we have publicly acknowledged on several occasions that the company did a poor job of communicating during the period preceding our recent recalls. We have subsequently taken a number of important steps to improve our communications with regulators and customers on safety-related matters to ensure that this does not happen again. These include the appointment of a new Chief Quality Officer for North America and a greater role for the region in making safety-related decisions. As part of our heightened commitment to quality assurance, we are fully committed to being more transparent.[110]

7. Responses of Toyota

7.1 Denial and Deception

Initially after the August 28, 2009 car crash in San Diego, Toyota's response to potential issues with SUA was limited to a recall of all-weather floor mats on September 29, an entire month after the accident, and public apologies to the Saylor family. However, these apologies came across as matter of fact alongside apologies for sputtering sales with no definitive and collective action taking place.[111] The first organized communication to Toyota owners occurred on October 30, exactly two months after the accident. A letter was sent to owners notifying them of an unspecified upcoming recall to fix the issue, claiming floor mats were the sole source of the problem and that "no defect exists."[112] In response to the letters, he NHTSA openly criticized the company for giving "inaccurate" and "misleading" statements, calling the proposed floor mat recall as an "interim" solution that didn't solve the underlying problem.[113]

Despite the NHTSA's claims, Toyota stood by their argument that all SUA cases were caused by floor mats entrapping the accelerator pedal. Throughout the months of October and November, Toyota communicated numerous conflicting messages that undermined their efforts to maintain trust with their stakeholders. Beginning with a *Los Angeles Times* story on October 18, a Toyota spokesperson admitted there was no safety override programmed into the vehicles' computers to disable the throttle pedal when the brake pedal is pressed.[114] Shortly thereafter, a November 8 *Los Angeles Times* article reported over 1,200 complaints of SUA had been ignored by Toyota over the past eight years. In the same story, a Toyota spokesperson admitted that the current brakes were "not capable of stopping a vehicle accelerating at wide open throttle."[115]

Toyota continued refuting claims by the *Los Angeles Times* and other media that a problem existed with their drive-by-wire electronic throttle system. The company took an active role in responding to media claims, which came across in some circles as overly defensive and aggressive, resulting in even more coverage and more attention to the issue. This all culminated with a letter written by Irv Miller to the *Los Angeles Times* on December 5 that reiterated the stance that floor mats were the root cause of the problem and defended the NHTSA and its methodology in a recent investigation on the matter.[116] Miller wrote:

> The issue of unintended acceleration involving Toyota and Lexus vehicles has been thoroughly and methodically investigated on several occasions over the past few years. These investigations have used a variety of proven and recognized scientific methods. Importantly, none of these studies has ever found that an electronic engine control system malfunction is the cause of unintended acceleration.[117]

While Toyota's response was delayed, it was sufficient at the time. That was until another event dismantled their floor mat defense and escalated this situation into a full-blown crisis. On December 26, a Toyota Avalon crashed after accelerating out of control in Southlake, Texas, killing all four passengers. The floor mats were found in the trunk of the car, as was instructed by Toyota, which ruled them out as a cause of SUA and raised serious issues concerning Toyota's credibility and transparency in communications.[118]

7.2 Action Promised but Not Delivered

After the Texas crash voided all claims that Toyota had fixed the problem of SUA, there was a total void in communication from Toyota. President and CEO Akio Toyoda was nowhere to be found, and there was still no plan of action set out by Toyota to actually solve the problem and ease the worries of Toyota drivers.[119] Toyota responded first by announcing that it would make its brake override software fix, which allowed the brakes to override the accelerator pedal when both are applied, global in all vehicles by 2011.[120] While this was a promising gesture, it did little to impact the issue at hand.

It wasn't until February 1, 2010, a full five weeks after the Texas crash, that Toyota announced that it had developed a fix for the accelerator pedals that could poten- tially stick in 2.3 million vehicles.[121] The announcement was made by Jim Lentz, a U.S. Toyota executive, and in the process raised even more questions as to why Mr. Toyoda or other Japanese executives were unable to address the crisis.[122] "By putting Mr. Lentz out front, Toyota was sending a regional sales executive to do a job that needed to be handled by the top management of the entire corporation," said Jeffery A. Sonnenfeld, a Yale University professor and president of the Chief Execu- tive Leadership Institute.[123] Mr. Lentz "is not a known quantity, and he wasn't able to reassure people that this problem was being addressed," said Arthur C. Liebler, a former Chrysler vice president and top communications adviser to Lee Iacocca.[124] Finally, on February 5, President Toyoda apologized for the car recalls and promised to beef up quality control within the company.[125]

7.3 A Clearer Picture

After the multiple recalls and the announcement of the accelerator pedal fix, Toyota implemented consistent action. A plan was developed to reassure the public that Toyota was committed to safety, and President Toyoda spotlighted the plan intended to rebuild its image and increase transparency in an editorial he wrote for the *Washington Post* on February 9, 2010.[126] In the letter, Toyoda stated:

> For much of Toyota's history, we have ensured the quality and reliability of our vehicles by placing a device called an andon cord on every production line—and empowering any team member to halt production if there's an assembly problem. Only when the problem is resolved does the line begin to move again. Two weeks ago, I pulled the andon cord for our company. I ordered production of eight models in five plants across North America temporarily stopped so that we could focus on fixing our customers' vehicles that might be affected by sticking accelerator pedals. Today, Toyota team members and dealers across North America are working around the clock to repair all recalled vehicles. But to regain the trust of American drivers and their families, more is needed. We are taking responsibility for our mistakes, learning from them and acting immediately to address the concerns of consumers and independent government regulators.[127]

The letter announced the launching of a "top-to-bottom review of global operations to ensure that problems of this magnitude do not happen again."[128] As part the review, he announced the establishment of "an Automotive Center of Quality Excellence in the United States, where a team of our top engineers will focus on strengthening our quality management and quality control across North America."[129]

The editorial also announced the establishment of what would become the North American Quality Advisory Panel, which would independently review the company's operations and make sure that any deficiencies were eliminated in its processes. The findings of these experts were stated be made available to the public, as will Toyota's responses to these findings, therefore increasing transparency and taking a tremendous step forward for the company in tackling this issue.[130]

Along with a promise to increase its outreach with government agencies and a pledge to implement steps to do a better job within Toyota in sharing important quality and safety information across global operations, the company made a vital move to bottle up the seemingly never-ending escapade. On April 8, the company announced it had established a new SMART (Swift Market Analysis Response Team) business process to quickly and aggressively investigate customer reports of unintended acceleration in Toyota, Lexus, and Scion vehicles in the United States.[131] As stated in a Toyota press release:

> The rapid-response **S**wift **M**arket **A**nalysis **R**esponse **T**eam will attempt to contact customers within 24 hours of receiving a complaint of unintended acceleration to arrange for a comprehensive on-site vehicle analysis ... There has been a great deal of confusion, speculation and misinformation about unintended acceleration in the past several weeks. We believe judgments should be based on reliable evidence, and our SMART business process is there to help provide information upon which such judgments can be made.[132]

7.4 Marketing Actions

In the U.S., Toyota launched a series of special television ads specifically created for the crisis that acknowledged the automaker had let down customers but emphasized that they were working "tirelessly to fix the problem." The company also announced a "blueprint for fixes" in regards to the problems through newspaper ads, television spots, and personalized letters to Toyota owners.[133] This "blueprint," developed and tested by Toyota engineers, involved "reinforcing the pedal assembly in a manner that eliminates the excess friction that has caused the pedals to stick in rare instances."[134]

This was crucial in that it was the first solution offered by Toyota to combat SUA. Toyota also announced plans to launch the company's most far-reaching sales program in its history in an effort to offset plummeting sales and to retain existing Toyota customers, offering numerous customer loyalty offers to existing Toyota owners.[135]

In addition, Toyota sought to reconnect with its customers. It began posting updates at Toyota.com regarding the recall and created a specific page dedicated to safety and recall information.[136] Toyota also began heavily leveraging social media outlets such as Twitter and Facebook to connect with the consumers. Toyota's top U.S. executive, Jim Lentz, also took a personal role in the efforts. Along with a personal apology posted to YouTube and the website, he held a live chat at Digg.com. In this venue, questions were posted by Digg.com users and were voted on, or "dugg," to determine which questions would be asked during the 30-minute interview, and in what order.[137] Other YouTube videos were posted that spotlighted real workers in the plants and dealerships demonstrating how the recall repairs would take place.[138]

The company realized that its ability to repair its reputation rested in large part on the level of service it provided. And realizing this on a local level, dealerships also took an active role in the rebound. Along with some dealerships staying open 24 hours to accommodate the demand for recall fixes, one dealership in El Monte, California took advantage of its surroundings and offered coffee, Subway sandwiches and even a shuttle service to a nearby movie theater if repairs were to last longer than three hours.[139]

8. The Toyota Way Back—What the Future Holds

8.1 Weathering the Storm

After the initial impact of the crisis passed, Toyota exhibited signs of economic recovery at a surprising rate. A February 11 report that took place during the recall efforts showed that a one-year-old Toyota Camry CE dropped $100 in value from February 1 to February 8 and a one-year-old base model Honda Accord coupe in the same book also dropped $100 in value from February 1 to February 8, and $500—or $100 more than the Camry—from the January 11 book. Even with Honda's reputation intact, it lost more value.[140] Another identifier that the recall woes were disappearing occurred in the sales reports from March 2010, where Toyota Motor Sales reported a 35.3% increase over the same period from the last year despite the multiple plant closings around the country.[141]

The final and clearest sign that Toyota was on the path to economic recovery was reported in early August 2010, one year after their troubles began. The company's second-quarter results included a $2.2 billion profit.[142] This eased fears in investors and allowed the company to raise predictions for annual vehicle sales to sell 7.38 million, up from an earlier forecast of 7.29 million.[143]

8.2 Critical Acclaim and Media Coverage

Despite the tremendous losses Toyota experienced throughout the SUA debacle, there was some much-needed good news delivered shortly after the peak of the problems. Not only did Toyota customers maintain a positive attitude toward the company throughout the recalls, but the company also continued to receive critical acclaim. Interbrand ranked Toyota 11th on its list of "Best Global Brands," placing it as the highest ranked automotive company.[144] *Consumer Report* also ranked Toyota as the "Most Highly Perceived Car Brand" in the market according to a survey that ranked brands across seven areas.[145] J.D. Power and Associates also awarded Toyota with four first place awards—more than any other brand.[146]

Another key development in the aftermath of Toyota's recalls would be reports on the validity of the coverage that took place throughout the crisis. According to an article in the August 2010 issue of *Forbes* magazine:

> Mounting evidence indicates that those Toyotas truly accelerating suddenly can probably be explained by sliding floor mats (since fixed) and drivers hitting the gas instead of the brake. That is, the media have been chasing a will-o'-the-wisp for the better part of a year, whipping car buyers and Congress into a frenzy.[147]

The NHTSA "complaint database," available on its website, was discovered to be very poorly monitored and resulted in many of the NHTSA "complaints" turning out to be merely comments. The NHTSA has no "sudden acceleration" category to select when reporting a claim on the database, but instead uses "speed control," meaning that some of the sudden-acceleration claims were combined with entries regarding vehicle sluggishness and a number of other subjects.[148] "In most stories referring to the NHTSA complaints," *Forbes* reported, "they all became runaway Toyotas."[149]

8.3 U.S. Government Developments

After the recalls, information also emerged that the U.S. government might have been withholding information from Toyota in regards to SUA during their investigations. A *Wall Street Journal* article stated that:

> The U.S. Department of Transportation has analyzed dozens of data recorders from Toyota Motor Corp. vehicles involved in accidents blamed on sudden acceleration and found that the throttles were wide open and the brakes weren't engaged at the time of the crash.[150]

Simply put, this suggests that some drivers who have claimed their Toyota vehicles suddenly accelerated out of control were mistakenly using the accelerator instead of the brakes. The initial findings of a recent NHTSA study of the data recorders are consistent with a 1989 government-sponsored study that blamed similar driver mistakes for a rash of sudden-acceleration reports involving Audi 5000 sedans.[151] The Toyota findings appeared to support Toyota's original position that sudden-acceleration reports involving its vehicles weren't caused by electronic glitches in computer-controlled throttle systems, as many alleged.[152]

9. Toyota's Challenge

The biggest concern facing Toyota in the wake of their communications crisis is whether they can continue their dominance in the automotive industry on the back of a reputation for quality and dependability when these very qualities have been compromised. This issue played out both externally, through the extensive media coverage, and internally, through the trials and tribulations brought forth through a breakdown in communication within the company. The events that transpired revealed many weaknesses within the automotive giant, but also presented just as many opportunities. Given the culture of Japanese corporations and the great pride they take in efficiency, acknowledging imperfections in their company was a huge step. During his Congressional testimony, Toyota President and CEO Akio Toyoda spoke of the future direction of Toyota:

> Toyota has, for the past few years, been expanding its business rapidly. Quite frankly, I fear the pace at which we have grown may have been too quick. I would like to point out here that Toyota's priority has traditionally been the following: First; Safety, Second; Quality, and Third; Volume. These priorities became con-fused, and we were not able to stop, think, and make improvements as much as

we were able to before . . . We pursued growth over the speed at which we were able to develop our people and our organization, and we should sincerely be mindful of that . . . I will do everything in my power to ensure that such a tragedy never happens again.[153]

Once Toyota's corporate leadership unified internally, the company was able to regain its footing, stand, and deliver. Albeit late, their efforts were fixated on the main goal: regaining trust. Toyota is now challenged to realign itself with the foundations that launched them to the level of success from which they ultimately fell. The issue of sudden unintended acceleration will not quickly go away. And while Toyota has made drastic strides in an effort to restore its once infallible reputation for safety and quality, each and every stakeholder and competitor will be watching to see if they will take the opportunity to use these events to their advantage and rediscover the Toyota way.

Chapter 1: Long Case Notes

* This case study was an entry for the Arthur W. Page Society 2011 Case Study Competition.

1 Channel 10 News, "4 Killed in Fiery Santee Crash Believed Identified," August 31, 2010. Accessed November 14, 2010 from http://www.10news.com/news/20609225/detail.html.

2 "Toyota Suspends Sales of Selected Vehicles," *Toyota USA Newsroom,* January 26, 2010. Accessed November 14, 2010 from http://pressroom.toyota.com/pr/tms/toyota/toyota-temporarily-suspends-sales-153126.aspx.

3 Strott, E., "Toyota Takes Sales Crown from GM," *MSN.com,* January 21, 2009. Accessed November 14, 2010 from http://articles.moneycentral.msn.com/Investing/Dispatch/Toyota-takes-sales-crown-from-GM.aspx.

4 Toyota Motor North America Inc., (n.d.), Toyota corporate website. Accessed November 14, 2010, from http://www.toyota.com/about/our_business/our_history/u.s._history/.

5 Toyota Motor North America Inc., http://www.toyota.com/about/our_business/our_history/u.s._history/.

6 Abilla, P., "Toyota Motor Corporation: Company History," Shmula.com, January 5, 2007. Accessed on November 14, 2010 from http://www.shmula.com/toyota-motor-corporation-company-history/291/.

7 "World Ranking of Manufacturers Year 2009," *Ocia.net.* (n.d.). Accessed November 14, 2010 from http://oica.net/wp-content/uploads/ranking-2009.pdf.

8 Abilla, "Toyota Motor Corporation: Company History."

9 Abilla, "Toyota Motor Corporation: Company History."

10 Abilla, "Toyota Motor Corporation: Company History."

11 Abilla, "Toyota Motor Corporation: Company History."

12 Toyota Motor North America, Inc. (n.d.) Toyota Corporate website. Accessed November 14, 2010 from http://www.toyota.com/about/environment/hybrids/.

13 Advance! Business Consulting, "The Rise of Toyota," (n.d.). Accessed on November 14, 2010 from http://www.advancebusinessconsulting.com/advance!/strategic-alignment/strategic-alignment-business-cases/the-rise-of-toyota.aspx.

14 "Toyota Production—A Brief Introduction," *Strategosinc.*com (n.d.). Accessed November 14, 2010 from http://www.strategosinc.com/toyota_production.htm.

15 Advance! Business Consulting, "The Rise of Toyota."

16 "2009 World's Most Ethical Companies," *Ethisphere.com* (n.d.). Accessed December 1, 2010 from http://ethisphere.com/wme2009/.

17 Toyota Motor North America, Inc. (n.d.) Toyota corporate website. Accessed November 15, 2010 from http://www.toyota.com/about/philanthropy/.

18 Toyota Motor North America, Inc., http://www.toyota.com/about/philanthropy/.

19 Toyota Motor North America, Inc., http://www.toyota.com/about/philanthropy/.

20 Pollard. J. & Sussman, E.D., "An Examination of Unintended Acceleration," autosafety.org. http://www.autosafety.org/sites/default/files/1989%20NHTSA%20SA%20Study%20Report%20&%20Appendices%20A-D(1).pdf (January 1989). [Original Source: An Examination of Unintended Acceleration (January 1989)].

21 Pollard & Sussman, "An Examination of Unintended Acceleration."

22 Linebaugh, K. & Searcey, D., "Cause of Sudden Acceleration Proves Hard to Pinpoint," *Wall Street Journal*, February 25, 2010. Accessed November 14, 2010 from http://online.wsj.com/article/SB10001424052748703510204575085531383717288.html?KEYWORDS=sudden+acceleration.

23 "A Timeline of Toyota Recall Woes," *CNN*, February 11, 2010. Accessed November 14, 2010 from http://blogs.hbr.org/research/2010/03/does-media-coverage-of-toyota.html.

24 Lavell, T., "Audi 1980's Scare May Mean Lost Generation for Toyota (Update1)," *Businessweek*, February 4, 2010. Accessed November 14, 2010 from http://www.businessweek.com/news/2010-02-04/audi-s-1980s-scare-may-mean-lost-generation-for-toyota-sales.html

25 Lavell, "Audi 1980's Scare."

26 Lavell, "Audi 1980's Scare."

27 Denning, S., "Toyota and the Strange Case of the Runaway Cars: Three Facts & Four Lessons," March 26, 2010. Accessed December 17, 2010 from http://www.stevedenning.com/slides/Toyota Mar22-2010.pdf.

28 Denning, "Toyota and the Strange Case of the Runaway Cars."

29 Phillips, M., "Getting Toyota Back on Track," *Newsweek*, February 10, 2010. Accessed December 16, 2010 from http://www.newsweek.com/2010/02/09/getting-toyota-back-on-track.html.

30 Pollard & Sussman, "An Examination of Unintended Acceleration."

31 Channel 10 News, "4 Killed in Fiery Santee Crash Believed Identified," August 31, 2010. Accessed November 14, 2010 from http://www.10news.com/news/20609225/detail.html.

32 Channel 10 News, "4 Killed in Fiery Santee Crash Believed Identified."

33 Channel 10 News, "4 Killed in Fiery Santee Crash Believed Identified."

34 Channel 10 News, "4 Killed in Fiery Santee Crash Believed Identified."

35 Ross, B., ABC News, "Expert Recreates Sudden Acceleration in Toyota." Accessed November 14, 2010 from http://abcnews.go.com/Blotter/video/testing-toyota-9914148 (February 22, 2010).

36 O'Donnell, J., "Toyota Executive Urged Board to 'Come Clean'," *USA Today*, February 26, 2010. Accessed November 14, 2010 from http://www.usatoday.com/money/autos/2010-02-26-toyota26_ST_N.htm.

37 "Comprehensive Analysis Raises Concerns About Gilbert Congressional Testimony, ABC News Segment," *Toyota Press Room*, March 8, 2010. Accessed December 1, 2010 from http://pressroom.toyota.com/pr/tms/electronic-throttle-control-154300.aspx.

38 Channel 10 News, "4 Killed in Fiery Santee Crash Believed Identified."

39 "Lexus ES 350 Accident Investigation," *Toyota USA Newsroom*, September 14, 2009. Accessed November 14, 2010 from http://pressroom.toyota.com/pr/tms/statement-from-toyota-motor-sales-101993.aspx.

40 "Toyota/Lexus Safety Advisory: Potential Floor Mat Interference with Accelerator Pedal," *Toyota Press Room*, September 29, 2009. Accessed November 14, 2010 from http://pressroom.toyota.com/pr/tms/toyota-lexus-consumer-safety-advisory-102565.aspx.

41 "Toyota Reports September Sales," *Toyota Press Room*, October 1, 2009. Accessed November 14, 2010 from http://pressroom.toyota.com/pr/tms/toyota-reports-september-sales-102662.aspx.

42 Moore, B., "Toyota Offers Very Public Remorse for Financial Results," *Autosavant*, October 2, 2009. Accessed November 14, 2010 from http://www.autosavant.com/2009/10/02/toyota-offers-very-public-remorse-for-financial-results/.

43 Vartabedian, R. & Bensinger, K., "Toyota's Runaway-Car Worries May Not Stop at Floor Mats," *Los Angeles Times*, October 18, 2009. Accessed November 14, 2010 from http://articles.latimes.com/2009/oct/18/business/fi-toyota-recall18.

44 "NHTSA Unwanted and Unintended Acceleration Investigation Summary," *Toyota Press Room,* October 25, 2009. Accessed November 14, 2010 from http://pressroom.toyota.com/pr/tms/document/NHTSA_filing_summary.pdf.

45 Vartabedian, R. & Bensinger, K., "New Details in Crash That Prompted Toyota Recall," *Los Angeles Times,* October 25, 2009. Accessed November 14, 2010 from http://articles.latimes.com/2009/oct/25/nation/na-toyota-crash25.

46 "Potential Floor Mat Interference with Accelerator Pedal Safety Recall Campaign," *Toyota Press Room,* October 30, 2009. Accessed November 14, 2010 from http://pressroom.toyota.com/pr/tms/document/Floor_mat_Owner_Letter_sample.pdf.

47 Ireson, N., "NHTSA: Toyota Floor Mat Statement 'Inaccurate and Misleading'," *Motorauthority. com,* November 5, 2009. Accessed November 14, 2010 from http://www.motorauthority.com/blog/1037688_nhtsa-toyota-floor-mat-statement-inaccurate-and-misleading.

48 Miller, I., "Toyota's Statement Regarding NHTSA News Release," *Toyota Press Room,* November 4, 2009. Accessed November 14, 2010 from http://pressroom.toyota.com/pr/tms/toyota-s-response-to-nhtsa-news-release.aspx.

49 Vartabedian, R. & Bensinger, K., "Toyota's Runaway Cases Ignored," *Los Angeles Times,* November 8, 2009. Accessed November 14, 2010 from http://articles.latimes.com/2009/oct/18/business/fi-toyota-recall18.

50 Lawson, H., "Toyota to Fix Accelerators in Huge US Recall – Kyodo," *Reuters,* November 13, 2009. Accessed November 14, 2010 from http://www.reuters.com/article/idUST12766820091114.

51 "Toyota Announces Details of Remedy to Address Potential Accelerator Pedal Entrapment," *Toyota Press Room,* November 25, 2009. Accessed November 14, 2010 from http://pressroom.toyota.com/pr/tms/lexus/lexus-consumer-safety-advisory-102574.aspx.

52 Editorial, "Toyota's Acceleration Issue," *Los Angeles Times,* December 5, 2009. Accessed November 14, 2010 from http://articles.latimes.com/2009/dec/05/opinion/la-ed-toyota5-2009dec05.

53 Miller, I., "A Healthy Discussion on Safety," *Toyota Press Room,* December 5, 2009. Accessed November 14, 2010 from http://pressroom.toyota.com/pr/tms/our-point-of-view-post.aspx?id=2331.

54 Diaz, M. & Trahan, J., "Four Dead After Car Plunges into Southlake Pond," *WFAA News,* December 27, 2009. Accessed November 14, 2010 from www.wfaa.com/news/local/accident-80138632.html.

55 Loh, E., "Toyota to Include Brake Override Function on Global Vehicles by 2011," *Motortrend. com,* January 11, 2010. Accessed November 14, 2010 from http://wot.motortrend.com/toyota-to-include-brake-override-function-on-global-vehicles-by-2011–7183.html.

56 "Toyota Files Voluntary Safety Recall on Select Toyota Division Vehicles for Sticking Accelerator Pedal," *Toyota Press Room,* January 21, 2010. Accessed November 14, 2010 from http://pressroom.toyota.com/pr/tms/toyota/toyota-files-voluntary-safety-152979.aspx.

57 "Toyota Suspends Sales of Selected Vehicles," *Toyota USA Newsroom,* January 26, 2010. Accessed November 14, 2010 from http://pressroom.toyota.com/pr/tms/toyota/toyota-temporarily-suspends-sales-153126.aspx.

58 Ellis, B. & Valdes-Dapena, P., "Toyota's Big Recall Halts Sales, Production of 8 Models," *CNNMoney.com,* February 10, 2010. Accessed November 14, 2010 from http://money.cnn.com/2010/01/26/news/companies/toyota_recall/index.htm.

59 Maynard, M. & Tabuchi, H., "Rapid Growth Has its Perils, Toyota Learns," *New York Times,* January 27, 2010. Accessed November 14, 2010 from http://www.nytimes.com/2010/01/28/business/28toyota.html.

60 Tibken, S., "Auto Shares with Toyota Exposure Drop," *Wall Street Journal,* January 27, 2010. Accessed November 14, 2010 from http://online.wsj.com/article/SB10001424052748704094304575029210878935490.html.

61 Tibken, "Auto Shares with Toyota Exposure Drop."

62 "Toyota Announces Comprehensive Plan to Fix Accelerator Pedals on Recalled Vehicles to Ensure Customer Safety," *Toyota Press Room,* February 1, 2010. Accessed November 14, 2010 from http://pressroom.toyota.com/pr/tms/toyota/toyota-announces-comprehensive-153311.aspx.

63 Tabuchi, H. & Vlasic, B., "Toyota's Top Executive Under Rising Pressure," *New York Times,* February 5, 2010. Accessed November 14, 2010 from http://www.nytimes.com/2010/02/06/business/global/06toyota.html?_r=2l.

64 Tabuchi & Vlasic, "Toyota's Top Executive Under Rising Pressure."

65 Toyoda, A., "Toyota's Plan to Repair its Public Image," *Washington Post*, February 9, 2010. Accessed December 1, 2010 from http://www.washingtonpost.com/wp-dyn/content/article/2010/02/08/AR2010020803078.html.

66 Crawley, J. & Kim, S., "Toyota Recalls New Prius in Latest Safety Fix," *Reuters*, February 9, 2010. Accessed December 2, 2010 from http://www.reuters.com/article/idUSTRE6133U820100209.

67 "Prepared Testimony of James Lentz," *Toyota Press Room*, February 21, 2010. Accessed November 14, 2010 from http://pressroom.toyota.com/pr/tms/document/Lentz_Testimony_to_House_Committee_on_Energy_and_Commerce.pdf.

68 "Prepared Testimony of Akio Toyoda," *Toyota Press Room*, February 23, 2010. Accessed November 14, 2010 from http://pressroom.toyota.com/pr/tms/document/A._Toyoda_Testimony_to_House_Committee_on_Oversight_and_Government_Reform_2–24–10.pdf.

69 "Former U.S. Secretary of Transportation Rodney Slater to Lead Independent North American Quality Advisor Panel for Toyota," *Toyota Press Room*, March 2, 2010. Accessed November 14, 2010 from http://pressroom.toyota.com/pr/tms/former-u-s-secretary-of-transportation-154569.aspx.

70 "Toyota Announces March Sales Event," *Toyota Press Room*, March 2, 2010. Accessed November 14, 2010 from http://pressroom.toyota.com/pr/tms/toyota-announces-march-sales-event-154598.aspx.

71 Thomas, K., "US to seek $16 Million over Toyota Recall," *msnbc.com*, April 5, 2010. Accessed November 14, 2010 from http://www.msnbc.msn.com/id/36181616/ns/business-autos/.

72 Associated Press, "Toyota Won't Contest $16.4 Million Civil Fine," *CBSNews.com*, April 18, 2010. Accessed November 14, 2010 from http://www.cbsnews.com/stories/2010/04/18/business/main6409394.shtml.

73 "Toyota Announces 'SMART' Business Process for Quick Evaluation of Unintended Acceleration Reports," *Toyota Press Room*, April 8, 2010. Accessed November 14, 2010 from http://pressroom.toyota.com/pr/tms/toyota-announces-smart-business-156380.aspx.

74 Guardian Research, "BP Oil Spill Timeline," *Guardian* [U.K.], July 22, 2010. Accessed November 14, 2010 from http://www.guardian.co.uk/environment/2010/jun/29/bp-oil-spill-timeline-deepwater-horizon.

75 Associated Press, "Toyota Pays Record $16.4 million Govt Fine," *Boston Herald*, May 18, 2010. Accessed December 4, 2010 from http://www.bostonherald.com/business/automotive/view/20100518source_toyota_pays_record_164m_govt_fine/srvc=home&position=also.

76 Tabuchi, H., "Toyota Recovers from a Slump to Record a $2.2 Billion Profit," *New York Times*, August 4, 2010. Accessed November 14, 2010 from http://www.nytimes.com/2010/08/05/business/global/05toyota.html?_r=1.

77 Mittal, V., Sambandam, R. & Dholakia, U.M., "Does Media Coverage of Toyota Recalls Reflect Reality?," *The Economist*, March 9, 2010. Accessed November 14, 2010 from http://blogs.hbr.org/research/2010/03/does-media-coverage-of-toyota.html.

78 Starkman, D., "Toyota No Longer Attacking the L.A. Times," *Columbia Journalism Review*, February 3, 2010. Accessed November 14, 2010 from http://www.cjr.org/the_audit/toyota_no_longer_attacking_the.php?page=1.

79 Susman, T., "Nonprofit Newsroom wins Pulitzer Prize," *Los Angeles Times*, April 13, 2010. Accessed December 2, 2010 from http://articles.latimes.com/2010/apr/13/nation/la-na-pulitzer-prizes13–2010apr1.

80 Hyde, J., "Toyota Safety Recalls were Years in the Making," *USA Today*, February 1, 2010. Accessed November 14, 2010 from http://www.usatoday.com/money/autos/2010–02–01-toyotafreep01_ST_N.htm.

81 Schumpeter, "Getting the Cow Out of the Ditch," *The Economist*, February 11, 2010. Accessed November 14, 2010 from http://www.economist.com/node/15496136.

82 Ireson, N., "NHTSA: Toyota Floor Mat Statement 'Inaccurate and Misleading'," *Motorauthority.com*, November 5, 2009. Accessed November 14, 2010 from http://www.motorauthority.com/blog/1037688_nhtsa-toyota-floor-mat-statement-inaccurate-and-misleading.

83 Autoevolution, "Customers Stay Loyal to Toyota Survey Shows," March 15, 2010. Accessed November 14, 2010 from http://www.autoevolution.com/news/customers-stay-loyal-to-toyota-survey-shows-18037.html.

84 Belsie, L., "Toyota Recall: Is This Any Way to Treat a Customer?," *Christian Science Monitor,* January 27, 2010. Accessed November 14, 2010 from http://www.csmonitor.com/Business/new-economy/2010/0127/Toyota-recall-Is-this-any-way-to-treat-a-customer.

85 Belsie, "Toyota Recall."

86 Ramsey, M. & Linebaugh, K., "Early Tests Pin Toyota Accidents on Drivers," *Wall Street Journal,* July 13, 2010. Accessed December 1, 2010 from http://online.wsj.com/article/SB10001424052748 703834604575364871534435744.html?mod=WSJ_hpp_LEADNewsCollection.

87 "Make or Brake," *The Economist,* January 27, 2010. Accessed November 14, 2010 from http://www.economist.com/node/15390573.

88 "Make or Brake," *The Economist.*

89 Bailey, D. & Krolicki, K., "Toyota U.S. Sales Reel from Crisis; GM, Ford Surge," *Reuters,* February 2, 2010. Accessed November 14, 2010 from http://www.reuters.com/article/idUSTRE6114BW2010 0203.

90 Haq, H., "Toyota Recall Update: Dealers Face Full Lots, Anxious Customers," *Christian Science Monitor,* January 29, 2010. Accessed November 14, 2010 from http://www.csmonitor.com/USA/2010/0129/Toyota-recall-update-dealers-face-full-lots-anxious-customers.

91 "Make or Brake," *The Economist.*

92 Bailey & Krolicki, "Toyota U.S. Sales Reel from Crisis."

93 Bailey & Krolicki, "Toyota U.S. Sales Reel from Crisis."

94 Bailey & Krolicki, "Toyota U.S. Sales Reel from Crisis."

95 Haq, "Toyota Recall Update."

96 Strott, E., "Toyota Takes Sales Crown from GM," *MSN.com,* January 21, 2009. Accessed November 14, 2010 from http://articles.moneycentral.msn.com/Investing/Dispatch/Toyota-takes-sales-crown-from-GM.aspx.

97 Strott, "Toyota Takes Sales Crown from GM."

98 National Highway Traffic Safety Administration, March 30, 2010. NHTSA website. Accessed November 14, 2010 from www.wfaa.com/news/local/accident-80138632.html.

99 Strott, "Toyota Takes Sales Crown from GM."

100 O'Donnell, J., "Toyota Executive Urged Board to 'Come Clean'," *USA Today,* February 26, 2010. Accessed November 14, 2010 from http://www.usatoday.com/money/autos/2010-02-26-toyota 26_ST_N.htm.

101 O'Donnell, "Toyota Executive Urged Board to 'Come Clean'."

102 LaBeau, P., CNBC, "Toyota's PR Blitz," CNBC, February 8, 2010. Accessed November 14, 2010 from http://classic.cnbc.com/id/15840232?video=1428263861&play=1.

103 Frean, A., "Death Toll Linked to US Toyota Faults Rises to 52," *Sunday Times,* March 2, 2010. Accessed November 14, 2010 from http://business.timesonline.co.uk/tol/business/industry_sectors/engineering/article7047177.ece.

104 Thomas, K., "US to Seek $16 Million Over Toyota Recall," *msnbc.com,* April 5, 2010. Accessed November 14, 2010 from http://www.msnbc.msn.com/id/36181616/ns/business-autos/.

105 Liker, J., *The Toyota Way* (2004) pp. 35–41. Accessed November 14, 2010 from http://icos.groups.si.umich.edu/Liker04.pdf.

106 Lewis, L., "Toyota Executive Urged Board to 'Come Clean'," *Sunday Times,* April 8, 2010. Accessed December 2, 2010 from http://business.timesonline.co.uk/tol/business/industry_sectors/engineering/article7091326.ece.

107 Lewis, "Toyota Executive Urged Board to 'Come Clean'."

108 Lewis, "Toyota Executive Urged Board to 'Come Clean'."

109 Lewis, "Toyota Executive Urged Board to 'Come Clean'."

110 "Toyota Statement on Internal Communications Regarding Our Recent Recalls," *Toyota Press Room*, April 8, 2010. Accessed November 14, 2010 from http://pressroom.toyota.com/pr/tms/toyota-statement-on-internal-communications-156383.aspx.

111 Moore, B., "Toyota Offers Very Public Remorse for Financial Results," *Autosavant,* October 2, 2009. Accessed November 14, 2010 from http://www.autosavant.com/2009/10/02/toyota-offers-very-public-remorse-for-financial-results/.

112 "Potential Floor Mat Interference with Accelerator Pedal Safety Recall Campaign," *Toyota Press Room,* October 30, 2009. Accessed November 14, 2010 from http://pressroom.toyota.com/pr/tms/document/Floor_mat_Owner_Letter_sample.pdf.

113 Ireson, N., "NHTSA: Toyota Floor Mat Statement 'Inaccurate and Misleading'," *Motorauthority. com,* November 5, 2009. Accessed November 14, 2010 from http://www.motorauthority.com/blog/1037688_nhtsa-toyota-floor-mat-statement-inaccurate-and-misleading.

114 Vartabedian, R. and Bensinger, K., "Toyota's Runaway-Car Worries May Not Stop at Floor Mats," *Los Angeles Times,* October 18, 2009. Accessed November 14, 2010 from http://articles.latimes.com/2009/oct/18/business/fi-toyota-recall18.

115 Vartabedian, R. and Bensinger, K., "Toyota's Runaway Cases Ignored," *The Los Angeles Times,* November 8, 2009. Accessed November 14, 2010 from http://articles.latimes.com/2009/oct/18/business/fi-toyota-recall18.

116 Vartabedian & Bensinger, "Toyota's Runaway Cases Ignored."

117 Vartabedian & Bensinger, "Toyota's Runaway Cases Ignored."

118 Diaz, M. & Trahan, J., "Four Dead After Car Plunges into Southlake Pond," *WFAA News,* December 27, 2009. Accessed November 14, 2010 from www.wfaa.com/news/local/accident-80138632.html.

119 Tabuchi, H. and Vlasic, B., "Toyota's Top Executive Under Rising Pressure," *New York Times,* February 5, 2010. Accessed November 14, 2010 from http://www.nytimes.com/2010/02/06/business/global/06toyota.html?_r=2l.

120 Loh, E., "Toyota to Include Brake Override Function on Global Vehicles by 2011," *Motortrend.com,* January 11, 2010. Accessed November 14, 2010 from http://wot.motortrend.com/toyota-to-include-brake-override-function-on-global-vehicles-by-2011–7183.html.

121 Tabuchi & Vlasic, "Toyota's Top Executive Under Rising Pressure."

122 Tabuchi & Vlasic, "Toyota's Top Executive Under Rising Pressure."

123 Tabuchi & Vlasic, "Toyota's Top Executive Under Rising Pressure."

124 Tabuchi & Vlasic, "Toyota's Top Executive Under Rising Pressure."

125 Tabuchi & Vlasic, "Toyota's Top Executive Under Rising Pressure."

126 Toyoda, A., "Toyota's Plan to Repair its Public Image," *Washington Post,* February 9, 2010. Accessed December 1, 2010 from http://www.washingtonpost.com/wp-dyn/content/article/2010/02/08/AR2010020803078.html.

127 Toyoda, "Toyota's Plan to Repair its Public Image."

128 Toyoda, "Toyota's Plan to Repair its Public Image."

129 Toyoda, "Toyota's Plan to Repair its Public Image."

130 "Former U.S. Secretary of Transportation Rodney Slater to Lead Independent North American Quality Advisor Panel for Toyota," *Toyota Press Room,* March 2, 2010. Accessed November 14, 2010 from http://pressroom.toyota.com/pr/tms/former-u-s-secretary-of-transportation-154569.aspx.

131 "Toyota Announces 'SMART' Business Process for Quick Evaluation of Unintended Acceleration Reports," *Toyota Press Room,* April 8, 2010. Accessed November 14, 2010 from http://pressroom.toyota.com/pr/tms/toyota-announces-smart-business-156380.aspx.

132 "Toyota Announces 'SMART' Business Process," *Toyota Press Room.*

133 O'Donnell, J., "Toyota Executive Urged Board to 'Come Clean'," *USA Today*, February 26, 2010. Accessed November 14, 2010 from http://www.usatoday.com/money/autos/2010–02–26-toyota26_ST_N.htm.

134 "Toyota Announces Comprehensive Plan to Fix Accelerator Pedals on Recalled Vehicles to Ensure Customer Safety," *Toyota Press Room,* February 1, 2010. Accessed November 14, 2010 from http://pressroom.toyota.com/pr/tms/toyota/toyota-announces-comprehensive-153311.aspx.

135 "Toyota Announces March Sales Event," *Toyota Press Room,* March 2, 2010. Accessed November 14, 2010 from http://pressroom.toyota.com/pr/tms/toyota-announces-march-sales-event-154598.aspx.

136 Toyota Motor Sales, U.S.A., Inc., "Important Message," February 5, 2010. Accessed November 14, 2010 from http://www.toyota.com/recall/videos/jim-lentz-important-message.html.

137 Talarico, D., "Toyota Recall, Spin & Social Media: A PR Crisis Case Study in the Making," *Social Media and PR: Class Blog,* February 5, 2010. Accessed November 14, 2010 from http://prandsocialmedia.wordpress.com/2010/02/05/toyota-recall-spin-social-media-a-pr-crisis-case-study-in-the-making/.

138 Toyota Motor Sales, U.S.A., Inc., "Toyota Team Members Discuss Toyota's Improvements," February 8, 2010. Accessed November 14, 2010 from http://www.toyota.com/recall/videos/kentucky-plant-improvements.html.

139 Wallace, E., "The Real Scandal Behind the Toyota Recall," *Businessweek,* February 11, 2010. Accessed November 14, 2010 from http://www.businessweek.com/lifestyle/content/feb2010/bw20100211_986136.htm.

140 Wallace, "The Real Scandal Behind the Toyota Recall."

141 Wallace, "The Real Scandal Behind the Toyota Recall."

142 Wallace, "The Real Scandal Behind the Toyota Recall."

143 Wallace, "The Real Scandal Behind the Toyota Recall."

144 Interbrand (September 2010). Interbrand website. Accessed November 14, 2010 from http://www.interbrand.com/en/knowledge/best-global-brands/best-global-brands-2008/best-global-brands-2010.aspx.

145 Consumer Reports Brand Perception Survey (January 2008). Consumer Reports website. Accessed November 14, 2010 from http://www.consumerreports.org/cro/cars/new-cars/news/2008/01/brand-perceptions/overview/brand-perceptions-top-5.htm.

146 "Toyota Motor Sales, U.S.A., Inc. Comments on J.D. Power and Associates 2010 Vehicle Dependability Study," *Toyota Press Room,* March 18, 2010. Accessed November 14, 2010 from http://pressroom.toyota.com/pr/tms/document/2010_JD_Power_VDS_TMS_Statement.pdf.

147 Fumento, M., "Why Didn't the Media Do a Better Job on Toyota," *Forbes,* August 9, 2010. Accessed November 18, 2010 from http://www.forbes.com/forbes/2010/0809/opinions-toyota-cars-acceleration-brakes-93-and-counting.html.

148 Fumento, "Why Didn't the Media Do a Better Job on Toyota."

149 Fumento, "Why Didn't the Media Do a Better Job on Toyota."

150 Ramsey, M. & Linebaugh, K., "Early Tests Pin Toyota Accidents on Drivers," *Wall Street Journal,* July 13, 2010. Accessed December 1, 2010 from http://online.wsj.com/article/SB10001424052748703834604575364871534435744.html?mod=WSJ_hpp_LEADNewsCollection.

151 Ramsey & Linebaugh, "Early Tests Pin Toyota Accidents on Drivers."

152 Ramsey & Linebaugh, "Early Tests Pin Toyota Accidents on Drivers."

153 "Prepared Testimony of Akio Toyoda," *Toyota Press Room,* February 23, 2010. Accessed November 14, 2010 from http://pressroom.toyota.com/pr/tms/document/A._Toyoda_Testimony_to_House_Committee_on_Oversight_and_Government_Reform_2–24–10.pdf.

APPENDIX 1.1
International Organization of Motor Vehicle Manufacturers World Ranking of Automotive Manufacturers for the Year 2009—Top 50 Shown

WORLD MOTOR VEHICLE PRODUCTION
OICA correspondents survey
WITHOUT DOUBLE COUNTS

WORLD RANKING OF MANUFACTURERS
YEAR 2009

Rank	GROUP	Total	CARS	LCV	HCV	HEAVY BUS
	Total	60,499,159	51,075,480	7,817,520	1,305,755	300,404
1	TOYOTA	7,234,439	6,148,794	927,206	154,361	4,078
2	G.M.	6,459,053	4,997,824	1,447,625	7,027	6,577
3	VOLKSWAGEN	6,067,208	5,902,583	154,874	7,471	2,280
4	FORD	4,685,364	2,952,026	1,681,151	52,217	
5	HYUNDAI	4,645,776	4,222,532	324,979		98,265
6	PSA	3,042,311	2,769,902	272,409		
7	HONDA	3,012,637	2,984,011	28,626		
8	NISSAN	2,744,562	2,381,260	304,502	58,800	
9	FIAT	2,460,222	1,958,021	397,889	72,291	32,021
10	SUZUKI	2,387,537	2,103,553	283,984		
11	RENAULT	2,296,009	2,044,106	251,903		
12	DAIMLER AG	1,447,953	1,055,169	158,325	183,153	51,306
13	CHANA AUTOMOBILE	1,425,777	1,425,777			
14	B.M.W.	1,258,417	1,258,417			
15	MAZDA	984,520	920,892	62,305	1,323	
16	CHRYSLER	959,070	211,160	744,210	3,700	
17	MITSUBISHI	802,463	715,773	83,319	3,371	
18	BEIJING AUTOMOTIVE	684,534	684,534			
19	TATA	672,045	376,514	172,487	103,665	19,379
20	DONGFENG MOTOR	663,262	663,262			
21	FAW	650,275	650,275			
22	CHERY	508,567	508,567			
23	FUJI	491,352	440,229	51,123		
24	BYD	427,732	427,732			
25	SAIC	347,598	347,598			
26	ANHUI JIANGHUAI	336,979	336,979			
27	GEELY	330,275	330,275			
28	ISUZU	316,335		18,839	295,449	2,047
29	BRILLIANCE	314,189	314,189			
30	AVTOVAZ	294,737	294,737			
31	GREAT WALL	226,560	226,560			
32	MAHINDRA	223,065	145,977	77,088		
33	SHANGDONG KAIMA	169,023	169,023			
34	PROTON	152,965	129,741	23,224		
35	CHINA NATIONAL	120,930		120,930		
36	VOLVO	105,873		10,032	85,036	10,805
37	CHONGQING LIFAN	104,434	104,434			
38	FUJIAN	103,171	103,171			
39	KUOZUI	93,303	88,801	2,624	1,878	
40	SHANNXI AUTO	79,026		79,026		
41	PORSCHE	75,637	75,637			
42	ZIYANG NANJUN	72,470	72,470			
43	GAZ	69,591	2,161	44,816	12,988	9,626
44	NAVISTAR	65,364			51,544	13,820
45	GUANGZHOU AUTO	62,990	62,990			
46	PACCAR	58,918			58,918	
47	CHENZHOU JI'AO	51,008	51,008			
48	QINGLING MOTOR	50,120	50,120			
49	HEBEI ZHONGXING	48,173	48,173			
50	ASHOK LEYLAND	47,694		1,101	28,183	18,410

Source: "World Ranking of Manufacturers Year 2009," *Oica.net.* (n.d.). Accessed November 14, 2010 from http://oica.net/wp-content/uploads/ranking-2009.pdf.

APPENDIX 1.2
Personal recall letter sent from Jim Lentz, President and CEO Toyota Motors U.S.A., Inc.

The letter asked owners to bring in cars if problems were experienced. It announced that the "entire organization" was involved in the effort.

Over the past few days, there has been a lot of speculation about our sticking accelerator pedal recall. Our message to Toyota owners is this—if you are not experiencing any issues with your accelerator pedal, we are confident that your vehicle is safe to drive. If your accelerator pedal becomes harder to depress than normal or slower to return, please contact your dealer without delay.

At Toyota, we take this issue very seriously, but I want to make sure our customers understand that this situation is rare and generally doesn't occur suddenly. In the instance where it does occur, the vehicle can be controlled with firm and steady application of the brakes.

Here's the update on the recall:

1. We're starting to send letters this weekend to owners involved in the recall to schedule an appointment at their dealer.

2. Dealerships have extended their hours—some of them working 24/7—to fix your vehicle as quickly as possible.

3. Trained technicians have begun making repairs.

We've halted production of these models this week to focus fully on fixing this problem for the vehicles that are on the road.

Our entire organization of 172,000 North American employees and dealership personnel has been mobilized. And we're redoubling our quality control efforts across the company.

Ensuring your safety is our highest priority. I will continue to update you with accurate and timely information about the status of the recall in the days and weeks ahead.

Sincerely,

Jim Lentz

Source: http://injury.findlaw.com/toyota/toyota-recall-letter-jim-lentz/.

APPENDIX 1.3
November 25, 2009 press release

Toyota Announces Details of Remedy to Address Potential Accelerator Pedal Entrapment

Torrance, Calif., November 25, 2009—Toyota Motor Sales, U.S.A., Inc. (TMS) announced today details of the vehicle-based remedy to address the root cause of the potential risk for floor mat entrapment of accelerator pedals in certain Toyota and Lexus models. Toyota issued a consumer safety advisory on September 29 on this issue and has, as an interim measure, commenced the mailing of safety notices to certain Toyota and Lexus owners on October 30.

The models involved are: 2007 to 2010 MY (model year) Camry, 2005 to 2010 MY Avalon, 2004 to 2009 MY Prius, 2005 to 2010 MY Tacoma, 2007 to 2010 MY Tundra, 2007 to 2010 MY ES 350, 2006 to 2010 MY IS 250, and 2006 to 2010 MY IS 350.

The specific measures of the vehicle-based remedy are as follows:

1. The shape of the accelerator pedal will be reconfigured to address the risk of floor mat entrapment, even when an older-design all-weather floor mat or other inappropriate floor mat is improperly attached, or is placed on top of another floor mat. For the ES350, Camry, and Avalon models involved, the shape of the floor surface underneath will also be reconfigured to increase the space between the accelerator pedal and the floor.

2. Vehicles with any genuine Toyota or Lexus accessory all-weather floor mat will be provided with newly designed replacement driver- and front passenger-side all-weather floor mats.

In addition, as a separate measure independent of the vehicle-based remedy, Toyota will install a brake override system onto the involved Camry, Avalon, and Lexus ES 350, IS 350, and IS 250 models as an extra measure of confidence. This system cuts engine power in case of simultaneous application of both the accelerator and brake pedals.

Toyota is in the process of completing development of these actions and for the ES 350, Camry, and Avalon will start notifying owners of the involved vehicles via first-class mail by the end of this year. The remedy process regarding the other five models will occur on a rolling schedule during 2010.

Dealers will be trained and equipped to make the necessary modifications to these models starting at the beginning of 2010. Initially, dealers will be instructed on how to reshape the accelerator pedal for the repair. As replacement parts with the same shape as the modified pedal become available, they will be made available to dealers for the repair, beginning around April 2010. Customers who have had the remedy completed will have the opportunity to receive a new pedal if they desire.

In the meantime, owners of the involved vehicles are asked to take out any removable driver's floor mat and not replace it with any other floor mat until they are notified of the vehicle-based remedy, as notified in the consumer safety advisory and the interim notice.

The brake override system will be made standard equipment throughout the Toyota and Lexus product lines starting with January 2010 production of ES 350 and Camry and is scheduled to be incorporated into new production of most models by the end of 2010.

The safety of our owners and the public is our utmost concern and Toyota has and will continue to thoroughly investigate and take appropriate measures to address any defect trends that are identified.

Source: "Toyota Announces Details of Remedy to Address Potential Accelerator Pedal Entrapment," *Toyota Press Room*, November 25, 2009. Accessed November 14, 2010 from http://pressroom. toyota.com/pr/tms/lexus/lexus-consumer-safety-advisory-102574.aspx.

APPENDIX 1.4
February 1, 2010 press release

Toyota Announces Comprehensive Plan to Fix Accelerator Pedals on Recalled Vehicles and Ensure Customer Safety

TORRANCE, Calif., February 1, 2010—Toyota Motor Sales (TMS) U.S.A., Inc., today announced it will begin fixing accelerator pedals in recalled Toyota Division vehicles this week. Toyota's engineers have developed and rigorously tested a solution that involves reinforcing the pedal assembly in a manner that eliminates the excess friction that has caused the pedals to stick in rare instances. In addition, Toyota has developed an effective solution for vehicles in production.

Parts to reinforce the pedals are already being shipped for use by dealers, and dealer training is under way. Many Toyota dealers will work extended hours to complete the recall campaign as quickly and conveniently as possible, some even staying open 24 hours a day. The company has also taken the unprecedented action of stopping production of affected vehicles for the week of February 1.

"Nothing is more important to us than the safety and reliability of the vehicles our customers drive," said Jim Lentz, president and Chief Operating Officer, TMS. "We deeply regret the concern that our recalls have caused for our customers and we are doing everything we can—as fast as we can—to make things right. Stopping production is never an easy decision, but we are 100% confident it was the right decision. We know what's causing the sticking accelerator pedals, and we know what we have to do to fix it. We also know it is most important to fix this problem in the cars on the road."

Lentz added: "We are focused on making this recall as simple and trouble-free as possible, and will work day and night with our dealers to fix recalled vehicles quickly. We want to demonstrate that our commitment to safety is as high as ever and that our commitment to our customers is unwavering."

On January 21, Toyota announced its intention to recall approximately 2.3 million select Toyota Division vehicles equipped with a specific pedal assembly and suspended sales of the eight models involved in the recall on January 26.

Toyota vehicles affected by the recall include:

- Certain 2009–2010 RAV4
- Certain 2009–2010 Corolla
- 2009–2010 Matrix
- 2005–2010 Avalon
- Certain 2007–2010 Camry
- Certain 2010 Highlander
- 2007–2010 Tundra
- 2008–2010 Sequoia

No Lexus Division or Scion vehicles are affected by these actions. Also not affected are Toyota Prius, Tacoma, Sienna, Venza, Solara, Yaris, 4Runner, FJ Cruiser, Land Cruiser, Highlander hybrids and certain Camry models, including Camry hybrids, all of which remain for sale.

Further, Camry, RAV4, Corolla and Highlander vehicles with Vehicle Identification Numbers (VIN) that begin with "J" are not affected by the accelerator pedal recall.

In the event that a driver experiences an accelerator pedal that sticks in a partial open throttle position or returns slowly to idle position, the vehicle can be controlled with firm and steady application of the brakes. The brakes should not be pumped repeatedly because it could deplete vacuum assist, requiring stronger brake pedal pressure. The vehicle should be driven to the nearest safe location, the engine shut off and a Toyota dealer contacted for assistance.

How Toyota Will Fix Recalled Vehicles

Toyota has pinpointed the issue that could, on rare occasions, cause accelerator pedals in recalled vehicles to stick in a partially open position. The issue involves a friction device in the pedal designed to provide the proper "feel" by adding resistance and making the pedal steady and stable. The device includes a shoe that rubs against an adjoining surface during normal pedal operation. Due to the materials used, wear and environmental conditions, these surfaces may, over time, begin to stick and release instead of operating smoothly. In some cases, friction could increase to a point that the pedal is slow to return to the idle position or, in rare cases, the pedal sticks, leaving the throttle partially open.

Toyota's solution for current owners is both effective and simple. A precision-cut steel reinforcement bar will be installed into the assembly that will reduce the surface tension between the friction shoe and the adjoining surface. With this reinforcement in place, the excess friction that can cause the pedal to stick is eliminated. The company has confirmed the effectiveness of the newly reinforced pedals through rigorous testing on pedal assemblies that had previously shown a tendency to stick.

Separately from the recall for sticking accelerator pedals, Toyota is in the process of recalling vehicles to address rare instances in which floor mats have trapped the accelerator pedal in certain Toyota and Lexus models (announced November 25, 2009), and is already notifying customers about how it will fix this issue. In the case of vehicles covered by both recalls, it is Toyota's intention to remedy both at the same time.

Source: "Toyota Announces Comprehensive Plan to Fix Accelerator Pedals on Recalled Vehicles to Ensure Customer Safety," *Toyota Press Room,* February 1, 2010. Accessed November 14, 2010 from http://pressroom.toyota.com/pr/tms/toyota/toyota-announces-comprehensive-153311.aspx.

APPENDIX 1.5
December 5, 2009 editorial from the *Los Angeles Times*

Toyota's acceleration issue

Blaming floor mats may not be enough; the automaker needs to look at its vehicles' electronics.

Editorial

December 05, 2009

Toyota did the right thing when it recalled more than 4 million cars and trucks in response to mounting reports of unexpected and uncontrolled acceleration. But rather than sticking to its argument that the malfunctions stem from poorly designed pedals that get entangled with floor mats, the automaker should consider what happened to Eric Weiss. Otherwise, it may never get to the root of a problem that has claimed 19 lives in recent years.

As *The Times'* Ken Bensinger and Ralph Vartabedian have reported, Weiss says he had stopped his 2008 Tacoma pickup at an intersection in Long Beach in October when the truck, on its own, suddenly accelerated toward oncoming traffic. He was able to avoid a collision by clamping on the brakes and turning off the engine, but the incident left him reluctant to get behind the Tacoma's wheel again. And Weiss says the mats weren't the problem—he'd removed them months ago on his dealer's advice. His experience, combined with similar complaints by other Toyota owners and additional pieces of evidence, points to a potential electronic problem, not a mechanical one.

Source: Editorial, "Toyota's Acceleration Issue," *Los Angeles Times,* December 5, 2009. Accessed November 14, 2010 from http://articles.latimes.com/2009/dec/05/opinion/la-ed-toyota5–2009 dec05.

APPENDIX 1.6
February 9, 2010 editorial by Akio Toyoda, *Washington Post*

Toyota's plan to repair its public image

By Akio Toyoda

Tuesday, February 9, 2010

More than 70 years ago, Toyota entered the auto business based on a simple, but powerful, principle: that Toyota would build the highest-quality, safest and most reliable automobiles in the world. The company has always put the needs of our customers first and made the constant improvement of our vehicles a top priority. That is why 80% of all Toyotas sold in the United States over the past 20 years are still on the road today.

When consumers purchase a Toyota, they are not simply purchasing a car, truck or van. They are placing their trust in our company. The past few weeks, however, have made clear that Toyota has not lived up to the high standards we set for ourselves. More important, we have not lived up to the high standards you have come to expect from us. I am deeply disappointed by that and apologize. As the president of Toyota, I take personal responsibility. That is why I am personally leading the effort to restore trust in our word and in our products.

For much of Toyota's history, we have ensured the quality and reliability of our vehicles by placing a device called an andon cord on every production line—and empowering any team member to halt production if there's an assembly problem. Only when the problem is resolved does the line begin to move again.

Two weeks ago, I pulled the andon cord for our company. I ordered production of eight models in five plants across North America temporarily stopped so that we could focus on fixing our customers' vehicles that might be affected by sticking accelerator pedals. Today, Toyota team members and dealers across North America are working around the clock to repair all recalled vehicles.

But to regain the trust of American drivers and their families, more is needed. We are taking responsibility for our mistakes, learning from them and acting immediately to address the concerns of consumers and independent government regulators.

First, I have launched a top-to-bottom review of our global operations to ensure that problems of this magnitude do not happen again and that we not only meet but exceed the high safety standards that have defined our long history. As part of this, we will establish an Automotive Center of Quality Excellence in the United States, where a team of our top engineers will focus on strengthening our quality management and quality control across North America.

Second, to ensure that our quality-control operations are in line with best industry practices, we will ask a blue-ribbon safety advisory group composed of respected outside experts in quality management to independently review our operations and make sure that we have eliminated any deficiencies in our processes. The findings of these experts will be made available to the public, as will Toyota's responses to these findings.

Third, we fully understand that we need to more aggressively investigate complaints we hear directly from consumers and move more quickly to address any safety issues we identify. That is what we are doing by addressing customer concerns about the Prius and Lexus HS250h anti-lock brake systems.

We also are putting in place steps to do a better job within Toyota of sharing important quality and safety information across our global operations. This shortcoming contributed to the current situation. With respect to sticking accelerator pedals, we failed to connect the dots between problems in Europe and problems in the United States because the European situation related primarily to right-hand-drive vehicles.

Toyota will increase its outreach to government agencies charged with protecting the safety of motorists and passengers. I have spoken with U.S. Transportation Secretary Ray LaHood and given him my personal assurance that lines of communications with safety agencies and regulators will be kept open, that we will communicate more frequently and that we will be more vigilant in responding to those officials on all matters.

In recent years, much has been written about what we call "the Toyota Way"—the values and principles at the heart of our company. Chief among these is our unwavering commitment to continuous improvement: going to the source of a problem and fixing it. While problems with our cars have been rare over the years, the issues that Toyota is addressing today are by far the most serious we have ever faced.

But great companies learn from their mistakes, and we know that we have to win back the trust of our customers by adhering to the very values on which that trust was first built. The hundreds of thousands of men and women at Toyota operations worldwide— including the 172,000 team members and dealers in North America—are among the best in the auto industry. Whatever problems have occurred within our company, the strength and commitment to fix them resides within our company as well.

You have my commitment that Toyota will revitalize the simple but powerful principle that has guided us for 50 years: Toyota will build the highest-quality, safest and most reliable automobiles in the world.

The writer is president of Toyota Motor Co.

Source: Akio Toyoda, "Toyota's Plan to Repair its Public Image," *Washington Post,* February 9, 2010. Accessed December 1, 2010 from http://www.washingtonpost.com/wp-dyn/content/article/2010/02/08/AR2010020803078.html.

APPENDIX 1.7
March 30, 2010 press release

Toyota Begins Radically Reshaping Operations to Meet Customer Expectations

—Company Holds Inaugural Meeting of Special Committee for Global Quality—

Tokyo—Toyota Motor Corporation (TMC) announces that today it convened the first meeting of its Special Committee for Global Quality. Chaired by TMC President Akio Toyoda, the committee will spearhead reforms to further instill the company's operations throughout the world with a customer perspective.

The committee members include newly appointed chief quality officers for North America; Europe; China; Asia and Oceania; and the Middle East, Africa, and Latin America, who will represent concerns of customers. Also present at the meeting were representatives from TMC's business operations and others.

TMC's global committee will investigate the causes of quality problems, including those that necessitate recalls, and reexamine the factors that affect quality in every phase of design work, manufacturing, marketing and service. By approaching the task of quality assurance from the standpoint of customers in each region, and by keeping in mind the need for strengthened global communication and for ensuring transparency, the committee decided on various improvement measures aimed at resolving current issues.

With today's meeting of the global committee as the start, the committee and the regional quality committees will continue to spearhead comprehensive improvements to the company's operations, and promote the strengthening of global quality improvement activities.

Summary of Quality-Improvement Measures Adopted by Committee

Recalls and other safety decisions
- On behalf of the chief quality officers (CQOs), safety executives will participate in recall and other safety decision-making on a global basis. This is aimed at establishing a system in which representatives from each region will voice customer concerns from their regions and participate in determining if and how to undertake recalls and other safety measures.
- The CQO teams and the other representatives who participate in recall decision-making will promptly share information on customer complaints, defects and recalls with the global team members.

By realizing the above, Toyota aims to structure an optimal and prompt recall decision-making process both globally and locally.

Strengthening information gathering

- Toyota (as a whole) will strengthen its onsite information-gathering capabilities in regard to suspected quality problems. For instance, in the United States, the Swift Market Analysis Response Team (SMART), a team of specially trained technicians, will conduct onsite inspections as promptly as possible. Toyota plans also to increase the number of technology offices in North America from one to seven and establish seven offices in Europe, six offices in China, and other offices in other regions.
- To support analysis of the causes of accidents, Toyota in North America will, in cooperation with the authorities, expand the use of event data recorders (EDRs), which can record data regarding vehicle condition and driver operation. Toyota will also cooperate with the authorities in other regions regarding the use of EDRs. In addition, Toyota will expand the use of remote communications functions, such as G-BOOK telematics to convey vehicular self-diagnostic information to drivers and will consider a framework for storing that information as a resource for making product improvements.

Timely and accurate disclosure

- Toyota will have third-party experts from each region evaluate quality-improvement measures on a regional basis. Toyota will also enlist four third-party experts to review the quality-improvement measures adopted by its Special Committee for Global Quality. Plans call for the initial review results to be released in June 2010.
- Toyota will work closely with Toyota and Lexus dealers to promote safer driving. They will provide customers with useful information about safety technology and safe-driving practices.

Product safety and assurance

- Toyota will establish a specialized organization on safety within technical divisions to promptly and accurately reflect customer feedback to strengthen vehicle development.
- For additional customer confidence, Toyota will incorporate—globally—a brake override system (BOS) into new production models, starting in 2010. The BOS will automatically reduce engine power when the brake and accelerator pedals are applied simultaneously.

Human resources

- Toyota will establish CF (customer first) training centers by July 2010 in Japan, North America, Europe, Southeast Asia, and China to cultivate quality assurance professionals in each region.

TMC Special Committee for Global Quality, Organizational Position

Committee chair: TMC President Toyoda	Auditor	N.A. CQO	N.A. Quality Taskforce

Regional Quality Taskforce

Uchiyamada EVP, Funo EVP, Niimi EVP, Ichimaru EVP, Ihara SMD, Hayashi D, BR-CK	Chair: Sasaki EVP	Euro. CQO	Euro. Quality Taskforce	
	Secretariat: Quality Group	China CQO (CQO team)	China Quality Taskforce	
R&D Group	CS Group	Dom. Sales Group	AP CQO (CQO team)	AP Quality Taskforce
PE Group	HR Group	Sales Planning Grp	M.A.M. CQO (CQO team)	M.A.M. Quality Taskforce
Mfg Group	PA Group			
Purchasing Grp	Finance Group		Japan CQO	Japan Quality Taskforce

Improve planning, control process ⇄ Confirmation and advice from outside experts → Public disclosure

Chief Quality Officers

North America	Steve St. Angelo, managing officer, TMC
Europe	Didier Leroy, managing officer, TMC
China	Masahiro Kato, managing officer, TMC

- Tian Congming, senior vice president, FAW Toyota Motor Sales Co., Ltd. (FTMS)
- Feng Xingya, senior vice president, Guangzhou Toyota Motor Co., Ltd. (GTMC)
- Godfrey Tsang, vice president, Toyota Motor (China) Investment Co., Ltd. (TMCI)

Asia and Oceania — Mitsuhiro Sonoda, managing officer, TMC

- Surapong Tinnangwatana, senior vice president, Toyota Motor Asia Pacific-Engineering and Manufacturing Co., Ltd. (TMAP-EM)

- Vince S. Socco, senior vice president, Toyota Motor Asia Pacific Pte Ltd. (TMAP-MS)

Middle East, Africa, and Latin America — Hisayuki Inoue, managing officer, TMC
Katsutada Masumoto, managing officer, TMC

Japan — Katsutada Masumoto, managing officer, TMC

Source: "Toyota Begins Radically Shaping Operations to Meet Customer Expectations," *Toyota Motors U.S.A. Inc., Newsroom*, March 30, 2010. Accessed December 17, 2010 at http://press room.toyota.com/pr/tms/document/GlobalQuality.pdf.

APPENDIX 1.8
Videos

Important Message: Apology video from Jim Lentz posted on Toyota Corporate Website

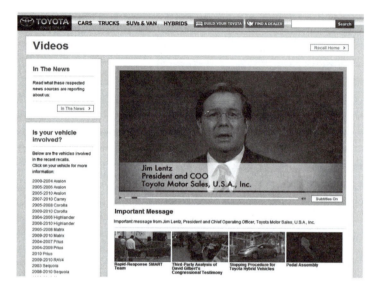

Toyota Team Members Discuss Toyota's Improvements: video spotlighting plan workers implementing the fixes for recalled vehicles

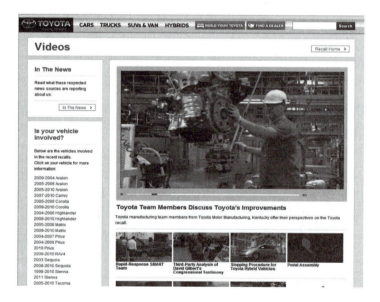

Source: Toyota Motor Sales, U.S.A., Inc., "Important Message," February 5, 2010. Accessed November 14, 2010 from http://www.toyota.com/recall/videos/jim-lentz-important-message.html.

LONG CASE QUESTIONS

1. Can simply seeking to embody the principles of *The Toyota Way* navigate the company back on the path of success?
2. Why is it to the company's advantage to take a proactive approach to issues impacting the company?
3. What proactive measures could Toyota have taken leading up to 2009 that would have allowed them to prepare for the events that took place?
4. What would be some necessary steps on strategic management plan for Toyota in the wake of the recalls?
5. How did the Japanese corporate culture come into play in the delayed action?
6. Will Toyota be able to improve its response in the future despite the cultural barriers?
7. How could it have helped Toyota in taking decisive and timely action in accepting the company's responsibility in the issue and finding a proven solution for SUA?

Chapter 2

Stakeholders

PREVIEW BUSINESS ETHICS INSIGHT

BP and the Oil Spill in Louisiana

In April 2010, a British Petroleum (BP) oil rig experienced a massive explosion that killed 11 workers. After the rig caught fire and sank, oil from the BP well started spilling into the Gulf of Mexico. Initial estimates suggest that around 10,000 to 15,000 barrels of oil were spewing into the sea.

The federal government's reaction was swift as they criticized BP's reaction to the scandal. At federal hearings, many BP officials admitted that the company was aware of the potential for this accident. BP ignored many warnings from its own engineers and proceeded with plans that seemed to ignore potential safety concerns. The hearings also revealed the massive lobbying resources BP invests in to influence the government.

The oil spill has had a tremendous impact on many levels. Many groups dependent on tourism in Louisiana and surrounding states have been affected as oil started appearing on the coastlines. Hundreds of individuals involved in the seafood industries in the Gulf region have been out of work. Furthermore, hundreds of other restaurants in the area have lost money as fewer tourists visit the area. Additionally, it is predicted that the price of seafood may rise as more and more restaurants avoid buying seafood from the Gulf. Restaurant owners report that customers are now becoming increasingly reluctant to eat seafood from the Gulf region because of the oil spill.

The disaster also seems to have had a severe impact on the ecological landscape. Many forms of wildlife have been severely affected, as the Louisiana marshes are crucial to many species including shrimp. Even a pelican species that had been rescued from the brink of extinction is now in catastrophic trouble.

The public and communities worldwide have also expressed anger at BP and its operations. Many groups are building boycott campaigns worldwide. Many consumer groups have also been appalled at BP's lack of preparation in the face of the spill. While no specific actions against BP have yet been taken by consumers, BP is well aware of the difficulties it faces ahead.

Minimization and stopping of the oil spill has also mobilized scientists' and countless individuals' solutions. For instance, a federally assembled group of scientists were the ones to recommend that a toxic chemical be sprayed (a dispersant) in the Gulf of Mexico to prevent the spilled oil reaching the coastal areas. BP engineers and scientists also proposed and tried many different solutions to stop the oil spill.

BP's share prices have also suffering from the oil spill. A month after the spill, BP's shares plunged over 12%. Many investors were panicking and feared that the oil spill could irreparably harm BP's chances of survival. These investors believed that the costs of the cleanup, as well as the mounting litigation and compensation claim, may become too much for BP to handle.

Based on Ball, J. 2010. "Scientists to back dispersant use, despite concerns." *Wall Street Journal* online; Chazan, G. 2010a. "BP shares under deeper pressure." *Wall Street Journal* online; Chazan, G. 2010b. "The Gulf oil spill: BP wasn't prepared for leak, CEO says." *Wall Street Journal*, A.5; Hughes, S. and Boles, C. 2010. "BP, Regulators Are Grilled On Hill Over Key Decisions." *Wall Street Journal* online; Isikoff, M. and Hirsh, M. 2010. "Slick operator: How British oil giant BP used all the political muscle money can buy to fend off regulators and influence investigations into corporate neglect." *Newsweek*, 155, 20; Weisman, J. 2010. "U.S. turns up heat on BP—Oil giant warns effort to plug well not a sure shot: Finger-pointing picks up." *Wall Street Journal*, A.1.

The Preview Business Ethics Insight on pages 70–1 shows the impact that the BP oil spill has had. The spill is turning out to be an even worse disaster than the *Exxon Valdez* oil spill. The *Exxon Valdez*, an oil tanker owned by Exxon, ran aground Alaska's coasts in March of 1989. The accident resulted in millions of gallons of crude oil being spilled along Alaska's coasts. The effect of the spill is still being felt today.

Both accidents show the extent to which different groups and entities can be affected by a company's actions. These groups or entities are commonly known as stakeholders. Most companies have to contend with more direct stakeholders such as customers or employees. However, the BP case described in the Preview Business Ethics Insight shows that stakeholders do not necessarily have to be directly linked to a company. Seemingly indirect groups such as restaurants and hotel owners are being affected by the spill. Any attempt by BP to deal adequately with the spill will be dependent on its ability to fully satisfy the needs and concerns of all stakeholders affected by the spill. This incident shows the critical need for companies to properly manage their stakeholders.

In this chapter, you will therefore learn about stakeholders and their implications for a company's strategic success. You will first read about the strategic need to understand and manage stakeholders. You will also learn about the various types of stakeholders and critical stakeholder attributes. In this chapter, you will also be exposed to stakeholder management and the many practical tools and techniques that are used for such purposes.

WHAT ARE STAKEHOLDERS AND WHY DO THEY MATTER?

The most accepted definition of a **stakeholder** is any group or individual that "can affect or is affected by the achievement of an organization's objectives."[1] Freeman, in his classic book *Strategic Management: A Stakeholder Approach*, is widely credited for introducing the business ethics and management field to the concept of the stakeholder.[2] As we saw in Chapter 1, stakeholder theory was introduced as an alternative to the then popular notion of stockholder theory. Rather than manage the organization solely in the interests of stockholders/shareholders, Freeman argues that a company should be managed taking into consideration the interests of all constituents or stakeholders.

Who are stakeholders? Exhibit 2.1 shows some of the more important stakeholders and the typical needs they have over a company.

As Exhibit 2.1 shows, there are many different types of shareholders. But why should a company be concerned about properly managing relationships with stakeholders? From a strategic management perspective, a strong stakeholder management approach is likely to help a company achieve and maintain strategic competitive advantage. For instance, a strong stakeholder management system means that a company has good relationships with its various stakeholders. Previous research suggests that such good relationships can increase a company's financial performance.[3] Furthermore, other research shows that a company's strong relationships with its stakeholders suggest that it has access to valuable, rare, inimitable, and non-substitutable resources that contribute to sustainable competitive advantage.[4] In other words, if a company is to

Stakeholder	Ethical Issue
Customers	• Product safety • Truth in advertising • Fair price
Shareholders	• Fair return on investment • Adequate management of company • Accurate financial reporting
Employees	• Discrimination • Sexual harassment • Child labor and sweatshops • Employee safety
Suppliers	• Impact of suppliers in environment • Exploitation of labor • Supply chain management
NGOs	• Environmental performance • Labor relations • Supplier sourcing issues
Host country	• Following local laws • Respecting local environment • Use of local labor
Government	• Lobbying • Regulation

EXHIBIT 2.1—Typical Stakeholders and their Needs

maintain competitive advantage, it needs access to resources that others cannot easily copy or imitate. A company's strong relationship with its stakeholders is something that is hard to replicate and can lead to success over the long term. Consider the Strategic Business Ethics Insight on page 74.

As the Strategic Business Ethics Insight shows, companies can benefit greatly from properly managing the relationship with their stakeholders. Strong relationships with various stakeholders can provide valuable information for companies. But does research mirror such strong relationships? Choi and Wang provide some insights into this question. They use large-scale data collected by a research firm on companies from the S&P 500 over an 11-year period ranging from 1991 to 2001. They found that good stakeholder relations are indeed related to superior company performance measured in terms of return on assets. However, most importantly, Choi and Wang found that positive stakeholder relations are even more critical for companies performing poorly. They found evidence that positive stakeholder relations can actually help such poorly performing companies recover.[5]

The above clearly shows that good stakeholder relationship management is critical. Next we consider key aspects of stakeholders in terms of categories and attributes.

STRATEGIC BUSINESS ETHICS INSIGHT

Unilever and Stakeholders

Unilever, a multinational based in Netherlands, is a market leader in industries such as the food, home, and personal care brands. Its brands include well-known products such as Bertolli, Lipton, Slim-Fast, Axe, Dove, and Pond's among others. It enjoys a strong reputation among its many stakeholders for being committed to sustainability. Furthermore, Unilever works hard to engage and develop relationships with its stakeholders. Such efforts have paid off, as the company has enjoyed sustainable competitive advantage.

An important component of Unilever's stakeholder management aspects is to engage and listen to stakeholders. For example, in May 2009, Unilever was presented with a damning report that raised serious concerns about its sourcing and working practices in its foreign operations. It took these allegations seriously and investigated the matter. It is now slowly implementing new measures to address these concerns.

In April 2008, Greenpeace issued a report detailing how Unilever's suppliers in Borneo were clearing land without permits in order to be able to grow palm trees. The cleared lands were often orangutan habitats, thus damaging many species' habitat. Unilever again responded to the report by commissioning its own reports. Its own independent report found that the Greenpeace allegations were indeed accurate. Unilever is now working with its suppliers to ensure that these practices end.

Unilever's stakeholder strategy has not been simply reactive to reports. It also actively engages with its suppliers to help these suppliers. Consider, for instance, Unilever's partnership with Ghana-based environmental and non-governmental organizations. It is working closely with these organizations to develop a way to accelerate the growth of the allanblackia tree. The allanblackia tree produces seeds that can be converted to oil. However, this oil is stable at room temperature and thus provides an important commercial advantage as the seeds do not need to be chemically processed. Furthermore, the oils in the allanblackia tree can make soaps harder, thus making these soaps more economical than the use of palm oil. Unilever's efforts have paid off and it has successfully developed a tree that grows faster. Such trees can provide new sources of income for farmers in Ghana. Furthermore, the program is being expanded to other African nations such as Tanzania and Nigeria.

Based on *Financial Times*. 2008. "Unilever's success with palm oil." *Financial Times*; http://www.unilever.com.

STAKEHOLDER CATEGORIZATION AND ATTRIBUTES

One of the critical aspects of properly managing stakeholders is the ability to identify these stakeholders. Being able to adequately identify critical stakeholders plays an important role in terms of how such relationships are managed and what impact such relationships have on any company. Furthermore, in such identification, critical attributes of these stakeholders have to be acknowledged. In this section, we discuss some of these key issues.

One of the most popular categorization of stakeholders is to classify them either as primary or secondary stakeholders. **Primary stakeholders** are typically directly linked to a company's survival and are either impacted by or impact companies directly.

BUSINESS ETHICS INSIGHT

Oil Companies and Host Communities in Nigeria's Delta Region

The commercial exploitation of Oil in Nigeria began in 1957 and is the largest business sector in the country. Oil revenues account for over 98% of Nigerian exports and over 80% of oil revenues. Most of the oil is extracted by oil multi-nationals such as Shell in partnership with Nigeria's national oil company, Nigerian National Petroleum Corporation, holding the majority stake.

However, despite the lucrative nature of oil extraction, most of these oil companies have ignored the host communities, resulting in very tense relationships. Oil companies have been accused of engaging in collusion with the government to appropriate ancestral lands for the purpose of oil extraction. Many of these companies have also been accused of damaging the environment irreversibly. Furthermore, there are allegations of human rights abuses and other discriminatory practices. With their primary focus on oil extraction, state security personnel and oil company security employees have also frequently clashed with members of the host communities.

This situation where oil companies have very hostile relationships with their host communities has been blamed on a blatant lack of concern for these stakeholders. Most of the oil companies have been more focused on oil extraction rather than working with the host communities to address their concerns. This lack of attention has also resulted in host community retaliation. Host communities in the Delta region have resorted to communal protests, hijacking of oil workers and even sabotage of oil equipment to protest against these companies. Most experts agree that these oil-producing companies will have to listen to the host communities if they want smoother relationships in the future.

Based on Ako, R.T., Obokoh, L.O., and Okonmah, P. 2009. "Forging peaceful relationships between oil companies and host-communities in Nigeria's Delta region." *Journal of Enterprising Communities: People and Practice in the Global Economy*, 3, 2, 205–216.

Examples of primary stakeholders include customers, suppliers, employees, and shareholders. These groups have a very strong and direct connection with a company. We will discuss some of these primary stakeholders in more detail in Chapter 3.

Ignoring primary stakeholders can be very disastrous for any company. Consider the Business Ethics Insight on page 75. As it shows, carefully responding to primary stakeholders' needs and concerns is critical to any company for survival. In this case, Shell ignored direct stakeholders such as the host communities and ran into consequent difficulties. Had the needs of these stakeholders been taken into consideration, Shell would not be facing such challenges today.

Another important stakeholder group is **secondary stakeholders**. In contrast to primary stakeholders, secondary stakeholders tend to be less directly linked to the company's survival and include the media, trade associations, and special-interest groups. We will discuss examples of key secondary stakeholders in more detail in Chapter 7.

Although it may seem that secondary stakeholders have less impact for multinational companies, recent examples show that secondary shareholders are as important as primary shareholders in terms of impact. Consider, for example, how the agricultural giant Monsanto has been forced to deal with secondary stakeholders such as Greenpeace and Friends of the Earth as it tries to develop agricultural biotechnology products. Similarly, the tobacco industry worldwide has been affected disproportionately by government and communities in an effort to lower smoking levels. Such examples show that, depending on the industry, secondary stakeholders may have critical influence on any company. Exhibit 2.2 gives some examples of primary and secondary stakeholders for a typical multinational.

Primary Stakeholders
Shareholders and investors
Employees
Suppliers
Local community
Secondary Stakeholders
Media
Special-interest groups
Non-governmental organizations
Labor unions

EXHIBIT 2.2—Primary and Secondary Shareholders for Typical Multinational

The above clearly shows that it is important to be able to clearly identify stakeholders. Any attempt to adequately manage stakeholders begins with proper identification. However, once the stakeholders have been identified, critical attributes of these stakeholders have to be assessed. Next, we examine stakeholder attributes.

Stakeholder Attributes: Power, Legitimacy, and Urgency

In addition to proper categorization of stakeholders in terms of the primary versus secondary types, it is important to examine the attributes of these stakeholders. In this section, we discuss three critical stakeholder attributes; namely, power, legitimacy, urgency and salience.[6] Each stakeholder attribute has the ability to influence an organization.

The first stakeholder attribute we consider is power. **Stakeholder power** refers to the ability of a stakeholder to exert pressures to force a company to make changes to accommodate such pressures. According to Mitchell, Agle, and Wood, power can take different forms.[7] Power can be of coercive, utilitarian, or normative forms.

Coercive power involves the use of force, violence, or other restraint to force a company to accommodate or respond to stakeholder needs. For instance, in the earlier Business Ethics Insight about Shell and its presence in the Delta region (page 75), host communities have frequently resorted to coercive means to force oil companies to halt their exploitative practices. As these oil companies have colluded with the state to appropriate land and have been more concerned about oil production at the expense of the environment, militant groups have mushroomed and have resorted to coercive power to force these oil companies to re-examine their practices.[8]

A second form of power is **utilitarian power**. Utilitarian power refers to the use of financial or other monetary means to force a company to accommodate a particular stakeholder need. Common manifestations of utilitarian power are use of money or boycott. Consider, for example, tobacco companies. For decades, they defended their products, arguing that the claims that tobacco can result in negative health effects were not true.[9] Many stakeholders, such as the government and states, used their utilitarian power to force tobacco companies to acknowledge the nature of their products and provide the means to start addressing problems associated with tobacco. Actions such as long lawsuits were only possible because the government has access to the necessary financial resources to face the tobacco industry.

Another example of utilitarian power is manifested in boycotts. Consider the case of Whole Foods and its CEO John Mackey. When the healthcare debates were ongoing in the U.S., he wrote an open letter to the *Wall Street Journal* arguing against government-run healthcare. A big majority of Whole Foods customers tend to be more liberal and they started organizing boycotts of the company.[10]

Finally, a third form of power is normative power. **Normative power** refers to the use of symbolic and other resources to force a company to accommodate stakeholder needs. As argued by Thorne, Ferrell, and Ferrell, actions such as letter writing campaigns and other advertising messages are examples of the use of normative power.[11] The advent of the internet also means that people can now easily vent about a company publicly. The internet and social media have therefore provided an important source of normative power.

It is critical for companies to properly assess the power of their stakeholders in order to adequately address their needs. If the extent of the power is not fully acknowledged, it can signal disaster for the company. Furthermore, companies need to be very aware of the power of social media. Consider the following Strategic Business Ethics Insight.

STRATEGIC BUSINESS ETHICS INSIGHT

Palm Oil, Nestlé, and Sinar Mas

Demand for palm oil continues to grow as it is used more and more as a biofuel and in household products. Most of the palm oil comes from countries like Indonesia and Malaysia. In December 2009, Greenpeace published a report blaming Sinar Mas, an Indonesian palm oil supplier, for severely contributing to deforestation. Sinar Mas was accused of clearing protected forests to make room for plantations. Furthermore, Greenpeace also released a YouTube video parodying one of Nestlé's KitKat chocolate commercials. In that commercial, an employee opens a KitKat bar and finds an orangutan finger. Greenpeace's commercial meant to show the connection between the use of palm oil in Nestlé KitKat bars and the resulting deforestation of orangutan habitat.

Nestlé's reaction to the video showed blatant disregard for the power of social media. When the video was released, Nestlé immediately emailed YouTube administrators to have the video removed because of copyright issues. The video was quickly removed. However, Greenpeace re-posted the video on other video-sharing websites and shared the censorship on Twitter. This resulted in increased attention to the video, which quickly went viral. However, this also initiated discussions on various social networks and some individuals even started discussing the issue on Nestlé's own Facebook page. Someone from the company started responding to the posts with very arrogant and angry rebuttals. This resulted in further consumers getting enraged as the issue was also discussed on Twitter.

As a result, Nestlé decided to boycott the palm oil supplier. Furthermore, many other major companies such as Cargill and Unilever decided to end their relationship with Sinar Mas. These companies decided to switch to suppliers with more sustainable practices.

Based on Deutsch, A. 2010a. "Cargill threatens palm oil supplier over deforestation." *Financial Times*, 50; Deutsch, A. 2010b. "Deforestation claims spur Cargill threat to switch palm oil supplier." *Financial Times*, 1; Mathieson, M. 2010. "Hit or Miss?" *PR Week*, 2.

As the Strategic Business Ethics Insight (page 78) shows, Nestlé simply ignored the power of social media. By reacting negatively, Nestlé invited ridicule from social savvy consumers. As you will see later in Chapter 7, properly assessing the power of the various forms of information technologies and social media is very important.

A second key stakeholder attribute we consider is **legitimacy**. A company behaves legitimately if it conducts itself in such a way that is consistent with widely held values and beliefs.[12] When a company behaves legitimately, it is more likely to be supported by society. Similarly, a stakeholder is considered to have a legitimate need if the actions of the stakeholder are considered reasonable and acceptable within a certain context.

A company is well advised to carefully consider the legitimacy of its various stakeholders. Ignorance of the legitimacy of some stakeholders can be disastrous. Consider the case of the public-sector healthcare reforms in Canada.[13] In 1994, the Canadian healthcare industry had to respond to the needs of the government-initiated efficiency reforms. The Canadian healthcare providers perceived the government as the only legitimate stakeholders. However, this focus on the government led to an important decline in quality and patient satisfaction. The Canadian companies simply ignored the legitimate demands of other stakeholders such as the employees and patients. The legitimacy of these other stakeholders had to be recognized as the companies also started addressing their needs.

A third critical attribute is urgency. **Urgency** refers to the degree to which a company needs to respond to stakeholder needs. The more urgent a stakeholder needs are, the more quickly a company has to respond to such needs. Similar to the other attributes, response to urgency is also critical.

One of the most urgent stakeholder claims that have emerged over the past decade is pressure on companies to be more environmentally sensitive. However, other urgent claims such as fair trade, human rights, and labor rights have also become very prevalent.[14] Many of these claims have resulted from the perceived growing power of large multinationals. This has also led to a number of non-governmental organizations making more urgent claims to counterbalance such power. The anti-global movement protests in Seattle during the World Trade Organization meeting and the disruption of the Olympic Torch Journey preceding the Olympic Games in China all reflect such urgent claims.[15]

As the above shows, it is extremely critical to properly assess stakeholder attributes. This points to the importance of adequately addressing stakeholder needs. Next we discuss stakeholder management.

STAKEHOLDER MANAGEMENT

Stakeholder management refers to the deliberate and purposeful process a company has devised to work with its stakeholders. As we saw in the many examples earlier, stakeholders often have disparate needs when they relate to companies. Companies have found that ignoring such needs can be very detrimental to their health. Having a systematic process to anticipate and address such needs is therefore critical.

79

Why is stakeholder management critical? As we saw earlier in this chapter, adequately dealing with stakeholders can be financially beneficial for a company. Having a strong stakeholder management system implies that a company has strong relationships with its stakeholders. Such relationships can provide the company with valuable, rare, and difficult to imitate resources. Such resources can thus lead to competitive advantage whereby companies have access to skills and capabilities that other companies do not have access to. Consider, for instance, the example of Nokia discussed later and how their strong relationship with the European Union has provided them with benefits that have allowed them to become strong environmental stewards. Such perceptions in the mind of consumers have also led to better phone sales, thereby benefiting the company.

Choi and Wang's study provides further evidence of the strong link between stakeholder management and competitive advantage.[16] Companies that have superior relationships with their workers tend to have employees that will work harder to help the company achieve its goals. Strong relationships with suppliers often result in greater willingness of suppliers to share knowledge with the firm. Furthermore, strong relationships with communities often mean that the communities may provide better terms for the use of local infrastructure. Thus, strong stakeholder management programs are likely to provide a company with resources that contribute to strategic competitive advantage.

How useful are strategic stakeholder management systems? Consider the Strategic Business Ethics Insight on page 81.

Next, we consider the various steps in the stakeholder management process. Exhibit 2.3 (page 82) shows the five steps of the process.

Step 1: Stakeholder Identification

A critical first step in the stakeholder management process is **stakeholder identification**, where the main focus is to properly identify stakeholders. A company needs to determine and understand which stakeholders have the ability to affect the organization. In that context, the earlier categorization of primary and secondary stakeholders is helpful. Companies can identify stakeholders based on the stakeholders' ability to directly (primary stakeholders) or indirectly affect (secondary stakeholders).

However, while the primary vs. secondary classification may work for most industries, it may not be necessarily useful for all industries. For some industries, the primary versus secondary categorization may pose peculiar challenges. Consider, for example, the construction industry where most projects are undertaken regularly on a contract level for a defined time period. In such instances, the industry has found it more useful to classify stakeholders in four categories based on the nature of the contract. Moodley, Smith, and Preece provide some insights for that industry.[17] They argue that those stakeholders that relate to construction firms directly on a contract basis are explicit stakeholders. Examples of explicit stakeholders include shareholders, alliance partners, and other contractors. However, although a construction firm may not have explicit

STRATEGIC BUSINESS ETHICS INSIGHT

Stakeholder Management in Sweden

How critical are stakeholder management systems? A comparison of railway construction projects in Sweden illustrates the importance of stakeholder management process. The first case involved the construction of 18km of tracks around the city of Malmö in Sweden. The project was necessary to take into consideration the large increase in traffic that was placing increased pressure on the Malmö tracks. The project involved the construction of two parallel tunnels under the city. The second case involved the expansion and improvement of tracks in the city of Lund. Because of projected traffic growth, there was a crucial need to expand and improve the tracks to cope with such growth.

An analysis of both projects shows the importance of stakeholder management practices. For example, surveys of the public and others affected by the Malmö project showed that around 68% of respondents had a very positive attitude toward the project and around 17% were neutral. Furthermore, of the 15% who had a negative perception of the project, 88% of them were comfortable with the project being built. In contrast, the Lund project ran into significant opposition and a delay before the project was completed.

The two projects were perceived very differently because the stakeholder management process was done differently. For the Malmö project, the project management team regarded stakeholder acceptance as extremely critical for successful completion of the project. Through surveys and other processes, the construction team identified six major critical stakeholder groups that could potentially influence the project. Using many of the methods described later, the construction company was able to proactively identify relevant stakeholder needs and respond to such needs. For example, project managers for the project met with members of the public on numerous occasions to provide open communication regarding seven critical areas where the project would most likely affect the public. Furthermore, the group communicated openly with the media to address any lingering issues. Members of the media then became the strongest advocate for the project.

The Lund project was conducted in almost opposite manner. No stakeholder management process was established and the construction company chose to ignore stakeholders. For instance, although the public is an external stakeholder, they had tremendous informal power on the projects. By ignoring the public, the company encouraged opposition, and politicians and the media soon formed coalitions with the public to oppose the project. While the public was considered as a legitimate stakeholder in the first project, it was completely ignored in the second project. This lack of a stakeholder management process resulted in a six-year delay. Furthermore, the project managers in the Lund project chose not to respond to negative criticisms from the media. This also resulted in negative articles promoting the views of opponents of the project only.

Based on Olander, S. and Landin, A. 2008. "A comparative study of factors affecting the external stakeholder management process." *Construction Management and Economics*, 26, 553–561.

EXHIBIT 2.3
Steps of the Stakeholder Management
Process

Explicit Stakeholders

Project financiers

Equity holders

Sponsors

Implicit Stakeholders

Suppliers

Regulators

Users

Consumers

Implicit Recognized Stakeholders

Community

Government

Local Government

NGOs

Unions

Unknown Stakeholders

Trade associations

Overseas government

Public-interest groups

EXHIBIT 2.4
Stakeholder Categorization for
Construction Industry

contracts with other groups such as regulators, they still need to abide by the demands of such groups. Such groups form part of the implicit stakeholder group and include regulators, employees of the company, and the consumers. Furthermore, construction firms have to contend with groups that may have no contracts but are interested in the company's projects. Such groups are the implicit recognized group and include activists, charities, and non-governmental organizations. These groups may not have a contract with the company but may have concerns about the construction project and its impact on the local community. Finally, the construction industry also recognizes "unknowns," which are groups whose interests or influence is unknown. Examples of the "unknowns" stakeholders include trade associations, overseas regulators, etc. Exhibit 2.4 shows examples of stakeholders for the construction industry.

As the above shows, it is important for companies to determine appropriate categorization of their stakeholders. Next we discuss stakeholder prioritization and mapping.

Step 2: Stakeholder Prioritization

After the company has identified its stakeholders, it needs to assess the attributes of these stakeholders. It is critical for any company to be concerned about the influence any stakeholder can have on its operations. This influence, also termed **salience**, will provide information on the degree to which managers need to give priority to competing stakeholder demands and claims.[18] The more salient a stakeholder is, the more likely the stakeholder has a potential to affect the company and the more priority the stakeholder needs.

According to Mitchell et al., stakeholder salience is based on a combination of the three attributes we discussed earlier.[19] Each combination of attribute strength results in a specific type of stakeholder demanding specific actions from the company. Exhibit 2.5 shows a combination of the various stakeholders' attributes.

The first groups of stakeholders we discuss are latent stakeholders. **Latent** stakeholders are those that possess only one of the three attributes and thus represent low salience. There are three types of latent stakeholders. The **dormant** stakeholders are those that possess power but have no legitimate claims or urgency. For instance, non-governmental organizations such as Greenpeace and others tend to have power. In such cases, it is advisable for companies to carefully monitor these stakeholders. The potential for dormant stakeholders to acquire another attribute is possible and careful attention needs to be paid to such stakeholders. A second form of latent stakeholder is the **discretionary** stakeholder, which has legitimacy but no power or urgency. Examples of discretionary stakeholders are philanthropic organizations such as the Red Cross and others. While a manager may not necessarily engage with such stakeholders, they may do so for strategic reasons to gain goodwill. The final form of latent stakeholders is the **demanding** stakeholders. Demanding stakeholders have urgency but do not have power or legitimacy. Companies are well advised to also monitor such stakeholders, as they are likely to generate much attention for their cause.

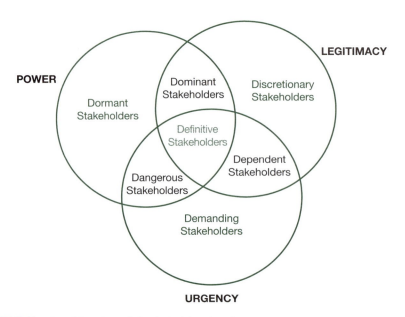

EXHIBIT 2.5—Combination of Stakeholder Attributes

While the above categories of stakeholders only require monitoring on the part of the company, the next category requires much closer attention and sometimes responses. The **expectant** stakeholders are those that possess two of the attributes discussed earlier. Such stakeholders are considered to have moderate salience.

Similar to latent stakeholders, there are three types of expectant stakeholders. The first type, known as **dominant** stakeholders, represents stakeholders that are both powerful and legitimate. Such stakeholders require formal actions as they are not only legitimate but they also have the ability to exercise power on a company. Examples of dominant stakeholders are employees or investors and most companies have formal structures (e.g., human resource department or investor relations) to tackle such stakeholders. **Dependent** stakeholders are those stakeholders that have urgency and legitimacy. For example, many stakeholders such as restaurant owners or fishermen or community residents are considered as dependent stakeholders in the BP oil spill as discussed in the Preview Business Ethics Insight (pages 70–1). Much of BP's response has been to cater to the needs of these stakeholders. Finally, the third form of latent stakeholders is **dangerous** stakeholders. Dangerous stakeholders have power and urgency but no legitimacy. An example of a dangerous stakeholder is the case of the fringe organizations in the Niger Delta involved in Shell employee kidnappings. While such groups may not be legitimate, they have been able to get Shell's and the world's attention because of their power and urgency.

The stakeholder that is most salient for any company is the definitive stakeholder. **Definitive stakeholders** have power, urgency, and are legitimate. For instance, in the case of Nestlé as discussed earlier, they failed to recognize Greenpeace as a stakeholder with power (it has access to resources and can force companies to make changes), urgency (it sees deforestation as a critical issue that needs to be addressed), and legitimacy (it is recognized as a credible environmental force). Thus, rather than address Greenpeace's concerns, Nestlé's ridicule of the Greenpeace report resulted in a major public relations nightmare for them. Not all companies react similarly. Consider the following Strategic Business Ethics Insight.

STRATEGIC BUSINESS ETHICS INSIGHT

Nokia and the European Union

Mobile communications equipment, such as mobile phones, contributes significantly to electronic scrap worldwide. Furthermore, companies such as Nokia and Motorola involved in manufacturing these products have a fairly large environmental impact by making these products. Such companies have had to respond to voluntary calls and legislative actions to minimize the impact of their actions on the environment worldwide.

The European Union has been very proactive in encouraging and enforcing actions to encourage companies to improve their environmental records. In that context, the 2003 Integrated Product Policy was adopted with the aim of reducing the environmental impacts of products at various stages of their lifecycles. More recent legislations such as the Waste Electrical and Electronic Equipment encourage companies to think of as many ways as possible of minimizing environmental harm. For instance, companies are required to manage end of life of the product by taking back and recycling such equipment.

Nokia is an important player in the mobile phone industry. Rather than wait for new legislations or try to fight new legislations, as is typical of many corporations, Nokia has taken a leadership role. They have worked hard to implement policies aimed at reducing environmental waste as well as minimizing use of toxic chemicals. Furthermore, they even piloted a project bringing the industry and non-governmental organizations to discuss ideas and actions dedicated to environmental issues. This project has resulted in a large group of corporations voluntarily committing to reducing waste and encouraging recycling.

Based on Paloviita, A. and Luoma-aho, V. 2010. "Recognizing definitive stakeholders in corporate environmental management." *Management Research Review*, 33, 4, 306–316.

As the Strategic Business Ethics Insight shows, Nokia's actions show that it recognized the European Union as a definitive stakeholder. The European Union has power (through legislations and other actions), legitimacy (it is regarded as a credible stakeholder), and urgency (environmental issues require quick actions). By addressing the European Union's concerns and being proactive, Nokia has considerably strengthened its environmental image and credibility. This has also led Greenpeace to rank them as the number one company in the "Guide to Greener Electronics." After the stakeholder salience is determined, the next step is to visualize and map the stakeholders.

Step 3: Stakeholder Visualization and Mapping

After the stakeholder salience is determined, the next step is to **visualize and map** the stakeholders. This step is necessary to determine the extent of claims, rights, and expectations stakeholders have and the appropriate response to these needs. Unmet stakeholders needs and expectations can be very disastrous and properly assessing these needs through visualization and mapping can be very helpful.

A simple way to visualize stakeholders to determine appropriate responses is to construct the power and urgency matrix. Rather than use all three attributes discussed earlier, most companies rely on a simpler consideration of only two attributes. Exhibit 2.6 displays the matrix with the corresponding company responses.

As Exhibit 2.6 shows, the attributes of power and urgency are often used to assess stakeholder influence.[20] The consideration of high and low levels of both power and urgency results in a four-quadrant matrix. Each quadrant recommends a specific action for the company. The quadrant that needs the most attention is the quadrant representing stakeholders with high power and high urgency. Such stakeholders need to be managed constantly to ensure that their needs are being met. In contrast, stakeholders with low power and low urgency do not place the same immediate need for concern for the company. Such stakeholders need to be monitored and their needs addressed when necessary. Furthermore, the appropriate response to those stakeholders that have high power and low interest is for the company to keep them satisfied. Finally, those stakeholders that have high urgency but low power should also be monitored and informed regularly of what is being done.

Once the stakeholder positions are visualized, a company can devise more complex matrices to gauge the degree to which they systematically need to respond to

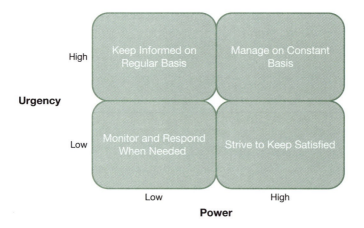

EXHIBIT 2.6—Power and Urgency Matrix

Stakeholders		Shareholders	Employees	Customers	Unions	Governments	Suppliers	NGOs	Key
Ethical Issues									Ranking 1 to 5 (Importance to stakeholder) ER: Ethical risk from stakeholder ES: Ethical support from stakeholder
Product	Product safety	5ER	5ES	5ER	2	5ER	2	5ER	
	Safety of materials	2	5ES	5ER	2	5ER	3	5ER	
	Pricing	2	3ES	5ER	2	3	2	3	
Environment	Compliance with local laws	5	3ES	3ER	2	5ER	5ES	5ER	
	Carbon footprint	5	3ES	4ER	2	5ER	5ES	5ER	
	Pollution	2	3ES	5ER	2	4ER	5ES	5ER	
	Waste	2	3ES	3ER	2	4ER	5ES	5ER	
	Water usage	2	3ES	4ER	2	5ER	5ES	5ER	
	Habitat destruction	2	3ES	5ER	2	5ER	5ES	5ER	
Labor and Human Rights	Collective bargaining	2	5ES	2	5ER	2	3ER	2	
	Forced labor	2	5ES	2	5ER	3	3ER	2	
	Child labor	2	5ES	3ER	5ER	5ER	4ER	2	
	Gender equality	2	5ES	3	5ER	3	4ER	2	
	Fair wage	2	5ES	3	5ER	4ER	5ER	2	
Community	Local causes	2	5ES	4ER	2	2	2	2	
	Charity	2	5ES	3ER	2	2	2	2	
	Employment	3	5ES	2	3ER	2	2	2	
	Social and economic impact	2	3ES	2	2	4ER	2	2	
Supply chain	Labor practice	2	5ES	3	5ER	3ER	5ES	2	
	Use of sustainable materials	2	3ES	3	2	2	5ES	5ER	
	Health and safety	2	5ES	3	2	4ER	5ES	5ER	
Conduct	Compliance with local codes	5ER	3ES	3	2	5ER	2	2	
	Corrupt practices	5ER	3ES	2	2	5ER	2	2	
	Competitive practices	5ER	4ES	2	2	5ER	2	2	
Suppliers	Use of sweatshops	2	5ES	3	5ER	5ER	5ES	5ER	
	Labor exploitation	2	5ES	3	5ER	5ER	5ES	5ER	
	Working conditions	2	5ES	3	5ER	5ER	5ES	5ER	

EXHIBIT 2.7—Stakeholder Ethical Responsibility Matrix for Puma

stakeholder needs. One example is the Stakeholder Ethical Responsibility Matrix as shown in Exhibit 2.7.[21]

Exhibit 2.7 shows the potential Stakeholder Ethical Responsibility Matrix (SERM) for a shoe manufacturing company such as the German Puma. Along the vertical axis are the many ethical issues that a company like Puma has to face. Along the horizontal axis are the stakeholders that were identified earlier. A company can then assess these various stakeholders based on 1) the importance of the stakeholder based on a rating of 1–5 obtained from the earlier matrix, 2) whether the stakeholder poses an ethical risk (ER), 3) whether the stakeholder will support the company (ES), and finally 4) whether the stakeholder will need to be consulted.

A well-constructed SERM serves many purposes for the company.[22] It should help a company identify the potential for ethical risks. However, it can also help the company identify areas for opportunities to enhance the company's ethics. For example, in the case of Puma, the potential to consult non-governmental organizations to develop better labor practices may be useful in improving ethical reputation. As a company strives to properly manage its stakeholders, the SERM can also help devise better training and policy to address stakeholder needs and expectations. Next we consider stakeholder engagement.

Step 4: Stakeholder Engagement

Stakeholders often have different claims, rights, and expectations of organizations. As we saw in many instances earlier, such demands often influence a company's operations. In extreme cases, such stakeholder demands can even pose severe threats to a company's survival. However, companies that engage their stakeholders are less likely to experience such threats. The next step in the stakeholder management process is **stakeholder engagement**. Stakeholder engagement refers to the deliberate attempt of a company to actively seek its stakeholders' inputs to better deal with their needs and also improve their operations. As we saw in the case of stakeholder management in Sweden, the project that actively engaged key stakeholders such as the media and the public were the ones that were perceived more positively.

According to Chinyio and Akintoye, companies that engage their shareholders enjoy significant advantages.[23] For instance, stakeholder management systems can provide companies with a broad idea of potential stakeholder problematic areas. However, by engaging these stakeholders, a company can find ways to alleviate such problems. Companies discover that stakeholder management not only develops a better ability for them to relate to their stakeholders but also results in significant reputational advantages. Such efforts help the company develop better public and community image.

Exhibit 2.8 lists the many advantages companies can reap from stakeholder engagement.

To develop an appropriate stakeholder management program, any company must actively engage with its stakeholders. The earlier steps discussed should provide important information about who the key stakeholders are. Depending on the company's

---

Advantages of Stakeholder Engagement

- Increased relationships with stakeholders

- Increase in process and organizational efficiency

- Stronger market positioning

- Reduced conflict with stakeholders and smaller risk of getting sued

- Better service to customers and other end-users

- Increased ability to identify new business potential

- Better ability to forecast future stakeholder demands

- Better organizational learning

EXHIBIT 2.8—Advantages of Stakeholder Engagement

mission and vision, the company should then devise an appropriate system to develop an ongoing dialogue with these stakeholders. Such systems can occur through a variety of methods and media. Consider the Ethics Sustainability Insight on page 90.

As the above shows, stakeholder engagement involves deliberate efforts on a company's part to involve stakeholders in uncovering problematic issues and opportunities in running the company. What are some of the key success factors in developing stakeholder management systems? Chinyio and Akintoye provide some insight in the process.[24] They argue that successful stakeholder engagement systems should be systematic, involve top-level support, and should be proactive. In practice, effective stakeholder engagement systems make heavy use of frequent and effective communication with stakeholders through meetings, workshops, and other communication methods. Effective stakeholder management systems also rely heavily on use of people skills to work with stakeholders.

Step 5: Stakeholder Monitoring

The final step in the stakeholder management process is that of **stakeholder monitoring**. At this stage, a company is interested in finding out how stakeholders are responding to stakeholder management issues and if further actions are necessary. A company can also determine the effectiveness of its communication strategies to gauge whether the appropriate message is being delivered to stakeholders.

An effective way to monitor stakeholders is to have regular meetings with critical stakeholders. Through the meetings, a company can determine whether stakeholder needs are continuously being met. Furthermore, a company can continue communicating its efforts to address stakeholder concerns. Finally, these meetings can reveal other new problematic areas where new stakeholders are identified and/or new visualization and prioritization is needed.

ETHICS SUSTAINABILITY INSIGHT

Stakeholder Management Process in New Zealand and India

Several New Zealand companies have developed different stakeholder management approaches to address specific needs. Consider the case of Vodafone. It typically runs stakeholder engagement workshops to engage with its stakeholders. However, most recently, it has been concerned about the role of telecommunications in a more sustainable future for New Zealand. To do so, it has invited its key stakeholders and organized their sessions around key questions such as what a sustainable New Zealand looks like, what the barriers to such a future are, and what telecommunications companies can do to overcome such barriers. This exercise has the potential not only to reveal new business opportunities to Vodafone but also to engage stakeholders in such discussions.

Urgent Courier is New Zealand's leading delivery services company. Recently, it engaged in a number of stakeholder engagement exercises as it continues its sustainability efforts. One of the most surprising results for it was to find that one of the biggest problem areas for its business was the earnings of its contracted drivers. They found that although drivers are extremely critical for their business, these drivers were not earning enough for them to attract and retain the best. Urgent Courier then embarked on a new pricing strategy to ensure that its prices would provide better earnings to its drivers while also remaining competitive. Urgent Couriers has now received workplace awards in an industry that is not often concerned about its drivers.

Stakeholder engagement has also played a key role in Titan of India. Titan, a joint venture involving the well-known Tata Group, manufactures watches for the growing Indian market. From its inception, Titan made corporate social responsibility a key aspect of its strategy. Through recent stakeholder engagement exercises, Titan realized that competition demanded more cost-efficient processes while the market provided significant business opportunities. Such factors forced Titan to engage in significant expansion. However, as it embarked on such expansion efforts, its stakeholder engagement exercises also provided impetus for Titan to further engage the community. It therefore conducted further stakeholder engagement exercises in the Hosur, where its main manufacturing facility is located. It found that significant gender inequality existed in the form of low literacy rates, female infanticide, and early marriages. Titan then partnered with other non-governmental organizations to create a micro-enterprise owned by poor women from the rural areas. Titan provided the technical training and expertise to run the micro-enterprise. Such efforts have provided income and power to an otherwise neglected group in India. However, Titan has also reaped the benefits of better engaging with the community.

Based on Brown, R. 2010. "Engaging your stakeholders." *NZ Business*, July, 24, 6; Kannabiran, G. 2009. "Sustainable stakeholder engagement through innovative supply chain strategy: An exploratory study of an Indian organization." *Asian Business & Management*, 8, 2, 205–223.

Consider the case of the rail track construction project in Sweden discussed earlier in this chapter. The Malmö project was extremely successful because the construction company continuously monitored its stakeholders (the public and the media) and devised ways to proactively address their needs. This regular monitoring showed to stakeholders that their views are valued. Through these efforts, the construction company was able to change these stakeholders' perceptions and encourage them to embrace the project. In contrast, the Lund project was conducted without any stakeholder input or monitoring. It is therefore not surprising to find that this project met with significant resistance and delays.

STAKEHOLDER IMPORTANCE WORLDWIDE

Most experts agree that the key to stakeholder management is to properly assess stakeholder needs and find appropriate ways to satisfy these needs. However, it may not always be possible for a company to satisfy all stakeholder needs. In such cases, it becomes more important to balance needs and to satisfy those needs that are most critical to the company's survival. Many companies develop missions and visions that suggest that some stakeholders are more critical than others. For instance, Starbucks considers its employees as important, if not more important, than customers.

Which stakeholders are considered most important? In this final section, we examine how stakeholders are viewed worldwide.

In a recent piece in the *Harvard Business Review*, Martin traces the evolution of stakeholder importance over history in the U.S. Martin argues that the U.S. business environment saw the birth of managerial capitalism around 1932.[25] Instead of having owner-CEOs run their companies, experts at the time suggested that there should be a separation between owners and managers. However, in 1976, another influential article suggested that owners were getting duped by managers. In the "Theory of the firm: managerial behavior, agency costs and ownership structure", Jensen and Meckling argued that managers were running companies for their own financial interest. Instead, Jensen and Meckling suggested that managers should run companies by focusing on the needs of shareholders.[26] This led to the age of stakeholder capitalism where stakeholder needs became the most important focus of any company.

Is this preference for stakeholders warranted? Martin rightly argues that a focus on shareholders may not always be beneficial for the company.[27] He argues that shareholder value maximization is not always within the control of managers. Managers may find ways to increase the value of shares by raising expectations about the future performance of the company. However, such expectations inevitably decline as it is impossible to continuously increase such expectations. In the light of such reality, managers may often resort to short-term and other misguided strategy to keep stakeholder expectations up. Unfortunately, this goal of putting shareholders first may end up hurting the firm.

Martin thus argues that a better way to benefit the company and shareholders is to put customers first.[28] By focusing on customer value, managers become free to manage and grow the business rather than manage shareholder expectations. Examples of companies such as Procter & Gamble and Johnson & Johnson are all provided to support this notion. Furthermore, even Unilever mentioned earlier in this chapter is known for its focus on customers. In fact, some companies have taken this focus on customers even further. Consider the following Business Ethics Insight.

BUSINESS ETHICS INSIGHT

Focusing on Emerging Markets' Poor Customer Needs

While some companies focus on putting customers first, other companies are taking this focus to the next level. Companies such as Nokia, Tata, and Unilever are all taking into consideration the needs of poor customers in emerging markets. Emerging markets represent tremendous potential and even poor customers are expected to eventually reach the middle class.

Consider some of the products that have been targeted for this segment. Nokia, for example, has developed a cheap handset that includes a flashlight (because of frequent power interruptions), multiple phone books to accommodate several users, and menus in different languages. Tata has developed a water filter that uses rice husks to purify the water. Because of the need for water purification, this very low-tech device can provide bacteria-free water to users. Finally, consider the case of General Electric, which has developed a portable electrocardiogram machine that can run on both batteries and power. This small device is very useful for the Indian market, where heart disease is prevalent and most patients cannot afford the costs associated with traditional electro-cardiogram machines.

This focus on poor customers is termed "frugal innovation." Rather than add new features to products, companies are working backwards to produce robust products that can satisfy customer demands.

Based on *The Economist*. 2010. "First break all of the rules." A special report on innovation in emerging markets. April 17, 6–8.

Although the above provides further proof of the importance of customers as stakeholders, this view is not necessarily shared by all societies. Although there are no recent studies that have investigated stakeholder preference worldwide, many societies are now embracing sustainability as the most important goal. Because of global warming and other potentially negative effects of companies on the environment, companies are also becoming more proactive and adopting corporate sustainability as a key goal.

While the environment may potentially be the most important stakeholder, it is necessary to also note that that importance varies for companies. Depending on their mission, some companies will consider key stakeholders such as customers, employees, and the environment as equally important. The major lesson in this chapter therefore is that, no matter which stakeholder or stakeholders a company holds as most important, these stakeholders need to be managed.

CHAPTER SUMMARY

In this chapter, you learned about the many key issues facing companies as they deal with stakeholders. Stakeholders are groups or individuals that can affect or be influenced by a company's goals. You read about the various classifications of stakeholders such as the primary and secondary classifications. You also learned that both secondary and primary stakeholders can have important influences on companies.

In the second part of the chapter, you learned about stakeholder attributes. You read about three important attributes; namely, power (the degree to which stakeholders can exert pressure on a company), legitimacy (the degree to which a stakeholder's needs are consistent with societal values and beliefs), and urgency (the degree to which stakeholder needs have to be prioritized). Each attribute's importance to the company was discussed and practical examples were provided.

An important message in this chapter is that stakeholders need to be managed. In the third section, key aspects of the stakeholder management process were discussed. The first step expanded on the adequate identification of stakeholders by discussing other available categorizations. In this step, the company needed to properly identify all of the stakeholders that have the potential to influence or be influenced. In the second step, the attributes of stakeholders discussed earlier could then be combined to provide the company with stakeholder prioritization. In other words, the combination of attributes revealed which stakeholders need to be catered to immediately and which other ones can receive attention later. The third step, namely stakeholder visualization and mapping, involved listing all identified stakeholders and corresponding issues associated with the stakeholder. The concept of Shareholder Ethical Responsibility Matrix was discussed in that context. In the fourth step, stakeholder engagement, you learned about the many efforts companies expend to involve their stakeholders in the company's operations and survival. By engaging stakeholders, a company can proactively gauge stakeholder needs and assess such needs before they become problematic. Finally, in the fifth and final step, a monitoring system was put in place to assess the degree of success of the stakeholder management program.

In the final part of the chapter, you read about stakeholder preferences worldwide. You learned about the importance of customers as the most important stakeholder. However, you also learned that customers may not be viewed as the most important stakeholder worldwide. Many examples discussed in the chapter point to the environment. Nevertheless, the important lesson of the chapter is that stakeholders need to be adequately managed.

NOTES

1   Freeman, R.E. 1984. *Strategic management: A stakeholder approach*. Boston: Pitman, p. 3.

2   Freeman, *Strategic management*.

3   Orlitzy, M., Schmidt, F. & Rynes, S.L. 2003. "Corporate social and financial performance: A meta-analysis." *Organization Studies*, 24, 403–441.

4   Hillman, A.J. & Keim, G.D. 2001. "Stakeholder value, stakeholder management, and social issues: what's the bottom line?" *Strategic Management Journal*, 22, 2, 125–139.

5   Choi, J. & Wang, H. 2009. "Stakeholder relations and the persistence of corporate financial performance." *Strategic Management Journal*, 30, 895–907.

6   Mitchell, R., Agle, B. & Wood, D.J. 1997. "Toward a theory of stakeholder identification and salience: Defining the principle of who and what really counts." *Academy of Management Review*, 22, 4, 853–886.

7   Mitchell et al., "Toward a theory of stakeholder identification and salience."

8   Ako, R.T., Obokoh, L.O. & Okonmah, P. 2009. "Forging peaceful relationships between oil companies and host-communities in Nigeria's Delta region." *Journal of Enterprising Communities: People and Practice in the Global Economy*, 3, 2, 205–216.

9   Armenakis, A. & Wigand, J. 2010. "Stakeholder actions and their impact on the organizational cultures of two tobacco companies." *Business and Society Review*, 115, 2, 147–171.

10 Sacks, D. 2010. "The miracle worker." *Fast Company*, 141, 83.

11 Thorne, D.M., Ferrell, O.C. & Ferrell, L. 2010. *Business and society. A strategic approach to social responsibility*. Boston: Houghton Mifflin.

12 Sonpar, K., Pazzaglia, F. & Kornijenko, J. 2010. "The paradox and constraints of legitimacy." *Journal of Business Ethics*, 95, 1–21.

13 Sonpar et al., "The paradox and constraints of legitimacy."

14 Fassin, Y. 2009. "Inconsistencies in activists' behaviours and the ethics of NGOs." *Journal of Business Ethics*, 90, 503–521.

15 Fassin, "Inconsistencies in activists' behaviours and the ethics of NGOs."

16 Choi & Wang, "Stakeholder relations."

17 Moodley, K., Smith, N. & Preece, C. 2008. "Stakeholder matrix for ethical relationships in the construction industry." *Construction Management and Economics*, 26, 625–632.

18 Mitchell et al., "Toward a theory of stakeholder identification and salience."

19 Mitchell et al., "Toward a theory of stakeholder identification and salience."

20 Chinyio, E. & Akintoye, A. 2008. "Practical approaches for engaging stakeholders: Findings from the U.K.." *Construction Management and Economics*, 26, 591–599.

21 Moodley et al., "Stakeholder matrix for ethical relationships in the construction industry."

22 Moodley et al., "Stakeholder matrix for ethical relationships in the construction industry."

23 Chinyio & Akintoye, "Practical approaches for engaging stakeholders."

24 Chinyio & Akintoye, "Practical approaches for engaging stakeholders."

25 Martin, R. 2010. "The age of customer capitalism." *Harvard Business Review*, January, 58–66.

26 Jensen, Michael C. & Meckling, William H. 1976. "Theory of the firm: Managerial behavior, agency costs and ownership structure." *Journal of Financial Economics*, 3, 4.

27 Martin, "The age of customer capitalism."

28 Martin, "The age of customer capitalism."

KEY TERMS

Coercive power: use of force, violence, or other restraint to force a company to accommodate or respond to their needs.

Dangerous stakeholders: have power and urgency but no legitimacy.

Definitive stakeholders: have power, urgency, and are legitimate.

Demanding stakeholders: have urgency but do not have power or legitimacy.

Dependent stakeholders: are those stakeholders that have urgency and legitimacy.

Discretionary stakeholder: stakeholder which has legitimacy but no power or urgency.

Dominant stakeholders: represents stakeholders that are both powerful and legitimate.

Dormant stakeholders: stakeholders that possess power but have no legitimate claims or urgency.

Expectant stakeholders: stakeholders are those that possess two of the attributes.

Latent stakeholders: are those that possess only one of the three attributes and thus represent low salience.

Legitimacy: company conducts itself in such a way that is consistent with widely held values and beliefs.

Normative power: refers to the use of symbolic and other resources to force a company to accommodate stakeholder needs.

Primary stakeholders: stakeholders directly linked to a company's survival and are either impacted or impact companies directly.

Salience: influence any stakeholder can have on a company's operations.

Secondary stakeholders: stakeholders that tend to be less directly linked to the company's survival and include the media, trade associations, and special-interest groups.

Stakeholder: any group or individual that can affect or is affected by the achievement of an organization's objectives.

Stakeholder engagement: deliberate attempt of a company to actively seek its stakeholders' inputs to better deal with their needs and also improve their operations.

Stakeholder identification: main focus is to properly identify stakeholders.

Stakeholder management: refers to the deliberate and purposeful process a company has devised to work with its stakeholders.

Stakeholder monitoring: determines how stakeholders are responding to stakeholder management issues and if further actions are necessary.

Stakeholder power: ability of a stakeholder to exert pressures to force a company to make changes to accommodate such pressures.

Urgency: refers to the degree to which a company needs to respond to stakeholder needs.

Utilitarian power: refers to the use of financial or other monetary means to force a company to accommodate a particular stakeholder need.

Visualizing and mapping stakeholders: necessary step to determine the extent of claims, rights, and expectations stakeholders have and the appropriate response to these needs.

DISCUSSION QUESTIONS

1. What are stakeholders? Why do stakeholders matter to companies?
2. What are primary stakeholders? How are primary stakeholders different from secondary stakeholders? Discuss your answer with examples.
3. What are the three types of stakeholder attributes? Illustrate your answer with one example for each stakeholder attribute.
4. What are the three different types of stakeholder power? How do these forms of power impact a company differently?
5. Compare and contrast stakeholder legitimacy and stakeholder urgency.
6. Briefly discuss the five steps of the stakeholder management process. Illustrate each step with examples.
7. What is stakeholder prioritization? How can companies identify which stakeholders need to be attended to quickly?
8. What are latent stakeholders? How are they different from expectant stakeholders?
9. What is stakeholder engagement? What are the steps companies can take to engage their stakeholders?
10. What is stakeholder monitoring? What steps can companies take to monitor their stakeholders?

INTERNET ACTIVITY

1. Go to the Unilever website: http://www.unilever.com.
2. Review the company's vision and goals. Discuss their purposes and principles and how they relate to the issues discussed in this chapter.
3. What do you learn about who Unilever's most important stakeholders are?
4. Describe in detail each of Unilever's important stakeholders. How do they address the needs of each stakeholder?
5. What are some of the codes that Unilever abides by as they deal with suppliers?

For more Internet Activities and resources, please visit the Companion Website at www.routledge.com/cw/parboteeah.

WHAT WOULD YOU DO?

Plant Closing in Wisconsin

You are the owner of a plant producing automotive parts in a small town in Wisconsin. Your plant is the main employer of the small town. You have lived in the town for your whole life. Your father operated the plant until you took over. Your family is well established in the town. You are involved in many charities in the town. Your children also attend the local schools.

The recent economic downturn has been very disastrous for your company, as you have suffered a significant decline in revenues. Despite these losses, you have not yet terminated any employee. You have been able to survive mostly because of your strong relationships with your customers. You are very reliable and have operated a very ethical company and most customers have stuck with you.

When you showed up to your office today, your assistant mentioned that the Chief Executive Officer of a German competitor called you. You call him back and he proposes to buy your plant for a very attractive price. However, you also learn that, if you sell, the German company will likely try to consolidate operations with another plant they bought in Pennsylvania. You find that all of your employees will be offered the option to move to the Pennsylvanian plant.

What would you do? Do you go ahead with the sale? Who is affected by such sale? How do you take into consideration the impact of your actions on the town if you sell?

BRIEF CASE: BUSINESS ETHICS INSIGHT

Taiwan's Sun Moon Lake

Taiwan's Sun Moon Lake is considered one of Taiwan's vacation spots. The lake, which originated as a Japanese era reservoir, is surrounded by beautiful mountain scenery. It is a preferred spot for both local and foreign tourists. The lake is also popular with the Chinese, as it is described in Chinese literature. Furthermore, the lake acquired even more mystique as legal barriers prevented the Chinese from visiting the lake. Now that such barriers are slowly being removed, there is strong desire for Chinese tourists to visit the lake as its beauty is perceived as unmatched on the Chinese mainland.

Recent indicators suggest that the popularity of Sun Moon Lake is indeed growing. For instance, the Sun Moon Lake International Fireworks Festival that was started in 2003 now draws hordes of people interested in both music and fireworks. Furthermore, recent official figures show that the number of Chinese tourists during the first week of October (a holiday to celebrate China's national day) of 2010 nearly doubled compared to the previous year. The Taiwanese government is continuing its sustained effort to advertise the lake in many nearby Asian countries such as South Korea and Japan.

However, not everyone is happy with the growing popularity of Sun Moon Lake. Many locals and environmentalists suspect that the continuing development will spoil the lake's natural beauty. Many hotels are being built at a very quick pace in anticipation of more affluent Chinese making visits to the lake. However, such construction is taking place without much planning. In fact, one of the hotels under construction will be 30 floors high, greatly exceeding the seven-floor limit. Furthermore, it is anticipated that more hotels will be built.

Locals are thus worried that such a construction boom will affect the region environmentally. The influx of tourists has already started to create traffic jams and other ills associated with more people. However, locals are also very worried that the growth of hotels and customers will cause increased pollution to the lake. With more tourists, local tourism officials believe that the lake water quality may go down. In 2007, four hotels were fined for improper waste treatment. However, as more hotels go up, it becomes very unlikely that local officials will still be able to properly manage the environmental impact of these hotels.

Sun Moon Lake officials thus have to properly manage the growth of the region. While increased tourism will bring in additional profits (it is estimated that tourists spent an average of $232 per day during the first "golden" week of October 2010), the impact on the environment will also need to be assessed.

Based on Anonymous. 2010. "Chinese visitors to Taiwan double in first October Week." *Asia Pulse*, October 8; Business Wire, 2010. "Sun Moon Lake International Fireworks music festival." *Business Wire*, August 19; Jennings, R. 2008. "Tourism brightens, darkens Taiwan's Sun Moon Lake." *Reuters*, online edition.

BRIEF CASE QUESTIONS

1. Who are the primary stakeholders in this case? Identify secondary stakeholders.
2. Who are most affected by the changes at Sun Moon Lake? How are they affected?
3. How would you compare the benefits of higher tourism profits with the environmental impact of increased tourism? What would you do if you were a local tourism official at Sun Moon Lake?
4. Assume that you are hired as a consultant by a hotel chain interested in building a hotel at Sun Moon Lake. What would you advise them? Describe the methodology you will use to provide advice.

LONG CASE: BUSINESS ETHICS

MERCK CO., INC.

In 1978, Dr. P. Roy Vagelos, then head of the Merck research labs, received a provocative memorandum from a senior researcher in parasitology, Dr. William C. Campbell. Dr. Campbell had made an intriguing observation while working with ivermectin, a new antiparasitic compound under investigation for use in animals.

Campbell thought that ivermectin might be the answer to a disease called river blindness that plagued millions in the Third World. But to find out if Campbell's hypothesis had merit, Merck would have to spend millions of dollars to develop the right formulation for human use and to conduct the field trials in the most remote parts of the world. Even if these efforts produced an effective and safe drug, virtually all of those afflicted with river blindness could not afford to buy it. Vagelos, originally a university researcher but by then a Merck executive, had to decide whether to invest in research for a drug that, even if successful, might never pay for itself.

River Blindness

River blindness, formally known as onchocerciasis, was a disease labeled by the World Health Organization (WHO) as a public health and socioeconomic problem of considerable magnitude in over 35 developing countries throughout the Third World. Some 85 million people in thousands of tiny settlements throughout Africa and parts of the Middle East and Latin America were thought to be at risk. The cause: a parasitic worm carried by a tiny black fly which bred along fast-moving rivers. When the flies bit humans—a single person could be bitten thousands of times a day—the larvae of a parasitic worm, *Onchocerca volvulus*, entered the body.

These worms grew to more than two feet in length, causing grotesque but relatively innocuous nodules in the skin. The real harm began when the adult worms reproduced, releasing millions of microscopic offspring, known as microfilariae, which swarmed through body tissue. A terrible itching resulted, so bad that some victims committed suicide. After several years, the microfilariae caused lesions and depigmentation of the skin. Eventually they invaded the eyes, often causing blindness.

The World Health Organization estimated in 1978 that some 340,000 people were blind because of onchocerciasis, and that a million more suffered from varying degrees of visual impairment. At that time, 18 million or more people were infected with the parasite, though half did not yet have serious symptoms. In some villages close to breeding sites, nearly all residents were infected and a majority of those over age 45 were blind. In such places, it was said, children believed that severe itching, skin infections, and blindness were simply part of growing up.

In desperate efforts to escape the flies, entire villages abandoned fertile areas near rivers, and moved to poorer land. As a result, food shortages were frequent. Community life disintegrated as new burdens arose for already impoverished families.

The disease was first identified in 1893 by scientists and in 1926 was found to be related to the black flies. But by the 1970s, there was still no cure that could safely be used for community-wide treatment. Two drugs, diethylcarbamazine (DEC) and Suramin, were useful in killing the parasite, but both had severe side effects in infected individuals, needed close monitoring, and had even caused deaths. In 1974, the Onchocerciasis Control Program was created to be administered by the World Health Organization, in the hope that the flies could be killed through spraying of larvacides at breeding sites, but success was slow and uncertain. The flies in many areas developed resistance to the treatment, and were also known to disappear and then reinfest areas.

Merck & Co., Inc.

Merck & Co., Inc. was, in 1978, one of the largest producers of prescription drugs in the world. Headquartered in Rahway, New Jersey, Merck traced its origins to Germany in 1668, when Friedrich Jacob Merck purchased an apothecary in the city of Darmstadt. Over three hundred years later, Merck, having become an American firm, employed over 28,000 people and had operations all over the world.

In the late 1970s, Merck was coming off a ten-year drought in terms of new products. For nearly a decade, the company had relied on two prescription drugs for a significant percentage of its approximately $2 billion in annual sales: Indocin, a treatment for rheumatoid arthritis, and Aldomet, a treatment for high blood pressure. Henry W. Gadsden, Merck's chief executive from 1965 to 1976, along with his successor, John J. Horan, were concerned that the 17-year patent protection on Merck's two big moneymakers would soon expire, and began investing an enormous amount in research.

Merck management spent a great deal of money on research because it knew that its success ten and twenty years in the future critically depended upon present investments. The company deliberately fashioned a corporate culture to nurture the most creative, fruitful research. Merck scientists were among the best-paid in the industry, and were given great latitude to pursue intriguing leads. Moreover, they were inspired to think of their work as a quest to alleviate human disease and suffering worldwide. Within certain proprietary constraints, researchers were encouraged to publish in academic journals and to share ideas with their scientific peers. Nearly a billion dollars was spent between 1975 and 1978, and the investment paid off. In that period, under the direction of head of research, Dr. P. Roy Vagelos, Merck introduced Clinoril, a painkiller for arthritis; a general antibiotic called Mefoxin; a drug for glaucoma named Timoptic; and Ivomec (ivermectin, MSD), an antiparasitic for cattle.

In 1978, Merck had sales of $1.98 billion and net income of $307 million. Sales had risen steadily between 1969 and 1978 from $691 million to almost $2 billion. Income during the same period rose from $106 million to over $300 million. (See Exhibit 1 for a ten-year summary of performance.)

At that time, Merck employed 28,700 people, up from 22,200 ten years earlier. Human and animal health products constituted 84% of the company's sales, with environmental health products and services representing an additional 14% of sales. Merck's foreign sales had grown more rapidly during the 1970s than had domestic sales, and in 1978 represented 47% of total sales. Much of the company's research operations were organized separately as the Merck Sharp & Dohme Research Laboratories, headed by Vagelos. Other Merck operations included the Merck Sharp & Dohme Division, the Merck Sharp & Dohme International Division, Kelco Division, Merck Chemical Manufacturing Division, Merck Animal Health Division, Calgon Corporation, Baltimore Aircoil Company, and Hubbard Farms.

The company had 24 plants in the United States, including one in Puerto Rico, and 44 in other countries. Six research laboratories were located in the United States and four abroad.

While Merck executives sometimes squirmed when they quoted the "unbusinesslike" language of George W. Merck, son of the company's founder and its former chairman, there could be no doubt that Merck employees found the words inspirational. "We try never to forget that medicine is for the people," Merck said. "It is not for the profits. The profits follow, and if we have remembered that, they have never failed to appear. The better we have remembered it, the larger they have been." These words formed the basis of Merck's overall corporate philosophy.

The Drug Investment Decision

Merck invested hundreds of millions of dollars each year in research. Allocating those funds amongst various projects, however, was a rather involved and inexact process. At a company as large as Merck, there was never a single method by which projects were approved or money distributed.

Studies showed that, on the average, it took 12 years and $200 million to bring a new drug to market. Thousands of scientists were continually working on new ideas and following new leads. Drug development was always a matter of trial and error; with each new iteration, scientists would close some doors and open others. When a Merck researcher came across an apparent breakthrough—either in an unexpected direction, or as a derivative of the original lead—he or she would conduct preliminary research. If the idea proved promising, it was brought to the attention of the department heads.

Every year, Merck's research division held a large review meeting at which all research programs were examined. Projects were coordinated and consolidated, established programs were reviewed, and new possibilities were considered. Final approval on research was not made, however, until the head of research met later with a committee of scientific advisors. Each potential program was extensively reviewed, analyzed on the basis of the likelihood of success, the existing market, competition, potential safety problems, manufacturing feasibility, and patent status before the decision was made whether to allocate funds for continued experimentation.

The Problem of Rare Diseases and Poor Customers

Many potential drugs offered little chance of financial return. Some diseases were so rare that treatments developed could never be priced high enough to recoup the investment in research, while other diseases afflicted only the poor in rural and remote areas of the Third World. These victims had limited ability to pay even a small amount for drugs or treatment.

EXHIBIT 1—10 Year Summary of Financial Performance (Marck & Co., Inc. and Subsidiaries)
(Dollar amounts in thousands except per-share figures)

Results for Year:	1978	1977	1976	1975	1974	1973	1972	1971	1970	1969
Sales	$1,981,440	$1,724,410	$1,561,117	$1,401,979	$1,260,416	$1,104,035	$942,631	$832,416	$761,109	$691,453
Materials and production costs	744,249	662,703	586,963	525,853	458,837	383,879	314,804	286,646	258,340	232,878
Marketing/administrative expenses	542,186	437,579	396,975	354,525	330,292	304,807	268,856	219,005	201,543	178,593
Research/development expenses	161,350	144,898	133,826	121,933	100,952	89,155	79,692	71,619	69,707	61,100
Interest expense	25,743	25,743	26,914	21,319	8,445	6,703	4,533	3,085	2,964	1,598
Income before taxes	507,912	453,487	416,439	378,349	361,890	319,491	274,746	252,061	228,555	217,284
Taxes on income	198,100	173,300	159,100	147,700	149,300	134,048	121,044	118,703	108,827	109,269
Net income**	307,534	277,525	255,482	228,778	210,492	182,681	151,180	131,381	117,878	106,645
Per common share**	$4.07	$3.67	$3.38	$3.03	$2.79	$2.43	$2.01	$1.75	$1.57	$1.43
Dividends declared on common stock	132,257	117,101	107,584	105,564	106,341	93,852	84,103	82,206	76,458	75,528
Per common share	$1.75	$1.55	$1.42½	$1.40	$1.40	$1.23½	$1.12	$1.10	$1.02½	$1.02½
Gross plant additions	155,853	177,167	153,894	249,015	159,148	90,194	69,477	67,343	71,540	48,715
Depreciation	75,477	66,785	58,198	52,091	46,057	40,617	36,283	32,104	27,819	23,973
Year-End Position:										
Working capital	666,817	629,515	549,840	502,262	359,591	342,434	296,378	260,350	226,084	228,296
Property, plant, and equipment net	924,179	846,784	747,107	652,804	459,245	352,145	305,416	274,240	239,638	197,220
Total assets	2,251,358	1,993,389	1,759,371	1,538,999	1,243,287	988,985	834,847	736,503	664,294	601,484
Stockholders' equity	1,455,135	1,277,753	1,102,154	949,991	822,782	709,614	621,792	542,978	493,214	451,030
Year-End Statistics:										
Average number of common shares outstanding (in thousands)	75,573	75,546	75,493	75,420	75,300	75,193	75,011	74,850	74,850	74,547
Number of stockholders	62,900	63,900	63,500	63,500	61,400	60,000	58,000	54,300	54,600	53,100
Number of employees	28,700	28,100	26,800	26,300	26,500	25,100	24,100	23,200	23,000	22,200

* The above data are as previously reported, restated for poolings-of-interests and stock splits.
** Net income for 1977 and related per-share amounts exclude gain on disposal of businesses of $13,225 and 18¢, respectively.

In the United States, Congress sought to encourage drug companies to conduct research on rare diseases. In 1978 legislation had been proposed which would grant drug companies tax benefits and seven-year exclusive marketing rights if they would manufacture drugs for diseases afflicting fewer than 200,000 Americans. It was expected that this "orphan drug" program would eventually be passed into law.

There was, however, no U.S. or international program that would create incentives for companies to develop drugs for diseases like river blindness, which afflicted millions of the poor in the Third World. The only hope was that some Third World government, foundation, or international aid organization might step in and partially fund the distribution of a drug that had already been developed.

The Discovery of Ivermectin

The process of investigating promising drug compounds was always long, laborious, and fraught with failure. For every pharmaceutical compound that became a "product candidate," thousands of others failed to meet the most rudimentary pre-clinical tests for safety and efficacy. With so much room for failure, it became especially important for drug companies to have sophisticated research managers who could identify the most productive research strategies.

Merck had long been a pioneer in developing major new antibiotic compounds, beginning with penicillin and streptomycin in the 1940s. In the 1970s, Merck Sharp & Dohme Research Laboratories were continuing this tradition. To help investigate for new microbial agents of potential therapeutic value, Merck researchers obtained 54 soil samples from the Kitasato Institute of Japan in 1974. These samples seemed novel and the researchers hoped they might disclose some naturally occurring antibiotics.

As Merck researchers methodically put the soil through hundreds of tests, Merck scientists were pleasantly surprised to detect strong antiparasitic activity in Sample No. OS3153, a scoop of soil dug up at a golf course near Ito, Japan. The Merck labs quickly brought together an interdisciplinary team to try to isolate a pure active ingredient from the microbial culture. The compound eventually isolated—ivermectin—proved to have an astonishing potency and effectiveness against a wide range of parasites in cattle, swine, horses, and other animals. Within a year, the Merck team also began to suspect that a group of related compounds discovered in the same soil sample could be effective against many other intestinal worms, mites, ticks, and insects.

After toxicological tests suggested that ivermectin would be safer than related compounds, Merck decided to develop the substance for the animal health market. In 1978 the first ivermectin-based animal drug, Ivomec, was nearing approval by the U.S. Department of Agriculture and foreign regulatory bodies. Many variations would likely follow: drugs for sheep and pigs, horses, dogs, and others. Ivomec had the potential to become a major advance in animal health treatment.

As clinical testing of ivermectin progressed in the late 1970s, Dr. William Campbell's ongoing research brought him face-to-face with an intriguing hypothesis. Ivermectin, when tested in horses, was effective against the microfilariae of an exotic, fairly unimportant gastrointestinal parasite, *Onchocerca cervicalis*. This particular worm, while harmless in horses, had characteristics similar to the insidious human parasite that causes river blindness, *Onchocerca volvulus*.

Dr. Campbell wondered: Could ivermectin be formulated to work against the human parasite? Could a safe, effective drug suitable for community-wide treatment of river blindness be developed? Both Campbell and Vagelos knew that it was very much a gamble that it would succeed. Furthermore, both knew that even if success were attained, the economic viability of such a project would be nil. On the other hand, because such a significant amount of money had already been invested in the development of the animal drug, the cost of developing a human formulation would be much less than that for developing a new compound. It was also widely believed at this point that ivermectin, though still in its final development stages, was likely to be very successful.

A decision to proceed would not be without risks. If a new derivative proved to have any adverse health effects when used on humans, its reputation as a veterinary drug could be tainted and sales negatively affected, no matter how irrelevant the experience with humans. In early tests, ivermectin had had some negative side effects on some specific species of mammals. Dr. Brian Duke of the Armed Forces Institute of Pathology in Washington, D.C. said the cross-species effectiveness of antiparasitic drugs is unpredictable, and there is "always a worry that some race or sub-section of the human population" might be adversely affected.

Isolated instances of harm to humans or improper use in Third World settings might also raise some unsettling questions: Could drug residues turn up in meat eaten by humans? Would any human version of ivermectin distributed to the Third World be diverted into the black market, undercutting sales of the veterinary drug? Could the drug harm certain animals in unknown ways?

Despite these risks, Vagelos wondered what the impact might be of turning down Campbell's proposal. Merck had built a research team dedicated to alleviating human suffering. What would a refusal to pursue a possible treatment for river blindness do to morale?

Ultimately, it was Dr. Vagelos who had to make the decision whether or not to fund research toward a treatment for river blindness.

LONG CASE QUESTIONS

1. What are the main ethical issues in this case?
2. Should Merck go ahead and develop the drug? How can Merck justify the decision?
3. Who are the stakeholders affected by the decision?
4. What can Merck do to allay the concerns of the main stakeholders if they decide to develop the drug?

Chapter 3

Building Ethics at the Individual Level

LEARNING OBJECTIVES

After reading this chapter you should be able to:

- Understand what individual ethics is
- Learn about the many aspects and factors that contribute to individual ethics
- Become aware of the concept of moral awareness to understand how individuals assess the ethical nature of situations
- Understand what moral judgment is
- Become aware of Kohlberg's cognitive moral development, moral philosophies, and moral theories
- Understand how companies can provide training to better equip their workers to deal with moral judgment
- Become aware of moral disengagement and other biases that encourage people to behave unethically
- Learn about the many steps companies can take to better prepare employees to be ethical

PREVIEW BUSINESS ETHICS INSIGHT

Individuals and Ethics

Examples of people behaving unethically and engaging in corruption are plenty. Consider the classic case of Enron. Although the Enron case tends to be used frequently to illustrate individual unethical behavior, it is important to appreciate how the company went from one of the most admired companies to oblivion. Enron collapsed in 2001 under a mountain of debt. Over time, several high-ranking officials in the company, including CEO Jeffrey Skilling, Chairman Ken Lay, and Chief Financial Officer Andrew Fastow, condoned a number of practices that concealed the debt. For instance, they created special-purpose entities to move its assets and losses, thereby showing cash flow in the company. Skilling was also instrumental in creating a rank and yank system that basically ranked employees every six months, whereby the bottom 20% of employees were fired. This also created an atmosphere where employees were ready to lie to keep their jobs. Furthermore, many accounting improprieties occurred whereby investors were being misled. This all came to a crash in 2001.

The case of Enron is not unique. Other companies such as WorldCom and Arthur Andersen also suffered considerable damage mainly due to individual misbehavior. These companies also had individuals who devised schemes for personal gains that ultimately led to the downfall of the companies.

However, although there are many examples of individuals perpetrating unethical behavior, there are others who are willing to take the risk and expose such practice. Consider the case of Enron Vice President Sherron Watkins. When she was given the task of finding more assets to sell by the CEO, she was troubled to find the many accounting irregularities at Enron. She then confronted CEO Skilling. However, Skilling decided to quit and Watkins then wrote a memo to the newly appointed CEO Ken Lay. Rather than investigate her suspicions, Ms. Watkins was demoted and moved from her plush executive office in the top floors of Enron headquarters to a more ordinary office in the basement of the building. Her hard drive was also confiscated, while the new tasks she was assigned became rather meaningless relative to the high-level projects she used to work on. Her testimonies eventually helped convict the high-ranking officials at Enron. Similar cases of whistle-blowers exist in many other companies.

Based on Herndon, N. 2011. "Enron: Questionable accounting lead to collapse." In Thorne, D.M., Ferrell, O.C., and Ferrell, L. 2010. *Business and society. A strategic approach to social responsibility*. Boston: Houghton Mifflin.

The Preview Business Ethics Insight above highlights the importance of individual actions with regards to unethical behavior. In the many examples discussed, single individuals or groups of individuals conspired and engaged in actions that resulted in major losses for large groups of people. For example, the fall of Enron resulted in tens of billions of losses for investors as well as employees. However, the examples also show that there were concerned individuals who eventually decided to blow the whistle. These individuals often felt that what they were observing went against their own principles and beliefs. Unlike others who either turned a blind eye or supported the unethical behavior, they decided to find ways to stop such unethical behaviors.

The Preview Business Ethics Insight provides evidence that unethical behavior starts with individuals within a company. Consistent with accepted practices, we define **unethical behavior** as any actions that violate accepted societal norms.[1] While many argue that the organizational culture can play an important role in promoting unethical behavior, the culture can partly be blamed on individuals supporting and enforcing the unethical norms of the culture. It therefore becomes very important to understand how and why individuals behave unethically. Furthermore, the examples show that some other individuals are less likely to conform to pressures around them and are more inclined to follow their own beliefs and principles. It also becomes crucial to understand why some behave unethically while others are more prone to follow their own ethical principles.

Why should companies attempt to understand individual ethics to reduce unethical behavior? Chapter 1 discussed the many benefits of ethical behavior for companies. Companies enjoy better financial results and many other side benefits. However, Giacalone and Promislo provide further evidence of the need of reducing unethical behavior.[2] They argue that unethical behavior can lead to a decrease in general well-being as a result of the trauma and stress associated with either being victimized or committing unethical behavior. Understanding individual ethics can thus help a company ensure its employees' well-being. Thus, from a strategic standpoint, reducing unethical behavior should result in more productive and happier employees.

In this chapter, we therefore consider the many critical aspects of ethics as they apply to individuals. To provide a systematic coverage of individual ethics, we frame our discussion within Rest's stages of ethical decision-making.[3] Rest argues that individuals go through several stages before they decide to commit an unethical behavior. We consider the relevant stages and the implications for understanding individual ethics. Specifically, we discuss both moral awareness and aspects of moral judgment. In doing so, we also discuss how companies can address these issues. Additionally, we consider moral disengagement and biases as a reflection of the factors behind why ethical individuals may still engage in unethical behavior despite having a strong moral code.

MORAL AWARENESS

One of the most important phases of understanding individual ethics is moral awareness. **Moral awareness** refers to the ability of an individual to understand the ethicality of a situation or behavior. It is considered as one of the most important aspects of ethical decision-making, since the ability to identify a situation as being ethical suggests that steps may be taken to ensure that consequent behavior is ethical.[4] Although appreciating the ethicality of a decision seems obvious, evidence suggests that people do not always properly understand such ethicality. Consider the Business Ethics Insight on page 108.

BUSINESS ETHICS INSIGHT

Hacking into MBA Admission Systems

Application into university programs always entails the long wait to hear about whether one has gotten admitted or not. However, for some applicants to some of the U.S. most prestigious MBA programs, the wait took a different turn. While visiting a Businessweek online messaging board, some applicants came across hacking instructions posted by an anonymous hacker. The hacking instructions basically gave access to the decision page to MBA programs at Harvard, Dartmouth, Duke, Carnegie Mellon, MIT, and Stanford. These universities were all using the same program, where students simply had to change the URL to add applicant specific details. This then gave access to whether they were admitted to the program or a blank page signifying that a decision had not yet been made.

In the time it took the company running the program to apply a patch, around 200 students were able to access the page. The universities were quickly given the names of those who hacked into the system. Harvard immediately took a stance reporting that they would deny admission to those 119 applicants who hacked into the system. The Dean of the School of Business stated that the hacking was clearly unethical. These applicants were gaining access to information to which they should not have had any access. Similar reactions occurred later at MIT and Stanford. Most of the other deans also saw the behaviors as unethical and dishonest.

However, these decisions, especially Harvard's, were criticized by some. The critics argued that the fault was with the company that did not safeguard its system from hacking. Furthermore, some suggested that these applicants were not really hackers. Rather they used their own account to access information that was ultimately going to be provided to them anyways. Additionally, the applicants could not really change any aspect of their file.

Interviews with applicants who hacked into the system were also fascinating. Many applicants felt offended, as their ethics were being called into question. They did not necessarily find any ethical aspect around the behavior, as they felt that they were only accessing their information and were not harming others. Another applicant apologized to Harvard, arguing that curiosity got the best of him. However, this applicant also did not feel that the behavior was unethical.

Based on Griffith, V. 2005. "Harvard hackers must await their fate." *Financial Times*, March 5, online version.

The above clearly shows that what many would perceive as unethical was clearly not seen as such by the applicants. Accessing the decision web page is equivalent to getting unauthorized access to restricted pages. Such a behavior is clearly unethical. However, many of the applicants failed to understand the unethical nature of their actions. Why did these applicants not see the ethics of their actions? Was it simply because they grew up in the internet age and do not see web snooping as an ethical issue? The case nevertheless suggests that companies need to work hard to train their employees to be able to properly identify the ethics of their behaviors.

How do individuals evaluate the moral intensity or ethicality of behaviors? According to Jones, people evaluate any situation according to six basic elements.[5] These elements include: 1) **magnitude of consequences**—refers to the degree of harm that the victims of an unethical choice will have to endure; 2) **social consensus**—the degree to which others agree that a specific behavior is wrong; 3) **probability of effect**— the probability that any action will result in harm to victims of the action; 4) **temporal immediacy**—the length of time between the action and the harmful consequences of such actions; 5) **proximity**—the psychological or cultural nearness to the victim; and 6) **concentration of effect**—the number of people affected by the act. According to Jones, the moral intensity of any action increases with any increase in one of the six elements.[6]

To gain better insights into the theory, Jones' six elements can be applied to the hacking case discussed earlier. Many applicants felt that their actions did not really harm anyone. Thus, the magnitude of consequences was negligible and the action not perceived as unethical. Furthermore, social consensus was low for the applicants. Experts argued that many of the applicants grew up in the internet age and did not believe that accessing a website was wrong. Furthermore, probability of effect, concentration of effect, and proximity were low simply because most applicants did not perceive that anyone was being harmed by their action. Finally, temporal immediacy was low because no harm was necessarily perceived.

As mentioned earlier, people will perceive moral intensity if any of the six elements is perceived at a high level. For example, it is likely that other applicants who had a chance to hack did not hack because they felt that the action of hacking is simply wrong. For these individuals, social consensus was at a high level. Furthermore, some applicants likely felt that the magnitude of consequences was high because, by getting an earlier decision, they could craft the next move ahead of others. Such a competitive edge would have "harmed" other applicants. Additionally, some applicants may have felt some form of proximity as it is likely that some of their close friends who were also applying to MBA programs would be at a disadvantage from their action. Thus, proximity for some individuals may have been high.

A recent review of published studies provides support for Jones' assertions.[7] Specifically, the review showed that all six elements were indeed negatively related to unethical choices. Such results are consistent with the main assertions that low levels of each of the six components should result in less unethical choices. Furthermore, the authors of the review also created a combined measure for all six elements. They found that the combined elements also resulted in reduced unethical choices.

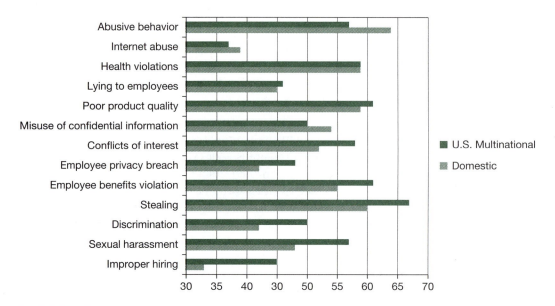

EXHIBIT 3.1 — Misconduct Reported in Survey (% of Respondents)

Given the above, companies can take the necessary steps to promote ethical behavior. First, it becomes critical for companies to provide training regarding proper identification of issues with moral implications.[8] For example, training can be provided to help employees see the harm they can inflict on victims (i.e., magnitude of consequences) or their closeness to potential victims (i.e., proximity). Second, companies can highlight issues with moral implications so as to create a norm that such issues are wrong. Consider Exhibit 3.1, which shows the results of the Ethics Resource Center survey of employees worldwide.

As Exhibit 3.1 shows, most companies, whether domestic or international, experience misconduct. Such misconduct can range from employee issues, such as discrimination and sexual harassment, to information technology issues, such as internet abuse. Companies can provide training to employees, sensitizing them to these many examples of unethical behavior. By providing such training, employees can be made aware of the unethical nature of such activities. By equipping workers to better identify behaviors with unethical consequences, it is more likely that employees will take the necessary steps to reduce the likelihood that the behavior occurs. Furthermore, for each of the misconducts discussed, the moral intensity of the actions can be clarified. Each of the six elements can be discussed within the context of each of the misconducts.

MORAL JUDGMENT

Once an individual has recognized an issue as having ethical implications, the next step is to understand how that individual deals with the situation. **Moral judgment** refers to the process by which someone reasons about how to deal with an ethical situation.

While there are many aspects of moral judgment, three aspects seem highly relevant to understand individual ethics. In this section, we therefore consider cognitive moral development, idealism/relativism, and ethical theories.

Cognitive Moral Development

Kohlberg's cognitive moral development theory remains one of the most important theories of ethical judgment.[9] To develop the theory, Kohlberg presented males in middle childhood to young adulthood with hypothetical moral dilemmas.[10] He then analyzed how his subjects responded spontaneously to these moral dilemmas. Kolberg found that individuals move through six stages of moral reasoning over time. As individuals move at higher levels, their ethical reasoning becomes more sophisticated.

Kohlberg's first stage is known as the obedience to **authority/fear of punishment stage** whereby the person defines right or wrong based on the obedience to rules from those in power. The primary rationale for someone at this stage is to avoid punishment by behaving consistent with expectations of those who have power. Kohlberg observed this mostly in the young children he studied. When applied to the organization, someone at this stage would decide not to bribe a foreign official because that person fears the potential punishment he/she may have to endure if his/her boss finds out.

The second stage of Kohlberg's theory is known as the **self-interest stage** where the person chooses the action that satisfies the person's self-interest the most. Instead of basing decisions on those who are in power, here the decision-maker makes the choice that is based on personal gains. As such, someone might decide to bribe in a foreign country because of the possibility of getting an order which will ultimately boost the person's income.

People who are at the third stage, known as **expectations of others** stage, now make their judgment about right or wrong based on the expectations of significant others and peers.[11] At this stage, rather than simply consider personal gains, an individual determines right or wrong based on the impact of the consequences of their actions on significant others. For instance, someone may decide not to bribe a foreign official because that action may eventually harm the organization through fines and the consequent loss of reputation. Such consequences may result in job losses for many.

At stage four of Kohlberg's theory, known as the **rules and laws stage**, an individual's moral judgment is externally oriented and based on whether the action respects rules and policies. At this stage, the decision-maker judges an action as right or wrong depending on whether such actions violate rules and regulations. For instance, an employee may decide not to bribe a foreign official because doing so would violate the company's code of conduct.

Individuals at stage five, or the **principled** stage, base their decisions on ethical principles of right and wrong and consider good to society. At this stage, the individual considers the impact of his/her actions based on the consequences for society and whether the action respects basic societal expectations. For instance, an individual may decide against bribing because such an action may violate local cultural norms.

111

The **universal ethical principles stage** is the last stage of Kohlberg's cognitive moral development theory. At this stage, the decision-maker determines whether an action is right based on universal ethical principles that everyone should follow. This stage is different from stage five in that the principles considered should apply to everyone rather than be specific to a country or culture. For instance, an individual may decide not to bribe because bribes are considered universally wrong.

According to the theory, people progress through these six stages as they mature and get ethics training. Furthermore, the higher the stage, the more sophisticated an individual's reasoning is about issues with moral implications. Research shows that most adults are at stages three or four.[12] However, only about 20% of adults are believed to reach the higher level stages (i.e., stages five or six). Additionally, it is believed that stage six is more of a theoretical stage, as very little empirical evidence has been found for that stage.

Despite the popularity of Kohlberg's theory, it has still received significant criticism. Critics have argued that people do not necessarily go through the rigid hierarchy as originally proposed.[13] Furthermore, some criticize Kohlberg's data collection methods arguing that he relied on self-reported data as the primary source for his study. Self-reports tend to be problematic as respondents may not always reveal their true details. In other cases, respondents may exaggerate or respond in ways consistent with the

Kohlberg (1969)	Rest (1986)	Examples
Stage 1: Authority/fear of punishment—You do what you are told to avoid punishment	Level 1: Pre-conventional level—Focus is on the self	Decision not to bribe foreign officials for fear of punishment if supervisor finds out
Stage 2: Self-interest—You scratch my back, I scratch yours		Decision to bribe because bribe results in personal gains
Stage 3: Expectations of others —Decisions are made to please other people and society	Level 2: Conventional level—Focus is on relationships and others' well-being	Decision not to bribe as bribe may hurt organization if sued
Stage 4: Rules and laws stage— Follow the laws and regulations		Decision not to bribe so as not to break company code of conduct
Stage 5: Principled stage—Base decisions on ethical principles of right and wrong	Level 3: Post-conventional level—Focus is on universal rules and regulations	Decision not to bribe as bribe breaks local cultural norms
Stage 6: Universal ethical principles—Follow universal ethical principles		Decision not to bribe as bribing is against universal ethical principles

EXHIBIT 3.2—Kohlberg's Cognitive Moral Development, Rest's Conceptualization, and Examples

interviewer's expectations. In such cases, the data collected may have been flawed. Furthermore, Kohlberg only studied males in crafting his theory, and questions arise as to whether the theory is generalizable to females.

In response to such critics, Rest, a former student of Kohlberg, developed an alternative to Kohlberg's theory.[14] Rest et al. suggest that the six stages can be conveniently collapsed into three levels.[15] Each of Kohlberg's two stages are combined to form one stage in Rest's application. At the **pre-conventional level** (stage one and two), decisions are typically driven internally by either reward or punishment. At the **conventional level** (stage three and four), decisions are made based on external rules and norms coming from family, friends, peers, and society.[16] Finally, at the **post-conventional level**, individuals are driven by consideration of universal principles and values. To give you further insights into Rest's conceptualization, Exhibit 3.2 shows the various levels, features, and examples when applied to organizational situations.

Rest et al.'s adaptation of Kohlberg's theory has received empirical validation.[17] It has been shown to be generalizable to different populations and cultures. In addition, higher levels of cognitive moral development have been shown to be related to less ethical choices.[18] Furthermore, studies over time have indeed shown that people progress through the various levels. Most importantly, studies have shown that people can be helped to progress to higher levels through ethics training.

How can companies benefit from using the theory? Consider the Business Ethics Insight on page 114.

As the Business Ethics Insight shows, companies can use the Defining Issues Test to gauge the moral development of their employees. The utility of assessing cognitive moral development stems from the fact that research shows that ethics training can help individuals to progress along the cognitive moral development levels. As such, understanding the cognitive moral development level can be useful on many levels, including:[19]

- Companies can gauge the level of cognitive moral development prior to hiring. They can potentially eliminate those applicants who are at lower levels and who may be of lower integrity. These individuals may be more likely to behave unethically. In fact, research by Venezia et al. shows that surveyed students who were at the pre-conventional level in their study were more likely to cheat than other students at higher levels.[20] This also provides support for the notion that those at the lower end of Rest et al.'s levels are more likely to engage in unethical behavior.
- Cognitive moral development of existing employees can be assessed. Those at lower levels can be provided with more extensive ethics training. Current research suggests that business ethics training provided over only a few weeks improved the cognitive moral development of students.[21] In both cases, students were simply presented with information pertaining to a typical business course. Both samples of students experienced improvements in cognitive moral reasoning. Similar types of ethics training can also be provided to employees and levels of cognitive moral development can be assessed regularly to determine progress.
- Companies can also provide very explicit training by having employees consider actual ethical dilemmas and assess how employees react to these dilemmas.

113

BUSINESS ETHICS INSIGHT

The Defining Issues Test

Rest et al.'s development of the Defining Issues Test provides the best way to measure the level of cognitive moral development for organizational use.[22] The approach asks respondents to activate their moral line of reasoning by presenting them with ethical dilemmas and potential solutions. In the test, respondents are presented with six hypothetical ethical dilemmas. For example, in one dilemma, respondents are presented with the case of a husband who has to buy a drug that has been recently developed and that has the best chances of saving his wife from dying from cancer. However, the druggist is charging ten times more than the cost of making the drug. The husband can only borrow half of the cost of the drug and asks the druggist to let him get the drug for half the price or allow him to pay later. The druggist refuses arguing that he needs to make as much money as possible, as he developed the drug. The husband then considers breaking into the pharmacy to steal the drug. Respondents are then presented three options: steal, do not steal, or cannot decide. They are then presented with considerations and are asked to rate and rank these considerations when making their decision. For instance, considerations such as whether it is right to steal for one's dying wife, or whether the druggist deserves to be robbed because he is greedy, or whether the law should be upheld are presented. Based on the ratings and rankings of the various considerations, the cognitive moral development level of an individual can be determined. For example, people at the post-conventional level may decide not to steal because the person believes the druggist's rights to his inventions have to be respected (potentially a universal principle).

Based on Kish-Gephart, J.J., Harrison, D.A., and Trevino, L.K. 2010. "Bad apples, bad cases, and bad barrels: Meta-analytic evidence about sources of unethical decisions at work." *Journal of Applied Social Psychology*, 95, 1, 1–31; Narvaez, D. and Bock. T. 2002. "Moral schemas and tacit judgment or how the Defining Issues Test is supported by cognitive science." *Journal of Moral Education*, 31, 3, 297–314.

Companies can then provide employees with the preferred way to react to such dilemmas by also discussing the considerations that need to be taken.

- The Cognitive Moral Development theory has also received cross-cultural validation. This suggests that training in multinationals may also be useful and can be approached uniformly worldwide.

Moral Philosophies: Idealism and Relativism

Beyond making a moral judgment based on cognitive moral development level, others argue that people's ethical decision-making is also influenced by their approaches to making ethical decisions.[23] In that respect, **moral philosophies** refer to the preferred way for individuals to approach ethical decision-making. In other words, the moral philosophy "refers to a system of ethics . . . which provides guidelines for judging and resolving behavior that may be ethically questionable."[24] Although there are many aspects of moral philosophies, two have received significant attention in the business ethics literature. We therefore consider idealism and relativism in this section. Forsyth argues that most people can be classified along these two continua.[25]

Idealism refers the degree to which an individual will minimize harm and maximize gain to others when making a decision. The more idealistic an individual is, the higher the concern for the welfare of others and the higher desire to minimize harm to others. For example, a manager high on idealism is less likely to give raises to high-performing employees if such raises mean that some employees will get laid off.[26] In contrast, less idealistic individuals believe that some decisions may unavoidably cause harm to some. These individuals are more likely to believe that they must sometimes choose between the lesser of two evils.[27]

Relativism, in contrast, refers to the degree to which individuals adhere to universal rules regardless of the situation when making decisions with ethical consequences. People highest on relativism believe that there are no universal rules, codes, or norms that need to be followed.[28] Relativist, for instance, may believe that sweatshops are acceptable because the pursuit of profits for shareholder gain is a situation that justifies employing workers in such conditions. In contrast, people who have low relativism believe that all situations should be guided by universal moral principles.

To give you further insights into idealism and relativism, Exhibit 3.3 shows the typical questions asked to respondents when assessing these two dimensions.

A recent review of research shows that, consistent with expectations, people with high relativism are more likely to make unethical choices at work.[29] This suggests that such individuals are more likely to use the situation to justify the unethical choices. Furthermore, the same review of a very large number of studies also shows that more idealistic individuals are less likely to make unethical choices at work. More idealistic individuals are more likely to be cognizant of the negative impact of their actions on others.

Other research also provides evidence of the utility of understanding relativism and idealism. Henle, Giacalone, and Jurkiewicz examined how idealism and relativism impacts workplace deviance.[30] Workplace deviance simply refers to behaviors that are in violation of company norms and policies that have the potential to threaten the organization or employee well-being. In a study of working individuals, Henle et al. show that idealism negatively affects workplace deviance. Furthermore, the study shows that relativism is also positively related to workplace deviance. The study again shows that people with high idealism and low relativism are less likely to behave unethically and commit workplace deviance. But is idealism and relativism relevant for other countries? Consider the Global Business Ethics Insight on page 117.

Clearly, the above shows that the idealism and relativism aspects are relevant in a cross-cultural environment. Further research provides support for the relevance of idealism and relativism in a cross-cultural environment. In a review of 139 samples

Relativism Questions

1. A person should make certain that their actions never intentionally harm another, even to a small degree

2. Risks to another should never be tolerated, irrespective of how small the risks might be

3. One should never psychologically or physically harm another person

4. One should not perform an action which might in any way threaten the dignity and welfare of another individual

5. If an action could harm an innocent other, then it should not be done

6. Deciding whether or not to perform an act by balancing the positive consequences of the act against the negative consequences of the act is immoral

7. The dignity and welfare of people should be the most important concern in any society

8. It is never necessary to sacrifice the welfare of others

Idealism Questions

1. Moral actions are those that closely match ideals of the "perfect" action

2. There are no ethical principles that are so important that they should be part of any code of ethics

3. What is ethical varies from one situation and society to another

4. Moral standards should be seen as being individualistic; what one person considers to be moral may be judged to be immoral by another person

5. Different types of moralities cannot be compared to "rightness"

6. Questions of what is ethical for everyone can never be resolved, since what is moral or immoral is up to the individual

7. Moral standards are simply personal rules that indicate how a person should behave, and are not to be applied in making judgments of others

8. Ethical considerations in interpersonal relations are so complex that individuals should be allowed to formulate their own individual codes

9. Rigidly codifying an ethical position that prevents certain types of actions could stand in the way of better human relations and adjustment

10. No rule concerning lying can be formulated; whether a lie is permissible or not "permissible" totally depends on the situation

11. Whether a lie is judged to be moral or immoral depends upon the circumstances surrounding the action

EXHIBIT 3.3—Relativism and Idealism Questions

GLOBAL BUSINESS ETHICS INSIGHT

Idealism and Relativism in China

According to the current practitioner literature, bribery and gift giving is a very common phenomenon in China. In fact, current research suggests that bribers are now offering officials not only money or other expensive home appliances but also stocks, houses, overseas travel, and even sexual services. However, the Chinese government has begun to crack down on bribery and there are now severe penalties for those caught bribing.

It is undeniable that a person's propensity to bribe will be dependent on that person's moral philosophy. In that context, a recent study examined how idealism and relativism affect 224 Mainland Chinese managers' perception of bribery and gift giving. Bribery is usually a gift large enough to affect the recipient's decision. In contrast, gift giving refers to gifts that reflect people's friendship with others.

Results of the study show that relativism positively affects bribery, while idealism negatively affects perceptions of bribery. In other words, people who are high on relativism are more likely to have a favorable perception of bribery. Furthermore, consistent with expectations, those managers high on idealism were more likely to have a negative perception of bribery. This provides further support for the utility of understanding relativism and idealism.

However, the results show that neither idealism nor relativism has an impact on gift giving. This suggests that gift giving is widely accepted as a business practice to show one's appreciation and friendship to others. Gift giving is an accepted practice in China and is thus not seen as an ethical issue.

Based on Tian, Q. 2008. "Perception of business bribery in China: The impact of moral philosophy." *Journal of Business Ethics*, 80, 437–445.

drawn from 29 different countries with 30,230 respondents, Forsyth et al. find that both relativism and idealism exist worldwide and that there are predictable variations in these concepts worldwide.[31]

Given the utility of both relativism and idealism, companies are well advised to do the following:

- At a fundamental level, research provides overwhelming evidence of the propensity for individuals with low levels of idealism and high levels of relativism to behave unethically. A company can therefore assess the level of relativism and idealism of potential new employees and consider only those who display higher levels of idealism and lower levels of relativism using the items showed in Exhibit 3.3. This will ensure that new employees are less likely to have attributes that lead to deviance.

- Although relativism and idealism are relatively stable in people, recent research showed that business ethics training in as little as a week altered relativism and idealism. In a study of around 100 German students taking a business ethics course, comparison of relativism and idealism before and after a business ethics course showed a significant increase in idealism and significant decrease in relativism.
- As shown in Exhibit 3.4, both relativism and idealism changed significantly after students took the business ethics course. Idealism went up while relativism came down as a result of the course. While it still needs to be determined whether such changes are permanent, this provides support for the assertion that business ethics training may be useful. Specifically, if companies provide training to emphasize the need to follow universal moral codes or the company codes and the need to not harm people in any circumstance, the company can potentially increase idealism and decrease relativism, at least in the short term.

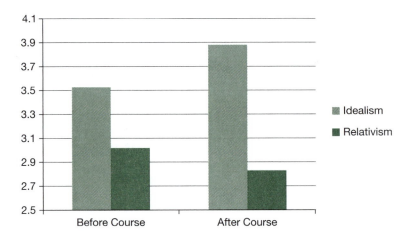

EXHIBIT 3.4—Relativism and Idealism Change after Business Ethics Course

Ethical Theories

A final aspect of moral philosophy we consider is ethical theories. Ethical theory refers to concerns regarding acceptable ways to solve ethical dilemmas. As managers face ethical issues, ethical theories provide insights into the processes behind ethical decision-making. By understanding how managers approach these decisions, companies can take steps to understand decision outcomes and ways to improve the decision-making process. We consider two of the more prominent ethical theories; namely, utilitarian theories and Kantian ethics in depth.

The basic premise of **utilitarian ethics** is that the moral worth of an action is based on the consequences of the action.[32] Specifically, when deciding among many potential options, an individual will consider the benefits and harm caused by the action.

The individual will then choose the option that maximizes good and minimizes harm. For instance, if a CEO is considering closing a plant in Germany and moving operations to China, the utilitarian CEO will consider the many gains and losses incurred by options of closing the plant and moving to China or keeping the plant in Germany. For the closing the plant option, gains may be the efficiency the company can achieve in China while losses would be the damaged reputation in Germany because of the plant closing. If the CEO considers keeping the plant, losses are the potential long run loss of competitive advantage while gains are the improved relations with workers. Thus, the utilitarian ethics CEO will choose the option that provides the most net gains.

Utilitarian ethics is thus based on the premise of maximization of benefits and minimization of harm. Furthermore, the theory accepts that harm can occur in any decision and focuses on the greatest good based on consequences of actions. Furthermore, utilitarian ethics accept that it is possible to measure everything.

Given the above, utilitarian ethics has many advantageous uses for organizational decision-making. It provides a simple way of gauging the impact of organizational decisions. By forcing decision-makers to consider the costs and benefits of various decisions, utilitarian ethics provide a convenient way to consider various alternatives. Furthermore, utilitarian ethics do not provide any special preference to any specific groups affected by decisions. This suggests a more objective way of making decisions.

However, despite these benefits, the basic premises of utilitarian ethics provide some of utilitarian ethics strongest criticisms. First, many argue that it is not always possible to precisely measure gains and losses.[33] Often, estimates are made based on different assumptions. However, making accurate estimations may not always be possible. For instance, going back to the earlier example, how can the CEO accurately gauge the reputational losses if the company moves the plant to China? How can the gains of improved relationship with employees be assessed?

Another important criticism of utilitarian ethics is that in the calculation of gains and losses, the needs of minorities are typically ignored. Justice is typically ignored. For instance, it is possible that the German company operates the plants mostly using German immigrants. In calculating the gains and losses from opening the plant in China, all considerations are considered equal. However, the losses associated with loss of jobs may be disproportionately higher if the German immigrants were to lose their jobs. However, they are considered as merely a number in the equation.

Finally, the most serious criticism of utilitarian ethics is that the rights of people are ignored.[34] To a utilitarian ethicist, violating someone's rights is irrelevant. The most important consideration is whether the good from the decision outweighs the bad. To give you further insights into utilitarian ethics, consider the Strategic Business Ethics Insight on page 120.

As the Strategic Business Ethics Insight shows, pushing utilitarian ethics to the limit can be dangerous. In trying to face competition and achieving its strategic objectives, Ford's employees made a number of assumptions and calculations that were ultimately very damaging.

Extant evidence suggests that there are other alternatives to utilitarian thinking. In that context, **Kantian ethics** "is about following universal norms that prescribe what

STRATEGIC BUSINESS ETHICS INSIGHT

The Ford Pinto

The Ford Pinto case is perhaps one of the examples of what can happen when individuals rely solely on utilitarian ethics when making decisions. In 1968, facing severe competition, Ford decided to start producing the Ford Pinto. The Ford Pinto was a subcompact car that was then retailing for around $2,000. To have the model ready by 1971, Ford hastened the design to make it to production. However, any changes to the design would have to be made during the production tooling process. During the design process, Ford was required to respect the new safety standard proposed by the National Highway Traffic Safety Administration (NHTSA) whereby cars could safely withstand rear impact without fuel loss at 20 mph. The Pinto failed and, although the problem could have been fixed with a rubber bladder in the gas tank for an additional $11, Ford decided against it. Engineers at the company engaged in utilitarian ethics to justify not adding the rubber bladder.

To make the decision, Ford engaged in the practical application of utilitarian ethics; namely, cost and benefit analysis. It estimated that the cost of adding the safety improvement would be around $137.5 million (11 million cars and 1.5 million trucks equipped with $11 per vehicle).

To estimate the benefits, Ford calculated the cost it would have to incur by not implementing the safety device. As such, it relied on the NHTSA estimation that the value of a life is $200,725, as society loses that amount when someone is killed in an accident. It also estimated that it would have to pay $67,000 per serious injury and $700 per burned vehicle. Assuming that 180 individuals would die from burn deaths (180 x $200,725), 180 (180 x $67,000) would have serious burns and 2,100 vehicles (2,100 x $700) would get burned, Ford estimated that the benefit would only amount to $49.5 million.

As the costs to Ford far outweighed the benefits, Ford decided not to implement the rubber bladder safety device. The decision proved very costly to Ford, as many of their assumptions were flawed. Many lawsuits were brought, with substantial damage given to the victims. Furthermore, Ford was even charged with criminal homicide in one case, when three teenagers died when the gas tank of their Pinto exploded on impact in an accident.

Based on Shaw, W.H. and Barry, V. 2011. "The Ford Pinto." In *Moral issues in business*, Florence, KY: Thomson-Wadsworth, p. 79.

people ought to do, how they should behave, and what is right or wrong."[35] Unlike utilitarian ethics, Kantian ethics see the consequences of an action as irrelevant. The moral worth of any action is the action itself and whether the action respects universal rules and norms.

Kant argues that universal rules and norms (or what he terms "categorical imperatives") should be based on pure reasoning and logic free from situational influences.[36] The notion of categorical imperatives suggests that they take the form of "do this" and that there are no exceptions to the rule. Kantian ethics thus argue that situations or consequences of actions have no relevance to the moral worth of a decision.

In making decisions, Kantian ethics suggest several categorical imperatives that should be followed. First, the decision should have universal acceptability. According to Kant, a person should "act according to that maxim whereby you can at the same time will that it should become a universal law."[37] In other words, if a person can act a certain way and is confident that such an action can become universally accepted, then Kant sees the action as moral. For instance, one would refrain from lying as lying can never become a universal law. If lying were to become universal, trust and other critical aspects of societal functioning would break down.

Second, a decision should respect the dignity of human beings such that a person acts "in a way that you treat humanity, whether in your own person or in the person of another, always at the same time as an end and never simply as a means."[38] Specifically, Kantian ethics believe that every human being has an inherent worth that should be respected and treated with dignity.

If we examine the earlier scenario regarding the decision to close a plant in Germany and move it to China, Kantian ethics would suggest that the plant remain open. Both categorical imperatives would suggest against closing the plant. A plant closure can never be considered a universal act and employees losing their jobs means that they are not being treated with respect and dignity.

Kantian ethics offers many benefits for organizational decision-making. First, by forcing decision-makers to only consider universal rules, Kantian ethics fosters universal decisions that are not guided by specific situations. Second, unlike utilitarian ethics, Kantian ethics emphasize treating human beings with dignity and respect. This humanistic aspect is a very valued aspect of the theory. Finally, Kantian ethics focus on principles rather than consequences of actions. Decisions are thus considered to be superior.

Despite the benefits, Kantian ethics has also been criticized. Kantian ethics do not provide as useful guidelines as utilitarian ethics. For instance, what does it mean not to treat people as means to an end? If we consider the case of the German plant, what about the location of the new plant and the potential new Chinese workers who are being denied a job. Furthermore, the neglect of situations may not always be practical. For instance, consider the case of a company that may decide to provide additional benefits or preferential treatment to regular customers. Examining the situation purely from a Kantian perspective would suggest that the company is being unethical. Preferential treatment does not necessarily reflect a universal moral code. Thus, in such cases, including the situation in the decision may be helpful. Finally, Kantian ethics place the responsibility on each individual to make the moral choice. This places responsibility only on the self and does not take into consideration social consensus and dynamics.

Nevertheless, as the above shows, utilitarian ethics and Kantian ethics provide different foci on which decisions can be made. Understanding which theory people adopt when making decisions is very useful. From an organizational standpoint, employees can be trained in both approaches and encouraged to combine these approaches when making decisions. As shown above, both approaches have strong benefits and these benefits need to be emphasized. Specifically:

- Employees can be trained in utilitarian ethics where the strengths of utilitarian ethics can be emphasized. Cost and benefit analysis is a very useful tool and can often provide very precise decision-making. By carefully considering the costs and benefits of any decision, the decision-maker can uncover unexpected issues that may also need addressing. Furthermore, utilitarian ethics encourages the decision-maker to think of all those affected by a decision.
- Employees can also be trained to use Kantian ethics, especially when decisions involve significant human costs. Specifically, Kantian ethics emphasize following universal rules and training can be undertaken through the adoption of universal rules as part of the code of conduct. For instance, Kantian ethics can help provide answers to questions when a decision may harm someone in a foreign country. The categorical imperative of treating human beings with respect can be useful in cases where there are human costs associated with decisions.

MORAL DISENGAGEMENT AND BIASES

The various issues discussed earlier provide some insights into what factors affect individual ethics. Companies routinely design ethics training and programs to address these factors and ensure that employees behave ethically. However, despite the training and despite people's best intentions, unethical behavior still occurs to a very large extent. Why do such unethical behaviors still occur? Why do people who consider themselves as being ethical still engage in clearly unethical behaviors? To examine some of the factors that encourage ethical individuals to behave unethically, let us consider the Business Ethics Insight on page 123 about the behavior of tobacco executives.

As the Business Ethics Insight shows, people will often engage in unethical behavior despite overwhelming evidence that the behaviors are wrong. How could the tobacco executives deny the link between smoking and cancer despite decades of evidence suggesting such a link? How could they belong to an industry that was clearly selling a harmful product? How could they deny that cigarettes are addictive? Despite strong internal ethical codes, these individuals willingly altered their own ethical values to justify their unethical actions. Thus, a big question for this part of the chapter is to understand why individuals engage repeatedly in unethical behavior despite clearly knowing that such activities are unethical. Why would tobacco executives engage in clearly unethical behavior and strongly believe that their actions are morally right? To understand why these situations occur, we consider moral disengagement and biases.

BUSINESS ETHICS INSIGHT

Tobacco Industry Executives and the Ethics of Cigarettes

While some industries receive frequent scrutiny, no industry has received more attention than the tobacco industry. For decades, people have examined the actions of the companies and their behaviors. Tobacco executives have also been subject to the same intense scrutiny. Examination of years of executive decision-making in the industry shows a pattern of deception and dishonesty. For decades, tobacco executives have defended the industry and its products under oath. These executives have publicly argued that tobacco is not addictive and not harmful to health if used properly. These executives engaged in many other behaviors that showed that they had cognitively justified these unethical behaviors. In other words, these executives developed mechanisms to justify their unethical behavior.

According to experts, the pattern of deceit started in December 1953, when the CEOs of five tobacco companies met and discussed strategy to defend themselves against scientific research that linked cigarette smoking with lung cancer. Because various stakeholders such as the government, consumers, and other tobacco control advocates were starting to demand tobacco control, the executives knew that the industry was in danger. They therefore decided to present evidence suggesting that the statistical link does not necessarily mean that smoking causes lung cancer. From a research standpoint, the only way to conclusively prove causation is through experiments where smokers and non-smokers were compared in controlled experiments. Such experiments are clearly impossible to conduct. Thus, the executives argued that, in the absence of such experiments, the statistical link should be discounted.

In addition to the denial that there is a link between smoking and lung cancer, tobacco executives engaged in many other clearly unethical behaviors. For instance, they argued that smokers have a choice and that they choose to smoke. Thus, rather than admit that the industry was responsible, the executives shifted the responsibility to the smoker's decision to smoke when justifying the product. In another case, tobacco executives were asked at a social reception why they chose not to smoke. The reply was, "We don't smoke the s..., we just sell it. We reserve that for the young, poor, the black, and the stupid."

Based on Armenakis, A. and Wigand, J. 2010. "Stakeholder actions and their impact on the organizational cultures of two tobacco companies." *Business and Society Review*, 115, 2, 147–171.

Moral disengagement was developed to explain how individuals can behave unethically despite having moral standards.[39] However, to understand moral disengagement, it is necessary to first understand social cognitive theory. Specifically, Bandura developed social cognitive theory, arguing that most people have developed "personal standards of moral behavior . . . that guide good behavior and deter bad behavior."[40] As individuals consider how to behave, they use these personal standards to monitor the morality of their actions. If they feel that their actions are against their personal standards, they will likely not engage in the behavior.

Bandura, however, argues that individuals have the ability to activate and deactivate this form of moral regulation.[41] **Moral disengagement** refers to this deactivation process where, when faced with potential behavior counter to their own personal standards, a person may choose to deactivate the standard and still engage in the behavior. Thus, moral disengagement helps individuals justify behaviors that may go against their moral standards.

Bandura argues that moral disengagement can occur through eight mechanisms categorized under three forms of justification of immoral behavior. The first type refers to cognitive reconstruction of behavior whereby people reconstruct behaviors cognitively to make them acceptable. Cognitive reconstruction includes three forms of moral disengagement; namely, moral justification, euphemistic labeling, and advantageous comparison. **Moral justification** occurs when individuals justify certain actions to make them seem more morally acceptable. For instance, a company CEO may justify employing child labor in a foreign plant on the basis that these children would otherwise engage in other more degrading forms of behavior to help their poor families.[42] **Euphemistic labeling** refers to the use of morally neutral language to make something seem less immoral. For instance, accidentally killing your own in a war is now called "friendly fire," while the killing of civilians is referred to as "collateral damage." In the mind of the decision-maker, this use of different terminology lessens the unethical nature of the action. **Advantageous comparison** occurs when someone compares a worse behavior with another behavior and rationalizes the behavior on that basis. As Detert et al. suggest, a student may ask about general content of an exam to a student who has inappropriately obtained the exam with the justification that it is less problematic to ask about the exam generally than it is to ask for an actual review of the specific exam questions.[43]

The second set of moral disengagement refers to mechanisms that minimizes one's responsibility for unethical behavior, and includes displacement of responsibility, diffusion of responsibility, and distorting consequences of the unethical behavior. **Displacement of responsibility** occurs when the perpetrator of an unethical behavior can attribute the behavior to other factors. For example, a person can blame the misreporting of sales figures for a quarter because the boss wanted the behavior. In such cases, the employee can attribute the action to his/her boss. Furthermore, **diffusion of responsibility** can occur if decisions are being made by a group. For instance, a specific member of a board of directors can attribute the decision to close a plant to the group rather than an individual decision. **Distortion of consequences** occurs when an individual can disconnect the actions from the harmful connections of the action. For example, a customer may return a used product by justifying that the unethical behavior will clearly not impact the large company from which the product was purchased.

The third and final set of moral disengagement mechanisms focus on the targets' unfavorable acts and includes dehumanization and attribution of blame. **Dehumanization** occurs when the target of the decision is derogated or is seen as lacking in human qualities. For instance, a company may justify dumping toxic pollutants in a river because the wildlife destroyed by the act may not be seen as worth saving because they are seen as subhuman. Finally, **attribution of blame** occurs when the decision-maker ascribes the blame for the decision to the target. As Detert et al. discuss, some have argued that torturing terrorists is acceptable, as they have brought such actions to themselves.[44] Exhibit 3.5 summarizes the types of moral disengagement and its application as executives of the tobacco industry justified their actions.

As Exhibit 3.5 shows, moral disengagement can be dangerous when carried to the extreme. As the exhibit shows and as discussed earlier in the Business Ethics Insight (page 123), tobacco executives relied on moral disengagement to justify their unethical decisions. For instance, the executives frequently used distortion of consequences to argue that the effects of smoking are not harmful to individuals. By arguing that statistical correlation (higher incidences of smoking is linked to more harmful health effects) is not necessarily causation (one leads to the other), the tobacco executives brought into question decades of evidence of the harmful effects of smoking. Research by Claybourn provides further evidence of the disastrous consequences of moral disengagement on workplace harassment.[45] Workplace harassment refers to problematic interpersonal relationships in organizations that lead to employees feeling victimized. Such harassment seems to be fairly prevalent. Claybourn finds that organizations that allow their employees to be harassed are also more likely to have these employees use moral disengagement to justify harming and harassing others. Thus, it seems like the feeling of being victimized can engender justification for harming others.

Taken together, the current research on moral disengagement suggests the latter can have very disastrous consequences for companies. It therefore becomes important for the company to find ways to limit the occurrence of moral disengagement. How can this be done? The following is suggested:[46]

- A company needs to create an ethical culture where employees do not feel harassed. As Claybourn argues, employees in an unhealthy culture are more likely to resort to moral disengagement in hurting others. You will read more about creating the ethical culture in Chapter 11.[47]
- Companies need to carefully screen new applicants to ensure that only those who are low on moral disengagement are hired. How can that be done? Exhibit 3.6 shows the typical questions that can be asked to assess the different moral disengagement mechanisms. Companies can thus assess their new hires.

Furthermore, Detert et al. (2008) show that people high on empathy and low on cynicism are less likely to adopt moral disengagement tactics.[48] Care must be taken to emphasize hiring of such individuals.

Moral Disengagement Mechanisms	Examples from Tobacco Industry
Moral Justification	Employees of tobacco industry focused on redefining their jobs as working in a rewarding environment rather than selling cigarettes. This quote is indicative: "I must tell you, the people you have around you everyday and the kind of environment you live in everyday, become an incredibly important part of the quality of your life … you deny the problems … It's the question of being very happy at doing what you are doing."
Euphemistic Labeling	Review of tobacco industry documents showed that there was strong effort to attract consumers younger than 18 years old. However, the documents showed that the industry used code words such as "new smoker," "presmoker," and "beginning smoker" instead of "underage smokers."
Advantageous Comparison	Tobacco executives from one company justifying their actions by arguing that others are also engaging in such behaviors.
Displacement of Responsibility	Tobacco executives using the argument that their actions are generally permissible as they do not break any rules or regulations. Fault is placed on regulators for not having the appropriate laws in place.
Diffusion of Responsibility	Scene of seven CEOs of the top tobacco companies appearing before U.S. Congress and swearing that tobacco is not addictive.
Distortion of Consequences	Open questioning of the "causation" hypothesis. Tobacco executives sought to sow seeds of doubts regarding the link between smoking and lung cancer, although statistics showed a strong link.
Dehumanization	Tobacco executives arguing that they do not smoke but that they leave the choice to the "poor, the black, and the stupid." A husband suing after his wife died was also told that he should not get any money as his wife admitted to enjoying smoking and that smoking made her feel glamorous.
Attribution of Blame	Blame smokers for making the choice, for enjoying smoking, for enjoying smoking as it made the smoker feel glamorous.

EXHIBIT 3.5—Moral Disengagement and Tobacco Industry

- Training can be given to those who are more prone to use moral disengagement tactics. Specific training can be developed to tailor one's own workplace environment. Examples pinpointing the various moral disengagement mechanisms can be provided to employees so as to make the training more relevant to their workplace. Employees should also be trained on the dangers of moral disengagement and the need for workers to guard themselves against such actions.
- Ethics officers can be appointed so that they can review decision-making processes across projects in the organization. The officer should have the ability to examine projects with potential ethical implications and determine whether moral disengagement is being used. Warnings such as "everybody is doing it" or "it doesn't

Moral Disengagement Mechanism	Moral Disengagement Questions
Moral Justification	• It is alright to fight to protect your friends • It's OK to steal to take care of your family's needs • It's OK to attack someone who threatens your family's honor • It is alright to lie to keep your friends out of trouble
Euphemistic Labeling	• Sharing test questions is just a way of helping your friends • Talking about people behind their back is just part of the game • Looking at a friend's homework without permission is just "borrowing it" • It is not bad to "get high" once in a while
Advantageous Comparison	• Not working very hard in school is really no big deal when you consider that other people are probably cheating • Compared to other illegal things people do, taking things from a store without paying for them is not very serious
Displacement of Responsibility	• If people are living in bad conditions, they cannot be blamed for behaving aggressively • If the professor doesn't discipline cheaters, students should not be blamed for cheating • If someone if pressured into doing something, they should not be blamed for it • People cannot be blamed for misbehaving if their friends pressured them to do it
Diffusion of Responsibility	• A member of a group or team should not be blamed for the trouble the team caused • A student who only suggests breaking the rules should not be blamed if other students go ahead and do it • If a group decides together to do something harmful, it is unfair to blame any one member of the group • You can't blame a person who plays only a small part in the harm caused by a group
Distortion of Consequences	• It is OK to tell small lies, because they really don't do any harm • People don't mind being teased because it shows interest in them • Teasing someone does not really hurt them • Insults really don't hurt anyone
Dehumanization	• Some people deserve to be treated like animals • It is OK to treat badly someone who behaved like a "worm" • Someone who is obnoxious does not deserve to be treated like a human being • Some people have to be treated roughly because they lack feelings that can be hurt
Attribution of Blame	• If someone leaves something lying around, it is their own fault if it gets stolen • People who are mistreated have usually done things to deserve it • People are not at fault for misbehaving at work if their managers mistreat them • If students misbehave in class, it is their teacher's fault

EXHIBIT 3.6—Moral Disengagement Questions

really hurt anyone" should be carefully scrutinized to ensure that project members are not engaging in moral disengagement mechanisms.

Unconscious Biases

While the previous section discussed some of the mechanisms as to how individuals cognitively justify unethical behavior, some experts argue that sometimes people commit unethical behavior without knowing it. As such, **unconscious biases** occur when the "most well-meaning person unwittingly allows unconscious thoughts and feelings to influence seemingly objective decisions."[49] In the final section of this chapter, we examine some of these unconscious biases and what companies can do to ensure that they do not occur.

According to Banaji et al. and Bazerman and Tenbrunsel, managers can engage in unethical behaviors through several potential biases.[50] **Implicit prejudice** occurs when people rely on unconscious biases and prejudice when people judge others. This occurs because people tend to make associations between employee characteristics and organizational outcomes that may not be accurate. For instance, consider the case of *Price Waterhouse v. Hopkins*, where a woman employee sued the company for not being appointed as a partner although she was a great employee. The court case revealed that many of the evaluators had serious implicit prejudice based on gender stereotypes. For example, the evaluators felt that she was being overcompensated for being a woman and that she needed training in charm school. Implicit prejudice can thus be very costly, as Price Waterhouse had to pay $25 million to Ms. Ann Hopkins.

Another unconscious bias that may affect employees is in-group favoritism. According to Banaji et al. (2003), **in-group favoritism** occurs because people tend to favor those individuals who share similar characteristics to their own, such as being from the same school, social class, or religion. For instance, a company executive may unconsciously prefer a job applicant who also holds an MBA from the same school that the executive went to. Thus, rather than objectively considering all candidates for the job opening, in-group favoritism may give an unfair advantage to another person because that person possesses certain characteristics.

Another important bias is termed motivated blindness. **Motivated blindness** takes place when people turn a blind eye to unethical behavior because such behavior is beneficial to them.[51] For example, a manager may turn a blind eye to a salesperson filing a fraudulent expense claim as the salesperson is one of the best performers in the company. In such cases, the manager may unconsciously ignore the unethical behavior and focus more on desired sales results. However, as we saw in the Preview Business Ethics Insight (pages 105–6), ignoring unethical behavior can be very disastrous. Turning a blind eye to audit improprieties at Enron led to the downfall of both Enron and Arthur Andersen the auditing company.

Finally, another unconscious bias that may affect decision-making is conflict of interest. **Conflict of interest** occurs when decision-making can be unconsciously affected because the decision-maker may benefit from the chosen decision. As Banaji et al. discuss, although Nasdaq fell by almost 60% in 2000, most brokerage firms advised their clients to buy or hold their stocks.[52] Why did this occur? Most of the brokers were compensated based on the extent of the relationship with customers. A sell recommendation would end the relationship. As a consequence, the broker may unconsciously recommend a buy or hold in order to prolong the relationship to get compensated.

Given these unconscious biases, it is important that companies take steps to reduce the likelihood of occurrences. It is therefore important for companies to consider the following steps:[53]

- First, it is important for companies to collect data to determine whether employees are engaging in implicit prejudice. If patterns of decision-making seem consistent with implicit prejudice, the necessary training must be given to employees to encourage them to abandon such biases. It is critical that employees be made aware of how these biases may be influencing them so that they can take a more deliberate look at future decisions. Furthermore, experts suggest that employees take the Implicit Association Tests to determine the presence of such biases (see Internet Activity, p. 135).
- Companies can also train their employees to be empathetic. When decisions are to be made, it is important to visualize how minorities or other disadvantaged groups might be affected by the decision. It is important for employees to realize how they may make different decisions if they belonged to a different group.
- Rather than focus on outcomes or ignore unethical behavior, employees should be trained to understand the process behind decision-making. Systems should be implemented so that employees do not ignore unethical behavior for the sake of performance outcomes. Companies thus need to sensitize employees to the importance of ethical behavior.
- Employees should also be trained to understand the presence of conflicts of interest. While decision-makers may be unconsciously influenced by such conflicts, companies can emphasize the presence of such conflicts by exposing workers to potential work dilemmas and sensitizing them to avoid such conflicts. Making employees aware of such conflicts of interest will push these issues into the conscious.

CHAPTER SUMMARY

In this chapter, you read about the many factors contributing to an understanding of individual ethics. To provide a pictorial depiction of the factors discussed, Exhibit 3.7 shows the various types of factors concerned.

As Exhibit 3.7 shows, the first set of factors considered is moral awareness. Research shows that people may not always readily understand the ethical implications of situations. To better understand such implications, you read about the six elements contributing to moral awareness. Research shows that higher degrees of the various characteristics contribute to higher moral awareness. Relevant steps companies can take to increase moral awareness were also discussed.

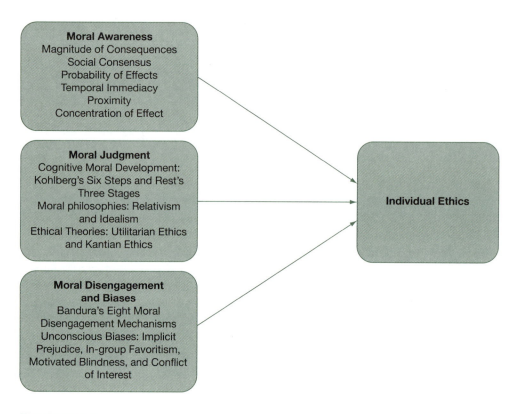

EXHIBIT 3.7—Factors Contributing to Individual Ethics

The second set of factors pertains to moral judgment. Specifically, moral judgment deals with the process behind how people make decisions with ethical implications. The first aspect of moral judgment you read about was Kohlberg's stages of moral development. Specifically, Kohlberg argues that people go through various stages of moral development in life. Higher stages typically imply superior ethical decision-making. You also read about moral philosophies and how people approach decisions with moral implications. You learned about both relativism and idealism and the implications of higher ratings on these dimensions. Finally, you also learned about ethical theories discussing how individuals approach decision-making. You learned about the many assumptions behind utilitarian and Kantian ethics and how these theories can be combined to make better decisions.

As Exhibit 3.7 shows, the third and final aspect of this chapter dealt with moral disengagement and unconscious biases. The third part of the chapter is concerned with how people may believe they are ethical and deliberately engage in unethical behavior. Moral disengagement is concerned with how people can cognitively justify unethical behavior through several mechanisms. In contrast, biases pertain to factors that may unconsciously influence people in making unethical decisions.

Taken together, the chapter discusses the most important factors determining unethical behavior. Companies that take the time and effort to properly understand these individual aspects of ethics can then implement the appropriate steps to ensure ethical behavior. However, as you will see later, the work environment also plays an important part in ethics. Designing appropriate systems to ensure that both individual and organizational culture aspects of ethics are addressed are necessary to encourage ethical behavior.

NOTES

1 Kish-Gephart, J.J., Harrison, D.A. & Trevino, L.K. 2010. "Bad apples, bad cases, and bad barrels: Meta-analytic evidence about sources of unethical decisions at work." *Journal of Applied Social Psychology*, 95, 1, 1–31.

2 Giacalone, R.A. & Promislo, M.D. 2010. "Unethical and unwell: Decrements in well-being and unethical activity at work." *Journal of Business Ethics*, 91, 275–297.

3 Rest, J. 1986. *Development in judging moral issues*. Minneapolis, MN: University of Minnesota Press.

4 Trevino, L.K., Weaver, G.R. & Reynolds, S.J. 2006. "Behavioral ethics in organizations: A review." *Journal of Management*, 32, 6, 951–990.

5 Jones, T.M. 1991. "Ethical decision making by individuals in organizations: An issue-contingent model." *Academy of Management Review*, 16, 366–395.

6 Jones, "Ethical decision making by individuals in organizations."

7 Kish-Gephart et al., "Bad apples, bad cases, and bad barrels."

8 Kish-Gephart et al., "Bad apples, bad cases, and bad barrels."

9 Kohlberg, L. 1969. "Stage and sequence: The cognitive-developmental approach to socialization." In Goslin, D.A. (Ed.), *Handbook of Socialization Theory and Research*. Chicago, IL: Rand McNally.

10 Trevino, L.K., Weaver, G.R. & Reynolds, S.J. 2006. "Behavioral ethics in organizations: A review."

11 Kish-Gephart et al., "Bad apples, bad cases, and bad barrels."

12 Trevino et al., "Behavioral ethics in organizations: A review."

13 Trevino et al., "Behavioral ethics in organizations: A review."

14 Rest, J., Narvaez, D., Bebeau, M.J. & Thoma, S.J. 1999. *Postconventional moral thinking: A neo-Kolhbergian approach*. Mahwah, NJ: Lawrence Erlbaum.

15 Rest et al., *Postconventional moral thinking*.

16 Narvaez, D. & Bock, T. 2002. "Moral schemas and tacit judgment or how the Defining Issues Test is supported by cognitive science." *Journal of Moral Education*, 31, 3, 297–341.

17 Rest et al., *Postconventional moral thinking*.

18 Kish-Gephart et al., "Bad apples, bad cases, and bad barrels."

19 Jones, D.A. 2009. "A novel approach to business ethics training: Improving moral reasoning in just a few weeks." *Journal of Business Ethics*, 88, 367–379; Jordan, J. 2009. "A social cognition framework for examining moral awareness in managers and academics." *Journal of Business Ethics*, 84, 237–258.

20 Venezia, C.C., Venezia, G., Cavico, F.J. & Mutjaba, B.G. 2011. "Is ethics education necessary? A comparative study of moral cognizance in Taiwan and the United States." *International Business & Economics Research Journal*, 10, 3, 17–28.

21 Jones, "A novel approach to business ethics training"; Ritter, B.A. 2006. "Can business ethics be trained? A study of the ethical decision-making process in business students." *Journal of Business Ethics*, 68, 153–164.

22 Rest et al., *Postconventional moral thinking*.

23 Forsyth, D.R., O'Boyle, E.H., Jr. & McDaniel, M.A. "East meets West: A meta-analytic investigation of cultural variations in idealism and relativism." *Journal of Business Ethics*, 83, 813–833.

24 Henle, C.A., Giacalone, R.A. & Jurkiewicz, C.L. 2005. "The role of ethical ideology in workplace deviance." *Journal of Business Ethics*, 56, 219–230.

25 Forsyth, D.R. 1980. "A taxonomy of ethical ideologies." *Journal of Personality and Social Psychology*, 39, 175–184.

26 Neubaum, D.O., Pagell, M., Drexler J.A., Jr., McKee-Ryan, F.M. & Larson, E. 2009. "Business education and its relationship to student personal moral philosophies and attitudes toward profits: An empirical response to critics." *Academy of Management Learning and Education*, 8, 1, 9–24.

27 Forsyth et al., "East meets West."

28 Neubaum et al., "Business education."

29 Kish-Gephart et al., "Bad apples, bad cases, and bad barrels."

30 Henle et al., "The role of ethical ideology in workplace deviance."

31 Forsyth et al., "East meets West."

32 Bentham, J. 1781/1988. *The principles of morals and legislation.* Amherst, NY: Prometheus Books; Mill, J.S. 1861/1979. *Utilitarianism.* Cambridge, U.K.: Hackett Publishing Company; McGee, R.W. 2009. "Analyzing insider trading from the perspective of utilitarian ethics and rights theory." *Journal of Business Ethics*, 91, 65–82.

33 McGee, "Analyzing insider trading."

34 McGee, "Analyzing insider trading."

35 Van Staveren, I. 2007. "Beyond utilitarianism and deontology: Ethics in economics." *Review of Political Economy*, 19, 1, 21–35.

36 Kant, I. 1785/1988. *Groundwork of the metaphysics of morals.* New York: Cambridge University Press.

37 Kant, *Groundwork of the metaphysics of morals*, p. 421.

38 Kant, *Groundwork of the metaphysics of morals*, p. 429.

39 Bandura, A. 1999. "Moral disengagement in the preparations of inhumanities." *Personal and Social Psychology Review*, 3, 193–209.

40 Bandura, A. 1986. *Social foundations of thought and action: A social cognitive theory.* Englewoods Cliffs, NJ: Prentice Hall; Detert, J.E., Trevino, L.K. & Sweitzer, V.L. 2008. "Moral disengagement in ethical decision making: A study of antecedents and outcomes." *Journal of Applied Psychology*, 93, 2, 374–391 (at 375).

41 Bandura, "Moral disengagement in the preparations of inhumanities."

42 Detert et al., "Moral disengagement in ethical decision making."

43 Detert et al., "Moral disengagement in ethical decision making."

44 Detert et al., "Moral disengagement in ethical decision making."

45 Claybourn, M. 2011. "Relationships between moral disengagement, work characteristics and workplace harassment." *Journal of Business Ethics*, 100, 283–301.

46 Claybourn, "Relationships between moral disengagement"; Detert et al., "Moral disengagement in ethical decision making."

47 Claybourn, "Relationships between moral disengagement."

48 Detert et al., "Moral disengagement in ethical decision making."

49 Banaji, M., Bazerman, M.H. & Chugh, D. 2003. "How (Un) Ethical are you?" *Harvard Business Review*, November, 56–64 (at 56).

50 Banaji et al., "How (Un) Ethical are you?"; Bazerman, M.H. & Tenbrunsel, A.E. 2011. "Good people often let bad things happen. Why?" *Harvard Business Review*, April, 58–65.

51 Bazerman & Tenbrunsel, "Good people often let bad things happen. Why?"

52 Banaji et al., "How (Un) Ethical are you?"

53 Banaji et al., "How (Un) Ethical are you?"; Bazerman & Tenbrunsel, "Good people often let bad things happen. Why?"

KEY TERMS

Advantageous comparison: occurs when someone compares a worse behavior with another behavior and rationalizes the behavior on that basis.

Attribution of blame: occurs when the decision-maker ascribes the blame for the decision to the target.

Authority/fear of punishment stage: the person defines right or wrong based on the obedience to rules from those in power.

Concentration of effect: the number of people affected by the act.

Conflict of interest: occurs when decision-making can be unconsciously affected because the decision-maker may benefit from the chosen decision.

Conventional level: decisions are made based on external rules and norms coming from family, friends, peers, and society.

Dehumanization: occurs when the target of the decision is derogated or is seen as lacking in human qualities.

Diffusion of responsibility: can occur if decisions are being made by a group.

Displacement of responsibility: occurs when the perpetrator of an unethical behavior can attribute the behavior to other factors.

Distortion of consequences: occurs when an individual can disconnect the actions from the harmful connections of the action.

Euphemistic labeling: refers to the use of morally neutral language to make something seem less immoral.

Expectations of others stage: judgment about right or wrong is based on the expectations of significant others and peers.

Idealism: degree to which an individual will minimize harm and maximize gain to others when making a decision.

Implicit prejudice: occurs when people rely on unconscious biases and prejudice when people judge others.

In-group favoritism: occurs because people tend to favor those individuals who share similar characteristics to their own, such as being from the same school, social class, or religion.

Kantian ethics: basic premise is about following universal norms that prescribe what people ought to do, how they should behave, and what is right or wrong.

Magnitude of consequences: refers to the degree of harm that the victims of an unethical choice will have to endure.

Moral awareness: refers to the ability of an individual to understand the ethicality of a situation or behavior.

Moral disengagement: refers to the process where, when faced with potential behavior counter to their own personal standards, a person may choose to deactivate the standard and still engage in the behavior.

Moral judgment: refers to the process by which someone reasons about how to deal with an ethical situation.

Moral justification: occurs when individuals justify certain actions to make them seem more morally acceptable.

Moral philosophies: the preferred way for individuals to approach ethical decision-making.

Motivated blindness: takes place when people turn a blind eye to unethical behavior because such behavior is beneficial to them.

Post-conventional level: individuals are driven by consideration of universal principles and values.

Pre-conventional level: decisions are typically driven internally by either reward or punishment.

Principled stage: decisions based on ethical principles of right and wrong and consider what is good to society.

Probability of effect: the probability that any action will result in harm to victims of the action.

Proximity: the psychological or cultural nearness to the victim.

Relativism: refers to the degree to which individuals adhere to universal rules regardless of the situation when making decisions with ethical consequences.

Rules and laws stage: moral judgment is externally oriented and based on whether the action respects rules and policies.

Self-interest stage: person chooses the action that satisfies the person's self-interest the most.

Social consensus: the degree to which others agree that a specific behavior is wrong.

Temporal immediacy: the length of time between the action and the harmful consequences of such actions.

Unconscious biases: occur when the most well-meaning person unwittingly allows unconscious thoughts and feelings to influence seemingly objective decisions.

Unethical behavior: actions that violate accepted societal norms.

Universal ethical principles stage: the decision-maker determines whether an action is right based on universal ethical principles that everyone should follow.

Utilitarian ethics: basic premise is that the moral worth of an action is based on the consequences of the action.

DISCUSSION QUESTIONS

1. What is moral awareness? Discuss the six basic elements contributing to moral awareness.
2. Briefly discuss Kohlberg's cognitive moral development theory. How can companies use Kohlberg's theory to better train their employees?
3. Discuss the first and second stages of Kohlberg's theory of cognitive moral development. How are the two stages different?
4. What are relativism and idealism? Discuss why it is important for companies to understand the relativism and idealism of their employees?
5. What is utilitarian ethics? What are some of the assumptions of utilitarian theory? Discuss some advantages and disadvantages of the approach.

6. Discuss the basic assumptions of Kantian ethics. What are the advantages and weaknesses of the theory?
7. What is moral disengagement? Briefly describe three moral disengagement mechanisms.
8. Discuss moral disengagement through the cognitive reconstruction mechanisms. Describe the three mechanisms pertaining to cognitive reconstruction. Provide some examples to illustrate your answers.
9. What are unconscious biases? Discuss four of the most popular unconscious biases.
10. Describe how companies can build individual ethics based on what you read in the chapter. Use at least two major factors to illustrate your answer.

INTERNET ACTIVITY

1. Go to the Harvard University Implicit Association Test at https://implicit.harvard.edu/implicit/demo/.
2. Review the background information and share that information with the class.
3. Take one of the tests from the various tests such as Disability-IAT, Religion-IAT, Arab-Muslim IAT.
4. What are the results of your test? What does it reveal about your biases?
5. Share your findings with others.

For more Internet Activities and resources, please visit the Companion Website at www.routledge.com/cw/parboteeah.

WHAT WOULD YOU DO?

The Salesperson

You have been recently hired as a salesperson by a well-known company that provides many services including uniforms, laundry services, document shredding, and a large number of other business services. Your job requires you to continue developing relationships with existing customers while also developing new customers. You realize that your district manager likes you much more than other salespersons hired with you. He wants to make sure that you succeed and provides you with many tips on how to develop new customers and what to do to keep existing ones.

After working for the company for several months, you realize that many of the tips that the district manager gives you are not ethical. For example, you find that some customers require that you report some products as being defective so that they can get reimbursed. However, you know that these products are not defective. Furthermore, you find that you can get new customers through existing customers. You discover that your predecessor would often take existing customers and their referrals for new customers to the local strip clubs. Moreover, you find that your predecessor would also often take existing customers and their family members to expensive restaurants if they happened to be at the same conference.

You realize that many of these practices are against company policy. However, at the same time, you also realize that your district manager/mentor condones such practices. What would you do? Do you report your district manager? Or do you do nothing? Why?

BRIEF CASE: BUSINESS ETHICS INSIGHT

Raj Rajaratnam and Insider Trading

Until recently, Raj Rajaratnam was considered to be a very successful hedge-fund manager. He founded the Galleon Group in 1997 and grew the company to an impressive $7 billion. He was considered a hero in his native Sri Lanka and also one of his native country's richest sons. However, the reason behind Rajaratnam's success unraveled after a lengthy government investigation. These investigations showed that Rajaratnam developed extensive contacts in many prominent companies. He provided benefits to these contacts in exchange for valuable company information that he used for investment purposes.

According to Mr. Kumar, one of Mr. Rajaratnam's classmates at the Wharton School of Business and a former McKinsey director, it all started when he saw Mr. Rajaratnam at a gala. During the gala, Mr. Rajaratnam pulled him aside and offered to pay him for his insights. Over time, he developed useful contacts with senior officials at many of the world's biggest companies including IBM, Goldman Sachs, McKinsey, and Akamai. While it is not illegal to have a network of contacts, Mr. Rajaratnam's actions regarding how he used his network is what sparked the investigation. Investors routinely use company information to make investment decisions. However, Mr. Rajaratnam used substantial and non-private information to trade and profit from the information. For example, through wiretaps of his phone conversations, the federal government showed that he was able to get confidential Goldman Sachs earnings information from Mr. Gupta, a board member of the company. He then used the information to trade and made a profit. The investigations revealed similar insider trading based on information provided by insiders from many of the U.S.'s largest corporations, such as Advanced Micro Devices, Moody's, IBM, Intel, etc.

After a lengthy seven-week trial, Mr. Rajaratnam was convicted of insider trading in May 2011. He now faces about 19 years of jail time. Furthermore, although experts believed that it would be difficult to prove insider trading, the government wiretaps of his phone conversations proved invaluable. However, many are still wondering why Mr. Rajaratnam was the only one who was prosecuted. Many of the company officials who provided such insider information also broke the law.

Based on Anonymous. 2011. "The fall of Raj." *Wall Street Journal*, May 12, A14; Scannell, K. 2011a. "Big names drawn into Galleon web." *Financial Times*, May 12, online version; Scannell, K. 2011b. "Rajarataram found guilty." *Financial Times*, May 12, online version; Scannell, K. 2011c. "Insider training was a drama worthy of Hollywood." *Financial Times*, May 12, online version. Rothfield, M., Pulliam, S., and Bray, C. 2011. "Fund titan found guilty." *Wall Street Journal*, May 12, online version.

BRIEF CASE QUESTIONS

1. Given what you know after reading this chapter, what are some of the reasons why Mr. Rajaratnam may have engaged in such widespread unethical behavior? Why were so many others accomplices in the schemes?
2. Looking at moral awareness, how likely did the people involved in the scandal see the moral aspect of the scandal? Be specific about each aspect of moral awareness.
3. How is moral disengagement relevant in this situation? Discuss how each of the moral disengagement aspects may have been activated to justify the behavior.
4. What can be done to ensure that such behaviors do not occur again?

LONG CASE: BUSINESS ETHICS

NEWS CORPORATION

Introduction

Rupert Murdoch is said to be television's most powerful man, with the capacity to reach more than 110 million viewers across four different continents. He is the Australian-born newspaper publisher and media mogul who is the head of the global media company News Corporation Limited, which holds the following companies: News Limited (Australia), News International (U.K.), and News America Holdings Inc. (U.S.). The company's interests are centered on newspaper, magazine, book and electronics publishing, television broadcasting, and film and video production.

Starting with a couple of small papers given to him when his father died, Murdoch has grown the News Corporation to a revenue of approximately $33 billion in 2010. The company owns many well-known interests such as the Fox News Network, the *New York Post*, and the Fox Cinema and Television Network. In addition to these, the company owns more than 175 different newspapers and magazines and publishes close to 40 million papers a week.

Rupert Murdoch

Rupert Murdoch was born in 1931 in Melbourne as the son of a famous Australian war correspondent and publisher. This is where his interest in media and journalism began. Rupert eventually studied at Worcester College in Oxford and briefly worked as an editor on Lord Beaverbrook's *London Daily Express*. This was Rupert's first real practical experience with journalism and would provide the inspiration for much of the success in his life.

When his father died in 1954, Rupert returned to Australia to receive the inheritance that his father had left for him. That inheritance was the *Sunday Mail* and *The News*. His passion for bold and interesting stories was realized through *The News* and the paper quickly became dominated by news of sex and scandals, with most of the headlines written by Rupert himself. The circulation of this paper increased dramatically, which provided the cash needed to purchase papers throughout Sydney, Perth, Melbourne, and Brisbane. With these new institutions under his control, he instituted similar writing and changes.

In 1969, Murdoch acquired his first British paper, called the *News of the World* (London). The following year he acquired another London paper, named *The Sun*. Both of these magazines received the proven formula, with an emphasis on crime, sex, scandals, and human-interest stories. The formula once again proved successful, providing Murdoch with his signature style.

The next frontier to conquer was the American market. Rupert made his play in the United States in 1973 when he purchased two San Antonio dailies, one of which he immediately turned into the sex and scandal format which soon dominated the city's afternoon market. Over the next 20 years, many tabloids, magazines, and papers such as the *Chicago Sun-Times*, the *New York City Village Voice*, *New York* magazine, the *Boston Herald*, the *TV Guide*, and the *Star Tabloid* were either started or bought by the company. Not all magazines and newspapers received the format that made his others so popular. Murdoch took residence in the United States in 1974 and finally became a U.S. citizen in 1985 based out of New York City.

In the 1980s and 1990s, Murdoch greatly diversified his company and began buying major holdings in radio and television stations. In 1985 he acquired Twentieth-Century-Fox Film Corporation along with several independent stations from Metromedia, Inc. He immediately consolidated these into what would become Fox, Inc., which has become a major competitor to the three major broadcasting networks ABC, NBC, and CBS. In addition to these, he also began acquiring a number of book publishing companies such as Harper & Row Publishers, Foresman & Company, and William Collins PLC.

This expansion left the company with a large amount of debt, which was reduced by selling off *New York*, *Seventeen*, and several other American magazines. The company also began to expand its internet presence with the purchase of MySpace.com. In 2007, the company acquired Dow Jones & Company, the publisher of *The Wall Street Journal*, for $5 billion.

Today, Rupert Murdoch is worth approximately $7.6 billion and is ranked number 122 on the Forbes list of billionaires worldwide (he is ranked number 36 in the United States). He continues to have residence in New York and is listed as number 13 on the most powerful people rankings. His total compensation in 2010 was $15.2 million.

News Corporation Structure

News Corporation is a diversified global company that is organized around eight different business segments. The eight business segments are identified as Filmed Entertainment, Television, Cable Network Programming, Direct Broadcast Satellite Television, Integrated Marketing Services, Newspapers and Information Services, Book Publishing, and Other. The Other segment is made up of a *Digital Media Group* that sells advertising, sponsorships, and subscriptions on the company's various digital media properties (i.e. MySpace.com, IGN.com, and Fox Audience Network) and *News Outdoor*, which sells outdoor advertising space primarily in Russia. As of fiscal 2010, the company's revenue totaled $32.7 billion with a net income of $2.5 billion.

The Filmed Entertainment business segment is the largest segment of revenue for News Corporation. This segment generates income through the production and distribution of feature motion pictures and television series. This business is very much affected by the timing of theatrical and home entertainment releases, which are driven by the timing of vacations, holiday periods, and competition in the marketplace. Examples of recent theatrical and home entertainment releases are *Avatar*, *Alvin and the Chipmunks: The Squeekquel*, *Ice Age: Dawn of the Dinosaurs*, and *Date Night*.

The second largest segment in terms of revenue is Cable Network Programming. This segment generates the largest amount of operating income for the business. It is primarily made up of the Fox News Channel, the FX Network, Regional Sports Network, National Geographic, SPEED, and the Big Ten Networks in the USA and the Fox International Channels (FIC) and STAR internationally. This segment derives the majority of its revenue from the monthly affiliate fees received from cable television systems.

The third largest business unit and most associated with News Corporation is the Newspapers and Information Services segment. This segment derives its revenue from the sale of advertising space, the sale of published newspapers, subscriptions, and contract printing. This segment continues to struggle as more online and electronic media formats come into the industry, shifting customer preferences.

Those three business segments (Filmed Entertainment, Cable Network Programming, and Newspapers and Information Services) make up over 63% of the company's revenues, with the remaining five segments (Television, Direct Broadcast Satellite Television, Integrated Marketing Services, Book Publishing, and Other) representing the remaining approximately 37%. For a more detailed overview, see Appendix 3.1.

While the company is public, it has a dual-class stock structure that consists of Class-A shares, which have no voting rights, and Class-B shares, which have voting power. There are currently 1.8 billion Class-A shares out in the market and 798 million Class-B shares. The Murdoch family trust owns 38.4% of the voting Class-B shares, which has led many institutional investors to accuse News Corporation of having poor corporate governance and structure. The Class-A investors really have no control over the CEO and the board. The only option they have is to sell the stock they own. Currently, there are several lawsuits in process over this structure.

News Corporation Political Contributions

News Corporation has long been criticized for its seemingly conservative bias in both its print and media coverage along with its contributions to political candidates and organizations. News Corporation maintains that the government plays a significant role in how their business operates and is therefore active in public policy and protecting their interests. Broadcast regulations, online advertising, intellectual property protection, and legislators at both the state and the federal levels are all seen as things that could limit the company's ability to achieve its goals. The company clearly states that it takes a three-tiered approach to its government relations strategy. This comprises operating a Political Action Committee (PAC), grassroots communications, and direct lobbying.

News Corporation's Political Action Committee (PAC) is called News America-FOXPAC, which is funded by voluntary contributions from eligible employees of the company. The company uses these funds to contribute at both the state and the federal level. While Rupert himself donates 100% to the Republican Party, the PAC contributed 58% to Democrats and 41% to Republicans in the 2010 election cycle, with a total of $485,909 donated. The number one recipient all time of News

Corporation is President Obama. Much of the money in 2009 and 2010 was donated to members of the Subcommittee on Communications and Technology and the Subcommittee on Intellectual Property, Competition, and the Internet. Both of these committees are seen as instrumental in deciding the regulations and oversight for News Corporation and its operations.

During the mid-term elections in 2010, News Corporation was highlighted for donating $1.25 million to the Republican Governors Association and $1 million to the U.S. Chamber of Commerce. Many have argued that News Corporation, who owns Fox News and the *Wall Street Journal*, should have made these donations more transparent, with disclaimers about each donation in the coverage of candidates by each organization. It has also been considered a move that has severely harmed the credibility of these organizations. Many shareholders were also concerned, as the decision to spend this money was not made available through the normal process, with shareholders instead learning of the expenditure through the media. In the spring of 2011, the board decided to begin publicly disclosing all corporate political donations.

News of the World Phone Hacking Scandal

In 1843, *News of the World* was launched and quickly grew in size and popularity in the British market. It was billed as the "Novelty of the Nation and Wonder of the World," regularly exposing scandals, crime, and writing of vices. By the 1950s it had grown to the largest English language paper in the world, with over 8.5 million copies sold per week. In 1969, Rupert Murdoch made a successful bid for the company and it became the cornerstone of his entire global empire. It was also the first British company he added to his conglomerate. The newspaper has appealed to the heart of Britain and has been well respected for the majority of its existence.

However, the paper came under immense criticism and public outcry during the summer of 2011, as it was revealed that phone hacking was used to attain private information. Victims of this scandal included celebrities, politicians, families of dead military troops, and crime victims. It also included involvement from senior executives in both the *News of the World* organization and News Corporation itself.

The paper has had quite a few cases of breaking into cell phone voicemail of celebrities, sports figures, and royal aides, admitting wrongdoing in these cases and paying financial settlements. It was an ongoing saga that not too many paid attention to until the case of a young girl named Milly Dowler. In 2002, Milly, a 13-year-old British girl, was abducted on her way home from school and murdered. At first police were unable to find her and there was a slight hope that she was still alive. The family was also given hope, as it was determined that there was activity on her cell phone voicemail, with messages being deleted. It was later learned that a private investigator hired by *News of the World* hacked into her voicemail and deleted some of the messages. This not only hampered the investigation but also gave her parents false hope that she was still alive. These details were finally brought to the public's attention July 4, 2011, which ignited a worldwide investigation of *News of the World* and News Corporation.

On July 5, 2011 it was reported that emails from *News of the World* appeared to show evidence that payments were made to police for information, with authorization coming from Andy Coulson, who was the editor at *News of the World*. The list of victims for which information was given included victims of the London Suicide Bombing in 2005 and Madeleine McCann, who disappeared in Portugal in 2007. The very next day, July 6, it was announced that *News of the World* had hacked into the phones of families members of soldiers killed in the Iraq and Afghanistan wars.

Executive Knowledge of Hacking Scandal

As with many corporate scandals, the top executives in the *News of the World* scandal all claimed innocence and pledged their full support in getting to the bottom of these allegations. Rupert Murdoch, James Murdoch (Rupert's son and head of European and Asian operations), and Rebekah Brooks (editor of *News of the World*) said they were not aware of these allegations until civil suits were filed in late 2010. Brooks stated publicly that the company acted "quickly and decisively" in dealing with these allegations. Rupert stated that he had clearly been misled by members of his staff and James has said that he was not aware of anything outside of one rogue reporter about whom he received an email.

As the scandal unfolded, many pieces of evidence began to support the fact that executives, including Rupert and James, were aware of these issues. Two former executives for *News of the World* have since issued official statements stating that James had received an email regarding the hacking. In addition, Rebekah Brooks resigned from her duties as the editor and was arrested immediately after on suspicion of phone hacking and bribes to the police. Rupert continues to maintain that he was not aware of the £600,000 and £1 million payments that were made to two different victims. James said he was aware but was not fully briefed on the reasons for these settlements. Both Rupert and James state they were not aware of the legal fees for Glen Mulcaire, a private investigator for *News of the World* who was convicted in 2007 of phone hacking, which were paid by the company.

In addition to Brooks' arrest, Andy Coulson, an ex-*News of the World* editor and communications chief of Prime Minister David Cameron, was also arrested. He was in charge at the paper when Glen Mulcaire was arrested and accused of phone hacking. Stuart Kuttner was also arrested and was the former managing editor at *News of the World*, retiring in 2009 after 29 years. Each of these former employees has been released on bail and has not been officially charged with a crime yet.

Scandal Fallout

A little more than a month after the scandal was first brought to the public's attention and News Corporation has already been feeling the sting. There has been a tremendous amount of fallout involving British politicians, business deals, and executive resignation and arrests. James and Rupert still maintain innocence amidst the massive backlash of the public, its shareholders, and the British government.

The biggest fallout thus far has been the withdrawal of a bid to purchase BSkyB, which is a pay-TV company. This deal, which was first started back in 2010, was the key strategy for U.K. corporate growth for the future and has now left that strategy in ruins. The deal was a proposed £8 billion deal and is likely one of the biggest setbacks Rupert has ever faced. The decision to withdraw the bid came amidst huge pressure from the public and parliament. All three main British political parties were prepared to call on News Corporation to abandon its deal.

The scandal has also led to heated criticism from shareholders and investors for the scandal itself, the way the company handled the scandal, and the botched deal. James was initially put in charge of the scandal but Rupert has had the sense to step in to help clean up the mess. This has tarnished James' reputation and called into question not only whether he is capable of taking over from his father but also whether he is capable of the current job he is in.

Rupert's political connections and ties have been damaged as well. He has long been seen as having the ability to wield strong political power. However, this scandal has severely strained his ties, especially with current British prime minister David Cameron. Cameron has come under immense criticism for his close links to the Murdoch family and especially for hiring Andy Coulson, who was later arrested as part of this scandal. He had very close ties to Rebekah Brooks, who resigned from *News of the World* and was later arrested. Ed Miliband, leader of the Labour Party, has also been greatly criticized for his relationship to Murdoch but has used this opportunity to attack Cameron and the BSkyB deal.

In addition, London's Metropolitan Police department has been greatly criticized, with numerous people resigning. Many of the reporters at *News of the World* have been linked to police officers, some of whom have been accused of providing telephone numbers of victims. John Yates, Assistant Commissioner, and Paul Stephensen, Britain's top police chief, have both resigned amid the controversy.

News of the World's Demise

The *News of the World* is now no longer trading, since News Corporation decided to close the newspaper. It remains in the middle of a giant international scandal that includes top executives, British police, the British government, and the company's leader, Rupert. This scandal has brought the worst out in any company and has called into question the News Corporation's corporate governance and structure.

APPENDIX 3.1
News Corporation Operation Overview

For the years ended June 30,	2010	2009	Change	%Change
	($millions)			
Revenues	$ 32,778	$30,423	$2,355	8%
Operating expenses	(21,015)	(19,563)	(1,452)	7%
Selling, general and administrative	(6,619)	(6,164)	(445)	7%
Depreciation and amortization	(1,185)	(1,138)	(47)	4%
Impairment and restructuring charges	(253)	(9,208)	8,955	**
Equity earnings (losses) of affiliates	448	(309)	757	**
Interest expense, net	(991)	(927)	(64)	7%
Interest income	91	91	–	–
Other, net	69	1,256	(1,187)	(95)%
Income (loss) before income tax expense	3,323	(5,539)	8,862	**
Income tax (expense) benefit	(679)	2,229	(2,908)	**
Net income (loss)	2,644	(3,310)	5,954	**
Less: Net income attributable to noncontrolling interests	(105)	(68)	(37)	54%
Net income (loss) attributable to News Corporation stockholders	$ 2,539	$ (3,378)	$ 5,917	**

For the years ended June 30,	2010	2009	Change	%Change
	($millions)			
Revenues:				
Filmed Entertainment	$ 7,631	$ 5,936	$ 1,695	29%
Television	4,228	4,051	177	4%
Cable Network Programming	7,038	6,131	907	15%
Direct Brodcast Satellite Television	3,802	3,760	42	1%
Integrated Marketing Services	1,192	1,168	24	2%
Newspapers and Information Services	6,087	5,858	229	4%
Book Publishing	1,269	1,141	128	11%
Other	1,531	2,378	(847)	(36)%
Total revenues	$32,778	$30,423	$2,355	8%
Segment operating income (loss):				
Filmed Entertainment	$ 1,349	$ 848	$ 501	59%
Television	220	191	29	15%
Cable Network Programming	2,268	1,653	615	37%
Direct Broadcast Satellite Television	230	393	(163)	(41)%
Integrated Marketing Services	(151)	353	(504)	**
Newspapers and Information Services	530	466	64	14%
Book publishing	88	17	71	**
Other	(575)	(363)	(212)	58%
Total segment operating income	$ 3,959	$ 3,558	$ 401	11%

For the years ended June 30,	2010	2009
	(in millions)	
Total segment operating income	$ 3,959	$ 3,558
Impairment and restructuring charges	(253)	(9,208)
Equity earnings (losses) of affiliates	448	(309)
Interest expense, net	(991)	(927)
Interest income	91	91
Other, net	69	1,256
Income (loss) before income tax expense	$3,323	$(5,539)

Chapter 3: Long Case Bibliography

BBC News U.K.. *Q&A: News of the World Phone-Hacking Scandal.* 17 August 2011. 21 August 2011. http://www.bbc.co.uk/news/uk-11195407.

Benner, K. *News Corp's Post Scandal Future Dims.* 13 July 2011. 21 August 2011. http://finance.fortune.cnn.com/2011/07/13/news-corp-s-post-scandal-future-dims/.

Burr, B.B. *Shareholders' Hands Tied By News Corp. Structure.* 25 July 2011. 20 August 2011. http://www.pionline.com/article/20110725/PRINTSUB/307259968.

Business Daily. *In Corporate Scandals, The Fish Truly Rots from the Head Down.* 21 August 2011. 2011 August 2011. http://www.businessdailyafrica.com/Opinion@UNCODED:Duff, Gordon. *Who is Rupert Murdoch.* 17 July 2011. 18 August 2011. http://coto2.wordpress.com/2011/07/17/who-is-rupert-murdoch/.

Easley, J. *Follow the Money: Why News Corp Donated to So Many Democrats.* 19 July 2011. 21 August 2011. http://www.politicususa.com/en/news-corp-donate-democrats.

Encyclopedia Britanica, Inc. *Rupert Murdoch Biography.* 2010. 18 August 2011. http://www.biography.com/articles/Rupert-Murdoch-9418489?part=1.

Forbes. *Rupert Murdoch.* March 2011. 18 August 2011. http://www.forbes.com/profile/rupert-murdoch.

Graves, L. *News Corp Faces Criticism Over New Political Contribution Policy.* 19 May 2011. 20 August 2011. http://www.huffingtonpost.com/2011/05/19/news-corp-political-contributions-new-policy_n_864254.html.

Katz, G. *News of the World Hacked into Abducted, Murdered Girl Milly Dowler's Phone.* 5 July 2011. 21 August 2011. http://www.huffingtonpost.com/2011/07/04/news-of-the-world-hacked-milly-dowler_n_889809.html.

Lawless, J. *Police Arrest Ex-*News of the World *Executive Over Phone Hacking; Murdoch Pie Attacker Jailed.* 2 August 2011. 21 August 2011. http://www.newser.com/article/d9os1dmg0/police-arrest-ex-news-of-the-world-executive-over-phone-hacking-murdoch-pie-attacker-jailed.html.

Lyall, S. *Murdochs Deny that They Knew of Illegal Acts.* 19 July 2011. 21 August 2011. http://www.nytimes.com/2011/07/20/world/europe/20hacking.html?pagewanted=all.

Moore, A. *Guess Who Has Received the Most Campaign Contributions from News Corp.* 25 July 2011. 21 August 2011. http://moorecommonsense.com/2011/07/25/guess-received-campaign-contributions-newscorp/.

News Corporation. *Annual Report 2010.* Annual Report. New York City: News Corporation, 2010.

—. *Investor Relations.* 2011. 18 August 2011. http://www.newscorp.com/investor/index.html.

—. *News Corporation Political Activities Policy.* 2011. 20 August 2011. http://www.newscorp.com/corp_gov/politicalactivities.html.

OpenSecrets.Org. *News America Holdings.* 20 May 2011. 20 August 2011. http://www.opensecrets.org/pacs/lookup2.php?strID=C00330019&cycle=2010.

Reuters. *News Corp Mulling Future without James Murdoch.* 18 August 2011. 21 August 2011. http://news.nationalpost.com/2011/08/18/news-corp-mulling-future-without-james-murdoch/.

—. *Timeline: Phone Hacking Scandal Hits News Corp.* 2 August 2011. 21 August 2011. http://www.reuters.com/article/2011/08/02/us-newscorp-hacking-events-idUSTRE7713R120110802.

Robinson, J. *News Corp Pulls Out of BSkyB Bid.* 13 July 2011. 21 August 2011. http://www.guardian.co.uk/media/2011/jul/13/news-corp-pulls-out-of-bskyb-bid.

Sandle, P. *Quick Guide to the News Corp Hacking Scandal.* 18 July 2011. 21 August 2011. http://www.reuters.com/article/2011/07/18/us-newscorp-quickguide-idUSTRE76H5SA20110718.

Stelter, B. *News Corp. Will Disclose Its Political Donations.* 14 May 2011. 20 August 2011. http://www.nytimes.com/2011/05/15/business/media/15newscorp.html.

—. *News Corp. Will Disclose Its Political Donations.* 14 May 2011. 21 August 2011. http://www.nytimes.com/2011/05/15/business/media/15newscorp.html?_r=1.

Stockdill, R. News of the World *History: All Human Life Was There.* 10 July 2011. 21 August 2011. http://www.guardian.co.uk/media/2011/jul/10/news-of-the-world-history.

Teinowitz, I. *Democrats: News Corp's $1M Gift to GOP Kill's Fox News' Credibility.* 17 August 2010. 21 August 2011. http://www.thewrap.com/media/column-post/news-corp-donation-gop-raises-ire-dems-20206.

LONG CASE QUESTIONS

1. Reviewing the case, which of the individual ethics concepts discussed in the case are applicable to Robert Murdoch? Why?
2. What are some of the factors that may have led Robert Murdoch to run the company the way he did?
3. Do you agree that the executives were aware of the phone hacking incidences? Why would these executives allow such unethical behaviors on the part of the journalists?
4. Which stakeholders have been affected by Robert Murdoch's actions? Why?
5. What can companies do to ensure that their executives behave ethically?

Part I: Comprehensive Case

SATYAM COMPUTER SERVICES LTD.: ACCOUNTING FRAUD IN INDIA

It was a warm day in Hyderabad, India. Ramalinga Raju sat in his corner office at Satyam's headquarters and looked around to see the company that he had built over the last 20 years. He remembered starting the company in 1987 with his brother, and the day in 1991 when he landed his first *Fortune* 500 client, John Deere & Co. He had singlehandedly turned Satyam from an unheard-of company to the fourth largest provider of information technology outsourcing in India. However, these were not happy thoughts. Raju watched the history of his career flash before his eyes because he knew that, once he mailed this letter, his career and reputation would be gone.

Raju knew this was the only thing that he could do. All of his attempts to cover up his transgressions had failed, foreign investors were dumping his stock, the Maytas deal had been effectively shelved, the Security and Exchange Board of India was conducting an investigation on his company, and Merrill Lynch had just snapped ties with Satyam, citing material accounting irregularities. So he put pen to paper and wrote down the story of how he managed to destroy a company that he himself had nurtured. Then he prepared himself for the worst.

Meanwhile, a first-year associate ran into Thomas Mathew's office at Pricewater-houseCoopers' (PwC) offices in India. The associate knew Mathew emphasized an open-door policy, but, as the head of PricewaterhouseCoopers' assurance wing, he at least expected people to knock. Mathew asked the associate what had happened, and she asked him if he had heard the news about Satyam. He replied no, even though he was vaguely familiar with the company, as it was one of his firm's largest clients. She then broke the news to him. Satyam's founder had admitted to orchestrating a massive accounting fraud, by which he overstated the company's cash balance by 45 billion Indian Rupees (US$1 billion) and, subsequently, its stock was in freefall.

Mathew knew this would be very bad for PwC, as Satyam's auditors they were responsible for detecting any material misstatements in the company's financial statements. Additionally, PwC had spent over a hundred years in the Indian financial services market, building the reputation it held today. He wondered what the backlash from this would be. Then the last, but most horrifying, thought ran through his mind. What would be the consequence that the partnership would have to face if its partners were involved in the scandal?

The account that had been overstated was cash. He knew that any auditor worth his salt could detect missing cash, because it was the only account for which two separate entities accounted for it: the bank and the company. He buried his head in his hands and thought hard. He tried to call his partners in charge of the Satyam audit, but their secretaries informed him that they had been arrested by the police.

The biggest financial fraud in the history of India had taken place. Some had likened it to the Enron scandal that happened in United States in the early 2000s. Both the company Enron and its auditor Arthur Andersen no longer exist as a result of the fraud. Whether or not Satyam and PwC were walking a similar path was yet to be determined. However, one thing was certain: fraud had occurred and now both firms had to deal with it.

THE HISTORY OF SATYAM

Satyam Computer Services Ltd. (NYSE:SAY) is a leading global business and information technology services company headquartered in Hyderabad, India. Satyam's core competencies are in consulting, systems integration, and outsourcing.[1]

As of 2008, Satyam serviced 690 clients, including 185 *Fortune* 500 companies, in 20 industries and more than 65 countries. Satyam employed more than 52,000 associates in engineering and product development, supply chain management, client relationship management, business process quality, business intelligence, enterprise integration and infrastructure management, among other key capabilities. Its revenues exceeded $2 billion, and Satyam became the first company to launch a secondary listing on Euronext Amsterdam under NYSE Euronext's new "Fast Path" process for cross listings in New York and Europe.[2]

Before 2008, Satyam's beginnings were quick and promising. On June 24, 1987, the company was incorporated as a Private Limited Company for providing software development and consultancy services to large corporations. The company was pro-moted by B. Rama Raju and B. Ramalinga Raju.[3] On August 26, 1991, Satyam was recognized as a public limited company after its Initial Public Offering; it was listed on the Bombay Stock Exchange (BSE). Also in 1991, Satyam obtained its first *Fortune* 500 customer in a software project with John Deere & Co.[4] By 1999, Satyam had established its presence in 30 countries. In the following year, the associate count within Satyam reached a new level at 10,000. In 2001, Satyam was listed on the New York Stock Exchange under the ticker symbol "SAY." Five years after listing on the NYSE, Satyam reported revenues that exceed US$1 billion.[5]

THE FOUNDER OF SATYAM

Byrraju Ramalinga Raju, the founder and chairman of Satyam Computers, was born in West Godavari, India, in 1954. He received his Bachelor of Commerce from Andhra Loyola College at Vijayawada prior to receiving an MBA degree at Ohio University. He also attended the Owner/President course at Harvard. Before Raju founded Satyam, he had tried his hand in other businesses such as textiles and real estate.

Satyam was initially an IT company with only 20 employees. The IT projects performed at Satyam were for contracts obtained from mainly U.S. companies. Over time, Satyam quickly emerged as a multinational corporation with thousands of employees and a presence in many countries.[6]

During his time at Satyam, Raju received many awards and distinctions, the most recent of which was the Ernst & Young Entrepreneur of the Year 2007 award.[7] Raju was also a philanthropist: he helped create a foundation that assisted in the building of progressive and self-reliant rural communities,[8] and furthered the cause of several not-for-profit institutions.[9]

However, there was another side to Raju. After his arrest, some interesting facts came to light that displayed his greed. According to the Andhra Pradesh police, Raju owned more than 1,000 designer suits, 321 pairs of shoes, and 310 belts. His desire to lead a lavish lifestyle drove him to own "palatial mansions and villas" in 63 countries.[10] Raju was truly living the lifestyle that any billionaire could.

THE BACKGROUND OF PWC INDIA

PricewaterhouseCoopers is the largest professional services firm in the world and employs over 155,000 people in 153 countries.[11] It was formed in 1998 from a merger between Price Waterhouse and Coopers & Lybrand. Not only did both firms share similar origins, starting in London in the 1800s, but they each also had a history in client services that dated back to the nineteenth century.[12]

In the United States, PwC is the third largest privately owned organization. It operates as PricewaterhouseCoopers LLP. PwC is a Big Four auditor in the U.S., alongside KPMG, Ernst & Young, and Deloitte Touche Tohmatsu. Along with being the largest professional services firm, PwC generated $28.2 billion in total worldwide revenues for its fiscal year 2008. The firm's dominant practice is auditing, which accounted for nearly 50% of PwC's total worldwide revenues in 2008.[13]

Currently PwC offers industry-focused professional services that are grouped into three main service lines. These service lines are assurance, tax, and advisory. The assurance service line is focused on the audit of financial statements. The tax service line is concerned with tax planning and the compliance with local, national, and international tax laws. The advisory service line primarily handles consulting activities such as transaction services, mergers and acquisitions, performance improvement, business recovery services, and crisis management. Not only does PwC work with corporations and large business structures, but they also work with educational institutions, governments, non-profits, and international relief agencies to address their unique business issues.[14]

PwC's Indian arm operates under the name Price Waterhouse. Price Waterhouse is the largest professional services firm in the country, with nearly 4,000 professionals. It has had a long history of involvement in India and has been there for over 128 years. PwC's Indian operations began in 1880 in the city of Kolkata. Since then, Price Waterhouse has expanded its offices to Bangalore, Bhubaneshwar, Chennai, Ahmedabad, Hyderabad, Mumbai, Delhi NCR, and Pune.[15]

In recently published research, India's economy is expected to grow to almost 90% of the U.S. economy by 2050. Nonetheless, PwC is already seeing amazing growth in India. In 2007, PwC India's revenues went up 36% from the previous year. In 2008, PwC India's revenues went up 44%.[16] The rapid growth in India's economy is something that PwC is aware of. It would like to continue to be the dominant leader in the professional services industry there. Any opportunity to expand and grow PwC is an opportunity not to be missed.

THE BACKGROUND ON INDIAN BUSINESS

India has long been known to be one of the most highly regulated economies in the world. With tariffs on imports over 32% and caps placed on foreign investments, the country was largely left out of participating in international trade. In 2002, the United States Secretary of Treasury, Paul O'Neill, stated, "India is rated among the most restrictive countries in the world in terms of its trade and investment rules."[17] The government of India, realizing a need for change, implemented various strategies by which it could open up the economy and liberalize trade. It effectively abolished the cap on direct foreign investment and drastically reduced tariffs on foreign goods coming into the country.[18] This was done in the hopes of a reciprocal response by foreign governments on Indian goods and services. The relaxed restrictions proved helpful to business in India, eventually leading to the information technology (IT) outsourcing industry's rapid growth. The major IT outsourcing companies in India are Wipro, Infosys Technologies, Tata Consultancy Services, and Satyam. The client list of these firms spans the breadth of *Fortune* 500 companies from General Electric to Lufthansa Airlines.

SATYAM-MAYTAS FIASCO

On December 16, 2008, Satyam announced that it would acquire a 100% stake in Maytas Properties Ltd. and a 51% stake in Maytas Infra, both of which are companies that develop properties in smaller cities in India. ("Maytas" is also "Satyam" spelled backwards.) The Raju family was the controlling shareholder in both Maytas Properties and Maytas Infra. Satyam stated that it would purchase Maytas Properties for $1.3 billion and pay $300 million for its stake in Maytas Infra. This decision was made without seeking the approval of minority shareholders, who controlled over 90% of the voting shares in Satyam.[19]

Management's rationale for the deal was to de-risk the business model for the company in light of slowing demand for the company's IT services. However, the acquisition itself would have netted the Raju family $570 million. The deal would have also drained Satyam of its excess cash, which was $1.1 billion, and would have caused the company to take on $400 million in debt financing. Investors retaliated by dumping the stock, which lost over 30% of its value in a single day of trading on the Bombay Stock Exchange (BSE). The company immediately withdrew the deal; however, the damage had already been done as investors had lost their faith in management.[20]

THE SECURITY AND EXCHANGE BOARD OF INDIA INITIATES AN INQUIRY

The Securities and Exchange Board of India (SEBI), the primary market regulator for the Indian capital markets, decided to investigate the corporate governance issues concerning the Satyam-Maytas deal. SEBI Chairman C.B. Bhave stated, "We do not want to react immediately to the incident (the acquisition bid that triggered investor outrage) . . . we will study issues involved and then come to a conclusion."[21]

WORLD BANK BAN

On December 22, 2008, a story broke on Fox News that the international outsourcing giant Satyam had been banned from providing services to the World Bank.[22] The reason for the ban was first reported to be due to Satyam employees installing improper backdoor software programs that were used to snoop on the bank's activities. However, a bank official later clarified that the reason for the ban was actually due to Satyam providing "improper benefits to bank staff." Satyam's contract with the World Bank exceeded $100 million in value and was awarded by the then-chief information officer for the bank, Mr. Mohamed Vazir Muhsin. However, the internal anti-corruption unit of the bank started looking at Mr. Muhsin's dealings and found that he had "purchased shares of stock in companies that had then current or prospective business interests"[23] with his department, including Satyam. The bank also found "reasonably sufficient evidence showing that [Muhsin] purchased some of the shares of stock under preferential terms,"[24] as he blatantly awarded major contracts to Satyam. Satyam shares traded on the BSE lost 13% of their value, bringing them to their lowest point in over four and a half years.[25]

This was a major blow to Satyam. It had already been hurt by investor discontent arising from the failed Maytas deal. Additionally, this was a smear on the company itself as it had been shown to be unethical. Harshad Deshpande, an IT analyst, said, "Once a firm is declared unethical, everyone doubts its credibility. Other clients could take a fresh look at their contracts."[26] A Satyam spokesperson stated, "As a matter of company policy we normally do not comment on individual customers, contracts and relationships."[27] This did nothing to allay the fear of the market, and hence most analysts put a "Sell" recommendation on the stock. Satyam's stock continued its freefall, eventually shedding 69% of its value from its 52-week high.[28]

MERRILL LYNCH RESIGNATION

In a bid to alleviate investor anger, Satyam hired DSP Merrill Lynch to explore strategic opportunities to enhance shareholder value. However, a week after being hired, the Merrill Lynch team found material accounting irregularities and resigned from the assignment. A spokesperson for DSP Merrill Lynch stated, "We, DSP Merrill Lynch Limited, have terminated our advisory engagement with Satyam Computer Services Ltd. for considering various strategic options on January 6, 2009 . . . In the course of such engagement, we came to understand that there were material accounting irregularities, which prompted our aforesaid decisions."[29]

THE LETTER

On January 7, 2009, Mr. Raju mailed a letter to the board members of Satyam, the Securities and Exchange Board of India, as well as the various stock exchanges at which Satyam traded, in which he detailed the massive fraud perpetrated by him. The letter states:

1. The Balance Sheet carries as of September 30, 2008
   a. Inflated (non-existent) cash and bank balances or Rs. 5,040 crore (as against Rs. 5361 crore reflected in the books)
   b. An accrued interest of Rs. 376 crore which is non-existent
   c. An understated liability of Rs. 1,230 crore on account of funds arranged by me
   d. An overstated debtors position of Rs. 490 crore (as against Rs. 2651 reflected in the books)[30]

The holes in the balance sheet were due to inflated profits recognized in the past several years. What began as a small gap between actual and reported performance soon swelled in size, and each failed attempt to cover up the scam resulted in a larger gap. In describing the scam, Raju stated, "It was like riding a tiger, not knowing how to get off without being eaten." He stated that "the aborted Satyam-Maytas deal was the last attempt to fill the fictitious assets with real ones." His final words in the letter were, "I am now prepared to subject myself to the laws of the land and face consequences thereof."[31]

PRICE WATERHOUSE'S INVOLVEMENT

Price Waterhouse had been the auditor for Satyam since 2000. Subramani Gopalakrishnan, Price Waterhouse's chief relationship partner, had signed off on all of the Satyam audits since 2000, except for the last one, which was signed off by Talluri Srinivas, the engagement leader.[32] After the news came out about the Satyam fraud, the board of directors at Satyam was replaced. The new board at

Satyam dropped Price Waterhouse and appointed Deloitte and KPMG as its auditors. The two Price Waterhouse partners mentioned previously were arrested.

Since Raju's shocking disclosures, Price Waterhouse has come under close scrutiny. The market regulator Securities and Exchange Board of India (SEBI) and the Registrar of Companies (RoC) have launched a probe into Price Waterhouse. The Andhra Pradesh police have also conducted raids at Price Waterhouse's office in Hyderabad. Price Waterhouse is under as much scrutiny as Satyam.[33]

In a statement that was released, PwC said that there is "not an iota of material to link them with the accusations leveled against them."[34] S. Gopalakrishnan and T. Srinivas also initially denied allegations brought against them. These Price Waterhouse partners were both arrested and charged with cheating, forgery, criminal breach of trust, and criminal conspiracy under the Indian Penal Code (IPC).[35] Following their arrests, PwC International Chief Executive Sam DiPiazza flew to New Delhi to talk with Prem Chand Gupta, the government minister in charge of corporate affairs, to discuss the firm's involvement in the scandal.[36]

Although PwC claims its innocence, there are some that think that Price Waterhouse was not completely blameless. Satyam's CFO Vadlamani Srinivas, who was also arrested, blamed Price Waterhouse for not pointing out the deficiencies in the company's accounts. He further said that, as Satyam's auditors, Price Waterhouse normally shared its audit findings but failed to play its role.[37] In a recent report, T. Srinivas and S. Gopalakrishnan told police that the agenda used to be clear in the meetings, though the word "fudging" was not used. Everyone present was aware of the motive of the meetings, which was to falsify the accounts.[38] They also told the Crime Investigation Department (CID) that they approved the accounts of Satyam because of Raju's "towering presence" and did so without ever questioning him. "We did not dare raise questions when the client was a reputed company."[39]

The Institute of Chartered Accountants of India (ICAI), a sort of AICPA of India, announced that it would take six more months to determine the extent of the involvement of the company's auditor in the Satyam fraud. Uttam Prakash Aggarwal, President of ICAI, said that whether the auditors (Price Waterhouse) are guilty of falsifying accounts or not will become clear as soon as the investigation is completed. According to Amarjit Chopra, Chairman of the Accounting Standards Board at the ICAI, "If the government decides against giving any consultancy work to Price Waterhouse until the investigations are completed, then it [the firm] will have problems."[40]

In addition to Satyam dropping Price Waterhouse as its external auditor, two software firms—Infotech Enterprises and Applabs—are evaluating options to replace Price Waterhouse as their statutory auditors.[41] A senior official at Infotech Enterprises is quoted as saying: "Though [S. Gopalakrishnan's] involvement in the Satyam-scandal is not yet proved, there's some amount of bad reputation and, certainly, no company would like to be associated with it for long." Meanwhile, Applabs, the world's third largest software testing company, will soon be replacing Price Waterhouse. "We are seriously looking at changing our auditors. We will soon start talking to other auditing firms," said Sashi Reddi, the founder and chairman at Applabs.[42]

It will be hard to believe that Price Waterhouse won't suffer a large loss of credibility from the Satyam scandal. Even if Price Waterhouse is proven innocent or that, at the very least, this fraud proves to be an isolated incident, the damage has already been done.

INDIAN GOVERNMENT RESPONSE

The financial crisis and tightened lending standards made it extremely difficult for Satyam to find liquidity. This put the company in a precarious situation, as it was quickly running out of cash. The corporate sector looked to the government to bail Satyam out, as they were the only ones who could raise the capital required in a short period of time. In response, Commerce Minister of India Kamal Nath stated, "We are considering all options and will soon announce definite steps to help the company overcome the current crisis as it is the question of saving jobs and an international brand."[43] These steps included dissolving Satyam's existing board of directors and appointing new candidates to these positions. The first thing the new government-appointed board did was to find sources of liquidity to meet approaching pay days for its staff both in India and overseas. However, a few days later Nath revealed that the government would not bail out Satyam. He also mentioned that even though there was a problem with liquidity, the company had engaged investment bankers to find the cash it needed to survive. He stated, "There is no question of bailing out Satyam. It has strong bankers who would look for investors."[44]

CONCLUSION

Satyam found itself in a precarious position. It had a global network of clients and a strategically sound business, but it was running out of cash. The government had appointed a Satyam veteran, A.S. Murthy, to the position of chief executive officer. As the new CEO, he promised to "restore Satyam to its well-deserved glory."[45] Satyam had managed to secure a loan for 6 billion rupees ($123 million) to fund its operations for the short term. However, clients were reconsidering renewing their contracts with Satyam, and this would put the long-term viability of the company in jeopardy. In the meantime, Satyam's bankers were looking for strategic partners to buy the ailing outsourcing giant. The government stated, "The next step of the government is to find out some suitable strategic investor who can take over the company."[46]

Halfway across the country, in Mumbai, Thomas Mathew knew that PwC's days in India might be numbered. Although he knew that he did not have anything to do with the Satyam scandal, he felt it was necessary to send an appropriate message to the rest of the firm. As he signed his own resignation letter as PwC India's audit head, he hoped that this act would help his fellow employees realize that personal accountability applies to everybody in an organization, even top management.

NOTES

1   "Satyam: About us—About." Satyam Computer Services. 30 September 2008. http://www.satyam. com/about/about_us.asp.

2   "Satyam: About us—About." Satyam Computer Services.

3   "Satyam: About us—About." Satyam Computer Services.

4   "Company history—Satyam Computer Services." 2007. http://www.moneycontrol.com/stocks/ company_info/company_history.php'sc_did=SCS.

5   "Satyam: About Us—About." Satyam Computer Services.

6   "Satyam stunner: Highs and lows of Raju's career." IBN. 7 January 2009. http://ibnlive.in.com/ news/satyam-stunner-highs-and-lows-of-rajus-career/82183-7.html?from=rssfeed.

7   Seth, K. "Satyam's Raju is E&Y Entrepreneur of the year 2007." 21 September 2007. http://www. topnews.in/satyam-s-raju-e-y-entrepreneur-year-2007-26759.

8   Byrraju Foundation. http://www.byrrajufoundation.org/.

9   "EMRI looking for corporates, donors to replace Raju family." 2008. Headlines India. 19 January 2009. http://www.headlinesindia.com/business-news/satyam-fraud/emri-looking-for-corporates-donors-to-replace-raju-family-5422.html.

10 "Raju owned 321 shoes, 310 belts, 1000 suits." *Times of India*. 4 February 2009. http://timesof india.indiatimes.com/articleshow/4073101.cms.

11 "Raju owned 321 shoes, 310 belts, 1000 suits." *Times of India*.

12 "PricewaterhouseCoopers Global home." PricewaterhouseCoopers.

13 "PricewaterhouseCoopers Global home." PricewaterhouseCoopers.

14 "PricewaterhouseCoopers Global home." PricewaterhouseCoopers.

15 "Empower poor." http://www.empowerpoor.com/pricewaterhousecoopers.asp.

16 "Empower poor."

17 "U.S. calls for reform in India." British Broadcasting Corporation. 22 November 2002. http://news. bbc.co.uk/2/hi/business/2501943.stm.

18 "U.S. calls for reform in India." British Broadcasting Corporation.

19 Aggarwal, A. "World Bank admits ban on Satyam for data theft." Merinews.com. 22 December 2008. http://www.merinews.com/catFull.jsp?articleID=154269.

20 Aggarwal, A. "World Bank admits ban on Satyam for data theft."

21 "Satyam fiasco puts Sebi on alert." *Telegraph*. 19 December 2008. http://www.telegraphindia.com/ 1081220/jsp/business/story_10278343.jsp.

22 Behar, R. "World Bank admits top tech vendor debarred for 8 years." 24 December 2008. http://www.foxnews.com/story/0,2933,470964,00.html'sPage=fnc/world/unitednations.

23 "Satyam: Govt looking for strategic investor, Hindujas interested." *Economic Times*. 12 February 2009. http://economictimes.indiatimes.com/Infotech/Software/Satyam_Govt_looking_for_strategic_ investor_Hindujas_interested/rssarticleshow/4120147.cms.

24 "Satyam: Govt looking for strategic investor, Hindujas interested." *Economic Times*.

25 Aggarwal, A. "World Bank admits ban on Satyam for data theft." Merinews.com.

26 "Satyam: Govt looking for strategic investor, Hindujas interested." *Economic Times*.

27 "Satyam: Govt looking for strategic investor, Hindujas interested." *Economic Times*.

28 Aggarwal, A. "World Bank admits ban on Satyam for data theft." Merinews.com.

29 "Merrill Lynch snaps ties with Satyam." *Financial Express*. 7 January 2009. http://www.financial express.com/news/merrill-lynch-snaps-ties-with-satyam/407864/.

30 Raju, R. "Satyam Raju letter." Scribd.com. 7 January 2009. http://www.scribd.com/doc/9812606/ Satyam-Raju-Letter.

31 Raju, R. "Satyam Raju letter." Scribd.com.

32 "Satyam scandal casts shadow over PwC India." *Accountancy Age*. 5 February 2009 http://www. accountancyage.com/accountancyage/news/2235787/satyam-scandal-casts-shadow-pwc-4463639.

33 "Satyam scandal casts shadow over PwC India." *Accountancy Age*.

34 Chatterjee, S. "Price Waterhouse India partners to remain in custody (Update1)." CAlclubindia. 3 February 2009. 6 May 2009 http://www.caclubindia.com/forum/messages/2009/2/24041_price_waterhouse_india_partners_to_remain_in_custody_updat.asp?quote=143753&.

35 "Two partners of PwC arrested, sent to judicial custody." Chennaionline New. 25 January 2009 http://news.chennaionline.com/newsitem.aspx?NEWSID=27acf181-f9dd-471d-9771-61c78a5c2579&CATEGORYNAME=NATL.

36 "Satyam scandal casts shadow over PwC India." *Accountancy Age*.

37 Kundu, S. "PwC dumped as Satyams auditors." *IT Examiner*. 22 February 2009. http://www.it examiner.com/pwc-dumped-as-satyams-auditors.aspx.

38 "Raju's agenda: Cook the books." *Times of India*. 8 February 2009. http://timesofindia.indiatimes.com/Home/Satyam-A-Big-Lie/Rajus-agenda-Cook-the-books/articleshow/4094116.cms.

39 "Raju's agenda: Cook the books." *Times of India*.

40 "ICAI wants 6 mths to determine PwC's involvement in Satyam." *Economic Times*. 13 February 2009. http://economictimes.indiatimes.com/News/News_By_Industry/Services/ICAI_wants_6_mths_to_determine_PwCs_involvement_in_Satyam/articleshow/4123010.cms.

41 "PWC finds itself in deep waters after Satyam fraud." *Express buzz*. 28 January 2009. http://www.expressbuzz.com/edition/story.aspx?Title=PWC+finds+itself+in+deep+waters+after+satyam+fraud&artid=5rR7aIxyTBQ=&SectionID=XT7e3Zkr/lw=&MainSectionID=XT7e3Zkr/lw=&SectionName=HFdYSiSIflu29kcfsoAfeg==&SEO=PwC,+S+Gopalakrishnan+and+Srinivas+Talluri.

42 "PWC finds itself in deep waters after Satyam fraud." *Express buzz*.

43 Simpkons, J. "Indian government ponders Satyam bailout to salvage corporate image." *Seeking Alpha*. 16 January 2009. http://seekingalpha.com/article/115111-indian-government-ponders-satyam-bailout-to-salvage-corporate-image.

44 "Govt not to bail out Satyam, reiterates Kamal Nath." *Times of India*. 19 January 2009. http://timesofindia.indiatimes.com/No_question_of_bailing_out_Satyam_Kamal_Nath/articleshow/4001432.cms.

45 Kripalani, M. "Satyam's new CEO: asset or liability." *Business Week*. 6 February 2009. http://www.businessweek.com/globalbiz/blog/eyeonasia/archives/2009/02/satyams_new_ceo.html?campaign_id=rss_daily.

46 "Satyam: Govt looking for strategic investor, Hindujas interested." *Economic Times*. 12 February 2009. http://economictimes.indiatimes.com/Infotech/Software/Satyam_Govt_looking_for_strategic_investor_Hindujas_interested/rssarticleshow/4120147.cms.

DISCUSSION QUESTIONS: RETROSPECTIVE

1. Although there weren't many options after the fraud had been committed, what could Satyam have done better to minimize the media attention?

2. In a unique crisis such as this, how did Satyam address the needs of its stakeholders? What could it have done better?

3. Both Satyam officials and Price Waterhouse officials have been blamed for the corporate scandal. In your assessment, who really deserves to take responsibility for the fraud?

4. If you had been the Price Waterhouse partner involved with the Satyam engagement, how would you have confronted an issue with Raju's accounting? What assistance might you have had available to you?

5. What responsibility does the Indian government and its respective agencies have to mitigate corporate fraud?

DISCUSSION QUESTIONS: PROSPECTIVE

1. Looking ahead, what challenges does Satyam face? Will it be able to re-establish itself in the world market and remain a viable business?
2. What challenges does Price Waterhouse face? Will it suffer a major loss of reputation in India? Will it be able to recover from this incident and remain in India?
3. What actions can Satyam take to regain the trust and confidence of its shareholders, clients, and the Indian government?
4. How will India, as an emerging market, be affected by the Satyam scandal? Is increased regulation due to come back in India?
5. What communication platform should the new board at Satyam use to convey to its stakeholders that it will succeed moving forward? What message can Price Waterhouse send to ensure its clients that their reputation can still be trusted?

Stakeholders

Chapter 4

Primary Stakeholders: Employees

PREVIEW BUSINESS ETHICS INSIGHT

The *Fortune* List of Best Performing Companies

On an annual basis, *Fortune* magazine ranks and announces the list of top performing companies on the basis of several criteria. For example, it publishes a list of the World's Most Admired Companies. Nestlé, the Dutch famous maker of chocolate and coffee, has been the leading company on the list for every year but one. It is the leading company because it has been able to adapt products to local niches despite its gigantic size. The company empowers its employees to make products that they see as most likely to succeed in local markets. Products like Nescafé were invented for places that lacked refrigeration. Nestlé also spends a proportionately large percentage of its revenues on research and development. This focus on research has helped the company develop products that tend to be preferred over competitors consistently.

Fortune magazine also publishes a *Fortune* 500 companies list. These companies are ranked in terms of revenues. The company 3M is listed at number 106 on that list. However, what makes 3M shine is the degree to which they innovate. It produces around 55,000 products, among which are the popular Post-it notes, Scotch tape, and Thinsulate insulation. Furthermore, long before Google gave their employees time off to pursue their own ideas at the workplace, 3M allowed their employees to do the same with around 15% of their time at work.

Finally, *Fortune* also publishes another list of the Top 100 Best Companies to Work For. In that list, companies are ranked based on their attractiveness to employees. American Express, the well-known credit card company, is listed at number 73. American Express is on the list because of the many benefits its employees have access to. In an effort to improve customer service, it decided to focus on making the lives of their 26,000 call-center employees better. Through surveys with these employees, it made changes to improve the pay, and to provide more flexible schedules and better career development. It implemented a new system where employees could modify their schedule remotely in order to accommodate a visit to the doctor or taking a sick child to the doctor. Others can then trade such hours. It also now provides on-site healthcare where nurse practitioners can see an employee and write prescriptions. Such changes have been very beneficial for American Express, as its service margins have improved by 10%.

Based on Gunther, M. 2010. "3M's Innovation Revival." *Fortune*, September 27, 73–76; Kowitt, B. 2010. "Top Performers: World's Most Admired Companies. Nestlé." *Fortune*, July 5, 20; Moskowitz, M., Levering, R., and Tkaczyk, C. 2010. "100 Best Companies: The List." *Fortune*, February 8, 75–88; Tkaczyk, C. 2010. "100 Best Companies to Work for: American Express." *Fortune*, August 16, 14.

The *Fortune* top performing companies list discussed in the Preview Business Ethics Insight above provides evidence of the importance of employees to any company. Most of the top performing companies have exceptional working conditions that attract and retain the best employees. **Employees** represent the human resources available to a company dedicated to achieving its goals. Additionally, many of these companies succeed because of their exceptional workforce. However, the list of the Top 100 Best Companies to Work For provides more evidence of the extent to which companies will go in order to keep their employees happy. The list is developed based on employee surveys on issues such as job satisfaction, camaraderie, pay and benefits, and diversity. Companies that are ranked highly are typically known for their great benefits and working conditions.

The *Fortune* lists show how critical employees are for companies. While experts regularly argue which stakeholders are most critical, many companies put their employees at the top of their priorities. From a strategy standpoint, most experts suggest that having the right types of employees is critical to build sustainable competitive advantage. As we saw in Chapter 1, sustainable competitive advantage relates to the ability of a company to create the right conditions where the company has access to critical competencies and skills to be able to succeed and be profitable over the long term. Employees provide such means and are influential in helping the company achieve its vision and mission. In the absence of employees who are supportive of the mission and vision of the company, the company will likely fail.

This chapter will therefore discuss employees as stakeholders. While there are many potential issues that can be discussed (e.g., occupational risk, workforce reduction, work–life balance), we focus on those issues that seem to be most relevant to multinationals today. In the next few sections, you will learn about hiring/firing of employees, diversity and affirmative action, sexual harassment, whistle-blowing, and unions. We note that critical employee issues such as gender equality and child labor, related to the hiring of cheap labor, will be discussed later in Chapter 10.

Next we discuss the hiring/terminating of employees.

HIRING AND TERMINATING OF EMPLOYEES

Hiring, Recruitment, and Selection

One of the most critical ways companies relate to employees as stakeholders is through the **hiring process**. Collins argues that the key to developing an ethical organization is by carefully selecting employees that display high ethics.[1] Potential employees who display the propensity to be unethical may eventually affect other employees and corrupt a culture of integrity. Care must therefore be taken to maximize the chances of hiring employees who are ethical. In that respect, Collins suggests the use of combination of integrity tests (asking employees whether they have committed unethical workplace behavior or whether they condone unethical behavior, personality tests, interviews, and other diagnostics to ensure that new employees display the highest level of ethics). The recruitment and selection process therefore becomes very important.

Recruitment refers to the process of identifying and attracting qualified people to apply for vacant positions in an organization. For all types of positions, U.S. companies use a variety of methods to recruit. These include, among others, applications and advertisements placed in newspapers or on the internet, internal job postings where companies post a list of vacancies on their websites or internally, use of private or public agencies, and use of recommendations from current employees. However, this preference for open forms of recruitment is not shared worldwide. For many of the collectivist societies such as Japan, South Korea, and Taiwan, referrals from friends or family tend to be much more important. Collectivistic societies place heavy emphasis on the family and friends compared to more individualistic societies like the U.S. where the focus is on the individual. Such practices are not surprising, as collectivist societies place emphasis on harmony and loyalty.

Selection also varies by country. While recruitment is concerned with attracting people to apply for jobs, **selection** is the process by which a company chooses a person to fill a vacant position. The U.S. selection process is guided by legal considerations, as employers need to ensure that they do not discriminate against job candidates based on race, color, religion, gender, national origin, age, or disability.[2] In the U.S., selection practices are focused on gathering credible information on a candidate's job qualifications. Previous work experience, performance on tests, and perceptions of qualifications from interviews help inform human resource managers about the applicant's qualifications.

Selection is also affected by cultural practices. One of the most critical differences pertains again to more collectivist countries. As Hofstede notes, "the hiring process in a collectivist society always takes the in-group into account. Usually preference is given to hiring relatives, first of the employer, but also of other persons already employed by the company. Hiring persons from a family one already knows reduces risks. Also relatives will be concerned about the reputation of the family and help correct misbehavior of a family member."[3] Thus, in selecting employees, collectivist cultural norms value trustworthiness, reliability, and loyalty over performance-related

Steps	Type	Activities
Step 1	Set legal ground rules	• Make sure that information gathered does not discriminate against job candidates based on protected classes (race, gender, etc.) • Respect all laws and regulations concerning recruitment
Step 2	Seek behavioral information	• Get as much review information from resumes and reference checks • Conduct background checks • Conduct integrity tests or other honesty tests
Step 3	Determine personality traits	• Conduct conscientiousness tests, as more conscientious employees are more likely to be ethical and perform at a high level • Evaluate organization citizenship behavior traits
Step 4	Conduct interview	• Interview candidates regarding ethics from previous jobs • Ask questions such as whether candidate saw unethical behavior (saw colleague steal, saw sexual harassment, etc.) and how candidate responded • Ask candidate about their response to potential ethical dilemmas • Interview about how candidate managed ethical dilemma
Step 5	Conduct other tests	Conduct other tests to determine ethics of candidate • Alcohol test • Drug test • Final integrity tests

EXHIBIT 4.1—Five-Step Job Screening Process

background characteristics. Personal traits such as loyalty to the company, loyalty to the boss, and trustworthiness are the traits that family members can provide. As such, in smaller companies, preference is given to family members.

The hiring process is thus extremely critical for any multinational intent on building an ethical organization. Careful attention has to be paid to assessing the ethical potential of employees. Exhibit 4.1 shows the five-step job screening process suggested by Collins.[4]

However, the multinational must also pay close attention to the recruitment and selection practices in the country. While the U.S. recruitment and selection process is heavily guided by legal considerations, other societies may present additional considerations. Careful attention must be paid to such issues.

Terminating Employees

Another critical issue related to employees is the **termination** of these employees. Bird and Charters (2004: 205) argue that such involuntary separation likely "represents one of the most dramatic events that can happen to an individual in his or her lifetime."[5] Terminations, in any form, affect the worker's well-being and the people in their families. Terminations have been an important component of the U.S. workplace environment since the beginning of the recession. Consider the Business Ethics Insight on page 166.

As the Business Ethics Insight shows, U.S. workers have seen extensive layoffs over the past few years. The recession has forced many companies to reduce costs. One of the ways that such costs reduction can occur is through layoffs. However, layoffs have dramatic consequences for both survivors and those who are fired. Understanding the ethical implications of the firing process is therefore very important.

In that context, U.S. companies have the legal ability to terminate employees at short notice. Such ease of firing is not the same in all countries. We therefore look at the employment environment in the U.S. and worldwide.

In the U.S., terminations are regulated by the employment-at-will doctrine. **Employment-at-will** means that "an employer may terminate its employee for a good reason, bad reason, or no reason at all."[6] As such, except for a number of reasons deemed illegitimate by the law (firing on the basis of race, religion, age, etc.) companies have significant discretion regarding the procedures and the reasons why employees are fired.[7] Werhane and Radin (2010) further argue that over 60% of employees in the private sector are at-will employees.[8]

This legal environment is one of the major reasons why the U.S. work environment sees regular mass layoffs as discussed in the Business Ethics Insight. Furthermore, employment-at-will also favors employers in that if an employee feels that he/she has been terminated unlawfully, it is his/her responsibility and burden to show that the termination was unlawful. Thus, while employees can win millions of dollars for unlawful termination, they also face significant upfront costs to fight any charges.

Proponents of employment-at-will provide a number of reasons to justify its use.[9] First, employment-at-will has been rooted in U.S. law since 1871 and is seen as being

BUSINESS ETHICS INSIGHT

Layoffs and Consequences of Layoffs

Since the beginning of the recession in December 2007, the U.S. has averaged over 1,900 mass layoffs per month. As of August 2010, these layoffs have affected over 198,000 workers. However, more recent figures suggest that companies are not firing as many workers as before. Around 1.83 million workers were laid off in August 2010 compared to 2.11 million in July the same year.

Large companies such as Pfizer Inc. have contributed to such mass layoffs. In an attempt to slash $4 billion in costs, they have closed many manufacturing plants and cut around 6,000 jobs. The company also wants to cut its research and development costs by around $3 billion. However, layoffs have not been limited to large companies. Smaller companies with fewer than 50 employees contributed to around 62% of all job cuts in the private sector in the fourth quarter of 2010. What is most troubling is that small companies made up a large percentage of net job creators. Coupled with the fact that larger companies are also not hiring, the U.S. will have to deal with the challenges of these layoffs for a long time.

What are the consequences of layoffs on the workplace? As mentioned earlier, people who are laid off and their families suffer considerably. However, Maertz et al. (2010) provide evidence of the devastating effects of layoffs on those who survive such layoffs.[10] In a representative sample of 13,683 workers, they find that survivors of layoffs tend to have lower perceptions of organizational performance and job security. Not surprisingly, such survivors also tend to feel less attached to their company and have higher desires to look for jobs elsewhere.

Evidence of the negative impact of layoffs on companies is also provided by Thurm.[11] Companies that tend to have the deepest cuts tend to be the ones who suffer the most. For example, Honeywell International lost most of its industrial base when it laid off a fourth of its workforce. Companies are now taking less drastic layoffs measures.

Based on Lahart, J., 2010. "U.S news: Layoffs ease but hiring sluggish." *Wall Street Journal* online, October 8; Murray, S. August 19, 2010. "U.S news: Small firms lagging, with bulk of job losses." *Wall Street Journal*, August 19; Maertz, C.P., Wiley, J.W., Lerouge, C., and Campion M.A. 2010. "Downsizing effects on survivors: Layoffs, offshoring, and outsourcing." *International Relations*, 49, 2, 275–285; Rockoff, J.D., 2010. "Corporate news: Pfizer details plan for 6,000 job cuts." *Wall Street Journal*, May 19; Siegel, G.E. 2010. "Mass layoffs in July total 143,703 lost jobs." *Bond Buyer*, 373, 2.

central to the free market economy where both employers and employees have the freedom to choose.[12] As much as employers have freedom to terminate employees, employees also have the right to freely choose who they work for. Employees can quit their jobs for any or no reason and do not have to give notice to their employers. Second, companies have the proprietary rights to be able to employ and fire whomever they want. Employees willingly choose jobs where they know that they can be fired at any time. Third, proponents also argue that due process (i.e., giving employees the opportunity to contest their termination) can often negatively impact a company's efficiency and productivity. Finally, some proponents also advance that the U.S. economy is already overregulated and there is no need for further regulation.

Despite the support, employment-at-will has an equal share of critics. By arguing that employers have proprietary rights to hire and fire employees as they see fit, employers are treating employees as inanimate property. However, many argue that employees should be treated with respect and dignity and be provided reasons for their termination.[13] Furthermore, it is routinely assumed that employment-at-will is desirable because both companies and employees have equal freedom. However, it is undeniable that most employees have more to lose when they are fired. An employment relationship also demands loyalty, trust, and respect from the employee. Employers thus have reciprocal obligations and should treat their employees similarly. Finally, Dannin also argues that employment-at-will is not always efficient for companies.[14] Employment litigation is now a major cost for many corporations as more employees file termination lawsuits.

While employment-at-will is widely practiced in the U.S., many other countries such as those found in the European Union and Canada use the **just-cause dismissal** approach.[15] Unlike employment-at-will where employees can be dismissed for "any reason or no reason," in just-cause dismissal, employers must provide reasonable notice of termination of an employee.[16] In other words, employers must have legitimate reasons to terminate an employee. Justifiable reasons include employee misconduct which negatively affects the employer's business. Such misconduct can include "habitual neglect of duty, incompetence, willful disobedience, insubordination, dishonesty or intoxication."[17]

To fulfill just-cause dismissal provisions, employers typically give reasonable notice to employees.[18] Reasonable notice is based on the premise that the employer must give enough time for the employee to find a new job. Just-cause requirements can be satisfied with two options. Either the employer gives notice to employees for a reasonable amount of time and allows them to work during that time. However, most employers prefer the second option whereby employees can be terminated immediately and provided for an amount of pay equivalent to the amount of time equivalent to the reasonable notice. According to Bird and Charters, the reasonable notice time is determined based on factors such as length of service, the character of the employee, the age, and availability of similar employment, as well as general environmental factors such as the general economic climate and industry custom.[19]

An interesting aspect of just-cause dismissal is that if employees are terminated, it is the employer's responsibility to provide adequate justification for such termination. The burden of proof thus rests with the employer. Most employers are therefore

167

required to have a system of regular feedback in place to let employees know the level of their performance. If employees are performing poorly, they need to have the chance to show improvement by being given feedback on how to improve. Failure to show improvement then becomes ground for fair dismissal.

The contrasting termination modes discussed above thus present different ethical dilemmas for companies. It therefore becomes imperative to decide which system to adopt to conform to ethical norms. Some argue that employment-at-will is necessary in order to provide companies with the means to freely participate in a capitalist system.[20] However, others argue that employment-at-will has many disadvantages that should encourage companies to adopt more of a just-cause dismissal approach.[21] Treating employees humanely and fairly, a reflection of ethical companies, seems more likely with a just-cause system. It is also important that many factors now prevent companies from adopting a strict employment-at-will policy. We discuss some of these factors next.

DIVERSITY AND AFFIRMATIVE ACTION

While employment-at-will remains the dominant firing method in the U.S., recent regulations have made certain grounds illegal for dismissal. Thus, companies can no longer fire on the basis of race, gender, age, or even if a potential employee is handicapped.[22] The relevant regulation enforcing prohibition of discrimination is the Title VII of the 1964 Civil Rights Act prohibiting discrimination that was due to race, color, religion, sex, or national origin.[23] These new regulations have encouraged some companies to strive for more **diversity** in their workforce. Diversity thus refers to hiring of workers who are different in race, color, or religion compared to the traditional Caucasian male workforce. However, as the Global Business Ethics Insight on page 169 shows, achieving diversity is not necessarily a U.S.-only phenomenon.

The Global Business Ethics Insight shows that achieving diversity is not confined to U.S. multinationals. Fearfull and Kamenou argue that reduction of inequality of all forms is an area of crucial importance for most societies.[24] For example, the European Union has drafted numerous legislations aimed at reducing discrimination based on gender, religious belief, sexual orientation, and age. However, such factors also represent "protected classes" that U.S. companies cannot discriminate against. In this section, we therefore look at diversity and the consequent affirmative action programs.

Diversity can take many shapes and forms. However, most U.S. companies have focused on increasing diversity on the basis of gender and race. These two groups of employees have been traditionally discriminated against and diversity efforts are necessary to provide more opportunities to these groups to succeed.

Why should companies be concerned about diversity? Consider the Strategic Business Ethics Insight on page 170.

Given the benefits of diversity and the legal requirements to encourage diversity, most companies have embarked on affirmative action programs. **Affirmative action** programs refer to "laws, policies, or guidelines that specify positive steps to be taken

GLOBAL BUSINESS ETHICS INSIGHT

Affirmative Action around the World

Brazil is among the most multiracial societies in the world. Around 44% of the population describe themselves as mixed. However, with a racially diverse population with descent from countries such as Italy, Germany, and Lebanon, Brazil's black population faces significant discrimination. Afro-Brazilians tend to earn almost half that of white people and have fewer years of schooling compared to their white counterparts. This has led some Brazilian universities to implement quota-based admission policies to allow black students to gain admission. However, as the country continues to experience a significant economic boom, it is investigating affirmative action models worldwide to decide which model to adopt.

India's caste system has for centuries sustained a stratified society where success is heavily dependent on what caste one is born into. Those from the lower castes (about 100 million untouchables) are only allowed to do the most demeaning jobs and face considerable challenges in improving their lot. The Indian government thus embarked on an affirmative action program to give preferential treatment to those from lower castes. Lower caste individuals were reserved seats in the parliament, admission in universities, and jobs in the public sector. While this program was originally created to last ten years, it still remains a controversial aspect of Indian society today.

The apartheid system in South Africa encouraged an environment where black people were discriminated against at all levels. When apartheid was abolished, the ruling African National Congress (ANC) brought in some new laws to eradicate such discrimination. However, the ANC has strived especially hard to improve women's rights. In a traditionally patriarchal society, the ANC decided that it was necessary to introduce numerous legislations to provide wider opportunities for women to succeed. Through such affirmative action programs, South Africa has progressed considerably and presents a significantly improved environment for women. For example, women hold around 44% of parliamentary seats, ranking South Africa third in the world in terms of gender parliamentary representation. However, progress in companies has been much slower.

Based on *The Economist*. 2010. "Walking several paces behind; Women in South Africa". 397, 8703, 68; Dalmia, S. 2010. "India's government by quota; The affirmative-action plan to eliminate caste discrimination was supposed to last 10 years. Instead it has become a permanent, and divisive, fact of life." *Wall Street Journal* online, April 30; Stillman, A. 2010. "Wealth is still unevenly distributed." *Financial Times*, November 15.

STRATEGIC BUSINESS ETHICS INSIGHT

Diversity and Benefits of Diversity

Proponents of diversity argue that diversity can be very beneficial to the organization. Diversity enriches the workplace whereby employees of different perspectives can interact to work on problems, thus offering more creative solutions to problems. The conflicting ideas inherent in diverse organizations can lead to broadening of perspectives and to a more complex environment that provides significant resources as companies craft strategies. Strategically, this can allow companies to find superior ways to address problems, thus out-competing the opponents.

The benefits of diversity are even more apparent considering recent research on competitive firms. Herring used large-scale data from the National Organizations Survey of for-profit organizations.[25] His results show that greater racial diversity is "increased sales revenue, more customers, greater market share, and greater relative profit," while gender diversity is associated with "increased sales revenue, more customers, and greater relative profits."[26] To provide further insights into these advantages, Exhibit 4.2 shows the differing levels of profits based on the level of diversity in companies.

Why is diversity associated with greater profits? More diverse companies tend to have broader perspectives that can help find better solutions to organizational problems. This not only helps employees feel more engaged but also helps companies better understand their markets. Consider that products such as Guacamole Burritos and Mountain Dew Code Red all come from Pepsi's diversity initiatives. These initiatives have paid off for them, as they found that around 8% of their revenue growth came from such initiatives. However, diversity also helps better understand the market. Consider that in the U.S. the African-American sector is growing at 34% faster than any other sectors. Furthermore, the growth of African-American households with income over $75,000 has grown over 47% in the past five years. Taking advantage of this $860 billion purchasing power is only possible if employees mirror the demographics. Such employees are more likely to be able to understand the needs of such customers.

However, diversity is also very beneficial for multinationals. As most companies enter foreign markets and engage in trade with such markets, a diverse workforce provides them with better ability to understand diverse cultures and global markets.

Based on Lencioni, P., 2010. "Power of diversity." *Leadership Excellence*, 27, 1, 15; Toland, S. "The diversity payoff." *Fortune*, November 1, 58; *Stanford Social Innovation Review*. 2010. "Diversity brings the dollars." Fall, 9–10.

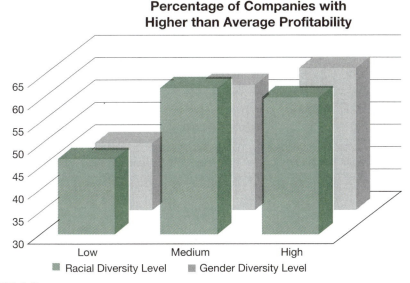

Percentage of Companies with Higher than Average Profitability

■ Racial Diversity Level   ■ Gender Diversity Level

EXHIBIT 4.2 — Diversity and Profits

to hire and promote persons from groups previously and presently discriminated against."[27] Specifically, companies endeavor to proactively recruit employees from groups that have traditionally been discriminated against. For example, many companies such as IBM and Johnson Controls focus their attention on recruiting, developing, and promoting women, minorities, and people with disability.

To help companies implement affirmative action, the U.S. Equal Opportunity Commission has issued various "Uniform Guidelines on Employee Selection Procedures." The major aspects of these guidelines are that companies need to publish an affirmative action policy to show their commitment. High-level employees need to be appointed to show the importance of affirmative action. Companies also need to assess the degree of diversity in the company and determine programs to address problematic areas represented by gender or racial diversity.

Proponents of affirmative action argue that the latter is necessary to counteract ingrained discriminatory practices. Furthermore, affirmative action is seen as necessary as compensation for the damages caused by discrimination over the past. Additionally, both minorities and women face glass ceilings and other barriers that keep them in lower paid and less prestigious jobs. Affirmative action is seen as a way to alleviate such barriers.

Despite the above reasoning behind affirmative action programs, such programs have encountered significant criticisms. Because specific races or gender are given preference, some critics see affirmative action as violating the principle of equality. Furthermore, others argue that white males tend to be discriminated against in what is termed "reverse discrimination." Finally, some argue that all should be viewed and seen equally if we want to have an equal and fair society.

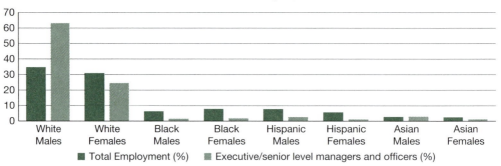

Comparison of Whites vs. Minorities in Terms of Employment

EXHIBIT 4.3 — Comparison of Whites and Minorities

While affirmative action has its critics, some argue that many companies have actually not gone far enough in their programs.[28] Consider that although Bank of America has a well-known diversity program, it was recently given a $60 million fine because it was found that the program was keeping black employees away from rich white customers. Similarly, KPMG's statistics show that its new hires include around 28% of minorities, while around 27% of promoted managers are also minorities. However, at the higher partner level, diversity metrics show that 93% of all KPMG partners are white. Examination of data from the U.S. Bureau of Labor Statistics shows the wide racial and gender disparity in the workforce. As Exhibit 4.3 shows, although white employees account for around two-thirds of all employment, they hold 90% of executive/senior level positions in companies.

Given the bleak picture painted by Exhibit 4.3, it becomes imperative for companies to implement strong affirmative action programs. In fact, Combs, Nadkarni, and Combs go as far as suggesting that multinationals need to implement affirmative action programs in their global operations.[29] Such recommendations are necessary given that vulnerable groups such as women or minorities tend to be discriminated against worldwide. Furthermore, as the Global Business Ethics Insight on page 169 showed, many other countries such as the U.K., Malaysia, India, Nigeria, South Africa, and Canada have all embarked on affirmative action legislation. Implementing affirmative action and diversity programs allow multinationals to be proactive by staying ahead of potential new regulations. Furthermore, global affirmative action programs allow these multinationals to reap the benefits of a more diverse and creative workforce while also projecting a socially responsible image.

While implementing affirmative action programs for domestic companies involves following the Equal Opportunity Uniform Guidelines and investing in other efforts such as 1) having a diversity advisory board and diversity officer, 2) establishing diversity networks for mentoring, 3) providing diversity training, 4) active diversity recruiting, and 5) establishing diversity scorecards for accountability and to gauge progress, most experts agree that multinationals face additional challenges when implementing such programs.[30] For instance, not all cultures readily accept implementation of affirmative action programs. As an example, the cultural dimension of power distance suggests that countries with high power distance have societal members who are more likely to accept and submit to authority. Previous research suggests that it is easier to implement programs in such countries. Additionally, legal frameworks may constrain the types of affirmative action programs that are implemented. Consider that both India and Malaysia have programs that require quotas in certain jobs. This suggests that multinationals will need to clearly understand the local requirements before implementing such programs.

Given the above constraints, Combs et al. suggest that the following be kept in mind when implementing global affirmative action programs:[31]

- The local requirements should dictate the appropriate form of affirmative action programs. Such programs fall within two categories: 1) opportunity enhancement plans whereby multinationals proactively hire and promote minorities and women without focus on rigid quotas; and 2) preferential treatment plans where multinationals adhere to strict quotas and hire on the basis of race, ethnicity, or caste. For instance, India has passed legislation to encourage companies to encourage more of a preferential treatment program.
- Multinationals need to clearly define the target groups of affirmative action program beneficiaries. For example, in Canada, affirmative action programs target four groups: women, racial minorities, aboriginal groups, and people with disabilities. In India, affirmative action programs target the lowest caste: untouchables.
- While customization to local needs is necessary, multinationals must also actively integrate the various affirmative action programs. Top management should play a key role in supporting such efforts. Liaison units should be created to coordinate the various efforts. Finally, networks should be established to help mentor disadvantaged groups worldwide. For instance, it is well known that women expatriates (employees who decide to take employment in a foreign subsidiary of a multinational) are rare and face significant barriers. Multinationals can thus work to establish female expatriate networks.

SEXUAL HARASSMENT

Sexual harassment is another critical issue most companies have to face as they relate to employees. **Sexual harassment** is defined by the Equal Employment Opportunity Commission as:

> Unwelcome sexual advances, requests for sexual favors, and other verbal or physical conduct of a sexual nature constitute sexual harassment when a) submission to such conduct is made either explicitly or implicitly a term or condition of an individual's employment, b) submission to or rejection of such conduct by an individual is used as the basis for employment decisions affecting such individual, and c) such conduct has the purpose or effect of unreasonably interfering with an individual's work performance, or creating an intimidating, hostile or offensive work environment.[32]

173

Given the above definition, sexual harassment is usually categorized in two forms. Sexual harassment can be seen as **quid pro quo** (i.e., this for that) where a person makes explicit requests for sexual favors in exchange for a workplace benefit such as a raise or a promotion. Often, the person making the request is in a position of power and has authority over the victim.[33] The second form of sexual harassment is referred to as the **hostile/poisoned work environment**, where sex-related behaviors and mores make individuals feel uncomfortable and abused in the workplace. Hostile environment sexual harassment can take the form of sexual jokes being told in the workplace, derogatory name calling where the victim is labeled with a sexual nickname, rubbing of buttocks or breasts, and other forms of more subtle harassment. Exhibit 4.4 lists the most frequent forms of harassment.

Most Common Forms of Sexual Harassment
1. Sexual teasing, jokes, or remarks
2. Pressure for dating
3. Letters, phone calls, or other materials of sexual nature
4. Sexual gestures or looks
5. Deliberate touching, leaning, or cornering
6. Pressure for sexual favors
7. Actual or attempted rape or sexual assault

EXHIBIT 4.4 — Most Common Forms of Sexual Harassment

Similar to affirmative action, sexual harassment is also a global issue. Consider the Global Business Ethics Insight on page 175, which provides some understanding of the prevalence of sexual harassment in Mexico and Nigeria. However, recent surveys published by the International Labor Organization reveal that sexual harassment is a worldwide phenomenon. Exhibit 4.5 summarizes worldwide surveys.

Clearly, sexual harassment is an issue that confronts most multinationals. Furthermore, the consequences of sexual harassment can be very devastating. A recent review of sexual harassment studies shows the extent to which sexual harassment can be destructive.[34] First, sexual harassment can have job-related consequences. For example, the review found that sexual harassment tends to negatively affect job satisfaction (the degree to which an employee is satisfied with his/her job) and organizational commitment (the degree to which an employee identifies with his/her employer company). Additionally, an international study done by Merkin in Argentina, Brazil, and Chile shows that the more sexually harassed employees feel, the more likely they were to look for other jobs.[35] Furthermore, more harassed workers were more likely to be late or absent. Given the high costs associated with both tardiness and absence, sexual harassment can thus be very costly for any multinational.

GLOBAL BUSINESS ETHICS INSIGHT

Sexual Harassment in Mexico and Nigeria

Maquiladoras are factories owned by corporations in foreign countries. In Mexico, many of these maquiladoras often have women form large proportions of their workforce. While the maquiladoras have provided women with the opportunity to work outside the home to be financially independent, they are often discriminated against and sexually harassed. These women are often hired based on gender stereotypes. While men are generally viewed as primary wage earners, women are often seen as docile, passive human beings who are easy to train. Owners thus subject these women to sexual harassment frequently. Supervisors use sexual harassment as a means to control and manipulate women employees. For example, they are often encouraged to attend company parties and dinners and to give in to the sexual advances of their supervisors in exchange for job benefits such as additional pay or vacation days. Furthermore, supervisors will also harass women employees to encourage them to compete against each other for affection and to lessen the likelihood of the formation of unions. Because these women are often expected to also fulfill female gender roles such as caring for children and cooking, they often do not have time to pursue sexual harassment claims.

In a field survey of employees in Nigeria, Johnson found that women are being sexually harassed on a regular basis.[36] Additionally, Johnson reported that many women were unwilling to complete the survey because of the lack of education regarding sexual harassment. More educated women were more likely to complete the survey and indicated that sexual harassment is pervasive in the Nigerian workplace. Many women mentioned that they were afraid to report the harassment for fear of losing their jobs. Sexual harassment included perpetrators asking for sexual favors, making sexual comments, grabbing the victim's buttocks, or kissing the victim.

Why is sexual harassment so prevalent in Mexico and Nigeria? Both societies embrace traditional gender roles where men are expected to be dominant providers while women are seen as submissive caregivers. Furthermore, attitudes toward sexuality are very different for males and females in Nigeria. Young men and men in general are encouraged to sexuality, while women are stigmatized if they engage in similar behaviors. This has also reinforced male sexual aggressiveness as normal and not worth reporting.

Based on Johnson, K. 2010. "Sexual harassment in the workplace: A case study of Nigeria." *Gender and Behaviour*, 8, 1, 2903–2918; Tanner-Rosati, C. 2010. "Is there a remedy to sex discrimination in maquiladoras?" *Law and Business Review of the Americas*, 16, 3, 533–557.

Country	Prevalence of Sexual Harassment
Hong Kong	Survey of employees in 2007 revealed that nearly 25% of workers were sexually harassed. One third of those harassed were men.
Italy	A 2004 report suggests that 55.4% of women in the 14–59 age group reported being sexually harassed.
European Union	Around 40–50% of women reported sexual harassment.
Australia	According to a survey carried out in 2004, 18% of interviewees reported being victims of sexual harassment.
Netherlands	Study published in 1986 reported that 58% of women interviewed had experienced sexual harassment.
United Kingdom	A 1987 study shows that 73% of women respondents felt sexually harassed during their occupational life.
Germany	In a study conducted in 1991, 93% of women reported sexual harassment.
Japan	In a large-scale study conducted among 6,762 employees, a third reported being sexually harassed at work.
South Korea	Two separate studies conducted found that between 64% and 70% of women reported being subject to sexual harassment at work.
Philippines	A survey of women workers revealed that at least 17% of the companies surveyed had sexual harassment cases.
Malaysia	Between 83% and 88% of women responding to a survey experienced some form of sexual harassment.

EXHIBIT 4.5 — Prevalence of Sexual Harassment Worldwide

Merkin also found that worker productivity can be greatly affected by sexual harassment.[37] Because employees feel abused or disempowered, they may develop personal animosities against other co-workers. Such an environment can be very hard for an employee to be productive. Roumeliotis and Kleiner (2005) also report that sometimes employees can become distracted from their task as a way to escape the harassment.[38] Furthermore, teamwork can suffer especially if an employee is being sexually harassed by another member of the team.

Beyond such work-related problems, sexual harassment can also be very disastrous for the harassed individual. Willness et al. argue that sexually harassed employees often suffer consequential poor mental health.[39] Some forms of sexual harassment can also be so traumatic that employees suffer from post-traumatic stress disorder. A recent survey in Asia and the Pacific showed that those that are sexually harassed can suffer from physical symptoms (nausea, loss of appetite, anger, fear, and anxiety) as well as emotional and physiological effects (humiliation, anger, powerlessness, depression, and loss of motivation). Furthermore, the survey reveals that women who are sexually harassed also face the possibility of unwanted pregnancies, sexually transmitted diseases

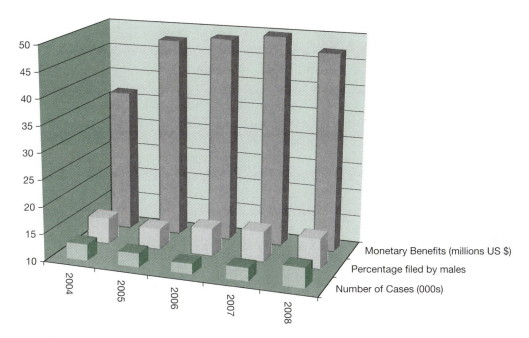

EXHIBIT 4.6—EEOC Statistics on Sexual Harassment

as well as HIV. The most extreme consequence is suicide. The International Labor Organization report suggests that women who are sexually harassed in some societies are seen as "tainted" or morally reprehensible women. There are therefore reports of such women attempting suicide in countries such as Bangladesh, Nepal, and Sri Lanka.

While employees suffer considerably from sexual harassment, research shows that the employers also suffer from rampant sexual harassment. Companies with cultures supporting sexual harassment tend to have employees with poorer productivity. Such companies may also have trouble retaining employees. Furthermore, the costs of litigation can be very high. According to statistics published by the Equal Employment Opportunity Commission, they received 13,867 complaints in 2008 and resolved 11,731 of those cases. In the process, the EEOC collected $47.4 million in damages. Exhibit 4.6 shows the number of cases filed and resolved and the amount of damages collected by the EEOC over the past few years.

Given the many negatives associated with sexual harassment, it is critical for multinationals to implement steps to reduce such incidences. Such steps must include the following:[40]

* *Determine the extent to which the problem currently exists.* Employees can be surveyed to determine the incidence of sexual harassment. The company should carefully look at gray areas where issues such as jokes are exceeding reasonable boundaries. Are employees too affectionate with each other? Carefully determining the extent of

inappropriate behavior will enable the company to determine the extent of the problem and the degree to which sexual harassment needs to be addressed.

- *Employee training and education.* Extant evidence suggests that people do not always view sexual harassment in the same light as the victim of the harassment. Employees may think that something is not offensive or that sexual harassment behaviors are acceptable because it is expected. It therefore becomes critical that employees be made aware of what constitutes sexual harassment and be given the means to end such abuses. Abusers can determine whether their behavior is appropriate by asking questions such as "Would you say it in front of your spouse or parents?," "How would you feel if your mother, sister, wife or daughter were subjected to the same behaviors or words?," or "Do such things really need to be said?" Making employees aware of what constitutes sexual harassment and the negative effects of sexual harassment is a good start to a healthy workplace environment.

- *Having the right sexual harassment officer.* A sexual harassment program is effective if a company chooses the right person to implement sexual harassment policies. This individual should be provided with ongoing training in harassment issues. The person should be able to listen, investigate, mediate, and counsel. Victims in a multinational should feel comfortable to talk to the officer without fear of retaliation. The officer should also have the appropriate training to be able to propose effective solutions to sexual harassment problems.

- *Having and communicating the right procedures.* The multinational should set up clear reporting procedures if employees feel sexually harassed. Managers and supervisors should be familiar with these procedures. Such procedures should also be clearly communicated to employees. Such policies should be regularly communicated to employees so that they feel that there is an outlet if they are sexually harassed. The worst outcome for a multinational is if the victim steps out of the company outlets to make such complaints.

- *Strong disciplinary action.* For the sexual harassment program to be effective, employees must perceive the program to be protecting them from sexual harassment while also punishing harassers. It therefore becomes critical for the multinational to take strong disciplinary action against the harasser if the sexual harassment incidences do not stop after training. This is especially critical in societies where strong gender roles exist and where women have been traditionally harassed.

- *Enforce and support national regulations and laws.* Multinationals have a critical role to play in enforcing sexual harassment laws and regulations worldwide. Most societies view sexual harassment negatively, although there is varying levels of support for the behavior. Multinationals can thus play important roles in enforcing healthy workplace environments in their foreign subsidiaries by clearly enforcing such policies.

As the above shows, sexual harassment is a key issue that affects most companies. Dealing appropriately with employees as stakeholders means providing a workplace environment free of sexual harassment. Next we discuss whistle-blowing.

WHISTLE-BLOWING

The final key employee issue we will examine in this chapter is whistle-blowing. **Whistle-blowing** refers to the activities involved "when current or former employees disclose illegal, immoral or illegitimate organizational activities to parties that they believe may be able to stop it."[41] Many recent high-profile ethical scandals at Enron and WorldCom came to light because of whistle-blowers who decided to publicize ethical wrongdoing. Whistle-blowing is therefore a key element of an ethical organization and its relationship to employees.

Is whistle-blowing a beneficial activity? Many argue that whistle-blowing has several advantages for society as well as the participating company. For example, whistle-blowing can benefit society as it can prevent faulty or dangerous products from reaching the marketplace. Furthermore, Verschoor reports that the U.S. Food and Drug Administration has received significant settlement from many pharmaceuticals companies for fraud.[42] For instance, Pfizer was involved in the illegal marketing of several drugs for unapproved uses. Such whistle-blowing has clearly benefited society in general.

However, whistle-blowing can also be beneficial to the organizations. As you read in Chapter 1, fraud is a significant problem for many companies. Whistle-blowing tips are often the primary way fraud can be detected and losses curbed. Furthermore, a good internal whistle-blowing program can enable a company to address some ethical problems before such problems escalate and cause significant losses and reputational damages to the company. Research reported in Miceli et al. also suggests that a strong whistle-blowing program should result in a workplace environment free of ethical wrongdoing.[43] Such an environment can lead to a very healthy culture that makes employees feel more committed to and satisfied with their employing organization. Finally, addressing whistle-blowing programs is now a legal requirement in the U.S. The Sarbanes-Oxley Act provides legal protection from retaliation to employees who whistle-blow.

Despite these advantages, many see whistle-blowing as an unethical behavior on the part of the employee. A company expects that its employees will be loyal and behave in ways that will protect the employing company's interests. For example, by exposing the fraudulent reporting at Enron, Sherron Watkins was perceived as being disloyal to Enron. However, recent arguments by Varelius suggest that whistle-blowing is not necessarily incompatible with being loyal to one's company.[44] In fact, whistle-blowing is beneficial to the company as it prevents further unethical wrongdoing that can hurt the company. Thus, it is possible to be loyal to a company and to whistle-blow on unethical wrongdoings.

While whistle-blowing is a key aspect of most U.S. companies' ethical programs, it is also practiced worldwide. Research documents whistle-blowing programs in countries such as Australia, Canada, Croatia, France, Hong Kong, India, Iceland, Jamaica, Japan, South Africa, and New Zealand among many others.[45] However, although whistle-blowing may be practiced in many countries, it is not necessarily as embraced as sexual harassment policies. In fact, the European Union has been problematic, as U.S. multinationals enforce whistle-blowing programs in their European subsidiaries. Consider the Global Business Ethics Insight on page 180.

GLOBAL BUSINESS ETHICS INSIGHT

Whistle-blowing in the European Union

U.S. companies listed on the U.S. Stock Exchange are required to establish a whistle-blower system to give employees the opportunity to anonymously report their concerns about wrongdoing regarding financial and accounting issues. Most U.S. multinationals thus encourage their European subsidiaries to establish internal whistle-blowing systems to give employees the opportunity to whistle-blow if needed. However, many countries in the European Union have strict laws and regulations that ban whistle-blowing. Such bans stem from the fact that the European Union has different views regarding data privacy protection rights and individual rights. For instance, the collection, registration, and storage of personal data related to an individual may fall foul of European Union laws governing the privacy of personal data.

Part of the fear of whistle-blowing comes from the experiences that Europe had to go through historically. For example, the Nazi regime forced German employees in Germany and other occupied countries to report misconduct during World War II. France and Eastern Europe also views whistle-blowing with suspicion given the concerns regarding political collaborators. Such experiences have produced a much different view of whistle-blowing from U.S. companies.

However, whistle-blowing has not been a failure in all countries of the European Union. For instance, a recent study of the Norwegian public sector showed that a very large proportion of employees blew the whistle when they observed misconduct. Surprisingly, a majority of these employees received positive reactions and helped improve the conduct that was whistle-blown. Authors of the study argue that the model of labor relations in Norway and the strong emphasis on collective arrangements provide for a healthy environment where employees are free to voice their opinions on misconduct and not fear retaliation.

Given the varying rules and regulations, it becomes difficult for any multinational to establish uniform worldwide codes of conduct for whistle-blowing. Astute multinationals will have to scan local laws and establish whistle-blowing programs in compliance with such rules and regulations.

Based on *Oprisk and Compliance*. 2009. "Global whistleblowing systems could fall foul of local rules." April, 11; Skivenes, M. and Trygstad, C.S. 2010. "When whistle-blowing works: The Norwegian case." *Human Relations*, 63, 7, 1072–1092; Wisskirchen, G. 2010. "The introduction of whistleblower systems in the European Union." *Defense Counsel Journal*, 77, 3, 366–383.

The above clearly shows the need for multinationals to be aware of local laws when implementing whistle-blowing programs. In some parts of the world, whistle-blowing may not be viewed as favorably. However, another key area of interest as it relates to employees as stakeholders is the consequences of whistle-blowing. Dasgupta and Kesharwani argue that one of the most damaging consequences of whistle-blowing has been retaliation against the whistle-blower.[46] Consider that Lee informed both the CEO and the chief financial officer of Lehman Brothers of senior management's violation of the company's code of conduct and the tens of billions of dollars that could not be substantiated on the balance sheet. Instead of taking Lee's report seriously, Lehman Brothers concluded that his report was unfounded and allegations baseless.[47] Mr. Lee was also fired. Retaliation can thus range from the employer attacking the whistle-blower on the basis of his/her credibility and sources, to subsequent poor performance evaluations, to eventually losing their jobs. Research also suggests that whistle-blowers suffer in their non-work lives though depression, divorce, and other personal life difficulties.

Given the importance of whistle-blowing to companies, recent regulation has been promulgated in the U.S. to protect whistle-blowers from retaliation. Specifically, the Sarbanes-Oxley Act (see Chapter 7) was passed to provide protection to whistle-blowers. A company is in violation if it takes wrongful action against an employee who whistle-blows about activities that the employee reasonably thinks that are in violation of laws or accounting practices. Furthermore, the law protects employees of public companies who whistle-blow about activities related to financial securities or shareholder fraud.

As whistle-blowing become a global phenomenon, more multinationals will be encouraged to establish whistle-blowing programs. As such, multinationals need to first establish some in-house mechanism for employees to whistle-blow. One of the popular ways to allow whistle-blowing is through the implementation of hotlines.[48] Employees should be made aware of such mechanisms, while new employees should be trained and informed of the existence of such mechanisms. Employees should also be aware that they will not be punished or retaliated against if they decide to whistle-blow. Some experts even argue for reward systems for those who whistle-blow.

The process by which multinationals deals with complaints is also an important factor in determining the effectiveness of a whistle-blowing program. Employees should have some reasonable assurance that their complaints will be dealt with seriously with no fear of retaliation. Managers and other supervisors should be properly trained in how to handle complaints. Furthermore, those participating in the violating activities should be punished. Employees need to know that their attempts to whistle-blow are taken seriously.

STRATEGIC ROLE OF HUMAN RESOURCE MANAGEMENT ENFORCING ETHICS

The **human resource management (HRM) department** has a strategic role in ensuring an ethical organization, as the organization deals with employees as stakeholders. Sloan and Gavin argue that around one third of ethics programs in *Fortune 500* companies are housed in the human resource management department.[49] The HRM department is the critical link between a company and its employees. The department is in charge of ensuring the welfare of employees while also ensuring that the rights of these employees are being respected. For instance, as you read in the opening paragraphs of this chapter, a company can maximize its chances of hiring employees with higher ethical dispositions by paying careful attention to the recruitment and selection process. Making sure that potential new employees are more likely to be ethical is a critical component of the ethical organization. In the final section of this chapter, we therefore look very briefly at the relevant HRM functions and how they contribute to ethics in any organization.

As you read earlier, if properly implemented, the HRM functions of recruitment and selection function allows the company to hire only those employees who have a higher likelihood of behaving ethically. However, the HRM recruitment and selection process can also play a critical role in ensuring that diversity and affirmative actions are met. The HRM department can take steps to encourage a multinational to pay attention to reaching out to potential candidates of prejudiced groups. The HRM department can find locally appropriate ways to recruit employees from these groups (e.g., advertising in different outlets). The HRM department can also ensure that there is fit between the potential new employee and the ethical values of the company.[50] Applicants should be surveyed to gauge their level of agreement with the ethical values espoused by the company. New employees should be committed to both enforcing ethics and discussing ethics issues.

Another critical function undertaken by a HRM department is performance appraisals. Performance appraisals relate to how employees' productivity and other performance components are assessed. For the ethical organization, the process by which performance takes place needs to embody ethical values.[51] The system should be transparent and provide for objective ways to assess how employees are doing.

The compensation area is also a critical area that embodies the ethical values of an organization. As Sloan and Gavin argue, this is an area that received considerable attention from both employees and society.[52] A multinational must therefore ensure that compensation and benefits are distributed in a fair and equitable manner. As you will see later in Chapter 10, the low wages paid in developing nations has always been a source of ethical controversy. Through compensation and benefits programs, a multinational must be ready and willing to address such controversies.

A final critical HRM function that we consider is **training**. This refers to the efforts by a multinational to impart new skills and capabilities in employees. However, many aspects of enforcing ethics in an organization involve training. Consider the Business Ethics Insight on page 183.

As the Business Ethics Insight shows, training is thus a critical function that HRM departments have to offer. For instance, consider that Howard suggests that while many companies offer training to their employees on how to detect sexual harassment, they often do not train workers to know how to stop such harassment or even deal with sexual harassment when it occurs.[53] Training is thus necessary to ensure that

BUSINESS ETHICS INSIGHT

Case of Discrimination at Auchan

Auchan, a French multinational, started in 1961 as a single supermarket. It now runs supermarkets and hypermarkets in over 12 countries with sales of 35 billion Euros. In 2004, when the Charte de la Diversité (Diversity Charter) passed in France, Auchan decided to examine diversity in its operations. Initial results revealed that the company had seemingly no problematic issues with diversity. Surveys showed that employees from around 30 countries worked in Auchan stores and that 75% of employees perceived no unequal treatment.

However, when the company decided to sign on the Charte de la Diversité, it elected to take a closer look at diversity in the company. Through internal surveys done by HRM, Auchan found that some level of discrimination did exist. To further confirm these beliefs, Auchan commissioned a series of experiments. An external team of consultants sent 280 fictitious applications for two types of jobs (technical jobs with little contact with customers and cashier jobs with contacts with customers) to 35 different supermarkets. Results showed that having North African names generally meant that there was a much less chance of getting invited for a job interview. The results were even more pronounced for cashiers, and the team sensed some form of reactive discrimination.

The diversity team thus found evidence of some form of implicit discrimination based on stereotypes. To address these problems, Auchan embarked on an ambitious diversity program. A major emphasis was placed on training employees to become more sensitive to unconscious discrimination. Auchan spent around 1 million Euros to provide 130 half-day training sessions to 5,500 of its employees. Employees had to confront their stereotypes through role-playing, and people from immigrant backgrounds, gays, and people with disabilities discussed how they cope with such discrimination.

Based on Demuijnck, G. 2009. "Non-discrimination in human resources management as a moral obligation." *Journal of Business Ethics*, 88, 83–100.

the many activities discussed in this chapter (affirmative action, sexual harassment, whistle-blowing) occur in ways that are consistent with the values of an ethical organization. Furthermore, training for the job must be offered in an equitable manner while also taking into consideration individual differences in abilities and learning styles.[54]

Finally, Krell argues that the HRM department is also responsible for conducting ethics audits.[55] Ethics audits ensure that prohibited behaviors and actions within the realm of ethics are not occurring in the organization. A recent report suggests that the most common ethics audits involve examining "conflicts of interest, access to personal

Human Resource Management Function	Ethics Activity
Recruitment and Selection	• Abide by all laws and regulations when soliciting candidates to ensure good representation in terms of traditionally prejudiced groups (race, gender) to meet all diversity and affirmative action goals • Respect local laws regarding recruitment and selection • Conduct extensive tests (integrity tests, interviews, honesty tests) to ensure that potential new employees are ethical • Ensure that potential new employees' values match those of the organization
Performance Appraisal	• Design system that embody the multinational's ethical norms and values • Ensure that system can objectively (as far as possible) assess performance and provide feedback • Ensure that performance appraisal is conducted in fair and objective manner
Compensation and Benefits	• Compensation and benefits must be distributed in a fair and equitable manner • Wage levels should be reasonable, taking into consideration local laws and norms • Address controversies surrounding low wages given in developing nations
Training	• Provide adequate training to ensure that employees can grow professionally • Provide sexual harassment, whistle-blowing, and other forms of needed training • Provide training in equitable manner while also taking into consideration personal needs and capabilities • Ensure that employees are trained to recognize prejudiced behaviors and/or use of stereotypes against protected classes (race, gender, etc.)
Other Activities	• Conduct ethics audit • Collect data regarding all ethics aspects in the organization (e.g., data regarding incidence of sexual harassment, data regarding discrimination, etc.)

EXHIBIT 4.7—HRM Functions and Ethics

information, bidding and award practices, giving and receiving gifts and employee discrimination issues."[56] Thus, the HRM department may be responsible for setting up mechanisms to gauge the level of behavior consistent with the espoused values of the organization.

Exhibit 4.7 summarizes the HRM functions and the critical role these functions play in enforcing ethics.

CHAPTER SUMMARY

In this chapter, you learned about the many key issues facing companies as they deal with employees. While it is debatable, employees may still be the most important stakeholder. Employees help implement the company's strategy. It therefore becomes critical to address such employee issues. You therefore read about four key aspects of the organization's relationship with employees; namely, hiring and firing, diversity and affirmative action, sexual harassment, and whistle-blowing.

The hiring process is a critical aspect of how any organization relates to employees. It represents the first point of contact between the company and a potential employee. Multinationals thus need to be sensitive to the cultural needs of the countries they operate in. However, the firing process also represents one of the most traumatic aspects of any employee's life. You therefore learned about the employment-at-will environment common in the U.S. and the contrasting just-cause employment system in countries such as Canada and those in the European Union.

As most multinationals strive for some form of diversity (race, gender, etc.), you read about the importance of diversity. You also learned about affirmative action and the importance of such programs in companies. You also read about the many issues to keep in mind when establishing such programs.

Sexual harassment remains one of the most critical issues facing multinationals as they relate to employees. You read about the types of sexual harassment and the potentially devastating consequences of sexual harassment for the victim, the employer, and society. You also learned about the steps multinationals can take to address sexual harassment problems.

You also learned about whistle-blowing and the critical role played by whistle-blowing. Unlike the other employee issues, you read about the need for multinationals to be sensitive to local rules and regulations. You also read about the steps a multinational can take to implement a strong whistle-blowing program.

Finally, the text concludes with a discussion of the critical role that the HRD department plays in implementing and enforcing ethics in the company. The critical HRD functions were discussed and the implications of these functions for the ethical company were emphasized.

NOTES

1   Collins, D. 2009. *Essentials of business ethics.* Hoboken, NJ: John Wiley and Sons.
2   Collins, *Essentials of business ethics.*
3   Hofstede, G. 1997. *Cultures and organizations: Software of the mind.* New York: McGraw-Hill, pp. 64–65.
4   Collins, *Essentials of business ethics.*
5   Bird, R.B. & Charters, D. 2004. "Good faith and wrongful termination in Canada and the United States: A comparative and relational inquiry." *American Business Law Journal*, 41, 2/3, 205–250 (at 205).
6   Bird & Charters, "Good faith and wrongful termination," 205.
7   McCall, J.J. 2003. "A defense of just cause dismissal rule." *Business Ethics Quarterly*, 12, 2, 151–175.
8   Werhane, P.H & Radin, T.J. 2009. "Employment at will and due process." In Beauchamp, T.L., Bowie, N.L. & Arnold, D.G. (Eds.), *Ethical theory and business*, Harlow, U.K.: Pearson Publishing, pp. 113–120.
9   Werhane & Radin, "Employment at will and due process."
10 Maertz, C.P., Wiley, J.W., Lerouge, C. & Campion, M.A. 2010. "Downsizing effects on survivors: Layoffs, offshoring, and outsourcing." *International Relations*, 49, 2, 275–285.
11 Thurm, S. 2010. "Recalculating the cost of big layoffs." *Wall Street Journal Online*, May 4.
12 Dannin, E. 2007. "Why at-will employment is bad for employers and just cause is good for them." *Labor Law Journal*, 58, 1, 5–16.
13 Werhane & Radin, "Employment at will and due process."
14 Dannin, "Why at-will employment is bad for employers."
15 McCall, "A defense of just cause dismissal rule."
16 Dannin, "Why at-will employment is bad for employers," 5.
17 Kaiser, D.M. 2005. "The implications of at-will versus just-cause employment." *Proceedings of the Academy of Organizational Culture, Communications and Conflict*, 10, 2 (at 34).
18 Bird & Charters, "Good faith and wrongful termination."
19 Bird & Charters, "Good faith and wrongful termination."
20 Werhane & Radin, "Employment at will and due process."
21 Dannin, "Why at-will employment is bad for employers."
22 Beauchamp, T.L., Bowie, N.L. & Arnold, D.G. 2010. *Ethical theory and business.* Harlow, U.K.: Pearson Publishing.
23 Owens, J.M., Gomes, G.M. & Morgan, J.F. 2008. "Broadening the definition of unlawful retaliation Under Title VII." *Employee Responsibility and Rights Journal*, 20, 249–260.
24 Fearfull, A. & Kamenou, N. (2010) "Work and career experiences of ethnic minority men and women." Introductory chapter for special issue, *Quality, Diversity and Inclusion: An International Journal*, 29, 4, 325–331.
25 Herring, C. 2009. "Does diversity pay? Race, gender, and the business case for diversity."*American Sociology Review*, 74, 2, 208–222.
26 Herring, "Does diversity pay?" 208.
27 Beauchamp et al., *Ethical theory and business*, p. 185.
28 Hansen, F. 2010. "Diversity of a different color." *Workforce Management*, 89, 6, 23–26.
29 Combs, M.G., Nadkarni, S. & Combs, M.W. 2005. "Implementing affirmative action plans in multinational corporations." *Organizational Dynamics*, 34, 4, 346–360.
30 Combs et al., "Implementing affirmative action plans."
31 Combs et al., "Implementing affirmative action plans."
32 Willness, C.R., Steel, P. & Lee, K. 2007. "A meta-analysis of the antecedents and consequences of workplace sexual harrasment." *Personnel Psychology*, 60, 1, 127–162 (at 131).
33 Smolensky, E. & Kleiner, B.H. 2003. "How to prevent sexual harassment in the workplace." *Equal Opportunities International*, 22, 2, 59–65.
34 Willness et al., "A meta-analysis."
35 Merkin, R.S. 2008. "The impact of sexual harassment on turnover intentions, absenteeism, and job satisfaction: Findings from Argentina, Brazil and Chile." *Journal of International Women's Studies*, 10, 2, 73–91.

36   Johnson, K. 2010. "Sexual harassment in the workplace: A case study of Nigeria." *Gender and Behaviour*, 8, 1, 2903–2918.

37   Merkin, "The impact of sexual harassment."

38   Roumeliotis, B.D. & Kleiner, B.H. 2005. "Individual response strategies to sexual harassment." *Equal Opportunities International*, 24, 5/6, 41–48.

39   Willness et al., "A meta-analysis."

40   Hunt, C.M., Davidson, M.J., Fielden, S.L. & Hoel, H. 2010. "Reviewing sexual harassment in the workplace—An intervention model." *Personnel Review*, 39, 5, 655–668; Johnson, "Sexual harassment in the workplace"; Smolensky & Kleiner, "How to prevent sexual harassment in the workplace."

41   Miceli, M.P., Near, J.P. & Dworkin, M.T. 2009. "A word to the wise: how managers and policy-makers can encourage employees to report wrongdoing." *Journal of Business Ethics*, 86, 379–392.

42   Verschoor, C. 2010. "Increased motivation for whistleblowing." *Ethics*, 16, 18, 61.

43   Miceli et al., "A word to the wise."

44   Varelius, J. 2009. "Is whistle-blowing compatible with employee loyalty?" *Journal of Business Ethics*, 85, 263–275.

45   Miceli et al., "A word to the wise."

46   Dasgupta, S. & Kesharwani A. 2010. "Whistleblowing: A survey of literature." *IUP Journal of Corporate Governance*, 9, 4, 57–70.

47   Jennings, M. 2010. "The employee we ignore, the signs we miss and the reality we avoid." *Corporate Finance Review*, 14, 6, 42–46.

48   Sweeney, P. 2008. "Hotlines helpful for blowing the whistle." *Financial Executive*, May 24, 28–31.

49   Sloan, K.A. & Gavin, J.H. (2010) "Human resources management: Meeting the ethical obligations of the function." *Business and Society Review*, 115, 1, 57–74.

50   Sloan & Gavin, "Human resources management."

51   Sloan & Gavin, "Human resources management."

52   Sloan & Gavin, "Human resources management."

53   Howard, L.G. 2007. "Employees poorly equipped to deal with sexual harassment." *Canadian HR Reporter*, 20, 6, 31.

54   Sloan & Gavin, "Human resources management."

55   Krell, E. 2010. "How to conduct an ethics audit." *HR Magazine*, 55, 4, 48–51.

56   Krell, "How to conduct an ethics audit," 49.

KEY TERMS

Affirmative action: laws, policies, or guidelines that specify positive steps to be taken to hire and promote persons from groups previously and presently discriminated against.

Diversity: hiring of workers who are different in race, color, or religion compared to the traditional Caucasian male workforce.

Employees: human resources available to a company dedicated to achieving its goals.

Employment-at-will: company may terminate its employee for a good reason, bad reason, or no reason at all.

Hiring: one of the critical ways that companies relate to employees as stake-holders.

Hostile/poisoned work environment: where sex-related behaviors and mores make women feel uncomfortable and abused in the workplace.

Human resource management (HRM) department: critical link between employees and company.

Just-cause dismissal: employers must provide reasonable notice of termination of an employee.

Quid pro quo sexual harassment: where a person makes explicit requests for sexual favors in exchange for a workplace benefit such as a raise or a promotion.

Recruitment: process of identifying and attracting qualified people to apply for vacant positions in an organization.

Selection: process by which a company chooses a person to fill a vacant position.

Sexual harassment: unwelcome sexual advances, requests for sexual favors, and other verbal or physical conduct of a sexual nature

Termination: involuntary separation of company from employee.

Training: efforts by a multinational to impart new skills and capabilities in its employees.

Whistle-blowing: disclosure by current or former employees of illegal, immoral, or illegitimate organizational activities to parties that they believe may be able to stop it.

DISCUSSION QUESTIONS

1. What are recruitment and selection? How do recruitment and selection differ by countries?
2. What are the main features of employment-at-will? Discuss arguments to support employment-at-will.
3. Discuss the just-cause dismissal approach. How is this approach different from employment-at-will?
4. What is diversity? How is diversity beneficial for a multinational?
5. What is affirmative action? How can companies implement affirmative action programs?
6. What is sexual harassment? Discuss the types of sexual harassment and provide examples?
7. What can companies do to implement effective sexual harassment programs?
8. What is whistle-blowing? What are the benefits of whistle-blowing? How can companies implement effective whistle-blowing programs?
9. Discuss the human resource management functions. How can each function help enforce ethics in a company?
10. Why is the human resource management department so critical to build an ethical organization? Defend your answer with specific examples.

INTERNET ACTIVITY

1. Go to the International Labor Organization (ILO) website: http://www.ilo.org.
2. Read about the organization and its many functions. Discuss these functions and the critical role played by the ILO.
3. Go to the "Topics" area. List the many activities the ILO is involved in.
4. Pick four of these topics. Read the latest reports on these four topics. What are some of the major areas of concern for each of the four topics you read about?
5. Read about "Child Labor." How prevalent is the problem worldwide? What solutions do the ILO suggest to address child labor issues?

For more Internet Activities and resources, visit the Companion Website at www.routledge.com/cw/parboteeah.

WHAT WOULD YOU DO?

Competitor's Products

You recently graduated from a prestigious university with a degree in marketing. You apply for several marketing jobs and eventually get the job that you wanted the most. You will be a salesperson in a pharmaceuticals company that has had several breakthrough drugs recently. You know that this job will give you significant experience but you are also aware that the job will require hard work and long days ahead. During the interview, you impressed many of the top executives in the company.

After several weeks at work, you are approached by the vice president of marketing, who invites you for drinks after work. You realize that several new employees who were hired at the same time as you often get invited for such events. However, you are unsure whether you should go or not. After giving the idea some thought, you decide to accept the invitation.

The event at the local pub starts out well. You are having a good time with your co-workers and several top executives of the company. During the conversation, you also reveal that your best friend works for a competitor. However, soon you find that some individuals are getting drunk and making uncomfortable sexual advances to you. The vice president (VP) of marketing also makes some advances to you and mentions that you will go far in the company. During the conversation, the VP also starts questioning you about information you gleaned from your best friend. The VP seems interested in new products being developed by the competitor.

What would you do? Do you leave the party and forget that anything happened? Or do you report the offending individuals the next day and run the risk of ruining your new career?

BRIEF CASE: BUSINESS ETHICS INSIGHT

WalMart and Healthcare Benefits

On Friday October 20, 2011, WalMart made some shocking announcements during a press conference. It announced that all employees who worked less than 24 hours per week for the company would no longer qualify for any of the company's health plans. This was a surprising turnaround from a few years ago when WalMart decided to become an advocate for larger companies providing healthcare to all of its employees, and to part-time employees in 1996. Under strong pressure from labor unions and many states, WalMart had agreed to provide healthcare to its part-time employees after these employees had worked one year on the job. WalMart's decision was praised, as more than half of larger employees did not provide any healthcare to part-time employees at that time.

WalMart claims that rising healthcare costs and declining profitability are some of the main reasons they have decided to reduce health benefits. Reports suggest that employer-sponsored health premiums are predicted to go up by 9% over the 2011–2012 time period. However, some WalMart employees will see premium growth of around 40% in 2012. Despite this growth, WalMart employees will still be paying less than plans offered by other employers.

One of the other controversial aspects of WalMart's new health offerings is that employees who smoke will be required to pay a significant penalty. Specifically, smoking employees will likely have to pay around $10 to $90 extra per pay period. For some employees, this premium increase will mean that they can no longer afford the health insurance from the company.

Based on Greenhouse, S. and Abelson, R. 2011. "WalMart cuts some healthcare benefits." *New York Times*, online edition, October 20; Kliff, S. 2011. "The health insurance plight of part-time workers." *Washington Post*, online edition, October 23.

BRIEF CASE QUESTIONS

1. Is it a moral obligation for companies to provide healthcare for their employees? Why or why not?
2. Is WalMart justified in cutting healthcare benefits for part-time workers?
3. Is it ethical for companies to ask employees who smoke to pay higher health premiums? Or are the companies infringing on an employee's right to privacy?
4. How should WalMart respond to critics who say that the company does not cover its fair share of healthcare costs?

LONG CASE: BUSINESS ETHICS

THE MARRIOTT CORPORATION HUMAN RESOURCES DEPARTMENT: MANAGING A LOW-WAGE WORKFORCE

In 1989, Marriott was at the top of the food and lodging business. Few companies, let alone family-operated ones, had achieved Marriott's stature and maintained a deeply felt sense of history and security. In its 62-year history, Marriott had earned a level of shareholder trust that no other hospitality company had even approached. Yet as a premier services company, Marriott's success depended on the people who actually delivered the service—the maids, janitors, kitchen workers, porters, waiters, delivery people, telemarketing representatives, and front desk clerks—the fastest growing and least appreciated segment of the U.S. labor force. Under pressure to please value-driven customers, Marriott was forced to scramble to hire, train, and retain average people capable of performing extraordinary service with a smile. To fill most of these low-level service jobs, Marriott did not need workers with high levels of education, experience, or technical expertise. Instead, in an era of flattening hier-archies and heightened expectations, Marriott needed low-wage-earning people who were also resilient and resourceful—skills previously demanded only of managers. In the 1990s, Marriott faced the challenge of not only finding, but also retaining, people willing to work for low wages with few benefits.

The major task facing Marriott's senior vice president for Human Resources, Clifford Ehrlich, was to help his people-dependent company ensure itself an abundant supply of well-trained, loyal, and content workers, dedicated to the overall success of their employer. This would not be an easy task, because his job as a human resources manager had undergone a transformation in the 1980s. Ehrlich stated:

> Ten years ago, there was still a large part of human resources that had a compliance (EEO compliance) cast to it, wage and hour compliance, compliance with the National Labor Relations Act . . . Then the world started to change . . . While you still had to have this compliance feature, you had to ask what are the things we can do to help create an environment in which people do get excited about coming to work? . . . As business strategies changed, you had to be sure that the human resource efforts were geared to the change.[1]

The son of a New York Telephone Company union organizer, Ehrlich was the first member of his family to go away to college (attending Boston College Law School at night). Ehrlich's personal values of hard work, personal accountability, self-reliance, and family values mirrored the Marriott corporate culture inspired by the Mormon roots of founder J.W. Marriott, Sr. These values played an important role in shaping Marriott's human resource policies for the 1990s. Ehrlich was faced with the dilemma of developing appropriate human resource policies for Marriott that would not only attract and maintain a large supply of relatively low-paid service employees, but would also fit the Marriott corporate culture without tarnishing the company's long-held reputation as a highly principled family-run concern.

Marriott History

As a recent transplant from Utah, John Willard (Bill) Marriott, Sr. founded what would become the Marriott Corporation in May of 1927, as a nine-seat A&W Root Beer stand in Washington, D.C. The Marriott root-beer stand evolved into a family restaurant chain called Hot Shoppes, which in turn expanded into in-flight airline catering in 1937. In 1957, Marriott went public and at the same time opened its first hotel in Arlington, Virginia. Over the next few years, the company opened a string of hotels and Hot Shoppe Restaurants. In 1964, with 45 Hot Shoppes, four hotels, and other successful businesses, Bill Marriott, Sr. handed the presidency of the company to his son, Bill Marriott, Jr. while retaining the office of CEO for himself.

Bill Marriott, Jr. accelerated the pace of the company's growth by focusing on the lodging segment of the business. Through acquisitions and new business start-ups, Marriott quadrupled in size between 1946 and 1970, surpassing its competitors Howard Johnson and Hilton Hotels in both revenues and profits. Marriott became international in 1966 by acquiring an airline-catering kitchen in Caracas, Venezuela. In 1967, Marriott acquired the Big Boy restaurant chain, and in 1968, the company started the Roy Rogers fast-food chain.

Succeeding his father as CEO in 1972, Bill Marriott, Jr., introduced new management techniques, dividing the company into three semi-autonomous groups: food operations, inflight service to airlines, and hotels and specialty restaurants. Presidents who reported directly to Marriott headed the groups, which were further divided into 16 divisions. Through this strategy, the company never depended on one segment for profits.

Between 1975 and 1984, Marriott increased its room capacity from 14,000 units to more than 60,000 units. This increase was the result of another of Bill Jr.'s innovative strategies—constructing hotels and selling them, while maintaining control over the properties through management contracts. This system created rapid profit growth, limited risk, and ensured the uniformity of Marriott service standards that would have been difficult to achieve in traditional franchising arrangements. In the 1980s, Marriott further expanded through the acquisition of Gino's Pizza, Host International (an airport food and merchandizing service), American Resorts Group (a time-share operator), the Howard Johnson Company, Cladieux Corporation, Service Systems, Inc., and the Saga Corporation. Anticipating the glut in luxury-end hotel rooms, in the late 1980s Marriott expanded into the middle-priced hotel market by creating the Courtyard Marriott chain and, with the creation of Marriott Suites, the all-suite hotel market.

The collapse of real-estate prices and the slowdown in the hotel industry in the early 1990s presented Marriott with new challenges. Much of Marriott's growth in the 1980s was debt financed. Marriott's debt:equity ratio increased from 1:1 in 1979 to 4.5:1 in 1989, with a negative surplus cash flow of $7.84 per share, excluding asset sales. Bill Jr.'s strategy was to downsize and restructure, thus slowing the pace of new hotel construction and decreasing capital expenditures from $1.5 billion in 1990 to $1 billion in 1991.[2] To isolate the debt load, the corporation split into two companies: the properties that Marriott owned were grouped within the Host Marriott Corporation, and its contract services were centralized in Marriott International, Inc.

Corporate Culture

Despite their wealth, the Marriott family (which owned slightly less than 30% of the company stock) always prided itself on a strong work ethic. Bill Marriott, Jr. stated: "I do what my father did, which is to teach my kids how to work." Bill Sr. and his wife expected their children to do housework when they were young and to work summers when they were older. Bill Marriott's younger brother, Steve, Marriott's director of sales, had started working in the family business at age 16, when he was hired to flip hamburgers at a Roy Rogers restaurant. Not only did he tithe his pre-tax income to the Church of Jesus Christ of Latter-day Saints, he also saved enough money to help with living expenses after his marriage. He did not believe that he should become president of the company "unless he earns it—and doing so will earn himself respect." In a 1987 *Forbes* interview, Bill Marriott, Jr. said that he ran the company with a very strong work ethic.[3]

On occasion, the Marriott family's Mormon beliefs conflicted with business decisions. In the name of business practicality and after much deliberation, the family decided to sell alcohol in its lodging facilities in the 1960s. A desire not to be associated with gambling, however, led to the family's decision not to have its company enter into the booming gaming business in the 1970s.

Labor Unions

Along with tight family and cost control, Bill Marriott, Jr. agreed with his father's philosophy that labor unions helped neither the worker nor the company. Marriott developed a tradition of working hard to keep unions out of all phases of the corporation. Its executives believed that the company could remain more flexible without union rules, and the reduced labor costs would enable them to offer better benefits to their employees. According to Bill Marriott, Jr.:

> Those who work for us must like us. If they like you and have respect for you then they will do almost anything for you. They will look after your customers properly, and a spirit of friendliness will pervade your whole organization.

As an expression of this corporate philosophy, Marriott instituted a profit-sharing plan and a system of bonus incentives. In place of union grievance committees and collective action, Marriott instituted a Guarantee of Fair Treatment policy, which promoted constructive engagement between employees and managers. Under this program, managers were expected to communicate regularly with employees, know about their ambitions, home lives, and work motivations, and involve employees in decisions that affected them. In 1990, only two of Marriott's 500 hotels were unionized. Marriott believed the fact that its employees had never formed a union was a testament to their fair treatment.

At Marriott, the anti-union culture was strong. So strong, in fact, that in 1992, labor union organizers found and made public a Marriott Human Resources anti-union manual that outlined interviewing techniques for human resources managers designed to weed out potential union sympathizers from among prospective employees.

The manual instructed managers to look out for "an applicant who wears an article of clothing or jewelry with union insignias. Be observant, you'll be surprised at what you see."[4]

In the late 1980s, when Marriott expanded into the northern industrialized union strongholds of New York, Chicago, and Boston, it met opposition from broad coalitions of community and labor leaders. This coalition sued Marriott over its practice of giving hiring preference to new employees from suburban areas outside the limits of cities that granted Marriott job-creation tax incentives. In 1989, in Boston a coalition consisting of the Community Task Force on Construction, Women in the Building Trades, and the Black Legislative Caucus protested Marriott's refusal to grant contracting work to minorities and women and its proclivity for hiring contractors from non-union southern states.

Structural Change in the American Labor Force

According to a 1994 Bureau of Labor Statistics Report, occupations with the largest growth projections were low-skilled: food service, retail sales clerks, truck drivers, childcare workers, nursing aids, and janitors. Service occupations accounted for 79% of all employment in the United States and 74% of U.S. GDP. This category was further projected to account for all net job growth in the coming decade. In 1994, the travel and hospitality industry alone employed 10.5 million people or 8% of the total U.S. labor force.

In the late 1980s, however, as the demand for service workers was increasing, the employable unskilled labor pool was shrinking. As the baby boomers aged, the number of people entering the job market to replace them was diminishing because of the decline in the birth rate during the 1960s and 1970s. In addition, many of these new entrants had such limited educational opportunities or work experience that they were ill equipped to enter the labor force. An estimated 25% of American high school graduates could not read or write at an eighth-grade level, and the high-school dropout rates in major cities ranged from 35% in New York City to 50% in Washington, D.C. Finally, more than 44% of the labor force were women, the majority of whom were of childbearing age; this percentage was projected to rise to 64% by the year 2000. Women with children under the age of six years were the fastest growing segment of the American workforce.

Until the late 1980s, Marriott had a convenient means of augmenting its demands on the shrinking unskilled labor pool. In Los Angeles and Miami, Marriott Corporation vans regularly stopped at designated street corners to pick up day workers to staff the banquet tables, dishwashers, and towel carts at local hotels. Peggy Pfeil, director of Human Resources for Marriott Corporation in 1987, stated: "It's a wonderful resource. These people need the work." Many of these day laborers picked up by the Marriott vans, however, were illegal aliens. Unfortunately for Marriott, the Immigration Reform and Control Act of 1987 enforced criminal penalties against companies with four or more employees who were illegal aliens. The law also required companies to verify the work permits for new employees. Marriott's short-term response to the new legislation was to attempt to shift its low-skilled employment burden in places like Los Angeles, Miami, and New York to private temporary contractors, as a means of transferring the liability for hiring illegal aliens to a third party.[5]

As American labor became increasingly deskilled and the traditional high-paying blue-collar jobs of the post-war era evaporated, the ranks of the low-wage labor pool began to swell. Because wages were so flat, however, these new workers had little allegiance to any particular job or employer. The tendency was for these workers to bounce from one minimum-wage job to another with few if any consequences, as the minimum-wage service sector jobs were plentiful.

Marriott faced the 1990s with the problem of not only hiring people willing to work for low wages, but also keeping them. Annual turnover rates of 100% or more were common in the hotel and restaurant industry. Until 1990, the tendency was to think of front-line service workers as a disposable commodity rather than as an economic resource. It cost Marriott as much as $1,100 to recruit and train each replacement—the total bill ran into millions of dollars each year. Ehrlich had to figure out how to recruit and maintain an effective workforce from a traditionally undependable low-skilled labor pool without dramatic wage increases.

Cliff Ehrlich took particular pride in the announcement that the *Personnel Journal* had awarded his company its 1993 Rebuild America Challenge Grant for the Chicago Marriott's innovative approaches to what the Hudson Institute called the problems associated with "Work Force 2000."[6] Under Ehrlich's leadership, Marriott created programs designed to break down the traditional barriers that had kept the "problem categories" of workers—former welfare recipients, single parents, teenagers, recent college graduates, high school dropouts, people with disabilities—out of the American workforce. Marriott's human resource programs focused on instilling a strong work ethic in its problem category employees, emphasizing job training, career development, reward incentives, and family services to not only attract new employees, but also to retain existing workers.

Under Ehrlich's leadership, Marriott developed a marketing approach to human resources based on the premise that Marriott should sell itself to prospective workers rather than the traditional reverse. Ehrlich adapted many of the same techniques used by marketers to build business—surveys, focus groups, and programs to enhance the company's reputation among customers—and applied them to current and future employees. "We're approaching it by saying we have jobs we're trying to sell, and the prospective workforce out there are the buyers." He also reasoned that instead of spending all of Marriott's money and attention going after new employees, an equal amount should be spent retaining old employees. Ehrlich believed that a large part of his job was to help employees feel good about working for Marriott: "That way they'll stay. And that way they'll spread the word . . . If all employees started their day with a little extra oomph, they would be willing to give their employer more than just what was written in their job description." He further stated that it was up to the employer to tap into what he calls "discretionary effort." The trick in management is to create a "work environment in which people do want to spend that discretionary effort . . . in which people contribute to the success of the business."[7] Ehrlich sought to challenge the traditional corporate paternalism of "we take care of our employees" and replace it with "we provide opportunities for our employees to take care of themselves." Ehrlich stated:

> Not only is it relieving the company of obligations that are not necessarily appropriate . . . It is also empowering the employee and recognizing that person as an adult responsible for managing his or her own life and job.[8]

He acknowledged that Marriott provided a lot less security to workers than in previous years due to the changing labor environment. Despite this fact, Ehrlich stated, "We still want loyalty. I believe that people come to work wanting to be loyal. They will exchange their loyalty not for security but for involvement." He saw his job as helping Marriott make the shift in employee management philosophy from the old paternalism to the new focus on individual self-help.

The Marriott human resource programs received a great deal of praise and publicity in the mid-1990s. The Marriott initiatives coincided with nationwide objectives to "eliminate welfare as we know it" and move the traditionally unemployable categories of workers into the workforce. As such, Marriott human resources became not only the industry leader, but also a model for other industries that depended on unskilled labor. Although Marriott managed to increase its retention rates, the rates never climbed above 60%. Despite the initial publicity blitz that surrounded new Marriott program announcements, several of the programs were never fully implemented. In addition, the Hotel and Restaurant Workers of the AFL-CIO began to take direct aim at the means through which Marriott maintained its non-union tradition, resulting in numerous lawsuits. Although Ehrlich received accolades for his innovative programs in 1996, he wondered how long this strategy could be sustained.

Pathways to Independence

In 1990, Marriott instituted the Pathways to Independence program, a six-week welfare-to-work course that included self-esteem training and basic communication and hospitality skills. Initially started in New Orleans, Pathways had expanded to 11 cities including Atlanta, Tampa, and Washington, D.C., by 1996. Six hundred workers, formerly on welfare, had been through the program. The result was higher retention rates and lower turnover for Marriott. The program was not without controversy, however, particularly because the training was government subsidized. See Appendix A for a 1997 interview with John A. Boardman, executive secretary-treasurer of the Hotel and Restaurant Employees Union, Local 25 of the AFL-CIO, Washington, D.C. Boardman was highly critical of Marriott's anti-union stance and its Pathways to Independence program.

Marriott's Workforce 2000 Programs

New Employee Orientation

Selecting employees who would stay beyond their first three months of employment was one of Marriott's biggest challenges. Until 1993, more than 40% of the new employees who left Marriott departed during the first three months on the job.

Marriott decided to focus on one of the most neglected areas of employment experience—orientation. Instead of hiring people and putting them immediately to work on a three-month "probationary" period, all fresh recruits attended an eight-hour initial training session, the highlight of which was an elegant lunch, served by hotel veterans. To guide them through the next 90 days, associates were assigned mentors (known as "buddies"). Every member of the entering class attended refresher courses after the second month. When these members reached their 90th day of employment, the hotel hosted them at a banquet. This program was based on the rationale that "You cannot expect your employees to delight your customers unless you as an employer delight your employees."[9]

"Partners in Career Management" Program

In 1994, Marriott instituted a workshop called "Partners in Career Management," a program designed to train its managers as "career coaches" capable of helping employees examine and manage their career options. All 6,000 management-level employees were slated to attend the course. The workshop would provide Marriott managers and supervisors with a four-step model to assist them in managing their own careers and prepare them to hold more effective career discussions with their employees. After attending the course, Marriott managers would be able to do the following:

1 Help employees identify skills, values, and interests, as well as answer the question, "Who am I?"
2 Offer ongoing feedback and help employees answer the question, "How am I seen?"
3 Help employees create a set of realistic career goals and answer the question, "What are my career alternatives?"
4 Help associates develop action plans and answer the question, "How can I achieve my goal?"

In addition, managers were expected to learn about career resources available within the organization, hold career discussions with employees on an ongoing basis, and identify developmental activities and experiences to help employees build their knowledge and skills and improve performance.

Marriott saw the creation of the workshop as a means of shifting the responsibility for career management away from the company and toward the employee. In accordance with this logic, at Marriott employees are officially responsible for:

- assessing their own skills, values, interests, and developmental needs
- determining long- and short-term career goals
- creating, with their manager, a career-development plan to reach their goals
- following through with their plan
- learning about and taking advantage of other career-management resources offered by Marriott, such as online job postings
- meeting their managers on a regular basis for career-development discussions
- recognizing that career discussions imply no promises or guarantees
- recognizing that their career development will depend directly on Marriott's needs and opportunities as well as their own performance and abilities

The J. Willard Marriott Award of Excellence

As a means of getting the best possible performance from each employee without excessive expenditure, Marriott established the J. Willard Marriott Award of Excellence, an engraved medallion bearing the likeness of the founder and the words expressing the basic values of the company: *dedication, achievement, character, ideals, effort,* and *perseverance*. Selection for this non-monetary award was based on remarks made by a nominator and the individual's length of service. The recipients represented a cross-section of the Marriott workforce: dishwashers, chefs, housekeepers, and merchandise managers. The Marriott Award was presented at a lavish awards banquet in Washington, D.C., attended by honorees, spouses, nominators, and top executives.

The Department of Work and Family Life

In 1989, to address the issue of employees' needs to balance the demands of home and work, Marriott created the Department of Work and Family Life. A 1989 *Harvard Business Review* article found that the labor force included more than 70% of all women with children between the ages of 6 and 17 and more than half the women with children less than one year old. With the two-income family becoming a norm and an economic necessity, Marriott began to realize the relationship between productivity and "family-friendly" policies. In 1996, *Business Week* announced:

> Work-family strategies haven't just hit the corporate mainstream—they've become a competitive advantage. The exclusive province of working mothers a decade ago, such benefits now extend to elder-care assistance, flexible scheduling, job-sharing, adoption benefits, on-site summer camp, employee help-lines, even—no joke—pet-care and lawnservice referrals.

Marriott additionally noted a direct correlation between family conflicts, particularly childcare issues, and retention levels and absenteeism. It also noted that even when work and family programs existed, they often exclusively focused on the needs of management-level employees.

Marriott sought to tailor these family related services to its low-wage workforce. A Marriott survey determined that 19% of Marriott hourly employees had considered leaving Marriott within the previous year because of work and family conflicts. Hourly employees also estimated they had missed an average of four days of work and been tardy seven days within the previous year, because of childcare demands.

Based on these findings, Marriott's Department of Work and Family Life developed a comprehensive plan of financial, research, and educational services for families. Among these initiatives was a nationwide referral service, Child Care Choices, which helped parents with children under age 13 to locate licensed providers in their communities. As of mid-1990, 80% of Marriott employees had used the service to find adequate childcare. The department also developed Family Care Spending Accounts to ease the economic strain on employees who were caring for dependants. These accounts allowed participants to take pretax deductions from their wages to pay for child and elder care.

Marriott's Participation in IAM CARES

Since 1985, Marriott participated in IAM CARES (International Association of Machinists Center for Administering Rehabilitation and Employment Services), an international nonprofit organization based in Maryland that teamed up with employers to train and help to secure employment for people with disabilities. The premier IAM CARES project was at the Chicago Marriott, which between 1987 and 1994 trained more than 131 individuals with disabilities.

As the Chicago program evolved, other special-interest organizations also became active partners: the Chicago Mayor's Office for People with Disabilities, the Illinois Department for Rehabilitation Services, and the Chicago Public Schools. The Chicago Marriott usually trained 30 people at the hotel each year. The bulk of IAM CARES funding came from the Department of Rehabilitation Services through Title I and Title II funds. The organization also received Job Training Partnership Act funding through the Chicago Mayor's Office on Employment Training. Participants received an on-the-job training wage of $4.25 per hour, paid by IAM CARES' funds.[10]

Marriott's Participation in the Private Industry Council

Located in every area of the United States, Private Industry Councils were the legal arm of the U.S. Department of Labor responsible for linking private industry with certain members of the local unemployed population. Private Industry Councils not only referred individuals for employment, but they also provided training funds under the Job Training Partnership Act (JTPA). Created in 1982, to replace the Comprehensive Employment and Training Act (CETA), in 1996, the JTPA was the federal government's largest job-skills training program. It had a $4 billion annual budget and had aided thousands of employers like Marriott in finding local disadvantaged and disabled individuals who needed job training assistance and who were likely to be qualified for jobs once they had been trained. Its primary goal was to move the jobless into permanent, sustaining employment.[11]

The program targeted educationally disadvantaged and displaced youths and adults, especially women, minorities, and the disabled. Once a candidate was referred, employers like Marriott signed a mandatory contract with the Private Industry Council that stipulated how long the company-specific training would last, what the training would entail, and how much the company would receive in reimbursement. Typically, an employer could not submit an invoice for wage reimbursement until the employee had been on the job for at least 30 days and more often 90 days.

Contracts could cover training for an individual or an entire group. A group's contract was called a customized-training contract and offered a slightly higher reimbursement because the employer also covered some initial costs, such as trainer's salaries, in addition to providing direct training.

Marriott's Participation in the Targeted Jobs Tax Credit (TJTC) Program

The TJTC provided an incentive for companies like Marriott to hire and train former welfare recipients. Marriott estimated that it cost approximately $1,000 to train an entry-level worker. The cost was even higher when training an individual with a poor educational background and sporadic job experience. According to Marriott, the TJTC subsidy enabled them to level the playing field for applications from these targeted populations. Through the TJTC, Marriott established relationships with various community-based organizations as a means of assuring a strong applicant flow.

The federal government discontinued this program because of criticism that some employers were receiving a windfall because eligibility standards were too subjective (i.e., the employer could categorize a prospective employee as "high risk" and receive the "wage subsidy"). The TJTC was replaced by the Work Opportunities Tax Credit Program, which more specifically limited eligibility to welfare recipients, ex-felons, economically disadvantaged veterans, youths in families receiving food stamps, and people with disabilities.[12]

Marriott was a major participant in the Work Opportunities Tax Credit Program, which subsidized the salaries of low-wage, difficult-to-employ categories of workers. These programs enabled Marriott to continue to use and keep a low-wage work-force.

APPENDIX:
A Case Note: Organized Labor

Interview with John A. Boardman, Executive Secretary—Treasurer of the Hotel and Restaurant Employees Union, Local 25 of the AFL-CIO, Washington, D.C.

The Union

In 1997, Local 25 of the Hotel and Restaurant Employees had over 6,000 members working in hotels, restaurants, private clubs, and caterers in the Washington, D.C., area. For over 50 years, Local 25 has advocated for "fair treatment, dignity, respect, and improved working conditions" for hotel and restaurant workers. Toward this end, in addition to its unionizing activities, Local 25 has also been politically active in the city of Washington, D.C., lobbying legislators and promoting a civil rights agenda.

Collective Bargaining

The unionization process involves employees in a given workplace electing Local 25 to "collectively bargain" on their behalf. Once elected, the union negotiates a contract between Local 25 and the employer, which guarantees wage rates, benefits, and working conditions. Contracts are usually for three years. Before negotiations begin with a given employer, members are asked to set the bargaining agenda, with the full understanding that not all labor demands will be met. Labor negotiation is a give-and-take process. Once Local 25 and the employer have come to an agreement, the contract only goes into effect after it is presented to the members for their balloted approval. If a contract is not approved, workers may vote to go on strike. The only way a strike can occur is if a majority of workers at a contract meeting vote for it.

Union members pay dues, which go toward maintaining the union. Dues are used to pay the salaries of union representatives, who negotiate on behalf of members, lawyers, and arbitrators; to educate and train members and shop stewards; and to pay for lobbying efforts to influence legislation that affects members and the communities in which they work.

In a unionized workplace, at least one employee is a designated "shop steward"— the on-the-job union representative. The shop steward is the first person to which a member can turn with grievances or job-related problems.

Benefits

Through their collective bargaining agreements, members are eligible for union-negotiated benefits generally after three months on the job. All benefits are provided by funds paid by the employers with some benefits administered by a joint union-management committee of trustees, and others purchase directly through various benefit providers. Benefits include:

- dental care
- eye care
- personal legal services

- pensions
- credit union benefits
- health care
- short- and long-term disability insurance
- life insurance
- 401k plan

Local 25 and the Marriott Corporation

As a company that prides itself on its "union free environment," the Marriott Corporation and various locals of the Hotel and Restaurant Employees Union across the United States have had a long and turbulent past. In numerous instances, particularly in traditional unionized cities, Marriott has signed "neutrality agreements" (in which Marriott pledges not to interfere with employee attempts to unionize) with municipalities in the interest of getting tax breaks for hotel construction and management and then completely ignoring them once the contract has been awarded.

John Boardman, executive secretary and treasurer of Local 25, described the Marriott Corporation as "Masters of Public Relations." Marriott has always defended its anti-union stance as being in the best interest of its employees. For Marriott, unionization represents increased costs to the employees and the corporation. By keeping unions out, Marriott claims that it can pass the savings on the employee in the form of increased hourly wages. While Boardman acknowledges that Marriott wage rates are comparable to union wage rates in markets where the union has contracts, the similarity ends there.

As opposed to union benefits paid by the employer, Marriott benefits are for the most part completely employee-funded.[13] At Marriott, the collectively bargained grievance process has been replaced by a "peer review" grievance system, embodied in the Partners in Management Program. According to Boardman, however, the major shortcoming of this internal review system is the fact that all decisions are reversible by Marriott management staff, particularly in firing decisions. Finally, despite the favorable publicity surrounding the institution of Marriott's Workforce 2000 programs, Local 25 asserts that low-wage employee turnover remains extremely high, especially when compared to the turnover rates at unionized shops.

What disturbs Boardman most is the Marriott "Pathways" program, which specifically targets welfare recipients and the chronically unemployed. Boardman and others at Local 25 see this program, for which Marriott receives federal government subsidies for hiring and training "problem categories" of workers, as an attempt to create a "docile" workforce. Although this program does seek to get the "unemployable" back to work, the federal government ultimately is subsidizing Marriott for hiring from a labor pool that it would have been hiring from anyway (i.e., low-skilled, poorly educated). In addition, the program subsidizes a minimum wage, which, without government interference (according to supply and demand in free market conditions), might have resulted in a natural increase in the wages of the unskilled. The situation has been exacerbated by the passage of the Welfare Reform Act, which essentially creates a labor pool composed of "conscripts."

John Boardman interprets the Marriott approach to its low-wage labor workforce as extremely paternalistic and anti-democratic. Marriott's "caring" approach treats its low-skilled labor as if they were children, and only bad, ungrateful children would attempt to unionize.

Industry Standards

Boardman also acknowledges that the Marriott approach using worker intimidation and reneging on municipal agreements has been extremely successful at confounding workers' unionization attempts. To his dismay, Marriott has been so successful that other hotel chains have been attempting to copy the Marriott model of violating the law. Boardman claims that over the past 20 years a cadre of "Labor Consultants" have emerged; these consultants are brought into workplaces at the time of union elections. He charges these "Labor Consultants" with utilizing unfair practices and worker intimidation. In addition, even when a workplace has voted in the union, employers have been able to use the judicial system to slow down the implementation process by tying up the union under the National Labor Relations Act in court for a number of years. In some instances, by the time the union ultimately wins a protracted legal battle, the hotel has been sold, and they are forced to repeat the process with a new owner.

In response, labor organizers like Boardman increasingly take a new approach: going outside the National Labor Relations Board process and utilizing other tactics such as protests at the homes of corporate board members, distributing leaflets to hotel guests, and proxy battles, all in the spirit of "If organizing is not war, I don't know what is."[14]

Chapter 4: Long Case Notes

1   Finney, M.I., "Fair Game: 'At Marriott, Clifford Ehrlich Bases Decisions on What's Fair,'" *Personnel Administrator* (February 1989): 46.
2   Raffio, R., "Company at the Crossroads: Marriott Corp.," *Restaurant Business* (June 10, 1991): 84.
3   McGough, R., "My son, I brought him up like an Immigrant," *Forbes 400* (October 26, 1987): 74.
4   "Labor's Love Lost," *Washington Post*, 17 February 1992, F3.
5   Walsh, S.W., "Firms Brace for New Law," *Washington Post*, April 30, 1987, 1.
6   Shannon Peters, "Personnel Journal Announces Grant Recipients," *Personnel Journal* (October 1993): 34.
7   Finney, 46.
8   Finney, 46.
9   Henkoff, R., "Finding, Training, and Keeping the Best Service Workers," *Fortune* (October 3, 1994): 116.
10 Laabs, J., "Individuals with Disabilities Augment Marriott's Workforce," *Personnel Journal* (September 1994): 46.
11 Laabs, J., "How Federally Funded Training Helps Business," *Personnel Journal* (March 1992): 35.
12 Prepared statement of Janet Tull, Marriott International, before the House Government Reform and Oversight Committee and Subcommittee on Human Resources and Intergovernmental Affairs on Work Opportunities Tax Credit as related to job training, April 18, 1996.

13 In Washington, union workers enjoy a 40–45% wage and fringe package advantage over their non-union counterparts. This is almost exclusively the result of the benefits provided in the collectively bargained agreements.

14 Perl, P., "Workplace Democracy American Style," *Washington Post Magazine*, April 6, 1997.

LONG CASE QUESTIONS

1. What are some of the unique ethical obligations and responsibilities facing Marriott Corporation as it deals with its employees?

2. Do you agree with Marriott's philosophy that labor unions do not necessarily help workers or the company? Why or why not?

3. Was it unethical for Marriott to take advantage of the Targeted Jobs Tax Credit? Why or why not? Why did the government discontinue the program?

4. Do you agree with John A. Boardman (Executive Secretary—Treasurer of the Hotel and Restaurant Employees Union — see Appendix) that Marriott Corporation is a "Master of Public Relations"? Or do you think they have dealt with their employees as ethically as possible?

5. What future employee ethical issues do you foresee Marriott corporation facing?

Primary Stakeholders: Customers

LEARNING OBJECTIVES

After reading this chapter you should be able to:

- Understand the general relationship of marketing's 4Ps for the ethical interface with customers
- Be aware of the ethical issues in pricing your products or services
- Understand what constitutes deception in advertising and be able to identify techniques used in deception
- Become aware of ethically sensitive issues in advertising such as the use of sexuality and advertising to children
- Understand a company's obligations to provide safe products in terms of buyer beware and the contract, due care, and strict liability views of product liability
- Become aware of the increasingly complex issues regarding consumer privacy

PREVIEW BUSINESS ETHICS INSIGHT

Advertising to Children: Potential Ethical Challenges

小儿科分

According to a recent policy statement by the American Academy of Pediatrics (AAP) children and adolescents see more than 300,000 ads per year on television, the internet, magazines, and billboards. Children are attractive targets in the U.S. because children younger than 12 spend an estimated $25 billion a year and their older teenage siblings spend an additional $155 billion. AAP estimate that an additional $200 billion comes from parental purchases influenced by children and teens. While many European countries limit or forbid advertising to children, this is not true in the U.S., and there may be consequences.

As a medical society, the AAP has particular concerns for health-related issues influenced by advertising.

- *Tobacco Advertising.* The AAP cites research showing that nearly one third of adolescent smoking is linked to tobacco advertising and promotions. Also noted is that the tobacco companies may specifically target teenagers with the advertisements.
- *Alcohol Advertising.* With young people in the U.S. exposed to as many as 2,000 beer and wine commercials a year, and research showing that adolescent drinkers are more often exposed to alcohol ads, the AAP is concerned that early exposure to alcohol ads is a significant risk factor for early-age drinking. They note that alcohol ads increase tremendously in sports programming where adolescents are more likely to be in the audience.
- *Drug Advertising.* The advertising of prescription drugs directly to con-sumers is a controversial practice that exists only in the U.S. While some question whether adults are capable of making or influencing the choice of the prescription drugs they take, the issue is more complicated for children. The AAP fears that children and teenagers may come to believe that there is a drug available to cure all ills and heal all pain.
- *Food Advertising and Obesity.* Of the estimated 40,000 ads per year that young people see on TV, half are for food. Most often these ads focus on sugared cereals and high-calorie snacks, potentially contributing to rising rates of childhood obesity. An additional practice of concern is the use of toy premiums where, for example, nearly 20% of fast food ads use toy premiums in their commercials.
- *Sex in Advertising.* The AAP cites research that shows teenagers' exposure to sexual advertising content may be responsible for earlier onset of sexual intercourse. In addition, they fear that the frequent use of female models who are anorectic in appearance potentially contributes to young women developing distorted body self-images and abnormal eating behaviors.

Based on Committee on Communications. 2006. "Policy statement, children, adolescents, and advertising." *Pediatrics*, 118, 2563–2569.

This chapter considers customers as stakeholders. Some might argue that customers are the primary stakeholders because, without customers, a business could not exist. That is, by purchasing products or services, customers are the stakeholders that provide the money necessary for the organization to exist and to serve other stakeholders.

In this chapter, we focus on points of contact between the company and the customer that raise the most important ethical issues for today's companies. The Preview Business Ethics Insight above shows one area of concern, advertising to children, where companies are attracted to the tremendous profit potential from purchases made or influenced by children. Yet, from an opposite perspective, children are vulnerable populations who are perhaps manipulated unethically to buy products with negative consequences for their health.

In the next few sections, you will learn about three important points of contact between the company and the consumer. The first relates to marketing and issues such as truthful advertising and fair pricing. The second relates to product safety and issues such as who is responsible when a product has a defect. The third section relates to privacy and issues such as the legal and ethical obligations for getting and protecting your customers' personal information. The correct ethical choice for how companies deal with customers as stakeholders is not always apparent and different perspectives are open to debate.

MARKETING

In this section, we are interested in how the marketing function affects customers as stakeholders. **Marketing** is the first level where the organization interacts with customers. There are various ways of looking at marketing, but most focus on how we communicate the nature of our product, how we identify what the customer values, and how we deliver the product to create an exchange between the customer and the company.[1] Formal definitions of marketing include:

> Marketing is the activity, set of institutions, and processes for creating, communicating, delivering, and exchanging offerings that have value for customers, clients, partners, and society at large.[2]

And:

> Marketing is the management process that identifies, anticipates, and satisfies customer requirements profitably.[3]

The functions of marketing are usually divided into the marketing mix, which is sometimes called the **4Ps**: product, price, promotion, and place. Each of these has different ethical challenges when considering the customer as a stakeholder. The 4Ps are:

- *Product*: the product or services offered by the company that meet the requirements of the customers
- *Price*: the process of setting the prices for the products/services
- *Promotion*: this includes the tools used by marketers to make potential customers aware of the company's products or services and the benefits to the customers of buying these products or services
- *Place*: this refers to the geographic areas to sell in and the channels selected to reach the market. For example, companies may sell directly to the end users or use distributors to get their product to the users

The American Marketing Association's Perspective on Marketing Ethics

Honesty – to be forthright in dealings with customers and stakeholders. To this end, we will:

- Strive to be truthful in all situations and at all times.
- Offer products of value that do what we claim in our communications.
- Stand behind our products if they fail to deliver their claimed benefits.
- Honor our explicit and implicit commitments and promises.

Responsibility – to accept the consequences of our marketing decisions and strategies. To this end, we will:

- Strive to serve the needs of customers.
- Avoid using coercion with all stakeholders.
- Acknowledge the social obligations to stakeholders that come with increased marketing and economic power.
- Recognize our special commitments to vulnerable market segments such as children, seniors, the economically impoverished, market illiterates and others who may be substantially disadvantaged.
- Consider environmental stewardship in our decision-making.

Fairness – to balance justly the needs of the buyer with the interests of the seller. To this end, we will:

- Represent products in a clear way in selling, advertising and other forms of communication; this includes the avoidance of false, misleading and deceptive promotion.
- Reject manipulations and sales tactics that harm customer trust.
- Refuse to engage in price fixing, predatory pricing, price gouging, or "bait-and-switch" tactics.
- Avoid knowing participation in conflicts of interest.
- Seek to protect the private information of customers, employees, and partners.

Respect – to acknowledge the basic human dignity of all stakeholders. To this end, we will:

- Value individual differences and avoid stereotyping customers or depicting demographic groups (e.g., gender, race, sexual orientation) in a negative or dehumanizing way.
- Listen to the needs of customers and make all reasonable efforts to monitor and improve their satisfaction on an ongoing basis.
- Make every effort to understand and respectfully treat buyers, suppliers, intermediaries, and distributors from all cultures.
- Acknowledge the contributions of others, such as consultants, employees, and coworkers, to marketing endeavors.
- Treat everyone, including our competitors, as we would wish to be treated.

Transparency – to create a spirit of openness in marketing operations. To this end, we will:

- Strive to communicate clearly with all constituencies.
- Accept constructive criticism from customers and other stakeholders.
- Explain and take appropriate action regarding significant product or service risks, component substitutions or other foreseeable eventualities that could affect customers or their perception of the purchase decision.
- Disclose list prices and terms of financing as well as available price deals and adjustments.

Citizenship – to fulfill the economic, legal, philanthropic and societal responsibilities that serve stakeholders. To this end, we will:

- Strive to protect the ecological environment in the execution of marketing campaigns.
- Give back to the community through volunteerism and charitable donations.
- Contribute to the overall betterment of marketing and its reputation.
- Urge supply chain members to ensure that trade is fair for all participants, including producers in developing countries.

EXHIBIT 5.1—The American Marketing Association's Perspective on Marketing Ethics

A general view, proposed by the American Marketing Association, of what is considered ethical in the marketing function is shown in Exhibit 5.1. We will consider some specific issues from the 4Ps that are most important for the customers as stakeholders. Because most of the "place" decisions relate to businesses dealings with other businesses, these aspects of marketing are not as important when considering the customer as a stakeholder.

Customer stakeholder issues regarding products tend to focus on issues related to product safety, which we will deal with in a separate section later in this chapter. However, two other important issues regarding products raise ethical concerns.

The first deals with the issue of whether the product meets a legitimate customer need. Many criticize controversial products such as casinos, tobacco, low mileage SUVs, and fast food as unethical because they do not satisfy legitimate needs but just customer wants. Such products have questionable value to the consumer and are particularly questionable if they appeal to vulnerable customer groups.

One classic example comes from Nestlé and its marketing of infant formula to mothers in Third World countries. Using free samples and paid workers looking like medical personnel, mothers were convinced to use the formula rather than breast-feed. For the target market, the formula was expensive and many mothers stretched the use by using more water than recommended. Additionally, local water supplies were often unsanitary and unfit for infant use and this unsanitary water was mixed with the formula. Although Nestlé profited greatly from this product, babies starved and often died, leaving a legacy that Nestlé has never fully overcome. How do you think Nestlé might have avoided this problem in the first place?

A second issue regarding products is that managers just ensure that the products they sell actually perform as claimed. There is an ethical obligation not to deceive the customer.[4] One type of product for which the evidence provides little support is the fitness device that proposes to reduce fat in specific areas. There is little scientific support for this claim, although many products purport to achieve fat loss in different parts of the body.[5] Ethical issues regarding deception of the customer often show up in advertising, which is covered in more detail below.

Ethical Issues in Pricing

Pricing is of concern to ethical marketers because we want to sell our products to consumers at a "**just price**." The concept of the just price is usually attributed to St. Thomas Aquinas. Following Aquinas' reasoning, a seller should not raise prices simply because a buyer has a strong need for a product.[6] Thus, for example, the high interest rate charged by payday loan companies would be unethical from Aquinas' point of view because the sellers (the lenders) are taking advantage of the short-term needs for cash of their customers. In a capitalistic market there is always some ambiguity over what constitutes a just price. However, several aspects surrounding pricing raise ethical concerns when dealing with the customer as a stakeholder.

These include:

- **Price gouging**. This occurs when sellers take advantage of situations like national disasters or shortages to raise prices during that situation. After Hurricane Katrina, WalMart, Home Depot, and Lowes took an opposite position by not only not increasing prices of high-demand products, but also giving some away free and using their distribution system to get people-needed goods. However, some might argue that companies should maximize their profits when they can, regardless of the reasons why. How can you argue for this point of view?
- **Predatory pricing**. Predatory pricing occurs when a company lowers it prices so far below competitors' that it drives the competitors out of the market. As a stakeholder, the consumer will later feel the effects because the predatory pricing company gains a more monopolistic power to set the prices.
- **Price fixing**. One type of price fixing, called horizontal, also has the effect of creating a monopoly effect when sellers agree with each other to sell at one price that is often above what they would have to do in a competitive market. Another type of price fixing is called vertical and occurs when sellers force the retailers to sell their products to consumers at specific prices. Horizontal price fixing is illegal in most countries but vertical price fixing has a more ambitious legal standard. In most cases, however, the consumer will pay more when competitive pricing is restricted.
- **Price discrimination**. This occurs when different groups are charged different prices. Youth or senior discounts or "ladies' nights" in nightclubs are types of price discrimination. Although most forms of price discrimination are considered ethical and legal, there are areas when the practice has a more ambivalent ethical foundation. For example, in upscale men's clothing stores the tailoring of suits is often considered as service without charge, whereas for women's clothes there is a much great chance of being charged for similar tailoring. Is this ethical? Is this fair?
- **Failure to disclose the full price**. This often occurs when listed prices do not include other fees or charges that the consumer will have to pay. For example, in 2010, U.S. Airways was fined $40,000 because when "consumers searched the carrier's website for one-way flights sorted by schedule, U.S. Airways provided a set of fares that did not include additional applicable taxes and fees, or any notice on that page that these additional charges would be required." This violated U.S. statutes on pricing.[7]
- **Bait-and-switch**. This is a sales tactic where a product is advertised at a low price, but when the consumer comes in he or she finds that the product is sold out (often there was only one in the store) or is pressured by sales people to look at higher-priced versions of the product.

Ethical Issues in Promotion

The objective of **promotion** is to make the customer aware of your product. Promotion involves an array of tools including, for example, advertising, sponsorships, coupons, and point-of-sale displays. Of most importance in dealing with ethical issues related to the consumer is the advertising function. The objective of advertising is to make customers aware of the product and to persuade them to purchase the product or service. The approach can appeal to rational self-interest (e.g., if you use this product you will be healthier or more physically attractive) or subtly to create an emotional tie to the product (e.g., Calvin Klein's controversial jeans advertisement that used 15-year-old Brooke Shields, in Calvin Klein jeans, with her saying: "Want to know what gets between me and my Calvin's? Nothing"). Can you think of any reasons why a company should not use beauty to sell?

Below we will discuss several issues regarding the nature and management of ethical advertising.

Ethical advertisements must be truthful and not deceptive. The U.S. Federal Trade Commission (FTC)[8] identifies criteria by which we can decide if an advertisement is not deceptive. To make this judgment one needs to consider the ad from the point of view of the typical person looking at the ad. One should ask what the words, phrases, and pictures convey to consumers. In making judgments about the legality of an advertisement, the FTC considers both **express** and **implied claims**. An express claim is stated directly in the ad. For example, "ABC tablets will reduce your weight by two pounds a week" is an express claim that you will lose weight if you take the pills. Implied claims for a product are made indirectly or by inference. "XYZ tablets reduce your appetite for fatty foods, a major contributor to weight gain" contains an implied claim that taking the pills results in your losing weight. Although the ad in this example does not claim directly that the pills cause weight loss, most reasonable consumers would conclude from the statement "reduce your appetite for fatty foods, a major contributor to weight gain" that the product will lead to weight loss.

Under U.S. law, advertisers must have evidence that supports both express *and* implied claims that advertisements make to consumers. If an advertisement makes health or safety claims, the company must support the claims with scientific evidence from studies evaluated by other professionals or scientists in the field.

Techniques for deceptive advertising include:[9]

- **Ambiguity in advertisements**. In ambiguous ads, the wording is sufficiently confusing and leads the consumer to make erroneous conclusions about the nature of the product. A classic example is Sara Lee's Light Classic desserts. Most consumers interpreted the word "light" to mean fewer calories. However, the State of Iowa confronted Sara Lee on the meaning of "light" when they found that the light products have almost the same calorie content as their regular desserts. When pressed under the requirement to provide evidence of the reduced calories, Sara Lee noted that this referred only to the texture of the products.
- **Concealing facts**. Advertisements that conceal facts often begin with truthful statements regarding the positive attributes of a product. For example, a company might state, "the ingredients in this car polish will result in a beautiful shine for your car." What the advertisement fails to note is that the car polish manufacturer uses the same ingredients as the other manufacturers. Consider Bayer Aspirin's scientifically factual claim that their aspirin "contains an ingredient doctors

recommend most." This advertisement, which ran for years, was designed to convince the consumer that Bayer Aspirin is preferable to other brands of aspirin. What Bayer did not say is that the ingredient doctors recommend most is aspirin.

- **Exaggeration**. Trident chewing gum is one example of an exaggeration in advertising. Described as a cavity fighting "dental instrument," this is a clear exaggeration of the benefits of Trident. Not only does the sugar substitutive used in Trident promote tooth decay, but all forms of sugarless chewing gum also help to prevent plaque formation by increasing salivary flow and prompting continuous chewing action. A step away from exaggeration is called "puffery." **Puffery** is an exaggeration so extreme that the assumption is that no reasonable person would believe the statement such as that BMW is unambiguously "the ultimate driving machine." As such, most government policymakers allow advertisers to use *puffery*. However, studies[10] show that, while consumers are able to identify exaggerated claims, continued exposure to puffed claims still increases the positive evaluation of the advertised brand.

Ethical advertisements should also not be manipulative. That is, they should not take advantage of giving false or misleading cues to manipulate the consumer psychologically. One ad that some might say used this tactic was employed by Michelin tires for many years. The visual presented by the advertisement shows a baby sitting on a Michelin tire. The quite simple slogan was "Because so much is riding on your tires." Of course, the implication was that if you do not buy Michelin tires, you are endangering your baby. Another insurance company ad showed a family in a dire economic situation because the chief breadwinner had not purchased life insurance, with the implication being you will fail your family if you do not buy our insurance.

Advertisements based on such emotional appeals are often not considered unethical and praised as effective advertising. However, they fall into a gray area between advertisements that provide consumers with the information to determine if they should purchase this product and the other extreme of coercion.[11] From the perspective of Kantian ethical philosophy, such manipulations are ethically questionable because they are a means to achieve the seller's ends and treat the consumer as an object. How would you respond to a Kantian objection to your company's advertisements that appeal to emotions?

Exhibit 5.2 gives examples of potential exaggeration or perhaps manipulation in advertisements for weight loss products.

Other Ethically Sensitive Issues: Sexual Appeals and Marketing to Children

Reichart et al. defined **sexual appeals** as "messages, as brand information in advertising contexts . . . that are associated with sexual information."[12] As anyone who watches TV or reads magazines knows, sexual innuendo in advertising content is quite common. Yet, to some people, it is considered immoral or a form of sexual harassment. Mark Levit,[13] managing partner of Partners & Levit Advertising and a professor of

A claim is too good to be true if it says the product will ...	Example Claims
Cause weight loss of two pounds or more a week for a month or more without dieting or exercise	• "I lost 30 pounds in 30 days even though I ate all my favorite foods." • "Lose up to two pounds daily without diet or exercise."
Cause substantial weight loss no matter what or how much the consumer eats	• "My 'formula for living' lets you eat: hamburgers, hot dogs, fries, steak, ice cream, sausage, bacon, eggs, and cheeses! And STILL LOSE WEIGHT!" • "Eat all the foods you love, and still lose weight (pill does all the work)."
Cause permanent weight loss (even when the consumer stops using product)	• "Thousands of dieters are already using it and losing weight faster than they have before ... and keeping the weight off." • "For 15 years, Mary yo-yo dieted without success. Fed up and desperate, she discovered a new miracle product to lose weight easily and permanently."
Block the absorption of fat or calories to enable consumers to lose substantial weight	• "Lose up to two pounds daily ... Apple Pectin is an energized enzyme that can absorb up to 900 times its own weight in fat. That's why it's a fantastic FAT BLOCKER." • "Brindall berries cause very rapid and substantial weight loss by reducing fat absorption by 76%."
Safely enable consumers to lose more than three pounds per week for more than four weeks	• "Lose 30-40-50 pounds. Yes! You can lose three pounds per week, naturally and without side effects." • "Neptune's Potion is safe and effective," with customer testimonials claiming more than 12 pounds of weight loss per month.
Cause substantial weight loss for all users	• "Lose excess body fat. You cannot fail, because no will power is required." • "Lose 10-15-20 pounds. Works for everyone, no matter how many times you've tried and failed before."

EXHIBIT 5.2—Suspect Advertisements for Weight Loss

marketing at New York University, agrees that sexual content of ads can increase their effectiveness because they attract the customer's attention. It is just human nature. However, when misused, sex appeal can be costly to companies. For example, nude or seminude pictures in Abercrombie & Fitch catalogues have led to customer boycotts.

According to Levit, ads that, for example, show an attractive model endorsing a product can lead to positive responses from consumers. However, more graphic sexual content often fails to do more than attract attention. Research[14] suggests that strong sexual messages, like strong violence content, tend to attract attention but reduce the consumers' intention to buy the product.

STRATEGIC BUSINESS ETHICS INSIGHT

Does Sex Appeal Advertising Work in China?

With the increased liberalization of China and access to Western media such as MTV, the use of sexual appeals has increased in print and television advertisements in China. This reflects, in part, the attempt by multinational companies to gain the efficiency of having similar promotional activities in all the countries in which they operate. However, the assumption that even mild forms of sexual innuendo that seem to work in the West with Heineken will work in an emerging market economy with an Eastern cultural tradition is not a sure thing.

A recent study by two marketing professors from Hong Kong casts doubt on the efficacy of using sexual innuendo in mainland Chinese advertisements. They found that Chinese consumers responded more favorably to ads with no sex appeal in terms of both their attitudes toward the advertisements and their intentions to buy the advertised products. They also found that Chinese consumers preferred Chinese models rather than Caucasian models, regardless of whether the ads contained high levels of sex appeal. The researchers recommend ``caution'' in using sexual messages to Chinese consumers as their findings suggest that Chinese consumers perceive such ads ethically less acceptable.

Based on Cui, Geng and Yang, Xiaoyan. 2009. ``Responses of Chinese consumers to sex appeals in international advertising: A test of congruency theory.'' *Journal of Global Marketing*, 22, 229–245.

One successful approach used by Heineken in "It's All About the Beer" campaign called "The Premature Pour," shows a man responding to a seductive woman by nervously pouring his beer so fast that it spills and dumps foam over him and the table. The sexual innuendo is clear but the ad worked. Targeted at young men, Heineken's beer sales jumped by over 10% in the U.S.

One strategic issue in the use of sexual innuendo in advertisements is the cross-cultural transferability of such ads. The Strategic Business Ethics Insight above looks at how sex appeal advertising works in China.

Advertising to Vulnerable Groups: Children

One of the most sensitive ethical topics in advertising is advertising to children. The Preview Business Ethics Insight (pages 205–6) showed some of the concerns for advertising to children. In addition, Gunilla Jarlbro[15] identifies four recurring themes in the literature on children's advertising. The first issue is the ability of children to recognize a marketing communication as advertising. Research on the issue at which age children can distinguish between advertisements and regular programs has mixed results. However, there seems to be agreement that a majority of children, by the age of eight, have developed the ability to distinguish commercials from programs. By the age of 10–12, nearly all children can make this distinction. One caveat for advertisers is that development of this ability varies by individuals and perhaps by cultural settings, as the research seems to find different abilities in different countries.

The second issue of concern for advertising to children relates to the age children develop the perceptual skills to understand the intent of the advertisement. However, for this issue, the level of the child's cognitive development seems most important and it is not clear that science can identify a specific age. Experts generally agree that the older the child, the more likely the child grasps the intent behind advertising.

The third issue concerns the extent that children influence their family's purchases, sometimes called "pester power." One recent review of the existing research[16]

Issue	Recommendation
Harm	• Children should not be shown in unsafe situations or behaving dangerously except for advertisements that promote safety • Children should not be shown using or in close proximity to dangerous substances or equipment without direct adult supervision • Children should be discouraged from copying potentially hazardous activities that may be displayed in ads
Credulity and Unfair Pressure	• Children should not be encouraged to feel inferior or unpopular if they do not buy the advertised product • Children should not be encouraged to feel that they are lacking in courage, duty, or loyalty if they do not buy the advertised product • Should be possible for children of the target age group to judge the size, characteristics, and performance of advertised products and to distinguish between real-life situations and fantasy • For complex or costly products, adult permission should be obtained before purchasing • Should not exaggerate what an ordinary child can do using the product being marketed
Price	• Should not lead children to an unrealistic perception of the product's value • Should not be presented that the price of the product is in the reach of every family
Parental Authority	• Should not undermine the authority and judgment of parents • Should not include appeals to children to persuade their parents to buy the advertised product
Skills and Age Levels	• Should not underestimate the degree of skill and age level needed to assemble or operate the products as shown
Social Values	• Should not suggest that the use of product will give a child physical or psychological superiority over other children

EXHIBIT 5.3—Example Standards for Advertisements to Children

Country	Advertising
Austria	None during children's programs
Belgium	None 5 minutes before or after programs for children under 12
Denmark	No program breaks for ads
Greece	Ban on ads for toys between 7 am and 10 pm; total ban on ads for war toys
Italy	No interruption of cartoons
Luxembourg	None pre and post children's programs
Norway	Cannot specifically target children or be included with children's programs
Sweden	Cannot specifically target children or be included with children's programs

EXHIBIT 5.4—National Differences in Regulations Concerning Advertisements to Children

concluded, at least in the area of food advertising, that advertising does result in pestering, leading to parents buying less healthy products that are higher in calories and often associated with obesity. They note that this conflicts with industry arguments that "pester power" is minimal in its effects.

The fourth issue concerns how advertisements to children work indirectly by influencing children as a group. Experts[17] agree that family, friends, and siblings have more influence over children's views on products than do advertisements. However, TV commercials can be a common source of conversation among school children, suggesting that age-group-targeted ads may work indirectly by stimulating peer group interest. In addition, promotions such as Barbie Clubs encourage peer groups to discuss and potentially purchase products associated with the clubs.

Exhibit 5.3 shows some general standards for advertising to children. These come from various codes of professional groups from around the world. In the next section, we will consider issues regarding product safety.

Some countries have additional restrictions regarding advertising to children that multinational companies need to be aware of. Exhibit 5.4 shows some examples.

PRODUCT SAFETY

Many products we purchase have some risks associated with their use. Whether it is the automobiles we drive, or the fertilizer we use on our lawns, harm will befall some users when using products, especially if the products are misused. A dilemma is that, even with improved safety for a product such as the automobile, can it be done at prices that consumers can afford? Thus, since many if not most products we use can potentially cause harm, the basic question is: Who has the responsibility for this harm?

There are several areas of concern regarding how defective products can cause harm to users. There can be design defects, material defects, manufacturing defects, the failure to warn with appropriate labels and warnings regarding potential product dangers, and notifications to users if faults are found in the future. Failure to warn is sometimes called a marketing failure.

One example of an apparent **design defect** was the sticking accelerator pedal that plagued a variety of Toyota models. This defect resulted in Toyota recalling millions of cars worldwide. In the U.S., courts assessed penalties totaling $48.8 million. Toyota was forced to pay $16.4 million to settle claims for fatal accidences caused by the defects based on allegations that the company hid the accelerator pedal defects initially. In an unprecedented step for a Japanese CEO, Toyota president Akio Toyoda, the grandson of the founder of the company, went to the United States early in 2010 to speak before Congress, Toyota workers, and dealers to apologize for Toyota's handling of the problems.[18]

In an example of a **material defect**, in 2007 the toy manufacturer Fisher-Price discovered that 21 million toys contained excessive amounts of lead and could endanger the lives of the children using the toys. Just three years later, the company faced a design defect forcing a recall for toddler's tricycles and high chairs with protruding parts that caused injuries when children fell against them. In an example of a manu-facturing defect, Fisher-Price recalled over three million toys due to choking hazards from small parts that fell off the toys.[19]

Laws in different states and countries determine how long a company is responsible for defects in their products. In the U.S., aircraft manufactures are responsible for design and manufacturing defects for up to 18 years. Automobile and boat manufacturers have a five-year window of responsibility. If defects are discovered, recall warnings might be mandated by governments or done voluntarily by companies.

Companies have both a moral and a legal duty to warn users of these potential dangers. This is why nearly all directions for product assembly and use contain a "read me first" section dealing with warnings. The obligation to warn consumers about potential dangers continues after the initial sale. That is, liability can exist even after purchase if manufacturers discover a defect or misuse of the product later.[20]

What should a warning say to the consumer? Experts[21] identify the following:

- Note the severity of the potential danger (e.g., death)
- Note the nature of the hazard (e.g., poisoning)
- Communicate the consequences of the hazard (e.g., potential choking)
- Explain how to avoid the hazard (e.g., wear protective gloves)

In addition, there are several issues to consider when evaluating warnings for product use:[22]

- What is the likelihood that the product can cause harm? Products that are more dangerous require more attention to warnings.
- Whether there is a reasonable likelihood that the consumer will use the product in a way not identified in the labeling and if such use could cause harm to the consumer.

In this case, companies should consider redesigning the product, if possible, to prevent such misuse.

- How serious is the potential harm? With greater potential harm, the obligation to provide warnings increases.
- What level of knowledge should the manufacturer expect from the users of a product? For example, a licensed pilot would be expected to have basic knowledge about dangers related to flying. People using fertilizers might not be aware of the potential dangers of exposure to the chemicals.
- Can the typical user of the product read and understand the warnings? Rather than technical language or translations into several languages, some companies will use pictorial warnings. IKEA provides directions on how to assemble its furniture, complete with safety warning information all through the pictures.

Perspectives on Product Liability

There are several perspectives regarding if or to what extent companies should assume liability for harm caused by the products they produce. These include the buyer beware view, contractual theory, due care, and strict liability.

Buyer Beware

The **buyer beware** perspective is sometimes called *caveat emptor*, which is Latin for "let the buyer beware." The legal definition is "A doctrine that often places on buyers the burden to reasonably examine property before purchase and take responsibility for its condition. Especially applicable to items that are not covered under a strict warranty."[23]

According to the buyer beware view, once a consumer purchases a product, the manufacturer has no responsibility for any risks associated with the product that they produced. Because it was a free market exchange, the purchaser and not the manufacturer must bear any costs with any injuries. It is the consumer's duty to research the product and the risks for harm prior to making the purchase. *The objection to this perspective is that consumers often do not have sufficient knowledge or expertise to identify any risks associated with a product.*

Contract View

According to the **contract view**, the relationship between the manufacturer and a consumer is based on a contract. The contract has both explicit (i.e., written) and implied claims regarding the product. The implicit or implied claims relate to the consumers' expectations regarding reliability (the probability that the product will function as expected), life of the product (expectations regarding the service life of the product), maintainability (the ease of keeping the product working), and product safety (the risk associated with using the product). There is an implied warranty that the product is fit for sale and is of acceptable quality for ordinary use.

The contract implies certain moral duties for the seller, including:

- Duty not to coerce—the buyer must enter the contract voluntarily
- Duty to comply with the terms of the contract regarding express and implied claims of reliability, product life, maintainability, and safety
- Duty not to misrepresent the product in any way
- Duty to disclose the nature of the product

As with the buyer beware approach to product safety, a problem with contract view is the assumption that consumers understand the products sufficiently to enter into a contract. For example, if you buy a car sold "as is" from a car dealer, there is an assumption that you understand automobiles sufficiently well to know that the car is safe to drive. In many instances, the buyer and seller are not equals in the knowledge required to understand the contract.

Due Care Theory

Due care theory addresses the weaknesses of the buyer beware approach by accepting that sellers and buyers do not have equality in knowledge and expertise regarding products. This is increasingly true, as products get more technologically complex. Thus, for example, few people have the engineering knowledge to assess all of the safety components of a modern automobile such ABS braking, frame construction to absorb impacts, or the workings of airbags. As such, since manufacturers have much greater knowledge than their consumers do, they assume an obligation to take reasonable precautions that their products do not harm the buyers. The more powerful and knowledgeable have more duties.

Legal wording emphasizes the actions of an *ordinary* and *reasonable* person to look out for the safety of others. If a manufacturer fails to use due care, then he or she is liable for negligence. If one uses due care, then an injured party cannot prove negligence. The "reasonable person" who exercises due care is not negligent. The issue most courts face is how to determine what a reasonable and ordinary person would do. Due care can apply to others besides the manufacturer, including retailers and wholesalers.

Critics of the due care view note that is difficult to determine when a company has shown sufficient "due care." There is also the issue of how the manufacturer can discover the problems with a product prior to its use if they followed all legal and industry safety standards. Can a manufacturer be negligent if they could not foresee that a product was dangerous or eventually misused in a way that was dangerous?

Consider the Business Ethics Insight on page 220, which shows how two boat manufacturers went beyond legal duties to protect their customers.

Strict Liability Theory

Under **strict liability**, if a product injures a user because it was defective, the manufacturer is responsible to compensate the user. This applies even if the manufacturers used due care in the production. That is, it applies even if a manufacturer was

BUSINESS ETHICS INSIGHT

A Tale of Two Voluntary Recalls in the Practice of Due Care

In spite of the fact that neither company was required to do so under U.S. law, two major boat manufacturers inspected and repaired hundreds of boats in voluntary recall campaigns. The companies warned owners of the 31-foot to 33-foot Tiara and Pursuit models built by Tiara/S2 Yachts and owners of 36-foot Outlaw models built by Baja Marine Corp. that their boats may be unsafe to use.

As with many products, U.S. federal law requires builders to recall boats when they contain manufacturer-generated defects that "create a substantial risk of personal injury." The Tiara/S2 boats faced potential fires from possible fuel tank leeks. The Baja boats had potential stress cracks in the boat hulls.

By U.S. law, marine manufacturers are responsible for defects only up to five years from the date boat construction began. Agreeing to repair boats much older than five years, Tiara/S2 went far beyond what the law required. Although some of the Tiara/S2 boat owners were willing to sign waivers releasing Tiara/S2 from liability, a Tiara/S2 representative said, "We are not suggesting this approach, this recall is an effort to protect our customers. Any waiver of liability would not address the safety issues."

Baja's action was equally extraordinary, as the company offered to reinforce hulls on 36-foot Outlaws that might fail when owners replaced factory-installed engines with heavier and higher horsepower models that "encroach on the upper limits of what our boats were originally designed for."

Baja discovered the problems when company president Doug Smith repowered his boat with a larger engine and then developed cracks. "We went back and looked at the product line. The boats were within the design scope and within our safety factor. But we decided to increase our upper margin of safety," James O'Sullivan, Baja's customer service manager, told *BoatUS*. "While we cannot force a customer to have the procedure done . . . we do strongly recommend that the procedure be performed as soon as possible." Costing the company around $5,000 per boat in factory modifications, but free to boat owners, the company reinforced hull panels below the engine compartment.

Based on *BoatUS Magazine*, May 2000. http://my.boatus.com/consumer/TaleRecalls.asp.

not negligent in producing the product based on the current knowledge at the time of production. For example, under strict liability, furnace manufacturers that built furnaces using asbestos insulation before it became known that asbestos was dangerous are still be held responsible for the sicknesses and deaths related to asbestos poisoning.

Many think that strict liability is not fair to companies and artificially increases costs to consumers, even though companies often exercise due care. If a product injured a

Greenman v. Yuba Power Products

In Greenman, Traynor cited to his own earlier concurrence in Escola v. Coca-Cola Bottling Co., 24 Cal. 2d 453, 462 (1944) (Traynor, J., concurring) stating:

Even if there is no negligence, however, public policy demands that responsibility be fixed wherever it will most effectively reduce the hazards to life and health inherent in defective products that reach the market. It is evident that the manufacturer can anticipate some hazards and guard against the recurrence of others, as the public cannot. Those who suffer injury from defective products are unprepared to meet its consequences.

The cost of an injury and the loss of time or health may be an overwhelming misfortune to the person injured, and a needless one, for the risk of injury can be insured by the manufacturer and distributed among the public as a cost of doing business. It is to the public interest to discourage the marketing of products having defects that are a menace to the public. If such products nevertheless find their way into the market it is to the public interest to place the responsibility for whatever injury they may cause upon the manufacturer, who, even if he is not negligent in the manufacture of the product, is responsible for its reaching the market. However intermittently such injuries may occur and however haphazardly they may strike, the risk of their occurrence is a constant risk and a general one. Against such a risk there should be general and constant protection and to afford such protection.

EXHIBIT 5.5—Strict Liability in U.S. Law—A Ruling by Justice Robert J. Traynor

member of your family, would you be willing to absolve the manufacturer from guilt if they designed and built the product to known safety standards but it still caused injury?

Exhibit 5.5 shows the major court decision in the U.S. supporting strict liability. Justice Traynor makes it clear that a company's liability for product defects goes beyond any warrantees. Following this famous *Greenman v. Yuba Power Products* case, the California Supreme Court extended strict liability to all parties involved in the manufacturing, distribution, and sale of defective products.[24]

One argument for strict liability is that by forcing producers to internalize all the costs of a product, manufacturers will then bear the full cost of production. Otherwise, manufacturers only cover their own production costs and not the costs to others from lost work, injury, or even death. Advocates argue that strict product liability gives manufacturers the incentive to maximize their efforts to produce the safest products possible to reduce the risks to consumers in order to lower their costs. Additionally, if the companies were not responsible for the costs associated with injuries, then the consumer bears all those costs.

However, strict liability may raise the costs of products for everyone, since manufacturers must either pay liability insurance or pay any potential damages from their earnings, both of which prompt price increases. In more extreme cases, companies may stop producing the product entirely, as happened in the small plane aviation market in the U.S. as explained in the Business Ethics Insight on page 222. Some also argue that strict liability is unfair to manufactures who exercise due care.[25] That is, manufacturers should not be at fault for things that are beyond their control, so they should not be penalized for non-preventable defects resulting in injuries. However, one might argue that even if the manufacturers used due care, there are some defects that were still preventable. While that may reduce the moral responsibility of the manufacturer, it still does not eliminate the fact that there was a failure to produce a product without defects when it was possible to do so. Hence, some would argue that the manufacturer still is accountable and thus obligated to compensate those who suffer injury.

The Business Ethics Insight below shows how the application of strict liability almost drove the general aviation companies out of business in the U.S. It also deals with

BUSINESS ETHICS INSIGHT

Downside of Strict Liability: How Long Should a Company be Liable? The Case of U.S. General Aviation

Spending over $20 million a year to defend product liability lawsuits, some that involved planes over 40 years old, and faced with soaring insurance costs, Cessna Aircraft Co. stopped producing propeller-driven airplanes in 1986. For a company that once produced about 6,500 small aircraft per year to suddenly stop building was a major shock to the general aviation industry. Other small airplane manufacturers faced similar product liability challenges. In just four years' time, Beech Aircraft spent over $100 million in legal fees from 203 liability suits. Piper Aircraft Corp. was forced into bankruptcy around the same time.

By 1994, the U.S. light airplane manufacturers produced only 444 planes. However, this was a year of turnaround when Congress passed the General Aviation Revitalization Act. This limited product liability to 18 years from the date of production. The reasoning is that if a product demonstrates its safety over an extended period, then it is no longer reasonable to hold manufacturers liable for defects or failure. In 1994, Cessna went back to producing light aircraft. In 2011, they produce a fleet of six different style single-engine aircraft. Beech no longer produces small aircraft but Piper offers seven different versions of single-engine planes.

In legal terms, limiting the amount of time that a product is open to strict liability is called a **statute of repose**. The only national statute of repose in the U.S. is the General Aviation Revitalization Act. Some people in the U.S. support a national fifteen-year time span for product liability. Some U.S. states have other statures dealing with product liability with statutes of repose ranging from seven to twenty years. Some have none. Japan and the European Union have a ten-year statute of repose.

Based on http://www.globalsecurity.org/military/world/general-aviation.htm; http://www.cessna.com/single-engine/stationair.html.

the issue of how long companies should be responsible for their products. In the next section, you will see how privacy issues impact on the relationships between the customer and the company.

PRIVACY

Modern economies generate extensive personal information on consumers. Every click of a mouse, credit card transaction, application for credit, or visit to the doctor creates a store of personal information. Of course, most companies use this information for legitimate reasons that benefit the consumer. However, beyond clearly illegal and unethical use of personal information such as identify theft, there are many gray areas regarding the use of customer information that confront companies in our increasingly digital business world.

Calls for protection of privacy have existed for some time. Consider the call by Samuel Warren and former U.S. Supreme Court chief justice Brandeis in an 1890 *Harvard Law Review* article:

> Recent inventions and business methods call attention to the next step which must be taken for the protection of the person, and for securing to the individual what Judge Cooley calls the right "to be let alone" . . . the question whether our law will recognize and protect the right to privacy in this and in other respects must soon come before our courts for consideration. Of the desirability—indeed the necessity—of some such protection there can, it is believed, be no doubt.[26]

In spite of this early call, that still sounds remarkably current, there is not nation-level comprehensive legislation protecting consumer privacy in the U.S. Instead, privacy legislation exists in specific industries or for specific types of transactions as, for example, the health insurance industry (Health Insurance Portability and Accountability Act), credit reporting industry (Fair Credit Reporting Act), telemarketing (National Do Not Call Registry), and Children's Online Privacy Protection Act (COPPA). At the state level, laws vary widely, with California having the most comprehensive privacy protection.

The prime method of monitoring consumer privacy in the U.S. falls on the Federal Trade Commission (FTC). The approach, however, is indirect. The duty of the FTC is to protect consumers against unfair or deceptive acts or practices in the marketplace. To protect consumers' privacy, the FTC monitors the promises that companies make to consumers regarding consumer privacy protection. While probably not as effective as a comprehensive law, the Business Ethics Insight on pages 224–5 shows how some penalties may make managers think twice when they do not live up to the promises made to their customers.

Unlike the U.S., consumer privacy laws in most countries, especially in the EU, Australia, New Zealand, and Canada, are more comprehensive. In Europe, privacy is considered a fundamental right, whereas in the U.S. there are competing views over who owns the information consumers provide to companies. As the Global Business

BUSINESS ETHICS INSIGHT

Consequences of Failure to Protect Customer Privacy: Rite Aid Settles a U.S. Federal Trade Commission Case

Rite Aid operates the third largest pharmacy chain in the United States, with about 4,900 retail pharmacies and an online pharmacy business. The FTC began its investigation following news reports about Rite Aid pharmacies using open dumpsters to discard trash that contained consumers' personal information such as pharmacy labels. At the same time, Health and Human Services began investigating the pharmacies' disposal of health information protected by the Health Insurance Portability and Accountability Act (HIPAA).

"Companies that say they will protect personal information shouldn't be tossing patient prescriptions and employment applications in an open dumpster," said Jon Leibowitz, Chairman of the FTC. "We hope other organizations will learn from the FTC's action against Rite Aid to take their obligation to protect consumers' personal information seriously."

According to the FTC's complaint, Rite Aid failed to use appropriate procedures in the following areas:

- Disposing of personal information
- Adequately training employees
- Assessing compliance with its disposal policies and procedures
- Employing a reasonable process for discovering and remedying risks to personal information.

Rite Aid made claims regarding its privacy policies such as, "Rite Aid takes its responsibility for maintaining your protected health information in confidence very seriously ... Although you have the right not to disclose your medical history, Rite Aid would like to assure you that we respect and protect your privacy." The FTC alleged that the claim was deceptive and that Rite Aid's security practices were unfair.

Rite Aid Corporation agreed to settle FTC charges that it failed to protect the sensitive financial and medical information of its customers and employees, in violation of federal law. In a separate but related action, the company's pharmacy chain also agreed to pay $1 million to resolve Department of Health and Human Services (HHS) allegations that it failed to protect customers' sensitive health information.

The FTC settlement order required Rite Aid to establish a comprehensive information security program designed to protect the security, confidentiality, and integrity of the personal information it collects from consumers and employees. It also required the company to obtain audits, every two years for the next 20 years, to ensure that its security program meets the standards of the order. In addition, the order bared future misrepresentations of the company's security practices. The HHS settlement required Rite Aid pharmacies to establish policies and procedures for disposing of protected health information, create a training program for handling and disposing of patient information, conduct internal monitoring, and get an independent assessment of its compliance for three years. Rite Aid also paid HHS $1 million to settle the matter.

Based on Press Release, "Rite Aid Settles FTC Charges That It Failed to Protect Medical and Financial Privacy of Customers and Employees." July 27, 2010 (FTC File No. 0723121).

Ethics Insight on page 226 shows, this difference in views regarding privacy has resulted in some mutual accommodation between the U.S. and the EU. With the increased ease of cross-border transactions, there is growing worldwide pressure to harmonize privacy standards.

Ethical Rationales for Consumer Privacy

Scholars have often debated the ethical rationales for keeping consumer information private.[27] Utilitarian theory offers support to a company perspective that the use of consumer information provides both the consumer and the company benefits because the company can better provide consumers with what they need and can be more efficient in doing so.

From the deontological viewpoint, Kant's[28] categorical imperative can support the gathering and use of consumer information if both sides accept equal rights and protections regarding the use of the information. This had led to the position that, as long as companies provide consumers with a detailed privacy protection policy statement and control over their information, the use of the information is ethical. Somewhat similarly, others argue that social contract theory[29] supports the idea of an equitable exchange between the consumer and the company. The consumer provides information in exchange for some benefit that the company provides by using this information. It is a social contract because there should be shared normative expectations regarding the use of the information.

Ethical perspectives concerning justice also apply to the use of consumer information. If consumers believe the company will use their personal information following practices that preserve their privacy, then the acquisition and use of the information is procedurally just. To be just from a distributive justice perspective, consumers must believe that what the company provides them in terms of products or services is a fair exchange for the personal information that they give to the company. When companies communicate their privacy policies to their customers and stick to those policies, they can build trust with the customer and appeal to interactional justice.

GLOBAL BUSINESS ETHICS INSIGHT

Privacy Views in Europe and the United States

In spite of some enforcement by the FTC to require companies to back up their privacy statements, European cultural norms regarding privacy and more stringent laws often shock U.S. companies doing business in Europe. Differing from the U.S., where privacy is a consumer protection issue, in the EU the privacy of personal data is a fundamental, human right. The EU's approach to privacy originates from Europe's history and legal traditions. In Europe, protection of information privacy relies on comprehensive lawmaking that seeks to guard against future harms, particularly where social issues are concerned. Thus, for companies in Europe, protection of the personnel data is required and expected, whereas, in the U.S., with the exception of some specific areas such as banking, many U.S. companies act on the assumption that once they acquire they data they own it and can do what they want with it.

However, to do business in Europe, U.S. companies must comply with EU standards. One system used by over 2,000 firms is a self-certifying scheme called "Safe Harbor." To meet EU concerns, the U.S. Department of Commerce (DOC) drew up the Safe Harbor Privacy Principles to comply with the EU's standard of "adequate privacy protection," as required by the EU Directive. The European Commission approved those principles in 2000 and the Safe Harbor program went into effect that year.

Although voluntary, if companies become Safe Harbor certified and violate the terms of the certification, the FTC can put companies under increased scrutiny for up to 20 years and even give fines. However, some critics, such as Adam Levitin from Georgetown Law School, see little enforcement and perceive U.S. companies using the data as they wish. Similarly, Edward Janger from Brooklyn Law School noted that "Nobody from the air sector is in Safe Harbor: Delta (DAL), American Airlines (AMR), none of them are. When you give them the information in Europe, I am sure beyond any doubt that the information goes to Atlanta (U.S.)."

Based on Pop, Valentina. "U.S. firms get privacy lessons from Europe." *BusinessWeek*. http://www.businessweek.com/print/globalbiz/content/jul2010/; *The Economist*. 2010. "Legal confusion on internet privacy: Sharply differing attitudes towards privacy in Europe and America are a headache for the world's internet giants." June 17; U.S. Department of Commerce. http://www.export.gov/safeharbor/eu/eg_main_018474.asp.

Emerging Challenges

There are several issues related to the ease of gathering information, particularly with the use of modern technologies, which should concern companies with an ethical focus on their customers as stakeholders. One area, **behavioral targeting**, monitors your web-browsing behaviors. Companies like Amazon.com use this information to select advertisements and product offerings that match their information on your tastes. Companies that use these techniques argue that they can better provide their customers with the content that fits their needs so there is a benefit to the consumer. The challenge from an ethical point of view as that companies often get such information without the customers' knowledge and without the customers realizing how others could use the information. Even if the site has a privacy policy that covers such issues, critics argue that few customers actually read the policies but simply check the acknowledgment box and go on. If you intend to use the information for better customer service, could you argue that getting the information without customers' knowledge is ethical?

RFID, or **radio-frequency-identifiers**, are very tiny computer chips with miniature antennae embedded in tags attached to physical objects. The data can be sent to computers over a range of just a few feet, or much longer if there is power in the tag. While acknowledging the ethical use of these devices such as for tracking pharmaceuticals, supply chain tracking, and the tracking of toxic substances, the Privacy Rights Clearing House[30] sees several threats to privacy and civil liberties. For example, the tags can be hidden from the people using the tagged products, such as being sewn into clothing. The readers of the information also can be hidden. The bottom line is that, if the data associated with the movement and use of a product are linked with other personal data, companies can profile individuals without their knowledge.

The Privacy Rights Clearing House recommends that the following should be prohibited:

- Forcing or coercing customers into accepting RFID tags in the products they buy
- Preventing people from disabling RFID tags and readers on items in their possession
- Tracking individuals without their informed and written consent.

Another area of sensitivity in the use of customer information focuses on children. In this U.S.-specific law, the Children's Online Privacy Protection Act (COPPA) focuses on companies that collect personal information from children under the age of 13.[31] The law requires operators to:

- Post a privacy policy on the homepage of the website and link to the privacy policy on every page where personal information is collected
- Provide notice about the site's information collection practices to parents and obtain verifiable parental consent before collecting personal information from children
- Give parents a choice regarding the disclosure of their child's personal information to third parties

- Provide parents with access to their child's personal information and the opportunity to delete the child's personal information and opt out of future collection or use of the information
- Note condition of a child's participation in a game, contest, or other activity on the child disclosing more personal information than is reasonably necessary to participate in that activity
- Maintain the confidentiality, security, and integrity of personal information collected from children.

Following such guidelines for any information collected from children is probably a good practice for companies. Similarly, the FTC has published general privacy guidelines that are similar to Chartered Institute of Marketing[32] in the U.K. Exhibit 5.6 shows these guidelines below. They provide good guiding principles for companies wishing to develop ethical privacy practices.

Principles	Explanation
Notice/ Awareness	Consumers should be given notice of an entity's information practices before any personal information is collected from them. • Identification of the entity collecting the data • Identification of the uses to which the data will be put • Identification of any potential recipients of the data • The nature of the data collected and the means by which it is collected • Whether the provision of the requested data is voluntary or required, and the consequences of a refusal to provide the requested information • The steps taken by the data collector to ensure the confidentiality, integrity and quality of the data.
Choice/ Consent	Choice means giving consumers options as to how any personal information collected from them may be used. Specifically, choice relates to secondary uses of information—i.e., uses beyond those necessary to complete the contemplated transaction. Opt-in regimes require affirmative steps by the consumer to allow the collection and/or use of information; opt-out regimes require affirmative steps to prevent the collection and/or use of such information.
Access/ Participation	Access refers to an individual's ability both to access data about him or herself—i.e., to view the data in an entity's files—and to contest the data's accuracy and completeness.
Integrity/ Security	To assure data integrity, collectors must take reasonable steps, such as using only reputable sources of data and cross-referencing data against multiple sources, providing consumer access to data, and destroying untimely data or converting it to anonymous form.

EXHIBIT 5.6—U.S. Federal Trade Commission Privacy Principles

CHAPTER SUMMARY

In this chapter, you learned about three of the many major issues companies face as they deal with customers. The three key points of customer interface include marketing, product safety, and privacy.

In the marketing section, you learned that the basic 4Ps of marketing are product, price, promotion, and place. Each of these basic functions has their unique ethical challenges. Most issues dealing with products related to product safety and the chapter devoted a separate section to that issue.

With regard to price, the chapter introduced the concept of the "just price." All companies need to make a profit to survive. However, there are unethical pricing practices in pricing. One is the "bait and switch," where the customer is lured to the store with a cheap price and then offered a more expensive alternative. Another is "price gouging," where businesses take advantage of situations like natural disasters to raise prices when customers are desperately in need of their products.

With regard to advertising, you learned that, under U.S. law, advertisers must have evidence that supports both express *and* implied claims that advertisements make to consumers. If an advertisement makes health or safety claims, scientific evidence from studies evaluated by other professionals or scientists in the field must support the claims. Ads that fail this test are considered deceptive. Techniques used in deceptive advertising include ambiguity, concealed facts, and exaggeration.

Two areas of special concern in advertising are the use of sexuality and advertising to children. With regard to sexuality, it seems that moderate levels of sexual innuendo can attract attention and possibly increased sales. However, you also saw that sexuality in advertisements might not work in all cultural settings.

Advertising to children is one of the more controversial issues in the ethics of marketing. The debate over advertising to children focuses on four areas: at what age children recognize an advertisement as such; at what age children understand the intent of the advertisement; the effect of "pester power" to influence parents; and indirect effects from peer groups. Children less than ten years old seem to be able to identify ads and understand the intent and this ability increases with age. Advertisements do seem to result in appeals to parents to purchase products and, similarly, ads that influence peer groups work indirectly through peer pressure. Exhibit 5.3 gives a guide for ethical ads to children.

In the section on product safety you learned that, even if the safety of a product such as an automobile can be improved, it is seldom possible to make a perfect product and do it at prices that consumers can afford. Thus, since many if not most products we use can potentially cause harm, the basic question is: Who has the responsibility for this harm? This section introduced you to various theories regarding how to determine product liability. These included the buyer beware view, contractual theory, due care, and strict liability. The most stringent is strict liability, in which the manufacturers are responsible for its products' safety regardless of reasonable efforts made to build a safe product and the customers' use of the product. A major issue here is how long liability should be maintained.

The chapter concluded with a section on consumer privacy. This is a growing area of ethical concerns for businesses because the same technologies that make business transactions faster and easier also generate much personal information on customers. Unlike for the EU, you learned that the U.S. does not have a general privacy protection law, although there are several statutes that protect privacy in particular or with particular customers such as children. There remains a debate in the U.S. considering whether privacy is a fundamental right or whether businesses have a degree of ownership over personal information. This section concluded by giving you a general guideline for managing consumer information that came from principles suggested by the U.S. Federal Trade Commission.

NOTES

1   Zinkhan, G.M. & Williams, B.C. 2007. "The New American Marketing Association definition of marketing: An alternative assessment." *Journal of Public Policy & Marketing*, 26, 2, 284–288.
2   American Marketing Association. 2007. http://www.marketingpower.com/AboutAMA/Pages/DefinitionofMarketing.aspx.
3   Chartered Institute of Marketing (CIM). 2011. http://www.cim.co.uk/resources/glossary/home.
4   Wicks, A.R., Freeman, E., Werhane, P.H. & Martin, K.E. 2010. *Business ethics*. New York: Prentice Hall.
5   Bryant, C.X. 2004. *ACE Fitness Matters*. January/February.
6   Friedman, D.D. 1980. "In defense of Thomas Aquinas and the just price." *History of Political Economy*, 12, 234–242.
7   U.S. Department of Transportation. 2010. "DOT fines US airways for violation of price advertising rules." Press Release, DOT 44–10 March 8.
8   U.S. Federal Trade Commission. 1998. "Children's Online Privacy Protection Act of 1998." http://www.ftc.gov/privacy/privacyinitiatives/childrens.html.
9   Shaw, W.H. 2008. *Business ethics*. Belmont, CA: Thomson.
10 Cowley, E. 2006. "Processing exaggerated advertising claims." *Journal of Business Research*, 59, 6, 728–734.
11 Beauchamp, T.L. 1984. "Manipulative advertising." *Business and Professional Ethics Journal*, 3, 1–22.
12 Reichert, T., Heckler, S.E. & Jackson, S. 2001. "The effects of sexual social marketing appeals on cognitive processing and persuasion." *Journal of Advertising*, 30, 1, 13–27 (at 13–14).
13 Levit, M. 2005. "Sex in advertising: Does it sell?" *Business: Advertising*, February 15.
14 Bushman, B.J. 2005. "Violence and sex in television programs do not sell products in advertisements," *Psychological Science*, 16, 9, 702–708; Prendergast, G. & Hwa, C.H. 2003. "An Asia perspective of offensive advertising on the web." *International Journal of Advertising*, 22, 393–411.
15 Jarlbro, G. 2001. *Children and television advertising: The players, the arguments and the research during the period 1994–2000*. Stockholm: Konsumentverket.
16 McDermott, L., O'Sullivan, T., Stead, M. & Hastings, G. 2006. "International food advertising, pester power and its effects." *International Journal of Advertising*, 25, 4, 513–539.
17 Jarlbro, *Children and television advertising*.
18 Associated Press. 2010. "Toyota's chief apologizes for global recalls." http://www.msnbc.msn.com/id/35254001/ns/business-autos/ February 5; Vartabedian, Ralph & Bensinger, Ken. 2010. "Doubt cast on Toyota's decision to blame sudden acceleration on gas pedal defect." *Los Angeles Times*, January 30.
19 Birchall, J. 2010. "Mattel forced to recall 11m products." *Financial Times*, September 30, 20, 40.

20 Schwartz, V.E. 1998. "Continuing duty to warn: An opportunity for liability prevention or exposure." *Journal of Public Policy & Marketing*, 17, 124–126.

21 McAlpin, R.J. 2000. "Failure to warn: A product liability issue." Speech presented at Boating Week. 2000, Annual meeting of the Recreational Boat Builders Association, Orlando, FL. http://www.rbbi.com/folders/show/bw2000/sessions/failure.htm.

22 McAlpin, "Failure to warn: A product liability issue"; U.S. Food and Drug Administration. 2002. "Determination of intended use for 510(k) devices; Guidance for CDRH staff (update to K98–1)." December 3. http://www.fda.gov/downloads/MedicalDevices/DeviceRegulationandGuidance/GuidanceDocuments/ucm082166.pdf.

23 Cornell Law School Legal Information Institute. 2011. *Greenman v. Yuba Power Products*, 59 Cal. 2d 57 (1963).

24 *Elmore v. American Motors Corp.*, 70 Cal. 2d 578 (1969).

25 Piker, A. 1998. "Strict product liability and the unfairness objection." *Journal of Business Ethics*, 17, 885–893.

26 Warren, S. & Brandeis, L.D. 1980. "The right to privacy." *Harvard Law Review*, IV, 195–96.

27 Caudill, E.M. & Murphy, P.E. 2000. "Consumer online privacy: Legal and ethical issues." *Journal of Public Policy & Marketing*, 19, 1, 7–19; Lanier, Clinton D. & Saini, Amit. 2008. "Understanding consumer privacy: A review and future directions." *Academy of Marketing Science Review*, 12, 2. http://www.amsreview.org/articles/lanier02–2008.pdf.

28 Kant, I. 1959. *Foundations of the metaphysics of morals*. Indianapolis: Bobbs-Merrill Company.

29 Dunfee, T.W., Smith, C.N. & Ross, W.T. 1999. "Social contracts and marketing ethics." *Journal of Marketing*, 63, 14–32.

30 Privacy Rights Clearing House. 2003. "RFID Position Statement of Consumer Privacy and Civil Liberties Organizations." http://www.privacyrights.org/ar/RFIDposition.htm.

31 U.S. Federal Trade Commission. 1998. "Children's Online Privacy Protection Act of 1998." http://www.ftc.gov/privacy/privacyinitiatives/childrens.html.

32 Chartered Institute of Marketing. 2011. (CIM) http://www.cim.co.uk/resources/glossary/home.aspx.

KEY TERMS

4Ps: product, price, promotion, and place.

Ambiguity in advertisements: advertisements with confusing wording that leads the consumer to make erroneous conclusions about the nature of the product.

Bait-and-switch: occurs when a product is advertised at a low price, but when the consumer comes in he or she finds, or is offered, only a higher priced version of the product.

Behavioral targeting: software that monitors web-browsing behaviors to track customer behaviors.

Buyer beware: a perspective that places the burden on the buyer for judging the value, safety, and characteristics of a product.

Concealing facts: advertisements that that leave out pertinent information regarding their products.

Design defect: a potentially harmful characteristic of a product that is related to how the product is designed or manufactured.

Contract view: a perspective where the relationship between the manufacturer and a consumer is based on a contract.

Due care theory: manufacturers have an obligation to take reasonable precautions that their products do not harm the buyers.

Exaggeration: advertisements that overstate the benefits of a product.

Express claim: expected performance of a product is stated directly in an advertisement.

Failure to disclose the full price: when listed prices do not include other fees or charges that the consumer will have to pay.

Implied claim: expected performance of a product is stated indirectly or by inference in an advertisement.

Just price: attributed to St. Thomas Aquinas and suggests a seller should not raise prices because a buyer has a strong need for a product.

Marketing: usually the first level where the organization interacts with customers.

Material defect: a potentially harmful characteristic of a product due the materials used in production.

Predatory pricing: when a company lowers its prices so far below competitors' that it drives the competitors out of the market.

Price discrimination: when different groups are charged different prices.

Price fixing: when sellers agree with each other to sell at one price that is often above what they would have to do in a competitive market.

Price gouging: when sellers take advantage of situations like national disasters or shortages to raise prices.

Promotion: activities like advertising, sponsorships, coupons, and point of sale displays that make the customer aware of your product.

Puffery: an exaggeration so extreme that the assumption is that no reasonable person would believe the statement.

Radio-frequency-identifiers: computer chips with miniature antennae embedded in tags attached to physical objects and which send information to others.

Sexual appeals: messages in advertisements and promotions that contain sexual imagery.

Statute of repose: limiting the amount of time that a product is open to strict liability.

Strict liability: the manufacturer is responsible to compensate the user for defective or unsafe products that potentially cause harm even if due care was used in the production.

DISCUSSION QUESTIONS

1. How can you determine if a customer has a legitimate need for your product? Should you care if he/she is willing to buy?
2. Consider the concept of a "just price." Contrast that with pricing based on supply and demand. Make an ethical argument for both perspectives.
3. Discuss whether price gouging is wrong.
4. Identify advertisements that conceal facts. Discuss whether customers are likely deceived by these concealments.
5. Identify advertisements that are exaggerations. Discuss whether different customer groups might be likely not to realize that these ads are exaggerations.
6. Is sexual appeal in advertisements a form of sexual harassment? Discuss the types of sexual harassment and provide examples.
7. Identify what special provisions should be made when advertising to children. Give an ethical argument as to why these provisions are considered, at least by some, as necessary.
8. Consider the amount of time manufacturers might be liable for product defects (in the U.S., 5 years for automobiles and 18 years for aircraft). Use due care theory and strict liability theory to justify a time period.
9. Develop and augment that the protection of consumer information is or is not a fundamental right.
10. Given what we know about advertisements to children, do you think such ads should be banned?

INTERNET ACTIVITY

1. Go to the internet and search on advertising ethical codes. You will find many codes from different professional societies and different countries, including the Vatican.
2. Compare the codes by country. How are they different? How are they similar?
3. Prepare recommendations for multinational companies that might want to use the same advertising copy around the world. Will they find different standards? Could they offend local customers?

For more Internet Activities and resources, visit the Companion Website at www.routledge.com/cw/parboteeah.

WHAT WOULD YOU DO?

Product Safety in Brazil

Your U.S. company has started producing all-terrain vehicles (ATVs) in Brazil for selling in the South American market. The company's strategy is to build a presence and market share in Brazil before moving to other countries. In your first international assignment, the company has appointed you the manager of the manufacturing plant. The sales staff is Brazilian.

After a year on the job, the manufacturing plant is running smoothly and sales are starting to grow. You are confident that this assignment will be a major career boost and, when you return to the U.S., you will receive a substantial promotion and salary raise.

Late one afternoon, Marcus Alves, your head of marketing, comes to your office. He tells you how happy he is to work for the company but he is worried that sales growth is slowing and if that continues the company may abandon its Brazilian investment. He tells you, "The real problem is that prices are a bit too high for the Brazilian market." He and the sales force have been discussing the problem and come up with an idea to cut manufacturing costs that can lower the price to a more affordable level.

Alves suggests that you abandon the four-wheel version of the ATV and produce a three-wheel version like the company did in the 1980s. You could save money by not having an extra wheel and the associated suspension, and the ATV would probably be lighter and go faster—something your target market of younger men would like.

You remind Alves that the industry stopped producing three-wheelers because they caused so many accidents and deaths. He counters, noting, "It's perfectly legal here in Brazil to sell these vehicles. All we would need to do is put a warning label and encourage people to wear helmets." You know that wearing helmets is not very popular among your customers, but he presses: "We need this to survive and people need the jobs."

What would you do? Do you manufacture the cheaper and affordable product or keep with the safety standards accepted in a much richer nation? What stakeholders are affected by your decision?

BRIEF CASE: BUSINESS ETHICS INSIGHT

Profits and People in the Drug Industry

Routinely, the drug industry reports the highest profit margins among all industries. A significant amount of this profit comes from the U.S., which is one of the few larger nations that does not regulate drug prices.

Particularly during economic downturns, shopping for prescription drugs in Canada has become popular for people living close to the border. The same multinational companies that sell in the U.S. make the drugs but the prices are much lower. The savings can be 25% to 80%. While it is technically legal to import prescription drugs into the U.S., the actual status of doing so is somewhat ambiguous, as the Federal Drug Administration has not implemented the law for fear of not controlling the quality of the drugs.

This has not stopped bus tours of seniors from buying drugs across the border and even some local governments working to make it easier. A recent *60 Minutes* report examined the program set up by former Springfield, MA mayor Michael Albano. This program works with a Canadian pharmacy to supply drugs to municipal workers in the city.

When the city of Springfield faced a budget deficit, Albano was forced to lay off firefighters, police officers, and teachers. Albano realized that the city could make substantial savings in healthcare costs if the 3,000 city employees, retirees, and family members bought Canadian drugs rather than drugs from the local pharmacy. Noted Albano, "We can save anywhere from $4 to $9 million on an annual basis if I get everybody enrolled and everybody goes to Canada. And that's a huge amount of money right now. If I can save $9 million for my city and put it back, redirect it back into police and fire and to public education, it'll make a world of difference. So it's a huge saving." Albano practices what he preaches, as his son is diabetic and he buys insulin from the Canadian pharmacy as well.

Naturally, U.S. Americans buying in Canada is bad for the pharmaceutical companies' business, although good for local Canadian pharmacies that often make up to 30% of revenues from U.S. customers. However, Canadian pharmacists risk alienating their suppliers. As the pharmacist that supplies the Springfield workers noted, "We've had several letters from the big multi-nationals, certainly threatening to cut off the drug supply very explicitly if you are supplying medications to U.S. patients."

Why are drug prices so high? Perhaps the most compelling argument made by the big pharmaceuticals is that they must cover the high costs of research and development (R&D) to make major advances in developing new drugs. Not all drugs succeed, and even if they work wonders it takes years for a drug to receive governmental approval for human use.

235

Some question this argument. A recent Bank of America study found that many companies spend more on paying dividends to stockholders and buying back shares to increase the prices of their stocks. These activities benefit the stockholders and not the people who need the drugs. The Bank of America figures are telling. The world's largest drug firm, Pfizer, spent $22.2 billion on buybacks and dividends. This equaled 210% of the amount spent on R&D. Similarly, British drug giant GlaxoSmithKline spent 122% of its R&D spending on buybacks and dividends and Merck spent 143% of its R&D budget.

Another recent report by the consumer health organization Families USA also questions the claim that high drug prices are necessary to support R&D. This study found that drug companies spent more than twice as much on administration, advertising, and marketing than they did on R&D. Among the nine companies examined in the study, which included Merck, Pfizer, Bristol-Myers Squibb, Pharmacia, Abbott Laboratories, American Home Products, Eli Lilly, Schering-Plough, and Allergan, only Eli Lilly spent less than twice as much on marketing, advertising, and administration than on R&D. In the year of the study, six of these firms reported higher net profits than spending on R&D.

Not all of the press is negative on big pharmaceuticals. Historically, pharmaceutical companies have aggressively used patents to protect their intellectual property rights for their drug creations and prevent other companies from copying the drugs and producing generic versions for a much cheaper price. The rationale behind this also rests on the return on R&D to the company that makes the investment.

However, this has placed many of the pharmaceuticals in the ethical dilemma of not providing drugs to people in desperate need, especially those from the poorer nations. Healthcare activists have long argued that drug patents deny the poor essential medicines. Whether responding to external pressures or internally derived concern for people, many drug companies are now relaxing their patent restrictions. For example, GlaxoSmithKline (GSK), a British drug company, waived patent restrictions and now allows generic drug firms to copy its HIV drugs and sell them in poor countries. The Swiss company Novartis shares propriety research in a partnership with the Institute for OneWorld Health, a non-profit research organization, to develop drugs for secretory diarrhea. Secretory diarrhea is a leading cause of death for children in poor countries. The institute also works with Roche, another Swiss company that waived patent restrictions to produce drugs targeted at common diseases in the poor nations.

Based on Off the Charts: Pay, Profits and Spending by Drug Companies. http://www.actupny.org/reports/drugcosts.html; http://www.cbsnews.com/stories/2004/03/12/60minutes/main605700.shtml; *The Economist.* "All together now, new initiatives to cure diseases of the poor world." July 16, 2009; Oliver Wagg, "Drug companies: Consumers or shareholders?" *Ethical Corporation*, November 18, 2004.

BRIEF CASE QUESTIONS

1. The pharmaceutical industry presents a complex case on how to balance the interests of stakeholders: the stockholders of the companies and the people who need affordable drugs to survive and life decent lives. Take the position of the company and counter the arguments from the groups discussed in the case.
2. Should drug prices be regulated in a rich country such as the U.S.?
3. From a justice point of view, discuss the issue of whether it is fair for people to pay for drugs (or other fundamental necessities) based on their income.

LONG CASE: BUSINESS ETHICS

MATTEL RECALLS 2007: IMPLICATIONS FOR QUALITY CONTROL, OUTSOURCING, AND CONSUMER RELATIONS*

During the summer and fall of 2007, international toy giant Mattel and childhood favorites Barbie® and Elmo® dominated media headlines for weeks. Reports talked not of Christmas sneak previews or of rising sales, but of recalls, lead poisoning, and deadly magnets. In total, an excess of 21 million toys were pulled from shelves in little over a month, either because they were coated in toxic lead paint or contained small, poorly designed magnets, just the right size to be swallowed by curious kids.

The voluntary recalls offered Mattel the opportunity to become a model of effective short-term crisis communication strategy. Working with the Consumer Product Safety Commission (CPSC) to execute the communication component of the recall at an accelerated pace, Mattel placed notifications in 20 languages on its website, sent personal letters to its entire customer database, sent letters and posters to its retailers, manned a hotline, placed full-page ads in major newspapers, and worked closely with the media.

However, the CPSC's subsequent revelation that Mattel first suspected lead contamination in early June, a good two months before it announced the first of four recalls on August 4, has overshadowed much of what the company claims it did right. The disclosure calls into question Mattel's prioritization of its customer's interests and the quality of its products over its business interests. According to CPSC regulations, companies must report suspected safety issues within 24 hours of detection, although companies do not often comply. For example, in 2001, Mattel waited more than three years to announce a Power Wheels® defect. Six years later, consumers and investors may question why the company still fails to comply with federal reporting regulations and why it still lacks the processes and infrastructure to prevent such crises from recurring.

Adding to the controversy surrounding Mattel's recalls is that the products were manufactured in China, a country recently under fire for exporting contaminated products such as pet food and toothpaste. In light of this, the Mattel case provides a unique opportunity to explore quality control, product safety, and reporting regulations in the context of a larger, global issue: outsourcing manufacturing to developing countries. Not only must Mattel regain the trust of consumers, investors, and regulators through transparent corporate communication and commitment to real change, but it must also regain the trust of the international community.

Accolades for Ethics

For more than 20 years, Mattel has incorporated social responsibility into its business practices. In 2007, *Business Ethics* magazine ranked Mattel number 92 of the top 100 Best Corporate Citizens, a list drawn from the country's largest 1,000 publicly listed companies.[1] The article praised Mattel for its Global Manufacturing Principles (GMP), a set of externally monitored ethical manufacturing standards first adopted in 1997. These principles require Mattel's supply chain partners to uphold its stringent standards for safe working conditions, employee health, fair wages, and environmental consciousness. To date, Mattel remains one of the only toy companies to have such checks in place.

The company also publishes an annual corporate social responsibility report for investors and claims that its product safety regulations either meet or exceed those set by the CPSC.[2] Likewise, Mattel prioritizes philanthropic work that benefits children. In 1978 it launched Mattel's Children's Foundation, a partnership with non-profits to fund children's projects using a percentage of pre-tax profits.[3]

Financial Performance and Annual Report (2006)[4]

As the world's largest toy manufacturer, Mattel has consistently performed well financially. From 2005 to 2006, for example, Mattel maintained the sales and profit growth depicted in Table 1.

TABLE 1 Financial Comparison, 2005 to 2006

	2005	2006	Increase
Net Sales	$5.18 billion	$5.65 billion	$0.47 billion
Net Income	$417 million	$592.9 million	$175.9 million
Cost of Sales	$2.81 billion	$3.04 billion	$232.2 million
Product Costs	$2.21 billion	$2.42 billion	$204.9 million
Gross Profit (as % of net sales)	45.8	46.2	0.4

http://www.shareholder.com/mattel/annual.cfm, Annual Reports: 2005 and 2006

According to its 2006 annual report, Mattel plans to maintain long-term business growth by reinvigorating the Barbie® brand, maintaining growth across core brands and non-traditional brands, and implementing lean supply chain initiatives to improve manufacturing, distribution, and sales.[5]

Toy Safety in the United States

Toy safety in the United States is monitored by the CPSC. Although corporations are expected to comply with its standards and regulations, they are encouraged to adopt more stringent regulations of their own, as has Mattel. This section explores both the CPSC's standards and Mattel's independent standards.

Consumer Product Safety Commission (CPSC) Standards

Congress established the CPSC as part of the Consumer Product Safety Act in 1972. Regulating more than 5,000 consumer products ranging from lawnmowers to children's toys, this independent federal agency protects the public from unreasonable injury and death.[6] Food, drugs, firearms, cars, and motorcycles lie outside its jurisdiction. In 2007, the CPSC negotiated 472 cooperative and voluntary recalls involving almost 110 million products.[7] Approximately 21 million of these products were toys from Mattel.

The CPSC has many responsibilities. It develops, issues, and enforces voluntary and mandatory industry standards. It can recall products and oversee repairs. It can ban consumer products proven to be so dangerous that no industry standard could realistically protect the public. The CPSC also inspects suspicious products and researches new hazards. It is responsible for communicating its findings to the media.[8] Using the CPSC's website or toll-free hotline, consumers can not only gather product safety information, but also report unsafe products.

Toy companies like Mattel and their foreign suppliers are expected to follow the CPSC's regulations and recall protocol. One of the most important regulations stipulates that a company must report a suspected defect or harmful product within 24 hours of discovery.[9] Unfortunately, companies often ignore this regulation. For instance, Mattel failed to comply during its recall of Power Wheels® in 1998 and again with the recalls in 2007.

Other regulations are specific to substances and materials. One example of a harmful substance is lead, which can cause neurological damage, learning disabilities, and hearing problems in children when ingested. To prevent such devastating consequences, the CPSC requires all American manufacturers, suppliers, importers, and retailers to abide by the provisions of the Federal Hazardous Substances Act (FHSA), which bans all children's toys containing hazardous amounts of lead.[10] The CPSC strengthened its guidelines in 1977 by lowering permissible lead levels from 0.5% to 0.06% to comply with the Lead Based Paint Poisoning Prevention Act.[11]

Other regulations apply to specific toy parts. In 1995, the CPSC applied the Child Safety Protection Act (CSPA) to all products sold in the United States.[12] The CSPA tightened restrictions on small parts and balls in children's toys to reduce choking deaths. If a company disregards these guidelines, the CPSC can seek civil penalties in court. In 2007, it recovered a total of $2.75 million in fines from companies that failed to report hazards within the 24-hour limit. Of this amount, $975,000 was meted to Mattel alone for a defect in Fisher-Price's Little People® Animal Sounds Farm™.[13] In 2001, Mattel paid $1.1 million—almost half of the total fines issued in 2007— for waiting more than three years to report a Power Wheels® fire hazard.

Many experts, including Pamela Gilbert, a former CPSC executive director, disparage the CPSC's penalties as too soft to deter large corporations from violating product safety laws.[14] Others add that the CPSC is weak and lacks funding to enforce its mostly voluntary regulations. Moreover, the CPSC does not have pre-market jurisdiction, which means it cannot test products before they hit store shelves.[15] Under pressure to respond, Congress is deliberating to increase the maximum monetary fee that can be slapped on companies.

Mattel's Independent Standards

Despite past fines, Mattel asserts it abides by CPSC regulations and follows its own Code of Conduct and Global Manufacturing Principles.[16] An excerpt from its Code of Conduct on product quality and safety, adopted in 2003, reads:

> Mattel's reputation for product quality and safety is among its most valuable assets ... Children's health, safety and well-being are our primary concern. We could damage our consumers' trust if we sell products that do not meet our standards. Our commitment to product quality and safety is an integral part of the design, manufacturing, testing and distribution processes. We will meet or exceed legal requirements and industry standards for product quality and safety. We strive to meet or exceed the expectations of our customers and consumers. Any compromise to product safety or quality must be immediately reported to Worldwide Quality Assurance.[17]

To meet this commitment, Mattel conducts periodic checks of toys pulled off production lines; new supplies, such as paint, are tested upon arrival.[18] Mattel has also set up testing laboratories for some of its contractors. Ironically, Mattel had built a lab for the supplier culpable in the 2007 lead paint crisis, suggesting that, "Even with regular inspections, breaches of codes of conduct in the supply chain become almost an inevitability." [19]

Some toy analysts are reluctant to blame the toy giant for the lead paint crisis. "If something like this can happen to Mattel, which has some of the most stringent standards in the industry, what does that mean for the other manufacturers of such products?" argues Richard Welford of *CSR Asia Weekly*.[20] "The recall is particularly alarming since Mattel, known for its strict quality controls, is considered a role model in the toy industry for how it operates in China," adds the Associated Press.[21] In fact, just weeks before the August recalls, Mattel was one of only two toy companies to allow the *New York Times* to visit its China plants. The *New York Times* article published on July 26, 2007, commended Mattel's product safety inspection procedures, which it maintained had improved since the Power Wheels® recall.

Issues in Outsourcing to China

The movement of manufacturing to developing countries such as China, where corruption is widespread and regulations are difficult to enforce, has arguably contributed to recent recall crises. This section looks at China's role as toy supplier to the world and to Mattel. It also analyzes the challenges of quality control and international communication.

China as the World's Workshop

Approximately 80% of toys bought in the United States today[22] are manufactured in factories scattered up and down China's east coast. Although American companies may own several factories in China, writes *Atlantic Monthly* reporter James Fallows in his article "China Makes, The World Takes," they mostly commission manufacturing to local subcontractors.[23]

TABLE 2 Chinese Toy Exports 2005

Region	Total # of Manu-facturers	Main Export Category	Export Value in 2005
Guangdong	>5,000	Plush toys, electronic toys, plastic toys	$11.934 billion
Zhejiang	>1,000	Wooden toys, baby bicycles	$871 million
Jiangsu	> 700	Plush toys	$850 million
Shanghai	> 700	Baby bicycles, strollers	$549 million
Shandong	> 550	Plush toys	$367 million
Fujian	> 500	Electronic toys, plastic toys	$226 million

China Toy Association, http://www.toy-cta.org/en/Introduction_1.asp

TABLE 3 China 2006 Main Export Destinations

Rank	Destination	Export Value
1	U.S.A.	6,553,321,398
2	Germany	1,469,936,169
3	Holland	1,055,340,703
4	England	1,040,271,120
5	Japan	718,578,989
6	France	230,893,819
7	Russia	216,180,371
8	Australia	213,071,333

http://www.toy-cta.org/en/Introduction_3.asp

The region with the largest production capacity is Guangdong province in southeastern China. In 2005, more than 5,000 manufacturers in Guangdong exported almost US$12 billion in plush, electronic, and plastic toys (see Table 2). The next largest exporters are Zhejiang, Jiangsu, Shanghai, Shandong, and Fujian provinces, which collectively exported more than US$2.8 billion in toys that same year. Of that amount, the China Toy Association estimates that an estimated US$6.5 billion in toys was exported to the United States, with Germany and Holland placing second and third (see Table 3).

Quality Control Challenges and Implications

Controlling the quality of products manufactured overseas remains a continual problem. For example, 177 recalls in the United States post-2006 have involved products manufactured in China. This is perhaps due to challenging operational and cultural differences.

"It is not easy to find the right factory, work out the right manufacturing system, ensure the right supply of parts and raw materials, impose the right quality standard, and develop the right relationships of trust and reliability," writes Fallows. He likens the supply chain to intellectual property in importance and writes that companies that have found a good chain will not divulge it to competitors.[24] In an interview with the *New York Times*, Dane Chamorro, regional director of global consulting company Control Risks, says that "The samples you get are always fantastic; but once they rope you in they can cut back. And a lot of Chinese companies will do anything to cut costs."[25] Andy Switky, managing director of California design firm IDEO, describes the general Chinese mentality as "happy with crappy," which makes it harder for Chinese suppliers to fully incorporate Western quality control standards.[26]

But some experts argue that corporations cannot possibly be held 100% accountable for slip-ups when hundreds of suppliers and thousands of employees are involved. Others say it is impossible for a company to test every batch of toys produced. The most a company can do is pick its suppliers carefully, strengthen communication, consistently implement rigorous inspections, and threaten to cease business with companies that fail to comply.

Mattel's China Operations

Mattel has a long history in China, where it has manufactured toys for 25 years.[27] The company owns five factories[28] and outsources 50% of production to third-party manufacturers[29] subject to quality control inspections. Together, these factories produce 65% of Mattel's toys.

In recent years, Mattel has transferred a greater portion of testing responsibility to manufacturers themselves. One example is batch testing. Ten to fifteen years ago, Mattel conducted the inspections itself. Now, to reduce costs, the company outsources testing to suppliers and manufacturers. But industry experts fear these contractors will cover up and cut corners.[30]

These experts also claim Mattel is inextricably tied to China. In a *Washington Post* article, Eric Johnson, a management professor at Dartmouth College and a specialist on the U.S.–China toy industry, says that Mattel is "dependent on Chinese industrial capacity for its toys . . . They have significant investment of their own capital . . . and don't want to lose it."[31] Coupling Mattel's dependence with its plans to expand into China's lucrative consumer market, Johnson concludes Mattel has a vested interest in maintaining good relations with China.

Managing International Communication

Managing complex international relationships during calm times and crises is a key communications challenge for corporations such as Mattel. For instance, the job involves being able to "sensitize managements and host governments to the mutual benefits of multinational capital, technology, and management-skills-providing jobs."[32] Additionally, corporate communicators must cultivate cross-cultural relationships based on respect for equals.[33] They must convince host countries that their goals are not imperialist and exploitative.[34] And because a company's reputation may be affected by its suppliers' business practices, corporate directives should be clearly communicated to suppliers at all times.

There are several trade groups that facilitate communication between China and the West. One Chinese organization that lobbies the Chinese government on toy industry interests is the China Toy Association, which works with the China National Standard Committee to revise toy safety standards, maintains communication with international media, and organizes international toy fairs and trade shows. The Toy Industry Association (TIA) likewise mediates conflict between China and its Western partners during times of crisis, while tactfully asserting the need for change, as it did during a toy safety conference held in Guangzhou, China, on November 15, 2007.

Industry experts claim both Chinese and American companies must increase collaboration. But ultimately American importers are responsible for the quality of imported goods.

Mattel's Recall History

Of the three billion toys sold in the United States each year, less than 1% is recalled.[35] But even just one recall can be incredibly damaging. It harms a company through lost sales, damaged reputation, diversion of resources, costly customer support, and the threat and expense of litigation.[36] It is clearly a crisis to avoid. Yet in spite of quality control efforts, Mattel has suffered 36 recalls since 1998 and two formal CPSC admonishments.[37] This section reviews Mattel's most controversial recall prior to 2007.

Power Wheels® Product Recall 1998–2001

The Power Wheels® crisis began in 1995, when parents began filing consumer complaints with the CPSC. In total, parents reported 71 accidents involving faulty brakes, 116 fires due to faulty electrical wiring, and 1,800 incidents of overheating, short-circuiting, or melting. Nine children suffered burn injuries.[38] In response, the CPSC independently investigated the ride-on toy vehicle from 1995 to 1998. The inquiry revealed that the affected models were manufactured as early as 1986, and although Mattel was aware of complaints it neglected to file a CPSC report for more than three years.[39]

Even after the CPSC stepped in, Mattel was uncooperative and refused to admit any wrongdoing. Anne Brown, the CPSC's then chairwoman, told the *Wall Street Journal* that "They didn't want to do a recall . . . It took way too long."[40] And Pamela Gilbert, the CPSC's executive director at the time, added that "Mattel was uncooperative in giving key documents over to them during the investigation."[41] In the end, the CPSC forced Mattel to implement a recall; however, the toymaker continued to blame consumers, who it claimed improperly used or tampered with the toys.[42] Mattel also strongly stated that the 24-hour reporting regulation was unreasonable and that it preferred to conduct an internal investigation before reporting to the public.[43]

The Competitive Environment

Though less than 1% of toys manufactured per year are ever recalled, a high-profile recall can result in industry-wide profit loss; this means that competitors are likewise affected.[44]

Toy Industry Overview

In the United States alone, approximately three billion toys are sold per year,[45] amounting to an estimated US$22 billion[46] in annual sales. And these numbers are growing. According to Table 4, annual toy sales for the period of July 2006 to June 2007 rose to US$22.5 billion from US$22.1 billion the previous year.

TABLE 4 State of the Toy Industry: 2005–2006 and 2006–2007

Category	July '05–June '06 (US$)	July '06–June '07 (US$)	% change
Action Figures and Accessories	1.3 billion	1.2 billion	−7
Arts & Crafts	2.5 billion	2.7 billion	8
Building Sets	686.8 million	684.3 million	0
Dolls	2.7 billion	2.7 billion	1
Games and Puzzles	2.4 billion	2.4 billion	0
Infant/Preschool	3.2 billion	3.3 billion	4
Youth Electronics	962.1 million	1.1 billion	17
Outdoor & Sports Toys	2.9 billion	2.8 billion	−5
Plush	1.3 billion	1.4 billion	3
Vehicles	2.0 billion	2.2 billion	9
All other Toys	2.1 billion	2.0 billion	−4
TOTAL	22.1 billion	22.5 billion	2

State of the Industry Report. http://www.toyassociation.org/AM/Template.cfm?Section=Industry_Statistics, accessed November 26, 2007, sourced from The NPD Group/Consumer Panel Tracking

Mattel Product Recalls 2007

The previous sections provide context for Mattel's four voluntary recalls that began in August 2007 just weeks after American toymaker RC2 recalled 1.5 million toy trains coated in toxic Chinese lead paint. Adding to the controversy was that all of Mattel's recalled products, like RC2s, were manufactured in China. Knowing it had to act fast, Mattel partnered with its old adversary, the CPSC, to implement a global crisis communication campaign. This section outlines the strengths and weaknesses of Mattel's communications strategy and also the responses of its affected publics, such as competitors, investors, parents, and the government.

Recall Timeline

To understand Mattel's communications strategy, it is helpful to review the events that transpired during the recall period. According to Table 5, the recalls started in August and continued into November, just in time for the holidays. As the holiday season is the most lucrative for toy companies, the third and fourth quarters of each fiscal year usually bring in the most sales.[47]

Therefore, a fast and transparent corporate response was imperative.

TABLE 5 Recall Timeline June–November 2007

Date	Event
June 8	Mattel is first alerted to possible lead paint contamination.
June 9	The CPSC deadline for Mattel to report the problem.
June 10	CPSC deadline passes; Mattel fails to act.
July 26	Mattel files full recall report with CPSC.
August 2	Mattel voluntarily recalls 1.5 million Fisher-Price® toys that are supposedly coated in paint containing dangerously high levels of lead.
August 7	Mattel identifies a Chinese factory as the source of the contamination scandal.
August 14	Mattel voluntarily recalls a further 17.4 million products containing loose nuts easy for children to swallow (Mattel Play Sets and Barbie® Doll & Tanner).
September 4	Mattel voluntarily recalls another 850,000 toys due to lead paint contamination (Barbie® Accessory Sets, It's a Big Big World™ and GeoTrax™ Engines).
September 11	CEO Robert A. Eckert publishes an opinion statement in the *Wall Street Journal*.
September 21	Mattel's Vice President Thomas Debrowski apologizes to China for blaming Chinese suppliers for the Mattel recalls.
October 25	Mattel voluntary recalls Go Diego Go!™ Rescue Boats coated in paint containing hazardous levels of lead.
November 6	Mattel voluntarily recalls 155,000 Laugh & Learn™ and Learning Kitchen™ toys, manufactured in Mexico, due to a choking hazard.

TABLE 6 "Fast Track" Tactics

	Mattel's "Fast Track" Recall Tactics
1	Staffed its call center, created a CPSC-approved script
2	Created a recall portion of its website
3	Sent notifications and posters to retailers
4	Gave retailers advance notice of recall so they could remove products from shelves even before logistics of recall had been finalized
5	Sent news releases to media
6	Started a toll-free, multilingual interactive voice response phone line to assist callers to determine if their product is an affected one
7	Launched a web-based recall identification tool on its website in more than 20 languages
8	CEO video posted on website
9	Allowed customers to register a product for recall online or over the phone
10	Mailed recall notification letters to customers who were in their customer relations database due to past recalls
11	Ran full-page ads in newspapers on August 14 and September 5: *USA Today, The New York Times, Los Angeles Times, Chicago Tribune, Washington Post*
12	Conducted print, online, and television satellite interviews
13	Posted ads on websites frequented by parents, such as Yahoo!, Disney, Nickelodeon, and Cartoon Network
14	Offered customers prepaid postage labels so that they could return the products
15	Compensated customers with vouchers equal to or greater than the retail price plus tax

Mattel's Response: Successful External Communication

On July 26, 2007, Mattel issued an official recall report to the CPSC. The regulatory agency agreed to help the toymaker alert the public. Together, they implemented the CPSC's "fast track" program[48] to communicate with parents and retailers using a mix of print, electronic, and new media. The tactics are outlined in Table 6.

As online communications facilitate quick and controlled corporate responses, Mattel's website played a leading tactical role. For example, the company posted a video of CEO Robert Eckert addressing parental concerns over the safety of Mattel's products.[49] His comments reinforced several key points.

1. He stressed the company's *commitment to children*. Eckert said, "Nothing is more important than the safety of children . . . we are confident our toys are the safest ever."
2. He emphasized the company's *dedication to open communication* with the public. "There's always room to be better . . . we are communicating frequently and openly."
3. He *assuaged parents' fears* over the company's inspections systems, saying that "All paint must be tested before it is used on toys, no exceptions. We've significantly increased testing and unannounced inspections at every stage of production . . . we are testing every production run of finished toys to ensure compliance before they reach consumers."
4. He then *praised Mattel's new three-point check system,* which he claimed had been followed by other toy companies.
5. Finally, he *reported* that Mattel had had *no further lead paint problems,* claiming success for the tighter inspection systems implemented after the August crisis.

Recurring themes included trust and child safety. Eckert personally thanked parents for putting trust in Mattel and reiterated that child safety is Mattel's number one priority.

The website also answered parent questions in a section called "What We're Doing and What You Need to Know." Queries such as "Are toys safe for the holidays?" and "How can I trust that Mattel's products are safe?" reinforced the themes of safety, commitment, and trust stressed in Eckert's video. A new topic that arose was parental self-efficacy, for example, "What can I do, as a parent, to ensure my child's safety?"[50] A page titled "Tips for Safe Toys This Holiday" guided holiday buying. What Mattel noticeably did not do, as it did during the Power Wheels® incident, was place blame on consumers.[51]

Mattel's Response: Internal Reorganization

Besides executing an external information blitz, Mattel reorganized internal operations to emphasize commitment to product safety. In the weeks following the recalls, Mattel established a corporate responsibility division to report to Eckert. The group, consisting of 500 employees worldwide, would monitor domestic and international vendor and manufacturer adherence to Mattel's toy safety standards. Eckert also announced a new Product Integrity Policy and Audit, "a function that will combine an internal audit organization and an independent audit organization to monitor Mattel and vendor facilities' compliance with Mattel's product integrity standards."[52] The company also instituted a three-point safety check system:

1. Mattel will only use paint from certified suppliers. Every single batch of paint at every single vendor will be tested. Paint that doesn't pass will be discarded without exception.
2. Mattel will increase unannounced testing and inspections at every stage of the manufacturing process.

3. Mattel will test finished toys from every single production run to ensure they meet accepted lead levels before being shipped to stores.[53]

Eckert attested to this system's success in an opinion piece he published in the *New York Times*:

> Mattel is conducting a thorough investigation, combing through our products to ensure that we identify and recall any product affected by lead paint, no matter how tiny the area . . . For example, we identified lead paint on the headlights of a three-inch train car—and we recalled it. If there is a needle in the proverbial haystack, we aim to find it. I encourage other companies to do the same.[54]

To reinforce this commitment, Mattel plans to apply American standards of lead toxicity levels to European Union countries, even if local EU standards are not as high.[55]

Analysts remain upbeat about Mattel's future. In a research report from the Bank of America, analyst Michael Savner estimates the total cost of the recalls at an "insignificant" US$24 million. Others predict that as Mattel advertises tighter testing regulations, parents will continue to buy its toys.[56] For example, though approximately 2.4 million defective Polly Pocket™ dolls were recalled in November 2006, Polly Pocket™ sales did not fall. The brand weathered on, and Mattel even expanded the line.[57] And if other toy companies disclose similar defects during the next few months, Mattel might be praised for getting the word out first.[58]

Mattel's Response: Shortcomings

Mattel's successful responses do not completely deflect its errors. First, the toymaker has on several occasions failed to comply with CPSC reporting requirements. Though Mattel was alerted to the Fisher-Price® paint contamination on June 8, it did not file a full report with the CPSC until July 26, more than a month and a half later.

Second, critics accuse the toymaker of expending a disproportionate amount of effort on preserving its reputation. For example, subsequent reports revealed that Mattel misled publics to believe its Chinese suppliers and manufacturers were responsible for both the lead paint *and* the magnets, when in fact the magnet hazard was an internal Mattel design flaw. This blame-shifting backfired as China retaliated, and on September 21 Mattel's executive vice president for worldwide operations admitted to China's product safety chief that the magnet recall should not have been associated with China; he also apologized to Chinese consumers.[59] Critics claim such pandering to corporate interests exposes excessive investment in public relations and the bottom line.

A third area where Mattel could improve is compensation. "Mattel is offering equivalent-value coupons good for other Mattel products in exchange for recalled products. Given the inconvenience caused to consumers and the need to motivate them to return the affected products, this offer may not be sufficient,"[60] says John Quelch, a senior associate dean at the Harvard Business School.

Industry Response

Industry groups responded to the crises by providing stakeholders with objective toy safety analysis. They also facilitated international communication and pushed for legislative change. "Our analysis of what had happened was that our toy safety standards were excellent, as they had been for years; but that the toy safety testing and inspection process had failed us," said Carter Keithley, president of TIA. "The U.S. toy industry has been very pleased with its China-based manufacturers for many years. The errors that resulted in lead paint and other hazardous materials being used on children's products were the acts and omissions of a very few," which he said did not reflect the standards maintained by the "vast majority" of their manufacturers.[61]

To cater to consumer concerns, the TIA's website posted the slogan, "Toy safety is our top priority, year-round." For the 2007 holiday season, the group offered extra services to parents, such as a new website (www.toyinfo.org) and a toll-free hotline (1–888–88–4TOYS), both of which provided safety tips, advice from experts, and objective recall information.

Members of the toy industry also collaborated with the Chinese government's General Administration of Quality Supervision, Inspection and Quarantine (AQSIQ) to force tighter testing protocols on Chinese manufacturers.[62] For example, on November 15, 2007, the TIA and the Chinese government co-hosted a toy safety conference in Guangzhou, China. Representatives from almost 300 Chinese toy manufacturers attended. At the conference, the TIA proposed a "conformity assessment" program to guarantee that all toys entering the United States are "in compliance with strengthened U.S. safety standards."[63] The projected program would include the following measures:

- Creating new procedures with the American National Standards Institute (ANSI) for sampling and testing products as they come off the production lines.
- Developing criteria to accredit testing laboratories or inspecting organizations. Only the accredited will be qualified to perform the above-mentioned conformity testing procedures.
- Drafting federal legislation that requires all toys sold in the United States to pass the revised tests to ensure they conform to safety standards.[64]

Industry analysts said it was imperative to act immediately. If toy companies did not enforce rigorous standards, then we would expect to see more frequent recalls in the future.

Investor Response

Unsurprisingly, the recalls shook investor confidence, as evidenced by the company's gradually decreasing stock price during the recall period. In August, for example, Mattel's stock price continued a downward trend that had begun as early as July. The price then slowly rose in September, even after the September 4 recall was disclosed, only to later drop again (see Table 7).

In addition, a large pension fund filed a shareholder's suit against Mattel in October 2007, alleging that the company's board of directors and executives purposely delayed announcements in order to sell as many faulty products as possible and to artificially increase stock shares. They claimed that company insiders dumped shares to increase profits in the months leading up to the recall, as share prices dropped 20% immediately after.[65]

TABLE 7 Mattel Stock Prices 2007

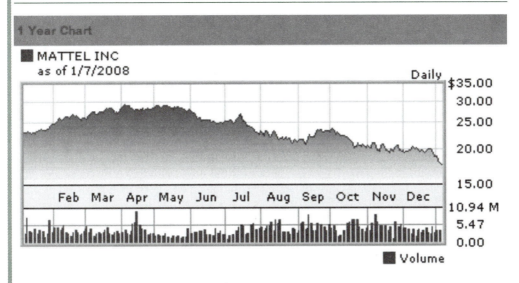

http://www.shareholder.com/mattel/graph2.cfm

Watchdog Response

The lead paint predicament extends beyond children's toys to products like jewelry and furniture. After the recalls, several groups, including the Ecology Center and the Center for Health, Environment and Justice, tested 1,200 children's products and found that 35% contained lead, while only 20% contained no lead. Tracey Easthope, Director of the Ecology Center's Environmental Health Project, said that lead levels in 17% of the children's products tested would likely trigger a recall. Jewelry products rather than toys most often contained high levels of lead.[66]

Parent/Consumer Response

According to a 2007 Harris Poll, the recalls could hurt the 2007 holiday toy market. For example, an increased number of American consumers reported being wary of products manufactured in China. One third said that they would likely buy fewer toys in December 2007, while 45% said they would outright avoid toys manufactured in China. Sixty-eight percent of consumers who had been directly affected by the recalls said they would also avoid toys manufactured in China during the holiday season.[67]

Government Response

In the wake of the year's recalls, the United States government elevated the importance of product safety. This was evidenced by a string of congressional hearings (at which Mattel's leadership has testified) and the fact that Speaker of the House Nancy Pelosi called for the resignation of the U.S. Product Safety regulator in November 2007. The outcome of such activities could mean stricter regulations for toymakers.

For instance, on September 12, 2007, Eckert appeared before the Senate Appropriations Committee to defend Mattel's outsourcing of manufacturing to countries like China. At issue was not just Mattel's three recent recalls, but that 177 products from China have been recalled since 2006, a staggering number compared to Taiwan (12) and Mexico (6). Senator Sam Brownback argued that American consumers and legislators were fed up with defective products. Though Mattel claimed it had strict safety inspection procedures, Brownback harangued the company for willingly choosing to manufacture in a country known for low standards and corruption.[68]

On September 20, 2007, both the CPSC and Mattel testified at a House Energy and Commerce Committee hearing investigating lead-tainted children's toys and product recalls. Testimonies are expected to guide lawmakers in discussing tighter import and export regulations.[69] At the hearing, Mattel was chastised by lawmakers. The CPSC will also investigate Mattel to determine whether it should levy fines against the toymaker.

Regulations born from these deliberations could include federally mandated inspections conducted by outside parties and higher penalties for those that fail to comply. Surprisingly, the regulations may receive a warm reception from the affected companies. Industry sources cited by ABC found that Mattel and Hasbro would actually support more stringent regulations enforced by an independent, international regulatory body.[70]

Current Dilemma

In the aftermath of Mattel's repeat recalls and failure to comply with CPSC reporting requirements, Mattel has been criticized for putting the bottom line ahead of customer safety. Parents are wary of toy quality and reportedly less likely to purchase toys manufactured in China during the 2007 holiday season. Working closely with its Chinese suppliers and government agencies operating within the toy industry, Mattel is focusing on realistic quality control solutions for which it can be held accountable. The company faces challenges such as reassuring the public that outsourcing to China is not a high-risk manufacturing move, and that Chinese suppliers and the Chinese government are likewise willing to cooperate. Regaining consumer confidence and controlling the dissemination of product safety information requires strong corporate communicators who can delicately and deliberately balance supplier, customer, governmental, media, and investor relationships.

Chapter 5: Long Case Notes

* This case was prepared by Courtney Woo while a student at the University of North Carolina under the supervision of Dr. Elizabeth Dougall. It was a 2008 Grand Prize winner in the Arthur W. Page Society Case Study competition. http://www.awpagesociety.com/site/resources/case_studies/.

1   "Business Ethics 100 Best Corporate Citizens 2007." *Business Ethics Magazine*, http://www. business-ethics.com/node/75, accessed November 17, 2007.
2   Corporate social responsibility, http://www.mattel.com/about_us/Corp_Responsibility.
3   Company history, http://www.mattel.com/about_us/history, accessed November 17, 2007.
4   Corporate information, Hasbro, http://phx.corporate-ir.net/phoenix.zhtml?c=68329&p=irol-news.
5   Corporate information, Hasbro, http://phx.corporate-ir.net/phoenix.zhtml?c=68329&p=irol-news.
6   "Who we are, what we do," http://www.cpsc.gov/pr/whoweare.html, accessed November 4, 2007.
7   "2007 Performance and Accountability Report," http://www.cpsc.gov/2007par.pdf.
8   "Who we are, what we do," http://www.cpsc.gov/pr/whoweare.html.
9   Section 15 (b) of the Consumer Product Safety Act, http://www.cpsc.gov/businfo/unreg.html.
10 "Guidance for lead in consumer products," http://www.cpsc.gov/businfo/leadguid.html.
11 "CPSC announces final ban on lead-containing paint," September 2, 1997, http://www.cpsc. gov/CPSCPUB/PREREL/prhtml77/77096.html, accessed November 4, 2007.
12 "For kids' sake: Think toy safety," http://www.cpsc.gov/CPSCPUB/PUBS/281.html.
13 O'Donnell, J., "Mattel recalls more toys for lead," *USA Today*, September 4, 2007, http://www. usatoday.com/money/industries/manufacturing/2007–09–04-mattel-toy-recall-lead_N.htm.
14 Jayne, "Mattel recalls more toys for lead."
15 Kavilanz, P.B., "Blame U.S. companies for bad Chinese goods," *CNNmoney.com*, August 14, 2007, http://money.cnn.com/2007/08/14/news/companies/china_recalls/index.htm.
16 "About us, product safety," http://www.mattel.com/about_us/Corp_Responsibility/cr_productsafety. asp.
17 "Code of Conduct," http://www.mattel.com/about_us/Corp_Governance/ethics.asp.
18 Barboza, "Toymaking in China, Mattel's way," *NYTimes.com*, July 26, 2007, www.nytimes.com/ 2007/07/26/business/26toy.htm?pagewanted=all.
19 "The stories behind the Mattel recall," *CSR Asia Weekly*, Vol. 3 Week 32, August 8, 2007, http://www.csr-asia.com/upload/csrasiaweeklyvol3week32.pdf
20 "The stories behind the Mattel recall," *CSR Asia Weekly*.
21 Associated Press, "Fisher Price recalls 1M toys," *CNN.com*, August 1, 2007, http://edition.cnn.com/ 2007/US/08/01/toy.recall.ap/index.html.
22 "The stories behind the Mattel recall," *CSR Asia Weekly*.
23 Fallows, J., "China makes, the world takes," *Atlantic Monthly*, July/August 2007, 48–72.
24 James, "China makes, the world takes."
25 Barboza, "Toymaking in China, Mattel's way."
26 James, "China makes, the world takes."
27 Media Statement, September 21, 2007, http://www.shareholder.com/mattel/downloads/09–21-07 %20China%20Meeting%20Media%20Statement.pdf, accessed November 29, 2007.
28 Merle, R. & Mui, Y., "Mattel and China differ on apology," *The Washington Post*, September 21, 2007, http://www.washingtonpost.com/wp-dyn/content/article/2007/09/21/AR2007092100330.html.
29 Kavilanz, "Blame U.S. companies for bad Chinese goods."
30 Kavilanz, "Blame U.S. companies for bad Chinese goods."
31 Merle & Mui, "Mattel and China differ on apology."
32 Cutlip, S., Center, A. & Brown, G. (2006) *Effective public relations*, Upper Saddle River, NJ: Prentice Hall, p. 407.
33 Fallows, "China makes, the world takes."
34 Cutlip et al., *Effective public relations*.

35   "Toy Info.org frequently asked questions," http://www.toyinfo.org/toy-safety-facts/faq.html#Q18, accessed on November 29, 2007.

36   "2006 Annual Report," http://www.shareholder.com/mattel/downloads/ar2006.pdf, p. 27, accessed November 29, 2007.

37   "Product Recalls," http://service.mattel.com/us/recall.asp.

38   News from CPSC, http://www.cpsc.gov/CPSCPUB/PREREL/prhtml01/01167.html.

39   Casey, N. & Pasztor, A., "Safety agency, Mattel clash over disclosures," *Wall Street Journal*, September 4, 2007, accessed on Factiva at http://wsjclassroomedition.com/monday/mx_07sep10.pdf.

40   Casey, N. & Pasztor, A., "Mattel takes a combative stance defending power wheels safety," *Wall Street Journal*, http://online.wsj.com/article/SB118885453709216163.html, accessed November 11, 2007.

41   Casey & Pasztor, "Mattel takes a combative stance."

42   Casey & Pasztor, "Mattel takes a combative stance."

43   "Mattel seen facing safety probe," *CNNmoney.com*, September 4, 2007, http://money.cnn.com/2007/09/04/news/companies/mattel_cpsc/index.htm.

44   "Toy industry stock prices as a whole decreased after the Mattel recalls in 2007," Toy Industry Association, Inc., http://www.toyassociation.org/AM/Template.cfm?Section=home&pagetype=home, accessed November 26, 2007.

45   Toy Industry Association, Inc., http://www.toyassociation.org/AM/Template.cfm?Section=home&pagetype=home.

46   Richtel, M. & Stone, B., "For toddlers, toy of choice is tech device," *New York Times*, November 29, 2007, http://www.nytimes.com/2007/11/29/technology/29techtoys.html, accessed November 29, 2007.

47   "2006 Annual Report," http://www.shareholder.com/mattel/downloads/ar2006.pdf, p. 6.

48   "Fast track product recall program brochure," http://www.cpsc.gov/businfo/fasttrk.html.

49   "Consumer Relations Answer Center," http://www.mattel.com/safety/us/ accessed November 4, 2007.

50   "Consumer Relations Answer Center," http://www.mattel.com/safety/us/.

51   Quelch, J., "Mattel, getting a toy recall right," *Harvard Business School Working Knowledge*, August 27, 2007, http://hbswk.hbs.edu/item/5755.html, accessed December 8, 2007.

52   "Mattel tackles crisis with solid communication," http://www.mmm-online.com/Mattel-tackles-crisis-with-solid-comms/article/96308/.

53   "Message from Bob Eckert," http://www.mattel.com/message_from_ceo.html, accessed November 29, 2007.

54   "Message from Bob Eckert," http://www.mattel.com/message_from_ceo.html.

55   Media statement, September 21, 2007, http://www.shareholder.com/mattel/downloads/09-21-07%20China%20Meeting%20Media%20Statement.pdf, accessed November 29, 2007.

56   Rooney, "Mattel's recall rebound," http:money.cnn.com/2007/10/12/markets/spotlight.mat/index.htm, *CNNMoney*, October 12, 2002.

57   Casey, N. & Zamiska, N., "China's export problems," *Wall Street Journal*, August 15, 2007, http://online.wsj.com/article/SB118709567221897168.html?mod=googlenews_wsj.

58   Quelch, "Mattel, getting a toy recall right."

59   Story, L., "Mattel official apologizes in China," *New York Times*, September 21, 2007, http://www.nytimes.com/2007/09/21/business/worldbusiness/21cnd-toys.html.

60   Quelch, "Mattel, getting a toy recall right."

61   "Toy safety conference opening remarks," http://www.toyassociation.org/AM/Template.cfm?Section=Toy_Safety&Template=/CM/ContentDisplay.cf m&ContentID=3811, accessed November 26, 2007.

62   "Toy safety facts," http://www.toyinfo.org/toy-safety-facts/faq.html#Q18, accessed November 29, 2007.

63   "Opening remarks, toy safety conference," http://www.toyassociation.org/AM/Template.cfm?Section=Toy_Safety&Template=/CM/HTMLDisplay.cfm&ContentID=3810, accessed November 26, 2007.

64   "Strengthening the toy safety assurance process," Toy Safety Conference, http://www.toyassociation.org/AM/Template.cfm?Section=Toy_Safety&Template=/CM/ContentDisplay.cfm&ContentID=3812.

65   "Grant & Eisenhofer brings investor suit in Delaware against Mattel over company's lapses in reporting problems with defective/hazardous toys," http://www.gelaw.com/Mattel.cfm.

66   "Cutting through the lead: New report says tainted paint very common on toys—Including those on retailers' shelves," *Bulldog Reporter*, http://www.bulldogreporter.com/ME2/dirmod.asp?sid=&nm=&type=Publishing&mod=Publications%3A%3AArticle&mid=8F3A7027421841978F18BE895F87F791&tier=4&id=599C3CE23A8E44D0BCE4233B560D8B6F.

67   "Recent toy recalls threaten sales of Chinese products this holiday season," http://www.harrisinteractive.com/harris_poll/index.asp?PID=833, accessed November 26, 2007.

68   Dart, B., "Mattel CEO defends toy manufacturing occupations in China," *Cox News Service*, September 13, 2007, http://www.coxwashington.com/hp/content/reporters/stories/2007/09/13/BC_CHINA_TOYS13_COX.html.

69   "Committee questions Consumer Product Safety Commission, Mattel on lead-tainted products and toy recalls," http://energycommerce.house.gov/Press_110/110nr89.shtml, accessed November 11, 2007.

70   Reuters, "EU, U.S. seek new global toy safety standards," *ABC.com*, November 9, 2007, http://www.abc.net.au/news/stories/2007/11/09/2086097.htm.

LONG CASE QUESTIONS

1.   Assume that Mattel's crisis is high level and requires "rebuilding" strategy. Did Mattel appropriately apply this strategy? If not, what should it have done differently?
2.   Has this issue been building over a long period of time?
3.   How can Mattel redirect negative media attention to ensure the recall crisis turns into a competitive advantage?
4.   Suppose that in 2008 a Mattel manufacturer operating in China is found to be using lead paint. How should Mattel respond from a corporate crisis communication standpoint?
5.   Did Mattel learn from past mistakes, like its handling of the Power Wheels® recall? Considering its history, was Mattel's 2007 communications plan for a quality control/product safety crisis adequate?
6.   To avoid repeat recalls, how should Mattel handle outsourcing issues? How should it manage Chinese suppliers and contractors?

Chapter 6

Primary Stakeholders, Shareholders and Corporate Governance

LEARNING OBJECTIVES

After reading this chapter you should be able to:

- Understand the types of shareholders and agency theory
- Be aware of the importance of corporate governance
- Appreciate the role played by board of directors and the steps needed to design an appropriate board
- Become aware of the controversial issues associated with executive compensation and the appropriate design of such compensation packages
- Understand the role of ownership structures in corporate governance
- Appreciate how national culture impacts corporate governance around the world
- Read about the future of corporate governance and shareholder rights

PREVIEW BUSINESS ETHICS INSIGHT

The Fall of Nortel

Nortel Network Corporations was a major player in the telecommunications industry in the 1990s. Headquartered in Canada, the company had capitalization in excess of C$350 billion in July 2000. Although a diversified company, Nortel focused primarily in the telecommunications industry. Using a very aggressive acquisition strategy, Nortel quickly grew worldwide acquiring companies linked to their business. Nortel was lauded for its performance and praised by analysts for its "solid sustainable growth." The CEO of Nortel was also praised for his visionary ideas and his deftness in growing Nortel. The company was seen as the pride of Canada as it continued its invincible ascent. Share prices of Nortel tripled in four years and were at a peak of C$200 in 2000.

However, reality soon hit Nortel as its fortune declined quickly in the early 2000s. Why did such a model of growth fall so fast? Why did the company's share fall from its high of C$200 to C$0.67? While thousands of workers were losing their job, Nortel was trying to find ways to prevent its U.K. subsidiary from taking its assets to pay for a shortfall in its pensions.

A look at the company's actions reveals many weaknesses that contributed to its dramatic downfall. However, a major contributing factor to the fall of Nortel was poor governance structure. First, Nortel suffered from overvaluation. Specifically, the company was manipulating accounting figures to inflate share prices way above its true underlying values. Furthermore, managers were smoothing earnings to provide a stable pattern of earnings for Nortel. However, financial analysts were also contributing to the decline. Rather than question high-priced acquisitions of overvalued companies, these analysts justified such prices. As a result, more investors were being duped.

A second major problem at Nortel was the weak role played by its board of directors. The board is typically in put in place by shareholders to monitor the actions of management. Furthermore, it is expected that a board will have individuals with financial expertise to monitor the financials of the firm. Unfortunately, Nortel's board of directors did not have such financial expertise. Furthermore, many of the members of the board had multiple memberships on other boards. As a consequence, they neither had the time nor expertise to perform due diligence in approving Nortel's strategic actions.

A third major factor that contributed to Nortel's decline was its ownership structure. Most companies rely on a combination of individual and institutional investors. However, a large proportion of Nortel's institutional investors were of the transient nature and were more interested in short-term earnings. To satisfy such short-term needs, the company management engaged in manipulation to continue providing the perception of growth at Nortel.

Finally, **executive compensation** played a big role in Nortel's decline. A big component of the executives' compensation level was stock options. However, because the value of stock options is tied to the market share price of a company, managers with stock options have every incentive to maximize the short-term price of a company's share. This was also the case at Nortel, where management were overly optimistic about the company's health and engaged in steps to keep the share price of Nortel growing.

Based on Cohen, T. 2010a. "Regulator acts as recession hits pensions." *Financial Times*, February 23; Duffy, J. and Greene, T. 2009. "Nortel's fall took years to hit bottom." *Network World*, January 19, 26, 3; Forgarty, T., Magnan, M.L., Markarain, G. and Bohdjalian, S. 2009. "Inside agency: The rise and fall of Nortel." *Journal of Business Ethics*, 84, 165–187.

The Preview Business Ethics Insight on pages 256–7 shows the impact of managerial actions on investor well-being. This and other high-profile examples such as Enron, WorldCom, and countless other companies worldwide show the ethical landscape facing investors. Investors or shareholders invest money in companies hoping for a return on their investments in the form of dividends and increased share prices. Managers are hired by shareholders to take the necessary steps to ensure that such benefits are produced for shareholders. However, as the above case illustrates, managers may not always act in the best interest of shareholders. These examples illustrate cases of companies where managers engaged in self-interested behaviors that destroyed shareholder wealth.

In this chapter, we therefore examine the shareholder as a primary stakeholder and the relationship of the shareholder with the company. We will examine the role of shareholders and the responsibilities companies have toward them. You will also read about the many mechanisms that can be put in place to ensure that managers behave in the interests of shareholders. Finally, you will also learn some of the rights shareholders have today.

Next, we examine the relationship between the company and a shareholder by understanding agency theory.

TYPES OF SHAREHOLDERS AND AGENCY THEORY

Shareholders are legal owners of business corporations. As mentioned earlier, shareholders invest their money in businesses hoping for a return on their investment. They believe that such returns will be higher than if they invest their money in alternative forms of investment. As a result, companies can decide to pay part of their earnings back to shareholders in the forms of dividends. However, shareholders also have a "residual claim on a firm's assets and earnings, meaning they get what's left after all other claimants—employees and their pension funds, suppliers, tax-collecting governments, debt holders, and preferred shareholders (if any exist) are paid."[1] In other words, the shares of shareholders are worth the future cash flows after all those payments. Thus, shareholders buy stocks in a company if they believe that the future cash flows will be greater than the payments to lead to an increase in the share prices. If they sell the shares in the future at a much higher price, shareholders also make money.

There are two main types of shareholders: individual shareholders and large shareholders. **Individual shareholders** include regular persons buying and selling shares of any company. Such transactions are usually done through a stockbroker and are typically held in brokerage accounts.

While individual shareholders used to traditionally make up a large proportion of shareholders, the past decade has seen a dramatic growth of large shareholders.[2] **Large shareholders** are typically grouped as blockholders and institutional shareholders. Blockowners are "individuals or corporations that buy firms' shares directly, not through an investment entity."[3] In the U.S., blockholders are defined as any investor with more than 5% equity stake in a firm.[4] We will discuss blockholders in more depth later.

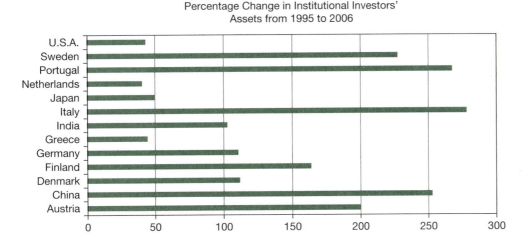

EXHIBIT 6.1—Growth of Institutional Investors Worldwide

In contrast, institutional investors are entities such as mutual funds, banks, pension funds, and insurance companies that invest money on other people's behalf. Extant research suggests that such institutional investors own around 65% of U.S. corporate equity. But is the importance of institutional shareholders only prevalent in the U.S.? Exhibit 6.1 shows the growth in institutional ownership in selected countries from 1995 to 2006.

As Exhibit 6.1 shows, the proportion of institutional investors has grown significantly worldwide. With blockholders, large shareholders constitute an important aspect of ownership structure worldwide. This has important implications for how companies are run. As you will see later, large shareholders can have significant influence on the way companies are run. Such shareholders can hold board of director seats and directly influence the company. However, other large shareholders can have indirect influence by threatening to liquidate their shares.

Given the nature and variety of shareholders and the fact that managers are hired to run companies, the differences in interests between the two groups (shareholders and managers) leads to problematic issues. Specifically, agency theory provides some understanding of how these problems arise. **Agency theory** views the firm as a "legal entity that serves as a nexus for a complex set of contracts among disparate individuals."[5] The contract is often between principals engaging agents to perform some service on behalf of their agents. More specifically, shareholders (the principals) hire top managers and the CEO (the agents) to manage the company. This relationship between shareholders and top management represents the agency problem whereby the interests of the shareholders may not necessarily coincide with the interests of top managers.[6]

According to Tosi,[7] owners of companies, specifically shareholders, face two problems with top management and the CEO. First, there is moral hazard whereby the top management does not put in the right effort or misuses the company resources

BUSINESS ETHICS INSIGHT

Examples of Recent "Moral Hazard"

Many experts see the recent financial institution crash in the U.S. as examples of moral hazard. Most of these institutions (JP Morgan Chase, Morgan Stanley, Goldman Sachs, etc.) had top management supporting the peddling of complex and toxic securities. Executives at banks supported loans to individuals and companies who could barely provide assets to back these loans. The results of such moral hazard have been serious concerns about financial stability in the U.S. and the accompanying housing market crash.

However, as the Preview Business Ethics Insight on pages 256–257 shows, moral hazard is not solely a U.S. phenomenon. The business environment worldwide has experienced serious consequences because of moral hazard on the part of companies. Consider the case of Satyam Computers, an Indian outsourcing company involved in computer systems for many *Fortune* 500 companies. The chairman and chief executive of the company admitted to committing a $1.47 billion fraud. Quarter after quarter, the chairman manipulated numbers to show a rosier picture at Satyam. He inflated profits, claimed cash reserves that did not exist, overstated the money it was owed. The scandal was revealed when he tried to buy two companies owned by his relatives. Shareholders were outraged, leading to a closer auditing of the company's finances and discovery of the elaborate scam.

The results of such moral hazard have been catastrophic for both India and Satyam. India took a large hit because many large multinationals rely on Indian companies for computer services. The reputation of these companies and India have been severely damaged. However, Satyam also suffered because shareholders lost large sums of their investments, while Satyam is still struggling to overcome the scandal. While rivals such as Infosys and Tata Consultancy services have taken advantage of a rebound in outsourcing services, Satyam's tarnished reputation discouraged multinationals from awarding contracts to the company.

Based on Leahy, J. 2009. $1bn fraud at India IT group. *Financial Times*, January 8, 13; Mehra, P. and Sharma, E.K. 2010. "The enemy within: Corporate fraud pops up across India suggesting corruption is rife and regulation needs strengthening." *Business Today*, December; Morrow, R. 2009. "Satyam scandal leaves no place for India to hide." *Asiamoney*, February; Thoppil, D.A. 2010. "Satyam sees U.S. revenues rising." *Wall Street Journal* online, November 29; Tripathi, S. 2009. "India faces an 'Enron moment'." *Wall Street Journal*, January 9, A11.

for their own interests. The Business Ethics Insight on page 260 provides some further insights into recent moral hazard problems.

As the Business Ethics Insight shows, the effects of moral hazard can be very catastrophic for both the company and its shareholders. As we saw in the Preview Business Ethics Insight (pages 256–257), Nortel also suffered considerably because of moral hazard. However, owners can also face an additional problem from CEOs; namely, adverse selection. According to Tosi,[8] adverse selection is the misrepresentation by the CEO of his/her ability to do the work that he/she is being paid for. Consider the case of a firm hiring a new CEO. Generally, candidates for the CEO position may have more information about their true competencies than the company. They may therefore misrepresent that information to be able to get the job. However, as research shows, many companies eventually find out that the new CEO misrepresented himself/herself. This explains the very high rate of dismissal of new CEOs as their companies become aware of their misrepresentation.[9]

As the above discussion reveals, because of the nature of the modern corporation whereby ownership is separated from management, owners face significant problems. Such problems stem from information asymmetry whereby the CEO has private information that is not accessible to the owners. Furthermore, CEOs and top managers can engage in self-interested behaviors that hurt shareholders. However, because owners are not always aware of managers' actions and the outcomes of such actions, it is critical to have systems in place to align the interests of both owners and managers. We therefore look at corporate governance and how its many aspects can solve the agency problem.

CORPORATE GOVERNANCE

Corporate governance refers to the many mechanisms that can be used to align managements' interests with owners' interests. Specifically, corporate governance refers to the system that controls and directs companies' and top managements' actions. How critical is corporate governance worldwide? Consider the Strategic Business Ethics Insight on page 262. It clearly shows the strategic importance of corporate governance, and companies need to ensure that appropriate governance systems are implemented. In the next few sections, we examine some of the key aspects of corporate governance.

Board of Directors

One of the key goals of corporate governance is how to solve the agency problem. Such problems arise because of the conflicts of interests between the principal (shareholders) and agents (top management). This separation of ownership and control often results in managers having increased power.

The **board of directors** is often seen as one of the primary mechanisms to monitor and control the conflict. A board of directors is expected to act in ways that puts

STRATEGIC BUSINESS ETHICS INSIGHT

Strategic Importance of Corporate Governance

Most companies and nations are now expected to have strong corporate governance in place to protect investors and others from corporate and top management misbehavior. In fact, the Organization for Economic Co-operation and Development, a global institution with membership from 34 of the world's wealthiest economies, sees corporate governance as critical to ethics. As sustainability and ethical behavior continue to grow in importance, it becomes a strategic imperative for companies to implement strong corporate governance programs. A key aspect of corporate governance is ensuring that shareholder needs and rights are respected.

Consider the many examples discussed earlier in this chapter. The U.S. banking industry has been very severely impacted by lack of good corporate governance and this has spilled into almost all industries, such as automotive and construction. Companies such as Satyam Computers in India and Nortel in Canada have both suffered financial consequences. Investors and societies have also suffered catastrophic consequences because of the lack of corporate governance. Corporate governance is thus a crucial factor in ensuring strategic success at the company level and survival of industries at the country level.

A recent study provides further insights into the impact of bad corporate governance on firms' strategic health. Investors provide capital to companies and companies are then required to be managed to satisfy investor rights. However, if this contract is violated, shareholders have the right to take the company to court. Bauer and Braun show that filing of large class-action lawsuits against companies has serious consequences for them.[10] A class-action lawsuit results in an immediate drop in stock price that a company never seems to recover from. Furthermore, class-action lawsuits result in declines in both short-term and long-term performance.

Another example of the strategic importance of corporate governance is provided by a large study of Chinese firms undertaken by Lu, Xu and Liu.[11] In that study, the authors find that stronger corporate governance such as more outsiders on the board of directors or appropriate executive compensation are both related to higher exports. This suggests that outside board of directors have potentially better views of the importance of internationalization. Furthermore, when the interests of both executives and shareholders are aligned through an appropriate compensation scheme, CEOs are more likely to see the importance of exporting to grow the firm. This study also shows the importance of strong corporate governance in a firm's future strategic health by going international.

Based on Bauer, R. and Braun, R. 2010. "Misdeeds matter: Long-term stock price performance after the filing of class-action lawsuits." *Financial Analyst Journal*, 66, 6, 74–92; Lu, J., Xu, B., and Liu, X. 2009. "The effects of corporate governance and institutional environments on export behaviour in emerging economies." *Management International Review*, 49, 455–478; Organization for Economic Co-operation and Development. 2010. "OECD Principles of Corporate Governance." http://www.oecd.org.

shareholder interests ahead of their own interests. Thus, a board has a duty of loyalty to shareholders. In fact, many of the corporate governance problems mentioned in this chapter, such as Satyam Computers and Nortel, were the result of a board of directors not properly fulfilling its functions. A board of directors thus fulfills many functions and these functions include:[12]

- Review and provide guidance on all aspects of strategic management such as reviewing the corporate strategy, monitoring and implementing corporate performance, and providing guidance on major strategic decisions such as major capital expenditures, acquisitions of new companies, and divestitures
- Provide guidance on tactical and operational planning such as annual budgets and business plans, setting goals in terms of performance objectives, and reviewing implementation
- Act as advisors to top management and CEO and provide guidance with respect to the above strategic, tactical, and operation issues
- Continuously monitoring the company's other governance practices and making changes as needed
- Providing human resource management expertise such as selection, recruitment, and performance appraisal of the CEO, top management, and other executives
- Performing the important task of determining the executive's compensation and benefits package to align the package with the company's long-term interests
- Assist in special investigations that question top management's integrity such as the recent investigation of the former CEO of Hewlett-Packard and sexual harassment or other major ethical violations on the part of the CEO or top managers
- Have the appropriate financial and accounting expertise to ensure the accurateness and integrity of the company's financial and accounting reporting
- Take steps to ensure that there is a transparent and formal mechanism to elect new board members
- Take every step to make sure that decisions that affect shareholder welfare are made on the basis of due diligence of gathering and considering the required material information
- Recent investigations also reveal that more boards of directors are playing a bigger role in risk management. Such roles involve understanding the many areas of risk for the company and the ways such risks can be minimized
- Conduct regular self-evaluations to ensure that the board is meeting its obligations.

A board of director is, thus, a critical corporate governance mechanism to ensure that interests of shareholders are met. If the above functions are conducted properly, most companies and their shareholders should be protected from managerial mischief. However, the composition of the board is also a key aspect of the effectiveness of a board of directors. We next consider the many issues relevant to the effectiveness of a board of directors.

A first critical issue in board composition is **board independence**. Specifically, many countries now prescribe that a number of the members of a board of directors should be independent.[13] The expectations are that outside boards of directors are more

GLOBAL BUSINESS ETHICS INSIGHT

Board Composition and Firm Performance in Malaysia

It is widely believed that having an independent board with outside board of directors is beneficial for a company. Outside directors have fewer conflicts of interest with current management and are more likely to bring new expertise to the board. In an interesting study of 277 Malaysian firms, Ameer, Ramli, and Zakaria examined the impact of the board of directors on firm performance.[14] The authors considered several types of directors. Specifically, they considered inside directors (those individuals who hold more than 5% of shares and who tend to be typically related to the founding family), non-independent directors (those individuals who are former employees of the company or any of its associated companies), outside directors (individuals who have no ties to the company but represent one of the major institutional shareholders), and foreign directors (director who is a foreign national).

Results reveal that companies with a high representation of outside directors or foreign directors tend to have better performance than those companies that have a majority of inside or non-independent directors. This result is even stronger when the majority of shareholders is made up of a combination of both independent and foreign directors. These results are therefore consistent with the view that outside directors represent a strong mechanism that can adequately solve the agency problems. In the case of Malaysia, foreign directors and those independent directors representing institutional investors are more likely to bring the outside expertise and due diligence required to ensure that management is on track.

Based on Ameer, R., Ramli, F., and Zakaria, H. 2010. "A new perspective on board composition and firm performance in an emerging market." *Corporate Governance*, 10, 5, 647–661.

likely to monitor management and represent shareholder interests. Because of their external nature, board members are less likely to be connected to the current firm's top management. This independence should therefore give such a board of directors a stronger ability to carefully monitor top management's actions without fear of hurting their relationships with the top management. Does the empirical evidence show that board independence is conducive to better protection of shareholder wealth? Consider the above Global Business Ethics Insight.

It clearly shows the benefits of board independence. However, a second critical aspect of a board of directors is the presence of **board diversity**. Most worldwide reforms in corporate governance now require that the different stakeholders are represented on a board of directors.[15] An important aspect of such calls for diversity has been to increase the number of women on such boards. In fact, a recent study of 4,200 global companies found that only 9.4% of directors on these boards are

Percentage of Women Board Members

EXHIBIT 6.2—Fortune Global 200 Companies with the Highest Percentage of Women on Board of Directors

women.[16] Furthermore, a recent study of the *Fortune* Global 200 companies shows that over 77.5% of these companies had at least one woman on their board of directors.[17] However, data from 2006 to 2009 shows that the percentage of women on a board of directors increased by only 1% to 12.2%. Thus, men still hold 87.8% of board seats in the world's largest corporations. Additionally, the study found that Asian companies were less likely to have women on their board of directors. U.S. companies led the world, with around 19.5% of women now holding board seats in U.S. *Fortune* Global 200 companies.

Exhibit 6.2 shows the *Fortune* Global 200 Companies (and their nationality) with the highest percentage of women on their board of directors.

Experts suggest that having women on a board of directors can be very beneficial for companies. In fact, the CEO of Pax World, a leading investor enterprise that undertook the first survey described above, believes that women tend to bring richer ideas to discussions and thus encourage better and more innovative management.[18] Women directors bring divergent experiences to boards and such experiences may help better understand different consumers. Furthermore, it is expected that women are more likely to carefully scrutinize management actions to ensure that the right actions are occurring.

It is generally accepted that the addition of women to a board of directors should positively affect firm performance. However, although the empirical evidence is not overwhelming for this position, recent research done in Singapore suggests that companies that added women to their board of directors experienced higher performance.[19] The same study also found that investors reacted very positively when companies in Singapore announced the addition of women to their boards. Investors also believe that the addition of women will positively affect the long-term prospects of the company.

A third critical aspect of the board of directors is **board size**. Board size is simply the number of members on the board of directors. Pozen mentions that the average board size for the Standard and Poor 500 companies is 11 members.[20] A large board size has many advantages. For example, as O'Connell and Cramer argue, a large board size provides wider expertise to a board of directors.[21] Furthermore, having a large board means having access to a wider network. Such access can also provide a board and its company with greater external linkages.

Despite these advantages, Pozen notes that many of the financial institutions that recently failed had very large boards.[22] For instance, Citigroup had 18 members. Having large boards does present some disadvantages.[23] First, large boards are more likely to have members engage in social loafing. In other words, some members may choose not to fully participate in board activities because they can "hide" behind the large number of members. Second, a large board may also result in higher levels of conflict. Such conflict may also make it more difficult for team members to develop the necessary cohesion they need to function effectively. Finally, large boards also make it much more difficult for team members to communicate and reach decisions. Larger sizes may make reaching consensus somewhat problematic.

Does board size thus negatively affect firm performance? In an interesting study, O'Connell and Cramer studied most of the Irish companies quoted on the Irish Stock Exchange.[24] They did indeed find that the larger the board size, the worse is a company's performance. However, this negative impact is much smaller for smaller companies. This lends support to the notion that large board sizes does impact performance negatively because of the many disadvantages. For smaller firms, larger board sizes may be necessary for them to take advantage of the network afforded by larger boards.

Given the above-mentioned problems associated with larger boards, Pozen argues that research on group dynamics suggests that the best group size is around six or seven.[25] A group this size can work together such that individual members are accountable for their contributions to larger decisions and can therefore take personal responsibility for group decisions. Furthermore, this size makes it easier for teams to reach consensus in a reasonable amount of time. Thus, critical decisions can still be made.

A final and generally ignored aspect of a board is **board expertise**. For a board of directors to operate effectively, the board needs the necessary expertise to understand the industry the company is operating in to have the ability to make decisions of strategic importance. Pozen further argues that many boards actually lack members with the sufficient expertise to adequately understand the business. He notes, for instance, that the board of Citigroup in 2008 had excellent board members from many other industries, such as a chemical company and a telecommunications company, but only one with expertise in financial services. This lack of expertise could have been a factor in the problems Citigroup eventually faced.

Given the above issues, what issues should a company take to form the best board? The following lists some of the key considerations based on Pozen and Waller:[26]

- Have a board with six to seven members. As argued earlier, larger boards have too many disadvantages that exceed the advantages brought by a larger group. A smaller size board has more chances at succeeding.

- Get the right mix by bringing in people with new expertise. It is important to have a strong balance of personalities and skills in the group. Furthermore, it is critical to have the right balance with independent directors to get outsiders' perspectives to objectively understand firm decisions.
- Have board members with sufficient expertise so that they can adequately understand the industry and ask the right questions. Board members with expertise can provide insights into new areas or niches that are not apparent to current management.
- Have board members representing the stakeholders the company will serve. Have an adequate number of women on the board.
- Have board members with accounting and financial expertise. Decisions often involve understanding financial implications of what will be done. Someone with the expertise to understand cash-flow statements and other financial reports is critical.
- Explore new channels when recruiting new board members. A company should make use of its professional network to make sure that the right candidate is hired.
- Encourage board members to commit their time to making meetings work. The necessary time needs to be invested so that the board member can understand the business and how both internal and external factors are affecting the company. Such deep understanding of a company can only come with significant study.

The above list describes some of the characteristics of the board that enhance success. However, a company also has several responsibilities to ensure that the board works well. First, the company should provide the board with the right types of information in a timely manner. The board should be fully informed of the company's health and where the company is going in terms of its strategy. Second, the board responsibilities and roles should be clearly defined. Be sure that board members know their roles and how to communicate with each other. Finally, a company should play an active role in the process. Boards are not created to rubber-stamp decisions. Rather, they should be made up of bold people with an understanding of the industry and visionary ideas of where the company should be going.

Executive Compensation

Executive compensation, which refers to the pay, perks, and benefits given to top executives in a company, is a second important aspect of corporate governance. As argued earlier, investors give top executives of a company control over their assets in the form of investments. Top managers can take advantage of investors because of information asymmetry.[27] Specifically, top executives have access to information about the company's situation and direction that investors do not generally have access to. Executives can thus use this information asymmetry to manipulate stock prices to give investors a rosier picture of the company. Executive compensation is thus a mechanism whereby the interests of shareholders can be aligned with the interests of top executives.

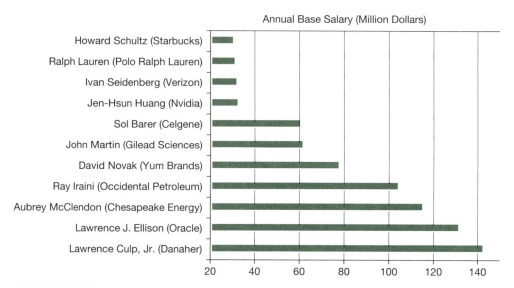

Annual Base Salary (Million Dollars)

EXHIBIT 6.3—U.S. Executive Compensation

Executive compensation remains one of the most controversial aspects of corporate governance. Critics routinely argue that executives earn too much money. This is further exacerbated by the recent banking crisis and the findings that banking executives continued to received very high bonuses despite accepting government bailouts. An examination of the latest data on executive compensation in the U.S. provides further insights into the issue. Exhibit 6.3 shows the executive compensation for the highest paid CEOs in the U.S.

Extant evidence suggests that such high levels of compensation are not limited to U.S. corporations. Consider the Global Business Ethics Insight on page 269.

Despite these examples, most experts still agree that U.S. CEOs make much more than their foreign counterparts. Strier mentions that in 2006 the average U.S. CEO earned 475 times the average employee pay.[28] However, this ratio is much smaller in other nations.[29] For instance, CEOs in Japan earn 11 times the average employee. For European countries such as France, Germany, Belgium, and Italy, the ratio is less than 40 to 1. Finally, a CEO in the United Kingdom earns around 22 times the average employee.

There is clearly a big difference between CEO pay and the average worker in most societies. This is one of the most important criticisms leveled against companies regarding executive compensation. Are CEOs really worth 475 average U.S. employees? Furthermore, given the many recent scandals and the banking crises, many believe that the high levels of compensation led to such excesses. Specifically, such high pays have encouraged CEOs to take excessive risks to keep companies growing.[30]

At a strategic level, high CEO pay is also very damaging to a company's shareholders. As Strier argues, the high salaries paid to executives represent losses in the form of lost dividends and earnings for shareholders.[31] Furthermore, the high disparity between

GLOBAL BUSINESS ETHICS INSIGHT

Executive Compensation Worldwide

While executive compensation receives significant attention in the U.S., high executive compensation is not limited to the U.S. In fact, shareholders and critics both decried the recent payment allocated to CEO Brady Dougan of the Credit Suisse Group. CEO Dougan received around $17.9 million in cash and stock for 2009. However, although the company argues that the CEO took the bank out of financial distress into a stronger position, critics have argued that such excesses are the main factors behind the recent financial crisis. Swiss lawmakers are thus discussing ways to legislate new salary rules to cap pay.

The Australian government has also decided to toughen rules on executive pay. It proposed a number of new reforms that are expected to keep executives' salary in check. For instance, shareholders will now have more power to be able to vote on executive compensation. Furthermore, measures will be implemented to force executives to return bonuses if financial statements done when the bonuses were given were misleading. Finally, companies that do not respond to shareholder concerns regarding salaries are expected to be penalized.

The European Union is also taking a tough stance on executive pay, especially those of bankers. The Committee of European Banking Supervisors helped draft the new legislation. For instance, banks are now required to limit executive bonuses to only a maximum of 20% as upfront cash. Other rules are being implemented to make executives' pay more reasonable.

Based on Curran, E. 2010. "Australia to toughen rules on executive pay." *Wall Street Journal* online, April 16; Mijuk, G. 2010. "Credit Suisse CEO earns $17.9 million." *Wall Street Journal* online, Mar 25; Munoz, S.S. 2010. "Europeans stay tough on pay rules." *Wall Street Journal*, December 1, B3.

CEO and average employees may result in a decrease in employee morale and thereby employee productivity. While most employees are currently experiencing pay decreases and even layoffs, employees become very resentful when CEOs continue to be awarded large salaries and benefits.

Despite these critics, some argue that high executive compensation is justified. For instance, Farid et al. mention that stock values have grown astronomically over the past 25 years, thereby justifying the increase in pay level to those who made such growth possible.[32] Furthermore, many argue that CEOs and top executives have rare skills and that they devote their entire lives to the company. These factors are also seen as justification for high pay.

Nevertheless, to fully understand the criticisms against executive compensation, it is also important to note the forms of CEO compensation. While most CEOs and

Bonus and Other Incentives as a Percentage of
Base Salary

CEO	Percentage
Lawrence Culp, Jr. (Danaher)	
Sol Barer (Celgene)	
Aubrey McClendon (Chesapeake Energy)	
David Novak (Yum Brands)	
John Martin (Gilead Sciences)	
Ivan Seidenberg (Verizon)	
Ralph Lauren (Polo Ralph Lauren)	
Jen-Hsun Huang (Nvidia)	
Howard Schultz (Starbucks)	
Ray Iraini (Occidental Petroleum)	
Lawrence J. Ellison (Oracle)	

100 200 300 400 500 600 700 800

EXHIBIT 6.4 — Bonus and Other Benefits as a Percentage of Base Salary for Top 11 U.S. CEO Earners

executives earn a base salary, they also earn significant bonuses and other benefits, such as club memberships, use of corporate jets, and tax preparation. Exhibit 6.4 displays the bonus and other benefits as a percentage of the base salary for the top 11 earning CEOs in the U.S.

As the exhibit shows, CEOs earn significantly more above and beyond their base salary. Experts believe that such bonuses are some of the main factors behind CEOs' extremely risky actions. One of the dominant forms of compensation on top of base salary is stock options. **Stock options** are stocks awarded to the CEO, who then has the ability to sell the stock at a future date. However, many companies have allowed their CEOs to backdate these stock options to enable the CEO to make more money when they sell their stocks. In other words, when the companies grant stock options to their CEOs, they allow the CEO to backdate the price of the stock to a much lower price. In fact, Collins, Gong, and Li report that the board of United Health allowed its former CEO to choose the day of the option grant and several stock options were dated back to the year's lowest price.[33] The CEO then sold the stocks at a much higher price and earned a significant profit.

Strier (2010) argues that stock options provide corrupting incentives to encourage CEOs to manipulate accounting figures ("cook the books") in order to boost the short-term price of stocks.[34] CEOs are thus encouraged to manipulate earnings, backdate options, and engage in unprofitable mergers. Such short-term actions are made at the expense of long-term profitability and growth. Although these actions may increase share price in the short term, they ultimately undermine shareholder wealth.

Executive compensation will continue receiving negative attention as critics continue decrying such excesses. For any multinational, it therefore becomes important to design a compensation package appropriate enough to retain the best CEOs but reasonable enough not to invite criticisms. However, such packages will likely remain very large relative to the average employee. Nevertheless, companies will need to address a number of issues as they devise such packages and these include:[35]

- Aligning COE incentives with long-term health and profitability of companies. Although this remains a difficult task, many companies are abandoning compensation practices that promote short-term gains. As an example, more companies are abandoning the use of stock options in favor of deferred stock units. Deferred stock units are said to more align investor and CEO interests because executives lose as much as investors if shares lose value. This loss is less apparent for stock options.

- Most compensations decisions are made by the board of directors. Boards of directors are therefore increasingly being asked to be fair, accountable, objective, and transparent about the determination of CEO and executive compensation. Experts agree that directors should be selected based on their loyalty to shareholders rather than the CEO.

- Become more aware of recent regulations. For instance, the U.S. saw the passing of the Dodd-Frank Act, which places many new boundaries on executive compensation. For instance, CEOs are increasingly being asked to hold on to their stocks until they retire. Many companies are adopting stock ownership guidelines for CEOs and executives to prevent focus on short-term gains. Furthermore, the Dodd-Frank Act contains "clawback" policies whereby executives are required to reimburse any compensation that was awarded as a result of erroneous financial results.

- Review perquisite policies of compensation packages. Because of shareholder and employee revolt, more companies are being asked to review their policies regarding generous perquisites provided to CEOs. Companies are finding it increasingly difficult to fund benefits such as expensive country club memberships and use of corporate jets when employees are being laid off.

- Adjusting pay plans in response to changing conditions. Many compensation plans were relatively inflexible in that executives would get the agreed-upon pay despite poor performance. Consider that former CEO Stan O'Neal of Merrill Lynch left the company with a retirement package worth $160 million although the company suffered one of its biggest losses.

- Give shareholders the means to vote on CEO and executive compensation. Shareholders should have some say in terms of generous compensation packages and the notoriously generous golden parachutes. This will then give shareholders an opportunity to express their approval (or disapproval) of a compensation plan.

Ownership Structure

While most of the corporate governance studies have focused on board of directors and executive compensation as main corporate governance mechanisms, **ownership structure** is also an important mechanism to control managers. Ownership structure refers to the primary way that ownership of shares of the company is structured. One way the interests of shareholders and managers can be aligned is where shareholders become large owners of the company. According to Connelly et al., such shareholders will often become owners to achieve key financial objectives.[36] There are many different types of ownership structures and we therefore examine some of these critical forms of ownership and the likely impact on the company.

The first form of ownership structure is **blockholders**. As we discussed at the beginning of the chapter, blockholders are those shareholders that have more than 5% equity stake in a company. A review of corporate governance worldwide shows that there are three main types of blockholders: corporate blockholders, family block-holders, and state blockholders. All three forms of ownership are guided by the owner's desire to better monitor management. However, some blockholders can also get access to private benefits that may not always be available to minority shareholders.

According to Connelly et al., corporations often acquire significant ownership in a company and become **corporate blockholders** as a prior step to actual taking over a target company. Consider, for instance, the case of the French luxury company Louis Vuitton Hennessy Moët (LVHM), which recently acquired a 17% stake in Hermès, the famous French scarf maker. LVHM hopes to eventually acquire the company. However, a corporation may also buy a minority stake in another company before selling the shares. Both forms of ownership provide the target firm with fresh capital. Nevertheless, the target company may also be subjected to more control from the firm buying the shares. Thus, there is potential for resources to be diverted to benefit the company acquiring the shares.

A second and very popular form of blockholder worldwide is the **family blockholder**, where a single family is a major owner of a company. While most share ownership in the Anglo countries such as the U.K. and the U.S. is more of the dispersed nature, whereby a large number of shareholders own small percentages of equity in a company, many European nations see a more dominant form of family ownership. Lazarides et al. thus report that, while only 11% of firms in the U.S. are owned by families, ownership percentage is more than 35% in Europe, with a family ownership percentage of 43% in Germany and 68% in Italy.[37]

Family ownership modifies the corporate governance issues discussed earlier. While dispersed ownership in the U.S. and the U.K means that the needs of shareholders and managers have to be aligned, family ownership poses a host of other problems.[38] Often, the family owners control managers through voting rights. Some family firms can also be managed by the family founders, thereby aligning interests of owners and managers. Furthermore, the family owners can use insider information to buy equity in other promising firms or redirect profits to their own affiliates.

The major challenge with regards to family ownership is the protection of minority shareholders. As Johnson et al. mention, minority shareholders often have no voting rights on how the company is managed and what strategic direction the company takes. Furthermore, majority shareholders have the ability to expropriate earnings through the form of profit reallocation, assets misuse, and selling parts of the firm to other firms at below market prices. Thus, the challenge for corporate governance with regards to family ownership is to ensure that the needs of the minority shareholders are not being subordinated to satisfy only majority shareholders. Nevertheless, Johnson et al. suggest that the influence and grip of a family on family-owned companies is very difficult to control and that minority shareholders will often endure such control.[39]

Consider the Global Business Ethics Insight on page 273.

GLOBAL BUSINESS ETHICS INSIGHT

Family Businesses and Shareholders

A majority of India's companies are family owned. However, family ownership comes with major risks for outside shareholders. Founders of these companies are often interested in seeking global sources of finances. But the founders are unwilling to give up control to others and often want the final say in cash flow matters. As a result, they often misstate financial reports and engage in complex transactions where subsidiaries are involved in questionable business with each other. Furthermore, outside auditors or outside directors are often appointed by the founding family and are reluctant to protect minority shareholders.

Consider the case of Satyam Computers mentioned earlier. The chairman stole profits from the company and tried to purchase other debt-laden companies owned by his sons. Furthermore, the auditors (Pricewaterhouse Coopers) turned a blind eye to these transgressions even though hundreds of millions of dollars were missing. The result of such unethical behavior resulted in a $1.5 billion loss for shareholders.

Family ownership is also the dominant form of company ownership in Japan. A 2009 study by the Tokyo Stock Exchange revealed that 54% of all listed companies did not have a single outside director working on their board. As a result, Japanese business culture has been very insular and companies have always been very secretive. Nevertheless, recent rules are now pressuring these companies to adopt better checks and balances.

The recent case of Seiko shows that family ownership does not hurt only the shareholders. Seiko, founded in 1881, has been family owned and controlled over the past 120 years. A look inside Seiko's culture revealed a very authoritarian and dominating top director, Ms. Unoura, who reportedly bullied executives. However, no one dared challenge that individual because she was protected by her mentor, Mr. Hattorri, the company chairman and grandson of Seiko's founder. Whenever Ms. Unoura had disagreements with an executive, she would inform Mr. Hattorri of her frustrations. Mr. Hattorri would then follow her advice of either firing or demoting the executive. As a result, the company had a mentally distressed workforce and talented executives were quickly leaving the company. Given these circumstances, the only outside director of Seiko recently teamed up with Mr. Shinji Hattori, a fourth-generation member of the founding family, to oust the elder Mr. Hattorri and Ms. Unoura. Such changes have proved tough but necessary for Seiko.

Based on Kripalini, M. 2009. "India Inc.'s murky accounting." *Bloomberg Business* Week online, January 15; Osawa, J. 2010. "Sahke-up at Seiko reflects changing culture." *Wall Street Journal*, June 23, B1.

A third and final form of blockholder ownership is **state ownership**. State ownership is more popular in emerging nations, whereby the government owns a significant percentage of a company. Consider that China, for instance, has transitioned from socialism to capitalism by keeping ownership interests in many companies. This has allowed the government to keep control over key business areas in the country.

However, developed nations like the U.S. and the U.K. have seen an increased growth in state ownership. Consider the U.S. government's decision to purchase shares of General Motors as a result of the financial crisis, thereby infusing some state-ownership in GM. According to Johnson et al., the motivation for governments to become part owner of companies is driven by a desire to correct market failures.[40] Such failures may occur in industries that are deemed too big to fail (e.g., banking or automobile in the U.S.) or in industries that are characterized as monopolies.

Existing research suggests that state ownership generally results in problems for a company's well-being. Connelly et al. discuss current studies that show that state ownership typically faces soft budget constraints.[41] Furthermore, state-owned companies suffer from a lack of innovation and suffer from poor financial performance and corruption.

Su, Li, and Li discuss why this occurs in Chinese state-owned enterprises.[42] China has a large number of state-owned enterprises. However, the government has tasked a smaller number of bureaucrats to monitor these state-owned enterprises. Unfortunately, because of the small number of officials, the close monitoring of the assets of these enterprises and their managers is impossible. As a result, monitoring of top management tends to be weak and these government officials generally do not place emphasis on profit maximization. Consequently, these state-owned enterprises are less likely to be run efficiently and there is higher likelihood of managers using the enterprises for their own benefits.

In addition to blockholders, another form of firm ownership that can be used for corporate governance purposes is **private equity**.[43] Private equity refers to the various forms of private funding that are available to companies that are not necessarily publicly traded. The forms of private equity vary greatly depending on the stages the company is at. Although there seems to be a number of types of private equity, Bruton, Filatotchev, Chahine, and Wright distinguish between two main types of private equity; namely, the business angel and the venture capital.[44]

When a venture is too small or risky, there are often "business angels" who provide private equity funds. Business angels tend to know the entrepreneur personally and thus invest their own money in the company. They are more likely to invest on the basis of trust with the entrepreneur.[45] Furthermore, business angels are more patient investors who do not necessarily have a timeline determining when they take their investments out if the company.

In contrast, venture capitalists are those individuals who invest money in a company on behalf of other companies. While business angels tend to rely on informal monitoring methods, venture capitalists emphasize more formal contractual methods of monitoring. Furthermore, the primary motivation for such professional investors is mostly capital gains.[46] Bruton et al. also note that venture capitalists are both principals (they invest their money in companies and expect management to run the company efficiently) and agents (acting as agents of their investors).[47] As agents, they face pressures to make the appropriate exit from the company to gain as many returns as possible on their investments. However, they also face long-term pressures to raise future funds.

Given the differences between business angels and venture capitalists, the corporate governance is also based on what each form of private equity is trying to achieve. As such, because business angels are more often interested in the long-term success of the company, they are more likely to use their long-term commitment and trust as the basis to influence management of the company. In contrast, venture capitalists are more likely to place direct control on management because of a firm's dependence on such sources of funding. Venture capitalists thus rely on more formal forms of monitoring.

CORPORATE GOVERNANCE AND GLOBALIZATION

As multinationals continue their global expansion in trading with new countries, it will become more critical to understand corporate governance worldwide. Corporate governance will remain a key aspect of how companies need to be governed in order to run a company efficiently and effectively.[48] Furthermore, corporate governance will be used as the means to ensure that the needs of all stakeholders and shareholders are met. In this section, we examine how corporate governance differs worldwide.

Research has devoted significant attention to how countries differ on corporate governance. However, a significant aspect of the research has been to examine how countries differ in terms of the structure and composition of the board of directors. Such an emphasis is not surprising given the critical role of the board of directors in corporate governance. In this context, research has examined how national culture impacts differences in boards of directors worldwide. National culture represents the beliefs, norms, and values of individuals within a country. Such values, norms, and beliefs are likely to affect how boards of directors are structured.

Hofstede argues that national culture can be represented by a number of ways in which countries are different.[49] According to Hofstede, power distance is an important aspect of national culture and refers to the degree to which a society accepts that power differences exist and that such power distance is distributed unequally. In such societies, people accept that there are individuals who have more power and authority and that these individuals have the right to exercise such authority.

In a large-scale study involving 399 multinational firms, Li and Harrison found that countries with high power distance are more likely to have a board of directors with consolidated leadership structures whereby the CEO is also the chair of the board.[50] This is consistent with the view that, in high power distance, few have authority and privileges that are accepted by others. Having a CEO who also serves as chairperson of the board is consistent with the CEO using his/her authority and stature on other board members. Furthermore, companies in high power distance societies are also more likely to have boards with a higher percentage of outsiders on the board of

Cultural Dimension	Level	Example of Countries	Corporate Governance Findings for High Levels
Power Distance	High	Malaysia, Guatemala, Mexico, India	Consolidated leadership structure where CEO is also chair of board
		Singapore, Brazil, France, Hong Kong	Higher percentage of outside directors
	Low	Austria, Israel, Denmark, Ireland	
		Sweden, Norway, Finland	
Uncertainty Avoidance	High	Greece, Portugal, Guatemala	Consolidated leadership structure where CEO is also chair of board
		Uruguay, Spain, France, Chile, Israel	More outsiders on board of directors
	Low	Singapore, Jamaica, Denmark, India	
		Hong Kong, U.K., U.S.A., Canada	
Individualism	High	U.S.A., Australia, U.K., Canada	Smaller number of board members
		Italy, Belgium, France, Norway	Consolidated leadership structure
	Low	Ecuador, Peru, Taiwan, South Korea	
		Singapore, Chile, Hong Kong	
Masculinity	High	Japan, Austria, Italy, Mexico, U.K.	Consolidated leadership structure
		Germany, U.S.A., Australia, Jamaica	Higher percentage of outside directors on board
			Larger size of board of directors
	Low	Sweden, Norway, Netherlands	
		Denmark, South Korea, Chile	

EXHIBIT 6.5—National Culture and Impact on Corporate Governance

276

directors. This is also consistent with the view that there should be an appropriate display of power within companies. Having outside directors reflects the influence of powerful individuals outside a company.

Uncertainty avoidance is another cultural aspect that has been studied. Uncertainty avoidance reflects the degree to which individuals within a country are comfortable with ambiguity and uncertainty. In high uncertainty avoidance countries, people are less likely to be comfortable with uncertainty. Rules and procedures are thus relied upon to reduce uncertainty and unknown situations.

Research shows that countries high in uncertainty avoidance tend to have boards where the CEO also acts as the chairperson of the board.[51] This is consistent with the view that having a CEO acting as chairperson of the board reduces ambiguity about the position. Furthermore, high uncertainty avoidance is also linked to having more outsiders on the board of directors. This increase in outsiders provides the company with added expertise and capabilities to reduce risks and ambiguities.

Another important national culture aspect is individualism.[52] Countries that are high on individualism tend to value individual freedom. In contrast, countries that are low on individualism tend to place emphasis on interpersonal relationships and group affiliations are highly preferred.

Research shows that countries that are more individualistic tend to have smaller boards, the CEO acting as chairperson of the board of directors, and a smaller percentage of outsiders on the board of directors.[53] Such results are consistent with the view of individual freedom (one person as both CEO and chairperson of the board) and less emphasis on group affiliations (higher percentage of insiders).

Finally, another cultural aspect studied is masculinity. More masculine societies tend to embrace values that are stereotypically male. As such, more masculine societies tend to value aggressiveness, competition, ambition, assertiveness, and the acquisition of material goods. In contrast, less masculine societies tend to be more concerned about quality of life and harmonious interpersonal relationships.

In the study of a large number of multinationals, Li and Harrison (2008, 2010) show that countries with high masculinity tend to have a board of directors with a higher percentage of outside directors (i.e., reflecting of power and ambition), consolidated CEO and chairperson position (again reflecting values of personal dominance and aggressiveness), and larger board of directors (i.e., consistent with the view that larger shows more power and ambition).[54]

As the above shows, there are clearly differences in terms of corporate governance worldwide. As multinationals engage in more cross-border trade, they will have to understand such differences to operate effectively worldwide. Exhibit 6.5 shows examples of countries on the above discussed national culture aspects and the implications for the board.

THE FUTURE OF CORPORATE GOVERNANCE

Corporate governance will continue to grow in importance. As more of the emerging nations strive to present an environment conducive to business, there will be an increased reliance on corporate governance to demonstrate that such aims are being achieved. Consider, for example, that India has been implementing many new corporate governance policies to ensure that shareholders do not lose their investments because of managerial misbehavior. Similarly, countries with dominant family owner-ship structures are also implementing measures to ensure that the needs of minority shareholders are heard and respected. It should also be noted that the Organization for Economic Co-operation and Development sees the failure of corporate governance as the root cause of the economic crisis in most Western societies. Implementing appropriate corporate governance measures is seen as a way to prevent such disasters occurring again.

Many countries have seen investors lose their investments as a result of management misbehavior. As a consequence, more countries are considering shareholders when they implement new corporate governance measures. It is therefore becoming more critical for multinationals to consider shareholder rights, which include the following:[55]

- Shareholders have the right to purchase shares. They should be able to secure registration for their shares. They should also be able to freely buy or sell such shares.
- Shareholders have the right to timely and accurate information from the company. Such information is necessary to allow shareholders to make informed decisions about what they want to do with their shares.
- Shareholders have the right to share in the profits of the corporation.
- Shareholders have the right to participate in key decisions related to new strategic directions of the company. Shareholders should be provided with accurate and timely information to help them make such decisions.
- Shareholders have the right to vote at board meetings. They should be informed of meeting times and agenda and be given the opportunity to voice their opinions on decisions being considered.
- Shareholders have the right in determining compensation packages for executives. They should be given the means to voice their opposition to compensation packages that they deem too excessive. In fact, more countries are now giving shareholders the right to also vote on compensation of the board of directors. Exhibit 6.6 shows selected countries and the rights shareholders now have.
- Shareholders have the right to participate in the nomination and election of board members. Information regarding new board election should be provided to shareholders in a timely manner.
- Recent regulation in the U.S. now allows large shareholders to nominate at least 25% of board members of a company. Such rights, known as proxy access, give large shareholders the right to have a say on who is nominated for board positions.
- Shareholders have the right to freely exercise their ownership rights. Such action should be facilitated by companies.

Finally, corporate governance is also seen by both investors and governments as a critical way to curb corruption. Companies with strong governance mechanisms are more likely to have systems in place to prevent misappropriation and misuse of assets. For instance, strong corporate governance can prevent corruption such as stock options

Country	Right to Vote On Renumeration of Board	Right to Vote On Renumeration of Management	Right to Vote On Stock and Option Plans
Austria	√		√
Denmark	√		√
France	√		√
Germany	√		
Netherlands	√		√
Norway	√	√	√
Sweden	√		√
Switzerland			
Canada			√
U.S.A.			√
Australia			
Japan			
U.K.			√
Italy	√	√	√

EXHIBIT 6.6 — Selected Countries and Shareholder Rights

backdating and self-dealings on the part of top executives.[56] Similarly, Halter et al. discuss how stockholders are now pushing for corporate governance in Brazilian firms.[57] Corruption is rife in Brazil and investors are wary of the risks of unethical behavior on the part of firms in which they own stocks. They are therefore pushing for more of these companies to adopt more ethical practices and implement strong corporate governance.

CHAPTER SUMMARY

In this chapter, you learned about shareholders as a primary stakeholder. You read about the types of shareholder. However, you were also exposed to agency theory and how the theory helps explain the problematic issues facing shareholders. Specifically, managers are hired to manage a firm by shareholders. Nevertheless, shareholders' and managers' interests may not diverge and managers can sometimes make self-interested decisions. Corporate governance is thus seen as a way to resolve this agency problem.

The first aspect of corporate governance discussed in this chapter is the board of directors. You learned about the critical role played by a board of directors and the many aspects of the board (board independence, board diversity, board size, and board expertise). Many experts see board diversity and specifically increasing women on such boards as a critical step to create the appropriate board. You also read about the issues that companies need to keep in mind when they design a board of directors.

The second critical aspect of corporate governance you learned about is executive compensation. You read about the controversial issues with executive compensation (high ration of CEO salary to average worker, large benefits package, stock options, etc.) and the extent of these problems worldwide. You also learned about the arguments for and against high executive compensation. Finally, you read about some of the issues companies should keep in mind when designing top executives' compensation. As executive compensation gets more attention globally, these issues will have to be paid attention to.

A final critical aspect of corporate governance discussed is ownership concentration. You read about the different types of blockholders (corporate blockholder, family blockholder, and state blockholder). You also learned about the many problematic issues associated with the family blockholder (minority shareholder rights not respected) and state ownership (lack of innovation and corruption). Finally, you also learned about the importance of private equity as a form of ownership.

Given the importance of corporate governance worldwide, you also learned about the impact of culture on corporate governance. You read about the different forms of cultural dimensions such as uncertainty avoidance, individualism, and masculinity and how they affect corporate governance.

In the final part of the chapter, you read about the future of corporate governance. You learned about the sustained importance of corporate governance worldwide. As more emerging nations try to shape an environment conducive to business, more of them will rely on stronger corporate governance mechanisms. Furthermore, given that many shareholders were severely impacted by the last economic crisis, you also read about the many shareholder rights being enacted worldwide. Finally, you also learned about the importance of corporate governance to curb corruption worldwide.

NOTES

1   Martin, R. 2010. "The age of customer capitalism." *Harvard Business Review*, January–February, 58–65 (at 61).
2   Johnson, R.A., Schnatterly, K., Johnson, S.G. & Chiu,S. 2010. "Institutional investors and institutional environment: A comparative analysis and review." *Journal of Management Studies*, 47, 8.
3   Pergola, T.M. & Verreault, D.A. 2009. "Motivations and potential monitoring effects of large shareholders." *Corporate Governance*, 9, 5, 551–563 (at 553).
4   Connelly, B.L, Hoskisson, R.E., Tihanyi, L. & Cresto, T. 2010. "Ownership as a form of Corporate Governance." *Journal of Management Studies*, 47, 8.
5   Fama, E.F. & Jensen, M.C. 1983. "Separation of ownership and control." *Journal of Law and Economics*, 26, 2, 301–325.
6   Nyberg, A.J., Fulmer, I.G., Gerhart, B. & Carpenter, M.A. 2010. "Agency theory revisited: CEO return and shareholder interest alignment." *Academy of Management Journal*, 53, 5, 1029–1049.

7 .Tosi, H.J. 2008. "Quo Vadis? Suggestions for future corporate governance research." *Journal of Management and Governance*, 12, 153–169.

8 Tosi, "Quo Vadis?"

9 Zhang, Y. 2008. " Information asymmetry and the dismissal of newly appointed CEOs: An empirical investigation." *Strategic Management Journal*, 29, 859–872.

10 Bauer, R. & Braun, R. 2010. "Misdeeds matter: Long-term stock price performance after the filing of class-action lawsuits." *Financial Analysis Journal*, 66, 6, 74–92.

11 Lu, J., Xu, B. & Liu, X. 2009. "The effects of corporate governance and institutional environments on export behavior in emerging economies." *Management International Review*, 49, 455–478.

12 Aguilar, M.K. 2010. "Special investigations 101: The board's role." *Compliance Week*, November, 48–49; Whitehouse. T. 2010. "Boards turn to self-evaluation to regain trust." *Compliance Week*, 49–50; Yammeesri, J. & Herath, S.K. 2010. "Board characteristics and corporate value: evidence from Thailand." *Corporate Governance*, 10, 3, 279–292.

13 Wagner, A.F. 2011. "Board independence and competence." *Journal of Financial Intermediation*, 20, 71–93.

14 Ameer, R., Ramli, F. & Zakaria, H. 2010. "A new perspective on board composition and firm performance in an emerging market." *Corporate Governance*, 10, 5, 647–661.

15 Francouer, C., Labelle, R. & Sinclair-Desgagne, B. 2008. "Gender diversity in corporate governance and top management." *Journal of Business Ethics*, 81, 83–95.

16 Governance Metrics International. 2010. "Women on boards." http://www.gmiratings.com.

17 GlobeWomen. 2010. http://www.globewomen.org.

18 Governance Metrics International. "Women on boards."

19 Kang, E., Ding, D.K. & Charoenwong, C. 2010. "Investor reaction to women directors." *Journal of Business Research*, 63, 888–894.

20 Pozen, R.C. 2010. "The case for professional boards." *Harvard Business Review*, December.

21 O'Connell, V. & Cramer, N. 2010. "The relationship between firm performance and board characteristics in Ireland." *European Management Journal*, 28, 387–399.

22 Pozen, "The case for professional boards."

23 O'Connell & Cramer, "The relationship between firm performance"; Pozen, "The case for professional boards."

24 O'Connell & Cramer, "The relationship between firm performance."

25 Pozen, "The case for professional boards."

26 Pozen, "The case for professional boards."

27 Ryan, L.V., Buchholtz, A.K. & Kold, R.W. 2010. "New directions in corporate governance and finance: Implications for business ethics research." *Business Ethics Quarterly*, 20, 4, 673–694.

28 Strier, F. 2010. "Runway CEO pay? Blame the boards." *The IUP Journal of Corporate Governance*, 3, 8–27.

29 Strier, "Runway CEO pay?"; Martin, "The age of customer capitalism."

30 Farid, M.; Conte, V. & Lazarus, H. 2011. "Toward a general model for executive compensation." *Journal of Management Development*, 30, 1, 61–74.

31 Strier, "Runway CEO pay?"

32 Farid et al., "Toward a general model for executive compensation."

33 Collins, D.W., Gong, G. & Li, H. 2009. "Corporate governance and backdating of executive stock options." *Contemporary Accounting Research*, 26, 2, 403–445.

34 Strier, "Runway CEO pay?"

35 Chodhury, D.S. 2009. "Director compensation: the growing popularity of deferred stock units." *Ivey Business Journal* online, January/February; Lynn, D.M., Parris, B.C. & Thorpe A.D. 2010. "Revisiting your key corporate governance and disclosure policies." *Corporate Governance Advisor*, 18, 6; Ryan, L.V., Buchholtz, A.K. & Kolb, R.W. 2010. "New directions in corporate governance and finance: implications for business ethics research." *Business Ethics Quarterly*, 20, 4, 673–694.

36 Connelly et al., "Ownership as a form of Corporate Governance."

37 Lazardies. T., Drimpetas, E. & Dimitrios, K. 2009. "Ownership structure in Greece: Impact of corporate governance." *IUP Journal of Corporate Governance*, 8, 3 & 4.

38 Johnson et al., "Institutional investors and institutional environment."

39 Johnson et al., "Institutional investors and institutional environment."

40 Johnson et al., "Institutional investors and institutional environment."

41 Connelly et al., "Ownership as a form of Corporate Governance."

42 Su, Z., Li, S.Y. & Li, L. 2010. "Ownership concentration and executive compensation in emerging economies: Evidence from China." *Corporate Governance*, 10, 3, 223–233.

43 Morrell, K. & Clark, I. 2010. "Private equity and the public good." *Journal of Business Ethics*, 96, 249–263.

44 Bruton, G.D., Filatotchev, I., Chahine, S. & Wright, M. 2010. "Governance, ownership structure, and performance of IPO firms: The impact of different types of private equity investors and institutional environments." *Strategic Management Journal*, 31, 491–509.

45 Bruton et al., "Governance, ownership structure, and performance of IPO firms."

46 Connelly et al., "Ownership as a form of Corporate Governance."

47 Bruton et al., "Governance, ownership structure, and performance of IPO firms."

48 Strange, R., Filatotchev, I., Buck, T. & Wright, M. 2009. "Corporate governance and international business." *Management International Review*, 49, 4, 395–407.

49 Hofstede, G. 1980. *Culture's consequences: International differences in work-related values*. Newbury Park, CA: Sage.

50 Li., J. & Harrison, J.R. 2008. "Corporate governance and national culture: A multi-country study." *Corporate Governance*, 8, 5, 607–621; Li., J. & Harrison, J.R. 2008. "National culture and the composition and leadership structure of boards of directors." *Journal of International Corporate Governance*, 16, 5, 375–385.

51 Li & Harrison, "Corporate governance and national culture"; Li & Harrison, "National culture."

52 Hofstede, *Culture's consequences*.

53 Li & Harrison, "Corporate governance and national culture"; Li & Harrison, "National culture."

54 Li & Harrison, "Corporate governance and national culture"; Li & Harrison, "National culture."

55 Organization for Economic Co-operation and Development (OECD). 2009. "Corporate governance and the financial crisis: key findings and main messages." http://www.oecd.org; Ryan et al., "New directions in corporate governance and finance"; Steinberg, R.M. 2010. "Shareholders, be careful what you wish for." *Compliance Week*, December, 46–47.

56 Bishra, N.D. & Schipani, C.A. 2009. "Strengthening the ties that bind: Preventing corruption in the executive suite." *Journal of Business Ethics*, 88, 765–780.

57 Halter, M.V., Coutinho, M.C. & Halter, R.B. 2009. "Transparency to reduce corruption?" *Journal of Business Ethics*, 84, 375–385.

KEY TERMS

Agency theory: views the firm as a legal entity that serves as a nexus for a complex set of contracts among disparate individuals.

Blockholders: shareholders that have more than 5% equity stake in a company.

Board diversity: reforms in corporate governance that require that different stakeholders, especially women, are represented on a board of directors.

Board expertise: the necessary expertise needed by the board to understand the industry the company is operating in to have the ability to make decisions of strategic importance.

Board independence: prescription that a number of the members of a board of directors should be independent from the company.

Board of directors: often seen as one of the primary mechanisms to monitor and control the agency conflict.

Board size: the number of members on the board of directors.

Corporate blockholders: corporations with significant ownership in a company.

Corporate governance: the many mechanisms that can be used to align managements' interests with owners' interests.

Executive compensation: refers to the pay, perks, and benefits given to top executives in a company.

Family blockholder: single family is a major owner of a company.

Individual shareholders: include regular persons buying and selling shares of any company.

Large shareholders: blockholders and institutional shareholders that buy firms' shares directly, not through an investment entity.

Ownership structure: primary way ownership of shares of the company is structured.

Private equity: various forms of private funding that are available to companies that are not necessarily publicly traded.

Shareholders: legal owners of business corporations.

State ownership: government owns a significant percentage of a company.

Stock options: stocks awarded to the CEO, who then has the ability to sell the stock at a future date.

DISCUSSION QUESTIONS

1. Briefly define shareholders. What are the two different types of shareholders? Which type has more control on a company and why?
2. What is agency theory? Discuss the two problems faced by shareholders as they deal with top management.
3. What is corporate governance? What are some of the major benefits of having strong corporate governance systems?
4. What is a board of directors? Discuss five important roles played by a board of directors.
5. Discuss three key aspects of a board of directors. How does each of these aspects contribute to stronger company performance?
6. What are some of the key issues a company needs to consider when designing a board of directors? Be as specific as possible.
7. Why is executive compensation worldwide such a controversial issue? Discuss two arguments to support the high levels of executive compensation.
8. What is ownership concentration? Briefly discuss each of the three types of blockholders and the challenges they present for corporate governance.
9. How is corporate governance different worldwide? Be specific by discussing the link between national culture dimensions and how they affect corporate governance.
10. What are shareholder rights? Discuss five rights shareholders should have.

INTERNET ACTIVITY

1. Go to the Organization for Economic Co-operation and Development website: http://www.oecd.org.
2. Find the general corporate governance report and the report for a specific region (e.g., Africa, Asia, or Latin America).
3. What do you learn about the importance of corporate governance from the general report?
4. Describe the situation in the region you researched. Why is corporate governance the way it is in that region?
5. Discuss some of the recommendations provided by the OECD to improve corporate governance in that region. Present some of your own recommendations to the class.

For more Internet Activities and resources, visit the Companion Website at www.routledge.com/cw/parboteeah.

WHAT WOULD YOU DO?

International Negotiations

You come to the U.S. to get your Bachelor's degree in International Business. After graduation, you get a job with a local company that is interested in expanding operations in your native country. You do very well during your first year and you are soon invited to meet with the CEO to discuss investment opportunities in your native country. You are very valuable to the company as you speak the local language and could also act as a trusted interpreter.

The CEO mentions that he has been approached by a company in your native country. The owner of that company is interested in selling the company. You therefore arrange for negotiations with the owner of the company. Your CEO and relevant personnel have done extensive research on the local company and strongly believe that acquisition would be very beneficial to your company. The local company has some technology that will allow your company to develop expertise in new areas.

Negotiations proceed smoothly and you have the impression that the deal will be concluded soon. However, the owner of the local company approaches you and mentions in your native language that he is willing to seal the deal if $1 million is transferred to a private bank account. He argues that he has run the family business for a long time and deserves an additional incentive compared to the other shareholders of his company. He also tells you that he will not sign unless he is given the money.

What would you do? Do you mention the $1 million to your CEO? Do you try to reason with the owner?

BRIEF CASE: BUSINESS ETHICS INSIGHT

The Olympus Scandal

On February 10, 2011, Olympus made a surprising announcement. Bypassing several domestic senior managers, the Japanese camera maker decided to appoint the 50-year-old Briton Michael Woodford as its company president. The outgoing president saw Woodford as the person who would be able to cut costs at Olympus and provide a more international perspective to the company. However, on October 14, 2011, Mr. Woodford was terminated at an Olympus board meeting. The board meeting only lasted ten minutes and Mr. Woodford was not even allowed to speak. One of his fellow board members even told him to "catch a bus to the airport"! Why did Olympus fire Mr. Woodford so soon after he was hired?

During his tenure, Mr. Woodford alleges that he discovered several irregularities and decided to investigate these issues. For example, he found that Olympus had paid over $2.88 billion for four small and midsize companies in businesses unrelated to their core camera business. Olympus predicted highly optimistic profits from these companies and ended up writing these companies off. However, most troubling was that Olympus paid about $2 billion for a U.K. company developing "non-invasive" surgical cameras. However, in making the deal, Mr. Woodford alleges that Olympus paid $678m fee to a financial advisor for help with the deal. Such a fee was seen as very unusual given that it represented almost seven times Olympus' profits in 2010. Furthermore, he believes that the money actually went to criminal organizations.

Major shareholders of Olympus are obviously very disturbed by these allegations. The value of the company has halved since the news broke out. Larger shareholders are demanding investigations into these acquisitions and why the company paid such high fees for these acquisitions. For instance, Nippon Life Insurance, Olympus' largest shareholder (with 8.3% shares) is requesting details about these deals. Such questioning is rare in the Japanese environment, where domestic investors are typically very passive.

Despite the scandal, many argue that the Japanese have been very sluggish in embracing progress in corporate governance. Olympus is still denying any wrongdoing and argues that they fired Mr. Woodford for his failure to master Japanese culture. Furthermore, the scandal was barely mentioned in Japan, and the Tokyo Stock Exchange has still not declared Olympus a candidate for delisting. As of October 25, 2011, none of the Japanese government officials have commented on the matter.

Based on *Financial Times*, 2011. "Olympus." Online edition, October 22; Inagaki, K. 2011. "Olympus is under pressure." *Wall Street Journal*, online, October 21; Soble, J., Soble, L., and Whipp, J. 2011. "A camera-maker obscurer: The Olympus affair." *Wall Street Journal* online, October 22.

BRIEF CASE QUESTIONS

1. Do you think that Olympus is justified in terminating Mr. Woodford? What other information do you need to make this determination?
2. Why do critics contend that the Japanese have been more reluctant to adopt progressive corporate governance practices? What Japanese cultural elements make such changes difficult?
3. Which elements of corporate governance were weak in this case and allowed the scandal to occur?
4. What changes would you suggest so that such corporate misbehavior does not occur again?

LONG CASE: BUSINESS ETHICS

HEBEI DAWU GROUP: BUILDING THE FIRST FAMILY BUSINESS CONSTITUTION IN CHINA

Background

Sun Dawu, the founder of Hebei Dawu Group, smiled after the third board of directors election was successfully held on December 16, 2008. It had been witnessed by many media. The day after the election at the Dawu Hot Spring Restaurant, Chen Jianfen, a reporter from *Chinese Entrepreneur*, saw Liu Jinhu asking one of the clients to tell the chief executive officer (CEO) that his salary and benefits were too low. Liu, a manager at Dawu Animal Feed Company, had been elected to the board of directors the day before. During the election, Sun used his preferential nomination right to nominate Sun Erwu and Liu Ping as the candidates for the positions of CEO and general manager (GM), respectively. Although those who had disagreed could vote for other candidates, both were unanimously elected. This triggered much discussion among the experts and journalists present. Facing the unexpected challenges, Sun Dawu, who was ready to retire after achieving his success in his career, pondered again about his "Family Business Constitution," the only one of its kind in China.

On June 6, 2004, Sun Dawu celebrated his 50th birthday. He wrote a poem to express his feeling: "I reflect after surviving the storm. The sun can travel in the sky because of blessings from all gods. I wonder how my fate will be. All that I can do is to pray for people who pass by!"

One year earlier, Sun had been deprived of his personal freedom because his "Grains Bank" was deemed to be involved in illegal fundraising. He spent his 49th birthday in prison. All senior executives in Dawu Group were arrested, and the government even urged the company to replace its legal representative. However, Sun was eventually released after six months. Why was he so sentimental on his 50th birthday? It seemed to be public knowledge that Sun's release was a result of an agreement among various parties. In fact, Sun's original three-year prison sentence with four-year probation indicated a somewhat relaxed policy toward private fundraising, and was also considered to be a signal of reform in China's financial industry.

Facing the unexpected imprisonment of Sun Dawu, the younger members of the Sun family including Sun Meng had decided to make some big changes to their future plans. Sun Meng was Sun Dawu's eldest son. He had recently graduated from college, and had already obtained his visa to pursue further education in Australia starting in July. Yet, with his father behind bars and his mother on the run, 25-year-old Sun Meng had to assume the critical appointment of acting president. He insisted on returning the position to his father upon the latter's release, yet this idea was rejected by Sun Dawu. It seemed obvious to everyone that it would only be a matter of time before Sun Meng took over the business, as this was the convention in Chinese families. However, for Sun Meng, who had not acquired enough working experience, managing a company worth several hundred million yuan was such a daunting task that the pressure became overwhelming. Thus, Sun Meng resigned from the position a few months later, showing his determination to acquire more front-line experience.

Sun Dawu realized that the problem was not only about his son's change in position, but also about the critical issue of selecting and developing his company successors, which was of great importance to the entire family group's sustainable development of the family business. Dawu Group had encountered major challenges in 2003 but had luckily survived. Reflecting on what he had experienced, Sun Dawu considered the succession issue and the prospects of his family business ever since 2004. Dawu Group was on the brink of a fateful revolution.

The Development of Dawu Group

Dawu Agriculture and Animal Husbandry Group Ltd. (Dawu Group) was based in Langwuzhuang Village, Xushui County, Hebei Province, 110 kilometers or a 90-minute drive from Beijing. It was a high-tech private enterprise with multiple businesses. Its founder, Sun Dawu, was from the farming and feed processing industries. As the leader of the Sun family, Sun Dawu had managed to make Dawu Group into one of the top 500 largest private enterprises in China after more than two decades of hard work. Industry authorities, including the All-China Federation of Industry and Commerce (ACFIC), rated Dawu Group as one of "China's Top 100 Most Vigorous Enterprises" for five consecutive years (from 2004 to 2008).

However, being a successful family business was not the only factor that made the Group legendary: it was also famous for its unique system, "Family Business Constitution." Sun Dawu created the system under the influence of both traditional Chinese Confucianism and Western political systems. The system had not only been functioning well, but with ongoing development and improvement had also attracted constant attention from local and international media.

Start-up Stage: From the Wife's Contracting and the Husband's Resignation to the Couple's Venture

In 1970, 16-year-old Sun Dawu started his eight-year military career. He joined the Chinese Communist Party after only two years due to his outstanding performance, and eventually became a battalion commander. Demobilized in 1978, Sun returned home to work in the Agricultural Bank of China and then the Rural Credit Cooperative (RCC) as a "civil servant."

In 1985, the Chinese economy was utilizing the popular "contract system." Bids were solicited for tracts of idle land. In Sun's village, the reduction of contract prices to six yuan per *mu* (about 667 square meters) had been broadcast for three months, but no one was willing to place a bid. Sun Dawu persuaded his wife, Liu Huiru, to seize the opportunity. They assumed the position of contractor under Liu Huiru's name, with four other farmers as joint investment partners, after collecting 10,000 yuan and raising another 20,000 yuan from loans.

Meanwhile, they set up Langwuzhuang Farm and a small feed processing plant, and hired more than 10 workers to raise 54 pigs and 1,000 chickens. The farm suffered a 16,000 yuan loss in the first year as a result of poor management. The other four shareholders decided to withdraw their money, but Sun Dawu insisted that his wife take over the business. The number of chickens on the farm steadily grew from 5,000 to 10,000, peaking at 300,000. As a consequence, not only was Liu Huiru able to repay the 20,000 yuan loan, she also earned 10,000 yuan as an initial net profit.

At the time, Sun was still working in an RCC branch. Sun decided to resign and help his wife, as he saw the business getting bigger and Liu Huiru becoming tired because of the heavy workload. Sun filed for a no-pay administrative leave in 1989, and eventually resigned the following year. Many people around Sun thought he was behaving foolishly, but Sun Dawu and his wife were determined to start their own venture.

Expansion and Rapid Development: From a Small Home Business to a Large Family Enterprise

Between January 18 and February 28, 1992, Chinese Premier Deng Xiaoping made a series of speeches in his Southern Tour, encouraging Chinese people to end the fights between the public and private sectors. Sun's business began to boom at that time. At the beginning, the couple kept their earnings of several hundred thousand yuan in a safe. When they made more money, they deposited it in banks. Over time, they became very successful. Sun Dawu's two younger brothers, in turn, also achieved local success. His younger brother, Sun Erwu, ran a prosperous small business, whereas another younger brother, Sun Zhihua, had a bright future as deputy head of Rongcheng County.

As far as Sun Dawu was concerned, the three brothers should have had bigger dreams than those minor accomplishments. He told his two brothers, "Let's work together and set up a great business! Individual wealth can never compare to prosperity in the community, so we should help all the people here to get rich as well." Sun's two brothers joined the group in July 1992. Other family members followed. Thus, Dawu Group was formed.

At this stage, Sun's business took the leap from a small home business to a rapidly developing family business. In 1994, Sun Dawu set up the Dawu Vocational School that provided free education to hone local talent, thus leading Sun to start his enterprise down a path where people who got rich earlier could help those who had not. In less than three years, more than 3,000 people received technical training in farming. In 1995, Sun Dawu was named the "Chicken-raising Champion of Hebei Province" and chairman of the Baoding Poultry and Egg Association. Dawu Group was ranked 224th in China's Top 500 Private High-tech Enterprises by ACFIC. Sun Dawu believed that "private businesses should not target merely at private prosperity; in fact only their form of production and management is private; what private businesses create should also be counted into social wealth." He likewise formulated his own philosophy of not aiming at profits, but at development.

Up until 1998, Dawu Vocational School had been a Provincial and Municipal Model School, National Training Base, and UNESCO's (United Nations Educational, Scientific and Cultural Organization) Corresponding Base for Research and Training Centre of Rural Education. In the same year, Dawu School was established. Within three years, the student enrolment increased from 165 to more than 1,800, and the school became a comprehensive one with a kindergarten, a primary school, a junior high school, and a senior high school. Many buildings were built, including a restaurant with a 1,000-seat capacity, a cafeteria, and teaching and dormitory buildings. It was then that some media started to name the village where Dawu Group was located "Dawu Village."

Unexpected Crisis and Critical Turning Point: The Suffering and Rebirth of Dawu Group

For 18 years after its establishment in 1985, Sun Dawu's business had never suffered any financial loss. By 2002, Dawu Group had more than 1,500 employees, with fixed assets worth more than 100 million yuan and more than 9.8 million yuan in profits. On May 27, 2003, Sun Dawu was arrested and was detained for 158 days, as his "Grains Bank" was suspected to have been involved in illegal fundraising.

With Sun having left, the machines ground to a halt, and the workers were forced to quit. An appalling disaster seemed to be awaiting Sun Dawu's family business. The winery and cornstarch plants had to shut down; the feed company witnessed a substantial reduction in customers. Even worse, a significant drop in enrollment in Dawu School (with only six pupils enrolled in the first grade) led to a halt of the jointly sponsored educational projects with Canada. With the business going downhill, some workers sought other jobs. Even those who chose to stay had to accept the fact that their salaries would be greatly cut. In fact, two-thirds of the employees in each section were laid off, the construction crew was dismissed, and more than 100 workers at the winery were forced to leave their positions.

Right after the inspection, the government's liquidation and auditing report showed that Dawu Group's fixed assets were valued of 110 million yuan. Nevertheless, after Sun Dawu's arrest, his business suffered a loss of 5.84 million yuan, which was the first financial loss in its history. In total, Dawu Group suffered a loss of almost 20 million yuan. Sun Dawu's business plummeted drastically.

To revitalize his business, Sun Dawu, after his release, started to give serious thought to the firm's reform plan. Hence, Sun's long-brewing plan of "Family Business Constitution" was implemented on a trial basis in November 2004. The same year, Dawu Group's sales went up to 84 million yuan, with 6 million yuan in net profit. In the following year, the business successfully passed the ISO9001:2000 international quality management system certification and ranked 52nd in the selection of "China's Top 100 Most Vigorous Enterprises," held by four industry authorities, including ACFIC. Its products were named "Hebei Province Brand Name Products." More than 20 scientists and technical experts served in Dawu Group's panel tasked with the breeding of "939 Chickens." The farm raised 55,000 sets of "Dawu Jingbai 939" progenitor chickens and sold 1.5 million sets of parent chickens annually across more than 10 provinces and regions in Northern, Eastern, Southern, Northeastern, and Northwestern China. In 2008, the Dawu hatchery boasted more than 100 sets of the most advanced hatching equipment in China and provided 18 million healthy commercial chickens every year. By the first half of 2007, Dawu Breeder Company had sold 11 million "939 Breeding Stock Chickens" to 106 cities and towns in 15 provinces.

The Increase of Community Wealth: From a Rural Dream to an Urban Legend

In 2008, there were eight subsidiaries and 17 factories under the governance of Dawu Group, including Dawu Feedstuff Co. Ltd., Dawu Poultry Breeding Co. Ltd., Dawu Food Co. Ltd., Dawu Fertilizer Co. Ltd., and Dawu Crop Breeding Company, as well as Dawu School, Dawu Hot Spring Holiday Resort, and Dawu Construction Company. The Group had established a vocational school, and a hospital, and had a fleet of company cars and trucks. By 2010, Dawu Group's comprehensive services had successfully covered the primary secondary, and tertiary education industries.

Sun Dawu categorized his business strategies into four stages: 1) making profit by combining breeding, raising, and processing; 2) developing by integrating poultry breeding, feed manufacturing, and food companies; 3) upgrading by covering primary, secondary, and tertiary education; and 4) increasing wealth for the community, that is, constructing the new homeland of Dawu City, an urban community where people could lead a peaceful and harmonious life. Sun Dawu hoped that his employees could consume in Dawu City instead of saving their money in banks. Therefore, people could turn individual wealth into community wealth shared by every member. He also wanted to attract new consumers from outside Dawu City who would substantially add to the wealth in Dawu City.

Enterprises might prosper and perish; however, it was believed that Dawu City would become a small but stable society once construction was completed. Dawu Hot Spring Holiday Resort was built in 2006. Dawu Sci-Fi Park, a 3D cinema, and a 4D cinema had all been put into use. A dome cinema was to be completed in 2009, as well as a golf course. All the new projects that Sun Dawu had carried out were taking him closer to his ideal society, which featured "harmony between labor and capital, the poor and the rich, government and citizens."

The Family Business Succession: The "Family Business Constitution"

The idea of the "Family Business Constitution" of Dawu Group was initiated during Sun Dawu's imprisonment in 2003. At that time, Sun had been mainly engaged in farming and the feed processing business, as there was great demand for grains. However, none of the local banks was willing to grant loans to Sun due to the high-risk nature of his business. There was once a very popular saying in the Chinese banking industry: "No matter how large the family fortune, never include those with fur and feathers!" Hence, raising funds turned out to be Sun's biggest obstacle.

To resolve the feed shortage, Sun Dawu began to borrow grains from the local villagers. They called on other villagers to deposit their corn in Sun's business, which made a convenient "Grains Bank" for the local people. Sun promised the villagers that they could withdraw their grains anytime within three months, while grains still kept in the bank after three months would be turned into the Group's borrowings from villagers, for which they could gain interest. In addition, if at the time of grains deposit the market price for the grains was 1 yuan per kilogram, and after three months the price rose to 1.6 yuan per kilogram, then the withdrawal price would be calculated as 1.6 yuan per kilogram. If, after three months, the prevailing grains price fell to

0.4 yuan per kilogram, then the "Grains Bank" would still pay the price of 1 yuan per kilogram to the villagers. Lending vouchers (or IOUs) would be recognized by the People's Court as evidence for "Deposit Receipts."

As the scale of Sun's business got bigger, the workers in his firm also started to deposit their salaries and grains in the firm, thus encouraging even more villagers to come to Sun with their money, with the understanding that the money they deposited was considered as lending to Sun's business. Then, Sun Dawu decided to raise more funds through the market. The Group recruited agents and set up a few financing agencies. From January 2000 to May 2003, by offering lending rates higher than bank deposit rates, the Group issued 1,627 IOUs and raised 13,083,161 yuan in finds, involving a total of 611 people.

On May 29, 2003, as president of Dawu Group, Sun Dawu was accused of "illegally withdrawing public deposits" and was arrested by local police. The borrowing activities were later determined by the People's Court of Xushui County as withdrawing public funds in a disguised form "without the approval of People's Bank of China." The Group had issued credentials under the name of IOUs, which were in essence "Deposit Receipts." Not only did the Group provide rates higher than bank deposit rates, but it also made promises to the public that no "interest tax" would be levied. The People's Court of Xushui County made the first judgment based on provisions of the Criminal Law of the People's Republic of China. Hebei Dawu Agriculture and Animal Husbandry Group Ltd. was found to have committed the offense of "illegally drawing public deposits" and was fined 300,000 yuan; Sun Dawu was also accused of illegal fund-raising and was sentenced to a three-year imprisonment with a four-year probation, as well as a fine of 100,000 yuan.

Sun never stopped worrying about the future of Dawu Group throughout the 158 days he spent in jail. At that time, all senior managers, including his two brothers, were put into prison, and the firm was temporarily taken over by the government. Three months later, however, the manager appointed by the government retired due to health problems. Sun Dawu's eldest son, Sun Meng, then only 25 years old and just graduated from college, had to take over the Group in this critical circumstance. Joining him in the management team was Sun Meng's cousin, Liu Ping (Sun Dawu's wife's niece, who was then the manager of the Breeding Stock Company).

When Sun Dawu was released half a year later, he was surprised to see that none of the members from senior management had left his Group; and when the accounts were reopened, there were very few mistakes. Sun and his wife were deeply touched. After the downfall and the rebirth of his business, Sun realized that he had to establish a management system that fitted Dawu Group better. Only this could ensure the business's prosperity in the long run. It took Sun a year to formulate the Group's future plan, including a system reform.

Tough Choice between "Splitting" and "Completeness"

As Sun was formulating a new management system, his family members' opinions about the Group's future diverged a lot. Sun Dawu was still serving his sentence, so he could not assume his post as the Group president. He had to step down aged 49.

Being young and inexperienced, Sun Meng felt inadequate to manage such a large enterprise worth tens of millions of Renminbi. The increasing pressure eventually turned him against the idea of continuing with the position. Sun Meng tried to resign several times.

Meanwhile, Sun Dawu's brothers, together with many other veterans in the Group, all favored a joint-share system. They disagreed with Sun Dawu on keeping the enterprise private. Sun had also tried introducing such systems as the senior joint-share system and family joint-share system, but he found all of them difficult to carry out because there would always be too many conflicts between individual interests and responsibilities. Due to the requests from companies' veterans and the disputes among family members, many family joint-share systems would eventually break down once the businesses were passed down to the succeeding generations. In Sun's eyes, a joint-share system would divide the enterprise's assets, resulting in not only family alienation but also losses of many development opportunities for the Group. It would be a shame if things had to turn out this way. Sun felt that he was in a big dilemma: whether to pass the business down to his son or to other family members.

Sun's wife asked him, "Can you find a way to keep what it is now and never, ever let it be split? If our sons are capable of establishing their own businesses, then let them do it on their own. If they're not capable enough, then just let them enjoy a cozy life in the family business." The very honest words of Liu Huiru inspired Sun Dawu, which made him think further whether the business should be kept whole or run under the joint-share system.

Enlightenment from History and Reference from China and Abroad

Sun Dawu was always interested in the studies of Chinese history and, in fact, was deeply influenced by Confucianism from ancient China. The "Incident at Xuanwu Gate" story shed light on his thinking. Li Yuan, the first emperor in the Tang Dynasty, had three sons: the eldest, named Li Jiancheng, the second, Li Shimin, and the youngest, Li Yuanji. Following the Chinese tradition of passing the throne down to the eldest son, Li Yuan proclaimed Li Jiancheng the new emperor. However, Li Yuan's second son, Li Shimin, had made a great contribution to the establishment of the new empire and had gained ample support from all generals and officials. Li Shimin killed his two brothers, forcing his father to abdicate, and then ascended the throne himself.

This episode in history about the discord in the imperial family made Sun Dawu consider the situation of his family business. He viewed his family as a country: there were many things in common between a family business and an emperor's big country. Looking back at the succession issues in many countries and families, all of them centered on whether to pass the throne to the eldest son or to the most talented. Sun regarded family businesses, especially large and medium-sized ones, as an integral part of society. Meanwhile, they also mirrored every aspect of a society. While a society was an eternal enterprise, people had to admit that a family was a miniature society. Only by getting rid of the inappropriate convention of choosing between the eldest son and the most talented executive, and combining the current social situation, could a business develop in a healthy and sustainable way.

Sun also studied carefully the "Constitutional Monarchy" in the United Kingdom, the "Separation of Powers" in the United States, and the "Central Government System of Three Councils and Six Boards" in the Sui Dynasty in ancient China. The "Constitutional Monarchy" promoted the separation of ownership and management control, imposing restrictions on imperial power and returning governance rights to the people. Meanwhile, the "Separation of Powers" practiced checks and balances among different power groups in order to maintain a stable system in administrating a country. The "Central Government System of Three Councils and Six Boards" in ancient China used a similar system of separation of powers to balance the powers of prime ministers and councils while protecting sovereignty (i.e., "Zhongshu Council" drafted the imperial edicts, "Menxia Council" reviewed the edicts, and "Shangshu Council" implemented the orders from the emperor).

Sun did a thorough study and analysis of references from historical stories and cases about the succession issue in many other companies. He also took into consideration the unique characteristics of Dawu Group. Then a brand-new concept began to emerge more clearly in his mind. That was how he created and established the "Family Business Constitution" in November 2004.

The Structure and Content of the "Family Business Constitution"

The core concept of Sun Dawu's "Family Business Constitution" was separating the rights of ownership, decision-making and operations, thus creating a stable system in which the three powers could co-exist while checking and balancing each other at the same time. The constitution was the foundation of the system and was placed at the top of the "Family Business Constitution" hierarchy. The board of supervisors, board of directors, and board of executives acted as the corresponding entities of the three powers. The centralization of the three powers took place under the control of the highest authority—the joint boards council. The three boards were all under this management system, each enjoying one and only one of the rights. They were also accountable for all the staff in the Group, as well as the enterprise and the society. Their rewards were closely related to the business's profitability. The Constitution could only be revised if the equity owners, the three boards, and 70% of the staff with more than five years' tenure unanimously approved. Sun Dawu and his wife, Liu Huiru, jointly possessed the equity, which would be inherited by their descendants. The Constitution also covered the production management and meeting systems.

Components, Functions, Rights, Benefits and Terms of the Three Boards

Under the Constitution, the components, functions, rights, benefits, and terms were formulated as follows.

The board of supervisors mainly consisted of the Sun family members, whose duty was to draft and revise general rules and regulations, as well as to monitor the board of directors and board of executives from legal, institutional, and moral perspectives. The supervisors were also responsible for overseeing finance and equities. Members of the board of supervisors, as supervisors of the other two boards, could enjoy supervisor subsidies, as well as year-end bonuses and performance-based commissions.

The board had ownership of the business, yet had no control over decision-making and operations. The general elections of the supervisors were held every three years. The chief supervisor (CS), vice-supervisor, and other supervisors could all participate in re-elections. The CS, who had the right to draw 10% of the Group's gross profit as public welfare funds, was to respect the decision-making rights of the CEO (the head of the board of directors) as well as the operational decisions of the general manager (the head of the board of executives). The administrative expense budget of the supervisors would be the same as that of the other two boards.

The board of directors was composed of directors elected by staff in the company. All directors were responsible for developing the strategic goals and direction of the Group, as well as making investment decisions of subsidiary companies. They were also responsible for selecting the top leaders for each subsidiary company, deciding on annual profit targets and making bonus allocation plans. Members of the board of directors could enjoy director subsidies as well as use both public and private cars. A CEO holding the position for more than two terms consecutively or accumulatively, and other directors holding the position for more than eight terms, would be entitled to retirement benefits. Dawu Group also encouraged the children of the directors to study abroad and to start their own businesses. Funds of 300,000 to 1 million yuan were reserved for their future education and businesses. The board of directors could make administrative and strategic decisions, but did not have any ownership or operational power. The directors' term was two years, whereas the CEO's was four years. All of them could participate in re-elections. In addition, the CEO could nominate several vice-directors as his assistants. The assets the CEO could deploy were not to exceed the total amount of the Group's profit plus depreciation in the past year. The CEO was monitored by the board of supervisors, and was to respect the operational decisions of the GM. The CEO had no right to dismiss the GM.

The board of executives was made up of the top leaders of subsidiary companies and office directors. All executive board members were to coordinate in raising and using funds and ensure the efficient implementation of projects and tasks, all in compliance with the decisions made by the board of directors. The executives on the board were entitled to performance-based bonuses and year-end bonuses. At retirement, a GM who had held the position for more than three terms would be able to enjoy the same benefits after his retirement. Board members who had made great contributions could also enjoy the pay level of directors. The board of executives only had power in operational issues with no ownership or administrative rights. The GM had a four-year office term and could be re-elected. He could also nominate several vice-executives as his assistants. The upper limit of funds the GM could deploy was 300,000 yuan. Signatures of two board chiefs were required if 300,000 to 1 million yuan was to be used. If it was more than 1 million yuan, then all three board chiefs needed to give consent.

The Implementation of the "Family Business Constitution"

Of the three boards, the CEO and the GM were elected, whereas the CS was appointed according to the succession system within the Sun family. By 2008, Sun Dawu was the CS, his brother Sun Erwu was the CEO, and Liu Ping, the niece of Liu Huiru, was the GM. The Dawu Group always held its elections in December. It was in this "Dawu Election Month" that the elections of all three boards were held. As of 2008, the board of supervisors had been in charge of organizing the election meetings for the last three years.

The first election, held on February 28, 2005, adopted an equal nomination system. The Group was divided into five constituencies. Each constituency nominated its own candidates and voted separately. Fifteen people were elected to form the board of directors. In the first directors' meeting that followed, the CEO and the GM were determined. This election marked the official implementation of the "Family Business Constitution" within Dawu Group. During the directors' meeting, Sun Erwu and Liu Ping were elected the CEO and GM, respectively.

The second election, held on December 16, 2006, was conducted in three steps: public selection, representative selection, and elite election. Thirteen directors, two replacement directors and seven subsidiary heads were elected from 26 candidates. (The CEO and GM were still in their office terms.) The three steps in the election ensured that top talents managed the company, which was in turn under the inspection of all staff. Jia Linnan and Li Aiming, reporters from the *Industrial and Commercial Times of China*, observed the election, and published their news report titled "Witnessing 'Family Business Constitution' of Dawu Group." In the report, they wrote, "Sun Meng, who had previously resigned, obtained 425 votes (only second to his uncle Sun Shuhua) and was thus reappointed as a member of the board of directors. Wang Caijin, chief manager of the department of power, Li Sixu, office director of the Feed Company, and Lu Huijie, office director of the Poultry Breeding Company, were elected as the youngest members of the board. The ages of member directors showed a normal distribution: the majority was between 30 and 50 years old, while there were approximately similar numbers of 25 to 30 year olds and 50 to 60 year olds."

The third election was held on December 16, 2008. The constituency system was also applied in this election. A total of 661 employees with more than three years' tenure in the company were eligible for voting. At the end of the election, 11 out of the 13 directors were re-elected. Another four members were elected from the 14 candidates. They formed the new 15-person board of directors. Two replacement directors were also elected. During this election, Sun Dawu kept the nomination rights as the chief supervisor. Nine members of the board of directors, including Sun Dawu, did not vote for Sun Shuo, Sun Dawu's second son, believing that Sun Shuo should gain experience for a few more years. However, votes from the public eventually placed him on the board of directors. Only 20 people had the right to vote at the election venue of the Hot Spring Centre, which Sun Shuo was in charge of; however, it turned out that he won more than 300 votes. Most votes came from ordinary employees in other subsidiaries.

Rules for the Family Members

Sun Dawu established a set of rules for the family members, hoping to ensure the integrity of assets and properties at the time of inheritance. The rules stated that the board of supervisors was the representative and custodian of the Sun family, serving to protect the family members' legal rights and benefits, such as housing, medication, education, international traveling, and entrepreneurial activities (1 million yuan).

The family members were entitled to monthly subsidies as much as two to three times the average salary of the employees, even if they did not work in the company. The family members claimed this right as the owners of the assets. In addition to the subsidies, salaries were paid to the family members who worked in the Group. The female members in the Sun family, even after they were married, would be entitled to the same benefits for their entire life, but their children would not. At all times, the family members were to act as models in conforming to and implementing the Constitution. They were also encouraged to run for the CEO, GM, and CS positions. The family members had the ownership of the rewards and bonuses related to the positions. All family members oversaw the CS. As to legacies, only a symbol of equity would be passed down to younger generations, which meant that they needed to be elected to the board of directors through public elections to obtain decision-making rights. Currently, the two sons of Sun Erwu, one studying abroad and the other, starting his own business, were examples of family members getting support from the Group.

The Challenges Ahead for the "Family Business Constitution"

In 2010, it had been six years since the Constitution was first implemented, and the output of Dawu Group had doubled, with annual profits increasing rapidly at a rate of 30%. Yet, for Sun Dawu, expanding the business was not all that concerned him. These days, he thought about the future direction of his enterprise, as well as that of his family. As a man who held traditional values, he believed that under no circumstances should a family be separated. He once said that it was his wish to see his parents enjoy long and healthy lives, his brothers enjoy harmony among each other, and his younger generations be nurtured. However, members of the family should not rest on the enterprise's laurels. They had to gain front-line work experience and fight their way up to gradually win the support and confidence of staff and voters.

The election system also needed to be improved. The re-election for directors was held every two years, and every four years for the CEO and the GM. Re-election and reappointment were allowed. If a director was impeached, his or her assessment report would be made public to all staff representatives. One third of the director positions would be changed every two years, and a contested election mechanism had been adopted to maintain the vitality and continuity of director positions. Sun Dawu was also considering the "withdrawal" mechanism. The tentative idea was that once a subsidiary was shut down two director positions would be eliminated. Should the whole business shut down, then all the director positions would automatically disappear.

Besides the unexpected internal and external challenges that emerged after the third election, some middle-level managers thought that, under the current situation, it was impossible for talented professional managers to enter the Group, and that it was impossible for the Group to retain those talents; in addition, the separation of the three powers depleted the motivation to achieve sustainable growth. As Sun Dawu admitted, "Under the constitution system, the weak link would not be able to ruin the business, and it's not easy for anybody to shine either." Therefore, Sun Dawu was again concerned that the "Family Business Constitution" would not support the sustainability of his family business. Only time would tell whether the "Family Business Constitution" he created could succeed or not.

LONG CASE QUESTIONS

1. What are some of the major factors that encouraged Sun Dawu to work on a family constitution for the Hebei Dawu group?
2. What issues the family constitution hopes to address? Are these issues internal or external? Why?
3. Discuss the key elements of the family business constitution. Assess these elements critically given your reading of the chapter.
4. How does the new corporate system address many of the problematic issues with a family business? Do you see any aspects of the family constitution counter to Chinese culture?
5. What future corporate governance challenges do you see the company facing?

Secondary Stakeholders: Government, Media, and Non-Governmental Organizations

LEARNING OBJECTIVES

After reading this chapter you should be able to:

- Understand the government and how the government influences corporations
- Appreciate how companies influence the government through corporate political activity
- Appreciate the role played by the media as a secondary stakeholder
- Become aware of media analysis and its importance in managing the media
- Understand the critical role played by non-governmental organizations (NGOs) and the strategies they use to influence corporations
- Comprehend how NGOs can be managed and appreciate the role of cooperation with these NGOs

PREVIEW BUSINESS ETHICS INSIGHT

Nike and Sweatshops

In 2008, an Australian TV reporter posed as a fashion buyer to gain entry into a Nike Malaysian factory. The investigation into the factory, which employed mostly foreign migrants, showed horrific working conditions. Large numbers of workers were living in cramped and filthy rooms and sharing toilets in very bad condition. Furthermore, these workers had to pay recruiting fees in order to get access to these jobs. Once they got to the Nike plant, their passports were seized so that they would not be able to escape. Additionally, their wages were being reduced to pay off the recruiting fees.

This case of the Nike Malaysian factory quickly reminded the public of similar ethical crises at Nike in the 1990s. Nike is widely known as the company that pioneered the outsourcing model whereby most of its products are contracted to manufacturers in developing nations. However, it was exposed in the early 1990s and quickly became the poster for sweatshops and corresponding bad working conditions. The media and non-governmental organizations exposed abuses such as child labor in Pakistan and these resulted in protests on university campuses and outside Nike stores. Nike remained the target of protests for most of the 1990s and quickly realized that such protests were taking their toll. In 1998, Nike's reported a 50% decline in profit over the previous year.

In addition to the protests, Nike also attracted the attention of non-governmental organizations interested in improving working conditions. For instance, Oxfam, a non-governmental organization working on aid and development issues, started targeting Nike. Its Australian branch set up a Nike Watch campaign where it called for clothing and footwear companies (and specifically Nike) to help eradicate sweatshops and to improve labor conditions. This activity brought significant negative publicity to Nike.

When Nike first confronted the abuse reports in the 1990s, it initially rejected responsibility, arguing that the subcontractors are the ones responsible for the abuses. However, Nike quickly realized that it had to take responsibility to turn its tarnished image around. It implemented a number of steps such as the development of a code for its vendors, while also setting up a monitoring system. However, the broadcast on Australian TV in 2008 showed that Nike had still not addressed the issue completely. When faced with the new report, they quickly took responsibility by admitting a serious breach of its code. Furthermore, it reimbursed the workers and helped them relocate back to their home country if they wanted to. The company also set up meetings with its subcontractors to address labor regulation.

While Nike admits that it will never be able to fully address sweatshop conditions, it has come a long way since the original abuses were reported. It now has a website dedicated to working conditions where it strives to be transparent about its list of factories, working conditions, and audit results. The company has also become a world leader in terms of sustainability and waste reduction.

Based on Brenton, S. and Hacken, L. 2006. "Ethical consumerism: Are unethical labour practices important to consumers?" *Journal of Research for Consumers*, 11, 1–4; Drickhamer, D. 2002. "Under Fire." *Industry Week*, 251, 5; Levenson, E. 2008. "Citizen Nike." *Fortune*, 158, 10, 165–170.

The Preview Business Ethics Insight on pages 299–300 shows the experience of Nike as they dealt with groups such as the media and non-governmental organizations (NGOs). Both groups played an important role in educating consumers about the abuses occurring at Nike and other clothing and footwear giants. Both groups represent examples of secondary stakeholders. Recall in Chapter 2 that **secondary stake-holders** were defined as those groups or entities that have an indirect impact on the company's survival and strategic activities. Thus, while secondary stakeholders may not necessarily have a direct impact on a company, they can still have a significant influence on how companies operate. For instance, Nike and most other clothing and footwear giants such as Puma and Reebok all responded by investing significantly in improving worker conditions. For many of these companies, secondary stakeholders had a significant impact on their bottom line and thus an important impact on their strategic health.

For a company to succeed and to gain a strategic competitive advantage, it needs to be able to strategically manage its secondary stakeholders. In this chapter, we there-fore consider secondary stakeholders in depth. While there are a number of entities or groups that may have indirect influences on a company, we discuss three second-ary stakeholders that seem most critical for companies. First, you will read about the role of the government as a secondary stakeholder. You will learn about the regula-tive power of governments and what companies can do to deal with such regulation. Governments play critical roles as secondary stakeholders and we devote a significant portion of this chapter to the government. Second, we will learn about the media and its impact on companies as secondary stakeholders. Third, and finally, you will learn about NGOs and their roles in effective business ethics functioning.

GOVERNMENT REGULATION

The government is one of the most important secondary stakeholders. **Governments** are considered as regulative institutions that can constrain and regularize behaviors and actions through its capacity to establish rules, to inspect and review conformity, and to manipulate consequences to reinforce behaviors. In other words, governments through **regulation** can create laws and regulations to force companies to behave in ways that are more ethical. Furthermore, companies can punish companies that deviate from respecting such norms.

Why is regulation necessary? Many argue that the recent economic crisis worldwide is the result of too much deregulation. The government is seen as an important antidote to markets that seemed to have promoted greed and unethical behaviors.[1] Markets may not always function as effectively as required and governments will need to intervene to influence the market forces in positive ways. Furthermore, company actions can also result in negative externalities such as pollution, which is then borne by consumers and societies. Governmental regulation can help prevent the impact of such negative externalities on other stakeholders.

An examination of the business ethics literature shows that the government can regulate companies in two ways. First, government regulation itself can create the conditions which make competition possible whereby companies can expect to be dealt with ethically. It seems feasible to assume that to encourage ethical behavior companies must first be presented with an environment that promotes ethics. For instance, the government can create rules and regulations to ensure that contracts are thoroughly enforced. In this case, government regulation pertains to making sure that companies can expect to be treated ethically by both the government and other entities. Second, the government can also create regulation to force companies to behave ethically or to engage in corporate social responsibility. We consider both aspects next.

The government has a key role in creating an environment where companies can operate ethically. Consider the following Global Business Ethics Insight.

GLOBAL BUSINESS ETHICS INSIGHT

Google and Yahoo! in China

China views the media as an important tool for political control. Flow of information is constrained, as the Chinese Communist Party believes that such information should be controlled. Foreign companies operating in China have therefore had to consider the ethical dilemmas of operating in such an environment. Media companies have to be especially careful given that they operate in the area of information flow and exchange.

Consider the case of Yahoo!. They entered the Chinese market in 1999 and, unlike other companies such as Google or Microsoft, they kept personal information of their members inside China. In doing so, they had to abide by the Chinese "Public Pledge on Self-Discipline for the Chinese Internet Industry." The pledge meant that Yahoo! basically agreed to having their data monitored. Furthermore, signing the pledge also means that Yahoo! needs to censor electronic communication if such communication could jeopardize state security.

Yahoo! came under intense criticism when it gave information about two Chinese citizens to the Chinese government. Both individuals were arrested, prosecuted, and sentenced to prison for emailing pro-democracy views from their accounts. Although Yahoo! has strict policies regarding privacy of its users, it had no choice but to divulge such information to the Chinese government.

In contrast, Google has taken a different path. Given their goal of making the world's information "universally accessible and useful," they decided that operating in China could jeopardize achieving such goals. Rather than agree to abide by Chinese regulations and violate its own ethical principles, Google has decided to abandon the Chinese market.

Based on Dean, J. 2010. "Ethical conflicts for firms in China." *Wall Street Journal* online, January 13, A6; Venezia, G. and Venezia, C.C. 2010. "Yahoo! And the Chinese dissidents: A case study of trust, values, and clashing cultures." *Journal of Business Case Studies*, 6, 2.

As the Global Business Ethics Insight on page 302 shows, the government has significant impact on the environment facing any organization. While free-flowing information and individual privacy are ethical ideals in most societies, the Chinese government sees such information flow as a threat to their stability. Multinationals operating in China thus have to consider whether they want to deal with such an environment. However, for many media companies, this has been a difficult situation given the potential offered by the Chinese market.

What other aspects of the ethical environment should multinationals consider? The World Bank Doing Business project, which studies business environments worldwide, provides some insights into ethical aspects of the business environment. The project was conceived to give an idea of the environment conducive to entrepreneurship in different societies. However, while the project considers nine areas, three of these are directly pertinent to government regulation promoting an ethical environment. We therefore focus on these three areas.

The first aspect of government regulation pertaining to the creation of an ethical environment is the registration of property. **Registration of property** refers to the "full sequence of procedures necessary for a business to purchase a property from another business and transfer the title to the buyer's name."[2] The ability to have formal property rights is a key aspect determining a company's ability to do business ethically. Formal property ownership enables a company to use such assets as guarantees for loans and other financial funds to facilitate economic growth. Furthermore, formal property rights allow companies to rightfully own property. However, if the environment in a country only allows informal property ownership, companies will not easily be able to use such property as guarantee to access more finance to experience further growth. In such societies, companies will not have the ability to grow and flourish as they should.

The World Bank notes that registration of property is especially critical for women starting their own businesses. In many developing countries, women are important sources of income for their families. However, if registration of property is very difficult, these women will often face insurmountable barriers in trying to access loans to start their businesses. In some economies, women often do not have the same rights as men with regards to mortgaging a property or even owning a property.

Given the above, a multinational should strive to operate in nations that make property registration possible. Exhibit 7.1 (page 304) shows the regional averages for three aspects of registration of property; namely, the number of procedures, the time it takes to register the property, and the cost of registration as a percentage of the value of the property. Multinationals can use such guides for location decisions.

A second aspect of the World Bank project that relates to ethics is the **protection of investors**. As we saw in Chapter 6, companies can often raise capital by selling shares to investors. In return, investors expect transparency and accountability from managers running the company. However, company insiders can often use such funds or corporate assets for their personal gains. Furthermore, as we saw in Chapter 6, concentrated ownership such as family ownership, for instance, makes it possible for controlling family shareholders to abuse company assets. Controlling shareholders can sell company assets at low prices, thereby hurting both the company's and the minority

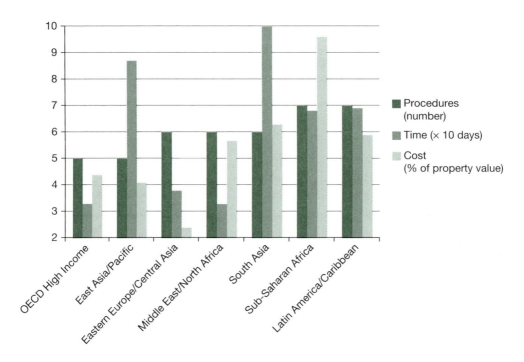

EXHIBIT 7.1—Property Registration Around the World

shareholders' financial health. In these cases, shareholder rights can be abused. This aspect of the World Bank project thus looks at the government regulation in place to ensure that such rights are respected.

Three main regulatory aspects are seen to contribute to investor protection. First, governments can mandate transparency in related-party transactions. For instance, if a company decides to sell company assets to a related company, it is necessary that shareholders are made aware of such transactions. Second, regulation can also hold company executives liable for self-dealing transactions. For instance, if executives used company assets for personal gains, regulations should hold these executives responsible for such transgressions. Finally, regulation pertaining to the ease with which shareholders can sue companies for mismanagement is also seen as an important aspect of investor protection. Minority shareholders should have access to a functioning legal system whereby they can defend their case and get retribution within a reasonable amount of time.

Exhibit 7.2 shows the countries with the highest and lowest level of investor protection. As companies consider expanding worldwide, such data can help regarding investment decisions in foreign companies.

Finally, a third aspect of the Doing Business project that sheds light on the ethicality of a business environment is **enforcement of contract**. If parties engage in contracts, they expect that the terms and conditions of the contract will be respected. Business transactions that take place between entities that do not fully know each other rely on the assumption that the parties will deliver on the agreed-upon aspects of contracts.

Top 10 Countries — Most Protected
New Zealand
Singapore
Hong Kong
Malaysia
Canada
Colombia
Ireland
Israel
U.S.
U.K.

Bottom 10 Countries — Least Protected
Guinea
Gambia
Micronesia
Palau
Vietnam
Venezuela
Djibouti
Suriname
Laos
Afghanistan

EXHIBIT 7.2 — Investor Protection: Top and Bottom Countries

Companies will thus less likely be able to engage in transaction with others if they do not feel that there are sufficient regulations to enforce contracts.

The World Bank project suggests that contract disputes have increased dramatically as a result of the economic crisis. Many large creditors such as utility companies have filed suits to try to recover money they are owed. Having an efficient system to ensure that such contract disputes are resolved is thus critical.

What contributes to adequate contract enforcement? The World Bank examines three indicators; namely, the time it takes to resolve a contract dispute, the number

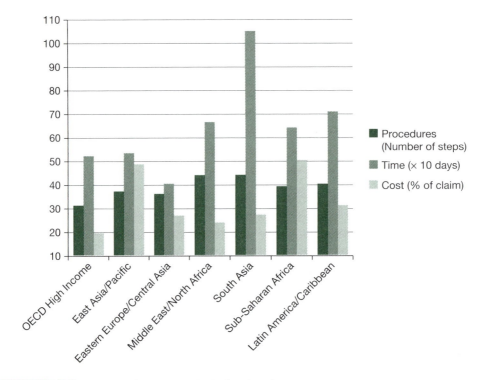

EXHIBIT 7.3—Regional Averages in Enforcing Contracts

of procedures needed to file such commercial suits, and finally the cost of the dispute as a percentage of the claim. Exhibit 7.3 shows the regional averages on these three aspects.

Similar to other exhibits, the data shows that the richer societies in the OECD group tend to have a better ethical environment. On all three aspects, the OECD has, on average, the smallest indicator. Furthermore, African nations tend to show some of the highest levels on these indicators, reflecting the less ethical environment.

The above regulatory aspects deal with the creation and enforcement of an environment where a company is confident that it will be dealt with in an ethical manner by both the government and other entities. However, government regulation can also take the form whereby they create rules and regulations to force companies to be ethical. For example, many of the recent U.S. legislations, such as the Sarbanes-Oxley Act and the Volcker Rule, were created to make it illegal for companies when they behave unethically. Consider the Ethics Sustainability Insight on page 309.

As the Ethics Sustainability Insight shows, government can regulate so that businesses behave in more ethical ways. Lawrence and Weber argue that there are two types of government regulation; namely, economic and social regulation.[3] Economic regulations are aimed at the modification of the free market to counter some negative aspects of the market. The aim of such economic regulation is to tackle market failures that occur, such as when firms have monopolistic power or when some consequences of company actions are thought to be undesirable. For instance, if firms have

ETHICS SUSTAINABILITY INSIGHT

Corporate Social Responsibility in Europe and Mauritius

Corporate social responsibility (CSR), which will be discussed in Chapter 12, suggests that companies have the duty to balance the interests of stakeholders while also keeping in mind the impact of their actions on the environment. The European Union started encouraging companies to take a proactive stance on CSR in 2001 when it published *Corporate Social Responsibility. A Business Contribution to Sustainable Development.* This report was the result of intense public consultation in the European Union and was written to provide some form of common grounds for CSR implementation in the European Union countries. Many companies located in the European Union then started implementing CSR programs. In fact a recent study showed that 90% of European companies on the Fortune Global 250 published sustainability reports. This suggests that the value placed on CSR by the European Union encouraged most companies to adopt such CSR practices.

While the European Union has taken a more passive stance on CSR, the Mauritian government has taken a much more aggressive posture to force companies to engage in CSR. Mauritius is a highly successful African island located off the East coast of Madagascar. In 2009, it passed legislation requiring for-profit companies to devote 2% of their after-tax profits to CSR efforts. Rather than rely on voluntary efforts of companies, the government effectively makes it illegal not to participate in the program. Furthermore, the government has provided very specific criteria on how the 2% can be used to contribute to CSR. For instance, it has approved a list of non-governmental organizations that can become recipient of such funds. Furthermore, the government has speci-fied that activities such as contributions to religious activities or contributions to political parties do not qualify as CSR activities. The Mauritian government has thus provided very clear guidance as to what constitutes CSR.

Based on Canto-Mila, N. and Lozano, J.M. 2009 "The Spanish discourse on corporate social responsibility" *Journal of Business Ethics,* 87, 157–171; http://www.nef.mu/csr; Liederkerke, L.V. and Dubbink, W. 2008. "Twenty years of european business ethics—past developments and future concerns." *Journal of Business Ethics,* 82, 273–280.

monopolistic power, they can restrict output and increase prices. Similarly, sometimes firms' activities can result in negative consequences, such as air or water pollution. In both cases, the government can step in and impose regulation to correct such market failures.

Steiner and Steiner argue that most regulation in the U.S. were historically economic in nature.[4] For instance, the late 1800s and early 1900s saw the public asking for more regulation of big businesses in the U.S. Such demands resulted in legislations such as railroad regulations and anti-trust laws. Such new economic regulation in the U.S. continued well in the 1950s. The 1960s to the present saw a severe decline in economic regulations.

Although there was a considerable decline in economic regulation after the 1950s, a significant economic regulation was passed in 2002. The Sarbanes-Oxley Act (SOX) was passed in 2002 as a result of the accounting scandals at companies such as Enron and WorldCom. The act was passed mostly to improve financial reporting to ensure that accounting practices were being rigorously followed. Such measures also aimed at restoring investor confidence in such reports. Among the many new conditions, SOX now requires that both CEOs and Chief Financial Officers certify financial reports to ensure honest and transparent reporting. Furthermore, SOX requires that internal controls are audited and documented. Exhibit 7.4 summarizes some of the main aspects of SOX.

The 1960s in the U.S. saw the growth of the second form of regulation; namely, social regulation. Social regulations are aimed at improving the lives of individuals in society. As such, social regulations have social goals such as protection of consumers, providing employees with a safe and healthy work environment, and providing workers with equal opportunity at work. In contrast to economic regulations more focused on correcting problems associated with the proper functioning of the market, social regulation emphasizes the improvement of the quality of life of individuals as members of society, employees, consumers, etc. To give further insights on social regulation, Exhibit 7.5 summarizes some of the recent social regulation coming from the European Union.

Exhibit 7.5 shows the many social regulations that the European Union has implemented. Taken together, the government has significant clout in terms of forcing

Sarbanes-Oxley Main Rules
Chief Executive Officers and Chief Financial Officers need to certify financial reports
Financial statements should fairly represent financial conditions of company
Pro Forma financial statements cannot contain fraudulent statements or misleading information
Filing schedules should be done in a more timely fashion
Internal controls need to be audited and documented
Auditors are prohibited from providing non-audit consulting services to their customers
Off-balance-sheets items need to be properly disclosed
Board of directors need to include independent members
Companies should not destroy, alter, or fabricate evidence when investigated for abuse
Whistle-blowers should be protected from company retaliation

EXHIBIT 7.4—Sarbanes-Oxley Act Summary

Consumers	• Consumers have the right to a safe product. A safe product is one that causes no harm when used the way it is supposed to be used.
	• Manufacturers should provide consumers with information so that they can assess the inherent threat of using a product.
	• Consumers should not be subject to misleading advertising. Advertising is misleading if it fails to provide a minimum standard of information to consumers prior to purchase.
	• Commercial practices such as pyramid schemes, bait advertising, or use of advertorial (advertising disguised as editorial) are prohibited.
Employees	• Employees cannot be discriminated on the basis of their disability, age, sexual orientation, religion, or beliefs.
	• Employers need to consult with authorities at the national level in case of mass layoffs. Reasons for the layoff, the length of the layoffs, the decision criteria for layoffs, and the compensations for the layoffs need to be presented.
	• Both men and women should be treated equally in all respects and specifically with regards to pay.
	• Employees have the right to a safe and healthy work environment.
Environment	• Member states should assess the level of pollution in their air. Measures need to be taken to ensure "Pure Air for Europe."
	• Member states agree to require car manufacturers to reduce carbon emissions progressively. For instance, 100% of cars in 2015 can only produce 130g of carbon dioxide per kilometers.
	• All member states will take every step necessary to measure noise levels across their boundaries. Steps need to be implemented to reduce or manage noise levels.
Human Rights	• All member states should enforce human rights based on six main principles, namely 1) dignity (the right to dignity and right to life), 2) freedoms (right to liberty and security, right to private life and family, right to safeguard of private data), 3) equality (equality before the laws, non-discrimination, right of the child), 4) solidarity (right of workers to engage in collective bargaining, fair and just working conditions, protections against unjustified firing), 5) citizens' right (right to vote, right to good administration, right to information), and 6) justice (right to fair trial, presumption of innocence, right not to be punished twice for the same offence).
The Information Society	• Members will strive to increase media literacy. Media literacy refers to the ability of citizens to access, understand, and critically assess media content.
	• Members should ensure that their citizens have equal access to computers, telephones, televisions, online administration, online shopping, call centers, self-service terminals, and automatic teller machines.
	• All member states should work towards the creation of a single market in creative content online. For instance, one of the aims is the creation of a single market for online music, films, and games.

EXHIBIT 7.5—European Union Social Regulation

companies to abide by such rules and regulations. But do companies always respond to such regulation? In the next section, we examine company reactions to regulations.

GOVERNMENT REGULATION AND COMPANY POLITICAL ACTIVITY

When government regulations are enacted, companies have two main choices. They can either abide by the new regulations or they can find ways to make the regulation less effective or delay the implementation of the new rules. If the company accepts the new regulation, they are effectively behaving legitimately to avoid prosecution. Institutional theory argues that the government is a key constituent in modern society forcing companies to adopt government mandate as a way to seek legitimacy.[5] In this respect, legitimacy refers to conduct of behavior in a manner that is consistent with widely held values and norms.

Why do companies seek legitimacy by adopting government mandates? From a strategic management perspective, legitimacy is critical. First, such behaviors reduce the need for managers to decide what is appropriate. As government regulations are adopted by more companies, they become institutionalized and taken for granted. Such norms reduce the need for managers to engage in complex decision-making processes. Second and most importantly, legitimacy shows that a company is abiding by governmental rules and regulations. This provides continued support from key stakeholders while also providing access to valued resources from key constituents. Legitimacy thus facilitates company survival. To get more insights into the legitimacy process, consider the Business Ethics Insight on page 311.

The Business Ethics Insight illustrates the attempt of the Canadian regional health authorities to seek legitimacy from the government. However, in seeking legitimacy, these authorities ignored the needs of other stakeholders. There are clearly limits to legitimacy. Furthermore, in some cases, companies may actively find ways to either change regulations or delay the implementation of new regulation. Next we look at corporate public activity.

Corporate public activity (CPA) refers to the attempt by a company to influence or manage the political entities and the government.[6] CPA includes activities such as lobbying, campaign contributions, operation of a government relations office, and contributions to industry trade groups. Lux et al. argue that business contributions have increased dramatically in the U.S. recently. For instance, business contributions to the Republican National Committee and House and Senate campaign committees increased 220% to $782 million in 2004, from only $358 million in 1994.

Companies engage in CPA for many reasons. First, they engage in CPA to influence legislation pertaining to their operations. For instance, lobbying is often seen as influencing the government to take into account company private interests while making public interest regulation.[7]

Second, companies also engage in CPA to get access to governmental resources. Consider, for instance, that in Chapter 5 on corporate governance we considered the role of the government in state-owned run companies. In such cases, the company can

BUSINESS ETHICS INSIGHT

Government Reforms in the Public Sector Healthcare in Canada

In 1994, the Canadian province of Alberta embarked on a reform of its public healthcare system. Major reforms and legislations were passed to encourage the public sector hospitals to be run more efficiently like "businesses." Around 200 hospital boards and health units were merged and combined to form nine regional health authorities. These new units were pressured to become much more efficient in an effort to save over $700 million over four years.

These regional health authorities had no choice but to adopt the government mandates to seek legitimacy. They operated under strict governmental regulations and received government funding to operate. Not respecting such mandates would surely have meant organizational death. In an effort to cut costs to respond to the legitimacy needs, administrative functions were centralized and restructuring led to savings through thousands of job cuts.

However, in respecting the wishes of the government to seek legitimacy, the regional health authorities ignored the needs of other stakeholders. While they were able to drive down costs, other outcomes such as patient satisfaction and quality of care were going down. This led to increased dissatisfaction from the community, nurses, and patients. Nurses started organizing activist demonstrations. Physicians also protested because they wanted higher pay and more authority in running the healthcare facilities.

While the Canadian authorities were originally defiant, they quickly had to give in to prevent further disruptions to the system. The government agreed to increased funding and many of the needs of the various stakeholders involved were satisfied.

Based on Sonpar, K., Pazzaglia, F., and Kornijenko, J. 2010. "The paradox and constraints of legitimacy." *Journal of Business Ethics*, 95, 1–21.

often derive significant funds from the government. Furthermore, in many countries, governments are significant business actors providing the opportunity to companies to make sales. The decision to award business to companies is usually made by specific government officials.[8] Thus, CPA may be a direct way to influence these government officials.

A final reason why companies engage in CPA is to positively affect its performance. Ties with the government provide a firm with the ability to ward off future negative attention while also providing access to government resources. Recent research provides support for this position. In a large-scale compilation of 78 studies, Lux et al. show that CPA indeed leads to higher firm performance.[9] However, Okhmatovskiy's study provides a more refined look at the relationship between government ties and firm performance.[10] Rather than merely looking at the direct ties with the government, Okhmatovskiy studied around 600 Russian banks and found that indirect connect with the government through ties with state-owned businesses resulted in higher firm performance. However, in this sample, direct ties with the government do not help performance.

In this section, you learned about the importance of the government as a secondary stakeholder. In the face of the recent economic crises, many have argued that the government should play an even bigger role in the future. This suggests that companies will have to contend with more expanded government influence in the future in devising their strategies. Furthermore, many of the emerging markets also have dominant governments that have significant influence on the business environ. As Google has found, it became difficult for them to operate freely once they decided to not abide by Chinese rules and regulations governing the internet. Astute companies intent on taking advantage of such emerging markets will face a definite dilemma as they decide between abandoning such markets or entering these markets and violating their own mission. This also suggests that governments will remain critical in the future.

THE MEDIA

The **media**, referring to the many avenues of information such as newspapers, television, and the internet, is also a powerful secondary stakeholder. Most people rely on the media to get information about companies and it is powerful because of such reach and prominence.[11] Furthermore, Donlon goes as far as claiming that the media has often created "headline-grabbing" cases that have brought down companies.[12] How companies and industries are perceived by the public thus becomes an important aspect of how these companies are viewed. In this section, we therefore consider media influence. We also note that internet media such as social media is also a powerful media form. However, we will cover internet and social media ethics in Chapter 8.

How powerful is the media? Consider the Strategic Business Ethics Insight on page 313.

As the Strategic Business Ethics Insight shows, the media can have a powerful impact on how companies and industries are perceived. This can have long-term effects on the survival of the industry. No one disputes the notion that the pharmaceutical industry has engaged in unethical behaviors. However, the study does put in question whether the industry has received fair coverage of issues. Another study by Kollmeyer also provides some insights into how the media portrays businesses.[13] In that study, Kollmeyer examined the news portrayed in the *Los Angeles Times* and compared such coverage with the objective performance indicators of the state of California. The study found that the newspaper was more likely to feature negative news about the economic elite such as corporations and investors. Although workers faced significant challenges in California, the *Los Angeles Times* was likely to feature disproportionately shorter stories about the workers, often in its back pages. This also suggests that the media may not necessarily portray all stories in a balanced manner. As the public relies on

STRATEGIC BUSINESS ETHICS INSIGHT

U.S. Newspapers and Ethical Issues in the Pharmaceutical Industry

The pharmaceutical industry is undoubtedly a very vital industry. It has significant economic impact for the U.S. economy. Furthermore, it has significant impact on the well-being and health of people at all levels. The industry continues to invest in research and development to develop new drugs to address new ailments to help people to live longer, healthier, and more productive lives.

Despite this importance, the pharmaceutical industry continues to be viewed very negatively in the U.S. An analysis of media portrayal of the industry in newspapers provides evidence of such a claim. Newspapers are considered very influential, as readers can still have access to newspaper articles even after the sound bites of the radio and television are gone. In an interesting study of the top five U.S. newspapers, the authors of the study examined a number of attributes of the portrayal of the industry in these newspapers. For example, they examined the nature of both headlines and the content of the articles about the industry. The authors classified the headline as negative, positive, or neutral toward the industry. They also considered whether the article's content took a positive, negative, or neutral position toward the industry.

Results of the study showed that 2004 and 2005 headlines and articles viewed the industry overwhelmingly as either negative or neutral. In 2004, only 18.1% of headlines were positive while only 9.2% of headlines were considered positive in 2005. As far as the articles are concerned, only 20% of articles were positive in 2004 and only 19.2% of articles were positive in 2005. These results clearly supported the industry's perception that they are unfairly portrayed negatively.

Is the portrayal of the industry really negative? The industry has certainly engaged in many unethical practices such as pricing issues, gift-giving, sales, and marketing practices. However, the industry also engages in positive actions but such actions do not get much press coverage. Consider that Merck's drug safety issues related to Vioxx received much more press coverage than its efforts to provide HIV treatment for patients in sub-Saharan Africa.

Based on Sillup. P.G. 2008. "Ethical issues in the pharmaceutical industry: An analysis of U.S. newspapers." *International Journal of Pharmaceutical and Healthcare Marketing*, 2, 3.

the information provided by the media, they may develop a perspective different from reality. It therefore becomes critical for a company to manage this aspect of media portrayal.

Recent research in the political arena has some implications for how businesses are portrayed.[14] For instance, in election coverage, it is found that the media is more likely to focus on campaign controversies. Rather than provide a balanced view of candidates, the media is more likely to create or emphasize controversial issues in such campaigns. Why this focus on controversy? Ridout and Smith argue that commercial pressures often compel the media to focus on the sensational rather than the routine. To attract large audiences to allow media companies to get more advertising funds, the media is more likely to focus on the sensation to attract attention. This is also true for businesses whereby the media is more likely to focus on a sensational story about the unethical behaviors of executives at a specific company rather than the charitable work of another company.

Understanding how the media influences the public is thus very critical. Andina-Diaz argues that the "media hold great power, as they transmit information to the public and are free to highlight certain news items and ignore others, setting the agenda of public life and creating consensus or disagreement on certain issues."[15] While the influence of the media has been the subject of a large body of literature, we focus only on those that are relevant to business ethics. In that context, Barber and Axinn (2004) provide some understanding of how the media can influence the public about businesses.[16] First, the media can affect the public's attitudes and behaviors simply by increasing knowledge about business ethics issues. However, as Andina-Diaz suggests, such information may sometimes reinforce people's already existing attitudes.[17] For example, if the public believes that businesses are unethical, they may be receptive to new information to confirm such pre-existing attitudes. Second, the media can also influence the public as the public identifies with the television or radio personalities communicating the message. For instance, people may be more likely to change their attitudes regarding global warming if such messages are coming from a known celebrity dedicated to environmental awareness.

Given the above, clearly the media affects how the public perceives businesses or specific companies. However, the mechanisms discussed mostly show direct effects of the media. The literature on the media also shows that indirect influences are also possible. One of the most prominent theories explaining indirect effects of the media is known as the "third-person" effect.[18] The third-person effect basically implies that people exposed to media generally think that such messages have much greater influence on others than themselves. However, such messages are likely to affect the person receiving the message. For example, it has been shown that teenagers are more likely to smoke when they felt that pro-smoking media messages influenced their peers. Similarly, doctors were less likely to prescribe direct-to-consumer drugs when they perceived that direct-to-consumer drug advertising adversely affects their clients. When applied to business ethics, the third-person effects occurs when, for instance, someone watches the news and learns about a company that deceived a customer and that person decides not to patronize the company for fear that the company will also deceive him/her.

Media Analysis and Business Ethics

The preceding paragraphs show that the media can be very powerful. Although the media may sometimes unfairly portray businesses, it is still an important source of information for most people. While research shows that companies often survive public revelations of ethical wrongdoing, experts argue that it is important to carefully monitor the media.[19] A company's reputation is an extremely important asset. Over time, media coverage often defines what people believe about companies.[20] If such beliefs project a bad company reputation and unethical activities, such effects can have very adverse effects on the company. Furthermore, the media provides the information that the public uses to decide whether they can trust a company.[21] Trust is also a critical aspect of a company's survival.

Despite the importance of understanding the media, fairly recent research suggests that not all companies routinely conduct media analysis. Consider Exhibit 7.6. As it shows, only 27% of companies in this sample conduct any form of formal media analysis. However, such **media analysis** when companies "routinely scan the media to discover what is being said about them" is extremely critical.[22] Media analysis can help companies assess the way the company is being portrayed in the media and address inconsistencies. Media analysis can also help a company understand what its competitors are doing. From a strategic management standpoint, media analysis of competitors can become an important source of competitive intelligence.[23]

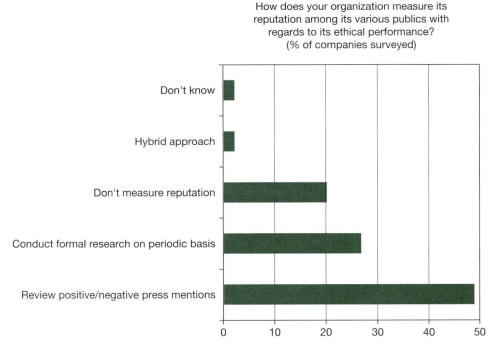

How does your organization measure its reputation among its various publics with regards to its ethical performance? (% of companies surveyed)

EXHIBIT 7.6—Percentage of Companies Conducting Media Analysis

Media analysis is typically done by third-party firms specializing in scouring the media for company coverage. As we will see later in Chapter 8, companies also now spend significant resources to understand what is being said about them on social media such as Facebook and Twitter. Furthermore, the high speed of information flow on social networks and other forms of social media suggests that companies need to also respond quickly to damaging information.

According to Dowling and Weeks, media analysis typically takes place in three forms.[24] First, media analysis can be of the **salience and sentiment analysis** form. Salience is measured by the number of times a company is mentioned in selected outlets. This can also take a more refined form if the prestige of the media is also taken into consideration. Sentiment analysis refers to whether the company is being portrayed in a positive, neutral, or negative way. Such salience and sentiment analysis can thus provide some idea of how the company is generally viewed. Tagging such analysis with events in the company can also reveal the impact of such events on the media.

A second form of media analysis is the **theme and contradiction analysis**. In such cases, the media can be analyzed to determine whether ongoing media coverage is portraying the company under some specific theme. For instance, Dowling and Weeks argue that the recent themes behind media coverage of the computer giant Apple has been decreasing customer satisfaction as the company keeps growing and seems less responsive to customer needs.[25] Uncovering this theme has enabled Apple to devise a concerted public relations strategy to address problematic issues. Additionally, contradiction analysis refers to the comparison of media portrayal of issues with what the company is itself saying. For example, the banking industry is currently fighting contradictions in that, while they say they are responding to foreclosures by being more careful about which homes are being foreclosed, media coverage seems to show recklessness with regards to foreclosure decisions.

Finally, media analysis can also take form of **problem and solution analysis**. Specifically, the above two forms of analysis can provide a company with many aspects of its media portrayal such as what is being said, whether the information is being portrayed positively or negatively, what themes are being reported, and how the company compares to rivals. This information can then be used to address issues that are seen as problems. According to Dowling and Weeks, from a strategic management standpoint, such media analysis should encourage companies to do the following:[26]

- *Reinforcing strong company messages*. A company should link its strengths to ongoing messages in the media. Consider how the U.S. company GE has shifted the company theme from being profit motivated to being a green company with the consistent "eco-imagination" advertising theme. Such consistency helps build new themes for companies.
- *Addressing negative information*. If a company is being portrayed in an unfairly negative way, the reasons for such portrayal should first be analyzed. It is possible that there are real problems behind such portrayals. A company should then address these issues and slowly communicate the new information to the media. For example, rather than deny reliability issues, Mercedes-Benz would have averted a public

relations disaster by addressing their customer needs (see Brief Case at end of chapter). Denial of negative information simply led to a catastrophic snowball.

- *Appreciating mixed messages.* A company should carefully analyze why it is being portrayed in both negative and positive messages. Careful analysis of the negatives may sometimes reveal important ethical areas that need to be addressed. It is therefore important for companies to address such contradictions.

- *Understanding missing messages.* A company also needs to consider whether some core company message is missing when conducting a theme analysis. For instance, if a company has embarked recently on a new environmental mission and finds that this has not been covered in the media, a more concerted effort is needed to get this message out. Similarly, if new ethical initiatives are not covered in much depth, it is important for a company to address such gaps.

The above discusses some of the more obvious steps a company can take after a media analysis. It is important that the right messages be consistently communicated to the media. Such consistency in communication is important to project the required ethical image. Furthermore, much of this can take place in a concerted public relations campaign. We discuss public relations later in the chapter.

NON-GOVERNMENTAL ORGANIZATIONS

The final secondary but influential stakeholders we consider in this chapter are **non-governmental organizations** (or NGOs). As the power of multinationals and companies have grown worldwide, NGOs have emerged as important counterbalances to such power.[27] For example, as we saw with the Preview Business Ethics Insight (pages 299–300), many NGOs kept strong pressure on Nike to address labor and other human rights. Without such consistent and strong NGO attention, Nike would probably not have responded quickly to the labor abuses.

"NGOs" is an umbrella term that includes "special interest groups, activist groups, social movement organizations, charities, religious groups, protest groups, and other non-profit groups"[28] organized around and committed to specific shared beliefs or principles. Exhibit 7.7 shows some of the more popular NGOs and the causes they believe in.

As Exhibit 7.7 shows, NGOs are organized around issues such as child labor, sweatshops, human rights, sustainable development, oil pollution, fair trade, and attention to future generations.[29] In such cases, NGOs are known as "social purpose" NGOs that are typically confronting organizations to tackle these issues.[30] Such NGOs are also known as "non-membership" organizations, whereby the interests of the members are represented by other individuals who contribute time and money. In contrast, there are NGOs that are known as "membership NGOs" that represent the interests of their members. Such NGOs are trade associations, industry groups, and labor unions. It is also important to note that the size and structure of NGOs can vary greatly. Some NGOs are smaller, informal, but very dynamic grassroot type organizations. Other NGOs can have very formal structures and be larger and more mature organizations.

Organization	Description and Causes
Amnesty International	• Founded in 1961, it is an organization with around 3 million members from around 150 countries • Works to end abuses of human rights and protect human rights according to Universal Declaration of Human Rights • See http://www.amnesty.org for more detail
Conservation International	• Founded in 1987 with around 900 employees in more than 30 offices globally • Uses a strong foundation in science to influence global development and to demonstrate that inherently caring and valuing nature is critical to humankind • See http://www.conservation.org for more detail
Fair Labor Association	• Founded in 1999, the Fair Labor Association is a collaborative effort of socially responsible companies, universities, and civic society organizations • Dedicated to ending sweatshop conditions and improving workers' rights and working conditions worldwide • See http://www.fairlabor.org for more detail
Greenpeace International	• Founded in 1971 and now has offices in more than 30 countries with funding coming from around 2.8 million members worldwide • Main mission is to campaign and fight for the earth by addressing threat of global warming, destruction of ancient forests, deterioration of oceans, and threat of nuclear disaster • See http://www.greenpeace.org for more detail
Oxfam International	• Founded in 1995 by a group of independent NGOs and is now a confederation of 14 organizations working in 99 countries • Works with over 3,000 local organizations to work with people living in poverty to exercise their human rights and assert their dignity as human beings. Main mission is to find solutions for poverty and injustice worldwide. • See http://www.oxfam.org for more detail
Transparency International	• Founded in 1993 and is a global network of more than 90 locally established chapters • Dedicated to fighting corruption by bringing awareness of corruption, reducing apathy and tolerance of corruption, and implementing actions to end corruption globally • See http://www.transparency.org for more detail

EXHIBIT 7.7 — Popular NGOs and their Causes

STRATEGIC BUSINESS ETHICS INSIGHT

NGOs and Influence

NGOs have had a major influence on how multinationals have operated in the last few decades. Consider, for instance, that many experts agree that the push for corporate social responsibility (CSR) has been mainly due to the strong and consistent pressures from NGOs. For example, in a study of the progression and adoption of CSR in Spain, Arenas et al. argue clearly that although NGOs are sometimes controversial, they played a big role in forcing Spanish companies to adopt CSR policies.[31] Furthermore, Sobczak and Martins illustrate the critical role of NGOs in CSR discourses in countries such as France and Brazil.[32] Such critical roles of NGOs in CSR are not surprising given the important role they played in keeping climate change prominent in discussions. Carpenter shows how the various climate conferences started seeing more and more NGOs with specific goals in mind.[33] As worldwide negotiations for the Kyoto Protocol continued, such negotiations had to increasingly contend with more powerful NGOs.

The above shows the role of NGOs in keeping the climate change and CSR debates at the national level strong. However, NGOs can also have an impact on specific companies. In a longitudinal study, Skippari and Pajunen show how the Finnish multinational Metsä-Botnia was unable to make foreign direct investments in Uruguay because they ignored the demands of NGOs.[34] Botnia wanted to make a pulp mill investment in Uruguay. However, although their assessment showed that the mill would not have had much environmental impact and would contribute to the economy, activist groups soon started opposing the mill. People from regions affected by the mill formed NGOs. At the national level, activist groups also started raising concerns about the groups. Because it strongly believed in its assessments, Botnia proceeded with the mill project. However, this resulted in more conflicts with the NGOs. At some point, the conflicts were so out of hand that it made reconciliation impossible. Botnia later agreed that they should have listened to the NGOs' demands much earlier.

Based on Arenas, D., Lozano, J.M., and Albareda, L. 2009. "The role of NGOs in CSR: Mutual perceptions among stakeholders." *Journal of Business Ethics*, 88, 175–197; Skippari, M. and Pajunen, K. 2010. "MNE-NGO—Host government relationships in escalation of an FDI conflict." *Business Society*, 49, 619; Sobczak, A. and Martins, L.C. 2010. "The impact and interplay of national and global CSR discourses: Insights from France and Brazil." *Corporate Governance*, 10, 4, 445–455.

How influential are NGOs on the strategic health of companies? Consider the brief cases in the Strategic Business Ethics Insight on page 319.

The Business Ethics Insight provides a very short description of the influence of NGOs on the strategic health of companies. The Finnish company Metsa-Botnia had to abandon a strategic project because it ignored the NGO demands early. Thus, similar to other stakeholders, NGOs also need to be appropriately managed. However, to understand how NGOs needs and demands can be satisfied, it is important to understand the various strategies they use to influence companies. We examine these issues next.

NGO Strategies

While there seems to be wide variations in terms of what NGOs can do, most experts agree that NGOs' strategies can range on a continuum from **active cooperation** and engagement to confrontation with threats and other adversarial behaviors. NGOs that cooperate typically assume that the multinational that they are working with will adopt some form of voluntary code of conduct.[35] In a study of Spanish firms and their interactions with NGOs, Valor and Merino provide evidence of cooperative strategies used by NGOs.[36] Their findings show that in the Spanish environment both companies and NGOs are actively seeking each other to establish partnerships. In fact, while there is evidence that many companies will seek NGOs to partner with, the findings also show that NGOs are equally likely to seek firms to work with. In seeking such companies, an NGO may identify key areas that a company must attend to. Such cooperation and engagement often results in a win–win relationship for both companies and NGOs.

However, NGOs can also adopt a **confrontational strategy**. In such cases, the NGOs assume that the offending multinationals are less likely to make changes to improve the cause they believe in. They therefore believe that being confrontational will likely affect the financial interests of the offending multinational and bring changes. In pursuing a confrontational strategy, NGOs may rely on symbolic damage strategies such as negative publicity or material damage strategies such as boycotts. In extreme cases, NGOs may also resort to vandalism and other property destruction strategies.

The above discusses some of the more direct ways that NGOs can interact with companies. However, Fassin argues that NGOs can also influence companies indirectly.[37] In such cases, NGOs can try to influence the company by targeting other stakeholders of the company and the media. Specifically, NGOs can indirectly influence the company by operating at three levels. First, NGOs can target primary stakeholders such as customers and employees. For example, consumers may be asked to boycott a specific company because of unethical practices. Second, NGOs can indirectly target companies by shaping public opinion. In such cases, the media can be used to change public opinion about a company. Letter-writing campaigns, denunciation campaigns, and other moral stigmatization tactics are the likely means. Third and finally, NGOs can influence companies indirectly by targeting regulators and lawmakers. Lobbying, discussed earlier, is a typical way that NGOs can use to encourage regulators to pass new laws and regulations to make specific company actions illegal.

Although NGOs play an important role to counterbalance company actions on society, it is important to note that they may sometimes engage in questionable practices. In a study of various cases of NGO practices, Fassin found evidence of the following questionable practices:

- *Distorted communication*. In some cases, NGOs may rely on unchecked information or distort information to make their point. If the media publicizes such information, it may sometimes be more difficult to correct errors.
- *Arbitrary attacks*. Because of their size and clout, multinationals may sometimes be arbitrarily targeted for attack campaigns. Consider that, for instance, the oil company Total was attacked by environmentalists when there was an oil disaster in Brittany in 1999. Although the responsibility for the disaster was largely attributed to the transport companies, Total was blamed for a lack of judgment in choosing companies to transport their products.
- *Conflicts of interest*. NGOs may not always fight for all stakeholders involved. In fact, some industry and trade group may fight for specific stakeholders. For instance, consider that when Dow Corning was faced with the breast implant scandal whereby silicon was leaking into women's bodies, one of its unlikely defendants was an NGO representing plastic surgeons. It defended the practice as necessary for women.
- *Fraud*. NGOs exist because of the funding they received from various sources. Fassin notes that there are numerous cases of NGOs receiving multiple sources of funding for the same project. Furthermore, some NGOs have submitted duplicate invoices for the same project and received funding multiple times from sources such as the World Bank and the European Union.

Despite these questionable practices, NGOs play an important role in today's business environment. In the final section of this chapter, we examine how companies can manage NGOs.

NGO Management

NGOs, similar to most other stakeholders, have to be managed. The many cases discussed in this chapter show that they can have significant influence on a company. For instance, the Preview Business Ethics Insight discussed at the beginning of the chapter on pages 299–300 showed how Nike received significant negative publicity that eventually affected their profitability. They gradually had to address the NGOs' demand for better work conditions. Furthermore the Strategic Business Ethics Insight on page 319 showed how Metsä-Botnia's ignorance of the demands of the NGOs resulted in irreversible damage that doomed the pulp mill project. It is therefore important that the presence and actions of NGOs be analyzed and be managed.

How should NGOs be managed? The techniques and tools discussed in Chapter 2 are very useful here. A multinational should conduct the many steps discussed in that chapter. Specifically, a company is expected to conduct stakeholder identification (which NGOs currently have impact for the company), stakeholder prioritization

STRATEGIC BUSINESS ETHICS INSIGHT

NGOs and Cooperation

For decades, companies and NGOs operated mostly in conflict with each other. The influential scholar C.K. Prahalad termed this as "co-existence." However, companies are now facing new challenges and, as they strive to embark on corporate social and environmental responsibility, they are now increasingly partnering with NGOs. This new era termed "co-creation" signals a new direction for company–NGO relationships. Consider the case of Danone and work with NGOs in developing countries to better understand the low-income but economically viable consumers in such countries. Similarly, FedEx partnered with Environmental Defense Fund, an NGO based in Washington, D.C., to launch its hybrid electric truck fleets. Both forms of cooperation resulted in significant strategic advantage for the company involved.

Aleman and Sandilands' study of cooperation between Starbucks and NGOs also show how cooperation and engagement can be beneficial to affected stakeholders.[38] As early as in 1994, NGOs started targeting Starbucks to pressure the company to set standards for the wages, benefits, housing, and health of its coffee suppliers. Although it initially resisted such NGO activism, it eventually started partnering with the various NGOs representing suppliers. Specifically, the relationship it built with the Conservational International NGO (see description in Exhibit 7.7) resulted in significant improvement in the lives of its suppliers worldwide. The partnership helped Starbucks identify problematic areas with its suppliers worldwide. In partnership with these NGOs, Starbucks developed solutions and a code of standards as it interacts with its suppliers. For instance, its suppliers must show how much of the money they are spending actually goes to farmers. Starbucks now purchases a high percentage of its coffee from sustainable and fair trade suppliers.

Companies are thus finding significant benefits when partnering with NGOs. Danone, for instance, was able to learn about the four billion people who are considered low income and earn less than $2 a day. By better understanding these individuals, Danone has been better able to devise products to satisfy their needs. Besides such marketing benefits, companies are improving their reputation while also earning improved returns in their research and development. In the process, companies are helping these NGOs better fulfill their missions.

Based on Auriac, J. 2010. "Corporate social innovation." *Organisation for Economic Co-operation and Development*, May, 279; Aleman, Perez P. and Sandilands, M. 2008. "Building value at the top and the bottom of the global supply chain: MNC-NGO partnerships." *California Management Review*, 51, 1, 24–49.

(which stakeholders have a combination of power, legitimacy, and urgency), stakeholder visualization and mapping (which stakeholders have the most power and urgency), stakeholder engagement (how to engage NGOs through dialogue and cooperation), and stakeholder monitoring (the nature of NGO actions). More extensive detail on these issues can be found in Chapter 2.

One of the key steps of the stakeholder analysis that experts suggest companies should adopt is stakeholder engagement. Valor and Merino go as far as arguing that most NGOs now have gone from confrontation to cooperation with the firms they target.[39] NGOs are now seen as becoming more practical and flexible and less ideological. NGOs also seem to be more willing to work with the companies they target to find solutions to problems. NGOs see such a path as a better way to become more credible among policy-makers, while also improving their reputations. Most multinationals are therefore well advised to adopt a more cooperative posture when interacting with NGOs. The final Strategic Business Ethics Insight (page 322) shows some of the benefits when companies and NGOs cooperate.

CHAPTER SUMMARY

In this chapter, you learned about three critical secondary stakeholders. For a company to survive, it has to adequately analyze its environment. Secondary stakeholders are extremely important elements of a company's strategic environment. While there are many stakeholders that can potentially influence a company's strategy indirectly, we emphasized three important secondary stakeholders.

First, you read about the government as an influential secondary stakeholder. You learned about the role of the government in both creating an environment leading to ethics and to enacting of rules and regulations to reinforce ethical behavior. You read about the World Bank Doing Business project and the various indicators of the extent of ethicality of the business environment. However, you also learned about the types of government regulation; namely, social and economic regulation. Furthermore, you learned how companies can react to the government either by adopting the rules or regulations or delay such rules through corporate political activity.

The second secondary stakeholder you learned about is the media. You read about the important influence the media plays on companies. You also learned about the direct influence the media have on public perception of companies. However, you also read about the "third-person" effect and the indirect ways the media can influence public perception of companies. To adequately manage the media, you also learned about media analysis and the strategic importance of the various steps inherent in media analysis. You also read about the various possible options available to companies based on media analysis.

Finally, you also read about non-governmental organizations (NGOs) as critical secondary stakeholders. You learned about the various strategies NGOs can use to influence companies. You read about the continuum ranging from active cooperation to open confrontation and the assumptions behind adoption of such strategies.

However, you also read about questionable NGO practices such as misinformation, conflicts of interest, and fraud. Similar to other secondary stakeholders, you learned about NGO management. You also learned about the importance and benefits of multinationals to actively cooperate and engage with NGOs.

NOTES

1   Verschoor, C.C. 2009. "Can government manage more ethically than capitalism?" *Strategic Finance*, October, 91, 4, 14.

2   World Bank. 2011. http://www.worldbank.org, 32.

3   Lawrence, A.T. & Weber, J. 2011. *Business & society: Stakeholders, ethics, public policy*. New York: McGraw-Hill Publishing.

4   Steiner, G.A. & Steiner, J.F. 2010. *Business, government and society: A managerial perspective, text and cases*. 12th ed. New York: McGraw-Hill.

5   DiMaggio, P.J. & Powell, W. 1983. "The iron cage revisited: Institutional isomorphism and collective rationality in organizational fields." *American Sociological Review*, 48, 147–160.

6   Lux, S., Crook, T.R. & Woehr, D. 2011. "Mixing business with politics: A meta-analysis of the antecedents and outcomes of corporate political activity." *Journal of Management*, 37, 1, 223–247.

7   Scheppers, S. 2010. "Business-government relations: Beyond lobbying." *Corporate Governance*, 10, 4, 475–483.

8   Okhmatovskiy, I. 2010. "Performance implications of ties to the government and SOEs: A political embeddedness perspective." *Journal of Management Studies*, 47, 6.

9   Lux et al., "Mixing business with politics."

10 Okhmatovskiy, "Performance implications of ties to the government and SOEs."

11 Dowling, G. & Weeks, W. 2008. "What the media is really telling you about your brand." *MIT Sloan Management Review*, 49, 3.

12 Donlon. J.P. 2009. "The criminalization of corporate conduct." *Chief Executive*, 241.

13 Kollmeyer, C.J. 2004. "Corporate interests: How the news media portray the economy." *Social Problems*, 51, 3, 432–452.

14 Ridout, T.N. & Smith, G.R. 2008. "Free advertising: How the media amplify campaign messages." *Political Research Quarterly*, 61, 4, 598–608.

15 Andina-Diaz, A. 2007. "Reinforcement vs. change: The political influence of the media." *Public Choice*, 131, 65–81 (at 65).

16 Barber. J.S. & Axinn.W.G. 2004. "New ideas and fertility limitation: The role of miss media." *Journal of Marriage and Family*, 66, 5, 1180–1200.

17 Andina-Diaz, "Reinforcement vs. change."

18 Tal-Or, N., Cohen, J., Tsfati, Y. & Gunther, C.A. 2010. "Testing casual direction in the influence of presumed media influence." *Communication Research*, 37.

19 Reuber, R.A. & Fischer, E. 2010. "Organizations behaving badly: When are discreditable actions likely to damage organizational reputation?" *Journal of Business Ethics*, 93, 39–50.

20 Dowling, G. & Weeks, W. 2011. "Media analysis: What is it worth?" *Journal of Business Strategy*, 32, 1, 26–33.

21 Ingenhoff, D. & Sommer, K. 2010. "Trust in companies and CEOs: A comparative study of the main influences." *Journal of Business Ethics*, 95, 339–355.

22 Dowling & Weeks, "Media analysis: What is it worth?".

23 Cullen, J. 2003. "A rounded picture: Using media framing as a tool for competitive intelligence and business research." *Business Information Review*, 20, 2, 88–94.

24 Dowling & Weeks, "Media analysis: What is it worth?"

25 Dowling & Weeks, "Media analysis: What is it worth?"

26 Dowling & Weeks, "Media analysis: What is it worth?"

27 Fassin, Y. 2009. "Inconsistencies in activists' behaviours and the ethics of NGOs." *Journal of Business Ethics*, 90, 503–521.

28 Fassin, "Inconsistencies in activists' behaviours," 503.

29 Arenas, D., Lozano, J.M. & Albareda, L. 2009. "The role of NGOs in CSR: Mutual perceptions among stakeholders." *Journal of Business Ethics*, 88, 175–197; Fassin, "Inconsistencies in activists' behaviours."

30 Arenas et al., "The role of NGOs in CSR."

31 Arenas et al., "The role of NGOs in CSR."

32 Sobczak, A. & Martins, L.C. 2010. "The impact and interplay of national and global CSR discourses: Insights from France and Brazil." *Corporate Governance*, 10, 4, 445–455.

33 Carpenter, C. 2001. "Business, green groups & the media: The role of non-governmental organizations in the climate change debate." *International Affairs*, 77, 2, 313–328.

34 Skippari, M. & Pajunen, K. 2010. "MNE-NGO—host government relationships in escalation of an FDI conflict." *Business Society*, 49, 619.

35 Fassin, "Inconsistencies in activists' behaviours."

36 Valor, C. & Merino, A. 2009. "Relationship of business and NGOs: An empirical analysis of strategies and mediators of their private relationship." *Business Ethics: A European Review*, 18, 2.

37 Fassin, "Inconsistencies in activists' behaviours."

38 Aleman, P.P. & Sandilands, M. 2008. "Building value at the top and the bottom of the global supply chain: MNC-NGO partnerships." *California Management Review*, 51, 1, 24–49.

39 Valor & Merino, "Relationship of business and NGOs."

KEY TERMS

Corporate public activity: attempt by a company to influence or manage the political entities and the government.

Enforcement of contract: expectation that the terms and conditions of a contract will be respected.

Governments: institutions that can constrain and regularize behaviors and actions through its capacity to establish rules, to inspect and review conformity, and to manipulate consequences to reinforce behaviors.

Media: many avenues of information such as newspapers, television, and the internet.

Media analysis: routine scan of media to discover what is being said about companies.

NGO active cooperation: engage with stakeholders to develop solutions.

NGO confrontational strategy: reliance on symbolic damage strategies such as negative publicity or material damage strategies such as boycotts.

Non-governmental organizations: umbrella term that includes special interest groups, activist groups, social movement organizations, charities, religious groups, protest groups, and other non-profit groups.

Problem and solution analysis: using information from salience/sentiment analysis and theme/contradiction analysis to formulate solutions to ongoing problems.

Protection of investors: expectations investors have of transparency and accountability from managers running the company.

Registration of property: procedures necessary for a business to purchase a property from another business and transfer the title to the buyer's name.

Regulation: laws and regulations to force companies to behave in ways that are more ethical.

Salience and sentiment analysis: the number of times companies are mentioned and whether they are portrayed positively or negatively.

Secondary stakeholders: those groups or entities that have an indirect impact on the company's survival and strategic activities.

Theme and contradiction analysis: analysis of media to determine whether ongoing media coverage is portraying the company under some specific theme.

DISCUSSION QUESTIONS

1. What are secondary stakeholders? How do they differ from primary stakeholders? How do they influence companies? Be specific with examples.
2. Discuss the role of the government as a secondary stakeholder. What are the various ways they can influence companies?
3. What is legitimacy in reference to the government as a secondary stakeholder? How can companies achieve legitimacy?
4. What is corporate political activity? Describe the various forms of corporate political activity. What purposes does corporate political activity serve?
5. Briefly define the media. How do the media influence perception of companies? Be specific about both direct and indirect influences.
6. Describe the various activities involved in a media analysis. Discuss the possible responses to the results of a media analysis.
7. Discuss the salience and sentiment media analyses. How are the salience and sentiment analyses different from themes and contradiction media analyses? How can the results of the above analyses be used for the problems and solutions media analyses?
8. What are NGOs? Discuss some of the strategies NGOs can use to influence companies.
9. Discuss some of the questionable practices NGOs sometimes engage in. Be specific with examples.
10. Why are more companies now cooperating with NGOs? What are the benefits of such NGO engagement and cooperation?

INTERNET ACTIVITY

1. Go to the World Bank website: http://www.worldbank.org.
2. Find the Doing Business Project Report for 2011.
3. What are the ten indicators of the Doing Business project? Which of these indicators are also relevant to ethics? Do you think that Paying Taxes should also be included in the ethics environment?

4. Research the "Enforcing Contracts" report. What are some of the major trends worldwide regarding contract enforcement? Which regions have the highest contract enforcement? Why?
5. Research the "Protecting Investors" report. What are the major trends? Which regions have made the most progress protecting their investors?

For more Internet Activities and resources, visit the Companion Website at www.routledge.com/cw/parboteeah.

WHAT WOULD YOU DO?

The Non-Governmental Organization

You start a Bachelor's degree in Business Administration at a prestigious university. However, you have always been very environmentally conscious and you are dismayed to find that so many companies end up being strong polluters of the environment. You are also unhappy with current environmental regulations being weakened in most parts of the country. You therefore become very frustrated with the field of business administration and vow to change things.

After graduation, you join a well-known non-governmental organization (NGO). The NGO's main aim is to scrutinize practices of multinationals with regards to the environment. The NGO will then publicize the actions of offending multinationals. However, similar to employment in many NGOs, you find that you are not getting paid as much as you could if you were in the private sector. You also know that there is lots of uncertainty regarding your position. Your position could easily be cut if the NGO does not get similar levels of donation.

You have been working very hard on a large multinational that is headquartered in your town. You discover that the multinational has a very poor environmental record and that they have engaged in many practices locally that have resulted in severe pollution. Before such actions are publicized, the NGO will typically share the findings with the company. This is done to give a chance to the offending organization to respond to such allegations.

You are asked to share your findings with the company. You arrange a meeting with the CEO to share these results. The CEO is actually very appreciative of your work and the findings. She asks you about your role in the NGO and about your educational qualifications. The CEO then proceeds to ask you to work for them. She assures you that they want to be more environmentally sensitive. She also believes that the company needs someone like you to determine what changes will need to occur and where.

What do you do? You have vowed to never work for a large corporation. However, you also know that the pay will be much better and you will have a more stable job. But if you take the job, you feel that you will be selling out your friends at the NGO. Do you still go along and take the job? Why or why not?

BRIEF CASE: BUSINESS ETHICS INSIGHT

Mercedes in China

As the Chinese enjoy increasing affluence, Mercedes-Benz cars are becoming important status symbols and signifiers of luxury. High-powered executives see Mercedes-Benz as the car of choice, while the average Chinese views the car as a glamorous vehicle. Mercedes-Benz vehicles are often sought to lead wedding processions. It is therefore not surprising to find that Mercedes-Benz has the highest sales figure among both domestic and international luxury car brands.

In 2002, Mercedes-Benz faced a major media nightmare that threatened to destabilize its image of luxury in China. The major incident that led to this nightmare was a press conference with around 50 journalists. During the press conference, six young individuals proceeded to destroy a Mercedes-Benz car with a sledgehammer. The car was completely decimated in less than ten minutes. Over the next months, Mercedes had to deal with the impact of the media repeatedly showing the event.

Why did the six individuals decide to destroy the car? A close examination of events leading to the destruction sheds some insight. The conflict between Mercedes-Benz and its Chinese consumers started when management of the Wuhan Wild Animals Zoo discovered numerous defects and other reliability issues in their newly purchased Mercedes-Benz vehicles. To repair the vehicles, the cars had to be towed to Beijing. There, they allegedly faced significant delays in the repair. Furthermore, Mercedes-Benz refused to cover the repairs, although these individuals had spent over $100,000 for each vehicle. Their frustrations continued after they met with further reticence on the part of Mercedes-Benz in assuming responsibility for the defects. Rather than trying to fix the problems, Mercedes-Benz blamed the problems on consumers, arguing that the cars were not being maintained as needed and the quality of gas not adequate to run the high-powered engines.

This case illustrates the dangers of not properly addressing customer needs in an emerging market. The widely publicized initial demolition led to similar stunts across China. These led to more unrest as more consumers confronted the company with similar grievances. Furthermore, the media continued their sensational coverage of the various events giving consumers a voice. Soon Mercedes-Benz was being seen as an arrogant company having double standards with regards to how they treated their consumers worldwide. Chinese consumers were frustrated that they were not being treated similarly to consumers in Western countries. Fueled by the media, this resulted in further controversy and outrage, seen as an affront to Chinese cultural identity.

Based on Tan, J. and Tan. A.E. 2009. "Managing public relations in a emerging economy: The case of Mercedes in China." *Journal of Business Ethics*, 86, 257–266.

BRIEF CASE QUESTIONS

1. What are some of the major factors that led to this media nightmare for Mercedes?
2. Why did the news spread so rapidly? Why did other consumers start engaging in similar demonstrations?
3. Do Western companies approach emerging market consumers with arrogance? Why or why not?
4. What should Mercedes do to ensure that similar events do not occur in the future? Illustrate with concepts discussed in the chapter.

LONG CASE: BUSINESS ETHICS

PROCTER & GAMBLE CONFRONTATION WITH PETA

On March 25, 2003, People for the Ethical Treatment of Animals held a press conference to announce findings of animal cruelty in an independent laboratory used by the Iams Company. PETA announced these claims as the result of a nine-month secret investigation of an independent research laboratory. The press conference was held in Dayton, Ohio, the home of the Iams Company and just down the road from Iams' parent company, Cincinnati-based Procter & Gamble (P&G).[1]

The chain of events leading up to this press conference started in September of 2001 when Iams executives met with PETA to discuss what PETA called "consumer concern" over testing conducted in Iams' independent laboratories.[2] While Iams has garnered praise from such organizations as the Humane Society of the United States and the American Veterinary Medical Association, PETA was concerned that Iams conducted tests that were unnecessary and under conditions that were cruel to the animal "research associates" that were the subjects of the testing. In 2002 and 2003, a representative of PETA was hired by Iams to work in its independent laboratory, the Sinclair Research Center, in Columbia, Missouri. While her exact role as an employee has been debated, she made observations of alleged animal abuse. PETA claims that 27 "research associates" were destroyed during the course of testing and that other inhumane practices such as debarking procedures and muscle removal surgeries were performed.[3] Iams claims that the inhumane procedures were directly tied to the investigator, while PETA claims that this is not true.[4]

While both sides dispute the actual role of the investigator and the degree of the abuse, if any, it was clear that Iams' reputation as a high-quality producer of pet products that had genuine concern for the well-being of animals was being called into doubt. Iams needed to act immediately to determine the validity of PETA's claims and to take any appropriate action to protect the well-being of their "research associates" in independent labs. Proper communication of their record on preventing animal abuse, the validity of PETA's claims and any actions taken as a result of these claims was imperative to protecting Iams' reputation.

A Company for Animal Lovers

The Iams Company was founded in 1946 by an animal nutritionist in 1946. Mr. Iams started operations in a modest feed mill outside Dayton, Ohio. Mr. Iams took on Clay Mathile in 1970 as a business partner. Eventually, Mr. Mathile purchased the company in 1982.[5]

The Iams Company sells under two brand names, Eukanuba and Iams dog and cat food. The company's mission is "to enhance the well-being of dogs and cats by providing world-class quality foods and pet care products." The company prides itself on being a collection of dog, cat, and animal lovers. The Iams Company markets itself as the maker of high-quality brands that are sold in specialty pet stores, veterinary offices and clinics, feed and grain stores, gourmet food stores and pet boarding and grooming locations, as well as commercial grocery stores.[6]

Iams conducts its research and development through the Paul F. Iams Technical Center. A significant part of this research revolves around dog and cat "research associates" which help test nutritional content and taste of new or modified products. Iams holds the research conducted with the help of dogs and cats to standards set forth by the Animal Welfare Act of the U.S., the U.S. Department of Agriculture, and Directive 86/609/EEC of the European Union.[7]

A Partnership is Born

P&G can trace its roots back to two European immigrants who intended to settle out west. However, due to unforeseen circumstances, the two men settled instead in the busy city of Cincinnati, Ohio. William Procter was an established candlemaker while James Gamble worked as a soapmaker. The two men met years later when they married sisters Olivia and Elizabeth Norris. Their father-in-law convinced the two men to become business partners and in 1837 the partnership Procter & Gamble was formed.[8]

P&G initially sold only candles and soap. During the Civil War, the partnership was awarded several contracts to supply Union soldiers with their products. Their reputation grew as Union soldiers returned home with their P&G products. In 1890, P&G incorporated to raise additional funds for the company. William Alexander Procter, the son of the founder, was named president. He set up an analytical lab to study and improve the soapmaking process. This was one of the first research labs in American industry, and helped build P&G's reputation for being an innovator and industry leader.[9]

International Expansion

P&G continued to grow for the next 120 years through research, innovation, and international expansion. They developed new product lines such as Tide detergent and Crest toothpaste and purchased similar companies throughout the world. P&G grew into a truly global company and, by 1993, their sales exceeded US$30 billion, with over half of their sales coming from outside the United States. In September of 1999, P&G purchased the pet food manufacturer Iams Company. Since then, Iams has grown to become the number one pet food manufacturer in the U.S. and, because of brands like Iams, P&G has grown into a major, multinational corporation with nearly 98,000 employees working in almost 80 countries worldwide. P&G's portfolio of brands is the envy of many corporations. They are recognized throughout the world, with 16 of the brands exceeding US$1 billion in annual revenues. P&G's total revenues for 2003 exceed US$51 billion and their net earnings were nearly US$6.5 billion.[10]

PETA: People for the Ethical Treatment of Animals

"People for the Ethical Treatment of Animals," better known as PETA, is a non-profit organization founded in 1980 and based in Norfolk, Virginia. PETA's mission statement is "animals are not ours to eat, wear, experiment on, or use for entertainment." They have spent the last 24 years working to protect the rights of all animals. PETA works through public education, cruelty investigations, research, animal rescue, legislation, special events, celebrity involvement, and direct action.[11]

PETA first gained national recognition in 1981 when they uncovered the abuse of animals in experiments. The organization's undercover investigation led to the precedent-setting Silver Springs Monkeys case. This case resulted in the first arrest and conviction of an animal experimenter in the United States on charges of cruelty to animals, the first confiscation of abused laboratory animals, and the first U.S. Supreme Court victory for animals in laboratories. As a result, PETA has had a major effect on the way U.S. corporations conduct their business. During the 1990s, PETA launched an international campaign against cosmetic companies that used animals for cosmetic testing. They convinced Benetton to halt their animal testing, and the major cosmetic corporations soon followed. PETA now lists 550 cosmetic companies that do not test on animals. Corporation after corporation has learned of PETA's power and influence the hard way. McDonald's, General Motors, Calvin Klein, and, most recently, Burger King have all acquiesced to the demands of a PETA-led campaign in one way or another.[12]

PETA has recently gained large support among many entertainers and celebrities in Hollywood. PETA compiled two animal rights albums, *Animal Liberation* and *Tame Yourself,* featuring artists such as Chrissie Hynde, Indigo Girls, Michael Stipe, and Belinda Carlisle. PETA also has held several "Rock against Fur" and "Fur is a Drag" benefit concerts featuring The B-52s, k.d. lang, and others. Long-time supporter Paul McCartney invited PETA to set up literature tables on his world tour.[13]

This Hollywood influence has led to a major problem in the fur industry. PETA has launched a major "I'd rather go naked than wear fur" campaign with models such as Christy Turlington, Tyra Banks, and Marcus Schenkenberg, actor Kim Basinger, among others, posing for the campaign. They have also received pledges from filmmakers including Oliver Stone, Martin Scorsese, and Rob Reiner to keep fur off movie sets. According to the *San Francisco Chronicle,* "Protests by groups such as PETA have hobbled the fur business." PETA's influence is continuing to grow as a result of the large number of Hollywood backers. In fact, Britain's *Time Out* magazine named animal rights the number one "hip cause," thanks largely, it said, to the high-profile campaigns of "super-trendy PETA."[14]

Regulation of Animal Testing

In 1966, Congress enacted Public Law (PL) 89-544, known as the Laboratory Animal Welfare Act. This law regulates dealers who handle dogs and cats, as well as laboratories that use dogs, cats, hamsters, guinea pigs, rabbits, or non-human primates in research.

The first amendment to the Laboratory Animal Welfare Act was passed in 1970 (PL 91-579) and changed the name of the law to the Animal Welfare Act (AWA). This amendment authorized the Secretary of Agriculture to regulate other warm-blooded animals when used in research, exhibition, or the wholesale pet trade.

An amendment was added to the AWA in 1985 as the Improved Standards for Laboratory Animals Act, which was part of the Food Security Act. These amendments required the Secretary to issue additional standards for the use of animals in research. This standard governs facilities such as the Sinclair Research Center.

The Regulations

The United States Department of Agriculture (USDA) is charged with developing and implementing regulations to support the AWA. These regulations (which appear in Title 9, Code of Federal Regulations [CFR], Chapter 1, Subchapter A, Parts 13) require the licensing of animal dealers, exhibitors, and operators of animal auction sales where animals regulated under the AWA are sold. The regulations also require all non-Federal research facilities to register with the Secretary of Agriculture.[15]

All licensees and registrants must provide their animals with care that meets or exceeds the USDA's standards for veterinary care and animal husbandry. These standards include requirements for handling, housing, feeding, sanitation, ventilation, shelter from extreme weather, veterinary care, and separation of species when necessary.[16]

Over the years, the USDA has made substantive changes to the AWA regulations. In the late 1980s, the USDA amended the requirements pertaining to the use of animals in research. These amendments, in response to the Improved Standards for Laboratory Animals Act, established standards for the exercise of dogs and psychological well-being of non-human primates. The amendments also set standards to minimize the pain and distress of animals; ensure the proper use of anesthetics, analgesics, and tranquilizers; and require researchers to consider alternatives to painful procedures.[17]

To ensure that these standards are met, the amendments require each research facility to establish an Institutional Animal Care and Use Committee to approve and monitor all research conducted at the institution. The regulations for this amendment were published February 15, 1991.[18]

The Investigation Unveiled

While March 25, 2003 was the official unveiling of PETA's claims against P&G subsidiary Iams, the course of action was set several years earlier. A United Kingdom animal rights group closely affiliated with PETA called Uncaged Campaign protested Iams in Europe in the late 1990s. They based their protests on 13 years of published Iams research which disclosed the euthanasia of some dogs and cats. This gained some publicity in European newspapers. After meeting with Uncaged Campaign, Iams announced that it would suspend any new research that resulted in the euthanasia of dogs and cats in March of 1999.[19]

As a reaction to the publicity generated in Europe by Uncaged Campaign, PETA began investigating Iams research policies. They had a meeting with Brian Brown, the Associate Director of Global External Relations for the Iams Company at the time, and Dan Carey, Iams Director of Research and Technical Development. PETA walked away from this unsatisfied with the progress of Iams' efforts to improve conditions for research on laboratory dogs and cats.[20]

This led to the now well-known undercover operation. According to Mary Beth Sweetland, PETA's Director of Research and Undercover Investigations, the non-profit organization had a budget of approximately US$3 million for undercover operations in 2002. Thus, the investigation into the Columbia, Missouri facility was well funded and supported by PETA. Sweetland said in a 2003 interview, "We see our undercover actions as helping the government do its job. The USDA visits for a day, while we stay for months."[21]

The exact nature of the position that the undercover PETA representative held is debated by both sides. Iams claims that the representative was hired by Iams as an "animal welfare specialist."[22] The representative's duties were focused on the testing environment and improving the lives of the testing subjects. However, Iams claims that the representative had a "clear conflict of interest," as PETA had spent time and money to place her inside the Sinclair Research Center. She was, thus, responsible for much of the abuse in order to produce video of suffering animals to advance PETA's cause. In fact, Dan Carey, Iams Director of Technical Research and Development, in a 2003 interview, said, "the PETA spy was the one that told the facility in question that debarking was an acceptable course of action."[23]

PETA vehemently denies these claims. They claim that the representative was a "study monitor" employed directly by Sinclair Research Center and any form of care for the animals was not included in her job description. PETA claims that the agent is an animal lover and tried to contact Liz Fuess, the supervisor of that particular Iams study, to alert her of the debarking procedure. PETA claims that the debarking was ordered by the facility director, Guy Bouchard.[24]

PETA also claimed that, in addition to the debarking procedures and the termination of 27 dogs, Iams dogs were dumped on cold concrete flooring after having huge chunks of muscle cut out of their thighs. They also claim dogs and cats were stir-crazy from confinement in "windowless, dungeon-like buildings." Allegedly, a co-worker instructed the PETA representative to hit the test dogs on the chest if they quit breathing and another co-worker talked about an Iams dog found dead in his cage, bleeding from the mouth. PETA claims cruel studies were done by Iams involving sticking tubes down dogs' throats to force them to ingest vegetable oil. These claims are just a few of the alleged findings from their investigation.[25]

Iams and P&G dispute these claims. They assert that, posing as an animal lover, the PETA representative captured sensational video that did not include any scenes of the socialization and enrichment activities she was being paid to develop and deliver. They claim her video also falsely attributed footage and stories of dogs and cats that were not a part of the Iams studies. Company literature clearly states, "Iams doesn't kill dogs or cats! It's against the research policy that has been in place for years."[26]

The Procter & Gamble Response

P&G is an international conglomerate that is no newcomer to external relations. However, Iams is an extremely valuable brand and the global leader in pet food supplies. The reputation of this valuable brand is at stake as it is built upon the ideal that "Iams is a company full of pet lovers who dedicate their lives to helping dogs and cats live longer, healthier lives.[27]

Chapter 7: Long Case Notes

1 Wilkinson, N., "Focus: PETA vs. Iams," *Dayton City Paper,* September 25, 2003.
2 Wilkinson, N., "Focus: PETA vs. Iams," *Dayton City Paper,* September 25, 2003.
3 Bolinski, Jayette, "PETA Calls for Boycott of Iams Over Allegations," *State Journal-Register* (Springfield, IL), November 4, 2003, Local; p. 11.
4 www.iamstruth.com.
5 www.iams.com.
6 www.iams.com.
7 www.iams.com.
8 www.pg.com.
9 www.pg.com.
10 Hoover's Company Records, "The Procter & Gamble Company," 2004.
11 www.peta.org.
12 Young, S.C., "PETA's Principles," *The Harvard Crimson,* March 8, 2004, Opinion Section.
13 www.peta.org.
14 www.peta.org.
15 Crawford, R.L., "Animal Welfare Act Interpretive Summaries," United States Department of Agriculture. www.nal.usda.gov.
16 Crawford, R.L., "Animal Welfare Act Interpretive Summaries," United States Department of Agriculture. www.nal.usda.gov.
17 Brown, J., "Animal Testing—The Facts and the Figures," *Independent (London),* July 30, 2004, NEWS, pp. 12–13.
18 Crawford, R.L., "Animal Welfare Act Interpretive Summaries," United States Department of Agriculture, www.nal.usda.gov.
19 Telephone correspondence with Kelly Vanasse, Associate Director for Global External Relations, The Iams Company.
20 Telephone correspondence with Kelly Vanasse, Associate Director for Global External Relations, The Iams Company.
21 Wilkinson, N., "Focus: PETA vs. Iams," *Dayton City Paper,* September 25, 2003.
22 Telephone correspondence with Kelly Vanasse, Associate Director for Global External Relations, The Iams Company.
23 Wilkinson, N., "Focus: PETA vs. Iams," *Dayton City Paper,* September 25, 2003.
24 Wilkinson, N., "Focus: PETA vs. Iams," *Dayton City Paper,* September 25, 2003.
25 www.iamscruelty.com.
26 www.iamstruth.com.
27 Telephone correspondence with Kelly Vanasse, Associate Director for Global External Relations, The Iams Company.

LONG CASE QUESTIONS

1. Who are the affected stakeholders? Who are the most important? Which stakeholder(s) should P&G communicate with first? How should communication goals be accomplished?
2. Is this only an external problem? How strong a response should P&G have for internal communication?
3. What are the risks and potential rewards of working with NGOs such as PETA? Can PETA ever be fully satisfied by Iams and P&G without sacrificing product quality and/or business goals?
4. Which side do you believe: P&G arguing that the PETA spy set up the company? Or PETA? Why?
5. How can companies work with NGOs to ensure that their needs are met?

Part II:
Comprehensive Case

BRISTOL-MYERS SQUIBB: PATENTS, PROFITS, AND PUBLIC SCRUTINY

"ALL THE WORLD'S A STAGE"

Bob Zito let out a deep breath as he hung up the phone in his office. It was 11:07 a.m. on Saturday morning, and the weather was perfect for the first college football game day of the season. He opened his office window to let in the brisk autumn air of September 2, 2006, and tried to relax for the first time in what felt like weeks. His corporate counsel had called to tell him that the U.S. District Court for the Southern District of New York had just granted Bristol-Myers Squibb a preliminary injunction against the Canadian generic drug producer Apotex.

Zito leaned back in his chair, thankful for the breathing space. In the past month alone, Apotex's generic version of Bristol-Myers' Plavix had siphoned off almost 75% of the $4-billion annual market for the blockbuster blood thinner. Many pharmacies had already stocked up multiple months' worth of the product, but this injunction would prevent Apotex from shipping any more of the generic until the patent-protection question was resolved.

Zito was grateful for the temporary respite, which he hoped to use to construct and implement a corporate communication strategy to help the embattled pharmaceutical giant. Such a strategy would have to be comprehensive and incredibly detailed, addressing the widely publicized Apotex negotiation scandal, the potential loss of patent protection (and revenues) for the company's best-selling drug, and the looming dismissal of Bristol-Myers' CEO, while simultaneously steering attention away from the company's past ethical troubles. Zito opened his laptop and checked the time. With a sigh, he resigned himself to the fact that he wasn't likely to make it home in time to watch the game.

THE HISTORY OF BRISTOL-MYERS SQUIBB

Bristol-Myers Squibb is the leading worldwide provider of anti-cancer therapies, as well as a leader in the discovery and development of innovative treatments to fight heart disease, stroke, and infectious diseases including HIV/AIDS. Its areas of specialization include most of the pharmaceutical spectrum, from oncology to cardiovascular disease to infectious diseases (including HIV/AIDS) and mental illness. The company enjoys a distinguished history: in the early 1960s Bristol-Myers produced its first anti-cancer medicine (still in use today), while the 1980s witnessed Squibb market the first of an important new class of medications, called ACE inhibitors, for the treatment of hypertension. In 1989, these two companies joined forces in one of the largest mergers in corporate history. During the 1990s, Bristol-Myers Squibb brought to market the first medicine specifically designed for the treatment of HIV/AIDS, as well as a breakthrough therapy "hailed as the most important cancer medication in 20 years."[1]

Bristol-Myers

In 1887, William McLaren Bristol and John Ripley Myers invested $5,000 into a failing drug manufacturing firm located in Clinton, New York. The company was officially incorporated on December 13, 1887, and in May 1898 changed its name to the Bristol, Myers Company (a hyphen would replace the comma when the company became a corporation in 1899).

The partners strove to grow the business in a challenging environment, maintaining two rules above all: an insistence on high-quality products and the maintenance of the firm's good financial standing at all costs. With these two priorities in mind, Bristol-Myers became profitable for the first time in 1900, and from 1903 to 1905 saw a tenfold increase in sales. Bristol-Myers was transformed from a regional to a national company, soon to become an international one. With the company's products being sold in 26 countries, gross profits topped $1 million for the first time in 1924. At the same time, "the shares held by John Myers's heirs became available for sale, triggering a series of moves that in 1929 turned Bristol-Myers into a publicly held company, listed on the New York Stock Exchange."[2] Subsequent business decisions saw Bristol-Myers take over smaller, well-managed pharmaceutical firms in a strategy of growth through judicious acquisition that has continued to this day.[3]

Squibb

Edward Robinson Squibb founded his pharmaceutical company in 1858, headquartered in Brooklyn, New York. He dedicated Squibb to the production of "consistently pure medicines", a cause that claimed his lifelong interest. In 1906, six years after Edward Squibb's death, Congress passed the Pure Food and Drugs Act. As related in company lore, the law still stands as the triumph of his lifelong crusade for safe, reliable pharmaceutical products.[4] In 1921, Squibb adopted a slogan that reflected the ideals of its founder: "The priceless ingredient in every product is the honor and integrity of its maker." The company enjoyed respectable growth, and the company expanded into South America and Europe. Squibb International was incorporated in 1946, and built manufacturing facilities in Mexico, Italy, and Argentina. Squibb researchers made a significant breakthrough in 1975 with the creation of Capoten®, the first of a brand-new class of antihypertensive agents called ACE inhibitors.

Bristol-Myers Squibb (BMS)

Bristol-Myers merged with Squibb in 1989, creating a global leader in the healthcare industry. The merger created what was then the world's second largest pharmaceutical enterprise. BMS core products include: Videx (1991), Monopril (1991), and Pravachol (1991, expanded usage granted in 1995 by the FDA), TAXOL Injection (1991), Glucophage (1993), Avapro (1997), Plavix (1997), Excedrin (1998), Sustiva capsules (2001), Coumadin Crystalline (2001), Abilify (2002), Reyataz (2004), Orencia (2005), EMSAM transdermal (2006), SPRYCEL (2006), and ATRIPLA (2006). Bristol-Myers Squibb received the National Medal of Technology in December 1998, an award widely respected as America's highest honor for technological innovation. The company received outstanding recognition "for extending and enhancing human life through innovative pharmaceutical research and development, and for redefining the science of clinical study through groundbreaking and hugely complex clinical trials that are recognized models in the industry."[5] BMS attempts to act as a good global corporate citizen and live the ideals of its founders through its outreach programs.

In 1999, the company announced Secure the Future, a $100 million commitment to advance HIV/AIDS research and community outreach programs in five southern African countries. In 2000, BMS and four other pharmaceutical companies and international agencies joined the UNAIDS "Drug ACCESS Initiative," which aims to make antiretroviral medicines and therapies widely available in African countries that have developed a coherent national AIDS strategy. As part of the program, the company offered to lower the prices of HIV/AIDS medicines in those countries by 90%.

More recently, Bristol-Myers Squibb took its access efforts a step further, offering HIV/AIDS drugs below cost in Africa. The company is also ensuring that its patents do not prevent inexpensive HIV/AIDS therapy in Africa.[6] BMS had 2005 revenues of approximately $19 billion, with profits of $3 billion. This is a 7.6% decrease and 25.6% increase, respectively, on 2004 results.[7] R&D expenditures in 2005 were $2.7 billion, up 10% from 2004. This included $2.5 billion in payments for in-licensing and development programs. The first quarter of 2006 saw $750 million spent on R&D, up 22% from the previous year.

BMS is determined to retain its position as a leader in drug development. Current strategies include: in-house development and collaboration, the acquisition of smaller dynamic pharmaceutical companies, the divestiture of non-core assets (including the May 2005 sale of BMS's Oncology Therapeutics Network distribution business, as well as the divestiture of the U.S. and Canadian Consumer Medicines business to Novartis).

BMS's forecast for the future is cautiously optimistic. New BMS blockbuster drugs may strengthen the company's financial position. In the first half of 2003 two major drugs were approved: Abilify, an antipsychotic, and Reyataz, the first once-daily protease inhibitor for the treatment of HIV/AIDS. The FDA also granted limited clearance to Erbitux, the sidelined cancer drug that BMS developed in conjunction with ImClone. Analysts at SunTrust Robinson Humphrey estimated that Erbitux sales could peak at more than $700 million. These promising drugs signal a potential new beginning for the company. Morningstar projects an average revenue growth rate of 3% through 2007. However, generic challengers continue to enter the market at a steady pace, and there is the constant threat of competition from the large drug developers (Merck, Novartis, and Pfizer) in BMS's core territories.

If the first quarter is a trend indicator, 2006 will be more profitable for BMS: the company reported a 34% increase in first-quarter profit to $714 million, helped by higher sales of heart and blood-pressure drugs, and a $200 million gain from the sale of assets. Erbitux sales were $413 million for the year up 58%. Plavix, Abilify, and Reyataz sales were up 15%, 54%, and 68% respectively—definitely a bright spot for the company. Nevertheless, revenues were up only 3% to $4.7 billion, while the average U.S. pharmaceutical industry revenues rose 7% to $2.1 billion.[8] In February 2001, *Fortune* magazine named Bristol-Myers Squibb "America's Most Admired Pharmaceutical Company." One month later, Peter R. Dolan, a 13-year veteran of the company, succeeded Charles A. Heimbold, Jr., as chief executive officer.[9]

PETER R. DOLAN

Peter R. Dolan was born on January 6, 1956, in Salem, Massachusetts. He received his BA from Tufts University in 1978, and his MBA from Dartmouth College in 1980. He began his career at General Foods from 1983 to 1987, but by 1988 had transferred to Bristol-Myers Squibb as Vice-President of Marketing.

Dolan served as president of the Mead Johnson Nutritional Group from 1995 to 1996. Under his direction, the company opened related manufacturing facilities in four countries and international sales climbed to 40% of the corporation's revenue by 1996.

Dolan was named CEO in February 2001 and made Chairman of the Board in 2002. He was infamous within the company for setting "Big Hairy Audacious Goals," such as his 2001 promise to double BMS revenues within five years. He would come to regret that particular statement, as 2002 sales totaled $18.1 billion, down 1% from 2000.

ROBERT ZITO AND BMS CORPORATE COMMUNICATIONS

Robert T. Zito joined Bristol-Myers Squibb as Chief Communications Officer (CCO) in June 2004. Zito received his BA in English from Fairfield University and is a 1998 Ellis Island Medal of Honor recipient.[10] He is responsible for implementing external and internal communications initiatives, as well as developing a long-term corporate strategic communications plan for BMS. He oversees all aspects of communication and public relations for the company, including corporate brand management, advertising, media relations, employee and policy communications, executive prep and communications, creative services, and community affairs.[11]

Before accepting his current position with BMS, Zito was the Executive Vice President of Communications at the New York Stock Exchange, where he was responsible for developing and building the NYSE's brand. He has also worked as VP of Corporate Communications at Sony (North America), VP of CN Communications, and as an account executive at the public relations firm of Hill and Knowlton.[12]

WHAT IS PLAVIX?

Plavix was a FDA-approved anti-platelet daily medication that reduced the risk of heart attack, stroke, or vascular death in patients with established peripheral arterial disease (PAD).[13] The drug had also been shown to reduce occurrences of peripheral artery disease and stroke. Plavix was brought to market through a partnership between Bristol-Myers Squibb and French drug maker Sanofi-Aventis, the world's third largest pharmaceutical company and the largest in Europe.

Plavix Function

Clot formation is a natural defense mechanism of the body that protects excessive bleeding in the case of an injury. When the skin is cut, particles in human blood called platelets bond together to form a clot. Clot formation can also be triggered by the rupture of plaque, which is a buildup of cholesterol and other materials in the walls of the arteries. When platelets clump together on or near the plaque, they can form a clot that may limit or completely stop the flow of blood to various parts of the body. If a clot forms in an artery leading to the heart, heart-related chest pain or a heart attack may occur. If a clot forms in an artery leading to the brain, it can cause a stroke. Plavix prevents platelets from sticking together and forming clots, which keeps blood flowing and helps protect against future heart attack or stroke.

Plavix Revenues

Plavix 2005 global sales were $5.9 billion, up more than 15% from 2004.[14] According to Pharmaceutical Business Revenue and Data Monitor, sales were expected to peak at $6 billion in 2011, when the Plavix patent was expected to expire. Bristol-Myers Squibb total 2005 revenues were $19.2 billion; Plavix sales thus represented 30% of the company's total revenues.

THE PHARMACEUTICAL INDUSTRY

The global pharmaceutical sales market in 2005 was $565 billion, growing at an estimated 7% per year.[15] Generic competition is currently the principal threat to branded drug makers. Between 2006 and 2010, at least 70 innovative brand name drugs are expected to go off-patent in the United States. Nineteen of these drugs are "blockbusters," meaning that they have annual sales of more than $1 billion. This accounts for $45 billion in revenues, or roughly 8% of the global market.[16]

GENERIC DRUG COMPETITION

A generic drug may be comparable to a brand name drug in dosage form, strength, performance characteristics, and intended use. Brand name drug patents are usually protected for 20 years from the date of the patent submission.[17] The patent protects the drug manufacturer that incurred the costs of researching, developing, and marketing the drug. Once a drug's patent has expired, any other drug company may release a generic version. Generic drugs tend to be drastically cheaper than brand-name drugs, with prices ranging from 20–70% of the brand-name version.

FDA APPROVAL: BRAND NAME AND GENERIC DRUGS

All new drugs must be approved for human use by the United State Food and Drug Administration. The approval process includes laboratory, animal, and human testing. Human testing is completed in three phases and may include data collected from thousands of patients. It is not uncommon for a drug to take as long as eight years to be approved.[18] Generic drugs must also obtain FDA approval. However, generic drugs may take advantage of an abbreviated process wherein they do not have to submit the generic drug for animal or human tests, as the drug's safety and effectiveness were already established in the initial clinical trials.

ACCOUNTING IRREGULARITIES: DOLAN'S TROUBLES BEGIN

On March 10, 2003, just over two years after Dolan took over as CEO, Bristol-Myers Squibb announced that it had overstated sales by $2.5 billion over a three-year period. The earnings overstatement was due to Bristol-Myers employing a "channel surfing" scheme in which the company used financial incentives that rewarded wholesalers for buying and holding larger prescription drug inventories. The scheme resulted in wholesalers acquiring almost $2 billion in excess inventories. Bristol-Myers eventually admitted that the incentives were designed to help the company meet its quarterly sales projections.[19]

Bristol's accounting troubles continued when former Chief Financial Officer Frederick S. Schiff and former Executive Vice President Richard J. Lane were indicted and charged with securities fraud for artificially inflating sales through the channel surfing scheme. Schiff and Lane were also charged with signing inaccurate SEC filings and purposely misleading investors through press releases and conference calls that masked the increasing wholesaler drug inventories. Both were asked to leave in 2001.

At the end of the scandal, Bristol-Myers Squibb reduced net sales figures by $1.4 billion for 2001, $678 million for 2000, and $376 million for 1999.[20] A total of $839 million was paid to shareholders harmed by BMS's fraudulent conduct.[21] The Department of Justice agreed to dismiss criminal complaints against the company if it cooperated with the legal investigation, admitted wrongdoing, and adopted strict internal compliance controls.

PLAVIX GENERIC DRUG AGREEMENT

In July 2006, BMS announced that the U.S. Justice Department was investigating the company's March 2006 agreement with Canadian generic drug manufacturer

Apotex. The agreement was intended to delay Apotex's release of an inexpensive generic version of Plavix. The investigation led FBI agents to search Dolan's office in New York the day before the announcement was made.

Under the terms of Bristol-Myers' ill-conceived agreement with Apotex, BMS offered Apotex $40 million to halt production of the generic Plavix until June 1, 2011. This date was five months before the Plavix patent was set to expire.[22] Bristol-Myers also agreed not to release its own non-branded Plavix until six months after Apotex began to sell its generic version of the blood thinner. When asked to approve the agreement, the U.S. Federal Trade Commission and state Attorneys General objected to these provisions. They labeled the Bristol-Myers concession anti-competitive because it assured that Apotex would be the sole market vendor of cheap, generic Plavix for at least six months.[23] Bristol-Myers Squibb agreed to remove the anti-competitive provision from the contract. Nevertheless, the Federal Trade Commission began questioning Apotex regarding the revised agreement. During these questioning sessions, Apotex told the federal regulators that Bristol-Myers had given Apotex private assurance that it would not release a general version of Plavix to the market.[24] These statements, which contradicted statements made by Bristol-Myers to the FTC, led the Federal Trade Commission to pursue a criminal investigation into the rejected contract.

When the agreement did not receive approval, Apotex quickly introduced its generic version of Plavix (which had obtained FDA approval earlier that year), and the drug became universally available in August 2006. While Plavix cost about $4 per dose in the U.S., Apotex priced the generic version at an estimated 10–20% discount.[25] Apotex's generic Plavix quickly gained 75% market share of new prescriptions.[26] Within the month, Bristol-Myers Squibb was able to get a United States District Judge to order a temporary injunction halting further sales of the generic Plavix. However, the judge did not order a recall of generic Plavix. The District Court set January 22, 2007 as the start of the patent trial. The Court required Bristol-Myers and Sanofi-Aventis (BMS's Plavix development partner) to post a $400 million bond to the court. The bond provided security to Apotex in the event that the Court ruled that Apotex had the legal right to sell its generic version of Plavix.

After only one month of generic Plavix competition, BMS was forced to reduce its 2006 earnings forecast by 25%. Bristol-Myers' reduced per share earnings estimate was below the company dividend, meaning that Bristol would be paying more to shareholders than it actually earned.[27] Citing the threat of generic competition, Moody's Investor Services downgraded Bristol-Myers' debt from A1 to A2. The BMS Board stated that it still intended to declare its regular 28 cents-per-share quarterly dividend, but some analysts predicted that the lost Plavix sales would force Bristol-Myers to slash the dividend in half. In sum, over the five years of Dolan's tenure, the stock price of Bristol-Myers Squibb had declined by more than 60%.[28]

THE BOARD DECIDES TO ACT

On September 12, 2006, CEO Peter Dolan and General Counsel Richard K. Willard were dismissed by the Bristol-Myers board. Dolan was replaced on an interim basis by James M. Cornelius, a Bristol-Myers director and former executive at Guidant Corporation. The board maintained that it would search both internally and externally for a permanent replacement, but Dolan's firing increased Wall Street speculation that Bristol-Myers would be acquired.

THE UNCERTAIN PATH AHEAD FOR BRISTOL-MYERS SQUIBB

As Dolan's rocky tenure came to a close, CCO Zito wondered what he needed to communicate to stakeholders to overcome Bristol-Myers' poor financial projections and questionable practices over the past five years. With the threat of acquisition looming larger, Zito began to brainstorm, crafting a communications strategy that would help retain investor, employee, and customer confidence in the pharmaceutical giant.

With the January 22, 2007 patent trial date approaching rapidly, Zito also knew he had to consider if and how corporate communication could help Bristol-Myers win its patent dispute with Apotex. If Bristol-Myers lost the legal case, it risked losing 30% of its revenues and would forfeit its share of the $400 million bond set by the U.S. District Court.

NOTES

1 BMS Official Site: Company History. Last updated: August 2006. Website: http://www.bms.com/aboutbms/content/data/ourhis.html.
2 BMS Official Site: Company History.
3 BMS Official Site: Company History.
4 BMS Official Site: Company History.
5 BMS Official Site: Company History.
6 Paraphrased from: Bristol-Myers Squibb Homepage. Last updated: August 2006. Website: http://www.bms.com/aboutbms/content/data/ourhis.html.
7 CNN Money.com, *Fortune* 500 2006 rankings.
8 Website: http://www.contractpharma.com/articles/2006/07/bristol-myers-squibb.php.
9 Quote from BMS Official Site: Company History. Last updated: August 2006. Website: http://www.bms.com/aboutbms/content/data/ourhis.html.
10 Biography of Robert Zito. Last updated 2006. Website: www.bms.com/news/pressroom/content/data/zito.pdf.
11 Biography of Robert Zito. Last updated 2006. Website: www.bms.com/news/pressroom/content/data/zito.pdf.
12 Adapted from Biography of Robert Zito.
13 Plavix Website (Bristol Myers Squibb). Last updated: 2006. Website: www.plavix.com.
14 S&P Market Insight: Pharmaceuticals Industry Survey.
15 S&P Market Insight: Pharmaceuticals Industry Survey.
16 Medco Health Solutions Inc. & S&P Market Insight.
17 Generic Drugs: Questions & Answers. Website: http://www.fda.gov/cder/consumerinfo/genericsq&a.htm.
18 "Solving The Drug Patent Problem." Last updated: May 2, 2002. Website: http://www.forbes.com/2002/05/02/0502patents.html.
19 "Bitter Pill? Bristol-Myers Squibb Off by $900 Million." Last updated: March 11, 2003. Website: http://www.cfo.com/printable/article.cfm/3008682?f—options.

20 "Bitter Pill? Bristol-Myers Squibb Off by $900 Million." Last updated: March 11, 2003. Website: http://www.cfo.com/printable/article.cfm/3008682?f—options.

21 "Bristol's Former CFO Indicted." Last updated: June 17, 2005. Website: http://www.cfo.com/article.cfm/4096065?f—related.

22 "Bristol Stock Hurt by Generic Plavix." Last updated: August 8, 2006. Website: http://money.cnn.com/2006/08/08/news/companies/plavix/index.htm?postversion=2006080812.

23 "Bristol-Myers Probed for Deceiving U.S. Regulators." Last updated: July 29, 2006. Website: http://www.investmentsmagazine.com/ManageArticle.asp?C=160&A=17351.

24 "Bristol-Myers Probed for Deceiving U.S. Regulators." Last updated: July 29, 2006. Website: http://www.investmentsmagazine.com/ManageArticle.asp?C=160&A=17351.

25 "Battle Over a Blood Thinner Goes to Court." Last updated: August 18, 2006. Website: http://www.npr.org/templates/story/story.php?storyld=5673477.

26 "Bristol-Myers Ousts CEO Dolan, Willard." Last updated: September 12, 2006. Website: http://www.wtopnews.com/?nid=111 &pid=0&sid=909672&page=2.

27 "Bristol-Myers Chief Fired Over Patent Dispute." Last updated: September 12, 2006. Website: http://www.nytimes.com/2006/09/12/business/13bristolcnd.html?pagewanted=l &ei=5088&en=829899f2l a96a8a2& ex=1315713600&partner=rssnyt&emc=rss.

28 "Bristol-Myers CEO Forced Out." Last updated: September 12, 2006. Website: http://news.yahoo.com/s/nm/20060912/bs nm/bristolmyers_dc.

DISCUSSION QUESTIONS

1. What are the critical issues facing Bristol-Myers Squibb in this case?
2. Who are the key stakeholders in this case? How would a patent case verdict for or against Bristol-Myers Squibb affect the stakeholders?
3. What messages does Zito need to communicate to the stakeholder groups? How should he deliver his message to them?
4. Does Bristol-Myers Squibb need to retain an external firm to help it craft an effective public response to Dolan's firing or the patent dispute?
5. What other actions (if any) should the board take in response to the accounting and patent protection scandals?
6. What mistakes did Dolan make while negotiating with Apotex? What else could he have done to protect the Plavix patent?
7. Can corporate communication play a role in helping Bristol-Myers Squibb win the upcoming patent protection trial? What can Zito and his team do?

The Environment

Chapter 8

Information Technology and Ethics

LEARNING OBJECTIVES

After reading this chapter you should be able to:

- Understand how the use of information technology is bringing about important ethical implications
- Learn about the various forms of social media and the ethical implications of such social media for company stakeholders
- Become aware of the need for properly managing the ethical implications of social media
- Understand the growth of e-commerce worldwide and the consequent ethical implications such as e-commerce privacy, e-commerce security, and e-commerce trust
- Learn about other IT ethical issues such as those occurring in global e-commerce and the global digital divide
- Become aware of the amount of waste created by IT and the steps companies can take to minimize the impact of such waste

PREVIEW BUSINESS ETHICS INSIGHT

Social Networking and Business Ethics

Consider the following short cases:

- Dawnmarie Souza, an employee of a Connecticut-based ambulance services company, was asked by her supervisor to prepare an investigative report concerning a customer complaint about her work. Before preparing the report, she requested but was denied union representation. When she got home, she posted a negative comment about her supervisor on the popular social media outlet Facebook. When she posted the comments, her co-workers responded in supportive fashion, leading to even more negative comments about the supervisor. However, when she went back to work, she was suspended and eventually terminated.

- In August 2010, a few weeks before a Canadian Mazda car dealership became unionized, two employees started posting disparaging comments about their employer and supervisor. One of the employees posted hostile comments about his supervisor, while the other employee started posting profanities about the company. The second employee went as far as advising his Facebook friends not to patronize the car dealership. Both employees were then fired. The company argued that their comments created a hostile work environment while also damaging the company's reputation and business interests.

- A *Fortune* 500 company recently found itself involved in a serious public relations nightmare as it had sponsored two freelance writers to pose as consumers and post entries related to their experiences using the company's products. Similarly, a New York-based company urged its employees to visit review sites and to post comments posing as satisfied customers. Both companies faced significant public relations nightmares as a result of these actions.

- Companies are finding that they can become more personable if the public and customers have easy and quick access to their CEOs. Many companies have thus started engaging in CEO blogging where the CEO can then become the "face" of the company, sharing the vision while also providing feedback to customers. However, companies are also finding that CEOs may not always have time to blog. Many companies are therefore engaging in ghostwriting whereby somebody else other than the CEO actually makes the blog posts.

Based on Aguilar, M.K. 2011. "Facebook firing tests social media policies." *Compliance Week*, 35, 71; Crawshaw, C. 2010. "Status update: 'You're fired.'" *Canadian HR Reporter*, 23, 21.

The Preview Business Ethics Insight above shows four short cases of the ethical issues presented by new **information technologies (IT)**. The internet and new forms of social media have brought a host of new ethical dilemmas that companies have to contend with. Companies are finding that using such new technologies can be very rewarding. However, the misuse of such technologies can also be very damaging, as such misuse gets communicated to thousands of individuals over the internet.

To understand the implications of IT, it is first necessary to examine how information gathering and storing has changed. Information collection is not new. According to Beauchamp et al., governments and private agencies have always been involved in collecting data and keeping such records.[1] However, IT has brought a number of changes that make data gathering and storing different. First, data can now be collected and stored on a very large scale. While data collected in the past was limited to physical paper storage, IT developments have made data storing and gathering extremely cheap. For example, a computer can easily store the web navigation of any individual. Second, the types of information that are being collected have also changed. As you will see later, companies now routinely scan their employees' e-mails and online activities and take actions on those. Such information can now be easily collected. Finally, it is also easy for companies to exchange information. Customer information collected by one company can easily be shared with other companies without the customers' knowledge and marketing decisions made on such information.

As more companies exchange information about transactions with their business partners, employees, customers, and other stakeholders, many more ethical issues are arising.[2] Today, most companies have to contend with IT ethical concerns such as confidence in customer online transactions, safeguarding threats to data integrity, safeguarding employee and customer privacy, while also protecting sensitive proprietary organizational information. Properly managing ethical aspects of IT is therefore becoming a critical aspect of any company's ethical program. This chapter will therefore examine the ethical aspects of IT.

From a strategic standpoint, it is also becoming more critical for companies to manage their IT ethics. Consider the first case discussed in the Preview Business Ethics Insight. After the company fired the employee, the National Labor Review Board filed a complaint against the company, arguing that the employee's Facebook postings are protected by the National Labor Relations Act. The company was also told that their social media policies were too restrictive, as they violated the law. The company had to therefore settle with the employee. The other cases also show the potential damage to a company's strategic health if they do not properly understand the ethical implications of their IT operations. Improper action can result in devastating losses that can put the company's reputation and financial health in danger. However, if properly implemented, IT ethical programs can also be a source of competitive advantage.

Given the above, we examine the ethical implications of IT for a multinational. We first discuss the ethical implications of social media. The explosion in use of social media has led to new ethical dilemmas for companies. We also look at the growth of e-commerce and the many ethical issues (consumer privacy, e-commerce trust) associated with such growth. Finally, we examine IT in a globalized world and the many ethical issues such aspects take. Specifically, we look at the ethics of operating e-commerce globally, the global digital divide, and the waste created by the use of IT.

SOCIAL MEDIA AND ETHICS

"**Social media**" is the popular term that refers to the advanced internet technology and applications that have largely enabled collaboration among internet users. Social media sites all form part of the new Web 2.0 phenomena. Unlike the Web 1.0, whereby few entities had control on the construction of websites and flow of information,

Social Media	Functions
Blogs	Blogs refer to a combination of the terms "web" and "log." Blogs give readers the ability to leave comments in an interactive format in response to other people's comments.
Video sharing sites	YouTube and others give users the ability to easily post videos for viewing by web users.
Social networks	Websites such as Facebook and LinkedIn give users the ability to connect and share personal information.
Wikis	Wikis are sites that allow the easy creation and editing of webpages. For example, Wikipedia allows users to post and update information about a large number of topics.
Augmented reality	Technology that blends the virtual world with reality.
Micro-blogging	Sites such as Twitter that allow people to share information based on a number of limited characters.
Massively multi-player online role-playing game	Site that allows large number of users to interact in a virtual world. An example is World of Warcraft.
WikiLeaks	Host of websites that leak information about governments or companies.

EXHIBIT 8.1 — Examples of Social Media

Web 2.0 is user-generated, allowing millions of individuals to interact. An important aspect of Web 2.0 is online social networking that allows the creation of virtual communities "which have opened up possibilities for rich, online human-to-human interactions unprecedented in the history of Internet communication."[3] Much of the Web 2.0 is thus based on exchange of personal information online. Examples of social media platforms include blogging, YouTube, Facebook, LinkedIn, Wikipedia, Twitter, and Yammer. Exhibit 8.1 shows some of the more popular social media websites and how they are used.

Why should companies be concerned about the ethical implications of social media? Consider the following Strategic Business Ethics Insight on page 353.

As the Strategic Business Ethics Insight shows, social media is critical for companies. Adequate use of social media can build a stronger brand and help address the needs of stakeholders in a more ethical manner. This need is even more critical considering that few companies devote attention to social media.[4] Two critical issues that companies need to pay attention to with regards to ethical implications of social media are privacy and transparency.

STRATEGIC BUSINESS ETHICS INSIGHT

Ethical Implications of Social Media

The four short cases discussed in the Preview Business Ethics Insight on pages 349–50 show that it is strategically important for companies to properly understand the ethical implications of social media for their operations. Failure to do so can result in serious damages that can hurt a company's finances and reputation. Recovering from such mistakes can be very difficult.

However, recent evidence also suggests that, when properly managed, social media can have important benefits for companies. Companies such as Comcast and Zappos are well known for engaging customers on Twitter. Furthermore, Zappos is known to respond to complaints posted on Twitter quickly. In another example, Southwest Airlines was able to respond quickly to complaints when Kevin Smith, the film director, complained that he was not allowed to board a Southwest flight because of his weight. Monsoon, a fashion retailer, used social media to fight inaccurate information about its supply chain. When stories came out about alleged use of child labor in its supply chain, it quickly used Twitter and its Facebook page to fight such false information.

The above three short examples provide some evidence of the importance of social media. In the first two cases, companies have been able to address customer ethical complaints against the company. In the third case, Monsoon used social media to fight back against misinformation. However, social media is useful for both large and small companies. Consider the case of New York Spot Dessert Bar bakery buried under snow during the December 2010 blizzard. Rather than let business slow to a crawl, it quickly got customers back by offering half-price hot drinks on Facebook, Twitter, and its blog. The company also offers visiting customers computers to create their own social media presence. Such approach has paid strong dividends for the company, as sales have increased between 15% and 20%.

Based on Baker, R. 2010. "Monsoon uses social media to fight claims." *Marketing Week*, November 25, 4; Brandel, M. 2010. "Are you listening?" *Computerworld*, July 12, 44, 13, 13.

Privacy refers to the ability of individuals to control or restrict access to information about them. In an influential paper, Rachels argue that privacy is extremely important because it allows people to maintain the diversity of relationships they value.[5] For instance, people at work should only act professionally and provide information that is professionally relevant. What the person does in his/her private life may not necessarily be relevant to the work environment. However, if information about different relationships is revealed (e.g., information about the person's partying habits), privacy of the individual is breached. Consider, for instance, when posted party pictures from Facebook are used to decide whether someone should be hired or promoted. Should such information be relevant to human resource management decisions?

Mooradian argues that computers have greatly modified people's privacy.[6] To appreciate the issue of privacy with regards to social media, Mooradian distinguishes among three forms of information; namely, institution specific personal information such as medical and financial information, socially sensitive personal information such as embarrassing information, and biographical personal information such as mundane facts about who a person is, etc. Mooradian further argues that there is ample regulation in the U.S. to limit access to institutional specific personal information. However, most access to biographical information remains virtually unregulated, whereby companies can easily access and use such information.

Mooradian continues by suggesting that most aspects of social media rely a lot on biographical personal information. For instance, blogging is a medium where people routinely disclose very personal aspects of their information. Furthermore, bloggers need to understand that blogs tend to be accessible to the public and their personal information is thus accessible to millions of internet users. Similarly, social networks provide users with pages where very personal information can be listed. In both cases, companies can have easy access to significant amounts of information and make use of such information.

Given the above and the cases discussed earlier, social networks present significant ethical risks to companies. Such risks exist for many stakeholders. However, it is most pronounced for employees. Companies therefore need to implement privacy policies for employees to avoid potential ethical risks and consequent legal repercussions of such risks. Furthermore, recent research suggests that few companies pay attention to social media. Consider Exhibit 8.2 opposite.

As the exhibit shows, only one third of companies surveyed had specific policies addressing employee use of social media at and outside of work. It is therefore very critical for companies to address such issues. As we saw earlier, breaching social media ethics can result in unnecessary negative publicity and legal costs as companies are sued by employees. To address ethical implications for employee use of social media, experts suggest the following:[7]

- Employees should be made aware that companies constantly monitor their social media postings for legitimate and business reasons. Because such information is publicly available, employees should not expect privacy. However, companies should not access other sources of information that may not be publicly available as this would violate privacy laws.
- Monitoring social media to ensure that employees are not creating social media communication that is supposed to represent the company. Employees should also be warned to properly inform viewers that postings represent their own views rather than the company's views. Furthermore, to avoid potential conflicts, employees should be encouraged to disclose their employment with the company when commenting on the company's products or services.
- Inform employees that all communications they make are public. Such communications should thus be made in good taste, living the company values. For

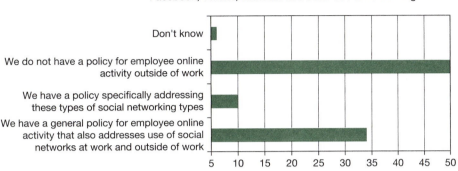

Does your company have policies specifically addressing use of Facebook, Twitter, LinkedIn and other social networking sites?

EXHIBIT 8.2—Employee Policy Regarding Social Media in Companies

instance, employees should be encouraged to avoid insulting co-workers or others or denigrating competitors. As such, employees should be informed that general policies regarding employee communication apply to social media too. As such, employees should refrain from harassment or discrimination. However, employees should also know that their rights to expression about discussion regarding their terms and conditions of employment and unionization is protected by law and that they have the ability to discuss such issues.

- Employees should also be encouraged to avoid posting sensitive information. Experts suggest avoiding identification and discussion of others such as competitors or co-workers. Employees should make sure that posted materials are not copyrighted. It is important for employees to know that posted information is often impossible to delete and all efforts should be made to protect such information.

- Employees should be discouraged from using social media during work times. Furthermore, to avoid potential ethical conflicts, employees should be warned of the potential risks of "friending" subordinates or supervisors. Some companies are going as far as prohibiting such relationships.

In addition to the employee social media ethical issues discussed above, most experts agree that another critical aspect of social media ethics is **information transparency**.[8] In fact, some have even argued that "transparency, as opposed to privacy, is the new ethical issue of the century."[9] Information transparency refers to the process of making information explicitly and openly available to concerned stakeholders. For example, as Turilli and Floridi argue, transparency for green and socially ethical banks has meant that these banks had to disclose information related to their investments and the way they treat customers.[10]

Vaccaro and Madsen suggest that companies need to take a corporate approach to information transparency.[11] Specifically, they argue that more companies will be required to provide access to information as they deal with their stakeholders. As such, information transparency will become increasingly important as more companies try to gain trust and collaborate with their stakeholders. In fact, we saw in Chapter 6 how many multinationals are now becoming more transparent about their suppliers to show their commitment to improving labor conditions of their suppliers. Such efforts have been necessary to build collaborative efforts with stakeholders such as non-governmental organizations.

How can companies use social media and IT to implement information transparency policies? Vaccaro and Madsen suggest three potential avenues. First, the internet and social media can be used as a repository of critical information. Stakeholders can then easily get access to information regarding their need in the level of detail and in the format they prefer. Second, transparency can also take the form of information-sharing and exchanges. Consider the case of Johnson & Johnson, which has a presence on Twitter, YouTube, and Facebook. They use all three formats to share information and to get customer feedback on products.[12] Finally, companies can also use both of the above to find better ways to improve their information transparency for the future.

It is likely that company use of social media will continue its growth in the near future. Similar to policies governing employees with regards to social media, it is also important for companies to develop programs to address social media use with regards to other stakeholders visiting a company's various social media websites. Experts suggest the following:[13]

- Most experts agree that companies need to be transparent and truthful. Using social media to influence public opinion about the company or its products can backfire. Companies need to disclose information about itself in a truthful and honest manner.
- Companies need to clearly inform users of how collected data is being used. How such data will be shared with other companies or sold to other entities needs to be clearly explained to both customers and others who surf a company's website.
- Social media communication should be timely. For instance, the growth of micro-blogging use such as Twitter has grown considerably. Customers expect that companies will respond quickly to their voiced concerns. If companies wait too long to respond to such concerns, these comments can quickly become mainstream issues. Consider the case of Domino's Pizza and the employee video that showed a distasteful look at how pizza is made. Domino's Pizza waited for more than 24 hours to respond to complaints on social media and faced a significant public relations nightmare.
- Implement policies to govern the use of all social media. For instance, Johnson & Johnson has created strict policies regarding live tweeting. While live tweeting can add to a company's efforts during a live event, such efforts can also be disastrous if not done properly. Experts suggest that all tweets be reviewed by the legal department to ensure that they comply with existing rules and regulations. Care must be taken when responding to customer tweets to ensure that information is protected when needed but also divulged in an honest manner. Tweets should also provide links to relevant information on the company's website.
- Finally, it is important for company employees to be respectful and tactful when responding to customer or other stakeholder complaints. Rather than negate such complaints or berate those posting such comments, it is more advisable to consider and respond to such complaints in a respectful manner.

ELECTRONIC COMMERCE AND ETHICS

Electronic commerce (e-commerce) refers to the selling and trading of goods and services over the internet. E-commerce can occur when companies buy products from online-only companies such as Amazon.com or from companies that also have brick-and-mortar outlets (e.g., Best Buy) and have the products delivered by mail. However, e-commerce can also take place fully online, such as when a customer buys software online. Most online transactions occur either in the B2B form (business-to-business representing selling among businesses) or in the B2C form (business-to-consumers).

Electronic commerce also brings a host of ethical implications for companies. However, to appreciate the necessity of addressing the ethical implications of e-commerce, it is first important to note the explosive growth of e-commerce both in the U.S. and worldwide. Consider the Global Business Ethics Insight on page 358.

As the Global Business Ethics Insight shows, e-commerce is predicted to grow dramatically in the future. Exhibit 8.3 shows the current internet penetration rate by world region and the growth rate between 2000 and 2010.

As Exhibit 8.3 shows, whether companies are operating in developed, emerging, or developing nations, they will have to contend with increased e-commerce. It will therefore become critical for multinationals to increasingly consider the ethical implications of their e-commerce operations. We consider three main interrelated areas in this section of the chapter; namely, e-commerce customer privacy, e-commerce security, and e-commerce trust.

Customer Privacy

In the section on social media, we discussed the privacy implications for employees. E-commerce also poses important ethical implications for **customer privacy**, the expectations that customers can protect their personal information. Why are consumers worried about privacy? While most individuals assume that surfing the web is anonymous, marketers are routinely watching every click an individual makes, every site that person visits, while also scanning every e-mail that is being written. Through such information collected, it is possible for web watchers to discover who a web user is, what the web user's interests are, and where they live. Furthermore, the seamless integration of global position satellite (GPS) technology also means that web watchers can know the exact location of any individual at any point. This has offered tremendous potential to marketers, as they engage in behavioral targeting whereby they monitor individual web surfing and provide more targeted advertising based on this information.

Pollach argues that customers are especially at risk for violation of privacy issues.[14] Consider that most online transactions require data that identifies the individual making the purchase. Use of a credit card implies disclosing information such as the buyer's home address, etc. However, through the collection of IP addresses, a company can easily match the web surfing information discussed above with the more personal information about purchases. By combining such data, companies can have access to very personal user profile.

GLOBAL BUSINESS ETHICS INSIGHT

E-Commerce Activity Worldwide

The growth of e-commerce is predicted to grow dramatically in the near future. Consider the following:

- Forrester Research group predicts that online retailing will continue on double-digit growth over the next few years. It is forecasted that the U.S. will see growth of 10% compounded between 2011 and 2015 reaching sales of $279 billion in 2015.

- Forrester Research also studied 17 Western European nations. It is predicted that these nations will also experience 10% growth. Online retail sales are predicted to reach 134 billion Euros in 2015.

- The most recent report suggests that the number of Chinese using the internet will reach 750 million individuals in 2015. Of these 750 million, the report also mentioned that 15% of the Chinese internet users (or Netizens) are serious users, including those living in big cities aged between 18 and 24 and those spending significant time on digital media. A further 25% are moderate users and include high-income professionals and managers. Both groups are expected to be important targets for marketing groups and companies.

- Despite an economic slowdown, South Korea has seen impressive growth in cyberspace sales. E-commerce sales for 2010 grew 23% from a year earlier. Business to business e-commerce also grew around 23% from 2009 levels.

- While growth of e-commerce in Africa has been low, it is nevertheless steadily increasing. As such, Africa is also seen as one of the world's last big emerging markets. Consumer spending has risen at a compounded rate of 16% between 2005 and 2008 and online shopping is expected to grow in a sustainable manner. Furthermore, McKinsey, the consulting firm, estimates that about 220 million Africans will join the middle class as consumers. South Africa provides a good glimpse of the potential of Africa. A recent report suggests that online retailing has grown at a compounded rate of 48% between 2004 and 2008. It is further predicted that online retailing will stay robust growing at 34% between 2010 and 2013.

- Experts also predict that Latin America will see tremendous growth in e-commerce. While the internet penetration rate is currently only 34%, it is expected to grow at a steady rate. Furthermore, while e-commerce is still in its infancy, online retailing in Latin America continues to grow.

Based on Anonymous. 2011a. "More double-digit growth ahead for online retail in U.S. and Western Europe." *Business Wire*, February 28; Anonymous. 2011b. "South Korea Q4 e-commerce jump amid economic recovery." *Asia Pulse*, February 25; Anonymous. 2011c. "Netizens will reach 750 million in China 2015." *Asia Corporate News*; Carrey, B. 2010. McClatchy. "Tapping Latin Americans who click." *Tribune Business News*, October 6; Childress, S. 2011. "Africa rising: Telecom giants battle for Kenya—India's Bharti, U.K.'s Vodafone trade barbs in fight for cellphone subscribers." *Wall Street*, January 14, B.1.

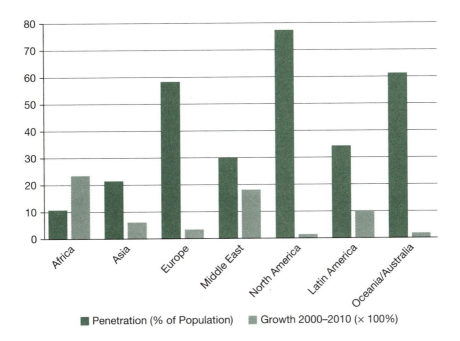

EXHIBIT 8.3—Internet Penetration Rate and Growth by World Region

Companies are now also increasingly relying on data mining companies to detect patterns in the data. For instance, Chiang discusses the case of Palantir, a company that created software that can integrate data from various sources and then create filters or other mapping processes for end-users.[15] For instance, data mining makes it possible for a bank to notice that many of its loans are not paid on time from customers in a specific geographic area. Is it ethical for the bank to then use this information to justify charging customers from the specific geographic area higher rates of interest?

The ethical implications of such data collection thus relates to how companies make use of the data.[16] For example, they can use the data to recognize their users and facilitate e-commerce transactions. However, companies can also share such information with other companies or use the information to send marketing e-mails or banner advertisements to users. Furthermore, because of the ease of the movement of data and access to such data, companies can either buy or sell such information. For instance, consider Facebook's recent decision to suspend some application developers from using its website. The developed "apps" which let users share information was also collecting identifiable information about Facebook users and selling such information to data brokers. Facebook found such activity in violation of its policies.

It is also important to note that privacy is viewed very differently globally. What is acceptable and legal in the U.S. may not necessarily be acceptable in other parts of the world. Consider the Global Business Ethics Insight on page 360 and the case of privacy in the European Union.

Privacy becomes more critical in the light of a recent study that showed that very few companies have comprehensive privacy programs despite the fact that most of them

GLOBAL BUSINESS ETHICS INSIGHT

Privacy in Germany and in the European Union

The earlier paragraphs discussing potential data that can be collected on the web suggest that companies run the risk of violating privacy laws regarding customers. In fact, the European Union is taking a much more stringent stance to protect customer privacy. For instance, recent agreements between Facebook and the German government will provide more protection to non-users. While in the U.S. users of Facebook can routinely invite non-users to join Facebook by using the non-user's e-mail address available from other e-mail websites such as Yahoo!, data of non-users in Germany will be protected. As such, non-users data cannot be freely imported into Facebook. Rather, Facebook will now provide non-users the option of never using their e-mail address again when inviting them to join Facebook. This change was made necessary after concerned Germans e-mailed the head of the data-protection agency in Hamburg complaining that they had been invited to join Facebook although they had never given their e-mail addresses to Facebook. Furthermore, Germany will be the only country in the world where residents were allowed to opt out of the Google Street View mapping services even before the product was launched.

Other e-commerce sites are also facing increased scrutiny by regulators in the European Union. Consider that, in November 2010, European Union regulators passed legislation requiring that social media websites such as Facebook and Google be required to get consent from users before their personal data is used for any purpose. Such new regulations will protect privacy rights of users in much stronger fashion than in other countries.

Based on Lawton, C. 2011. "Facebook alters tool in German privacy deal." *Wall Street Journal*, January 24.

---

claim that it is an ethical imperative to address privacy concerns. In that study, Pollach reviewed the corporate social responsibility disclosures of the largest IT companies in the world.[17] She finds that very few companies have comprehensive online privacy programs although most companies see it as a moral imperative to protect customer privacy. Furthermore, she found that most companies address online privacy issues more from a compliance perspective rather than embracing such policies.

Given the above, it is important for companies to address consumer privacy. Experts suggest that customers should be made aware of the types of data that a company is collecting and how such data will be used. Companies should inform customers whether collected data is also being sold or shared with other companies. Furthermore, as the above Global Business Ethics Insight shows, privacy is not viewed similarly worldwide. Companies are therefore strongly advised to respect local laws and

Internal	External
Physical protection of data	Privacy newsletter for customers
Privacy policy	Resources for parental guidance and child safety
Privacy employee training	Guidance for customers
Privacy board	Privacy e-mail address
Disciplinary action for privacy breach	Privacy blog
Employee monitoring	Involve stakeholders in design of privacy policy
Privacy office	Working with industry, government, and trade group
Privacy hotline	Publishing privacy research papers
Online reporting of privacy statements	Supporting IS education
Regular review of privacy policy	Working with NGOs and think tanks
Internal privacy campaign	Privacy seal
Privacy newsletter for employees	Compliance and exceeding privacy laws
Online privacy resources for employees	Self-regulation

EXHIBIT 8.4—Content of Corporate Privacy Programs

traditions when implementing policies regarding customer privacy. What are some of the ways companies address privacy issues? Exhibit 8.4 provides further insights into the content of corporate privacy programs.

E-Commerce Security

E-commerce security refers to the degree to which stakeholders feel that the data collected online by companies is safe. For instance, data collected for e-commerce transactions involve very personal information such as credit card information, home addresses, and phone numbers. The degree to which a company can ensure that such information is kept safe and private reflects the company's effort at e-commerce security.

Gordon and Loeb provide some insights into the many components of e-commerce security.[18] A company needs to be concerned about 1) **confidentiality** (making sure that private information is protected and such information is not made available to unauthorized parties), 2) **availability** (ensuring that information is made available in a timely manner to authorized users), 3) **integrity** (protecting and ensuring that data collected is accurate, reliable, and truthful), 4) **authentication** (ensuring that those who are using the data are really who they claim to be), and 5) **non-repudiation** (making sure that authorized users are not denied access to data).

E-commerce security is becoming increasingly important as the amount of online fraud grows. Bell argues that, although online purchases from 2009 to 2010 grew 30% in the U.S., fraud attempts increased by 78%.[19] Fraudsters are becoming more sophisticated at stealing credit card and other personal information. Consider the recent indictment of three individuals who stole information from over 130 million debit and credit cards from five corporations including 7-Eleven.[20] The anonymity of online purchasing provides these fraudsters with the ability to use such credit card and debit card information for online purchases without fear of detection. However, e-commerce security violations are not limited to cyber-criminals attempting to steal data from corporations. Consider the following Business Ethics Insight.

BUSINESS ETHICS INSIGHT

WikiLeaks and E-Commerce Security

WikiLeaks, the website that became famous recently for revealing government secrets, is also a source of fear for companies. Many companies are realizing that they can become the target for damaging information leaks. Consider the case of Shell and its Nigerian oil operations. Recent cable leaks suggest Shell is afraid of losing its oil licenses in Nigeria. Furthermore, the cables also revealed that the Nigerian government may have been sending Shell information to both China and Russia. However, the cables also revealed that Shell may have planted its own employees in many of the relevant Nigerian ministries. The cable leaks thus revealed embarrassing Shell information that may not necessarily help its effort to keep its oil operations in Nigeria.

Another company that is being seemingly targeted by WikiLeaks is Bank of America. The founder of WikiLeaks suggested that WikiLeaks had very damaging information about the company and that such information could potentially lead to the resignation of the company's head. WikiLeaks has repeatedly threatened to release the information.

Based on Herron, J. and Connors W. 2010. "Wikileaks touches Shell." *Wall Street Journal*, December 9; Ryst, S. 2011. "Wikileaks fuels data breach fears." *Business Insurance*, 45, 1, 1.

The above provides some evidence as to why companies need to pay stronger attention to e-commerce security. However, a recent study shows that e-commerce security breaches at companies can be strategically damaging to a company. Yayla and Hu examined stock market reactions to information-security breaches.[21] The

Security Breaches Description	Cost
Denial of service attack where web server or order processing slows down	Loss of revenue
Virus attacks shut down e-mail or networks and employees must spend time to restore system	Loss of productivity
Virus attack damages hardware or file servers	Cost of replacing software or hardware
Denial of service attack or virus lead to customers not trusting company's ability to protect data	Loss of revenue, customer trust, and loyalty
Virus attack encourages customers to switch to competitors	Loss of revenue and loss of competitive advantage
Security breaches cause investors to sell shares or stop buying shares	Loss of investor confidence

EXHIBIT 8.5 — E-Commerce Security Breaches and Costs

researchers found that both traditional brick-and-mortar stores and pure e-commerce companies experienced negative market reactions. However, the effect was much stronger for pure e-commerce companies. Furthermore, the study shows that denial of service attacks where access to a website is denied tends to have the most negative impact on market reactions. The study shows that information security breach thus has important strategic implications for companies, as such breaches can have a damaging impact on the company's share prices and financial health.

E-commerce security breaches can thus be very disastrous for companies. Exhibit 8.5 shows some of the costs associated with information breaches.

As Exhibit 8.5 shows, e-commerce security breaches can be very costly for companies. It is therefore critical to first identify the types of e-commerce and information security breaches to be able to address such breaches. Yayla and Qu's study provides some insights into the many forms of e-commerce security breaches.[22] At a basic level, e-commerce security breaches occur when unauthorized users gain access to customer, company, or employee data. These breaches can be disastrous, as the fraudsters can use such information for personal gain. Customer information can be used for illegal online purchases while company data can reveal proprietary information. However, e-commerce security breaches can occur also when unauthorized individuals either deny access to a company's website (denial of service attacks) or find ways to alter a company's website. Both breaches can result in significant public relations nightmare.

To ensure e-commerce security, companies are now strongly advised to take a strategic approach to data management. Simply using firewalls or anti-virus programs are no longer sufficient. Companies need to implement an overall program starting with an inventory of collected data. Experts thus suggest the following:[23]

- Conducting an inventory of data and keeping only data that is needed—companies need to know what data has been collected and where such information is stored. Companies often collect more data that is needed. In the current world of information overload, it is important for companies to decide what information they really need to collect. Furthermore, once data is no longer needed, it is important to purge the data. The less data a company has at any point in time, the less disastrous the potential for information leaks.

- Protect the data—efforts have to be taken to ensure that the data is protected. Firewalls and anti-virus programs need to be implemented. However, recent evidence suggests that companies have a variety of approaches to protect data. Content management systems allow a company to control acquisition of data, to classify the data, and to control who has access to such data. Data loss prevention takes a different approach to protecting data. Such systems are placed on the boundary of a firm's network to monitor outgoing data. If the system detects sensitive information is being leaked, it can block such information from leaving the organization. Finally, network forensics systems examine a company's digital operations and report any suspicious activity or patterns that diverge from the past. Companies need to thus decide on which of the three approaches works best for their situation.

- Control access to data—data access also needs to be controlled. It is critical for the company to determine which employees will have access to which types of data. Key aspects of data access control such as user account management (providing appropriate user identity and password), password management (creation and protection of passwords), data encryption (protection of data flowing through the company's network), user access policies (policies governing responsibility of user are needed), and monitoring access have to be dealt with. Furthermore, the physical aspects of the data, such as tapes, etc., need to be controlled. For instance, data needs to be in a secure building so that the data is not easily accessible to all.

- Create data management policies and train employees on such policies—while data leakages can occur because of malicious activities, some data leakage can also occur inadvertently because of the increased exchanges of data outside of the company's confines. Employee collaboration software, mobile devices, video teleconferencing, and online chats are all examples of data exchanges and sharing that occur outside of the boundaries of the organization. Employees should thus be reminded of their responsibilities when using data outside of the company. Appropriate precautions should be taken to avoid leakages. For instance, it may be possible for employees to download critical data on their smartphones. Policies have to be enacted to ensure that such data is safeguarded, especially when the employee loses the smartphone. Companies may also decide to implement policies whereby no company data is allowed to be downloaded on a smartphone.

- Create a contingency plan—companies should have systems in place to enable them to deal with any e-commerce security breaches. A sound incident management system needs to be in place, as such breaches need to be dealt with in a very timely manner.

E-Commerce Trust

A final ethical aspect of e-commerce we consider in this chapter is **e-commerce trust** (**e-trust**). E-trust refers to the confidence that a buyer has that an online transaction will occur according to expectations. For instance, if someone decides to buy a product from Amazon.com from a third party vendor, e-trust refers to the expectation that the buyer will receive the product after payment. McCole, Ramsey, and Williams[24] argue that there are three main components of e-trust: namely, 1) trust in the internet—the perceived ability of the internet to perform what it is supposed to perform such as speed and integrity of the system, 2) trust in the vendor—trust in the company selling the products, and 3) trust in other parties, such as third parties certifying that a vendor has pledged integrity and honesty.

Why is e-trust important? Most experts agree that customers will not engage in online commercial transactions with a company unless they have trust.[25] Furthermore, in the light of the many new potential e-commerce problematic issues that companies are facing today (i.e., information breaches, denial of service attacks, identity theft, etc.), it is important for stakeholders to perceive a company as trustworthy in order to entice the stakeholder to develop a relationship with the company. From a strategic standpoint, e-trust is thus very critical as it forms the backbone of business-to-consumer trade.

Recent research provides evidence of some of the factors that promote e-trust in a company. Academic research suggests that the following main factors promote e-trust:[26]

- Previous transaction experience—the more buyers have engaged in online transactions before, the more likely they are to e-trust.
- Disposition to trust—some people seem more likely to trust than others.
- Perceived security protection—how much security is perceived?
- Familiarity—are users familiar with aspects of the website? The more the familiarity, the higher the e-trust.
- Company reputation/brand—does the company have a strong reputation?
- Referral and word-of-mouth—what are others saying about transactions with the company? Positive word-of-mouth engenders e-trust.
- Privacy concern—does the company address all privacy concerns?
- Trusted third parties—is there an organization that provides a privacy seal to reduce fear about online security and privacy? Privacy or other seals encourages e-trust.
- Social influence—users are more likely to trust a company if their friends or family have engaged in a transaction with the company before.
- Structural assurance—the basic internet structure needs to function as expected. Companies therefore need to provide technological safeguards such as data encryption, etc.

Recent research by Yang, Lin, Chandlrees, Lin, and Chao provides some evidence that the perceived ethics of shopping websites also contributes to ethics.[27] In that study, the researchers found that individuals were more likely to trust a website if the website

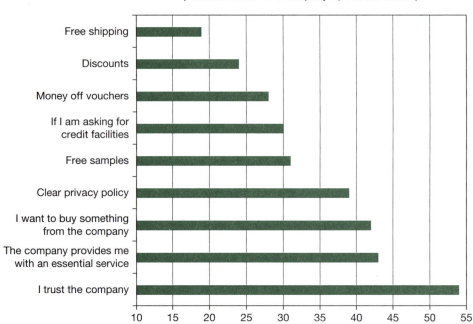

Which of the following would prompt you to give your
personal details to a company? (% of customers)

EXHIBIT 8.6—Factors Promoting E-Trust

maintains a good ethical performance. To be perceived as being ethical, a company needs to clearly practice posted privacy policies while also describing products and services in an appropriate way. This research provides evidence of the connection between perception of ethics of online companies and trust in the company.

More recent practical research provides further evidence of the importance of the above factors in promoting e-trust.[28] The study found that the most important factor is whether the company is well known or not. Eighty-four percent of respondents suggested that they are more likely to give personal data to a company they already know, as they are confident that such companies will protect their data. The next most important factor promoting e-trust is whether the company has websites with very obvious security features. Eighty-one percent of surveyed customers indicated that they are more likely to give personal information to companies that have such websites. Exhibit 8.6 summarizes the results of the study.

Building e-trust is thus a critical aspect of a company's strategic health. Online transactions tend not to require the same investments as typical brick-and-mortar stores and are thus more efficient. Companies that want to succeed will therefore be increasingly pressured to grow their online sales and increase e-trust. One of the most critical aspects of e-trust is providing users with the guarantee that their data will be safe with the company. As such, protecting data privacy and building e-security are all intertwined. The many steps discussed earlier to protect customer privacy and strengthen e-security apply here too. Furthermore, as Exhibit 8.6 suggests, taking steps to build online branding is critical. Companies need to ensure that they are perceived as having a strong reputation through transparency and the ethics of their online transactions.

OTHER IT ETHICS ISSUES

In the final section of this chapter, we examine three remaining IT ethics issues. First, we look at global e-commerce and the consequent ethical issues arising from such operations. We emphasize ethical issues related to operating in a specific culture. Second, we also examine the global digital divide and the role multinationals are playing in addressing this divide. Finally, we also discuss the amount of waste generated by IT operations and what responsible companies are doing to address such issues.

Ethics and Global E-Commerce and the Global Digital Divide

The inherent features of the internet make it possible for companies to easily have a global presence. However, operating globally is fraught with ethical dilemmas. Consider our earlier consideration of how privacy may not be viewed similarly worldwide. To avoid ethical violations, companies need to ensure that they operate within acceptable limits. Consider the case of Yahoo!, which was forced to give names of individuals voicing pro-democracy views on its Chinese website (see page 379). While Google has refused to behave similarly, Yahoo! has decided to embrace Chinese demands as a condition of doing business there. Yahoo! has received a significant public backlash for its role in helping the Chinese government arrest those voicing pro-democracy views. Yahoo! had to choose between enforcing its own privacy rules in the U.S. or those enforced by the Chinese government. Most experts agree that China offers significant potential as the number of citizens having access to the internet and disposable income grows. Yahoo! therefore decided to respect the local laws at the expense of its reputation in the Western world.

Operating globally in an IT environment thus poses significant risks. A company cannot be viewed as ethical if it breaches local culture or norms. As you will see in Chapter 10 on global ethics, companies can approach operations in other countries either through a universal lens (doing the same thing in all countries) or a relativist approach (responding to local conditions). Current research reports significant differences in cross-cultural aspects of IT that necessitate a relativist approach. We discuss the many IT aspects that differ by culture.

Similar to online retailing within local contexts, companies need to be trusted in order to encourage users to engage in transactions with them.[29] A critical component of the trust will emerge from the user's interaction with a company's website. However, most research has assumed that online trust is built similarly across cultures. Nevertheless, recent research by Sia et al. shows that online trust varies by culture. In that research, the authors examine two of the most important ways companies build trust; namely, **reputable website affiliation** (unknown website affiliating itself with a more reputable website to build online trust) and **peer endorsement** (existing customers providing feedback encouraging new customers to trust the website). They find that individualistic cultures such as the U.S. are more likely to build trust through reputable website affiliation. However, in more collectivistic cultures such as Hong Kong and South Korea, where the needs and values of the group takes precedence over the individual, peer endorsement is much more critical. This research suggests that companies need to adopt the appropriate web strategies based on the culture to be viewed as ethical and trusted.

Further current research suggests that companies need to provide consumers with website elements that are consistent with local norms and culture.[30] For example, at a basic level, websites should not offend local norms. Culturally inappropriate images should not be displayed on a company's local websites. However, cultural customization goes beyond merely adapting physical imaging. There are many other subtle aspects that need to be catered to.

Wurtz provides some interesting insights into the other many factors that contribute to a culturally appropriate website.[31] In that study, she examines the websites of McDonald's in the 119 countries they operated in at the time of study. To examine the cultural appropriateness of the various websites, she examines differences between high-context (e.g., Japan, Arab countries, Greece, Spain, Italy) and low-context cultures (e.g., German-speaking countries, Scandinavian countries, U.S.A.). People in high-context cultures communicate extensively using non-verbals such as body language, silence, and gestures. In contrast, people in low-context cultures tend to communicate more directly and explicitly.

Wurtz finds that McDonald's websites in high-context cultures tend to have much more animation. This is consistent with the notion that high-context communication is much more complex than low-context communication. High levels of animation indicate preference for the situation to play a role in the communicated message. Additionally, high-context websites are more likely to have embedded links whereby website surfers are more likely to try to find information. In contrast, low-context cultures feature much more explicit information on the home page. Furthermore, Wurzt found that McDonald's websites in more collectivistic countries are more likely to feature families or friends or other activities spent with others. In contrast, more individualistic websites feature individuals engaging in activities such as listening to music or relaxing.

The above clearly shows that some form of cultural customization is indeed necessary to ensure that a company does not break local norms and views as unethical. While it is outside of the scope of this chapter to discuss all culture customization aspects (see Singh et al., for example, on how to customize 36 aspects of websites to make them culturally appropriate[32]), companies will need to understand whether their e-commerce policies and practices are consistent with local norms. Issues such as privacy, appropriateness of website, and safeguarding data will all have to be dealt with. However, one of the other key issues that multinationals have to contend with in the global e-commerce environment is the global digital divide.

The **digital divide** refers to the "gap between the more privileged who have access and the less privileged who do not have access to information and communication technology."[33] As the internet and communication technology continues to play an increasingly important role both in terms of economic development and human interaction, countries and companies are increasingly focused on reducing the digital divide.

Why is a reduction in digital divide important? Most experts agree that access to internet technologies has a strong link with economic development.[34] The internet provides the infrastructure that is minimizing costs and uncertainty of distribution of goods and services in most societies. For instance, a farmer in rural India can quickly access the internet to check the prices of agricultural products before deciding on pricing. However, the internet is also playing a societal function in terms of the strengthening of civil societies. The internet provides access to information regarding constitutional rights, social movements, etc. that plays a key role in terms of democratic societal functioning.[35]

Recent research suggests that the digital divide between countries is narrowing. Exhibit 8.7 (overleaf) shows the inequality ratio of specific world region to North America for 1995 and 2007. The score reflects the ratio of internet users in the region to internet users in the U.S. and Canada. The higher the ratio, the higher is the equality in terms of internet access and use.

As Exhibit 8.7 shows, the digital divide is indeed falling worldwide. For instance, North Africa has seen a 104,007% increase of internet users per 1,000 individuals. It is important to note that the digital divide does not only apply to individuals. Chang, Wu, and Cho show how digital divide can also exist for companies.[36] They examine small and medium enterprises in the Taiwanese manufacturing industry. They find that there is a digital divide for these companies. From a strategic perspective, the digital divide means that companies that do not have access to digital technologies are likely to be less competitive and miss the benefits of strategic IT utilization. Furthermore, given the importance of small and medium companies to most countries' economy in terms of job creation and innovation, a big digital divide can hurt innovation and economic development.

Given the above, it is important for multinationals to play a key role in reducing the digital divide. While governments typically provide the internet backbone, research by Chen, Lin, and Lai (2010) of China's urban–rural digital divide suggest that users may not always take advantage of infrastructure because of limited internet literacy skills and computer skills.[37] Multinationals are thus well advised to provide opportunities for their employees to get internet-related training. Furthermore, multinationals may have a critical role to play in less developed societies by also providing the equipment to reduce the global digital divide. For instance, computer equipment can be donated to local community centers to ensure that disadvantaged locals have access to some minimal internet access. Additionally, Wresch's essay suggests that multinationals can play a big role in encouraging the creation of local websites.[38] Local websites can be an important repository of locally relevant medical information. Furthermore, the worldwide access to locally created websites can make such countries visible. The web is now dominated by websites from mostly Western countries, thus dominating the web culture.

369

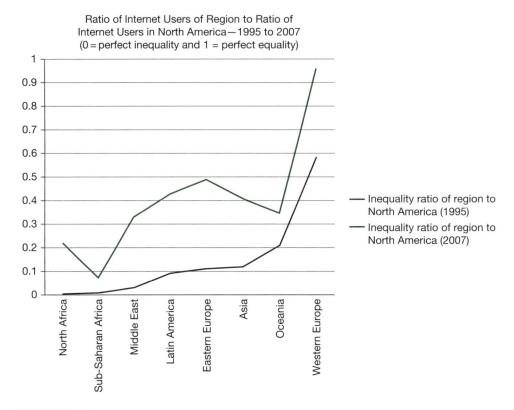

Ratio of Internet Users of Region to Ratio of
Internet Users in North America—1995 to 2007
(0 = perfect inequality and 1 = perfect equality)

— Inequality ratio of region to
North America (1995)
— Inequality ratio of region to
North America (2007)

EXHIBIT 8.7—Ratio of Internet Users by Region to Internet Users in North America

Electronic Waste

In the final section of this chapter, we examine electronic waste or e-waste. **E-waste** refers to the waste stream that occurs as a result of a company's use of information technology. Davis and Heart argue that e-waste is forecasted to grow at a steady rate of 3% to 5% annually.[39] A major reason behind the sustained growth of e-waste is the constant availability of new products with better design and technology. Furthermore, products are becoming obsolete faster. Consider, for instance, that the average lifespan of a new computer has fallen from 4.5 years in 1992 to around 2 years in 2005. Additionally, the price of IT equipment has steadily fallen over the past decade. This has led experts to estimate that the world generates around 40 million tons of waste annually.[40] Why should companies be concerned about e-waste? Consider the Ethics Sustainability Insight on page 371.

As the Ethics Sustainability Insight shows, it is very critical for multinationals to manage their IT operations in order to reduce the environmental and human impact of their IT operations. More experts are encouraging companies to engage in green IT initiatives to achieve such goals.[41] Such efforts seem to be geared either toward reduction of energy use or more efficient use of existing equipment. These include:[42]

ETHICS SUSTAINABILITY INSIGHT

E-waste and the Environment

It is estimated that IT contributes to around 2% of global dioxide emissions. Most of this comes from the use of IT products such as data centers, servers, and personal computers. Operation of these equipments is heavily dependent on energy which often originates from non-renewable sources such as fossil fuels. However, 25% of the ecological footprint comes from the materials used in such IT equipment. Furthermore, it is predicted that such IT-related global carbon emission will keep growing at around 6% per year. This growth thus is placing significant pressure on the IT industry to find ways to reduce its ecological footprint.

An important aspect of e-waste is what is done with the large amount of e-waste generated annually. For instance, a recent report suggests that India generates around 300,000 tons of e-waste annually and around 15% to 20% of the e-waste is collected for recycling. However, the way the e-waste is recycled is very problematic. Around 80,000 Indian workers in the informal sector collect and dismantle the e-waste. In the process, these workers are exposed to a host of toxic by-products as they do most of the work by hand and do not have the necessary safety equipment. Most IT equipment includes known carcinogenic and toxic elements such as lead, mercury, and cadmium. As these workers handle the e-waste, they are thus being exposed to toxic products that are known to cause brain damage in children, kidney damage, and even abnormal hormonal function. Furthermore, the informal nature of the work means that no effort is being made to protect the environment. The recycling process involves the disposal of these toxic products in the environment. For example, the disposal of used circuit boards, which are often melted in open fires, releases toxic flames in the environment.

An added aspect of e-waste that produces another ethical dimension to the problem is that most e-waste generated in the developed world is exported to developing nations for recycling. For instance, a recent report suggests that 80% of collected e-waste in the U.S. is exported. As the pace of e-waste grows in both Europe and the U.S., e-waste exports to less developed countries will mean that poor workers are being exposed to toxic materials in very dangerous environments and significant harm is being done to the environment.

Based on Davis, G. and Heart, S. 2010. "Opportunities and constraints for developing a sustainable e-waste management system at local government level in Australia." *Waste Management & Research*, 28, 705–713; Lawhon, M., Manomaivibool, P., and Inagaki, H. 2010. "Solving/understanding/evaluating the e-waste challenge through transdisciplinarity?" *Futures*, 42, 1212–1221; Rahman, N. and Akhter, S. 2010. "Incorporating sustainability into information technology management." *International Journal of Technology Management & Sustainable Development*, 9, 2, 95–111; Sohrabji, S. 2010. "End of life." *India-West, San Leandro*, 35, 19, A1, 5.

- More companies are experimenting with ways to reduce their IT-related energy use. For instance, techniques such as virtualization, cloud computing, and PC power management software are common techniques. Virtualization involves running multiple computers on a single computer. This reduces the need for hardware while also reducing the need for energy. Furthermore, the use of cloud computing involves placing data on the web as opposed to on in-house servers. For instance, companies that have moved their e-mail services to cloud computers save by eliminating the need for servers. Finally, companies are also purchasing software that lets companies control and reduce energy use centrally on their network. By optimizing energy use, companies can enjoy energy savings without loss of productivity.
- Companies are also analyzing their data to maintain only the needed data. Redundant data is being eliminated, while redundant databases are being combined. Such efforts reduce the need for servers that consume large amounts of energy to run and to be kept cool.
- Companies are also finding ways to extend the lifecycle of the products they use. More companies are participating in renewing, reusing, and refurbishing of personal computers. Furthermore, computer makers are increasingly considering personal computers that are easily upgradable with interchangeable parts, etc.
- More companies are considering the recycling options when making purchase decisions. One of the more recent developments in design is the cradle-to-cradle approach. Such products are designed to allow products to be produced waste-free. Thus, products can be designed so that all the types of materials used can be separated and recycled at all stages of the products' lifecycles. The cradle-to-cradle approach thus reduces the need for critical landfill space.
- Green IT initiatives also include companies managing the IT recycling process. Companies keep track of recycling rates of their own products. Furthermore, when making purchase decisions, companies can only purchase those products that have a minimum use of other recycled materials.

CHAPTER SUMMARY

In this chapter, you learned about IT and the ethical implications of IT. As more companies rely on IT for most aspects of their operations and as IT becomes ever present in most aspects of people's lives, the ethical aspects of IT will become more critical. Furthermore, the ease and scale of information collection has changed dramatically. Understanding and managing IT ethics will therefore become more critical.

First, you read about the types of social media and the ethical implications of such social media. You learned about the importance of managing social media and the inherent privacy issues raised by social media. The social media section also discussed some of the best practices regarding how companies can manage their social media for employees. Furthermore, prescriptions for social media were discussed for other stakeholders.

In the second part of the chapter, you read about electronic commerce and the tremendous global growth in e-commerce. You learned about a number of e-commerce ethical issues such as customer privacy, e-commerce security, and e-commerce trust. You read about the many steps companies can take to boost these three aspects of e-commerce.

In the final part of the chapter, you learned about a number of remaining IT ethical issues. First, you learned about the importance of access to IT and the role of such access in furthering both personal and economic growth. You read about the global digital divide and the role multinationals can play in addressing such a divide. You also learned that the global digital divide exists for small and medium companies and can actually have negative implications for the strategic health of such companies.

A second critical aspect discussed in the last part of the chapter is e-waste. As hardware becomes cheaper and lifecycles of such hardware become shorter, e-waste is growing at a dizzying rate every year. The ethical implications of such e-waste pertain to the appropriate disposal and recycling of such waste. Most of the e-waste generated in the Western world ends up being processed by workers in very poor conditions in less developed nations. Reducing and managing e-waste is therefore a critical consideration for most multinationals today.

NOTES

1 Beauchamp, T.L., Bowie, N.L. & Arnold, D.G. 2010. *Ethical theory and business*. Harlow, U.K.: Pearson Publishing.

2 Sipior, J.C. 2007. "Ethically responsible organizational privacy protection." *Information Resource Management Journal*, 20, 3, i–iii.

3 Grabner-Krauter, S. 2009. "Web 2.0 social networks: The role of trust." *Journal of Business Ethics*, 90, 4, 505–522 (at 505).

4 Aguilar, M.K. 2009. "How companies are coping with social media." *Compliance Week*, 56, 57, 71.

5 Rachels, J. 1975. "Why privacy is important." *Philosophy and Public Affairs*, 4, 323–333.

6 Mooradian, N. 2009. "The importance of privacy revisited." *Ethics Information Technology*, 11, 163–174.

7 Aguilar, "How companies are coping with social media"; Aguilar, M.K. 2011. "Facebook firing tests social media policies." *Compliance Week*, 35; 71; Palm, E. 2009. "Securing privacy at work: The importance of contextualized consent." *Ethics Information Technology*, 11, 233–241.

8 Turilli, M. & Floridi, L. 2010. "The ethics of information transparency." *Ethics Information Technology*, 11, 105–112.

9 Vaccaro, A. & Madsen, P. 2009. "Corporate dynamic transparency: The new ICT-driven ethics?" *Ethics Information Technology*, 11, 113–122 (at 113).

10 Turilli & Floridi, "The ethics of information transparency."

11 Vaccaro & Madsen, "Corporate dynamic transparency."

12 Aguilar, M.K. 2010. "Compliance and social media: Yes, it can be done." *Compliance Week*, 50–51.

13 Aguilar, "How companies are coping with social media"; Brandel, M. 2010. "Are you listening?" *Computerworld*, July 12, 44, 13, 13; Kaplan, A.M. & Haenlein, M. 2011. "The early bird catches the news: Nine things you should know about micro-blogging." *Business Horizons*, 54, 105–113.

14 Pollach, I. 2011. "Online privacy as a corporate social responsibility: An empirical study." *Business Ethics*, 20, 1, 88–102.

15 Chiang, O. 2011. "Super Crunchers." March 14, Forbes.com.

16 Pollach, "Online privacy as a corporate social responsibility."

17   Pollach, "Online privacy as a corporate social responsibility."

18   Gordon, L.A. & Loeb, M.P. 2006. "Budgeting process for information security expenditures." *Communication of the ACM*, 49, 1, 121–125.

19   Bell, S. 2011. "Shopping rises online, as do attempts to commit fraud." *Cardline*, January 28, 11, 4, 3.

20   Krol, C. 2009. "Breached spotlight data security." *DM New*, August 31, 2.

21   Yayla, A.A. & Hu, Q. 2011. "The impact of information security events on the stock value of firms: The effect of contingency factors." *Journal of Information Technology*, 26, 60–77.

22   Yayla & Hu, "The impact of information security events on the stock value of firms."

23   Anderson, S. & McClendon, T. 2011. "Data, data everywhere." *Risk Manager's Forum*, February, 30; *The Economist*. 2011. "The leaky corporation: Companies and information." *The Economist*, February 26, 398, 8722, 75; Nash, K.S. 2011. "Forget WikiLeaks: Your CEO maybe paranoid about Wikileaks, but his mobile device and cloud computing are the real threats to corporate security." *CIO*, 24, 10; Stelter, L. 2011. "Physically protecting data." *Security Systems News*, 14, 1, 15.

24   McCole, P., Ramsey, E. & Williams, J. 2010. "Trust considerations on attitudes towards online purchasing: The moderating effect of privacy and security concerns." *Journal of Business Research*, 63, 1018–1024.

25   McCole et al., "Trust considerations on attitudes towards online purchasing."

26   Kim, Y.H., Kim, D.J. & Hwang, Y. 2009. "Exploring online transaction self efficacy in trust building in B2C e-commerce." *Journal of Organizational and End User Computing*, 21, 1, 37–59; Sinclaire, J.K., Simon J.C. & Wilkes, R.B. 2010. "A prediction model for initial trust formation in electronic commerce." *International Business Research*, 3, 4, 17–27.

27   Yang, M., Lin, B., Chandlrees, N., Lin, B. & Chao, H. 2009. "The effect of preceived ethical performance of shopping websites on consumer trust." *Journal of Computer Information Systems*, 50, 1, 15–24.

28   Mortimer, R. 2010. "Customer data: Only trust can overcome data privacy fears." *Marketing Week*, 26.

29   Sia, C.L., Lim, K.H., Leung, K., Lee, M.K.O., Huang, W.W. & Benbasat, I. 2009. "Web strategies to promote internet shopping: Is cultural-customization needed?" *MIS Quarterly*, 33, 3, 491–512.

30   Cyr, D., Head, M., Larios, H. & Pan, B. 2009. "Exploring human images in website design: A multi-method approach." *MIS Quarterly*, 33, 3, 539–566; Singh, N., Zhao, H.X. & Hu, S. 2003. "Cultural adaptation on the Web: A study of American companies' domestic and Chinese websites." *Journal of Global Information Management*, 11, 3, 63–81.

31   Wurtz, E. 2005. "A cross-cultural analysis of websites from high-context cultures and low-context cultures." *Journal of Computer-Mediated Communication*, 11, 13–40.

32   Singh et al., "Cultural adaptation on the Web."

33   Huang, C. & Chen, H. 2010. "Global digital divide: A dynamic analysis based on the bass model." *Journal of Public Policy and Marketing*, 29, 2, 248–264 (at 248).

34   Chen, D., Lin, Z. & Lai, F. 2010. "Crossing the chasm—Understanding China's rural digital divide." *Journal of Global Information Technology Management*, 13, 2, 4–34.

35   Robinson, K.K. & Crenshaw, E.M. 2010. "Reevaluating the global digital divide: Socio-demographic and conflict barriers to the internet revolution." *Sociological Inquiry*, 80, 1, 34–62.

36   Chang, S., Wu, H. & Cho, C. 2011. "The development of digital divide assessment mechanism for SMEs: A perspective from the Taiwan manufacturing industry." *Journal of Global Information Technology Management*, 14, 1, 6–34.

37   Chen et al., "Crossing the chasm."

38   Wresch, W. 2009. "Progress on the global digital divide: An ethical perspective based on Amartya Sen's capabilities model." *Ethics Information Technology*, 11, 255–263.

39   Davis, G. & Heart, S. 2010. "Opportunities and constraints for developing a sustainable E-waste management system at local government level in Australia." *Waste Management & Research*, 28, 705–713.

40   Davis & Heart, "Opportunities and constraints."

41   Jain, R.P., Benbunan-Fich, R. & Mohan, K. 2011 "Assessing green IT initiatives using the balanced scorecard." *IT Pro*, January/February, 26–32.

42   Jain, R.P. et al., "Assessing green IT initiatives"; Rahman, N. & Akhter, S. 2010. "Incorporating sustainability into information technology management." *International Journal of Technology Management & Sustainable Development*, 9, 2, 95–111.

KEY TERMS

Authentication: ensuring that those who are using the data are really who they claim to be.

Availability: ensuring that information is made available in a timely manner to authorized users.

Confidentiality: ensuring that private information is protected and such information is not made available to unauthorized parties.

Customer privacy: the expectations that customers can protect their personal information.

Digital divide: gap between the more privileged who have access, and the less privileged who do not have access, to information and communication technology.

E-commerce security: refers to the degree to which stakeholders feel that the data collected online by companies is safe.

E-commerce trust (e-trust): refers to the confidence that a buyer has that an online transaction will occur according to expectations.

E-waste: waste stream that occurs as a result of a company's use of information technology.

Electronic commerce (e-commerce): refers to the selling and trading of goods and services over the internet.

Information technologies (IT): refers to the internet and new forms of social media.

Information transparency: process of making information explicitly and openly available to concerned stakeholders.

Integrity: protecting and ensuring that data collected is accurate, reliable, and truthful.

Non-repudiation: making sure that authorized users are not denied access to data.

Peer endorsement: where existing customers provide feedback to encourage new customers to trust the website.

Privacy: ability of individuals to control or restrict access to information about them.

Reputable website affiliation: where an unknown website affiliates itself with a more reputable website to build online trust.

Social media: popular term that refers to the advanced internet technology and applications that have largely enabled collaboration among internet users.

DISCUSSION QUESTIONS

1. What are some of the major changes that have occurred over the past decade regarding how information is collected? What are some of the ethical implications of these new data collection procedures?

2. What is social media? What are some of the main ethical issues companies face as they deal with social media?

3. What is privacy? Why is privacy important? What can companies do to protect employee privacy?

4. What is customer privacy? How does IT put customer privacy in danger? What can companies do to protect customer privacy?

5. Discuss the five components of e-commerce security; namely, confidentiality, availability, integrity, authentication, and non-repudiation. Give examples of how each of the five components is breached.

6. What are some of the key aspects of e-commerce security? What are some of the costs of e-commerce security breaches? What can companies do to protect its e-commerce security?

7. What is e-commerce trust? Why is e-commerce trust important? What are some of the major factors encouraging e-commerce trust?

8. What is the global digital divide? Why is reduction of the global digital divide important? What can multinationals do to reduce the divide?

9. What is electronic waste? Why is e-waste predicted to grow significantly in the future?

10. What are some of the ethical implications of e-waste? What can companies do to reduce e-waste?

INTERNET ACTIVITY

1. Go to the World Internet Usage Statistics Website: http://www.internet worldstats.com.

2. Review the data for the different regions of the world.

3. Which region of the world is experiencing most growth in internet usage? What are the factors that explain such growth?

4. Review the top 20 countries with the highest number of internet users. Which countries are on the list? Which country has the highest penetration rate? What led to such high penetration rates in that country?

5. Review broadband internet statistics. Which countries have the highest penetration rate using broadband? Why is broadband penetration considered a better indicator of internet penetration?

For more Internet Activities and resources, visit the Companion Website at www.routledge.com/cw/parboteeah.

WHAT WOULD YOU DO?

The IT Job

You complete a Bachelor's degree in Information Technology. After graduating, you get a job with a local company. Your main responsibility will be to manage the servers holding critical data and e-mails for the company. You start the job and feel very satisfied with the work. The company is moderate in size and you have the opportunity to learn most aspects of the company. You also like the company culture, as the latter values integrity, strong work ethic, but also a balance of work and family.

After several months on the job, you are asked to meet with the CEO. During the meeting, she mentions that she has read recently about software that allows the company to monitor productivity and the extent to which employees are accessing non-work sites such as Facebook and news site. You are asked to investigate the possibility of installing such software.

During the conversation, you also find that the CEO also suspects some employees of unethical behavior. While you don't know the nature of the unethical behavior, the CEO asks you to provide access to these employees' e-mails. You personally know many of these employees.

What would you do? Do you go along with the software monitoring employee use of the internet? Do you also provide access to these employees' e-mails? Why or why not?

BRIEF CASE: BUSINESS ETHICS INSIGHT

Alibaba.com and Online Fraud

Alibaba.com, founded in 1998, is the leading business-to-business retailer in China. It acts primarily as a directory of sellers offering products in bulk to other businesses. Alibaba.com was the first company created by well-known Chinese entrepreneur and former English teacher Jack Ma. After Mr. Ma created Alibaba.com, he went on to create Taobao, China's largest online retail website. Recent report suggests that Taobao accounted for 75% of all online transactions in China.

In early 2011, Alibaba.com had to face a major scandal. Investigation of the scandal started when an employee noticed suspicious activity and reported the activity to the company. An internal staff investigation revealed that over 2,300 sellers had committed fraud on the site, sometimes with the help of Alibaba.com staff. Would-be suppliers are required to provide business registration documents in order to set up a store front on the site. However, around 100 internal

Alibaba.com staff helped around 2,300 sellers to evade such business verification paperwork. With the help of the staff, these vendors were able to bypass the verification process and became listed on Alibaba.com. In some cases, these companies also provided fake paperwork that the staff accepted. The result was that many companies became listed despite any lack of authentication. Unfortunately, the result was that many buyers were tricked into doing business with fraudulent companies. Furthermore, many of these buyers ended up paying for products they did not receive.

Jack Ma is obviously very disturbed by the scandal. Like many of his companies, he places much premium on values such as "integrity," "ethics," "commitment," and "passion." This scandal has led a major blow to the company's credibility as a reliable source of goods. Furthermore, the scandal is ill timed as Alibaba.com is now facing an ever-increasing base of aggressive competitors. Mr. Ma has vowed to improve internal fraud detection processes. In addition, two of the senior executives of the company have accepted responsibility for the scandal, although they were not directly involved in such systematic breakdown. One of these executives, Mr. Wei, was a major force behind the company's long-term strategy and was instrumental in boosting Alibaba.com as the leading place for online business-to-business transactions.

Based on Chao, L. 2011. "Alibaba starts to repair reputation." *Wall Street Journal*, online edition, February 23; Chao, L. and Lee, Y. 2011. "Alibaba.com CEO resigns in wake of fraud by sellers." *Wall Street Journal*, online edition, February 21.

BRIEF CASE QUESTIONS

1. What are some of the factors that led to this scandal? What aspects of the online environment explain the scandal?
2. Do you think the company was justified in accepting the resignation of key executives such as Mr. Wei? Do you think people should be allowed to resign although they are not personally aware of unethical behaviors on the part of their subordinates?
3. What changes would you recommend to Alibaba.com internal processes to make sure that such fraud does not occur again in the future?
4. What should Mr. Ma do to restore confidence in Alibaba.com?

LONG CASE: BUSINESS ETHICS

INTERNET CENSORSHIP IN CHINA

Introduction

Freedom of Speech and the ability to express ideas is an ideal that certainly defines the culture of many Western nations. In these cultures, the internet is largely unregulated and unblocked, allowing users to look up information on politics, wars, religion, and even pornography. However, this freedom is not shared throughout many countries, with China being a prime example. The Communist government sensed the potential dangers of complete freedom as it relates to the internet and took many measures to ensure that internet did not create discontent among its citizens. As of November 16, 2006, China has had an active filter that is referred to as the Great Firewall of China in place. This blocks sites deemed illegal, along with filtering words, images, and videos it deems as inappropriate and forbidden. Well-known topics that are blocked by the firewall include Taiwan's Independence, Falun Gong, the Dalai Lama, and Tiananmen Square.

In addition to its own filter and moderation of internet content, the Chinese government requires that companies operating within its borders provide their own censorship and moderation. It is estimated that search engines that operate in the country maintain lists of thousands of words, phrases, and web addreses that are filtered out even if the sites may be blocked at the backbone or ISP level. Even e-mail and chat services are filtered, with many instances of messages being sent that never reach the recipient. China's internet has been called the most over-regulated system in the world, with at least twelve different government bureaus that have some authority over the internet, including the powerful State Council Information Office, the Ministry of Public Security, and the Ministry of Information Industry.

Despite these measures, China's internet usage and popularity have grown to record numbers. The number of net users in 2002 was estimated to be 59 million, with that number growing to 457 million at the end of 2010. In 2010 alone, 73.3 million more people gained access to the internet, representing a staggering 19.1% increase. The popularity rate of the internet has risen to an all-time high of 34.3%. The huge gains seen are attributed to the advance of network infrastructure and rapid development of mobile internet sources.

Chinese censorship has created lots of criticism and outrage toward companies who have partcipated in the government's attempt to squash freedom of speech. Three such companies are Yahoo!, Microsoft, and Google. Each of these companies have different philosophies when it comes to operating in China and each have come under scrutiny for its operations in China. The following discusses each company's struggles as it relates to the internet in China.

Yahoo! in China

Yahoo! is perhaps the most scrutinized and criticized company for its censorship of sensitive materials in China. The company has stated publicly that it is abiding by and cooperating with local authorities and regulations in addition to pointing out that it is the world's largest internet market. It cannot be ignored and the regulations must be followed. In addition to operating in China, Yahoo! also physically locates its servers with user profiles, locations, and data in the country allowing it to be at risk for requests from the Chinese government for the information.

In addition to filtering content and websites, it has been shown that Yahoo! has provided user information from its services to the Chinese government on two different occasions. These led to the imprisonment of these individuals. The first case involves a man by the name of Jiang Lijun, who was a Chinese freelance writer. Back in November of 2002, Lijun posted articles on the internet suggesting political reform was needed in China. This gained a lot of attention from the Chinese government, who ultimately ended up arresting him. What ultimately led to his arrest was a document that was produced by the government that was a draft e-mail from his personal computer named "Declaration." This e-mail had yet to be sent or posted on the internet. Lijun was eventually convicted in November 2003 and sentenced to four years in prison. A group named Reporters without Borders accused Yahoo! of providing the information and produced evidence of them doing so. Lawmakers also accused Yahoo! of helping China crush dissent in return for the ability to have access to its lucrative market.

In addition to Lijun, Yahoo! also came under scrutiny in the case of Shi Tao. Tao took a copy of a government document that was provided to journalists named "A Notice Concerning the Work for Maintaining Stability" and sent it to an organization named Asia Democracy Foundation using his personal Yahoo! e-mail account. In the notice, the media was asked not to report on the 15th anniversary of Tiananmen Square, Falun Gong, or any other people calling for social reform. When the Chinese government found out the information had been leaked, they immediately demanded that Yahoo! provide the sender's personal information. Yahoo! provided this information to the government which ultimately led to Tao's arrest in December of 2004 along with the confiscation of his computer and all documents without proper documentation or permits. Tao was sentenced to ten years in prison and his lawyer was stripped of his license to practice law and put under house arrest. Once again, Yahoo! was strongly criticized by the media, lawmakers, and Reporters without Borders.

Yahoo! to this day still operates in China. However, its Chinese operations are managed by its partner Alibaba Group, which operates completely inside the country of China. In 2005, Yahoo! handed its operations over to them in exchange for a 40% stake in the company. Alibaba and Yahoo! continue to assist the government to this day, claiming they are following local laws and regulations. The corporation continues to take criticism for assisting the Chinese government. Additionally in 2007, Yahoo! settled with the two families of the people it helped imprison, along with establishing a human rights fund to help all dissidents imprisoned due to censorship. Yahoo! continues to struggle with its image and many feel the brand and company have a huge public relations crisis that needs to be dealt with before they can regain international respect.

Microsoft in China

In 1992, Microsoft established its first presence in China by opening an office in Beijing. While the majority of its interests are in the sale of its Windows software, Servers and tools, Business Solutions, and Home and Entertainment products, it does operate its search engine and MSN products in the country as well. MSN products include e-mail service, Spaces, blogging, chat service, and other similar services. Unlike Yahoo!, Microsoft keeps its servers with account information outside of the China borders so they are less likely to be pressured into giving up users' information.

While Microsoft has taken steps to help prevent exposing users' information, it has taken the stance that it is a multinational business and as such needs to manage the reality of operating in different companies through the world. To them, that means operating under the local and national laws that apply to its many locations. Because they operate in China, they chose to follow the censorship guidelines and regulations imposed by the Chinese government.

One of the regulations for blogs in China is that they must first be registered with the government and be given approval before content can be posted. Blogs are one of the areas where Microsoft has come under scrutiny. It actively filters words such as "freedom," "democracy," and "demonstration" from its MSN site in China. In addition, it also shut down the blog site of a well-known Chinese blogger who used its MSN online service in China.

Zhao Jing was a well-known blogger who worked as a research assistant in Beijing for the *New York Times*. Mr. Jing discussed a high-profile newspaper strike that broke out on December 29, 2005 when the editor of the *Beijing News* was fired. One hundred journalists at the paper decided to go on strike in an unusual show of solidarity for a Chinese news organization that has very strict restrictions. Upon Zhao posting his report, the site was immediately pulled down by Microsoft. Microsoft released a statement that the site was taken down after Chinese authorities made a request that it be removed.

To this day, Microsoft still maintains word, image, and website filtering on its internet services provided in China. Just like Yahoo!, Microsoft continues to take criticism from human rights groups such as Human Rights Watch and Reporters without Borders. In addition, Microsoft linked a deal with China's largest search provider, Baidu, in July 2011. Microsoft will be providing English language search queries on various Baidu websites. With Baidu representing 85% of the current Chinese search market, Microsoft is clearly attempting to increase its market presence. Many are concerned about the details of the agreement as it relates to censorship but no information has been made public.

Google in China

Google's history in China is perhaps the most well known of any internet search company and service provider. The company prides itself on providing access to information all over the world and leading the charge on freedom of speech. This is why it was such a surprise when the company announced it was going into China and going to cooperate with the government on censorship.

On January 27, 2006, Google.cn went live and is headquartered in the northern part of Beijing. In typical Google fashion, its offices were outfitted with outrageous frills, entertainment, and free meals in its cafeteria. The major difference between this location and that of any other was that it would have to censor its activities and presence in accordance with the government of China. While Google agreed and knowingly knew it would need to censor itself, the hope was that operating this way would be equal to the constraints placed on its competition, especially the Chinese company Baidu.

This assumption was instantly challenged when Google.cn began experiencing unexplained outages while Baidu experienced none. In addition, Google lost its operating license, with the Chinese government claiming it was not clear whether Google was an internet service provider or a news portal. The loss of their license began a year-and-a-half-long project to get it restored and have its level of service restored. Even though service was restored, the Chinese market had already made up its mind that the service provided by Google was unreliable and many had moved to another provider.

Along with the service outages and concern over censorship, Google was very concerned about storing its users' data in China for fear of having to turn over the data. Because of this, users did not have access to services like Gmail, Blogger, Picasa, and YouTube. Many other services were offered but significantly altered.

The final incident that would ultimately cause Google to leave was the security hack and break-in that happened in December of 2009. In addition to some of Google's intellectual property and code being stolen, the accounts of Chinese activists were compromised with all of their contacts, plans, and private information being taken by the intruders. Google was able to determine that the geographical location of the attack was from China and, due to the sophistication of the attack, they were convinced it was likely government-sponsored at a minimum. The company not only felt threatened but felt it had been used to identify and silence critics of what they saw as a repressive government.

While Eric Schmidt, the current CEO, was against no longer carrying out censorship, he was outvoted and the company decided to no longer provide censorship for the Chinese government. On January 10, 2010, Google posted a note saying it would no longer help the Chinese dictatorship do its dirty work. Within a couple of months, Google closed its internet search service in China and began directing users to its uncensored search engine in Hong Kong.

Google continues to maintain its uncensored service by directing users to its Hong Kong site. Since it began redirecting users to Hong Kong, its market share in the Chinese market has declined from 35.6% in 2009 down to 18.9% in the second quarter of 2011. In addition, Google has accused the Chinese government of a Gmail phishing attack and blocking Gmail accounts. And, while its Android operating system represents about half of the phones in use in China, Baidu is the default search engine on 80% of those. With Microsoft joining forces with Baidu and Yahoo! in an agreement with Alibaba, it's not clear how Google plans to regain its once strong position in the Chinese search market.

Chapter 8: Long Case Bibliography

ABC News. "Yahoo! Settles Lawsuit with Chinese Dissidents." 2007. 12 July 2011. http://abcnews.go.com/Technology/story?id=3862513&page=1.

Associated Press. "Yahoo! Helped China, Again." 19 April 2006. 2 July 2011. http://www.wired.com/techbiz/media/news/2006/04/70698.

Barboza, M. and Helft, D. "Google Shuts China Site in Dispute Over Censorship." 22 March 2010. 25 June 2011. http://www.nytimes.com/2010/03/23/technology/23google.html.

Barboza, D., Jr. and Zeller, T. "Microsoft Shuts Blog's Site After Complaints by Beijing." 6 January 2006. 22 June 2011. http://www.nytimes.com/2006/01/06/technology/06blog.html.

BBC News. "Microsoft Censors Chinese Blogs." 14 June 2005. 29 June 2011. http://news.bbc.co.uk/2/hi/technology/4088702.stm.

——. "Timeline: China and Net Censorship." 23 March 2010. 28 June 2011. http://news.bbc.co.uk/2/hi/asia-pacific/8460129.stm.

——. "Yahoo! Helped Jail China Writer." 7 September 2005. 29 June 2011. http://news.bbc.co.uk/2/hi/asia-pacific/4221538.stm.

China Internet Network Information Center (CNNIC). "The 27th Statistical Report on Internet Development in China." 2011.

CIA. Central Intelligence Agency. 15 June 2011. 23 June 2011. https://www.cia.gov/library/publications/the-world-factbook/geos/ch.html.

Gunther, M. "Yahoo!'s China Problem." 22 February 2005. 30 June 2011. http://money.cnn.com/2006/02/21/news/international/pluggedin_fortune/.

InformationWeek. "Microsoft Strikes Search Deal with China's Baidu." 5 July 2011. 13 July 2011. http://www.informationweek.com/news/windows/microsoft_news/231000965.

Jacob, J. "How Internet Censorship Works." 17 February 2011. 26 June 2011. http://www.ibtimes.com/articles/113590/20110217/china-internet-censorship-great-firewall-us-hillary-clinton-communist.htm.

Jacobs, A. "Follow the Law, China Tells Internet Companies." 10 January 2010. 30 June 2011. http://www.nytimes.com/2010/01/15/world/asia/15beijing.html.

Levy, S. "Inside Google China's Misfortune." 15 April 2011. 23 June 2011. http://tech.fortune.cnn.com/2011/04/15/googles-ordeal-in-china/.

Microsoft. "Microsoft in China." 2006.

Reporters without Borders. "Yahoo! Implicated in Third Cyberdissident Trial." 25 January 2007. 26 June 2011. http://en.rsf.org/china-yahoo-implicated-in-third-19-04-2006,17180.html.

Riley, D. "Yahoo! in China: An Unfair Attack." 8 November 2007. 27 June 2011. http://techcrunch.com/2007/11/08/yahoo-in-china-an-unfair-attack/.

Search Engine Watch. "In China, Baidu Continues Search Market Domination Over Google." 15 July 2011. 15 July 2011. http://searchenginewatch.com/article/2094469/In-China-Baidu-Continues-Search-Market-Domination-Over-Google.

Washington Post. "Google vs. China." 14 January 2010. 1 July 2011. http://www.washingtonpost.com/wp-dyn/content/article/2010/01/13/AR2010011302908.html.

LONG CASE QUESTIONS

1. Should internet users expect privacy when surfing the web? Why or why not?
2. Was Yahoo! and Microsoft right in providing the data that the Chinese government requested? Should companies abide by local regulations even if such regulations violate other country's regulations?
3. If you were a Google stakeholder, would you have been disappointed when they decided to leave the Chinese market?
4. What future ethical issues do you anticipate for companies like Yahoo! and Microsoft, which still operate in China?

The Environment and Sustainability

LEARNING OBJECTIVES

After reading this chapter you should be able to:

- Understand what is sustainability
- Learn about the arguments for and against sustainability from a company perspective
- Become aware of the environment and key aspects of environmental degradation
- Learn about the many steps that lead to the successful sustainable company
- Become aware of the many benefits accruing to companies that are sustainable

PREVIEW BUSINESS ETHICS INSIGHT

WalMart and Sustainability

WalMart is not seen as a model environmentally friendly company. It is known for its size, achieving a billion dollars of sales per day. It has a global workforce of more than two million employees and is connected to over 100,000 businesses worldwide. Many are therefore surprised to hear that WalMart has actually been a world leader among the *Fortune* 500 companies pushing for sustainability and environmental responsibility. It has pioneered a number of environmental standards that have become targets in many industries. Because of its size, it has the ability to influence many of its partners to become more environmentally friendly.

The push for sustainability came with a speech made by the CEO Lee Scott in 2005. In that speech, he acknowledged the size of WalMart and the ability to use that size to positively impact the world. Environmentalists were then surprised to hear that CEO Scott wanted to make WalMart the greenest company on earth. The ultimate goal for WalMart in its greening efforts is to only use renewable energy to power its operations, reduce waste to zero, and sell only those products that sustain the environment.

To embark on its sustainability mission, WalMart started working with many of the world's leading environmental organizations. It brought in organizations such as Rocky Mountain Institute, Patagonia, and Seventh Generation, and even hired a former president of the Sierra Club to help the company improve its environmental performance. These individuals and organizations helped WalMart set industry-wide standards for sustainability.

WalMart also created a questionnaire that was sent out to thousands of suppliers in 2009. Through the questionnaire, WalMart surveyed its suppliers' every aspect of operations from energy use to level of waste. With such information, WalMart has created a "sustainable product index" that puts a green ranking on all of the products they carry. WalMart is pushing its suppliers to continue modifying their operations to improve on that index.

The ultimate indicator of its greening efforts is the new warehouse that was recently opened in Balzac, Canada. The warehouse is the model green building and it is estimated that the building will save around $5 million over the next five years. While the building is the typical large WalMart building, it has many features that reduce both waste and energy use. For example, the building is equipped with LED lighting using less energy while also lasting longer than fluorescent or other bulbs. Most of the lights are motion activated. This leads to huge savings as most warehouses have lights that are either on or off all the time. Lighting often makes up around 75% to 90% of a warehouse's costs. The doors leading to freezers have special air curtains to prevent the cold air from rushing outside to the warmer temperatures. The doors on the loading docks have motion sensors that open only when the trucks are parked on the loading bays. This also saves energy as it prevents chilled air from escaping. The wasted heat from the large refrigerators keeping the warehouse chilled is piped to areas where heat is needed. The building also has two wind turbines and solar panels that are used to heat the water the warehouse needs. The vehicles used in the building are also very environmentally friendly as they are all powered by hydrogen. Furthermore, the hydrogen is generated by renewable-power plants rather than the usual more polluting coal plants. Finally, the roof of the warehouse was painted white in order to reduce heat gain.

Based on Turner, C. 2010. "How WalMart is saving the world." *Canadian Business*, November 23–December 6, 83, 20, 44–49; Dutton, G. "Sustainable Warehousing." *World Trade 100*, November, 28–34.

The Preview Business Ethics Insight on pages 385–6 highlights the importance of sustainability and environmental responsibility to WalMart. **Sustainability** "refers to capacity of healthy ecosystems to continue functioning indefinitely"[1] or "economic development that meets the needs of the present generation without compromising the ability of future generations to meet their needs."[2] A core aspect of sustainability is the ability to make judicious use of current resources to ensure that such resources are available in the future.

As the world faces climate change, air and water pollution, and other environmental changes, sustainability is becoming more critical. **Sustainable or environmentally responsible organizations** are seen as those that are gradually modifying their operations in order to have less impact on the environment while also making better use of resources. However, as the Preview Business Ethics Insight shows, for WalMart, sustainability is going beyond mere window dressing. Authentic green organizations are those that are critically examining all operations and devising ways to have minimal impact on the environment.

But do companies have a special obligation to the environment? In an important piece, Bowie argues that companies have no special obligations to protect the environment above and beyond what the law prescribes.[3] This view is consistent with the view that the only responsibility for companies is to pursue profits while respecting the law. He argues that the only moral obligation of companies is to ensure that they do not intervene in the political arena to help defeat or weaken environmental laws. However, as long as a company is obeying the law, it has no special moral obligation to protect the environment. Furthermore, Bowie argues that businesses can only help solve environmental problems if they have the expertise to do so. In reality, most companies are not necessarily experts in the environment and should focus mostly on respecting the appropriate laws and avoiding negligent behaviors. Additionally, Bowie argues that customers are the ones that are responsible for environmental protection by paying higher prices if they want more environmentally conscious products.

Many experts have since argued that Bowie's views are based on erroneous assumptions. According to Desjardins,[4] Bowie's solution for environmental damage is either consumer action or legislation. However, Desjardins argues that the consumerist culture is placing severe pressures on the earth's biospheres. As the new economies of China, India, and others continue to grow, the earth will not be able to sustain the carbon dioxide emission that could potentially come from these new customers. Furthermore, not all societies have democratic institutions to enact laws to pressure companies to be more environmentally sensitive. Additionally, Desjardins argues that a business case can be made for sustainability. Contrary to the view that sustainability always incurs expense, Desjardins suggests that sustainability can actually be profitable for a company.

Most experts currently side with the latter view. Sustainability and environmental responsibility are among the most important goals as perceived by top executives in companies.[5] In fact, while world leaders were unable to reach a consensus on ways to mitigate climate change at the 2011 World Climate Summit in Cancun, business executives agreed that meeting needs of stakeholders will increasingly mean investing in environmentally sustainable practices to reduce carbon emissions and reducing waste

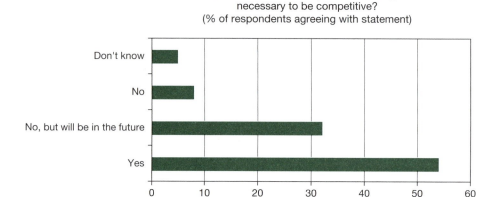

Is pursuing sustainability-related strategies
necessary to be competitive?
(% of respondents agreeing with statement)

EXHIBIT 9.1—Sustainability Strategies and Competitive Advantage Across Industries

while also maintaining profitable operations.[6] Furthermore, recent surveys across industries (i.e., automobiles, commodities, construction, financial services, etc.) suggest that most see sustainability as critical to achieving sustainable competitive advantage. Exhibit 9.1 shows the percentage of respondents who agreed with the statement "Is pursuing sustainability-related strategies necessary to be competitive?"

Given the critical importance of sustainability, this chapter will therefore discuss the key aspects related to sustainability. First, we discuss issues such as air pollution, land pollution, and water pollution. We also discuss water issues, as many are predicting that water will become increasingly scarce in the future and need to be managed. Second, we discuss the many aspects of the model sustainable company. We use a strategic approach and discuss the many aspects of the successful companies pursuing strategic environmental sustainability. In the final section of the chapter, we discuss the many benefits companies can reap from sustainability.

ENVIRONMENTAL DEGRADATION

One of the most important reasons why multinationals are getting so much attention for their environmental performance is because of the impact they have on the environment. Companies are important contributors to many aspects of environmental degradation. In this section of the chapter, we look at aspects of environmental degradation, specifically air pollution, land pollution, and water pollution. We also address critical water issues.

Air Pollution

Air pollution occurs when the release of materials to the atmosphere cannot be safely disposed of by natural processes. While some air pollution is caused by natural events such as forest fires and volcano eruptions, most air pollution is caused by human activity. Furthermore, companies contribute significantly to air pollution. A recent study of 230 of the Standard and Poor's 500 companies showed that these companies released around 1.4 billion metric tons of carbon dioxide or 30% of all carbon dioxide from industrial sources in the U.S.[7]

What contributes to air pollution? The Environmental Protection Agency (EPA), which regulates environmental quality in the U.S., lists six common **air pollutants**.[8] These are particulate matter, ozone, lead, carbon monoxide, sulfur dioxide, and nitrogen oxide. Particulate matter refers to those small particles that occur because of dusty industries and smoke. Ozone refers to the combination of three atoms of oxygen that occurs in the atmosphere. At high levels in the atmosphere, ozone is considered beneficial as it protects the earth from the sun's rays. However, ozone occurring at lower levels due to vehicle and industrial emissions is very harmful as it is a primary factor for smog. Carbon monoxide is an extremely dangerous odorless gas that comes mainly from vehicle emissions. Sulfur dioxide refers to the group of highly reactive gases that come mainly from power plants using fossil fuels. In contrast, nitrogen oxide is also a highly reactive gas coming from vehicle emissions. Finally, lead is a metal that is found naturally in the environment. Most lead came historically from vehicle emissions but has reduced considerably with the EPA's efforts to remove lead from gasoline.

The major concern with the six common air pollutants is that they contribute to major health problems. For instance, high levels of ground ozone have been linked to various respiratory ailments. High exposure to particulate matter has also been linked to respiratory ailments, as well as heart disease, such as irregular heartbeat and heart attacks. Carbon monoxide is an extremely dangerous gas that reduces the ability of the body to deliver oxygen to the heart and the brain. High levels of carbon monoxide are often fatal. To give you more insights into the health effects of these pollutants, Exhibit 9.2 (overleaf) shows the sources of the various types of pollutants and the likely health effects.

As Exhibit 9.2 shows, the common air pollutants can be very harmful to humans. Presence of the six pollutants can result in significant health problems ranging from respiratory difficulties to heart disease. However, another area of concern is acid rain. **Acid rain** occurs when both sulfur dioxide and nitrogen oxide combine with air vapor in the atmosphere and return to earth in the form of acid rain. Acid rain has also been shown to be a pollutant, contributing to acidification of lakes while also contributing to degradation of buildings.

Another important issue that is contributing to the discussion of air pollution is **greenhouse gases**. According to scientific evidence, life on earth is possible through energy from the sun. The earth absorbs energy from the sun and also radiates some energy back to space. However, the presence of greenhouse gases in the atmosphere traps the energy going to space. Such energy is then radiated back to earth, keeping the earth warmer. Without such greenhouse gases, the earth would be around 60°F colder, making life on earth impossible. Unfortunately, recent human activity has increased the level of greenhouse gases dramatically through the increased use of fossil fuels such as gas, coal, oil, and others. These activities release both carbon dioxide and

Pollutants	Sources	Health Effects
Ozone	Emissions from industrial facilities, motor vehicle exhaust, gasoline vapors, and other chemical solvents	People with lung problems, children, and older adults are affected when breathing unhealthy levels of ozone. These include • Wheezing and breathing difficulties when exercising or outdoors • Airway irritation and coughing when breathing deeply • Permanent lung damage with repeated exposure
Particulate matter	Found near dusty roadways, smog, and haze	• Irritation of the airways, coughing, difficulty breathing • Decreased lung function and aggravated asthma • Cardiovascular disease and non-fatal heart attacks • Premature death of individuals with heart or lung disease
Carbon monoxide	Emitted from combustion processes	• Reduces oxygen-carrying capacity of blood to organs • Causes harmful effects when less oxygen carried to organs such as brain and heart • Is particularly harmful to people with heart disease • Causes death at extremely high levels
Nitrogen oxides	Major sources are emissions from cars, trucks and buses, power plants, and off-road equipment	• Airway inflammation in healthy people • Increased respiratory problems in people with asthma • Breathing elevated levels of nitrogen oxides is linked with emergency room visits for respiratory issues • Specially harmful to children, older adults, and adults with respiratory disease
Sulfur dioxide	Major sources are from fossil fuel combustion at power plants and other industrial facilities	• Adverse respiratory effects including bronchoconstriction and increased asthma symptoms • Interacts with other small particles in the air and can cause lung damage and premature death for those with heart disease
Lead	Major sources used to be car emissions. Most are found now near lead smelters	• When ingested, is distributed in the body and accumulates in bones • Affects the nervous system, kidney function, immune system, reproductive and developmental systems, and the cardiovascular system.

EXHIBIT 9.2—Pollutant Types, Sources, and Health Effects

methane which are known to contribute to greenhouse gases. The enhanced greenhouse gases are believed to be contributing to the global climate change.

While there are still political debates about whether climate change is actually occurring or not, scientific evidence shows that the earth is indeed becoming warmer. According to data reported by the Environmental Protection Agency, the earth is currently warming about 0.29°C per decade. Further evidence is provided by the widespread melting of snow and ice and the consequent rise in sea level.

The consequences of the climate change for the earth are both direct and indirect. According to the EPA, the direct effects of climate change for individuals include more heat waves and fewer cold weather spells.[9] This can affect people, directly causing deaths among the elderly. Heat waves can also make smog more dangerous. The dangerous indirect effects of climate change include more extreme weather events. While scientific evidence does not yet provide definite claims of the link between climate change and weather events, data shows more extreme hurricanes and extreme heat and floods. Furthermore, some areas are expected to experience more droughts. Climate change is also expected to result in changes to the earth's ecosystem thus affecting some species.

Given the dire consequences of climate change for the earth, most companies are being pressured to reduce their emission of greenhouse gases. As discussed earlier, companies contribute significantly to emission of greenhouse gases.[10] Such emissions occur directly as a result of the company's fuel combustion or use of other industrial processes that emit carbon dioxide. However, carbon emissions can also occur indirectly through purchasing electricity made from fossil fuels or from other suppliers that provide goods and services to the company. Exhibit 9.3 shows the average emissions per company in various industrial sectors, based on the study of Standard and Poor's 500 companies.

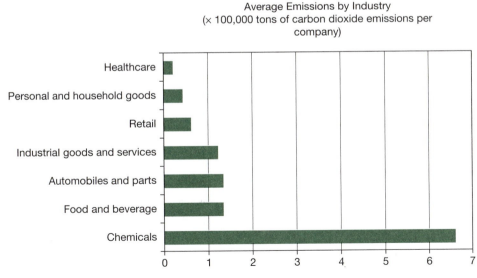

EXHIBIT 9.3—Average Carbon Emissions based on S&P 500 Companies

As Exhibit 9.3 shows, the chemicals sector has the highest level of carbon emissions. This is not surprising, because chemicals involve very energy-intensive processes. The other leading industries are food and beverage and automobiles and parts. The major sources of direct carbon emissions from the food and beverage industry comes from energy use and refrigerants.

Given the relatively high contribution of companies to overall carbon emissions, many countries are experimenting with regulation to reduce such emissions. One such mechanism is the cap-and-trade method where the government will impose a limit on carbon emissions while also allowing companies to trade such allowances. In the U.S., a recent attempt to impose cap-and-trade legislation failed.[11] The legislation, known as the Waxman-Markley Bill, would have proposed a target of greenhouse gas reduction of 17% from 2005 to 2020. However, critics have argued that the U.S. economy is heavily dependent on fossil fuels and such rules would result in severe loss of jobs.[12] Nevertheless, experts predict that cap-and-trade will likely be implemented and that those companies that are striving to reduce their greenhouse gases will likely enjoy a competitive advantage.

Land Pollution

Another important aspect of environmental degradation is land pollution. **Land pollution** refers to the contamination that occurs when toxic waste and other waste material that do not belong on land are disposed of on land. Such materials then are either consumed by plants or animals, which are then consumed by humans. Land pollution also occurs when toxic materials seep into the ground and affect the soil. Such pollution can affect individuals living in the area of the polluted land for decades.

Land pollution occurs because of many factors. For example, the growth in the use of fertilizers, pesticides, and insecticides to satisfy human demand for food has resulted in both land and plant absorption of such material. Human consumption of such plants can result in birth defects and other disease. Heavy metals can also cause land pollution. Such heavy metals (e.g., cadmium) are often dumped on land in industrial waste. However, these metals can be consumed by animals and plants and consequently get consumed by humans. Gradual increase of heavy metals in humans can eventually result in various forms of illnesses and cancer.

Another big factor resulting in land pollution is disposal of garbage. As many societies such as India, China, and Russia experience rapid economic growth, there is a consequent growth in waste. As more individuals in industrialized societies experience higher purchasing power, they are able to consume various new types of products.[13] However, as these products become obsolete and as more products are designed with shorter life spans, disposal of such products is adding to more complex and heterogeneous waste. Consider the Global Business Ethics Insight on page 393.

As the Global Business Ethics Insight shows, garbage disposal is also a significant contributor to land pollution. For instance, as we saw in Chapter 8 on Information Technology, disposal of electronic waste in less developed societies often put low paid

GLOBAL BUSINESS ETHICS INSIGHT

Sustainable Landfilling in Malaysia and Indonesia

Both Malaysia and Indonesia are relatively small nations with significant population densities. Furthermore, as the standard of living in both nations has been growing, more individuals have the means to consume a wide range of products. Unfortunately, disposal of waste created by increased use of these products have not been very efficient. Consider that Malaysia generates more than 30,000 tons of waste daily, while Indonesia generated around 38.5 million tons of waste in 2006.

Both countries had fairly low population density in the 1970s and landfill use was not a problem. Additionally, most of the landfills were of the most basic classes, whereby the landfill was simply fenced and perimeter drains installed. However, as the demand on such waste facilities has increased, use of these facilities have resulted in serious environmental damage as the waste seeps into the streams and other water areas. Furthermore, both countries have very little regulation regarding waste disposal. As a result, both households and companies have disposed of waste without concern for the environment. Consider the case of illegal dumping at many landfill sites in Malaysia. Malaysian companies have routinely dumped toxic and other caustic materials at these illegal dumpsites.

Both countries have therefore recently enacted legislation to manage waste disposal. However, both countries face significant barriers in ensuring that the law is followed. For instance, recent reports suggest that the Malaysian general population have not had very positive attitudes toward these new environmental efforts. Furthermore, the lack of financial assistance from the government means that only few landfills have the financial means to operate at sustainable levels. Both countries will therefore face significant difficulties as they implement such laws.

Based on Agamuthu, P. and Fauziah, S.H. 2011 "Challenges and issues in moving toward sustainable landfilling in a transitory country." *Waste Management and Research*, 29, 1, 13–19; Meidiana, C. and Gamse, T. 2011. "The new waster law: Challenging opportunity for future landfill operation in Indonesia." *Waste Management and Research*, 29, 1, 20–29.

workers' health at risk while also damaging the land. Some of the types of garbage generated by high-income countries may often pollute land in poorer countries.

Weber, Watson, Forter, and Oliaei also discuss another aspect of landfill use that may become problematic in the long term.[14] Persistent organic pollutants (POPs) are chemical products such as polychlorinated biphenyls (commonly known as PCPs) and hexachlorocyclohexane (HCH) that are increasingly being produced. Such POPs are commonly used in a wide variety of consumer goods. However, as these consumer goods are disposed of at landfills, the POPs they contain tend to degrade very slowly.

As the number of products containing POPs grows at landfills, POPs concentration will likely grow. Degradation of concentrated levels of POPs will likely build up in the food chain as animals and plants are exposed to POPs. This will also eventually affect humans.

In sum, similar to air pollution, companies are often significant contributors to land pollution in terms of both the way their operations pollute the land and the amount of waste they generate that ends up in landfills. Additionally, multinationals are also often criticized for taking advantage of poor or non-existent regulations to dump their waste. Consider the case of Shell in Nigeria, which is often blamed with poor operations and significant damage to the land.[15] Shell's poorly run and sometimes sabotaged oil extraction in the Niger Delta has resulted in significant damage to the land and waterways around their operations. This has negatively impacted the communities surrounding their operations. Many fishing communities have been decimated, while some residents of the local communities are suffering. Companies will therefore have to play an important role in reducing land pollution.

Water Pollution

Water pollution refers to the contamination of water sources such as lakes, streams, wells, and oceans by substances that are harmful to living organisms. Water is one of the most critical resources that sustain life. Humans need access to clean water for drinking on a daily basis. Lacking such access, humans eventually get sick and die. In fact, it is reported that around 5,000 children die daily due to dirty water, while it is estimated that around 1.8 million individuals die annually from diarrheal diseases linked to lack of access to clean water.[16] Ensuring that water is accessible and not polluted is therefore a critical endeavor.

Similar to other forms of pollution, companies contribute significantly to water pollution. This is especially salient for companies operating in new markets such as China and India. Consider the Global Business Ethics Insight on page 395.

The Global Business Ethics Insight reveals the two major problems facing most societies as they deal with water issues. Water pollution is clearly a major issue that many societies are facing.[17] Facing weak regulations, companies routinely dump pollutants that affect water sources. However, a second water-related problem facing most societies today is scarcity of water. While experts generally agree that the earth is not necessarily running out of water, water remains scarce for a sizable proportion of the world's population.[18] Companies are therefore already playing a critical role in promoting water conservation.

To understand the severity of the scarcity, it is important to examine some of the most important water-related statistics:[19]

- Although the earth is covered with water, less than 3% of the water is fresh and drinkable. The rest is seawater and undrinkable. Of the 3%, 2.5% is frozen, thereby providing less than 0.5% for human use.

GLOBAL BUSINESS ETHICS INSIGHT

Water Pollution in China

As China continues to experience economic growth, it is grappling with severe environmental problems. Experts report that pollution in China is costing the economy around 10% of gross domestic product. The various forms of pollution are resulting in around 400,000 deaths every year. Furthermore, such environmental disasters are resulting in a very large amount of environmental protests. However, one of the most problematic pollutions China faces is related to water.

China faces water-related challenges on two levels. First, environmental regulation is very weak in China and companies routinely pollute water sources. A prominent Chinese environmental organization released a list of multinationals that are believed to be contributing to water pollution.[17] This list includes companies such as PepsiCo, DuPont, Nestlé, and even Suzuki. More recent incidents also show that local companies are contributing to water pollution. For instance, in 2010, the Zijin Mining Company accidentally released 2.4 million gallons of acidic waste water in the Ting River in Fujian. Around 2,000 tons of fish perished and 60,000 individuals lost their source of safe water. A chemical spill near the city of Jilin resulted in around 3,000 barrels dumped in the Songhua river. The situation is so dire that it is reported that around 40% of surface water is so polluted that it is unusable.

A second water-related problem facing China is access to safe water. As demand for adequate usable water grows, the country is facing a severe shortage. It is reported that two-thirds of China's 650 or more cities do not have enough access to water. Furthermore, as the middle class grows, there is increased demand for water. More affluent individuals want to water their lawns while also making use of equipment using water such as dishwashers and washing machines. Additionally, China wastes more water than most countries as over 25% of water transmitted through pipes is lost through leakage.

As these two factors project a very bleak water situation in China for the future, more effort is being made to ensure that solutions are implemented to improve the situation. For example, more environmental groups are now taking steps to shame companies that are water polluters. Furthermore, the government is taking steps to strengthen and improve regulation. However, experts predict that it will take some strong effort to avert future water disasters.

Based on Economy, E. and Lieberthal, K. 2007. "Will environmental risks in China overwhelm its opportunities." *Harvard Business Review*, June, 88–96; Oxford Analytica Daily Brief Service. 2010. "China: Awareness is up but pollution is problematic." September 22, 1; Spencer, J. 2007. "Chinese activists launch drive to shame polluters." March 28, online edition.

- There is high inequality regarding water distribution. Fewer than ten countries (Brazil, Canada, China, Colombia, Democratic Republic of Congo, Indonesia, India, Russia, and the U.S.) have 60% of the world's access to freshwater. There is also wide variation in water consumption.
- 1.8 million individuals die yearly from diarrhea and other water-related illnesses because of lack of access to safe water. Exhibit 9.4 shows the number of people worldwide by region who do not have access to clean water for drinking and other uses.
- Humans are putting incredible stress on water supply because of excessive use of water as well as pollution and inefficient use of such water. Furthermore, around one fifth of the world's population live in areas where water is scarce.
- A recent study forecasts that demand for water in 2030 will grow from 4,500 billion meter cube today to around 6,900 million meter cube. This represents a 40% jump above our current water reserves.
- Over 90% of usable water is used in agriculture in developing nations. However, after agriculture, industry is the next biggest user of water.
- Waterways are routinely used for waste disposal. Although nature can often break down some waste quantities, current levels suggest that the water ecosystems are severely threatened.

Given the above dire statistics regarding water, more companies will be asked to play a critical role in preserving water in the future. In fact, one of the most important water initiatives taken by companies recently is known as the "CEO Water Mandate." As part of the United Nations Global Compact (see Chapter 1), companies are now launching initiatives to help face the water challenges.[20] Business leaders met and developed six key areas which companies can voluntary adapt to. These include: 1) direct operations (conduct water footprint to assess water use and find ways to reduce such water use), 2) supply chain water management (find ways to work with others in the supply chain to improve water use), 3) collective action (work with local and national organizations to address water challenges), 4) public policy (working with

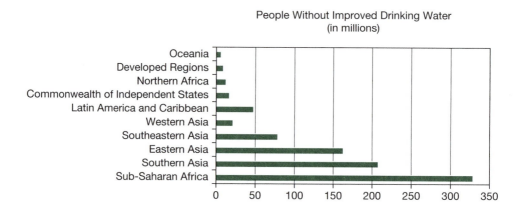

EXHIBIT 9.4—Number of People without Access to Improved Water by Region

governments to influence water policy), 5) community engagement (work with local communities to improve water use), and 6) transparency (be truthful about water use and strategies). More companies are joining this initiative, recognizing the urgency and extent of the water challenges facing the world today.

The above sections on environmental degradation show the extent of challenges facing companies today. Many companies are important contributors to such degradation. They will therefore be required to play an important role in helping address such challenges. Next we consider how to build the sustainable company.

BUILDING THE ENVIRONMENTALLY SUSTAINABLE COMPANY: A STRATEGIC APPROACH

The above sections of this chapter provide strong evidence of the need for companies to become more environmentally sensitive in the future. In this section, we discuss the many steps companies can take to become more environmentally sensitive. In doing so, we propose a strategic framework consistent with the theme of this text.

Top Management Support

Extant research suggests that **top management support** is extremely critical in implementing sustainability.[21] Without such support, it is unlikely that employees and others will buy into the effort. Most examples of successful environmental organizations tout leaders who were willing to engage employees and support the initiatives that will make sustainability a priority. Consider the Business Ethics Insight on page 398.

The Business Ethics Insight clearly shows that committed top management is critical to implement sustainability initiatives. In fact, recent research conducted in England suggests that top management mindset regarding sustainability is often a key barrier as to why sustainability efforts are not always successful. In interviews with executives from a variety of industries such as telecoms, food wholesaling, and banking, they found evidence of four types of top management sustainability mindsets.[22] Understanding the mindset of top management will provide important clues as to potential success of sustainability efforts.

According to Ahern,[23] there are four top management mindsets regarding sustainability. The first type known as the **"corporate conventionality"** mindset places strong emphasis on profit making. This type of mindset suggests that top management is unlikely to see much benefit from sustainability initiatives. Rather, these executives believe that the company's sole focus is to make profits and, if the company goes bankrupt because of sustainability efforts, the company does not really serve any purpose. A second type of mindset is the **"new sustainability paradigm"** view. Such executives see the need for a new way of measuring the success of sustainability efforts. However, these executives do not necessarily believe that sustainability can be profitable for the company. Rather, they see such efforts as not profitable for shareholders. The last two types tend to be more sympathetic to sustainability. Specifically, the third type, known as **"reconciliation,"** believes that it is possible to

BUSINESS ETHICS INSIGHT

Top Managers and Sustainability

There is ample evidence that sustainability efforts at many successful companies started with determined top managers willing to champion sustainability causes. In the Preview Business Ethics Insight (pages 385–6), we discussed how WalMart's sustainability efforts began with an influential speech by the CEO. He engaged consultants and other stakeholders to find ways to implement sustainability initiatives. WalMart's success was largely due to such support.

Consider the case of CEO of PepsiCo, Indra Nooyi. Even before she became CEO, she was an avid support of PepsiCo's green efforts. Executives remember how she loosened capital expenditure requirements to fund water- and heat-related conservation projects at an important meeting early in her career at PepsiCo. However, when she became CEO, she pushed for a new visionary strategy called "Performance with Purpose." The strategy basically links all green efforts in the company to the bottom line. This strategy has resulted in most employees participating in efforts to help PepsiCo become greener. Consider, for instance, that potatoes are 80% water. Through collaborative efforts with local universities and research institutes, PepsiCo is attempting to condense the steam from its chip-making plants in Leicester in order to return the water back to the plant. It has the world's seventh largest private fleet truck and recently put 176 all-electric trucks in its fleet. Such efforts would not have been possible without the support of its CEO.

Another example of a company that is now moving toward sustainability is Shell Oil. In a recent interview with Marvin Odum, the president of the company, he details the many factors that are forcing Shell to orient toward sustainability. While the company is in the very early stages of implementing sustainability, it is clear that the message sent when the CEO is in charge of such efforts is very powerful.

Based on Hopkins, M.S. 2011. "From 'trust me' to 'show me': Moving sustainability from 'priority' to 'core value.'" *MIT Sloan Management Review*, March, 1–6; Morris, B. 2008. "The Pepsi Challenge." *Fortune*, March 3, 54–66; Stanford, D. 2011. "Why sustainability is winning over CEOs." March 31, online edition.

reconcile sustainability with profitability. Such managers believe that sustainability can be profitable and beneficial to the organization despite the difficulties of getting there. Finally, the **"pragmatism"** mindset suggests that these executives take a more pragmatic view of sustainability. These executives are often involved in implementation of sustainability initiatives.

While the above research about mindsets is mostly practical, a lesson for most companies is that top management can have better appreciation for sustainability efforts if they move beyond understanding performance outcomes merely in terms of financial indicators. Specifically, those top managers comfortable with sustainability understand that sustainability cannot always be measured in terms of its impact on profits. Profits remain an adequate measure of success for shareholders. However, comprehensively understanding the impact of sustainability often means understanding the impact of actions on both social and environmental performance. As we will see later, measuring the impact of sustainability efforts in terms of social and environmental outcomes implies departure from conventional thinking regarding how project success is measured.

Another critical aspect of top management support is the role of top financial executives in ensuring that sustainability efforts go as planned. Consider, for instance, some of the "biodiversity" offsets that are being proposed where companies can counterbalance the environmental impact of one business activity in a region by preserving natural habitat in another area. Shell is currently engaged in this approach, where it is preserving antelopes and other natural habitat in one area of Qatar while developing a new natural gas facility in another.[24] Properly evaluating the trade-offs of such a project will require top financial executives with the ability to properly evaluate such a project. Financial executives need to have the skills to evaluate sustainability initiatives, set budgets, and track progress of such initiatives. Ultimately, the company will need the skills of someone who can effectively communicate the impact of such sustainability initiatives in terms of their impact on the environment.

Assessing Current Sustainability Situation

Once a company has the necessary support from top managerial levels, it is important to start assessing where the company stands with regards to the sustainability. This is conceptually similar to asking the "Where are we now?" question typical of strategic management practice. In this phase, the company examines the many aspects related to its business. Careful examination of the many areas will reveal potential avenues to implement sustainability initiatives.

Experts agree that one way that companies initially examine their activities to implement sustainability initiatives is by focusing on waste reduction and resource efficiencies.[25] Rather than embark immediately on full-fledged sustainability, companies will often adopt "low hanging fruits" that are easy to implement. For instance, for WalMart, understanding how to deal with its waste was a big factor to drive sustainability in the organization. It discovered that it was paying tens of millions of dollars to use 10-ton semi-compactors in order to get rid of the trash generated from its 4,400 locations. This realization led to the decision to start finding ways to reduce the amount of trash it was generating. Similarly, for Clorox, understanding the "low hanging fruit" activities that could help reduce waste and boost resource efficiency provided the means to convince others of the need for sustainability.

In assessing the current level, it is important to understand the types of companies engaged in sustainability. A recent report suggests that companies can be of the **embracer types** where such companies fully embrace sustainability efforts.[26]

However, some companies are **cautious adopters** where they see sustainability as limited to those activities that are linked to short-term efficiency. Embracer types are more likely to see the business case for sustainability and see sustainability as key to competitive advantage. As such, they are more likely to see and implement a stronger link between sustainability and profit and market share. In contrast, cautious adopters are less likely to take leaps of faith if they do not see properly quantified benefits of sustainability. Cautious adopters are obviously less enthusiastic of sustainability initiatives if they cannot see the monetized benefits of sustainability.

Either type of company will likely determine the extent to which assessment of the current situation is approached. Cautious adopters are more likely to adopt the "low hanging fruits," as these efforts are more easily quantifiable. However, embracers are more likely to look at the organization more strategically to find ways to make the company become more sustainable. For instance, WalMart embarked on its sustainability journey by working closely with consultants and outside experts to help it identify areas where sustainability initiatives could be implemented. These outside experts helped WalMart systematically analyze its operations to become more sustainable.

One of the more systematic ways to understand a company's operations is by conducting a value chain analysis. According to strategic management experts Gamble and Thompson Jr., the **value chain** of a company consists of the various activities that a company performs internally to create value for consumers.[27] Value chain analysis provides a systematic method to identify the many activities that are necessary to create the final product. To understand the value chain concept, Exhibit 9.5 shows the typical value chain and an illustrative example for the popular clothing retailer Gap.

Primary Activities

Supply Chain Management

Gap: Receiving and storing inputs from suppliers

Operations

Gap: Dealing with subcontractors

Distribution

Gap: Costs and activities dealing with physical distribution of products

Sales and Marketing

Gap: Activities and costs related to sales force efforts and marketing

Service

Gap: Costs and activities related to providing service to buyers

Support Activities and Costs

Product R&D, Technology and Systems Development
Gap – Product R&D, computer systems to run company, telecommunication systems

Human Resource Management
Gap – Costs associated with training, recruiting, and compensation of employees

General Administration
Gap – Costs associated with general management, finance, accounting, etc.

EXHIBIT 9.5—Value Chain and Example of Value Chain for Gap

As Exhibit 9.5 shows, the value chain consists of both primary activities and support activities. **Primary activities** are those activities directly linked to creating the product. Primary activities include:

- *Supply chain management.* The many activities and costs incurred in securing the raw materials and other energy requirements needed for production. This aspect may not be as relevant for Gap as they outsource most production. However, finding ways to work with these external contractors has been a critical aspect of Gap's sustainability strategy.
- *Operations.* This pertains to the many activities and costs that are necessary to convert the raw materials into finished products. While this may not be a critical activity for Gap, it is a critical aspect for other companies such as Procter & Gamble and others.
- *Distribution.* This pertains to the many costs and activities that are involved in physically distributing the products to buyers. For Gap, this involves the shipping and trucking of the clothing items to its stores.
- *Sales and marketing.* The activities and costs involved in the marketing and sales of the product, For Gap, this involves the advertising and other sales training their sales people receive.
- *Service.* The activities and costs associated with providing after-sales service to buyers. For Gap, this would involve the many activities related to returns.

The value chain also consists of **support activities** that are provided to support the primary activities. These include:

- *Product research and development, technology and systems development.* These include the costs and activities related to R&D as well as the development of appropriate information systems to support primary activities. For Gap, this would involve the use of computers for data analysis processes to determine buyer patterns.
- *Human resource management.* The activities and costs related to the hiring and firing of employees. For Gap, this would relate to training and other activities provided to support its workforce.
- *General administration.* These are activities and costs associated with the general management of the company. For Gap, this would involve the costs associated with activities such as finance, accounting, general management, and other management functions needed to adequately manage the company.

The value chain is thus a very systematic way in which companies can analyze their activities to determine where sustainability initiatives can be implemented. However, it should be noted that the value chain will differ by industry. For instance, a manufacturer will most likely be concerned about primary activities such as supply chain management and distribution. In contrast, a hotel chain is more concerned about primary activities such as sales and marketing.

GLOBAL BUSINESS ETHICS INSIGHT

Volkswagen and Sustainability

For the German automotive company Volkswagen, the supply chain aspect of its value chain is a very important aspect of its operations. Volkswagen has therefore taken many initiatives to reduce the environmental impact of its supply chain. By carefully analyzing its value chain activities, it determined areas where sustainability initiatives could take place. For instance, it not only has sustainability requirements for its suppliers but also provides them with environmental and sustainability training. Furthermore, it is very aware of the potential for the high environmental impact of its logistics. As such, the company is now aiming to reduce reliance on road transport to the more efficient rail and sea transport. The company has also developed software to ensure that fewer empty containers are being used during transport. Additionally, through analysis of its internal supply chain, it is now analyzing its in-house logistics to reduce the use of packaging and plastics when spare parts are moved to locations. Volkswagen has also implemented many initiatives aimed at the reduction of water use and air emissions. Furthermore, it has developed an extensive recycling system to go beyond manufacturing. It is aiming to recycle 95% of vehicles at the end of their lives to reduce the pressure on landfills, where a significant percentage of old cars end up.

Based on Nunes, B. and Bennett, D. 2010. "Green operations initiatives in the automotive industry." *Benchmarking: An International Journal*, 17, 3, 396–420.

Despite the differences by industry, the value chain is a critical mechanism to help a company understand the activities that contribute to environmental degradation. Consider the above Global Business Ethics Insight.

As you can see from the Global Business Ethics Insight, properly analyzing a company's value chain is critical to implement sustainability initiatives. By focusing only on some of its core aspects, Volkswagen was able to determine which areas to address.

Setting Sustainability Goals

An important aspect of a strategic approach to sustainability is to set **sustainability goals**. This is important as it will provide the focus for the company's sustainability efforts. Such goals will influence how new activities take shape in the company. It is likely that embracers are more likely to set sustainability goals for the whole organization, while cautious adopters may focus more on specific areas or set goals mostly focused on cost reductions. Consider, for instance, the case of Burt Bee's, the manufacturer of personal care products. Being a sustainability embracer, it has set an ambitious goal of "zero waste, zero carbon company, operating on 100% renewable energy" by the year 2020.[28]

From a strategic standpoint, an important aspect of a company's sustainability effort is the setting of its strategic vision. The **strategic vision** describes a company's aspirations about "where it is going," thus helping steer the company in that direction. Setting a strategic vision is a logical outcome of assessing where the company first stands on sustainability. By understanding the current situation, a company can then decide to what extent it will address sustainability issues. As such, it is likely that most embracers will incorporate sustainability at the strategic vision level to ensure that such efforts influence every aspect of a company's operations. However, cautious adopters may be less likely to set goals at the strategic vision level. In such cases, sustainability goals may be set at lower levels of the organization.

For sustainability goals to work, they must cascade down the organization and influence what each worker is doing. For instance, to show its support for sustainability, Burt Bee's provides paid time for its employees to volunteer for sustainability and other causes. In an effort to achieve its zero waste goal, it holds an annual dumpster dive where employees will go through the trash the company has generated to identify missed recycling opportunities. When the program started in 2007, Burt Bee's was generating around 40 tons of waste on a monthly basis. However, through the annual dumpster dive efforts, it reduced its waste to zero in 2009.

However, to set goals, companies need to be able to measure their sustainability efforts. **Measurable sustainability goals** provide a company with the needed benchmarks to determine whether it is successful in its sustainability efforts. Measurement also creates awareness around key issues and focuses energies toward improving such issues. The measurement process should also logically evolve from the value chain analysis. For each set of activities, the company can assess the level of energy consumption, water use, and waste created. Furthermore, companies can assess the level of land resources use.[29] These sustainability goals can then become benchmarks that the company can use to assess whether it is successful in its sustainability efforts.

Which sustainability goals should a company adopt? The types of goals adopted will likely depend on whether the company is an embracer or a cautious adopter. Embracers are more likely to adopt goals that cover the company's activities comprehensively. In contrast, cautious adopters may pick specific activities to achieve efficiencies or reduce waste. Furthermore, there are several organizations that provide guidance regarding sustainability. For instance, the International Organization for Standardization (ISO) provides very specific guidance regarding particular environmental indicators, thereby allowing companies to gauge their progress on environmental goals. Similarly, the Global Reporting Initiative (GRI) provides guidance regarding specific sustainability goals. To get a better understanding of sustainability goals, Exhibit 9.6 shows some of the environmental measures as used by the Global Reporting Initiative.

Category	Examples
Materials	Materials used by weight or volume
	Percentage of materials used that are recycled
Energy	Direct and indirect energy consumption
	Energy saved due to conservation and efficiency measures
	Energy sourced from alternative or other sources of energy
Water	Total water use by source
	Percentage of water recycled and reused
Biodiversity	Percentage of land owned, used, or managed in or near protected lands with high biodiversity
	Habitats protected or restored
	Strategies in place to manage impact of activities on biodiversity
Emissions	Direct and indirect greenhouse gas emissions by weight or volume
	Significant pollutant emissions by weight or volume
	Emissions of ozone-depleting materials by weight or volume
Waste	Total weight of waste by type and disposal method
	Total water discharge by quality and destination
	Total number and volume of significant spills
Products and Services	Initiatives to reduce environmental impact of products
	Percentage of products sold and packaging materials reclaimed or recycled
Compliance	Amount of fines and number of non-monetary sanctions for breaking laws and regulations
Transport	Impact of transporting materials
	Impact of transporting organizational members

EXHIBIT 9.6—Sustainability Goals

Reporting and Feedback

Another important component of any sustainability efforts is reporting. **Sustainability reporting** refers to the efforts by the company to report its sustainability efforts and the progress made on such efforts. Reporting is essential as it can provide the justification for sustainability choices while also addressing stakeholder concerns.[30] Many companies are engaging in reporting to show their efforts in addressing stakeholder sustainability issues. In doing so, companies are also relying on third-party institutions such as the International Organization for Standardization (ISO) or Global Reporting Initiative (GRI) to provide legitimacy regarding their claims.

In addition to reporting, a company also needs to provide **sustainability feedback** to all concerned parties and decide which areas need further improvements. Many of the companies discussed in this chapter will let employees know where they stand with regards to sustainability efforts and what will need to happen in the future. This "closing the loop" aspect of sustainability is consistent with the strategic management thinking that feedback is critical to improvement.

Other Success Factors

The above provided a strategic oversight of a successful sustainability program in a company. However, best practices suggest that a number of other factors contribute to success. These include:[31]

- Be a first mover. Surveys of successful companies attest to the need of being first movers. By being a first mover, a company can more quickly navigate the challenges associated with implementation of sustainability. Such knowledge can be very helpful as competitors attempt to mimic sustainability efforts.
- Balance visionary thinking with "low hanging fruits." While a long-term strategic view is necessary if a company is serious about sustainability, experts suggest that short-term projects with tangible benefits be integrated within the long-term plans of the company. Short-term projects can provide evidence of quick success that will convince skeptics about the benefits of sustainability.
- Balance between top-down and bottom-up. While CEO and top management support and communication regarding sustainability are important, experts also agree that employees need to be involved in the process. They are often more aware of places where sustainability steps can be taken. For instance, many sustainability ideas came from workers at Burt Bee's.[32] Involving workers also make it more likely that they will embrace sustainability.
- Devise and measure intangible benefits. As you may have realized, sustainability often involves benefits that may not always be tangible. It is therefore critical for companies to develop measures for those intangible benefits. For instance, Unilever's efforts to develop products that use less water may not provide direct benefits. However, the ability to evaluate the goodwill and other benefits from such an action needs to be developed in order to adequately quantify the benefits of sustainability.

- Educating consumers. Successful companies are also keen on educating their customers about the benefits of sustainability. For instance, WalMart is now only stocking fluorescent bulbs and educating its consumers about the benefits of such bulbs compared to traditional bulbs. Unilever is also encouraging its consumers to use products that are better for the environment.
- Role of Human Resource Management (HRM) department. Experts agree that the HRM department has a critical role to play to build a sustainability culture. HRM can play a critical role in hiring those employees who are more likely to embrace sustainability. However, HRM also has an important role in educating existing employees about the importance of sustainability and how such efforts can benefit the wider society.

BENEFITS OF SUSTAINABILITY

In the preceding section, we discussed the many steps to build the successful sustainable organization. But why should companies engage in operations that may be costly? Unfortunately, companies are important contributors to the many environmental problems we are facing and should therefore play a critical role in implementing changes to address such issues. Large multinationals have specially been targets for such calls and have been criticized for their lack of concern for the impact of their activities. This is exemplified in cases such as Shell Nigeria or, more recently, British Petroleum (BP), which have both been under tremendous pressure to improve their environmental performance. However, as we see below, **sustainability benefits** include many key advantages for companies.

An important benefit of sustainability today is avoiding the public relations nightmare that can occur when damages to the environment occur. Consider, again, the case of BP. While it took many years for the company to build its seemingly environmentally friendly image, the oil spill revealed the weaknesses of its environmental policies. BP had to face significant consumer backlash in many countries. It now has to toil in order to rebuild its reputation.

A related benefit of sustainability is avoiding fines and other legal costs associated with violating regulations. Most societies now have significant regulation enforcing environmental sustainability. Companies that break such environmental laws are often fined and may have to endure frequent inspections to satisfy regulators. Furthermore, companies that choose to fight the fines usually incur substantial legal costs as they endure years in the courtroom. Being environmental thus avoids incurring such costs.

An important benefit of sustainability is cost reduction. As the Preview Business Ethics Insight showed (pages 385–386), WalMart is expected to save significantly from the green warehouse. Pursuing sustainability efforts enables a company to identify areas where waste can be reduced and resources used more efficiently. In fact, the traditional view is that greening is costly and unprofitable for companies.[33] However, recent experiences at major companies such as Dow Chemical and United Technologies show that investments in green technology can help reduce costs and improve profits. In fact, Hopkins reports that some green investment can have a payback period as short

BUSINESS ETHICS INSIGHT

Sustainability in the Agricultural Industry

While the examples discussed in the chapter so far have pertained to companies, the agricultural industry has also been pressured to be more sustainable. Consider, for instance, the use of fertilizers and the traditional view that the more fertilizer is used, the higher the crop yield. However, as the cost of fertilizer is increasing, more farmers are paying attention to fertilizer use. Furthermore, fertilizer waste can trickle down to rivers and other water sources, thereby resulting in pollution.

In an interesting study of crop practices in Colorado, a team of researchers studied crop rotation, fertilizing, and irrigation practices of farmers growing vegetables, watermelons, wheat, corn, and alfalfa in rotation. Results of the study were very surprising. First, they found that some crops such as onions only used 12–15% of the fertilizers applied to the field. Given such low use, the researchers predicted that a significant amount of fertilizer applied actually stayed in the ground. They therefore recommended planting corn on the unfertilized land the next year. They were then very surprised to find a very high yield for unfertilized land. Over the years, heavy fertilizing had left significant deposits of nitrites in the ground. Furthermore, the researchers recommended growing alfalfa the following years with low levels of fertilizing. The alfalfa harvest was also very significant given the low levels of fertilizing that was used.

Given the scarcity of water, the researchers compared drip irrigation and the traditional overhead irrigation. They again found that the drip method used less water for onions while also resulting in the same yield. Taken together, the results of the study have thus been of help to farmers, who have been able to become more sustainable. The results have been very helpful, as farmers can now achieve the same product yield using less fertilizers and water. When applied to the large areas under cultivation for the agricultural industry, such results have resulted in significant savings.

Based on McGinnis, L. 2009. "Lowering nitrogen rates to increase profit, environmental sustainability." *Agricultural Research*, February, 20–21.

as two to three years. This is much shorter than the typical payback period expected for technology investment. However, sustainability does not only reduce costs for manufacturing or service industries. Consider the above Business Ethics Insight.

As the above shows, sustainability can have a clear impact on costs for the organization. Companies can reap benefits from ways to lower costs. However, sustainability efforts can also result in higher revenues. Research suggests that customers are more likely to purchase from companies that they perceive as being more sustainable relative to companies that have less perception of sustainability.[34] Additionally, research shows that customers tend to be more loyal to companies that have sustainable practices. Thus, sustainability can affect the revenue side of companies. Furthermore, consider the experiment discussed in Chapter 1 where it was found that customers are willing to pay higher prices for products that are considered more sustainable.[35] Such studies provide support for the notion that sustainability can result in higher sales.

Another important benefit of sustainability is improved relationships with stakeholders and improved brand reputation. As more multinationals are scrutinized for their practices, adopting sustainable practices can provide a positive perception to stakeholders. For instance, as we saw in Chapter 7 on secondary stakeholders, actively engaging stakeholders such as non-governmental organizations can provide companies with the ability to proactively deal with potential future environmental problems. Furthermore, sustainability projects a positive image in the community the company is located in. Such image can help the company develop a better relationship with the local community. Wexler argues that sustainable companies can have a positive influence on their industries.[36] Consider the case of Levi's, which partnered with other companies like IKEA and Marks and Spencer. By partnering with these companies and demanding more sustainable cotton (reduced water use, reduced pesticide, and improved working conditions), Levi's is influencing the cotton industry to become more sustainable.

Another benefit of sustainability is enhanced relationships with employees. Employees are more likely to feel committed and engaged with companies that demonstrate concern for the earth and the environment. Consider the case of Burt Bee's, maker of natural personal care products that has made sustainability its core reason for existence.[37] On an annual basis, employees gather to go through the trash to come up with more ways to reduce waste. Such concern for the environment has resulted in increased engagement with the company. Furthermore, such enthusiasm for sustainability has translated into further ideas for Burt's Bees to become more sustainable and profitable. Furthermore, employees have started changing their behaviors to reduce waste.

A final benefit of sustainability is enhanced relationships with shareholders. There is more evidence that investors are increasingly paying attention to environmental performance. Any impending environmental disaster is likely to send share prices tumbling. In contrast, companies that have engaged in sustainable paths have had more stable share prices.

From a strategic management standpoint, achieving the above advantages can also lead to increased competitive advantage. Pursuing sustainability can be a good source of innovation as companies not only discover new way of doing things but also new markets. Through cost reductions and better resource use, a company can become a cost leader in the market. Such efforts can thus provide important sources of competitive advantage.

To better appreciate these benefits, Exhibit 9.7 shows the percentage of executives who agreed with the types of benefits sustainability brings to their organizations.

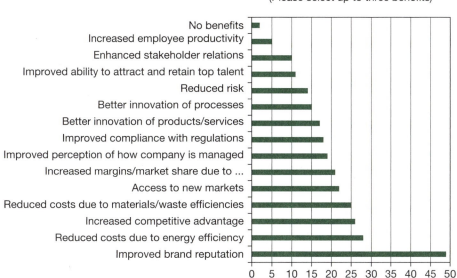

What are the greatest benefits to your
organization in addressing sustainability? (%)
(Please select up to three benefits)

EXHIBIT 9.7—Benefits of Sustainability

CHAPTER SUMMARY

In this chapter, you read about the importance of sustainability for companies. You learned about the many changes that are occurring that makes addressing sustainability issues critical. You read about the many forms of environmental degradation including air pollution, land pollution, and water pollution. You also became aware of how multinationals are important contributors to such problems and should therefore play important roles in addressing such problems.

In the second part of the chapter, you read about the many steps to a successful sustainability program. You learned about the importance of top management support and financial executives. You read about assessment of current sustainability efforts as well as the need to measure and set sustainability goals. You also became aware of the need to provide feedback while also reading about several other key factors that ensure success.

In the final part of the chapter, you read about the many benefits of sustainability. You learned about the cost benefits as well as avoiding significant fines and costs because of regulation. You also read about how sustainability can benefit a company by improving relationships with stakeholders. Sustainability efforts can demonstrate caring for the community and other stakeholders thus improving relationships with such stakeholders. Sustainability can also improve relationships with shareholders, as

409

many shareholders now pay attention to the sustainability records of the company they invest in. Finally, you learned that sustainability efforts can lead to improved competitive advantage.

NOTES

1 Unruh, G. 2008. "The biosphere rules." *Harvard Business Review*, 86, 2, 111–117 (at 111).

2 Epstein, M.J. 2008. *Making sustainability work*. Sheffield, U.K.: Greenleaf Publishing, p. 20.

3 Bowie, N. 1990. "Morality, money, and motor cars." In W.M. Hoffman, R. Frederick & E.S. Petry (Eds.), *Business ethics, and the global environment*. New York: Quorum Books, pp. 89–97.

4 Desjardins, J.R. 2007. "Sustainability: Business's new environmental obligation." In *Business, ethics, and the environment: Imagining a sustainable future*. Upper Saddle River, NJ: Prentice Hall.

5 Thomason, B. & Marquis, M. 2010. "Leadership and the first and last mile of sustainability." http://iveybusinessjournal.com.

6 Starbuck, S. 2011. "Why business needs to care." *Financial Executive*, March, 27, 2, 52–55.

7 Trucost. 2009. "Carbon risks and opportunities in the S&P 500." http://www.trucost.com/published-research/6/carbon-risks-and-opportunities-in-the-sp-500.

8 EPA. 2011. http://www.epa.gov.

9 EPA, http://www.epa.gov.

10 Trucost. "Carbon risks and opportunities in the S&P 500."

11 Power, S. 2011. "Senate halts efforts to cap CO_2 emissions." *Wall Street Journal*, July 23, http://online.wsj.com/article/SB10001424052748703467304575383373600358634.html.

12 Power, "Senate halts efforts to cap CO_2 emissions."

13 Agamuthu, P. & Fauziah, S.H. 2011 "Challenges and issues in moving towards sustainable landfilling in a transitory country." *Waste Management and Research*, 29, 1, 13–19.

14 Weber, R., Watson, A., Forter, M. & Oliaei, F. 2011. "Persistent organic pollutants and landfills— A review of past experiences and future challenges." *Waste Management & Research,* 29, 1, 107–121.

15 Warder, A. 2009. "Delivering the Delta from the spills of Shell." *Women in Action*, 2, 33–35.

16 World Business Council for Sustainable Development. 2009. "Water: Facts and trends." http://www.wbcsd.org.

17 Spencer, J. 2007. "Ravaged rivers. China pays steep price as textile booms." *Wall Street Journal*, August 22, A1.

18 World Business Council for Sustainable Development. "Water: Facts and trends."

19 World Business Council for Sustainable Development. "Water: Facts and trends"; United Nations Global Compact. 2010. http://www.unglobalcompact.org.

20 United Nations Global Compact. http://www.unglobalcompact.org.

21 Epstein, *Making sustainability work*, p. 20.

22 Ahern, G. 2009. "Improving environmental sustainability in ten multinationals." *Corporate Finance Review*, 13, 6, 27–31.

23 Ahern, "Improving environmental sustainability."

24 Etzion, D. 2009. "Creating a better environment for finance." *MIT Sloan Management Review*, Summer, 50, 4, 21–22.

25 *MIT Sloan Management Review*. 2011. "Sustainability: the 'embracers' seize advantage: the survey." Winter, 23–27

26 *MIT Sloan Management Review*. "Sustainability."

27 Gamble, J.E. & Thompson, Jr. 2011. *Essentials of strategic management*. New York: McGraw-Hill.

28 Thomason & Marquis, "Leadership."

29 Shaw, S., Grant, D.B. & Mangan, J. 2010. "Developing environmental supply chain performance measures." *Benchmarking: An International Journal*, 17, 3, 320–339.

30   Thomason & Marquis, "Leadership."

31   *MIT Sloan Management Review.* "Sustainability"; Thomason & Marquis, "Leadership"; Sroufe, R., Liebowitz, J. & Sivasubramaniam, N. 2010. "HR's role in creating a sustainability culture: What are we waiting for?" *People and Strategy, 33*, 1, 34–42.

32   Thomason & Marquis, "Leadership."

33   Hopkins, M.S. 2009. "8 reasons sustainability will change management." *MIT Sloan Management Review,* 51, 1, 27–29.

34   Manget, J., Roche, C. & Munnich, F. 2009. "Capturing the green advantage." *MIT Sloan Management Review,* online edition, http://sloanreview.mit.edu/special-report/for-real-not-just-for-show/.

35   Trudel, Remi and Cotte, June. 2009. "Does it pay to be good?" *MIT Sloan Management Review,* 50, 2, 61–68.

36   Wexler, E. 2010. "Talking 'bout my (green) reputation." *Strategy,* May 1, 13.

37   Thomason & Marquis, "Leadership."

KEY TERMS

Acid rain: occurs when both sulfur dioxide and nitrogen oxide combine with air vapor in the atmosphere and return to earth in the form of acid rain.

Air pollutants: six materials that contribute to air pollution.

Air pollution: when the release of materials to the atmosphere cannot be safely disposed of by natural processes.

Cautious adopters: sustainability is limited to those activities that are linked to short-term efficiency.

Corporate conventionality: mindset places strong emphasis on profit making.

Embracer types: where such companies fully embrace sustainability efforts.

Greenhouse gases: gases in the atmosphere that trap heat.

Land pollution: contamination that occurs when toxic waste and other waste material that do not belong on land are disposed of on land.

Measurable sustainability goals: provides a company with the needed benchmarks to determine whether it is successful in its sustainability efforts.

New sustainability paradigm: executives with this view see the need for a new way of measuring the success of sustainability efforts.

Pragmatism: mindset suggests that these executives take a more pragmatic view of sustainability.

Primary activities: those activities that are directly linked to creating the product.

Reconciliation: executives with this view believe that it is possible to reconcile sustainability with profitability.

Strategic vision: describes a company's aspirations about "where it is going," thus helping steer the company in that direction.

Support activities: activities that are provided to support the primary activities.

Sustainability: capacity of healthy ecosystems to continue functioning indefinitely.

Sustainability benefits: the many advantages companies enjoy as a result of their sustainability efforts.

Sustainability feedback: feedback regarding sustainability provided to all concerned parties regarding the company's progress toward achieving sustainability goals.

Sustainability goals: sustainability targets that companies set to achieve.

Sustainability reporting: efforts by the company to report its sustainability efforts and the progress made on such efforts.

Sustainable or environmentally responsible organizations: those companies that are gradually modifying their operations in order to have less impact on the environment while also making better use of resources.

Top management support: support for sustainability from top management.

Value chain: the various activities that a company performs internally to create value for consumers.

Water pollution: contamination of water sources such as lakes, streams, wells, and oceans by substances that are harmful to living organisms.

DISCUSSION QUESTIONS

1. What is sustainability? Do companies have any special obligations to the environment? Why or why not?
2. Defend the argument that companies have no special obligations to the environment.
3. What is air pollution? What are the six forms of pollutants? What types of dangers do these pollutants cause?
4. What is land pollution? What are the factors contributing to land pollution?
5. Why is it critical to address water pollution issues? How does the United Nations Global Compact help address such challenges?
6. What are some of the critical factors in building the environmentally sustainable organization? Which factor is most important? Why?
7. What is the value chain? What are the key components of the value chain? How can the value chain help companies assess their sustainability efforts?
8. What are the four top management mindsets regarding sustainability? What are the implications of such mindsets for the company?
9. What are sustainability goals? Why are measuring and setting sustainability goals critical in building the sustainable company?
10. Discuss five important benefits of sustainability.

INTERNET ACTIVITY

1. Go to the International Standards Organization website: http://www.iso.org.
2. Review ISO 14000: the environmental management aspect of ISO.
3. Describe the ISO 14000 standards. What are some of the major features of the ISO 14000?
4. What are some of the major areas that the ISO 14000 covers?

5. How can a company get the ISO 14000 certification? What steps are needed to get such certification?
6. Discuss some of the advantages of companies receiving the ISO 14000 certification.

For more Internet Activities and resources, visit the Companion Website at www.routledge.com/cw/parboteeah.

WHAT WOULD YOU DO?

Environmental Management

You are hired by a multinational as an environmental manager. Your task is to review the company's efforts toward sustainability and to provide suggestions on improvement. You conduct a sustainability analysis and quickly come up with many "low hanging fruit" suggestions. For example, you suggest that water taps in the company's stores be replaced with more efficient taps that can reduce water consumption for the company. You also embark on an energy-saving campaign whereby employees are encouraged to turn off lights and laptops when not in use. You also suggest a bike incentive program to encourage workers to use their bikes to come to work. Furthermore, you implement a new software program that facilitates car pooling among workers.

As you start considering more involved and drastic measures, you learn about a new packaging material that could result in significant carbon emission reduction for the company. The new material is lighter and is also better for the environment. However, you also learn that this new material could be more costly than the one you currently use. Furthermore, you recall reading about the fast-food company McDonald's efforts to change from polystyrene (foam) packaging to paper packaging and the resulting challenges, as it turned out that paper takes more energy to produce and is much harder to recycle than foam. Despite these misgivings, you believe that the new material will also endear the multinational to environmental groups.

What do you do? Do you recommend the new packaging? How do you take into account the costs of the new material and unanticipated challenges associated with the use of the new material?

BRIEF CASE: BUSINESS ETHICS INSIGHT

Unilever and Sustainability

Unilever is a successful global Anglo-Dutch multinational selling products in over 180 countries. Famous brands of the company include Dove, Lux, Pond's, and Lipton. Unilever has also been a strong supporter of sustainability. In fact, the CEO recently announced that Unilever has ambitious growth plans. However, the company has set numerous goals to ensure that such growth does not come at the expense of the world's scarce resources. The company recently released its "Sustainable Living Plan" whereby it has set goals of halving its environmental footprint by 2020. To achieve this goal, Unilever has conducted a value chain of its activities. It has also analyzed 1,651 products and their use in 14 countries to determine the environmental impact of these products. Based on these analyses, it has developed key areas and has set goals based on these areas.

The first area that Unilever has set goals for is to halve greenhouse gases by the year 2020. Through a comprehensive analysis, Unilever developed a carbon dioxide emission per consumer use based on its products. It also discovered that most of its carbon emissions came from consumers' use of hot water when using their products. To achieve its goals, Unilever is working to both reduce the carbon emissions of its factories that produce the products. However, it is also working to produce products that need less energy to be used. Furthermore, it is encouraging consumers to do their part for the environment. For instance, it is now encouraging consumers to do their laundry using colder water.

Another key area for Unilever is halving the waste with the disposal of its products. It measures waste based on the waste per consumer use in terms of packaging and product leftovers. To address this goal, it has implemented a number of steps aiming at reducing packaging, reusing, and recycling, while also reducing waste from its manufacturing process. To give you further insights on Unilever's overall sustainability goals, and the consequent metrics and sub-goals, Exhibit 9.8 illustrates Unilever's goals and how they connect across the organization.

BRIEF CASE QUESTIONS

1. What are some of the main components of Unilever's sustainability goals? How will the company achieve its main sustainability goals?
2. Discuss how the various goals are related.
3. Why do you think Unilever places so much emphasis on consumer education? Do you think they will be successful in these efforts?
4. Draw a tentative value chain for Unilever. Are there other areas they could address to achieve their sustainability goals?
5. What are some benefits Unilever is achieving through its sustainability efforts?

Unilever Overall Goal: Halve the Environmental Footprint of making and using Unilever Products by the year 2020

Greenhouse Gas Sub-goals: Aim to halve the gas impact of products across the lifecycle by 2020	Water Use Sub-goals: Halve the water associated with consumer use of products by 2020	Waste Sub-goals: Halve waste associated with disposal of products by 2020

How will Unilever achieve sub-goals?

Develop products that will use less water and energy	Focus on countries where water scarcity is a problem	Reduce size of packaging
Convince 20 million consumers to cut their shower time by 1 minute	Work with farmers to ensure water is being used sustainably	Use lightweight materials for packaging
Develop laundry products that use minimal energy	Use drip irrigation and low-pressure irrigation whenever appropriate	Eliminate unnecessary packaging
Move to concentrated products to minimize packaging, etc.	Harvest water during rainy season for use later	Reuse as much of packaging coming into factories
Double use of sustainable energy in manufacturing facilities	Reformulate all products so that they require less water	Encourage reuse of primary products packaging
Newly built factories will aim at half the emissions of old ones	Inform consumers of most efficient way to use products	Educate consumers about the benefits of packaging reuse
Use lower-emission vehicles for transportation	Educate consumers of the benefits of reduced water footprint	Increase use of recycled material to the maximum extent possible
Use rail or ship as more efficient transportation	Persuade consumers to take shorter and less intense showers	Use materials that best fit end-of-life material treatment facilities
Use freezer cabinets that use climate-friendly refrigerants	Continue identifying ways to reduce water consumption during manufacturing process	Encourage consumers to get recyclable material to recycling centers

EXHIBIT 9.8—Sustainability Goals at Unilever

Based on http://www.sustainable-living.unilever.com.

LONG CASE: BUSINESS ETHICS

PROCTER & GAMBLE: CHILDREN'S SAFE DRINKING WATER

In 1995, Procter & Gamble (P&G) scientists began researching methods of water treatment for use in communities facing water crises. P&G, one of the world's largest consumer products companies, was interested in bringing industrial-quality water treatment to remote areas worldwide, because the lack of clean water, primarily in developing countries, was alarming.[1]

In the latter half of the 1990s, approximately 1.1 billion (out of a worldwide population of around 5.6 billion)[2] people lacked access to clean drinking water or sanitation facilities. An estimated 6 million children died annually from diseases, including diarrhea, hookworm, and trachoma, brought about by contaminated water.[3] One report estimated that "about 400 children below age five die per hour in the developing world from waterborne diarrheal diseases"[4] and that, "at any given time, about half the population in the developing world is suffering from one or more of the six main diseases associated with water supply and sanitation."[5]

Procter & Gamble[6]

The Procter & Gamble company dated back to 1837, in Cincinnati, Ohio, when William Procter and James Gamble, married to sisters, started a soap and candle business with $3,596.47 each. By 1859, P&G sales reached $1 million, the company had 80 employees, and it was supplying the Union Army during the Civil War. Gamble's son, a trained chemist, created an inexpensive white soap in 1879 that they named "Ivory" from the Biblical phrase "out of ivory palaces." Ivory soap became one of the first nationally advertised products. In the late 1880s, during a time of labor unrest throughout the country, P&G developed a pioneering profit-sharing program for factory workers, giving them a stake in the company. By 1890, P&G sold more than 30 different types of soap. The company also set up one of the first product research laboratories in the United States. In 1911, P&G developed Crisco, the first all-vegetable shortening, less expensive and considered healthier than butter.

In 1915, P&G built its first manufacturing facility outside the United States, in Canada, and established its chemicals division to formalize research procedures and develop new products. In 1919, Procter revised its articles of incorporation to include the directive that the "interests of the Company and its employees are inseparable." The 1920s saw several marketing innovations: P&G's Crisco was the sponsor of radio cooking shows; the company created a market research department to study consumer preferences and buying habits; and the company developed a brand management system.

As the twentieth century progressed, P&G rolled out a number of new and eventually successful products and expanded its product lines through regular acquisitions of well-known and long-standing consumer brands as well as lesser-known products that showed considerable development potential. Products included Camay (1926); Dreft, the first synthetic detergent intended for household use (1933); Drene, the first detergent-based shampoo (1934); Tide detergent and Prell shampoo (1946); Crest, the first toothpaste with fluoride (1955); Charmin toilet paper (a 1957 acquisition); Downy fabric softener (1960); Pampers (1961); Folgers Coffee (a 1963 acquisition); Pringles Potato Crisps, named for a street in Cincinnati (1968); Bounce fabric softener sheets (1972); Always feminine protection (1983); Liquid Tide (1984); Vicks and Oil of Olay (separate 1985 acquisitions); Pert, a combination shampoo/conditioner (1986); Ultra Pampers and Luvs Super Baby Pants, thinner than traditional diapers (1986); Noxell, whose products were CoverGirl, Noxzema, and Clarion (a 1989 acquisition); Febreze, Dryel, and Swiffer, introduced and distributed globally in 18 months (1998); Iams canine products (a 1999 acquisition); and ThermaCare air-activated HeatWraps (2002).

Along the way, P&G celebrated its 100th anniversary in 1937 with sales of $230 million, then its 150th anniversary in 1987 as the second-oldest company among the 50 largest *Fortune* 500 companies. P&G created its first division, drug products, in 1943, and in 1978 introduced its first pharmaceutical product, Didronel (etidronate disodium)—a treatment for Paget's disease. P&G was also a leader in environmental and solid waste prevention practices. In 1988, Germany's retail grocers called P&G's refill packs for liquid products, which reduced packaging by 85%, the invention of the year. In the early 1990s, the company began using recycled plastic for more and more of its products, and in 1992 it received the World Environment Center Gold Medal for International Corporate Environmental Achievement. P&G was also recognized for its affirmative action programs by the U.S. Department of Labor, in 1994, with its Opportunity 2000 Award for commitment to instituting equal employment opportunities and creating a diverse workforce. In 1998, P&G began to implement Organization 2005, designed to "push the often slow-moving P&G to innovate, to move fast with product development and marketing and with this, grow revenues, earnings, and shareholder value."[7]

The Global Water Crisis

As the twentieth century came to a close, there was general agreement that the characteristics of a developed country included "improved longevity, reduced infant mortality, health, productivity, and material well-being."[8] But none of these was easily attainable unless the country had a supply of safe, drinkable water and a successful means of disposing of the household and industrial waste that often contaminated the drinking supply in developing countries.

Many of the deaths attributed to contaminated water were preventable, if a product that sanitized water was paired with effective systems of education and distribution. Most of the communities without access to clean water sources lacked the infrastructure to build large municipal water treatment facilities; often, if these facilities existed, they were hard to maintain. Inhabitants of these areas used wells or local surface water for bathing, drinking, and cooking. In addition, animals (both domesticated livestock and those that were wild) frequented the water sources, contaminating them with their feces. Heavily populated areas in some countries were susceptible to natural disaster, which often produced safe drinking-water crises. Floods, monsoons, and earthquakes often led to the contamination of local water sources when "large runoffs of silt and clay [ran] into the catchment areas of municipal water supplies, which overwhelm[ed] routine sedimentation and filtration methods"[9] and overwhelmed efforts to obtain and then to distribute safe water.

The metal contaminants in water could impair the mental development of children who drank it. The main diseases that resulted from contaminated water included:

- Diarrhea, which occurred when microbial and viral pathogens existed in either food or water. Diarrheal diseases were the big killer and, if they did not result in death, brought about malnutrition and stunted growth in children, because the diseases left the body unable to absorb important nutrients long past the period of the actual diarrhea.
- *Ascaris, Dracunculisis*, Hookworm, and *Schistosomiasis* were caused by infestations of different kinds of worms. Ultimately, people suffering from them experienced disability, morbidity, and occasionally, death.
- Trachoma, which was caused by bacteria and often resulted in blindness.

In addition to the deaths and physical illnesses caused by unsafe drinking water, there were larger economic consequences. These included "economic and health costs of about 10 million person-years of time and effort annually, mostly by women and girls, carrying water from distant, often polluted sources."[10] Entire households suffered financially when the primary breadwinner became ill. Boiling water as a purification technique was time-consuming, often eating up hours each day that could better be spent raising crops as food or, for children, attending school. In short, a shortage of safe drinking water could stunt the growth of a community just as it could stunt the growth of sick and malnourished children.

The Search for a Solution

In the mid-1990s, a number of companies, such as Mioxx Corporation, Innova Pure Water, Pall, CUNO, Millipore, Ionics, and Clorox's Brita, were already in the water-purification business. Their products covered a range of needs, including household, municipal, and military. As the global water access crisis grew, however, there was greater pressure to address the needs of developing countries though new water sanitation products and the alteration of existing technology. Crucial to the success of any water purification program was developing effective models for distribution and combining them with effective education about the use of potential products. A successful program would feature a product that could offer:

- inexpensive, on the spot, or "point-of-use" treatment
- ease of use, requiring no more than simple educational demonstrations
- potential to fit into a long-term, sustainable distribution system flexible enough to be utilized in disaster relief efforts.

With a long history of scientific research and innovation in health, hygiene, and nutrition, P&G, with more than 200 scientists, considered ways the company could address the safe drinking-water crisis as the millennium approached. The United Nations was drafting its Millennium Development Goals, which would be presented for resolution by the General Assembly in 2000. Included in the draft document was a 2015 goal to cut by half the world population that currently did not have access to safe drinking water. Although P&G had a vast array of successful products, the company did not offer anything that involved water purification, either domestically or in developing countries where poverty, lack of infrastructure, and inaccessibility of remote communities made the prospect of cleaning up the water more difficult.

In 1999, P&G purchased—through the acquisition of Recovery Engineering in a $265 million deal—PUR Water Filtration System, a point-of-use water filtration system. Harvard graduate and entrepreneur Brian Sullivan had founded Recovery in 1986 and, by 1999, the company had 550 employees, annual sales of $77 million (in 1998),[11] and was the number two water filtration product in the United States behind Clorox Company's Brita.[12] Sullivan said that his company's mission had always been "to solve the world's drinking water problems"[13] and that P&G's marketing clout would help expand sales of the product globally. PUR products had only been distributed domestically, and Sullivan said that "it would take us a long time to have a global impact . . . The technology . . . is very powerful, with fantastic potential, and it's something that can best be leveraged under the umbrella of a global consumer products firm."[14]

This was a new product category for P&G, said a spokesperson, but—referring to the company's detergent, hair and skin-care products—"we've been in the water management business for a long time . . . We've learned a lot about water—how to manage it well—so there is some synergy."[15] With this acquisition, P&G took a huge first step toward supplying drinkable water to areas throughout the world.

Development of PUR

The PUR water filtration system used a combination of the flocculant iron sulfate, an agent that caused particles suspended in water to bind and form sediment, and calcium hypochlorite (chlorine), a disinfectant. After acquiring the product, P&G began to develop and expand it. Over the next several years, the PUR product line included home faucet mounts, refrigerator pitchers and dispensers, portable water bottle systems, and, eventually, optional flavor packets that created gallons of clean, flavored water through specialized pitchers. P&G also began to experiment with a small point-of-use purifier: small sachets of flocculant-disinfectant. These sachets were approximately the size of a "pack of coffee creamer" and could "suck out dirt, bacteria, and parasites from 10 liters of water."[16] They were simple and easy to demonstrate, as well as inexpensive to produce, affordable to purchase (approximately $0.10 a unit), and easy to distribute. The user would mix a small packet of powder in a container of water. After stirring, the contaminants separated out and fell to the bottom of the container as visible sediment. These contaminants included "dirt, pesticides, toxic heavy metals, such as arsenic and lead, as well as bacteria, viruses and protozoa that [were] resistant to chlorine alone."[17] P&G called this system PUR Purifier of Water.

Strategic Partnerships

In 2001, to combine "a wide range of health-care research into one research institute,"[18] and broaden its philanthropic reach, P&G created the Procter & Gamble Health Sciences Institute (PGHSI), which was "dedicated to identifying, developing, and using leading health care technologies in the development of effective products for both the developing and developed world."[19] PGHSI partnered with the non-profit International Council of Nurses (ICN) and the U.S. Centers for Disease Control and Prevention (CDC) to improve the technology for use in developing nations. The Switzerland-based ICN, a federation of 124 national nurses' associations that represented millions of nurses globally, had made universal access to clean water a priority, with the following statement:

> ICN believes that the right to water is non-negotiable. Secure access to safe water is a universal need and fundamental human right; an essential resource to meet basic human needs, and to sustain livelihoods and development . . .
>
> ICN also believes that with commitment and political will by governments and others, clean and safe water can be made accessible to all people at low cost using appropriate technology.[20]

The Atlanta-based CDC was part of the U.S. Department of Health and Human Services. Its Safe Water Systems (SWS) program was "a water quality intervention that employ[ed] simple, robust, and inexpensive technologies appropriate for the developing world."[21] This intervention involved point-of-use treatment of contaminated water, safe water storage in containers, and behavioral techniques to educate the affected populations about the importance of, among other things, hygiene and proper use of water storage vessels.

In April 2001, at the CDC's annual Epidemic Intelligence Service Conference, PGHSI unveiled its small sachets of flocculant-disinfectant, or what it called PUR Purifier of Water. Between 2001 and 2003, the strategic partners conducted part of the PUR development process in parts of Guatemala and Haiti that suffered from a lack of clean drinking water. The studies they carried out tested the utility of PUR in large-scale water relief programs. After several years of testing, an impact study linked the use of four-gram sachets of PUR to a significant decrease in the occurrence of diarrhea. The 20-week study that comprised more than 600 families linked the use of PUR sachets to a 25% decrease in instances of diarrhea among children younger than two.[22] The *American Journal of Tropical Medicine and Hygiene* published an article, based on the studies in Guatemala, about the success of PUR in significantly reducing diarrheal illness in children. In January 2003, the *Journal of Water and Health* published an article called "Evaluation of a New Water Treatment for Point-of-Use Household Applications to Remove Microorganisms and Arsenic from Drinking Water," also describing the efficacy of the PUR system. PUR not only removed microbial contaminants, but also heavy metal contaminants such as chromium, lead, arsenic, and nickel.

At that point, P&G had spent $20 million developing PUR,[23] although it claimed that the product was "a social marketing breakthrough rather than a commercial initiative."[24] With glowing reports about the water purifier, various non-profits began purchasing and shipping it all over the globe. The International Rescue Committee in 2003 shipped 350,000 packets to Iraq, where fighting had destroyed or damaged many of the water systems. Relief agency AmeriCares delivered more than a million PUR sachets to Sudanese refuges in Chad. In 2003, the product had been used in Botswana, Malawi, Liberia, and Zimbabwe as well.

Children's Safe Drinking Water

With the success of PUR Water Filtration System, PGHSI and its partners created the Children's Safe Drinking Water (CSDW)[25] campaign in 2003. But there were obstacles to expanding the program effectively in developing countries and to persuading people in target water crisis areas to use it, so PGHSI needed seasoned strategy and expertise. PGHSI found that Population Services International (PSI) and the Aquaya Institute were organizations that were both experienced in the methods of social marketing and disaster relief planning.

Population Services International (PSI)

Founded in 1970 as a non-profit organization focusing on family planning and reproductive health, PSI expanded to operate programs promoting oral rehydration therapy and HIV awareness in the developing world. PSI utilized social marketing models to promote products that could improve health conditions for the poor. The PSI approach to social marketing "engaged private sector resources and used private sector techniques to encourage healthy behavior and make markets work for the poor" and focused heavily on combining measurable results and private sector operational efficiency.[26] This often included finding members of target communities to act as contacts for the program and to sell the water treatment systems. These local contacts had access to potential end users, understood local customs, and would be more likely to achieve product acceptance. PSI used performance metrics and review processes to create a level of operational efficiency comparable to a successful for-profit corporation. The organization operated water treatment programs in 23 countries, and used the social marketing model for successful distribution of PUR water treatment sachets in five countries.[27]

Aquaya Institute and PURelief

The Aquaya Institute offered consulting services to organizations planning and implementing safe water programs. It conducted original research on the technology, distribution systems, and impact of safe water programs. Supported by the Procter & Gamble Fund, the institute began developing a geographic information system that would help create sales strategies for communities reliant specifically on surface water. The Aquaya Institute joined the Johns Hopkins University School of Public Health to investigate methods of marketing and distributing PUR in Indonesia in 2004 with funding and support provided by the Procter & Gamble Fund. The program expanded after the December 26, 2004 Asian tsunami, which greatly exacerbated existing water

EXHIBIT 1 Blogging from Borneo[28]

In 2005, industrial toxicologist Dr. Greg Allgood, executive director of Procter and Gamble's Health Sciences Institute (PGHSI), began a blog to tell the story of his travels through the Tsunami-ravaged regions of Southern Asia. The December 26, 2004, tsunami killed hundreds of thousands of people and created water shortages throughout the affected areas, leaving millions without access. As part of PGHSI's Children's Safe Drinking Water Program, Allgood assisted in providing safe, clean drinking water to regions that had lost the ability to maintain the sanitation of water sources in the wake of the disaster. Along the way, Allgood worked to educate the people of each region about the dangers of unsafe drinking water. Over the next three years, Allgood's travels would take him from Sri Lanka to Pakistan, India, parts of Africa, Vietnam, and, in late 2007, into Indonesia.

In November 2007, Allgood and representatives from Aquaya Institute, a research and consulting NGO and the Dian Desa Foundation, a well-established Indonesian non-profit, entered the Indonesian region of Borneo. The trip was organized to promote safe water education in rural parts of the island and to investigate local acceptance of water treatment products. Experiencing the region's torrential downpours, Allgood and his team covered miles of rain-battered roadways, reaching the town of Batulicin and nearby villages. There they offered demonstrations of the PUR Water Filtration System.

Allgood joined a local PUR distributor, Heini, to tour nearby villages and demonstrate the water sanitizing properties of the product. Heini, a local, was chosen by the Dian Desa Foundation to assist Allgood and Aquaya Institute's Jeff Albert in documenting the acceptance of PUR by regional consumers. Using water taken from a river nearby, Heini's demonstrations convinced a number of locals to begin using PUR to sanitize their drinking water. Unfortunately, many potential PUR consumers had difficulty accepting the product, preferring instead to use decades-old purification techniques.

In a community along the route, Allgood watched locals pulling water from irrigation ditches. The water looked clear, but Allgood worried that it was contaminated nonetheless. Surprisingly, villagers preferred the taste of the unpurified water to sanitized water in a blind taste test. When members of his crew paused to join men from the village at a local mosque, they participated in ritual absolution before prayers. "They wash and cleanse their mouths from the irrigation ditch water," Allgood worried, "and I hope they don't get sick from it."

To demonstrate the product, Heini would draw 10 liters of water in one or more vessels from a contaminated local source. After reiterating the threat posed by unsafe water, Heini introduced a single sachet of PUR powder to each vessel, often inviting locals from the audience to participate in the treatment process. After stirring the water for five minutes, they allowed it to sit for another five minutes as the formerly turbid water visibly cleared. When the water was clear, they poured it into another vessel through a piece of cotton fabric, and allowed it to sit for another few minutes before drawing the now purified water into several clear cups. The audience was invited to comment on the clarity and flavor of the water.[29] Reactions varied greatly in each region in which PUR was introduced, as hesitant locals experienced a totally new flavor of water. Reluctance to stray from traditional sanitation methods and familiar flavors would become a major hurdle to acceptance of PUR in some areas.

Local Networks

The final stop in Allgood's tour of Borneo was a village that had only recently been introduced to PUR. The village, located in a swampy region where the well water was saturated with mud, had a tradition of boiling drinking water. Residents had a mixed response to PUR; some preferred to keep old habits of boiling, and others warmed up to the relative ease of cleansing water in this novel way. One villager, a tea and snack merchant named Sutyami, had been using PUR for a week. She was hesitant to use the product at first, but chose to test it to save time and money. Boiling, her habitual method of water sanitation, was expensive and time-consuming. She agreed to become a local distributor of PUR, and began selling the sachets alongside her regular wares. Like many other distributors in rural areas, she made a good local contact to provide the sachets to her community, and also generated extra income from selling them. With assistance from programs such as PGHSI's Children's Safe Drinking Water, local distributors like Heini and Sutyami are able to create sustainable water safety outlets for their communities, bringing affordable safe water practices to those most in need.

shortages. P&G joined local government organizations, as well as leading NGOs, to provide disaster relief in the form of PUR treatment. Indonesians in disaster areas received a portion of 15 million sachets of PUR, saving thousands of lives. Later, in 2007, the Aquaya Institute joined PSI in a PUR distribution program in Kenya.[30]

With the help of PSI and the Aquaya Institute, P&G expanded the use of PUR to many developing countries. P&G also worked with other organizations and non-profits, including the Johns Hopkins University School of Public Health, CARE, UNAIDS, WHO, and UNICEF, in supplying and distributing the water purification product. See Exhibit 1 for a description of travels made by PGHSI Executive Director Greg Allgood, to various regions around the world to observe the implementation of and response to the PUR product.

The Economics of PUR

Many of the PUR programs operated either on partial cost recovery, where the user paid only for the product and donor funds subsidized other program costs, or—in the case of emergencies, such as the Asian tsunami, flooding in Haiti, or cholera epidemics in Africa—as fully subsidized free distribution. In general, each PUR sachet was provided to relief or NGOs at a cost of $0.035, but program costs also included "transport, distribution, education, and community motivation."[31] Most often, sachets were sold at product cost recovery for $0.10 each, which translated to $0.01 per liter of treated water.

PUR Expands Globally

In June 2004, P&G's PUR Purifier of Water won the International Chamber of Commerce (ICC) World Business Award in support of the Millennium Development Goals. This was part of the first annual worldwide business awards to "recognize the significant role business can play in the implementation of the UN's targets for reducing poverty around the world by 2015." P&G's Children's Safe Drinking Water program went on to win other awards: the Stockholm Industry Water Award (2005), the Ron Brown Presidential Award for Corporate Leadership (2007), the EPA Children's Health Excellence Award (2007), and the Grainger Challenge Bronze Award (2007). Throughout the Children's Safe Drinking Water program from 2003 to 2007, P&G had sold the sachets at no cost, made no profit on PUR sales, and donated programmatic funding to some of the projects. Between 2003 and 2007, 85 million sachets of PUR, treating 850 million liters of water, had been distributed globally in emergency response or sold through social marketing projects. With the help of its various partners, PGHSI had made the product available in 23 countries.

Chapter 9: Long Case Notes

1 "Safe Drinking Water," P&G Health Sciences Institute, http://www.pghsi.com/pghsi/safewater (accessed 15 February 2008).

2 U.S. Census Bureau, International Data Base, "Total Midyear Population for the World: 1950–2050," 16 July 2007, http://www.census.gov/ipc/www/idb/worldpop.html (accessed 28 February 2008).

3 Hawkes, N. and Nuttall, N., "Seeds Offer Hope of Pure Water for the Developing World," *The Times* (London), 15 September 1995.

4 Gadgil, A., "Drinking Water in Developing Countries," *Annual Review of Energy and the Environment* 23 (November 1998): 254.

5 Gadgil, 254.

6 "Our History," P&G website, http://www.pg.com/company/who_we_are/ourhistory.jhtml (accessed 15 February 2008).

7 Nugent, M., "P&G CEO Sees Transformation in Five Years," Reuters News Service, 12 October 1999.

8 Gadgil, 264.

9 Gadgil, 264.

10 Gadgil, 256.

11 P&G had sales of $38.1 billion and net earnings of $3.76 billion in 1998.

12 In the first quarter of 1999, PUR had 21.2% of the market, compared with Brita's 66.2%, and had gained 49% of the market in the month of July 1999, according to Susan E. Peterson, "Pretty Price for Recovery Engineering," *Minneapolis Star-Tribune*, 27 August 1999, 1-D.

13   Peterson, 1-D.

14   Peterson, 1-D.

15   Peterson, 1-D.

16   Coolidge, A., "P&G Water Purifier Aids Third World," *Cincinnati Post*, 19 June 2003, B6.

17   Procter & Gamble Press Release, "New P&G Technology Improves Drinking Water in Developing Countries," 24 April 2001, http://www.pginvestor.com/phoenix.zhtml?c=104574&p=irolnewsArticle &ID=628966&highlight= (accessed 25 February 2008).

18   "Global Joint Program Partners," Health Communication Partnership, http://www.hcpartnership. org/Partners/gjpp.php (accessed 25 February 2008).

19   "Mission," P&G Health Sciences Institute, http://www.pghsi.com/pghsi/mission/ (accessed 25 February 2008).

20   "Universal Access to Clean Water," ICN Position Statement, 1995, http://www.icn.ch/pswater. htm (accessed 25 February 2008).

21   "Safe Water System," Centers for Disease Control and Prevention, http://www.cdc.gov/safewater/ (accessed 25 February 2008).

22   Crump, J.A., Otieno, P.O., Slutsker, L., Keswick, B.H., Rosen, D.H., Hoekstra, R.M., Vulule, J.M. & Luby, S.P., "Household Based Treatment of Drinking Water with Flocculant-Disinfectant for Preventing Diarrhoea in Areas with Turbid Source Water in Rural Western Kenya: Cluster Randomised Controlled Trial," *British Medical Journal (BMJ)*, 2005, 331; 478, published online 26 July 2005, http://www.bmj.com/cgi/reprint/331/7515/478 (accessed 19 February 2008).

23   Coolidge, B6.

24   "Financial Express: P&G May Test Waters With PUR," *Financial Express*, 26 May 2004.

25   "Children's Safe Drinking Water," Procter & Gamble, http://www.pg.com/company/our_commitment/ drinking_water.jhtml (accessed 25 February 2008).

26   "About PSI," Population Services International, http://www.psi.org/about_us (accessed 21 November 2007).

27   In 2006, PSI estimated that it had treated over 8.6 billion liters of water, averted 4.1 million cases of diarrhea, and prevented 6,000 child deaths that year. "Water/Child Survival: Safe Water and Diarrheal Disease Control," http://www.psi.org/child-survival (accessed 18 December 2007).

28   Source: Greg Allgood blog at http://childrensafedrinkingwater.typepad.com/pgsafewater/2007/11/ boiling-in-born.html (accessed 20 November 2007).

29   A video of a typical PUR product demonstration, produced by members of the non-profit Other Paths, may be seen at http://www.youtube.com/watch?v=mij0-3hBKs8&feature=related (accessed 25 February 2008).

30   "Aquaya to Assist PSI in Community Targeting for the Social Marketing of PUR in Kenya," Aquaya Institute press release, http://www.aquaya.org/news.php#010807 (accessed 4 December 2007).

31   "Household Water Treatment Options in Developing Countries," Centers for Disease Control, January 2008, http://www.ehproject.org/PDF/ehkm/cdc-options_pur.pdf (accessed 15 February 2008).

LONG CASE QUESTIONS

1. Discuss some of the factors that led P&G to work on a solution to the water problem worldwide.
2. What are some of the consequences of a lack of clean drinking water?
3. Discuss some of the essential features of any water purification program that P&G would deem critical to be successful. Why are these features so important?
4. The Children's Safe Drinking Water program is obviously a costly program with little potential for return. As a shareholder of P&G, would you oppose such a program? Why or why not?
5. What are some of the non-financial advantages of the P&G Children's Safe Drinking Water program?
6. Review the Children's Safe Drinking Water program at http://www.csdw.org/csdw/index.shtml. What are some of the new features of the program?

Chapter 10

Global Ethics

LEARNING OBJECTIVES

After reading this chapter you should be able to:

- Understand what global business ethics is
- Understand why there are differences in ethics worldwide
- Be aware of the approaches to global ethics
- Appreciate the key ethical issues facing multinationals today
- Understand what companies can do to address global ethical issues

PREVIEW BUSINESS ETHICS INSIGHT

Ethical Scandals at Nike and Toyota

In the 1990s, Nike was criticized by activists for its harsh labor practices. Stories surfaced of child labor in Pakistan and workers working in very inhumane conditions in many of its plants. Even the founder acknowledged in 1998 that Nike was synonymous with slave wages, forced overtime, and abuse. Nike then started implementing many measures to become more socially responsible. But did things change? The answer emerged with a broadcast aired on an Australian channel. Posing as a fashion buyer, an Australian reporter got access to a Nike plant operating in Malaysia. The reporter was shocked to find workers living in extremely bad conditions. They had to work for very long hours with very little pay. Worst of all, many of them were Bangladeshi and came to Malaysia for employment. However, as soon as they arrived, their passports were confiscated and they had to work long hours to pay for recruiting fees. The broadcast showed that Nike has seemingly not addressed the earlier labor problems. In fact, the 2008 broadcast made it seem like no progress had been made regarding the worker issues.

Launched before the Second World War, the Japanese car company Toyota built a car business that became synonymous with reliability, quality, efficiency, and longevity. Competitors feared Toyota because of its attention to quality and detail. In fact, many competitors copied the various aspects that made Toyota such a powerhouse in the industry. Toyota pioneered many new manufacturing techniques, such as just in time, lean manufacturing, and even introduced groundbreaking technology to the industry. However, the recent safety issues with Toyota cars are starting to damage Toyota's reputation and the industry is beginning to question the many Toyota achievements.

Recent reports suggest that Toyota was aware of sticky pedal problems with some of its models. In fact, other reports suggest that the problems were not limited to the U.S. It was reported that Toyota was aware of similar sticky pedal situations but did not report those problems to British government officials until prompted. Furthermore, these problems were reported in the U.K. almost six months earlier than in the U.S. Initially, Toyota asserted that these problems were rare and did not warrant a recall. However, with growing reports of sticking pedals and cars out of control at 100 mph, Toyota initiated a massive recall that extended to a large number of its models. New braking problems are now emerging with the Prius and faulty brakes in these cars and the next few months will show how Toyota deals with these new challenges.

Based on Booth, R. 2010. "Toyota under fire for its handling of safety recall." *Guardian* online; Levenson, E. 2008. "Citizen Nike." *Fortune*, 158, 10, 165–170; Reed, J. and Simon, B. 2010. "Toyota's long climb comes to an abrupt halt." *Financial Times*, 9; Reed, J. and Simon, B. 2010. "Viral element spins events out of control." *Financial Times* 16; Shirouzu, N. 2010. "The Toyota recall: Toyota acted first in Europe—scarcity of complaints is blamed for lag in fixing sticky gas pedals in U.S." *Wall Street Journal*, B2; Shirouzu, N. 2010. "Why Toyota took longer to fix pedal flaw in the U.S. than Europe." *Wall Street Journal* online; Takahashi, Y. and Kachi, H. 2010. "The Toyota recall: Action is likely on Prius." *Wall Street Journal*, B2.

The Preview Business Ethics Insight above shows that it is extremely critical for companies to manage their ethics worldwide. Consider the case of Nike and the workers in the plants in Malaysia. While Nike was not directly employing these workers, the media blamed Nike for the horrible working conditions. Is Nike to blame if their subcontractors decide to have bad working conditions for workers? How can they counteract weak government regulations in most of the emerging countries (Vietnam, China, Indonesia, and Thailand) where most of their shoes are made? The constant attention paid to Nike and the bad publicity with such reports suggest that multinationals have to strive very hard to be ethical. Nike admits that it is their responsibility to monitor and ensure that their suppliers have humane working conditions.

The Toyota example discussed in the Preview Business Ethics Insight provides more evidence of the need for large multinationals to behave ethically. By claiming that the acceleration problem was only isolated and not necessarily a safety issue, Toyota projected an image of insensitivity and neglect. Furthermore, as Reed and Simon note, information spreads rapidly today.[1] Although Toyota's recall is large, such recalls do occur. However, Toyota's denial that the braking problem was a major safety issue and the subsequent announcement of the recall has had a viral element that has quickly gotten out of control. This example also shows the critical need for large multinationals to adequately manage their ethics.

WHAT IS GLOBAL BUSINESS ETHICS?

In Chapter 1, we defined business ethics as the principles and standards that guide business. However, when applied to the global environment, **global business ethics** apply to the myriads of ethical issues any company faces when operating in the global environment. Companies have to deal with questions such as "Should we bribe knowing that we would not get the contract without bribes?" or "Should we locate a plant in a country because of cheap labor?" or "Should we dump wastes in the local river knowing that such actions are illegal in the home country?" Answering such questions provides insights into how multinationals approach ethics.

Why should companies be concerned with global ethics? In Chapter 1, we saw the many benefits pertaining to companies that pursue ethical goals domestically. Many of these benefits also accrue to companies pursuing ethics globally. However, as we saw from the Preview Business Ethics Insight on pages 427–8, large multinationals are constantly scrutinized for their ethical practices. Any ethical violations can be quickly reported and these companies can suffer serious reputational damage. Because of their size and extent of operations, global multinationals are often the subject of criticism. Consider Exhibit 10.1, where we compare some of the world's largest multinationals' revenues with selected countries' gross domestic product.

As Exhibit 10.1 shows, there are many multinationals that are larger than some countries. Such large firms have access to vast financial, capital, and human resources,

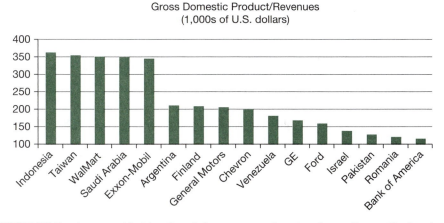

Gross Domestic Product/Revenues
(1,000s of U.S. dollars)

EXHIBIT 10.1—Largest Multinational Revenue vs. Country Gross Domestic Product

and such access provides power that limits the ability of the developing countries' governments to regulate these companies. In some cases, the governments of developing countries are not willing to regulate because they are competing for foreign investment. Because of their power and clout, the action of these companies are often carefully watched. Multinationals are thus well advised to implement proactive ethical programs to ward off such scrutiny.

Furthermore, in Chapter 1, we discussed the many reasons why domestic companies should be ethical. However, society also expects multinationals to display high levels of ethics. Part of these expectations comes from the power yielded by multinationals. In fact, there is strong evidence that multinationals have significant political power that can influence policies in a society. Consider the following Ethics Sustainability Insight.

ETHICS SUSTAINABILITY INSIGHT

Multinationals and Political Power on Climate Change

Multinationals have played important roles in terms of acceptance of the realities of climate change. For instance, a newspaper report showed that the initial U.S. position on climate change came from the Global Climate Coalition. However, further analysis showed that Exxon-Mobil was an important member of the coalition. This membership confirmed the suspicion of many that Exxon-Mobil had an important role in shaping the U.S. government's reluctance to embrace the Kyoto Protocol to reduce greenhouse gases.

A recent review of Global *Fortune* 500 firms by Kolk and Pinkse provides further evidence of the political power yielded by multinationals.[2] The review showed that when climate change started becoming an important issue in the 1990s, multinationals initially opposed the idea. There were significant financial and human resources devoted to shaping the conclusions of the debate aimed mainly at opposing climate change measures. However, as countries adopted the Kyoto Protocol in 1997, many multinationals started to change their stance. More and more multinationals began using their political clout to embrace climate change. In fact, the day after the Exxon-Mobil story was released, a number of U.S. companies, including Hewlett-Packard and Ford, issued a statement supporting climate change measures while also pressuring the G8 to adopt measures to curb emissions in the long term.

Based on Kolk, A. and Pinkse, J. 2007. "Multinationals' political activities on climate change." *Business & Society*, 46, 2, 201–228.

As the above shows, multinationals have strong political power that has attracted intense attention from the public and the media. Multinationals are expected to use such power wisely if they do not want to suffer negative backlashes. However, another reason why multinationals are expected to be more ethical is the increasing similarity of ethical practices or **convergence**. Experts believe that many management practices, including those related to ethics, are becoming more similar.

Many forces are pressuring this need for convergence. For example, agreements among countries, such as regional trade agreements and membership in the WTO, provide supranational regulatory environments that affect ethical practices. Cross-border competition, trade, mergers, and acquisitions provide more opportunities to learn about and copy successful managerial practices from anywhere in the world. Furthermore, other factors such as global customers and products and growing levels of economic development are all creating the pressures for convergence.

This chapter will therefore provide you with a solid background in global ethics. To understand global ethics, we must first determine if ethics is approached differently around the world. In doing so, we examine the nature of these differences. For instance, why are people more likely to tolerate bribery in some cultures than others? After we discuss the nature of such differences, you will read about ethical approaches adopted by multinationals. Finally, the chapter will consider some of the most pressing global ethical issues and conclude with what multinationals can do to build their global ethics program.

WHAT IS THE NATURE OF DIFFERENCES IN ETHICS?

In the Preview Business Ethics Insight on pages 427–8, you read about the ethical scandals at Nike. However, although Nike had implemented strong policies aiming at monitoring suppliers, the 2008 scandal shows that it is difficult to be able to monitor all suppliers. In fact, Levenson argues that many of Nike's plants are in emerging countries with weak governments.[3] In the absence of strong regulation, companies need to be even more forceful to ensure that the suppliers abide by ethical regulations. This implies that it is critical to understand whether ethics are viewed differently and the nature of such differences. For instance, why would any society allow its workers to work in harsh conditions? Why do some societies tolerate and participate in bribery? These examples suggest that there are varying degrees of what are considered unethical behaviors. In this part, we discuss the extent and nature of such differences.

What is the nature of differences in ethics **cross-nationally**? Many aspects of ethics have been studied in various nations. We consider the major approaches and discuss the explanations for these differences.

One of the most widespread surveys of ethics worldwide is undertaken by the Inter Consortium for Political and Social Research. In their last World Values Survey, respondents from over 40 nations were asked the degree to which they justify unethically suspect behaviors, such as claiming government benefits to which they are not entitled, cheating on their taxes, or accepting stolen property. Exhibit 10.2 shows the scores for selected countries.

The exhibit shows that there are indeed differences between societies regarding how much people justify ethically suspect behaviors. How can these differences be explained? Cullen, Parboteeah, and Hoegl argue that national cultural differences

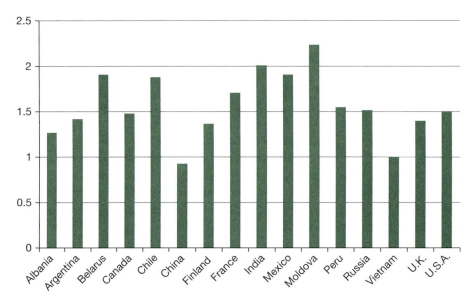

EXHIBIT 10.2—Justification of Ethically Suspect Behaviors for Selected Countries

(differences in what people think is the right way to do things) and social institutions (differences in educational systems, religion, etc.) are likely to encourage people to break norms and thereby justify ethically suspect behaviors.[4] Societies with national cultural dimensions such as values of high achievement (i.e., people value achievement), high individualism (i.e., people value their own personal freedom), high universalism (i.e., people are more ambitious because they expect to be treated fairly), and high pecuniary materialism (i.e., people have high materialist tendencies) are likely to have a greater number of people engaging in deviant acts such as crime, as these cultural dimensions are more likely to encourage people to be ambitious and want to achieve. In the process, they are more likely to break norms. In addition to these national cultural values, the authors specified that societies with relatively high levels of industrialization, capitalist systems, low degrees of family breakdown, and easily accessible education should encourage more deviance. Testing their theory on 3,450 managers from 28 countries, the researchers found support for most of their hypotheses.

The above study shows that national cultural and social institutional differences explain the degree to which people are willing to tolerate unethical behaviors. Other studies have focuses on alternative aspects of business ethics. Recall that in Chapter 1 we discussed that there are differences in corruption level worldwide. Why is understanding differences in corruption important? Consider the Global Business Ethics Insight on page 433.

As the Global Business Ethics Insight shows, understanding corruption and the nature of differences cross-culturally is important. Seleim and Bontis provide some understanding of how culture affects corruption.[5] They use the Corruption Perception Index (as reported in Exhibit 1.2 in Chapter 1) and examine how national culture dimensions influence the index for 62 countries. They find that specific cultural values

GLOBAL BUSINESS ETHICS INSIGHT

BAE Systems and Bribery

BAE systems, is Britain's leading defense company producing a variety of combat equipment. It is currently under investigation for corruption charges, with Britain's Fraud Office alleging that BAE gave millions of pounds of bribes to win contracts. However, the company has always had a strong corporate social responsibility program and, although these allegations have not yet been verified, they are troubling.

A look at the countries they allegedly won contracts in shows why it is critical to understand corruption levels. Specifically, BAE is blamed for bribing officials in Tanzania, the Czech Republic, Romania, and South Africa. An examination of the Corruption Perception Index (http://www.transparency.org) shows that these countries have very high levels of corruption. It therefore seems logical that any multinational would take additional measures to ensure that bribery does not occur in such countries. Such efforts were not really apparent at BAE and they are now fighting these charges.

Based on http://www.transparency.org and *Professional Engineering*. 2009. "BAE looks set to face prosecution on corruption charge." October 7, 8.

such as uncertainty avoidance (the degree to which people prefer certainty and order in their lives), individualism (the degree to which people are focused on themselves), and future orientation (the degree to which people are focused on the future) all promote higher corruption. In contrast, cultural dimensions such as gender egalitarianism (degree to which people promote gender equality in a society) is related to less corruption.

The above two studies provide some explanations of the nature of differences among countries on ethics. As the studies show, both culture and social institutions such as industrialization, economic development, degree of wealth, and religion have important influences on how people perceive ethics. Such findings are critical for multinational managers as they work to reduce unethical behavior. Specifically, managers making location decisions can assess the emphasis on cultural dimensions to gauge the degree to which unethical behavior will be tolerated. Research has shown overwhelmingly that some cultural dimensions such as high masculinity (people are more focused on work than quality of life), achievement and performance orientation (degree to which people are focused on achievement and performance in a society), and uncertainty avoidance are all related to higher corruption. Managers can assess these cultural dimensions and determine people's approach ethics. Furthermore, managers can often use only their own knowledge of a country's social institutions and culture to make inferences about which ethical issues are important and how they are best managed.

GLOBAL BUSINESS ETHICS INSIGHT

Ethical Relativism Worldwide

There is strong evidence to suggest that following ethical relativism principles may be the only way to do business in certain countries. Consider the impact of religion on business ethics rules in some countries. Islam, currently the world's second largest religions, with adherents in Africa, the Middle East, China, Malaysia, and the Far East, provides many ethical guidelines for business operations. For instance, Islam prohibits paying of interest. In other cases, Islam also prohibits the employment of women or encourages segregation based on gender. Multinationals may sometimes have to be cautious about posting women in such societies.

Hinduism, the religious traditions followed by around 760 million people in countries such as India, Nepal, and Sri Lanka, also provides moral guidelines for businesses. For Hindus, the caste system whereby people at birth are segregated into occupational groups is sacred. Often, multinationals have to consider whether they can have a person from a lower caste lead others from higher castes. While the caste system may be disappearing, it is still an important aspect of the ethical environment in India.

Besides religion, other aspects of the business environment may be indirectly affected by religion. Consider the case of *guanxi* prevalent in many of the Pacific Rim countries such as China and Taiwan. *Guanxis* generally refer to the social networks or relationships that companies in these countries develop to do business. *Guanxi* is based on the patient development of relationships between businesses to reach a point where businesses trust each other completely and have faith that businesses will look out for each other and reciprocate on favors. *Guanxi* has been a feature of Chinese society for more than 2,500 years and evolved from Confucianism and the latter's emphasis on harmony, loyalty, benevolence, and trust.

Many experts agree that having the right *guanxi* is essential for any multinational doing business in the Pacific Rim region. However, companies from Western societies have often argued that such arrangements lead to unethical behaviors, bribery, and corruption. In fact, *guanxis* have been getting negative publicity. In the absence of a good legal infrastructure, *guanxis* can sometimes lead to unethical behaviors because members within the same network engage in under-the-table dealings and give preferential treatment to each other.

Based on Hwang, D., Golemon, P., Chen, Y., Wang, T-S., and Hung, W-S. 2009. "Guanxi and business ethics in Confucian society today: an empirical case study in Taiwan." *Journal of Business Ethics*, 89, 235–250.

In addition to differences in the ways of tolerating or engaging in unethical behavior, the methods people and multinationals use to approach or resolve ethical dilemmas is worth exploring. Specifically, the concepts of ethical relativism and ethical universalism are important. Next, we discuss these concepts.

Ethical relativism is an ethical viewpoint based on the assumption that there are no objective and universal moral standards. Rather, the relativist sees morality as subjective and moral standards as different between cultures or groups within a single culture. For example, if the people in one country believe that abortion is morally wrong, then for the relativist abortion is morally wrong. If, on the other hand, people in another country believe that abortion is morally correct, then for the relativist abortion is correct. For multinational companies, ethical relativism means that managers need only follow local ethical conventions. Thus, for example, if bribery is an accepted way of doing business in a country, then it is okay for a multinational manager to follow local examples, even if it would be illegal at home. The opposite of ethical relativism is **ethical universalism**, which holds that basic moral principles transcend cultural and national boundaries. All cultures, for example, have rules that prohibit murder, at least of their own people. In such cases, the multinational manager will follow moral standards coming from the headquarters.

Why is it important to understand these ethical positions? Consider the Global Business Ethics Insight on page 434.

As the Global Business Ethics Insight shows, understanding ethical relativism and countries where it is followed is important. In other cases, ethical universalism should prevail. For the multinational company, however, there are problems following either approach. Some argue that a universalist approach may be insensitive and, as we see above, may go against well-established cultural norms. Other ethicists argue that cultural relativism cannot be applied to ethics. Thomas Donaldson, a famed business ethicist, argues that multinational companies have a higher moral responsibility than ethical relativism.[6] He argues that the extreme form of ethical relativism, namely convenient relativism, can occur when companies use the logic of ethical relativism to behave any way they please, using differences in cultures as an excuse. However, such approaches may backfire.

In sum, in this section we argued that it is necessary to understand the differences in ethics worldwide and the nature of these differences. Multinationals can use such understanding to refine their approaches to ethics in different societies. Next, we consider some of the major international ethics issues facing multinationals.

KEY GLOBAL ETHICAL ISSUES

In Chapter 1, you read about the many ethical issues facing the domestic company. When applied to the global level, companies also face many ethical issues. Exhibit 10.3 illustrates the many issues facing any company operating in the international environment today based on how stakeholders are affected.

While the global company faces a range of ethical issues in the international environment, two of the most important global ethical issues are labor issues and bribery. We consider these two in depth.

Employees	• Discrimination, diversity, and sexual harassment • Working conditions • Gender equality • Compensation
Shareholders	• Shareholder interests • Transparency in accounting • Transparency in shareholder communications • Executive salaries and compensation • Corporate governance
Government	• Respecting rules and regulations • Practices in foreign nations with weak governments • Lobbying
Country	• Respecting local laws • Influence on political climate • Bribery and corruption • Lobbying and other influence

EXHIBIT 10.3 — Global Ethical Issues

Labor Issues

It is undeniable that many companies choose to source to other countries to benefit from lower labor costs. Low wages, weak unions, and corrupt governments often encourage Western-based multinationals to have their products manufactured in developing countries in both Asia and Latin America.[7] However, this approach has also resulted in **labor issues** and many ethical dilemmas that have brought attention to multinationals. For instance, is it wrong to pay market wages to individuals in developing nations when such wages amount to a pittance locally? How should a company deal with child labor when children in these societies have no alternative? Should companies pay the same wage to women as men when there is a plentiful supply of female workers? Addressing these challenges has been the focus of many companies in the retail sector.

One of the major labor issues challenge facing multinationals is **women workers and their rights**. Women workers provide the bulk of labor in developing nations in export-oriented sectors, often in factories in export processing zones or in agriculture. However, in most cases, women workers are paid very low wages for insecure work in poor working conditions.[8] Furthermore, women are often paid lower wages than men. Additionally, fieldwork has shown that women work in such factories that often reflect patriarchal subordination. Men typically tend to be disproportionately represented in the managerial level relative to women. Women are also considered

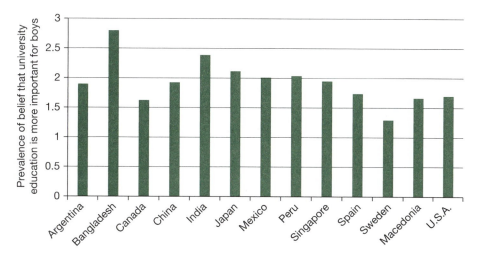

EXHIBIT 10.4 — Traditional Gender Roles

flexible labor and can easily be fired if they become pregnant or sick. Finally, women may also have to juggle both unpaid domestic work with paid work.

The current research suggests that how women are treated is mainly dependent on how gender roles are viewed. In that respect, the World Values Survey has collected valuable data to understand how the role of women is viewed in different societies. Some societies have very traditional views of gender roles where women are expected to stay at home and take care of children. In other societies, people share less traditional views where both men and women are expected to share in household chores.[9] Exhibit 10.4 shows country scores of traditional gender roles in selected countries. This was assessed by asking respondents the degree to which they believed that university education is more important for boys than girls.

Clearly, there are important differences regarding gender roles around the world. Some countries, such as Bangladesh and India, perceive women's role as very traditional. Countries such as Sweden have more modern views. Multinationals can rely on such scores to determine how to address women's ethical labor issues. For instance, when operating in societies with more traditional gender roles, multinationals must take more deliberate efforts to facilitate entry of women in the workforce. Stronger efforts must be exerted to provide mechanisms to change such traditional views. Multinationals should provide fair wages and also ensure that women have equal rights to men in terms of promotion and success at work.

Although such industrialization has had negative effects on women, there is also evidence that entering the workforce has been beneficial for women. Prieto-Carron reviews work suggesting that, despite the bad working conditions, women often benefit from having access to such jobs.[10] Employment alternatives for these women workers are often worse than the factory jobs and wages for such jobs still tend to be higher than in other sectors. Furthermore, being employed means that women have access to other female companies and the opportunity to be financially independent. Jobs also mean the ability to achieve greater equality in the household and more personal freedom. Finally, recent evidence suggests that women's employment allows them to organize collectively to better their working conditions.

Despite the benefits, it will take time before women workers' conditions are significantly improved. Multinationals will thus need to continue working hard to improve women's working conditions and facilitate their entry into the workforce. Next we discuss another important aspect of the labor ethical issues.

A related labor force issue is **child labor**, the practice of employing children. Even companies such as Apple and Nike have occasionally been hit with allegations of child labor. Critics condemn such companies for supporting exploitation of children. These children often work in very poor conditions and are paid very low wages. Such practices are threats to these children's development and their health and safety. As such, various organizations and child advocates are working tirelessly to convince governments and multinationals to aggressively address child labor and to ban such employment.

While most multinationals are working hard to ban child employment, some argue that child labor is not necessarily as simple as it seems. For instance, French suggests that such views ignore the complex environment such children employees face.[11] For instance, children sometimes have to work to help their families cope with poverty. If these children do not work, they may not have the means to get access to education. Second, it is also typically assumed that work is devastating to children. However, there is some evidence that child labor can provide children with psychosocial benefits and provide some education that a formal education system does not provide.

Despite these benefits, the reality is that children do work in less regulated and less visible areas of most economies. As such, rather than take a more complex look at child labor, many multinationals have created codes of conduct that ban any form of child labor. Next we consider worker safety.

Another critical labor issue that multinationals have to contend with is **work safety**, pertaining to the many steps multinationals take to ensure that their workers operate in an environment free of harm. Such safety can take many dimensions. First, multinationals have become more concerned about the safety of their workers in foreign plants. For instance, there is increased pressure for multinationals in the retail sector, such as Gap and Levi Strauss, to ensure that their employees work in safe conditions. A second key aspect is safety issues faced by expatriates. Consider the Global Business Ethics Insight opposite.

As the Global Business Ethics Insight shows, ensuring expatriates' safety is a critical ethical aspect of many multinationals. Another ignored but critical aspect of expatriate safety is road safety.[12] Consider that oil multinationals such as British Petroleum, Shell, and Total have all lost employees in road fatalities. In fact, in 2003, 6 out of 11 fatalities for Total were road accidents. Clearly, adequately assessing the potential for road fatalities in different societies is important. Exhibit 10.5 provides an idea of the trend in road fatalities in selected Southeast Asian countries which have the highest incidences of such fatalities worldwide.

As Exhibit 10.5 shows, there is a trend toward higher fatalities in many of the Southeast Asian societies multinationals are located in. In fact, a recent report by the World

GLOBAL BUSINESS ETHICS INSIGHT

Expatriate Safety

Expatriate safety is becoming a core issue for many multinationals. Consider the potential for violence and unrest in many countries where expatriates are posted. For instance, Mexico has seen over 5,400 people slain in the drug-fueled war in 2008. The recent bombing in Mumbai, India has also shed light on the potential for terrorism. Many companies lost employees and others could not account for their foreign employees for days. Yet another critical safety issue in India is the potential for kidnappings. Executives for companies such as Adobe and Satyam have all been kidnapped in high-risk areas. Others have been blackmailed or forced to withdraw money from ATMs in high-risk countries. Another case involves an expatriate's child who had powdered lime thrown in her eyes. The child was taken to the hospital and discharged quickly.

How responsible are multinationals for their expatriates' safety? Most companies are actually legally responsible to ensure their employees' safety. For instance, a company in the U.S. faces significant liability if it does not implement risk management plans. Employers are responsible for providing employees with the education and means to protect themselves against such situations in remote or dangerous locations.

How can multinationals prepare for such situations? Various companies provide intelligence services for $6,000 to $10,000 per year. Such reports can document potential risks in dangerous locations and also provide some ideas for preventive strategies. Other companies purchase annual membership for emergency medical services in situations where employees have to be returned home for emergency medical care.

Based on Lorenzo, O., Esqueda, P., and Larson, J. 2010. "Safety and ethics in the global workplace: Asymmetries in culture and infrastructure." *Journal of Business Ethics*, 92, 87–106.

Health Organization thus argues that multinationals need to adequately prepare for such realities.[13] In fact, it is clear that people living in high-fatalities countries see such fatal accidents as normal events. Having accepted such situations as normal, expatriates may be less attentive to potential safety rules that may prevent serious accidents. It is therefore imperative for multinationals to adequately prepare their employees for such situations. Later in this chapter, you will read about the importance of developing a safety culture.

In addition to expatriate safety, more multinationals are concerned with plant worker safety. In that context, Tulder, Wijk, and Kolk discuss that many of the world's largest multinationals are implementing codes of conduct to emphasize

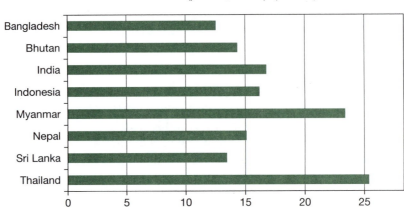

Road Fatalities (per 100,000 of population)

EXHIBIT 10.5—Road Fatalities for Selected Southeast Nations

occupational health and safety.[14] There is indeed strong interest to ensure that employees operate in a safe environment.

Next, we discuss the issue of bribery.

Bribery

One of the most pressing global ethics issues facing most multinationals is bribery. As you saw in Chapter 1, bribery and corruption occur to some varying degrees in most societies. In that context, corruption is the "misuse of entrusted power for private gain" (see http://www.transparency.org). Corruption occurs when someone receives a bribe and does something that they are legally prohibited from doing. **Bribery** also refers to gifts or payments to someone to expedite a government action or to gain some business advantages. Furthermore, as both Exhibits 1.1 and Exhibit 1.2 from Chapter 1 showed, there are significant differences in corruption worldwide. Earlier in this chapter, we discussed the nature of these differences.

Why should companies be concerned with bribery and ethics? There seem to be two major reasons for concern for ethics. First, companies put themselves at serious financial risk if they engage in bribery. As you will see later, there are many regulations that have been implemented to curb bribery. Consider the Business Ethics Insight on page 441.

As the Business Ethics Insight shows, one important reason for multinationals to implement anti-bribery measures is to avoid the potential of future fine. However, recent research provides a startling view of how bribery can have devastating effects on the firm. In that study, Fisman and Svensson examine the impact of bribery on firm growth.[15] They argue that bribery is detrimental to the firm because it diverts scarce resources away from critical business growth and innovation. The researchers find that increases in bribery in firms indeed resulted in lower annual growth rates for the firms. In fact, the researchers found that a 1% increase in rate of bribery results in 3.3% drop

BUSINESS ETHICS INSIGHT

Bribery Fines Worldwide

As mentioned in Chapter 1, the German multinational Siemens had to pay serious fines to both U.S. authorities and the European Union. The trend now is that anti-bribery authorities worldwide are becoming more likely to enforce anti-bribery laws. For instance, the U.K. joined the anti-corruption efforts as its Financial Services Authority fined Aon, a major insurance brokerage firm, £5.25 million for failing to implement initiatives to curb bribery and corruption. Aon is accused of giving over $7 million bribes to various individuals worldwide. Furthermore, the U.S. authorities are becoming more aggressive to combat corruption. For example, the Department of Justice is trying to seize $3 million in bank accounts held in Singapore. It is believed that these funds were paid to Bangladeshi officials and their family members as bribes. Furthermore, the Department of Justice is also eyeing the possibility of holding top executives' personal finances and freedom responsible if these executives either promote or turn a blind eye to bribes.

Based on Treanor, J. 2009. "FSA fines insurer AON 5.25 million pounds for corruption control failures." *Financial Times*, Jan 8.

in the annual company growth rate. Thus, these results also suggest that bribery not only increases the potential of fines that can bankrupt a company but also reduces growth rate. Multinational managers are therefore well advised to avoid bribes.

The above pertained to the impact of bribery on the company. However, many studies have also shown the devastating effects of bribery on societies. Bribery, in contrast to taxes, represents private goods that benefit few government officials at the expense of the wider society. Blackburn and Forgues-Puccio further provide a good review of studies that have examined the negative effects of bribery and corruption on countries.[16] Some studies have shown that bribery has negative effects on country growth rate. Rather than investing in development, bribes go directly to the private individuals who are being bribed.

The World Bank (http://www.worldbank.org) also argues that bribery often creates obstacles to doing business. As multinationals consider foreign investment decisions, they may be dissuaded because of bribery demands. Such decisions thus reduce the flow of foreign investment, thereby hurting a nation's growth. Thus, bribery may also become an important obstacle to doing business. Corruption and bribery may also discourage entrepreneurship because of the inherent obstacle creation. Furthermore, bribery may cause misallocation of public expenditure. Bribery may often encourage officials to favor specific pet projects or divert resources from more necessary projects.

Compte, Lambert-Mogiliansky, and Verdier also suggest that companies typically make up for bribery by increasing the contract price by the amount of the bribe.[17] As such, many developing countries suffer because they are charged higher prices. However, companies also routinely use poorer-quality products or materials to make up for the bribe, thus putting out inferior products. Furthermore, corruption can result in collusion among firms, resulting in even higher prices. As a result, corruption and bribery usually result in higher public spending, lower-quality projects, undermined competition, and the inefficient allocation of resources.

Despite the evidence that bribery is devastating for many nations, it is nevertheless important to note that not all societies are affected similarly. For instance, as Blackburn and Forgues-Puccio report, many countries such as China, Indonesia, South Korea, and Thailand have a reputation of being more corrupt but have yet enjoyed considerable economic growth.[18] However, the authors show that in such countries government bureaucrats tend to be more organized in corruption networks. In contrast, in countries where bureaucrats are less organized in networks, they are more likely to seek bribes to maximize their own income without regard to the effect of such bribes on other officials. In contrast, well-organized networks act as monopolies that minimize the extent of bribery while maximizing the provision of public goods. Thus, such networks have less damaging effects on the country's growth.

Given the widely acknowledged disadvantages associated with bribery, it is not surprising to note that many organizations worldwide are attempting to eradicate it. One of the more well-known efforts is led by the Organization for Economic Co-operation and Development (OECD). The OECD is an association of 30 of the world's largest economies in terms of gross domestic product, including countries such as Belgium, Canada, Ireland, South Korea, New Zealand, Spain, U.K., and the U.S. It was originally created in 1960 with 20 members and added ten new members over time.

The OECD members have ratified guidelines to combat bribery (http://www. oecd.org). Specifically, the members agree to take measures to make bribery a criminal offence. Furthermore, members are expected to provide legal assistance to each other to prosecute nationals who are engaged in bribery. Additionally, members are also expected to collaborate to prevent or tackle money laundering related to bribery. Members have to provide mutual legal assistance and can be asked to extradite foreign officials for prosecution.

In addition to providing clear guidelines regarding the eradication of bribery, the OECD has also enacted regulations to address bribery in companies. As such, multinationals operating in OECD and other countries are expected to have adequate accounting practices and internal controls and audits to ensure that they are complying with anti-bribery laws. In fact, the OECD has also proposed six guidelines that multinationals are widely expected to follow. Exhibit 10.6 shows these guidelines.

While the OECD guidelines were ratified in May 1997, the U.S. made bribery illegal in 1977. In that year, in response to widespread allegations of bribery in various agencies, President Carter passed the Foreign Corrupt Practices Act (FCPA). The FCPA forbids U.S. companies from making or offering payments or gifts to foreign government officials for the sake of gaining or retaining business. However, not all

Enterprises should not, directly or indirectly, offer, promise, or demand a briber or other undue advantage to obtain or retain business or other improper advantage. Nor should enterprises be solicited or expected to render a bribe or other under advantage. In particular, enterprises should:

1. Not offer, nor give in to demands, to pay public officials or the employees of business partners any portion of a contract payment. They should not use subcontracts, purchase orders or consulting agreements as means of channeling payments to public officials, to employees of business partners or their relatives or business associates.

2. Ensure that remuneration of agents is appropriate and for legitimate services only. Where relevant, a list of agents employed in connection with transactions with public bodies and state-owned enterprises should be kept and made available to competent authorities.

3. Enhance the transparency of their activities in the fight against bribery and extortion. Measures could include making public commitments against bribery and extortion and disclosing the management systems the company has adopted in order to honor these commitments. The enterprise should also foster openness and dialogue with the public so as to promote its awareness of and cooperation with the fight against bribery and extortion.

4. Promote employee awareness of and compliance with company policies against bribery and extortion through appropriate dissemination of these policies and through training programs and disciplinary procedures.

5. Adopt management control systems that discourage bribery and corrupt practices, and adopt financial and tax accounting and auditing practices that prevent the establishment of "off the books" or secret accounts or the creation of documents which do not properly and fairly record the transactions to which they relate.

6. Not make illegal contributions to candidates for public office or to political parties or to other political organizations. Contributions should fully comply with public disclosure requirements and should be reported to senior management.

EXHIBIT 10.6—OECD Bribery Guidelines for Multinationals

forms of payment are forbidden by the FCPA. Payments made under duress to avoid injury or violence are acceptable. For example, in an unstable political environment, a company may pay local officials "bribes" to avoid harassment of its employees. Furthermore, similar to the OECD guidelines, small payments that are needed for officials to do their legitimate and routine jobs are legal. For instance, small payments to induce officials to do their functions, such as issuing licenses or permits, are legal.

The FCPA has a tricky component known as the reason-to-know provision. This provision means that a firm is liable for bribes or questionable payments made by agents hired by the firm, even if members of the firm did not actually make the payments or see them being made. To take advantage of a local person's knowledge of "how to get things done" in a country, U.S. multinational managers often use local people as agents to conduct business. If it is common knowledge that these agents use part of their fees to bribe local officials to commit illegal acts, then the U.S. firm is breaking the law. If, however, the U.S. firm has no knowledge of the behavior of the agent and no reason to expect illegal behavior by the agent, then the firm has no liability under the FCPA.

As the above shows, bribery is an unethical behavior that most societies take seriously. However, as Exhibit 10.3 shows, there are many ethical issues that a multinational has to contend with. You learned about two of the most pressing of these ethical issues. Next, we discuss how multinationals can approach ethics.

MULTINATIONAL ETHICS: GOING LOCAL OR GLOBAL?

As we discussed in the opening paragraphs in this chapter, multinationals are constantly faced with ethical decisions. Such ethical decisions can sometimes result in cross-cultural ethical conflicts in which the company's business practices may be different from the host country's accepted business practices. For instance, if sweatshops are accepted business practices in some societies, should a multinational engage in such practices although it has specific policies prohibiting such practices? Because multinationals face constant scrutiny for such practices, they need to make the right decisions in these situations.[19] Specifically, these multinational managers frequently need to decide which set of business practices should prevail when cross-cultural conflicts occur. In this section, we consider the various approaches available to multinationals to make such decisions.

Several approaches rooted in ethical universalism whereby multinationals are expected to follow universal principles have been proposed. For instance, Donaldson offers an approach where the ethical decisions are made based on fundamental international rights.[20] Specifically, he argues that three moral languages of avoiding harm, rights, and duties, and the social contract, should guide multinational companies. He thus advocates prescriptive ethics for multinationals; that is, multinational companies should engage in business practices that avoid negative consequences to their stakeholders (e.g., employees, the local environment). Donaldson believes that these moral languages are the most appropriate for managing ethical behaviors among culturally heterogeneous multinationals; that is, regardless of their national culture, companies can agree with their stakeholders on the basic rules of moral behavior.

A more recent universalist approach is the **Integrated Social Contracts Theory**.[21] In this approach, multinationals are expected to make decisions that recognize universally binding ethical practices known as "hypernorms." They argue that **hypernorms** are norms that are accepted by all cultures and organizations irrespective of local cultures. Examples include the freedom of speech or freedom of association. In turn, business practices such as bribery or censoring of the internet violate such hypernorms. Multinationals are therefore advised to base their decisions on whether such decisions violate hypernorms. One source of such hypernorms is the United Nations Global Compact, providing guidelines addressing many areas of operations. Exhibit 10.7 shows some elements of the Global Compact.

Wood, Logson, Lewellyn, and Davenport propose a similar universalist approach.[22] However, instead of focusing on transnational rights or hypernorms, Wood et al. argue that multinationals should use their core values as the fundamental principles on which local ethical decisions can be made. This approach focuses on aiding the company in adjusting its practices to reflect local culture. However, when such adaptations are

Human Rights	• Principle 1: Businesses should support and respect the protection of internationally proclaimed human rights; and • Principle 2: make sure that they are not complicit in human rights abuses.
Labor Standards	• Principle 3: Businesses should uphold the freedom of association and the effective recognition of the right to collective bargaining; • Principle 4: the elimination of all forms of forced and compulsory labor; • Principle 5: the effective abolition of child labor; and • Principle 6: the elimination of discrimination in respect of employment and occupation.
Environment	• Principle 7: Businesses should support a precautionary approach to environmental challenges; • Principle 8: undertake initiatives to promote greater environmental responsibility; and • Principle 9: encourage the development and diffusion of environmentally friendly technologies.
Anti-Corruption	• Principle 10: Businesses should work against corruption in all its forms, including extortion and bribery.

EXHIBIT 10.7 — United Nations Global Compact

needed, there is strong emphasis on ensuring that these local adaptations are accommodated in such a way that the adaptations contribute to the company's culture. Thus, this approach focuses more on the company values rather than the local values.

While the above approaches provide some insights into ethical decision-making, multinationals may not always be able to follow universal approaches. In some cases, it is critical to respect local norms. For instance, Google decided to accept the Chinese requests of censoring the internet in order to be able to operate in China and take advantage of the potential offered by the Chinese market. In such cases, multinationals may need to assess their decisions to determine whether they want to implement such decisions. In that respect, Hamilton, Knouse, and Hill offer an ethical decision-making approach, referred to as the **HKH**, based on key questions.[23] They propose three possible outcomes: do business the firm's way, do business the host's way, or leave the country altogether. We discuss this approach next and which outcomes to adopt based on these questions.

The first step of the decision-making process in the HKH model is to determine whether the decision being pondered is actually a questionable practice. In such cases, the multinational has to determine whether the practice represents a conflict between the company's own values and the host country's accepted business practices. For instance, consider the case of Google's decision to do business in China. At the outset, there was a definite conflict between their corporate values (freedom of expression and "do no evil") and the Chinese demands for censorship. This gap between the company's business practices and the country's requests suggests that a questionable practice does exist.

In the second step of the model, the multinational needs to ask whether the questionable practice breaks any laws or regulations. This is critical as it allows the company to determine the legality of any decision. Furthermore, the multinational needs to consider whether the practice breaks both home and the host country's laws. For instance, in the case of bribery, a U.S. multinational needs to be aware that bribery is illegal under the Foreign Corrupt Practices Act. However, laws in the host country must also be considered. If the questionable practice breaks any laws, the multinational should rightly decide not to engage in the questionable practice. However, if no laws or regulations are broken, the multinational needs to subject the practice to the next question.

In the third step of the HKH model, the multinational needs to consider whether the questionable practice is simply a cultural difference or could represent a potential ethics problem. It is critical to make the distinction so that the multinational can determine whether they can adopt the host business practices as an acceptable way to do business. According to Hamilton et al., one way to determine whether a questionable practice represents a cultural difference is whether the practice in question does not harm anyone and represents a valid way for the culture to achieve an important cultural goal.[24] However, a questionable practice represents an ethics issue if the practice violates acceptable ethical practices such as those represented by hypernorms. For instance, if the behavior violates human rights, then it poses an ethical issue to the multinational. Thus, by assessing whether the questionable practice represents a genuine cultural difference or an ethics issue, the multinational can decide on the appropriate response.

After a multinational has determined whether a questionable practice represents a cultural difference or an ethics issue, the multinational needs to determine whether the practice violates any of its core values or some industry code of conduct. For example, if it is determined that a practice represents a cultural difference, it is also important to determine whether the practice goes against some corporate values. Consider the decision of promoting a woman manager in Saudi Arabia. While this practice is reflective of cultural differences due to the influence of Islam on the workplace, a multinational cannot simply decide to not promote the woman because it runs the risk of violating a cultural difference. It is critical for the multinational to also consider whether the practice is consistent with its own corporate culture or other aspects of the industry culture. Thus, if the questionable practice represents a cultural difference that does not violate any codes of conduct, the multinational can adopt the host's way of doing business. This principle would apply even if the questionable practice is a potential ethics issue. However, if the questionable practice violates industry codes of conduct or its own core values, the multinational needs to subject the practice to the next step.

In the fifth step of the HKH model, a multinational needs to determine whether it has leverage to do business its own way. Leverage refers to the ability of the multinational to have clout based on its reputation or ability to provide jobs or train employees in the host country. A company that has strong leverage is more likely to

BUSINESS ETHICS INSIGHT

Google in China

It is widely claimed that Google entered the Chinese market for 400 million reasons—equivalent to the number of potential customers Google could reach in China. It therefore initially decided to abide by the Chinese requests to censor its search sites so that those websites with offending material to the government would not be available. Google accepted requests counter to its corporate values in order to secure access to the market.

However, recent events suggest that Google may abandon its Chinese presence. There have been claims that its e-mail system was hacked in order to get access to the e-mails of individuals linked to opposition to the government. Furthermore, its search results are being subject to strong censorship and the state-controlled press has become extremely hostile to Google.

Why is Google now deciding to leave China? Part of the reason is because of Google's leverage in China. Google found that most of its revenues came from Chinese companies advertising on its Chinese website. Furthermore, many of these companies have enjoyed increased revenues because of such advertising. Thus, if Google leaves, many of these companies will still need to advertise on Google's website if they want to get exposure. Google therefore has strong leverage, as it sees that China and Chinese companies have more to lose if it leaves the country.

Based on *The Economist*. 2010. "Google ponders leaving China." March 2010.

be able to do business its own way in the host country. Consider the Business Ethics Insight above.

The Business Ethics Insight shows how Google can now use its leverage to make the decision to leave China. Multinationals can also make similar decisions. For example, if they have significant leverage, they could decide to do business their own way even if such decisions are counter to local cultural norms. This assumes that the multinational's way is ethically superior relative to the local way of doing business. However, if the multinational finds that it has no leverage to enforce its own way of doing things, the best option is to leave the host.

The HKH approach thus provides insights into the key questions multinationals need to ask before they decide whether they want to adopt their own way of doing business or follow the host's way.

Next we consider some of the major aspects of a multinational's ethics program.

WHAT CAN MULTINATIONALS DO TO BECOME MORE ETHICAL?

In Chapter 11, you will learn about how companies can become more ethical. You will read about the many aspects that need to be implemented to build an ethical culture (e.g., codes of ethics, ethics training, presence of ethics officers, ethics measurement and monitoring). We will not repeat these aspects here. However, because of the global nature of the environment facing a multinational, multinationals face some unique conditions compared to domestic-only firms. While it may seem easier to build an ethical culture for domestic firms, a multinational has to face multiple national cultures that may not view ethics similarly. As we saw earlier in this chapter, some societies tend to have higher tolerances for unethical behavior. What can a multinational do to ensure that it is behaving ethically worldwide? In this chapter, we consider two key aspects of a multinational ethics program; namely, code of ethics and whistle-blowing programs.

Code of Ethics

One of the key aspects of any multinational's ethics program is a code of ethics. The **code of ethics** is a formalized public statement that articulates the rules and regulations that will guide organizational practices with ethical consequences.[25] A code of ethics is a guide that governs both present and future employee behaviors as these employees interact with each other and with their stakeholders. A code of ethics implicitly assumes that the multinational will use universalistic standards that transcend the local cultural norms.

While you will read about the importance of codes of ethics in building the socially responsible firm in Chapter 11, a code of ethics is also extremely critical for multi-nationals. As multinationals get more media exposure, they are becoming increasingly responsible and visible when they break ethical norms in other societies. As we saw in the opening Preview Business Ethics Insight (pages 427–8), Nike suffered significant publicity backlash after it was revealed that its subcontractor had employees working in very poor conditions. A code of ethics thus allows a multinational to specify conditions and rules that all employees and stakeholders should follow worldwide. Furthermore, because of their size, multinationals cannot rely on their corporate cultures to ensure that similar behaviors are occurring worldwide. It therefore becomes important to specify appropriate behaviors worldwide in the code of ethics to ensure that all employees behave similarly. How critical is a code of ethics? Consider the Business Ethics Insight about GE on page 449.

Given the importance of code of ethics, what is the nature of such codes? Stohl, Stohl, and Popova provide some interesting insights on global codes of ethics.[26] They studied the code of ethics of 157 corporations of the Global *Fortune* 500 list. They classify codes of ethics as **first generation** (focus on the legal responsibility of the company), **second generation** (focus is on the responsibility to stakeholders), and **third generation** (focus on responsibilities grounded in the wider interconnected environment). Not surprisingly, they find that codes of ethics are becoming a more widespread aspect of a company's communication feature across regions and industries. However, findings also reveal that third generations are becoming more widespread, as over three-quarters of the companies studied had such codes that transcend profit motives. Furthermore, the authors found that only companies located in the European Union show a stronger degree for concern for the global environment and their ability to respond to such challenges.

BUSINESS ETHICS INSIGHT

Codes of Ethics at GE

GE is a global company engaged in a variety of industries ranging from finance and media, global infrastructure to jet engines. It operates in more than 100 countries, employing around 300,000 employees worldwide. GE is very dedicated to being a responsible global corporate citizen and sees a global code of ethics as critical to achieve that goal. It has developed a set of global standards that is more rigorous than the financial and legal requirements in place in any particular country. Although there are wide variations in terms of local conditions, GE sees the global code of ethics as a simpler way to ensure that its employees are all aware and can follow the values that the company stands for. For instance, GE has global standards specifying how to prevent money laundering and standards expected of their suppliers regarding worker exploitation and the environment.

How has GE been able to develop these global standards? First, GE has made the development of standards a corporate activity. It has a set of dedicated corporate officers who regularly review key activities to determine which activities need new standards. Second, it also involves experts at all levels. These experts review potential new laws and regulations to determine whether new standards are needed. As such, it can stay ahead of potential new regulations and even foresee potential areas where unethical behavior is likely.

GE makes sure it lives by these standards. For example, it will regularly terminate senior managers for failing to abide by company rules. This was the case with a senior manager who failed to properly conduct due diligence on suppliers in an emerging nation. GE terminated the manager, although that individual had rare extensive knowledge and experience in a difficult market. Furthermore, GE has also terminated senior leaders who failed to create the right culture. In several cases, the senior leaders were not personally aware of the failings of their subordinates (e.g., an employee agreeing to falsify supplier documents for a customer). However, they were deemed responsible for creating the right culture and were fired.

Based on Heineman, B.W. 2007. "Avoiding integrity landmines." *Harvard Business Review*, April, 100–108, http://www.ge.com.

Despite the popularity of codes of ethics, it is important to note that imposing the universalism inherent in such codes may be problematic in some countries. Talaulicar documents such challenges in the case of two U.S. multinationals implementing the U.S. codes of ethics in Germany.[27] The first example details WalMart's efforts to implement its statement of ethics in Germany. However, the law allows most German companies to establish work councils that are granted certain rights guaranteeing the welfare of its workers. By imposing the statement of ethics, the workers felt that WalMart violated their rights, as they were not consulted in determining these rights. WalMart fought these claims several times in court but was found to have indeed violated these rights. However, although WalMart could have appealed, the subsequent appeals were not heard, as WalMart sold its German stores in 2006 and exited the market. Similarly, Honeywell's implementation of its code of business conduct met similar resistance. The German courts argued that workers' co-determination rights are violated in some cases when foreign codes of ethics are unilaterally imposed without giving workers some voice in the matter.

As the above shows, multinationals have to be aware of cultural constraints when implementing in foreign locales. However, codes of ethics will likely remain as one of the key aspects of building a global ethical culture. Next, we discuss whistle-blowing.

Whistle-Blowing

A code of ethics regulates ethical behavior through control. In contrast, **whistle-blowing programs** shift ethics monitoring to employees. This is based on the assumption that employees know the most about unethical behavior and should therefore be involved in any ethics program. As such, ethics hotlines have become important mechanisms to reduce the probability of unethical behaviors. By providing employees with the means to report on the ethical violations, multinationals expect to detect such behaviors before it is too late. Prominent multinationals such as British Petroleum (Open Talk), Philips (Ethics Line), and P&G (Alert Line) all make use of ethics hotlines to reduce unethical behavior. Furthermore, Vodafone has gone one step further and has an online whistle-blowing system in addition to the traditional ethics hotline to detect ethical violations.

Multinationals are increasingly adopting ethics hotlines for many reasons.[28] First, because of their size, multinationals find it difficult to use only internal controls to control ethical behavior. By providing employees the opportunity to report violation, a multinational hopes to increase the likelihood of reducing unethical behavior. Second, there have been many new legal developments that now require companies to have ethics hotlines. For example, new European Union regulations require companies to have such mechanisms. Third, as we have discussed numerous times in this chapter, multinationals often face multiple cultural norms and rules. By including an ethics hotline, it can determine the potential to encounter conflicts in implementing its own corporate values with respect to local cultural norms.

How prevalent are whistle-blowing programs? Caldenon et al. provide some insights into ethics hotlines worldwide.[29] They reviewed the ethics policies of the 150 transnational companies on the United Nations Conference on Trade and Development (UNCTAD) rankings. The ranking includes both the top 50 financial transnational and top 100 non-financial transnational companies from a wide variety of locations, including the NAFTA region, Europe, and Asia, and a variety of industries ranging from media to finance to telecommunications. The authors carefully studied the website of each company to gauge their ethics policies.

Results show that ethics hotlines are becoming very prevalent: 101 of the 150 firms showed that they had some form of ethics hotline. The researchers also reviewed the terminology which was used to indicate the existence of these hotlines. It is widely assumed that employees can gauge the importance of an ethics program through the language that is used. Results show that around 57% of the firms use the term "hotlines" to denote some form of reactive response to ethics violations. However, for the 43% of firms not using the word "hotline," the ethics whistle-blowing program is described in terms of corporate values such as "helpline." Furthermore, the authors show that there are wide variations regarding to which employees are required to report wrongdoing if they observe such behaviors. Firms located in North America are more likely to require their employees report ethical wrongdoing compared to firms located in Europe. Finally, the authors also reviewed the mechanisms through which hotlines are implemented. They find that a majority of companies use a combination of both traditional systems such as mail and phone and new technologies such as e-mail and web. Furthermore, the findings show that financial firms are less likely to use new technologies such as e-mail to implement their hotlines. Exhibit 10.8 provides overall detail on these results.

As the above shows, ethics hotlines and whistle-blowing programs are very prevalent and likely to become more widespread in the future. We will revisit this issue again in Chapter 11 as we discuss some of the ethics hotlines' best practices.

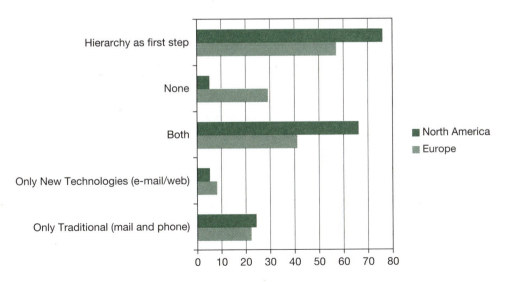

EXHIBIT 10.8—Ethics Hotlines Implementation Mechanism

CHAPTER SUMMARY

In this chapter, you learned about the many ethical aspects facing multinationals. You first read about the various factors determining why ethics differ between countries. You learned that national culture plays an important role in determining how people view ethics in a society. You also read about social institutions such as education and religion and how they also affect the way societies view ethics. The section also discussed the approaches to ethics for multinationals. Some multinationals respect local norms in their ethical decisions and follow ethical relativism. However, others are more likely to adopt a universalist approach and apply the same ethical standards worldwide.

The chapter discussed two of the key ethical issues facing multinationals: labor issues and bribery. You read about the many facets of labor issues such as women workers and child labor. You learned that such issues are not always as black and white as portrayed. For instance, child labor does provide some benefits to children workers. Furthermore, you read about safety issues as related to employees worldwide. The chapter also discussed bribery and the many devastating effects of bribery on societies. Furthermore, you also learned about the many factors motivating multi-nationals to fight bribery. Important regulations regarding bribery were also discussed.

In the last section of the chapter, you read about the many aspects of an ethical multinational. You read about an approach that provides answers to one of the key ethical questions for multinationals: whether to adopt home ethical country standards or to follow local norms and values. Furthermore, you learned about two unique aspects regarding a multinational's approach to ethics. You read about codes of ethics and the importance of such codes. You also learned about the difficulties of implementing global ethical standards worldwide. In the final section, you read about whistle-blowing and the usefulness of whistle-blowing programs for multinationals. Recent research on the use of ethics hotlines in some of the world's largest multi-nationals was also reviewed.

NOTES

1   Reed, J. & Simon, B. 2010. "Toyota's long climb comes to an abrupt halt." *Financial Times*, 9; Reed, J. & Simon, B. 2010. "Viral element spins events out of control." *Financial Times*, 16.

2   Kolk, A. & Pinkse, J. 2007. "Multinationals' political activities on climate change." *Business & Society*, 46, 2, 201–228.

3   Levenson, E. 2008. "Citizen Nike." *Fortune*, 158, 10, 165–170.

4   Cullen, J.B., Parboteeah, K.P. & Hoegl, M. 2004. "Cross-national differences in managers' willingness to justify ethically suspect behaviors: A test of institutional anomie theory." *Academy of Management Journal*, 47, 3, 411–421.

5   Seleim, A. & Bontis, N. 2009. "The relationship between culture and corruption: A cross-national study." *Journal of Intellectual Capital*, 10, 1, 165–184.

6   Donaldson, T. 1989. "The ethics of international business." In *Ethics and governance*, New York: Oxford University Press, 39–43.

7   French, L. 2010. "Children's labor market involvement, household work, and welfare: A Brazilian case study." *Journal of Business Ethics*, 92, 63–78.

8   Prieto-Carron, M. 2008. "Woman workers, industrialization, global supply chains and corporate codes of conduct." *Journal of Business Ethics*, 83, 5–17.

9   Parboteeah, K.P., Hoegl, M. & Cullen, J.B. 2008. "Managers' gender role attitudes: A country institutional profile approach." *Journal of International Business Studies*, 39, 795–813.

10 Prieto-Carron, "Woman workers."

11 French, "Children's labor market involvement."

12 Lorenzo, O., Esqueda, P. & Larson, J. 2010. "Safety and ethics in the global workplace: Asymmetries in culture and infrastructure." *Journal of Business Ethics*, 92, 87–106.

13 Lorenzo et al., "Safety and ethics in the global workplace."

14 Tulder, R., Wijk, J. & Kolk, A. 2009. "From chain liability to chain responsibility." *Journal of Business Ethics*, 85, 399–412.

15 Fisman, R. & Svensson, 2007. "Are corruption and taxation really harmful to growth? Firm level evidence." *Journal of Development Economics*, 83, 1, 63–75.

16 Blackburn, K. & Forgues-Puccio, G. 2009. "Why is corruption less harmful in some countries than in others?" *Journal of Economic Behavior & Organization*, 72, 797–810.

17 Compte, O., Lambert-Mogiliansky, A. & Verdier, T. 2005. "Corruption and competition in procurement auctions." *RAND Journal of Economics*, 35, 1, 1–15.

18 Blackburn & Forgues-Puccio, "Why is corruption less harmful in some countries?"

19 Hamilton, B., Knouse, S. & Hill, V. 2009. "Google in China: A manager-friendly heuristic model for resolving cross-cultural ethical conflicts." *Journal of Business Ethics*, 86, 143–157.

20 Donaldson, "The ethics of international business."

21 Donaldson, T. & Dunfee, T.W. 1999. *Ties that bind: A social contracts approach to business ethics.* Boston: Harvard Business School Press.

22 Wood, D.J., Logsdon, J.M., Lewellyn, P.G. & Davenport, K. 2006. *Global business citizenship: A transformative framework for ethics and sustainable capitalism.* Armonk, NY: M.E. Sharpe Co.

23 Hamilton et al., "Google in China."

24 Hamilton et al., "Google in China."

25 Stohl, C., Stohl, M. & Popova, L. 2009. "A new generation of corporate codes of ethics." *Journal of Business Ethics*, 90, 607–622.

26 Stohl et al., "A new generation of corporate codes of ethics."

27 Talaulicar, T. 2009. "Barriers against globalizing corporate ethics: An analysis of legal disputes on implementing U.S. codes of ethics in Germany." *Journal of Business Ethics*, 84, 349–360.

28 Calderon, R., Alvarez-Arce, J., Rodriguez-Tejedo, I. & Salvatierra, S. 2009. "Ethics hotlines in transnational companies: A comparative study." *Journal of Business Ethics*, 88, 199–210.

29 Calderon et al., "Ethics hotlines in transnational companies."

KEY TERMS

Bribery: refers to gifts or payments to someone to expedite a government action or to gain some business advantages.

Child labor: the practice of employing children.

Code of ethics: a formalized public statement that articulates the rules and regulations that will guide organizational practices with ethical consequences.

Convergence: belief that many management practices including those related to ethics, are becoming more similar.

Cross-national ethics: the differences that exist between countries when considering ethical issues.

Ethical relativism: ethical viewpoint based on the assumption that there are no objective and universal moral standards.

Ethical universalism: approach based on the notion that basic moral principles transcend cultural and national boundaries.

First generation code of ethics: focus on the legal responsibility of the company.

Global business ethics: apply to the myriad of ethical issues any company faces when operating in the global environment.

HKH: ethical decision-making approach based on key questions.

Hypernorms: norms that are accepted by all cultures and organizations irrespective of local cultures.

Integrated Social Contracts Theory: in this approach, multinationals are expected to make decisions that recognize universally binding ethical practices known as "hypernorms."

Labor issues: the many ethical dilemmas pertaining to labor.

Second generation code of ethics: focus is on the responsibility to stakeholders.

Third generation code of ethics: focus on responsibilities grounded in the wider interconnected environment.

Whistle-blowing programs: shifts ethics monitoring to employees by providing the means to report ethical violations.

Women workers and their rights: key ethical issues pertaining to the employment of women by multinationals.

Work safety: steps multinationals take to ensure that their workers operate in an environment free of harm.

DISCUSSION QUESTIONS

1. What is global business ethics? How is global ethics different from domestic ethics?
2. Discuss some of the factors explaining why global ethics differ worldwide. Explain the cultural and social institutional approach.
3. What are some of the ways multinationals approach ethical decision-making? What are some of the dangers of a relativist approach?
4. What are some of the key ethical issues facing multinationals?
5. What are some of the major challenges facing women workers worldwide? Why do such challenges exist?
6. What is bribery? How is bribery different worldwide? What are some disadvantages of bribery for both multinationals and the societies they operate in?
7. Discuss the key steps in deciding whether a universalist approach or a relativist approach should be used. What important questions does a multinational need to ask?
8. What is a code of ethics? How prevalent are codes of ethics worldwide?
9. What is whistle-blowing? Why do multinationals need a whistle-blowing program?
10. Discuss recent research regarding adopting of ethics hotlines in multinationals worldwide. What are some major lessons?

INTERNET ACTIVITY

1. Go to the Vodafone website: http://www.vodafone.com.
2. Review the company's corporate responsibility program.
3. What are some of the major elements of Vodafone's effort to implement a global ethical program?
4. Which important stakeholder areas do Vodafone address? What are the important requirements for each area?
5. What lessons do Vodafone provide for multinationals? Is it possible for a multinational to adopt global ethical standards?

For more Internet Activities and resources, visit the Companion Website at www.routledge.com/cw/parboteeah.

WHAT WOULD YOU DO?

A Job in Saudi Arabia

You finish your degree in business administration and are hired to work in the marketing department of a multinational. You perform extremely well two years into the job. Your work ethic and performance stand out among those who were hired at the same time as you. You are personally commended by your supervisor and others at the executive level. You are at a crossroads and need to make the next move to continue your ascent in the company.

You chat with numerous individuals and with your mentor and learn that most successful employees had to work for a few years in a foreign subsidiary of the company. You learn that your company is seriously considering entry into Saudi Arabia. Any employee who can take charge and make the subsidiary successful in Saudi Arabia will likely do very well in the company.

You are seriously considering taking the position. However, as a woman, you know that the work environment in Saudi Arabia for women is not necessarily ideal. You talk to others who have worked there and find that business is divided along gender lines and that it is sometimes tough for women to do business. However, you also hear from others that such attitudes are changing and that women can also be successful in Saudi Arabia.

What do you do? Do you take the challenge and work hard to overcome such attitudes? Or do you seek a global posting in a subsidiary where women are more easily accepted? Why?

BRIEF CASE: BUSINESS ETHICS INSIGHT

Ernst Lieb and Mercedes-Benz

In September 2006, Daimler appointed Ernst Lieb, a German national, to the post of CEO for Mercedes-Benz USA. Prior to coming to the U.S., Mr. Lieb was head of then Daimler Chrysler Australia/Pacific after being CEO of Mercedes Canada. Mr. Lieb was hired to bolster Mercedes cars in the U.S. Upon his arrival, he travelled the U.S. and listened to customers and dealers. He encouraged customers to discuss their problems with him. Dealers were also amazed that he was willing to listen and talk with them for hours. Because most dealers liked him, he was able to push most dealers to adopt a new controversial facilities improvement for the Mercedes dealerships. As of October 2011, he was able to get 300 out of 355 Mercedes-Benz dealerships to adopt new standards or build new stores, spending a combined $1.4 billion since 2008.

According to most dealers, Mr. Lieb was the best thing that happened to Mercedes-Benz USA. Through his leadership, Mercedes-Benz was able to close the gap with its main rival, BMW. While BMW outsold Mercedes by around 40,000 units in 2007, the gap was only around 3,738 vehicles in 2010. Many experts predicted that the gap would get even smaller. Furthermore, Mr. Lieb was the major force behind the push for the C-class compact vehicles as well as the C-class coupes. These moves have been hailed as major successes for Mercedes-Benz USA.

However, despite these successes, the automotive community was shocked to hear that Mr. Lieb was fired in October of 2011. While Daimler has yet to comment on the matter, the media suggests that Mr. Lieb was fired for repeatedly violating Daimler ethical rules. In one report, Mr. Lieb is accused of taking a personal trip to Australia at company expense. He is also alleged to have used company funds for private expenditures, such as golf club fees as well as building his house in New York. After Daimler had paid $185 million fines to the Department of Justice, Chairman Dieter Zetsche instituted a zero tolerance policy for ethical violations. Mr. Lieb probably violated this policy.

Based on Kurylko, D.T. 2011. "Leib's fall stuns Mercedes-Benz dealers." *Automotive News*, October 24, 86, 6487 ; Roberts, G. 2011. "Lieb firing reasons emerge in media." *Just-auto Global News*, online edition, October 20; Schulz, J. 2011. "Mercedes fires chief and cancels dealer meeting." *New York Times* online, October 31.

BRIEF CASE QUESTIONS

1. Do you think Daimler is justified in firing Mr. Lieb given his success in the U.S.?
2. What message does the firing send to Mercedes-Benz USA employees and other stakeholders?
3. Mr. Lieb was well liked by most Mercedes-Benz dealers in the U.S. and they were shocked by his firing. What should Daimler do to calm dealer anger?
4. Was there some other way Daimler could have dealt with this issue?

LONG CASE: BUSINESS ETHICS

SHELL OIL IN NIGERIA

Introduction

Nigeria is a country that is slightly more than twice the size of California. In July 2011, its population was estimated at just over 155 million people, making it the eighth most populated country in the world. It is Africa's most populous country and is composed of more than 250 ethnic groups. The country has the second highest rate of HIV/AIDS deaths and is ranked number three with respect to total number of people living with HIV/AIDS in the country.

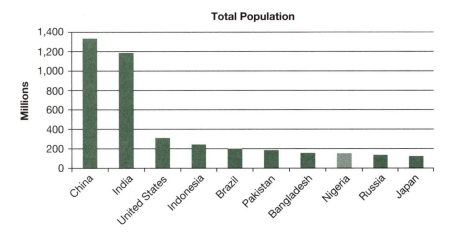

The country itself is full of rich natural resources such as natural gas, petroleum, tin, iron, coal, and limestone. Despite these rich resources, the country has been crippled by civil wars, military rule, religious tensions, and corruption. Even more devastating was the poor macroeconomic management that has left the country completely dependent upon its number one resource, which is petroleum. Petroleum provides 95% of the foreign exchange earnings and close to 80% of its budgetary revenues. In 2010, Nigeria surpassed Iran to become the second largest oil producer behind Saudi Arabia. It shipped 2,464 million barrels of oil per day compared to Iran, who shipped 2,248 million barrels per day.

The United States imports 17% of its petroleum from West Africa, with Nigeria being the key supplier. That number is estimated to rise to over 25% in the year 2015. Despite the potential for oil to change the lives of this resource rich country, the majority of Nigerians live on less than US$1 per day. The poor living conditions, low wages, and lack of quality of life improvement is attributed to the large amount of corruption by the citizens, politicians, and companies who exist within the country.

A History of Corruption

While petroleum drives the majority of the economy, it also drives the majority of the corruption. Nigeria has long been considered the most corrupt country in the world. Its citizens, government, and corporations have been party to and involved in political corruption, bureaucratic corruption, electoral corruption, embezzlement, and bribery. In fact, it has been said the corruption is actually a viable enterprise in society with no way to trace these activities or prosecute those involved.

The companies operating in this region have long been blamed for allowing, participating, and even creating the corruption that has taken place. Not only have they failed to engage reformers but they have also been accused of doing things like bribing officials, obscuring oil revenue figures, and failing to invest in the infra-structure and improvement of the people in the country. While the oil companies point to millions of dollars of investment into the region, one look at the impoverished conditions common to the people of Nigeria and it's difficult to say it was enough.

An estimated $200 billion in revenue is planned to go to African treasuries in the next ten years as new oil fields are opened throughout this region. This oil will bring the largest influx of revenue in the continent's history and more than ten times the amount Western donors give each year in aid. There is great concern about what countries like Nigeria will do with this money and the potential corruption that will take place.

Oil giant Royal Dutch Shell Group stands to benefit the most from these new oil fields as they are the largest producer of oil in the region. The company produces more than one million barrels of oil per day. With that said, there is much concern due to Shell's storied past in this country.

Shell Operations in Nigeria

The Royal Dutch Shell Group, more commonly referred to as Shell, is a group of more than 1,700 companies all over the world. Sixty percent of the company is owned by Royal Dutch of the Netherlands and 40% is owned by Shell Transport and Trading Group of Great Britain. The full merger between these two companies was official in 1907. This conglomerate of companies includes companies such as Shell Petroleum of the U.S.A., Shell Nigeria, and Shell Argentina. The company's mission was to bulk-ship and export oil, revolutionizing the transport of this precious resource. Soon after the merger was complete, the company rapidly expanded across the world with both marketing offices and exploration and production facilities. Within 12 months, both of the struggling entities were transformed into successful ones.

In 1937, Shell entered Nigeria, making it the first energy company to enter the market in this country. By 1938 they were granted an exploration license that allowed them to prospect for oil in the region. It was not until January of 1956 that the company drilled its first well. Later that year, the company changed its name to Shell-BP Petroleum Development Company of Nigeria Limited (SPDC). Over the course of the next 20 years Shell entered into a number of agreements with the Nigerian government that gradually increased the government's ownership of the company from 35% all the way up to 80% in 1979.

As it stands today, Shell operates two businesses related to the exploration, production, and transportation of oil and gas within Nigeria. The SPDC still exists and is the largest private sector oil and gas company in Nigeria. It is a joint venture between the government-owned Nigerian National Petroleum Corporation (NNPC) which owns 55% Shell (which owns 30%), Elf Petroleum Nigeria Limited (which owns 10%), and Agip (which owns 5%). The other business operated by Shell in Nigeria is called Shell Nigeria Exploration and Production Company (SNEPCO), which was formed in 1993 to develop deep-water drilling resources. It operates two deep-water licenses and a production sharing contract with the NNPC.

The SPDC's operations are spread over a 30,000 square kilometer area in the Niger Delta. Its network consists of 6,000 kilometers of flowlines and pipelines, 90 oil fields, 1,000 producing wells, 72 flowstations, 10 gas plants, and 2 major oil export terminals. This business unit is capable of producing up to one million barrels of oil per day on average. The SNEPCO is committed to the discovery of new resources and sources of oil and is charging toward the goal set by the Nigerian government of being able to have a capacity of four million barrels per day.

While Nigeria was once the shining star of Shell's portfolio, it is now a large black cloud that hangs over the entire organization. Shell Nigeria has been accused of pollution, collusion, corruption, bribery, and false accounting. Every time the company settles a claim or accusation, another one pops right up. The following provides an account of the accusations and corruption that have scarred this organization throughout its history.

Ken Saro-Wiwa

Shell's first problems began in the early 1990s when criticism of human rights policies and the destruction of the environment in Nigeria became a hot topic. Ken Saro-Wiwa was a leading environmentalist and author who happened to be a Nigerian native and part of the Ogoni tribe. He was one of the more determined and articulate critics of the government and Shell Oil's destruction of his homeland. He argued that neither party had appropriate regulations for protecting the Ogoni people's land and did not return any of the immense wealth that was taken from their region.

Saro-Wiwa organized a group called the Movement for Survival of the Ogoni People, which quickly grew to be the largest political organization in the region. This group began to protest and demonstrate for an end to destructive behaviors such as oil spills, gas flaring, and the destruction of property to make way for pipelines that Shell was building. They also began demanding they be given a share of the revenues from the land Shell was using. Shell denied these claims and stated that the group was greatly exaggerating their claims.

Nigeria's military began to respond to the group's claim through a strategy that has been referred to as a "scorched earth campaign against the Ogoni," which included burning villages and committing rapes and murders. Shell refused to get involved, stating that the company does not get involved in politics. This led to Saro-Wiwa and eight other Ogoni members being arrested on charges that Western governments and human rights groups called "trumped up." The Nigerian government ultimately executed all nine, with Saro-Wiwa's body being burned with acid and buried in an unmarked grave.

This event ignited worldwide protests and criticism against Nigeria, the African oil industry, and Shell. Shell was sued in a New York court by Saro-Wiwa's family and was accused of bribing soldiers who carried out human rights abuses in addition to playing a role in the capture and execution of the nine. Shell eventually settled this case out of court for $15.5 million.

Oil Spills

Oil spills are quite prevalent in the Niger Delta and it is estimated that the equivalent of the *Exxon Valdez* spill has occurred every year for the past 50 years. There is no other place in the world that has been as battered by oil as this region. The Nigerian government and international environmental groups sponsored a report in 2006 that concluded that as many as 546 million gallons of oil have spilled into the region over of the past five decades. This has led to the destruction of swamps, aquatic life, and the main food source for many of the tribes.

Shell is the major player with thousands of miles of pipes that have been laid through the swamps and fertile land. The majority of the spillage is attributed to poorly maintained and aging pipes; however, Shell maintains the position that the majority of the spills are due to oil thieves and sabotage. A spokesperson for Shell stated that the company does not discuss individual oil spills but only 2% of the total spills are due to equipment failure. Richard Steiner, a consultant on oil spills, concluded in a 2008 report that historically "the pipeline failure rate in Nigeria is many times that found elsewhere in the world." He also noted that almost every year Shell has acknowledged a spill due to corroded pipes.

Shell has repeatedly received pressure from the Niger Delta people and internationally to clean up its processes and spills. In 2008, there were two major oil spills that occurred. One of the spills was due to a leak in a major pipeline that went undetected for close to four months before something was done about it. This completely devastated the 20 square kilometer network of creeks and inlets in which the Bodo people inhabit. The company initially offered the people £3,500 along with 50 bags of rice, 50 bags of beans, and a few cartons of sugar, tomatoes, and groundnut oil. The offers were rejected and the Bodo filed a class action lawsuit.

Shell finally admitted that the spills were due to operational issues and stated that it will take full responsibility for these two spills in accordance with Nigerian law. Many estimate that Shell's exposure could be close to a $100 million for the cleanup and potentially take up to 20 years to fully revive this area. They are also responsible for paying compensation to those that are entitled to receive such under the Nigerian law.

Bribery

As discussed previously, bribery is common in Nigeria especially in doing business with the government. Shell has long been suspected of using bribery as a way of securing new territories, new licenses, and circumventing customs laws. However, up until recently no one was able to provide any proof that these things were happening.

In 2007, the SEC learned that Shell was doing business with a company named Panalpina. Panalpina was doing business with lots of different organizations that operated in high-risk countries as a freight forwarder. It was learned that Panalpina was bribing the Nigerian government on behalf of several companies, including Shell. The bribes went to the government to secure preferential treatment when moving rigs, ships, workboats, and other equipment throughout the country. It was learned that the money was used to go around the customs process, allowing Shell to benefit from faster movement of goods, using military aircraft to transport special goods, over-looking visa inspections, and avoiding employees being deported for overstaying visas. Panalpina provided information that Shell specifically requested for fake invoices to be drawn up to mask the nature of the bribes and avoid any suspicion in case of an audit.

In addition to Panalpina confirming the bribes on behalf of Shell, Shell also admitted to separate incidents of paying $2 million in bribes to Nigerian sub-contractors on its deep-water Bonga Project. It is estimated that Shell profited about $14 million because of these payments. Because of these two incidents, Shell has been ordered to pay fines of $48.1 million.

Shell Today

Even with all of these accusations, bad press, fines, and unethical issues surrounding the company, Shell continues to do business in Nigeria. The company maintains that it continues to support and improve the communities of the Niger Delta region through the taxes and royalties they pay to the Nigerian Federal Government. Shell claims to have contributed approximately $31 billion to the government over the past five years and that the government receives 95% of the revenue after costs from the SPDC joint venture.

In addition to generating revenue, the company actively promotes projects in the region. These projects support small businesses, agriculture, training, education, and healthcare throughout the region, with many of the details of each being available from the company's Nigeria website. Education is a strong part of their contributions as they pay a portion of their profit into an educational fund for the restoration and consolidation of education in Nigeria.

Long Case Bibliography

BBC News. Ogoniland Oil Spills: Shell Admits Nigeria Liability. 3 August 2011. 5 August 2011. http://www.bbc.co.uk/news/world-africa-14391015.

Blackden, R. & Mason, R. Shell to Pay $48M Nigerian Bribe Fine. 4 November 2010. 5 August 2011. http://www.telegraph.co.uk/finance/newsbysector/energy/oilandgas/8111277/Shell-to-pay-48m-Nigerian-bribe-fine.html.

Bloomberg. Nigeria Exported More Than Second Largest OPEC Nation Iran. 18 July 2011. 21 July 2011. http://www.bloomberg.com/news/2011-07-18/nigeria-exported-more-than-second-largest-opec-nation-iran-1-.html.

Calkins, D.V. & Brubaker, L. Shell Bribes Among "Culture of Corruption" Panalpina Admits. 5 November 2010. 5 August 2011. http://www.businessweek.com/news/2010-11-05/shell-bribes-among-culture-of-corruption-panalpina-admits.html.

CIA. The World Fact Book. 5 July 2011. 21 July 2011. https://www.cia.gov/library/publications/the-world-factbook/geos/ni.html.

Donovan, J. $15.5M Settlement: Shell Has Another Day in Court. 13 June 2009. 4 August 2011. http://royaldutchshellplc.com/2009/06/13/155m-settlement-shell-has-another-day-in-court/.

Investigative Africa. Shell to Pay $30M in Nigeria Corruption Settlement. 17 October 2010. 3 August 2011. http://investigativezim.com/2010/10/17/shell-to-pay-30-million-in-nigeria-corruption-settlement/.

New York Times. Far from Gulf, a Spill Scourge 5 Decades Old. 16 June 2010. 2 August 2011.http://www.nytimes.com/2010/06/17/world/africa/17nigeria.html.

——— . Ken Saro-Wiwa. 22 May 2009. 3 August 2011. http://topics.nytimes.com/topics/reference/times topics/people/s/ken_sarowiwa/index.html.

Shell Global. The Beginnings. 2 August 2011. http://www.shell.com/home/content/aboutshell/who_we_are/our_history/the_beginnings/.

Shell Nigeria. Shell At a Glance. 30 July 2011. http://www.shell.com.ng/home/content/nga/aboutshell/at_a_glance/.

Shell Oil. SNEPCO. 30 July 2011. http://www.shell.com.ng/home/content/nga/aboutshell/shell_businesses/e_and_p/snepco/.

Telegraph. Shell Execs Accused of ''Collaboration'' Over Hanging of Nigerian Activist Ken Saro-Wiwa. 31 May 2009. 2 August 2011. http://www.telegraph.co.uk/news/worldnews/africaandindianocean/niger/5413171/Shell-execs-accused-of-collaboration-over-hanging-of-Nigerian-activist-Ken-Saro-Wiwa.html.

UPI.com. Shell Admits to Oil Spills in Nigeria. 4 August 2011. 5 August 2011. http://www.upi.com/Business_News/Energy-Resources/2011/08/04/Shell-admits-to-oil-spills-in-Nigeria/UPI-6983 1312459493/.

Vidal, J. Shell Accepts Liability for Two Oil Spills in Nigeria. 3 August 2011. 5 August 2011. http://www.guardian.co.uk/environment/2011/aug/03/shell-liability-oil-spills-nigeria.

LONG CASE QUESTIONS

1. Why is corruption and bribery so rampant in Nigeria? Why has Shell not taken a stand against such corruption?
2. What were some of the factors that led to the killing of poet Ken Saro-Wiwa? Do you think that Shell was an accomplice in his murder?
3. Why do so many oil spills occur? Why has Shell not taken stronger steps to end such spills?
4. Do you think it is the international community's responsibility to get involved when local laws are not strong enough to prevent pollution on the part of multinationals like Shell?
5. What can Shell do to repair its image and reputation?

Part III:
Comprehensive Case

INTRODUCTION

Tetsuro Ishikawa, the president of Snow Brand at that time, had to raise his voice. He shouted at the Osaka plant manager at the press conference. "You, is that true?"

On July 1, 2000, Snow Brand Milk Products Co. Ltd., the top company in the Japanese milk product industry, held its fourth press conference about the food poisoning it caused on June 27. This was President Ishikawa's first appearance in public and he apologized for the failure along with accounting for the cause. He mentioned part of the production process was contaminated with the *Staphylococcus aureus* toxin but the reason for it was unclear. However, on this occasion, the Osaka plant manager exposed the fact that contamination was due to the negligence of routine cleaning which had already been found on June 29, two days after the poisoning happened. Neither the president nor the public relations manager who attended the press conference knew about the larger picture or the incident.

HISTORY OF SNOW BRAND

Snow Brand started in 1925 as a sales guild for dairy products in Hokkaido, the northernmost part of Japan. A big earthquake occurred two years before, in 1923, and it led to a supply shortage, and a large number of foreign-made dairy products flowed into Japan due to the abolishment of tariffs by the government. The origin of Snow Brand was to help dairy farmers in Hokkaido suffering from a fall in milk prices to become independent. Snow Brand's crystal mark (logo), a logo familiar to the Japanese public, was designed in 1926. The mark symbolizes stark white and purity, and the Pole Star in the center of the mark signifies Hokkaido. Torizo Korosawa, one of Snow Brand's founders, advocated *Kendo-Kenmin*, which means "dairy fertilizes earth and enriches people." This "spirit of establishment" has been the base of the corporate philosophy of Snow Brand.

After several changes to its name and organization, Snow Brand Milk Products Co., Ltd. was incorporated in 1950 and its business grew. However, Snow Brand caused a serious food-poisoning case in 1955. Over 1,900 students in nine elementary schools in Tokyo came down with food poisoning after drinking skim milk made at Snow Brand's Yakumo Plant in Hokkaido. *Hemolytic staphylococcus* was breeding in a portion of fresh milk made at the Yakumo Plant where germicidal treatment had been held up because of mechanical troubles and a power outage. Snow Brand's employees' response to the food poisoning was prompt and appropriate. Mitsugi Sato, the president at the time, immediately directed employees to stop distribution and ordered a recall of the products, published an apology in the newspapers, and took the lead in an investigation into the causes at the plant. In addition, he made apology visits to many of those who had been poisoned, to business partners, and to the dairy farmers. Other plants were also rechecked and drastic measures for preventing a recurrence of food poisoning were worked out. For example, departmental self-dependence of hygiene management and examination and reinforcement of the inspection process were implemented. Sato issued a document titled as "Announce-ment to all employees" regarding the Yakumo case and distributed it to all employees. It included these statements, "It takes long time to gain credit and no time to lose it. Additionally, we cannot buy credit" and "It is only quality improvement that can result in regaining the honor lost due to quality contamination."[1] It was also handed out to new employees from 1956 until 1985 during their hygienic management training.

After the food poisoning incident, Snow Brand afterwards started to pursue quality and credibility by developing technical capabilities and expansion of its plants by bringing the nationwide market into view. However, it also resulted in increasing the distance between Snow Brand and dairy farmers in Hokkaido who had been working together toward the progress of dairy food product manufacturing in Hokkaido. Before the 1960s in Japan, sales outlets of dairy food manufacturers that offered home delivery service supported the milk industry since milk is perishable and could not suitably be shipped in the distribution channel like other common foods. When Snow Brand expanded its market nationwide, its competitors had already set up their distribution networks. Snow Brand's weak distribution network allowed it to ride the wave of marketing revolution by moving into supermarkets without disturbing the existing distribution channels. By taking the largest share in the supermarket and convenience store channels, combined with technological advancements, Snow Brand became the leading company in the market. Specifically, the outstanding technology of Snow Brand generated high-quality dairy food products and it succeeded in building an excellent brand image along with the perception of snow's purity and fertile farmland in Hokkaido. Snow Brand remained at the top of the dairy food product industry for years. Nevertheless, the company had to deal with price competition, international trends toward free trade, and increased demand for freshness by consumers.

MILK IN THE JAPANESE MARKET

Milk has a special status in the Japanese product market. Because of its historical and social background, people from various age groups drink milk on a daily basis. Many consumers believe that milk is nutritious and healthy.[2] At the time of the food poisoning incident by Snow Brand, consumers did not imagine that milk could be bad for them.

Milk was introduced in Japan in the seventh century. Since only the aristocracy drank milk mainly for medical purposes, milk did not appear in the Japanese mass market till 1863. In 1871, the media reported that the Emperor drank milk twice a day; therefore, drinking milk became popular. In 1954, after World War II, the school lunch program was officially regulated by the government. Most Japanese children suffered from malnutrition at the time. Based on this program, all children in mandatory education schools were provided with lunches. The Japanese government included powdered milk into the school lunch program, provided by the U.S. government. In 1963, the school lunch program now included real daily milk and it became the fundamental drink for all children. The product volume of milk increased by 1,822% between 1948 and 1964. After they graduated from their mandatory schools, they continued to drink milk at home to maintain a healthy and balanced diet. The consumer milk market increased. The Japanese government also encouraged drinking milk by protecting the milk industry.[3] In 1985, product volumes of milk exceeded 4 million kiloliters, and then it grew to 5 million kiloliters in 1994[4] (see Exhibit 1). After that, as demands for milk based on the school lunch program declined because of low birthrates, the product volume was decreased. However, in the twentieth century, many people still include milk in their dairy diet.[5]

SEQUENCE OF THE FOOD POISONING EVENT

The Snow Brand Company received the first report about food poisoning on the morning of June 27, 2000. The West Japan Branch got a phone call from a consumer whose children showed significant symptoms after they drank Snow Brand's low-fat milk at dinner on June 26. An employee of the company immediately visited the consumer's house and asked several questions. The employee did not think that Snow Brand's Milk was the source of the children's symptoms. He told the consumer that the company had received no similar reports. However, the employee, just in case, took the remaining milk cartons from the house to have them inspected.[6]

Osaka City Hall also received several reports from local public health centers about food poisoning symptoms, which were possibly caused by Snow Brand's low-fat milk. Based on a previous experience with a food poisoning outbreak caused by 0-157 bacteria in 1996, officials from City Hall responded to the situation promptly and conducted an on-site investigation at Snow Brand's Osaka Plant on the afternoon of June 28. While conducting their inspection, City Hall continued to receive complaints from consumers about possible food poisoning from Snow Brand Milk. At 11 p.m. on June 28, employees at Osaka City Hall asked a representative of the Snow Brand West

Japan Branch to conduct a recall of its products and make a public announcement to tell consumers about the food poisoning immediately; however, the Osaka plant manager thought that seven complaints out of hundreds of thousands of products was usual. He believed that a public announcement would just confuse the consumers.[7]

On the 28th, Snow Brand also held a general stockholder meeting at its headquarters in Sapporo, with the executives and many of the directors at this meeting. They were not told about the possible food poisoning and the inspection of the Osaka Plant by Osaka City Hall until 1 a.m. on June 29. At 8 a.m., Snow Brand's executives finally decided to voluntarily recall the products in Western Japan, but did not make a public announcement. Tetsuro Ishikawa, the president of Snow Brand who used to be the financial director of the company, was informed about the recall one hour later. After the stockholder meeting, Ishikawa visited several stockholders in Sapporo; therefore, he was not included in the decision-making process. When the decision to make a public announcement was made, it was already 2 p.m.

At 4 p.m., Osaka City Hall held a press conference to report the food poisoning by Snow Brand's Milk. At 9:45 p.m., the general manager of the Snow Brand West Japan Branch called a press conference to explain its product recall. Approximately 58 hours had passed since the first phone call reached Snow Brand.[8]

On July 1, the number of food poisoning cases had risen to 6,121 in eight of the 47 prefectures (a prefecture is similar to one state in the United States) in Western Japan. Snow Brand Milk Products Company held two press conferences on July 1, 2000. The president, Ishikawa, attended the second press conference along with the Osaka plant manager to apologize to the public. In that conference, the plant manager disclosed that there were contaminants in the valves of the milk products line when the equipment was checked on June 29. Ishikawa shouted at him, "Is that true?" The director of the public relations department also shouted at the plant manager in a loud voice, "Is it a fact or your guess?" Moreover, the contamination of the valves for the milk products line was confirmed before the first press conference that day; however, that fact was not reported at the conference. The Osaka Plant was shut down the same day.[9]

On July 4, the number of cases reported was 9,394. Snow Brand published its official announcement in newspapers, but the manufacture date of possible poisoned products was mistakenly reported in the announcement. In another press conference, held on the 4th, a managing director replied to the questions about that mistake about the product date. "There is chaos in the company. It is very difficult to manage accurate information." In addition, it was found that two other milk products caused the food poisoning as well. First, Snow Brand denied that, but the inspection by Osaka City Hall confirmed the product lines for those two products were contaminated. Osaka City Hall ordered Snow Brand to recall those two products and strongly recommended a voluntary recall of all of the products, 56 items, produced at the Osaka Plant. During the press conference, media reporters asked Ishikawa many questions. He replied saying, "I do not know details about the manufacturing. I feel displeased because information did not reach me." Then, finally, Ishikawa shouted at the reporters, "I have not slept!!" His comments were aired on nationwide television.[10]

Osaka Prefecture Police conducted an investigation on the grounds of professional negligence resulting in food poisoning. A police executive commented, "Each person at Snow Brand told a different story. It seems that they do not share information among the plant, the branch and the headquarters. Accurate information from the production front-line may not be reported to the executives."[11]

On July 5, the number of cases finally exceeded 10,000. The next day, Ishikawa announced his resignation. During the press conference, he said, "I sincerely apologize that Snow Brand jeopardized its consumers and society," and "this incident happened because of our overconfidence in our policy and product quality." Ishikawa replied to the questions about the crisis management of Snow Brand by saying, "We have a crisis management manual, but in reality, it was difficult to follow the situation based on the manual." He also admitted that part of the reason may have been due to the company's conceit as the top selling brand. On the other hand, he insisted that the problem was only at the Osaka plant, and did not affect all Snow Brand plants and products. Ishikawa asserted, "We are sure about the quality of our other products."[12]

On July 10, however, Osaka City Hall confirmed that Snow Brand's Osaka Plant recycled its returned and outdated products to manufacture new products. Although technically this practice was not the source of the food poisoning, this finding damaged the entire image of Snow Brand's products.[13]

On July 11, at 11 p.m., Snow Brand announced its decision to voluntarily shut down its 21 plants nationwide. In dual press conferences, originally scheduled for 5 p.m. and conducted at 11 p.m. at the Western Japan Branch and Snow Brand headquarters in Tokyo,[14] reporters' questions were answered. However, at the conference in the West Japan Branch, a spokesperson from Snow Brand replied to questions suggesting that reporters ask for details from the headquarters in Tokyo. On the other hand, at the Tokyo headquarter's conference, a spokesperson suggested that reporters ask for details from the Western Japan Branch. Criticism by the media heated up because of Snow Brand's disorganized media relations.[15]

In addition, since the media could not get a timely response from the company or even fundamental explanation, the reporters tried to collect information from other sources, such as those who had been poisoned, Osaka City Hall or the Osaka Prefecture Police. Both accurate and inaccurate information was reported by the media and led to employee confusion regarding the internal communication from the company.[16] As a result, the employees of Snow Brand did not have the same level of information as the consumers, retailers and media.[17] The tone of media coverage changed. It became sloppy, careless, and insincere. The media started to report the organizational problems of the company, not just the technical mistakes of the company.[18]

On August 4, Kouhei Nishi, who had worked in the company's sales department, became the president. In a press conference, he explained the company's rebuilding plan. Nishi used a different approach with the media and included many visual aids to explain the plans well to the media.[19]

Despite Snow Brand's hopes, on August 18, Osaka City Hall pointed out that one of the sources of the food poisoning came from the Taiki Plant in Hokkaido. City Hall officials concluded that the contaminated milk products were manufactured with powdered milk made at the Taiki Plant. The Taiki Plant was the flagship plant of Snow

Brand. The next day, the Hokkaido government conducted an on-site inspection of the Taiki Plant. The inspectors found that there was an electric power outage accident on March 31, 2000, because freezing snow fell on the electric powerhouse for the plant. During the electric outage, raw milk material for the powdered skim milk remained on the line for three hours. At the time, *staphylococcus aureus* bacteria proliferated, and enterotoxin grew in the milk. However, the plant produced powdered milk as usual after the electric outage. Although plant workers found that the high bacterial count exceeded the company's own safety standards during the quality examination, the plant employees shipped the powdered milk to the Osaka Plant. It is common knowledge for someone who has studied food sanitation that *staphylococcus aureus* bacteria could proliferate during an electric outage in food plants, but the staff of the Taiki plant had not realized that risky connection between the electric outage and the proliferation of *staphylococcus aureus* bacteria until the Hokkaido government and the Hokkaido Prefecture Police confirmed the linkage. On August 23, Snow Brand held a press conference and admitted the contamination of the powdered milk made in the Taiki Plant. Hokkaido Prefecture Police had started an investigation of the Taiki Plant on the grounds of professional negligence resulting in milk poisoning.[20]

On September 26, Snow Brand submitted its business reconstruction plan, but the company was forced to revise the plan several times. Snow Brand's fiscal earnings were expected to show a deficit on March 31, 2001. The number of food poisoning cases was 13,000 in 15 prefectures. Snow Brand's milk poisoning incident was recorded as the worst case of food poisoning in Japanese history.[21] (See Chart 1 and Exhibit 2.)

PROBLEMS

Business Problem—Snow Brand as a Gigantic Top Brand

Snow Brand was a giant in the Japanese Milk Product Market. Although the market was very competitive, the brand image of Snow Brand was well established, and it strongly supported the company's sales. The brand image was composed of two main factors: a high level of manufacturing control process and its birthplace, Hokkaido.

Marketing research shows Snow Brand's high level of manufacturing control processes. The product blind recall survey by Hokuren, which is an association of Hokkaido Agricultural Cooperatives, indicated that Snow Brand placed second in any area in Japan. In each area, the first-place company varied, but Snow Brand always came in second. A director of Hokuren pointed out that this stability was the strength of Snow Brand. He insisted that it was very hard for the milk product companies to provide such a high-quality product in such a wide area. An executive of Meiji, one of Snow Brand's competitors, observed that 70% of respondents in a marketing survey indicated that Snow Brand Milk was the best when they knew the product's name. On the other hand, 70% of respondents indicated that the Meiji product was the best when they did not know the product's name.[22]

Another component of Snow Brand's strong brand equity was its birthplace, Hokkaido. In contemporary Japanese society, Hokkaido is regarded as a beautiful, broad, exotic northern place, which is one of the largest Japanese islands. Hokkaido was famous for its agriculture and fisheries. Hokkaido is also a very popular destination for domestic tourists. Like Florida in the United States, Hokkaido has a high recognition factor. Since the livestock industry is one of the representative industries of Hokkaido, milk products made in Hokkaido or the companies from Hokkaido are attractive to consumers in nationwide markets. As explained in the previous section, Snow Brand was born in Hokkaido, and that fact is widely recognized by consumers. Snow Brand utilized the brand equity of Hokkaido well to strengthen its marketing position.

Snow Brand became a giant brand; however, the company suffered from several problems because of its strong brand equity.

Competition as a Top Brand

Snow Brand owned its distribution company and earned a good reputation through good responses and flexibility in the market. Utilizing that distribution system, Snow Brand established its channels in supermarkets.[23] In the 1970s, milk products companies jumped into tough competition to gain shares of distribution channels in supermarkets, when the number of supermarkets bloomed. After successfully winning the competition, Snow Brand rapidly increased its sales. In 1996, the share of distribution channels for milk products held by Snow Brand were 82.3% for supermarkets, 8.6% for retailers which mainly delivered products door to door, and 9.1% for school lunch programs. Among the top three makers of milk products, Snow Brand, Meiji, and Morinaga, Snow Brand was slightly higher in terms of sales volume supported by its sales in supermarkets. On the other hand, maintaining its share of sales in price-competitive mass merchandise channels put a lot of pressures on Snow Brand. It is necessary for manufacturers to keep providing an enormous volume of products and discounting the trade price to maintain an advantage over the competition. Without following a low margin, high volume policy, Snow Brand could not maintain its share on shelves at supermarkets. This policy overwhelmed the production process. In 1999, Snow Brand fell into second place in the milk market. It was the first time in history for Snow Brand to be beaten by its competitors. Snow Brand became very aggressive in order to regain to the top position, and the quality control was gradually forgotten.[24]

Inertia at the Top

In 1999, Snow Brand was the largest milk product company in the industry, with 6,678 employees. Snow Brand had been the long-term defending champion in the market, even though the competition was tough.[25] This may have fueled overly optimistic thinking among its employees regarding the business. Many of the employees were aware of the company's history, but did not understand the challenge of starting a business in the market. They just knew their company was a strong establishment with a beautiful brand image and well-known products. Arrogance in the company could be one of the reasons why Snow Brand ignored the most fundamental rules for food product safety.[26]

Communication Problem

Physical Factors

It is said that the delay of the initial response to this milk poisoning was due to the absence of executives who were attending a shareholders' meeting in Sapporo (the capital of Hokkaido) on June 28, the day after the occurrence of the event. According to the Public Communication Division, at that time Snow Brand had four branches (Hokkaido, Eastern Japan, Central Japan, and Western Japan) and six regional offices (Hokkaido, Tohoku, Kanto, Chubu, Kansai, and Kyushu) belonging to each branch. For instance, the Western branch contained two regional offices (Kansai and Kyushu) and two quality assurance centers (Kansai and Kyushu); moreover, the Kansai regional office had area marketing and sales divisions with respect to each market: milk, dairy food, frozen food, ice cream, and baby food. Each regional office had a customer service division responsible for certain areas. At the time of the incident, information channels were extremely complicated within the company. An official at the Osaka City Public Health Office stated that "We couldn't understand which office was in charge because of getting faxes from both the Tokyo headquarters and the Western Branch."[27] Takafumi Isomura, Mayor of Osaka City at that time, complained that Snow Brand's announcements were incoherent.[28] For example, when the press required Snow Brand to hold a news conference, the responses of Snow Brand were: "We can't figure out whether the skim milk was made in the Taiki Plant [Tokyo headquarters]" or "We cannot deal with the issue of Taiki Plant since it is under the control of the dairy production division at the Tokyo headquarters [Western Branch]."[29] When the president of Snow Brand at the time, Tetsuro Ishikawa, was informed of the valve contamination in the Osaka Plant at the press conference, this was clear evidence of the confusion in the information channels (see Exhibits 3 and 4).

Structural Factors

Generally in Japan, personnel are moved between divisions every two to four years in order to foster executive trainees as generalists in business. The Japanese tradition of lifelong employment allows for this rotation system. For example, it is not unusual for cadres to transfer from sales to public relations, and then to the legal section. New recruits who are expected to be executives in the future are also required to train for approximately six months, which allows them to understand the overall business. For instance, a newspaper writer would receive on-the-job training and would be expected to deliver the newspaper. In this way, cadres get to grasp their company's main and related business, to share the basic knowledge about them, and to build a personal connection for information exchange within their organization. This rotation system contributed to the high growth of Japanese companies after World War II. However, this system has disadvantages. It is difficult to train specialists and thus the management cannot obtain professional advice.[30] Therefore some Japanese firms have begun to train professionals due to the competition in the global market. At Snow Brand, according to a former employee, personnel exchanges between different departments were seldom done because of the rationale that the staff should display its originality in each profession.[31] This may result in overvalue of an employees' profession, ignorance of their outside domain within the company, and loss of organizational flexibility. While generalist-oriented personnel strategy anticipates sharing information through experience and networking, specialist-oriented strategy needs more internal communication, such as training, education, and information exchange, for figuring out the organization and sharing of knowledge and information.

Some point out the lack of the sales experience of President Ishikawa, whose only experience was in financial affairs, as the reason for a sequence of failures in response to the food poisoning. In 1986, Snow Brand also stopped the tradition of handing out Sato's "Announcement to all employees" to newcomers. Consequently, "the lessons of Yakumo" were not utilized and all of Snow Brand's employees became overconfident and dependent on technology. After the 2000 food poisoning incident, Snow Brand decided to start dairy practical training for new employees because it realized that employees needed to have basic knowledge related to hygiene management and production processes.[32]

Cultural Factors

The fundamental causes of the food poisoning incident were that the plant manager and manufacturing chief in the Taiki Plant did not follow basic food safety rules established by the company and shirked the responsibility of disposing of the tainted dry milk. This led to the reuse of the tainted dry milk, covering-up of the facts, and intentional record alteration. The media leveled accusations against Snow Brand for its lack of flexibility due to its corporate culture. Favors were exchanged between the employees to improve their communication. The lack of flexibility and the exchanging of favors which created a better working environment may be related to Japanese general cultural aspects, such as collectivism, high levels of Uncertainty Avoidance, tendency of large Power Distance and emphasis on harmonization.[33] Then, emphasizing of using non-verbal communication, people encouraged maintaining harmonious interpersonal relations and group solidarity and discouraged self-assertions.[34] Warnings, concerns, or negative comments against the organization are perceived as a violation of harmonization, and this superior manner results in organizational inflexibility. The behavior of the staff in the Taiki Plant previously mentioned can be considered part of Uncertainty Avoidance. Favor exchanging is what has become of collectivism where a group is given priority over an individual. Although they normally do not emerge, these organizational dispositions of Snow Brand seriously affect its business once a problem happens.

It would be fair to say that the food poisoning would not have spread and the number of people poisoned could have been minimized if Snow Brand's communication process worked. What were the fundamental mistakes in terms of its communication? What kind of organizational culture should the company have? What did the company not prepare for the crisis?

APPENDIX

CHART 1—Sequence of the food poisoning event

2000

June 27 a.m.	•	First phone call from a victim's family reached Snow Brand Western Japan Branch
	•	Osaka City Hall received several reports about food poisoning
June 28 a.m.	•	Snow Brand general stockholders meeting at Sapporo, Hokkaido
p.m.	•	On-site investigation of Osaka Plant by Osaka City Hall
evening	•	Osaka City Hall asked Snow Brand to conduct a recall
June 29 8 a.m.	•	The recall of the production was decided in Sapporo
2 p.m.	•	Executives decide to make a public announcement
4 p.m.	•	Press conference by Osaka City Hall to report the food poisoning case of Snow Brand
9:45 p.m.	•	Press conference by Snow Brand Western Japan Branch
July 1 a.m.	•	Snow Brand confirmed the existence of contaminated valve in Osaka plant on June 29, but did not report it at the first press conference
p.m.	•	The CEO, Ishikawa, attended the second press conference of the day
	•	Osaka Plant was shut down
	•	6,121 victims were reported
July 4	•	Snow Brand published an official announcement in the newspapers
	•	All products made by the Osaka Plant were recalled
	•	9,394 victims were reported
July 5	•	Number of victims exceeded 10,000
July 6	•	The CEO, Ishikawa, resigned
July 11	•	Snow Brand announced 21 plants nationwide were shut down
Aug. 4	•	The new CEO, Nishi, takes over. He held a press conference and explained the rebuilding plan of the company
Aug. 18	•	Taiki plant in Hokkaido was pointed out as one source for food poisoning
Aug. 19	•	Hokkaido government and Prefecture Police conducted an on-site investigation of Taiki Plant
Aug. 23	•	Snow Brand admitted contaminated skim milk was shipped from Taiki Plant before the food poisoning outbreak
Sep. 26	•	Snow Brand released the business reconstruction plan
2001 **March 31**	•	Snow Brand reported fiscal deficit

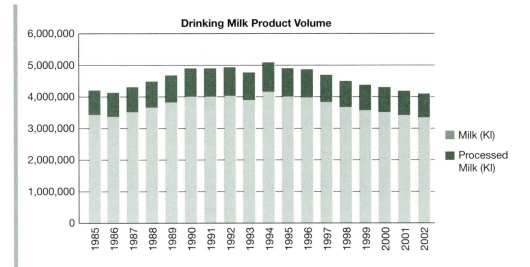

EXHIBIT 1 — Drinking Milk Product Volume

Source: Ministry of Agriculture, Forestry and Fisheries of Japan, 2003. *Gyunyu Nyuseihin Toukei* [Milk product statistics]. Retrieved January 1, 2004, from http://www.maff.go.jp/www/info/bun05.html.

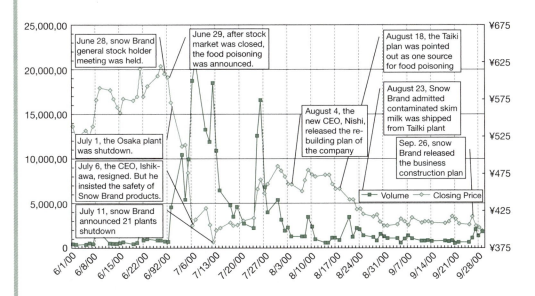

EXHIBIT 2 — Snow Brand Stock Price and Volume

Source: Toyo Keizai Inc., 2003. *Kigyu JhoHo 2262, Yukijirushi* [Corporate Information 2262, Snow Brand]. Retrieved January 1, 2004, from http://profile.yahoo.co.jp/biz/independent/2262.html.

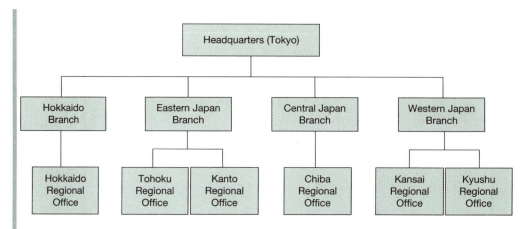

EXHIBIT 3—Snow Brand Organizational Structure

Source: Snow Brand Public Communication Department.

EXHIBIT 4—Japan Map

Years ended March 31					
(Millions of Yen)	2003	2002	2001	2000	1999
Net Sales	727,071	1,164,716	1,140,763	1,287,769	1,263,727
Cost of Sales	584,170	929,072	914,475	980,912	958,383
Net Income (Loss)	−27,091	−71,741	−52,925	−28,545	3,079
Total Assets	284,910	581,356	567,914	576,766	543,122
Stockholders' Equity	34,396	30,371	64,506	118,608	139,807
Number of Employees	4,591	12,404	15,326	15,127	15,343

EXHIBIT 5—Financial Highlights (Consolidated)—Snow Brand Milk Products Co., Ltd., and its Consolidated Subsidiaries

Notes: Snow Brand Milk Products Co., Ltd. conducted a stock binding (reverse stock split), binding two shares into one share of common stock, on August 1, 2002. The following per share figures are computed as if the stock binding (reverse stock split) had been conducted on April 1.

Source: Snow Brand Milk Product Co., Ltd. (2003). Annual Report 2003. Retrieved January 1, 2003, from http://www.snowbrand.co.jp/ir/index.htm.

NOTES

1 Sankei Shimbun Shuzaihan. (2002). *Brand wa naze ochitaka: Yukijirushi, Sogo, Mitsubishi Jidousha, jiken no shinso* [Why did the brand reach the bottom?: the truth of Snow Brand, Sogo, and Mitsubishi Motors Cases]. Tokyo: Kadokawa-shoten, pp. 44 and 45.

2 Milk Museum, *Statistics and history of milk* by Naraken Nyu Gyou Shogyou Kumiai. Retrieved January 1, 2004, from http://www.asm.ne.jp/~milknara/milktown/museum/museum.htm.

3 Milk Museum, *Statistics and history of milk*.

4 The Ministry of Agriculture, Forestry and Fisheries of Japan. (2003). *Gyunyu Nyuseihin Toukei* [Milk product statistics]. Retrieved January 1, 2004, from http://www.maff.go.jp/www/info/bun05.html

5 Milk Museum, *Statistics and history of milk*.

6 Hokkaido Shinbun Shuzaihan. (2002). *Kensho, "Yukijirushi" houkai: sonotoki, naniga okottaka* [Investigation of Snow Brand's disruption: What happened at that time]. Tokyo: Kodansha; Sankei Shimbun Shuzaihan. *Brand wa naze ochitaka*.

7 Hokkaido Shinbun Shuzaihan. *Kensho, "Yukijirushi" houkai*; Sankei Shimbun Shuzaihan. *Brand wa naze ochitaka*.

8 Hokkaido Shinbun Shuzaihan. *Kensho, "Yukijirushi" houkai*; Sankei Shimbun Shuzaihan. *Brand wa naze ochitaka*.

9 Hokkaido Shinbun Shuzaihan. *Kensho, "Yukijirushi" houkai*; Sankei Shimbun Shuzaihan. *Brand wa naze ochitaka*.

10 Hokkaido Shinbun Shuzaihan. *Kensho, "Yukijirushi" houkai*; Sankei Shimbun Shuzaihan. *Brand wa naze ochitaka*.

11 Hokkaido Shinbun Shuzaihan. *Kensho, "Yukijirushi" houkai*; Sankei Shimbun Shuzaihan. *Brand wa naze ochitaka*.

12 Hokkaido Shinbun Shuzaihan. *Kensho, "Yukijirushi" houkai*; Sankei Shimbun Shuzaihan. *Brand wa naze ochitaka*.

13 Hokkaido Shinbun Shuzaihan. *Kensho, "Yukijirushi" houkai*; Sankei Shimbun Shuzaihan. *Brand wa naze ochitaka*.

14 Hokkaido Shinbun Shuzaihan. *Kensho, "Yukijirushi" houkai*.

15 Ono, T. (2001). *Naze Fushoji wa Okoruka* [Why do scandals happen?]. *Jissen Kigyo Kouhou* [Practice: Corporate Public Relations], pp. 39–51. Hyogo, Japan: Kwansei Gakuin University Press.

16 Ono, T. *Naze Fushoji wa Okoruka.*

17 Takahashi, J. (2000, September 18). *Yukijirushi Shain no Atsuku Nagai Natsu* [A long, tough summer for Snow Brand employees]. *Asahi Shimbun Weekly AERA,* 30–33.

18 Ono, T. *Naze Fushoji wa Okoruka.*

19 Sankei Shimbun Shuzaihan. *Brand wa naze ochitaka.*

20 Hokkaido Shinbun Shuzaihan. *Kensho, "Yukijirushi" houkai*; Sankei Shimbun Shuzaihan. *Brand wa naze ochitaka.*

21 Hokkaido Shinbun Shuzaihan. *Kensho, "Yukijirushi" houkai*; Sankei Shimbun Shuzaihan. *Brand wa naze ochitaka.*

22 Sankei Shimbun Shuzaihan. *Brand wa naze ochitaka.*

23 Kaneda, S. (2000, June 7). *Yukijirushi Shokuchudoku jiken wa "Kozo fushoku" da* [The food poisoning by Snow Brand is because of the company's structural decay]. *Nikkei Business,* 8–10.

24 Hokkaido Shinbun Shuzaihan. *Kensho, "Yukijirushi" houkai*; Sankei Shimbun Shuzaihan. *Brand wa naze ochitaka.*

25 Inoshita, K. & Hasegawa, T. (2000, August 5). *Sochiki wo Ohu Kinou Fuzen. Kyoko no Brand "Yukijirushi"* [A functional disorder over companies. A fictitious brand "Snow Brand"]. *Shukan Toyo Keizai,* 62–68.

26 Sankei Shimbun Shuzaihan. *Brand wa naze ochitaka.*

27 Inoshita & Hasegawa. *Sochiki wo Ohu Kinou Fuzen,* p. 63.

28 Hokkaido Shinbun Shuzaihan. *Kensho, "Yukijirushi" houkai.*

29 Sankei Shimbun Shuzaihan. *Brand wa naze ochitaka,* p. 23.

30 Inoue, T. (2003). An overview of public relations in Japan and the self-correction concept. In K. Sriramesh & D. Vercic (Eds.), *The global public relations handbook: Theory, research and practice,* pp. 68–85. Mahwah, NJ: Lawrence Erlbaum Associates.

31 Sankei Shimbun Shuzaihan. *Brand wa naze ochitaka.*

32 Sankei Shimbun Shuzaihan. *Brand wa naze ochitaka,*

33 Hofstede, G. (2001). *Culture's consequences, comparing values, behaviors, institutions, and organizations across nations* (2nd ed.). Thousand Oaks, CA: Sage Publications.

34 *Japan: An Illustrated Encyclopedia.* (1996). *Keys to the Japanese Hearts and Soul.* Tokyo: Kodansha International.

DISCUSSION QUESTIONS

1. Why do you think it took Snow Brand executives so long to recall their poisoned milk?

2. What actions would you take if you had discovered contamination in the values of the milk product line?

3. What pressures do workers face that might encourage them to continue to produce a product when they knew it exceeded the company's safety levels for bacteria and fail to report it?

4. What would you recommend to Snow Brand regarding how to rebuild their reputation after this product failure?

5. Did Snow Brand suffer from an ethical problem or an organizational problem? Explain your answer.

6. The case attributes part of the failure of Snow Brand to respond to the contamination crisis as originating from Japanese culture. What is your assessment of this position? Do you see any parallels with other recalls for Japanese companies, such as the recent recalls by Toyota?

Building the Ethical Company

Building Ethics at the Corporate Level: Managing the Ethical Climate

LEARNING OBJECTIVES

After reading this chapter you should be able to:

- Understand the concept of ethical climate as a type of work climate
- Identify the different types of ethical climates and be able to explain how each type works
- Understand how ethical climates affect ethical decision-making and behaviors in organizations
- Explain the differences between the general organizational culture and the ethical climate
- Know how to create and maintain different ethical climate types
- Understand how to identify the ethical climate in your organization

PREVIEW BUSINESS ETHICS INSIGHT

Caring Climates: General Mills and Synovus

How do companies promote a caring climate? A caring ethical climate is when a company values the welfare of people, both inside and outside the organization, more than other organizational objectives.

For over 20 years, Synovus, a financial holding company, has been on *Fortune*'s "100 Best Companies to Work for" list. Synovus has over 13,000 employees in 700 locations throughout the U.S. yet they manage to create a team feeling that makes work have a family atmosphere. Creating this climate starts at the top with Senior Vice President Marty Grueber, who is responsible for external community involvement and for the quality of the work lives of team members. Symbolizing this team climate is the Synovus motto: "It's a team and we love each other." Consider these values from their website:

Putting People First. Passion. Humility. Values. Family: These are not just words to us, but a way of life at Synovus. We call it the "Culture of the Heart," and we believe it is the key to being a great company. It's a special spirit and a way of work that leads each of us to do great things each day.

People First: People are our top priority. This is what makes the Synovus family special. It is what makes us a great place to work. Our number one responsibility is for our team members. If we take care of our people, our people will take care of the business.

According to SVP Grueber, about putting people first: "it's the right thing to do, but it's the smart thing to do."

General Mills, a multinational food company, also strives to create a caring climate. Its focus is on a holistic view of the employees that takes the person into account for all decisions. For example, they encourage employees not to always put work first but to consider family needs. According to Sand Ohlsson, the Vice President of Human Resources, the key factor in considering someone for a promotion is to ask the person, "What impact will this have on your family?" Ohlsson describes General Mills as a "very nurturing" climate. The belief that a caring climate increases commitment to the organization is one reason why its turnover is less than half the industry average.

Based on http://www.synovus.com/index.cfm; Great Places to Work Institute, Inc. "Family feelings: General Mills and Synovus," December 1, 2006.

The Preview Business Ethics Insight above shows how companies can create different types of climates or cultures that influence ethical decision-making. For General Mills and Synovus it is clear that people in the company are expected to have a high concern for others. The leadership supports this view and the employees react with loyalty to the company. The Preview Business Ethics Insight shows how critical it is for companies to encourage an organizational culture that emphasizes caring.

Given the importance of ethical climate and culture, in this chapter we will learn about both. First, you will learn about ethical climate and the various types of climate in existence. You will see that there are varieties of ethical climate types that organizations have. Each type provides the members of the organization guides to how to make ethical decisions. Second, you will also read about organizational culture and how it differs from ethical climates. You will also become aware of the many ways of promoting the right types of ethical culture in the organization.

AN OVERVIEW OF ETHICAL CLIMATE

An Ethical Climate Model

Ethical climate is a type of work climate. **Work climates** represent the shared perceptions of procedures, policies, and practices, both formal and informal, of the organization.[1] Researchers have identified an assortment of work climate such as climates for innovation,[2] creativity,[3] and warmth and support.[4] Ethical climate is a work climate that reflects the organizational procedures, policies, and practices with moral consequences.

The **ethical climate** represents what organizational members believe are the forms of ethical reasoning or behavior and the expected standards or norms for ethical decision-making within the company.[5] That is, the ethical climate tells you what constitutes right behavior, and thus becomes a psychological mechanism through which ethical issues are managed. Ethical climate not only influences which moral criteria members use to understand, weigh, and resolve ethical dilemmas but also tells organization members which stakeholders to consider in ethical decision-making.[6] As such, the ethical climate in your organization is part of the organizational culture that represents how people in the organization believe ethical decisions are made and how ethical decisions should be made.

Formally, ethical climate is defined as "the shared perception of what is considered correct behavior in the organization, and how ethical situations should be handled in the organization."[7] It is important to remember that the idea of an ethical climate as used here is not what an employee believes is ethical for him/herself but what is expected of them by the organization—the leadership, colleagues, and friends. Thus, climate represents shared norms and values of what you "should" do and what you are expected to do in your organization when confronted with an ethical dilemma.

An ethical climate can differ by team, department, or the whole organization. Sport teams and social organizations also have ethical climates. Think about the organizations where you have worked or joined. To get a picture of an ethical climate you can consider questions like the following:

- What behaviors do organizational members believe are ethical in the company?
- What issues do people consider relevant to guide their ethical decision-making?
- What criteria do people use to understand and resolve these issues?
- How similar are the organizational members in their behaviors and decision-making styles related to ethics.

Ethical Climate Types

An organization's ethical climate is more complex than a single perspective on how to behave ethically in the organization. Rather, an ethical climate can be mapped into a variety of different sub-dimensions, the mixture of which is unique to each organization.

481

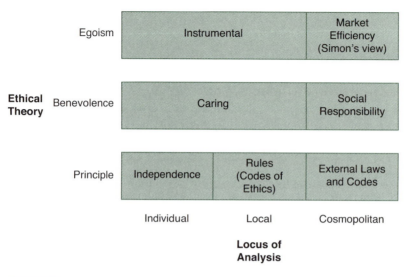

		Individual	Local	Cosmopolitan

	Egoism	Instrumental		Market Efficiency (Simon's view)
Ethical Theory	Benevolence	Caring		Social Responsibility
	Principle	Independence	Rules (Codes of Ethics)	External Laws and Codes

Locus of Analysis

EXHIBIT 11.1—Ethical Climate Types

Nearly 25 years ago, Victor and Cullen introduced what is perhaps the most famous model of the types of ethical climate. Since then it has been the dominant way researchers have looked at ethical climate. Exhibit 11.1 shows a diagram of the types of ethical climates based on their work and the numerous research studies done since the model was developed.[8] These ethical climates represent the different ways employees identify the forms of reasoning they are expected to use in organizational decision-making.

To understand how Exhibit 11.1 maps ethical climates types you need to look at each axis. In the vertical axis you see the ethical criteria that help guide possible ethical decision-making in the organization. These very much match the major ethical theories of egoism, benevolence, and deontology (principle). Basically, these criteria mean that, when faced with an ethical issue, you can take into account what is good for one's self (egoism), take into account what is good for others (benevolence), and take into account rules of behavior (principles). The horizontal axis further defines the ethical climate types by identifying the groups that are considered when making ethical decisions in the organization. Using the ethical criteria, people can make ethical decisions taking a personal perspective (individual), a local perspective (such as the team or the company), or an external perspective, what we call the cosmopolitan. Next we describe each climate type in a little more detail.

Principled climates occur when the organization has norms that encourage people to make ethical decisions based on a set of standards. In terms of the reference level, people in some organizations may make ethical decisions based on external codes such as a professional code of conduct. For example, you can see the classic ethical code of physicians, called the Hippocratic Oath, in the Business Ethics Insight on page 483. Although the Hippocratic Oath has evolved to deal with modern medicine, it still provides guiding principles for those who work in the medical profession. So, for example, the ethical climate of a hospital may be represented by values from the

BUSINESS ETHICS INSIGHT

Hippocratic Oath: Ethical Principles for a Physician's Work

I swear by Apollo the Physician and Asclepius and Hygieia and Panaceia and all the gods, and goddesses, making them my witnesses, that I will fulfill according to my ability and judgment this oath and this covenant:

To hold him who has taught me this art as equal to my parents and to live my life in partnership with him, and if he is in need of money to give him a share of mine, and to regard his offspring as equal to my brothers in male lineage and to teach them this art—if they desire to learn it—without fee and covenant; to give a share of precepts and oral instruction and all the other learning to my sons and to the sons of him who has instructed me and to pupils who have signed the covenant and have taken the oath according to medical law, but to no one else.

I will apply dietic measures for the benefit of the sick according to my ability and judgment; I will keep them from harm and injustice.

I will neither give a deadly drug to anybody if asked for it, nor will I make a suggestion to this effect. In purity and holiness I will guard my life and my art.

I will not use the knife, not even on sufferers from stone, but will withdraw in favor of such men as are engaged in this work.

Whatever houses I may visit, I will come for the benefit of the sick, remaining free of all intentional injustice, of all mischief and in particular of sexual relations with both female and male persons, be they free or slaves.

What I may see or hear in the course of treatment or even outside of the treatment in regard to the life of men, which on no account one must spread abroad, I will keep myself holding such things shameful to be spoken about.

If I fulfill this oath and do not violate it, may it be granted to me to enjoy life and art, being honored with fame among all men for all time to come; if I transgress it and swear falsely, may the opposite of all this be my lot.

Based on Translation from the Greek by Ludwig Edelstein. From *The Hippocratic Oath: Text, translation, and interpretation, by Ludwig Edelstein*. Baltimore: Johns Hopkins Press, 1943. http://www.pbs.org/wgbh/nova/doctors/oath_classical.html.

Hippocratic Oath or its more modern renditions. Other cosmopolitan principles that may guide ethical decision-making in organizations might include following national law or religious laws such as the Muslim *Sharia* or the Christian Bible. Consider the Business Ethics Insight on page 483.

To the degree that a hospital, for example, has expectations that physicians follow codes like the Hippocratic Oath, this would represent a principled ethical climate based on **law and code**.

Companies also develop their own **ethical codes** conduct in an attempt to identify the ethical principles that are used to guide the ethical decision-making within their organizations. In this sense, for a local principled ethical climate people are expected to follow the company's code of conduct. For example, with regard to bribery, if the code says one cannot take a gift worth more than $10, the "right" thing to do when offered something more expensive by a possible supplier is to refuse the gift. Codes of conduct increasingly being implemented by organizations in the contemporary corporate landscape appeal primarily to this dimension of ethical climate, which we call the rules of ethical climate.

Professor Charles Kerns categorizes company ethical codes into three types:[9]

- Type 1. **Inspirational–Idealistic** codes focus on broad virtuous themes such as "Be honest," "Show integrity in all matters," "Practice wise decision-making." They do not identify specific behaviors or situations but instead give broad guiding principles that can be applied when faced with an ethical dilemma. Perhaps the most famous of this type of principle guide is the Johnson & Johnson Credo shown in Exhibit 11.2.
- Type 2. **Regulatory** codes of conduct to specify how to behave in specific situations. This is what Kerns calls a "do and don't" approach. The Coca-Cola code shown in Exhibit 11.3 represents this type of code.
- Type 3. **Educational/Learning-Oriented** codes of conduct are something of a cross between the inspirational–idealistic code and the regulatory codes. It suggests guides for decision-making and behavioral reactions when faced with ethically challenging situations.

Codes of ethical conduct help establish the local principled ethical climate in organizations. However, without managerial leadership, example-setting, and enforcement they will not be very effective in creating a principled ethical climate.

The last principal ethical climate, called **independent**, has norms that support ethical decision-making based on personal morality. In this sense, each individual is expected to behave in a way that he or she personally considers ethical. Organizations that promote this type of climate often attempt to recruit people who are similar in terms of what they believe are the correct ways to behave ethically.

Caring climates occur when the organization has norms that encourage people to make ethical decisions based on looking out for the welfare of others, particularly for team members and those within the company. In most organizations with caring climates, people believe that the right thing to do is to look out for the welfare of friends and co-workers. The Preview Ethics Insight showed two companies that are

Our Credo

We believe our first responsibility is to the doctors, nurses and patients,
to mothers and fathers and all others who use our products and services,
In meeting their needs everything we do must be of high quality.
We must constantly strive to reduce our costs
in order to maintain reasonable prices.
Customers' orders must be serviced promptly and accurately.
Our suppliers and distributors must have an opportunity
to make a fair profit.

We are responsible to our employees,
the men and women who work with us throughout the world.
Everyone must be considered as an individual.
We must respect their dignity and recognize their merit.
They must have a sense of security in their jobs.
Compensation must be fair and adequate,
and working conditions clean, orderly and safe.
We must be mindful of ways to help our employees fulfill
their family responsibilities.
Employees must feel free to make suggestions and complaints.
There must be equal opportunity for employment, development
and advancement for those qualified.
We must provide competent management,
and their actions must be just and ethical.

We are responsible to the communities in which we live and work
and to the world community as well.
We must be good citizens—support good works and charities
and bear our fair share of taxes.
We must encourage civic improvements and better health and education.
We must maintain in good order
the property we are privileged to use,
protecting the environment and natural resources.

Our final responsibility is to our stockholders.
Business must make a sound profit.
We must experiment with new ideas.
Research must be carried on, innovative programs developed
and mistakes paid for.
New equipment must be purchased, new facilities provided
and new products launched.
Reserves must be created to provide for adverse times.
When we operate according to these principles,
the stockholders should realize a fair return.

Johnson & Johnson

EXHIBIT 11.2—Johnson & Johnson Credo

- Employees must follow the law wherever they are around the world.

- Employees must avoid conflicts of interest. Be aware of appearances.

- Financial records, both for internal activities and external transactions, must be timely and accurate.

- Company assets, including computers, materials, and work time, must not be used for personal benefit.

- Customers and suppliers must be dealt with fairly and at arm's length.

- Employees must never attempt to bribe or improperly influence a government official.

- Employees must safeguard the Company's non-public information.

- Violations of the Code include asking other employees to violate the Code, not reporting a Code violation, or failing to cooperate in a Code investigation.

- Violating the Code will result in discipline. Discipline will vary depending on the circumstances and may include, alone or in combination, a letter of reprimand, demotion, loss of merit increase, bonus or stock options, suspension, or even termination.

- Under the Code, certain actions require written approval by your Principal Manager. The Principal Manager is your Division President, Group President, Corporate function head, or the General Manager of your operating unit.

- For those who are themselves Principal Managers, written approvals must come from the General Counsel and Chief Financial Officer. Written approvals for executive officers and directors must come from the Board of Directors or its designated committee.

- If you have questions about any situation, ask. Always ask.

EXHIBIT 11.3—Coca-Cola Code

BUSINESS ETHICS INSIGHT

Malden Mills: Too Much of a Caring Ethical Climate?

Malden Mills, a family-run and -operated company in Malden, Massachusetts, grew by 200% in the 1980s and 1990s as Polarfleece, a 100% polyester, capable of wicking moisture away from the body while still providing warmth, drove up sales. As Polarfleece became a popular fabric for high-performance athletic and aerobic apparel, outerwear producers such as L.L. Bean, Eddie Bauer, and Patagonia flooded Malden with orders. The product was even adapted for military use. *Time* magazine named Polartec, the trade name for Polarfleece, as one of the greatest inventions of the twentieth century.

At a time when the textile industry in New England was in sharp decline, Malden Mills was booming. While outdated factories and increased labor costs led many companies to abandon the area and relocate to lower-cost countries, Malden had over 2,000 employees and contributed approximately $100 million a year into the local economy.

Unfortunately, on December 11, 1995, while owner Aaron Feuerstein was celebrating his 70th birthday with family and friends at a Boston restaurant, a devastating fire destroyed much of the factory and injured 33 employees. The explosion-sparked fire destroyed three of the company's nine buildings and caused an estimated $500 million in damages. The fire was not only a disaster for Malden but it was also a potential disaster for an entire community.

Many predicted that Aaron Feuerstein would take the $300 million insurance money and relocate or dissolve the business. This was an opportunity to follow the industry to lower-cost areas with cheaper labor or for the 70-year-old Feuerstein just to retire. Feuerstein shocked many when he immediately vowed to rebuild and announced just three nights later that Malden Mills would reopen on January 2. Moreover, he intended to pay all employees their regular salaries (at a cost of $1.5 million per week) for the next 30 days, possibly longer, and that he would continue health benefits for 90 days. This choice gained him international and national recognition for putting employees first.

It cost Feuerstein $25 million to keep his employees on the payroll. In spite of Malden's continued support of health benefits and exoneration from blame, the injured employees also sued the company and Feuerstein settled for an undisclosed amount. Rebuilding a state-of-the-art plant, the first new textile mill in New England in more than 100 years, cost an additional $100 million. This was all too much for Malden. By 2001, Feuerstein was forced to file for bankruptcy due to the cost of financing the rebuilding project. He struggled until 2003 to maintain family control of his company. Although he failed, he told reporters, "We insist the business must be profitable . . . But we also insist a business must have responsibility for its workers, for the community and the environment. It has a social obligation to figure out a strategy, which will be able to permit workers to make a living wage. There's a responsibility to the workforce, to this community." By July of 2004, Aaron Feuerstein, at 78, was fired as Malden Mills' CEO by the new owners.

Based on http://www.fundinguniverse.com/company-histories/Malden-Mills-Industries-Inc-Company-History.html; *Boston Globe,* December 12, 13, 14, 1995; September 14, 2003; January 29 and July 27, 2004; *Lawrence Eagle Tribune,* November 15, 2001; *Forward,* "Fabled mill owner works to manufacture a miracle," July 25, 2003; Diesenhouse, Susan, "A textile maker thrives by breaking all the rules," *New York Times,* July 24, 1994: Herszenhorn, David M., "A plume of hope rises from factory ashes . . ." *New York Times,* December 16, 1995; Teal, Thomas, "Not a fool; Not a saint," *Fortune,* November 11, 1996; Owens, Mitchell, "A mill community comes back to life," *New York Times,* December 26, 1996: Rotenier, Nancy, "The golden fleece," *Forbes,* May 24, 1993; Lee, Melissa, "Malden looks spiffy in New England textile gloom," *Wall Street Journal,* November 10, 1995: Goldberg, Carey, "A promise is kept," *New York Times,* September 16, 1997.

dominated by caring climates. In addition, an organization may have a climate that supports caring for stakeholders outside of the organization. Recent research[10] suggests that organizations with more caring cosmopolitan climates—that is those with norms and values for caring directed outside their organization—are more likely to see social responsibility as something done to benefit people rather than help make the organization more profitable.

The Business Ethics Insight on pages 486–7 discusses Malden Mills and its CEO owner Aaron Feuerstein. Mr. Feuerstein had perhaps one of the most caring organizations and he held to those expectations under the most trying times by keeping his employees on the payroll even after his factory was destroyed by fire. However, perhaps because he failed to keep an eye on the bottom line, Malden Mills eventually was forced into bankruptcy and employees and other stakeholders eventually lost out. After reading the Business Ethics Insight, how do you react to Mr. Feuerstein's approach to his organization?

Organizations having an **instrumental ethical climate** see their organizational unit as having norms and expectations that encourage ethical decision-making from an egoistic perspective. What is more, the actor perceives that self-interest guides behavior, even to the possible detriment of others. One believes that decisions are made that serve the organization's interests or provide personal benefits.[11] Even when considered in a variety of contexts, studies consistently show that instrumental climates are the least preferred.[12]

Instrumental ethical climates occur when the organization has norms that encourage people to define right and wrong in terms of the consequences to one's self. Thus, when faced with an ethical dilemma people are expected to make decisions based on what best serves self-interest. Researchers have found that, within organizations, one's self most often means the organization rather than the individual. As such, an instrumental ethical climate often means what you are expected to do is to look out for what is best for company profit.

An instrumental climate is actually close to what the Nobel-Prize-winning economist Milton Friedman argued: the only moral obligation of business is to make a profit and the only constraint is to obey the law.[13] Although on first glance such an ethical climate may seem inherently unethical, free market economists such as Friedman argue that, when acting under the rule of law, companies acting in their own self-interest create an efficient economic system. The market selects out the best companies that survive and profit, and everyone is better off.

BUSINESS ETHICS INSIGHT

Enron's Instrumental Ethical Climate

Enron is a classic business ethics case where questionable and extremely complicated financial practices first created a company that seemed impervious to failure and eventually imploded as revelations of debt and lack of transparency caused its stock to become worthless. The pain for many stakeholders is still felt today in lost pensions, investments, and jobs. However, our concern here is the culture that led to such practices. Insights from some of those commenting on Enron's culture reveal a highly instrumental ethical climate with perhaps the worst outcomes from such climates.

Jeffrey Skilling, the author of many of the complex and questionable financial deals, encountered Enron first as a consultant, and then, after being hired by the company, eventually became CEO. Skilling started early to change the corporate culture of Enron. The company hired the brightest and best graduates from top MBA schools. Skilling wanted extremely aggressive and competitive people who prosper in a "win at all cost" environment with little concern for rules. If you performed, regardless of methods, rewards were extremely high. As a former Enron vice president described it: "The moral of this story is break the rules, you can cheat, you can lie, but as long as you make money, it's all right"

To cement this culture, Skilling formed the performance review committee (PRC), which many felt was the harshest employee-ranking system in the country. Some called it the "rank and yank" system—ranking ten employees and yanking, or dismissing, the bottom three. Most associates felt that the only real performance measure was the profits they produced. Employees' ratings were based on a scale of 1 to 5. Getting a 5 pretty much meant you were fired within six months. Not only was that pressure-laden, but also performance reviews were public. Poor performance resulted in public ridicule and likely later firing through the "rank and yank" system. Turnover was nearly 15% every year.

To achieve top rankings and keep their jobs, employees became very motivated to "do deals" and increase earnings. The result was a corporate culture of fierce internal competition that prized immediate gratification over long-term results. Paranoia and secrecy flourished. For high performers, Skilling used merit-based bonuses without any cap, permitting traders to "eat what they killed." With this selection and compensation system, the team approach previously part of the Enron culture deteriorated. Self-interest becomes the dominant climate.

According to Wharton ethics professor Thomas Donaldson, "These practices built up a culture of backbiting and a very destructive atmosphere." The result was that, in spite of supplications that the company was going down, "a lot of people did not want to hear the straight truth" with the company eventually collapsing.

Based on Diane Huie Balay. n.d. "Close-up: Failed ethics: Enron debacle offers lessons." United Methodist News Service; David Burkus. 2011. "A tale of two cultures: Why culture trumps core values in building ethical organizations." *Journal of Values Based Leadership*, 4, Winter/Spring. http://www.valuesbasedleadershipjournal.com/issues/vol4issue1/tale_2 culture.php; A.J. Schuler. n.d. "Does corporate culture matter? The case of Enron." www.SchulerSolutions.com; Sims, R.R. and Brinkman, J. 2003. "Enron ethics (or: Culture matters more than codes)." *Journal of Business Ethics*, 45, 3, 243–256; C. William Thomas. 2002. "The rise and fall of Enron: When a company looks too good to be true, it usually is." *Journal of Accountancy*, April. http://www.journalofaccountancy.com/Issues/2002/Apr/TheRiseAndFallOfEnron.htm

Country	Summary of Findings
Belgium	Ethical climates have organizational influences
Canada	Existence of ethical climates in non-profit organizations
China	Ethical climates affect personal ethical decisions
Denmark	Concept of ethical climates validated in Danish sample
Hong Kong	Ethical climates affected organizational citizenship behaviors
India	Ethical climates affect manager manipulative behaviors
Israel	Ethical climates affect employee work misconduct
Japan	Comparison of ethical climates between U.S.A. and Japan
Mexico	Ethical climates influence commitment to companies
Nigeria	Ethical climates exist in Nigerian banks
Philippines	National and professional culture influence ethical climates
Russia	Ethical climates affect success and ethical behavior
Singapore	Ethical climates affect job satisfaction
South Korea	Ethical climates affect job satisfaction and commitment
Taiwan	Ethical climates affect job satisfaction
Turkey	Ethical climates affect both commitment and bullying

EXHIBIT 11.4 — Ethical Climates in the Global Environment

However, an instrumental climate comes with risks. Consider the Business Ethics Insight on pages 488–489, which looks at some of instrumental climate characteristics of Enron, perhaps one of the more classic cases of ethics failure.

As the Business Ethics Insight shows, an instrumental ethical climate comes with severe risks to the company. Because of the emphasis on the self, such climates can encourage very self-interested behaviors that may hurt the organization. Later you will see that different ethical climate types can have widely different consequences for companies. Think about what you would have done if you worked for Enron.

Although the ethical climate has received significant attention within mostly Western nations, is it relevant in a global environment? Exhibit 11.4 shows the list of countries that ethical climates have been studied in and some of the findings.

As Exhibit 11.4 shows, clearly the ethical climate is relevant to the global environment. The exhibit confirms the universal nature of these climate types, as many of the same findings in the U.S. or Europe have been reproduced in other countries, such as Nigeria and Singapore. This also confirms the utility of ethical climates for multinationals as they operate worldwide.

Next, we look at organizational culture.

ORGANIZATIONAL CLIMATES AND ETHICAL CULTURE

As you saw in the opening pages of this chapter, the organizational culture is a critical aspect of a company's long-term survival. **Organizational culture** refers to the general beliefs and views of how things are done in an organization. Organizational climates, including ethical climates, are reflections of the basic organizational culture. **Ethical culture** refers more specifically to the norms and values that guide organizational members when faced with ethical dilemmas. Cultural norms and values related to ethics are reflected in the ethical climate or the employees' shared perceptions of how to deal with ethical dilemmas. The degree to which employees agree on their perceptions of the ethical climate indicates the strength of the ethical culture and how likely it is that the ethical culture will affect behaviors. The relationship between organizational culture and ethical climate is shown in Exhibit 11.5.

Organizational cultures are very important for understanding ethics in companies. Organizational cultures often define what is right and wrong in companies and such aspects clearly govern how people behave in organizations. Furthermore, companies can impart employees with the essential moral principles and values that are conducive to ethics. Consider the Strategic Business Ethics Insight on page 492.

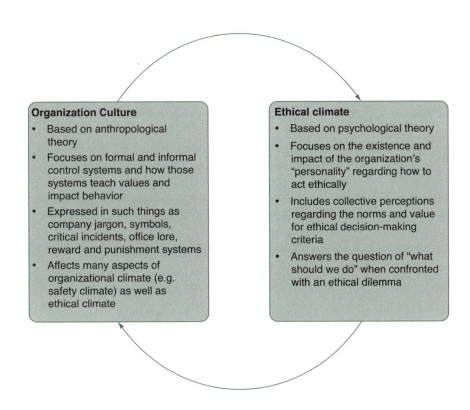

EXHIBIT 11.5—The Relationship between Organizational Culture and Ethical Climate

STRATEGIC BUSINESS ETHICS INSIGHT

Johnson & Johnson: Decline of its Ethical Culture

Johnson & Johnson (J&J) used to be seen as the model iconic U.S. company that most parents trust enough to give J&J products to their children. This had been a strategic aspect of doing business for J&J for decades. For instance, in 1982, facing a catastrophe where seven people died from using extra-strength Tylenol, J&J quickly tackled the crisis. Although someone laced the Tylenol with cyanide, J&J took responsibility for the crisis and quickly recalled the medicine and devised tamper-proof packaging. Furthermore, the company CEO made several TV appearances to reassure the public and its customers about the safety of their products. Although the recall cost J&J over $100 million, it quickly recovered and continued making a safety and ethical culture as the cornerstone of their strategy and competitive advantage.

Unfortunately for J&J, many changes occurred in the past decade and these changes have quickly demolished J&J's ethical culture. First, like most companies, J&J faced serious cost-cutting. This was manifested in the laying off of experienced staff in favor of new employees in the safety department. This quickly led to changes that affected the safety culture at J&J. Employees would routinely ignore safety concerns and pass drugs that had red flags. Second, facing serious competition, J&J acquired Pfizer's consumer division, makers of products such as Listerine, Sudafed, etc. This merger also meant that several key positions such as quality and R&D had to be centralized to achieve cost savings. This also led to J&J staffers losing their independence and pride. Furthermore, consumer executives at Pfizer were requesting ill-advised operation reductions that hurt J&J's safety culture. Third, J&J had to also lay off around 4,000 employees across the company in 2007. This meant that seasoned floor employees left with their expertise. Such layoffs resulted in a dilution of the company's ethical culture and increased safety concerns on the floor. Finally, instead of its usual approach to recalls, J&J started engaging in unusual recall operations that led to admonishment from the FDA. For instance, in 2009, it was reported that J&J relied on contractors who acted as regular customers to purchase all of the Motrin they could find. Rather than recall the products publicly, the company decided to do a quiet recall.

Based on Kimes, M. 2010. "Why J&J's headache won't go away." *Fortune*, September 6, 101–108.

As the Strategic Business Ethics Insight shows, having organizational culture that fits the challenges in your industry is extremely important. Without the right elements, a company will likely fail. Furthermore, in the case of Johnson & Johnson above, they allowed an excellent organizational culture that emphasized ethics to slowly erode. In that context, recent research suggests that a variety of ethical cultures can exist in different companies. Some types of cultures have helped organizational leaders and members to overcome ethical challenges, while other types of cultures have supported actions of questionable legal and ethical behaviors.[14]

In the case of J&J discussed above, the ethical culture emphasized safety for decades. However, as the emphasis on safety declined, J&J's ethical culture also declined.

What are the components of an ethical culture? Researchers argue that ethical cultures have two main components.[15] The formal components include elements such as the mission and vision, codes of conduct, and the socialization process that new and existing employees go through. However, the informal components are usually harder to observe. These include such aspects such as beliefs in heroes, myths, and stories discussed in the organization about how ethical dilemmas should be dealt with.

Extant evidence suggests that both formal and informal aspects of the ethical culture are important. For example, the formal component of an ethical organization will socialize members in the need of being ethical. Such companies are likely to emphasize key aspects of stakeholder ethics such as health and safety of employees, safe product, and community involvement. These companies are also more likely to focus on fairness. However, as examples of companies such as Enron have shown, the informal aspects of ethical culture are also important to promote ethics. Although Enron had all the key elements of the formal aspect of an ethical culture, such as a strong code of conduct and employee training, it still experienced significant ethical disasters that led to the downfall of the company. Thus, the informal aspects are also very important.

The researchers also mention that companies with strong informal ethical culture aspects are more likely to have organizational rituals that emphasize ethical behavior.[16] Furthermore, such companies are also more likely to have top executives and other leaders who talk about ethics regularly. When facing situations and dilemmas, such companies are more likely to engage in ethics-oriented conversations to help find solutions.

The above clearly shows that both formal and informal aspects of ethical cultures are critical. How can companies build their culture? Edgar Schein, a leading organizational culture expert, has identified several steps that managers can use to create their organizational cultures and hence their ethical climates.[17] These include:

* *What managers pay attention to, measure, and control.* What managers pay attention to communicates to the people in the organization the beliefs and values that dominate the leadership. This is not necessarily done formally. Employees notice comments made and casual questions and remarks. For example, if the management team pays attention to individual achievement and individual and unit competition, the ethical climate that results will likely reflect more egoistic norms and values. Conversely, if managers pay more attention to following the law, the ethical climate will more likely reflect a law and code orientation.

- *Manager reactions to critical incidents and organizational crises.* At some point in its life every organization will face a crisis. This might be, for example, a failed product, a natural disaster, a product recall, or a severe drop in demand. How managers deal with crises goes a long way to showing the dominant values of the leadership and the organization. Because crises heighten anxiety, they often help encourage culture change or are very important in the development of a new culture. Consider the Global Business Ethics Insight below regarding Toyota CEO Akio Toyoda's response to the recalls Toyota faced when accelerators stuck in some of its models.

GLOBAL BUSINESS ETHICS INSIGHT

Toyota's CEO Apologizes: A Critical Incident for Toyota?

Toyota CEO Akio Toyoda is the grandson of the car company's founder. He has publicly criticized Toyota's prioritization of profits during the last decade, perhaps seeing the ethical climate of Toyota becoming more instrumental. After Toyota's major recall crisis in late 2010, where a defect found in eight of its models involving a sticky gas pedal led to massive recalls throughout the world, his first public statement was to say "I am deeply sorry" in an interview with the Japanese television network NHK. He went on to say, "Truly we think of our customers as a priority and we guarantee their safety." Later, while testifying in front of a U.S. government committee, he apologized again. Prior to his testimony the company released the statement: "[In] the past few months, our customers have started to feel uncertain about the safety of Toyota's vehicles, and I take full responsibility for that. Today, I would like to explain to the American people, as well as our customers in the U.S. and around the world, how seriously Toyota takes the quality and safety of its vehicles." Toyoda, a trained test driver, also went on to note: "I drove the vehicles in the accelerator pedal recall as well as the Prius, comparing the vehicles before and after the remedy in various environmental settings. I believe that only by examining the problems onsite can one make decisions from the customer perspective. One cannot rely on reports or data in a meeting room."

This is a critical incident in the history of Toyota that may foster the creation of a more caring climate for customers as stakeholders. However, some skeptics see apologizing as just a reflection of Japanese culture. When a leader apologizes, he takes responsibility for the action and does not blame others. Such apologies are considered a virtue. However, an apology to a foreign government may be more than a ritual and still affect the Toyota climate for years ahead. As Japan's *Asahi Shimbun* newspaper noted in an editorial, Toyoda's testimony in the U.S. "not only determines Toyota's fate, but may affect all Japanese companies and consumer confidence in their products. President Toyoda has a heavy load on his shoulders."

Based on http://abcnews.go.com/Blotter/toyota-ceo-apologizes-deeply/story?id=9700622; pressroom.toyota.com; miamiherald.com.

- *Observed resource allocation and criteria for resource allocation.* In all organizations, there are public goals (what is stated publicly) and what are called operational goals (what is the organization's real concerns). One way to tell the operative goals and policies of an organization is what projects, people, units, etc. get resources. This communicates to the people in the organization "what really counts." For example, if donating time to community organizations gets recognized and rewarded, it signals that external caring is part of the organization's culture and ethical climate. Additionally, how managers make the decisions to allocate resources communicates which stakeholders are important. If only stockholders count, then the organization will likely have a more instrumental ethical climate.

- *Deliberate role modeling, teaching, and coaching.* How managers behave communicates values and assumptions to others in the organization. It is often not what managers say but what they do that sends the most powerful messages. Professors Sims and Brinkmann described the organizational culture of the now defunct Enron as "the ultimate contradiction between words and deeds, between a deceiving glossy facade and a rotten structure behind." Enron executives created an organizational culture with an instrumental organizational climate where profits (the bottom line) were valued over ethical behavior and doing what is right.[18]

- *Observed criteria for allocation of rewards and status.* Employees learn a lot about the organizational culture from their personal experiences in the organization. Performance appraisals, promotions (or lack of them), raises, and informal discussions with superiors send strong messages to employees regarding organizational values. What is rewarded or punished sends a message about organizational values.

- *Observed criteria for recruitment, selection.* Beyond formal qualifications, organizations usually strive to hire people who "fit"; that is, those who have similar values and beliefs. Current employees see the criteria used for recruitment and eventual selection. These observations communicate to them if the culture is changing or maintaining. For example, a disproportionate hiring of men might communicate that female employees have less value. Or, more positively, a firm that recruits college graduates with some experience in philanthropic work communicates that caring is important.

COMMUNICATING THE DESIRED ETHICAL CLIMATE IN YOUR ORGANIZATIONAL CULTURE

Schein's model tells us generally how organizational cultures get formed and changed. Many of his ideas can be applied to managing your organization's ethical climate. As such, we now need to look specifically at what strategies you can use to build and strengthen the ethical climate in your organizational culture.[19] Here are some practical suggestions:

- *Walk the walk.* When subordinates see managers demonstrate high ethical integrity, it sends a positive message to all employees about the importance of organizational values.

- *Keep people in the loop.* Keeping employees informed about what goes on in the organization builds trust in the openness and fairness of the organization's value system.
- *Encourage thoughtful dissent.* When employees can disagree with management they are more likely to identify potential ethical problems. Research shows that empowerment of subordinates by management increases the existence of caring climates and reduces the existence of egoistic climates.[20]
- *Show them that you care.* Research shows that caring organizations are less likely to have ethical problems, and also have more committed employees.
- *Don't sweep problems under the rug.* Ethical issues and problems should be addressed directly and consistently with the organization's values. Employees must see that management deals effectively with ethical issues.
- *Celebrate the successes.* More than talk or formal statements, the recognition and rewards for ethical behavior build a stronger climate that supports the organizational value system. Managers can make this happen by recognizing the ethical heroes as well as the business superstars.
- *Be fair.* Ethical standards must be applied consistently to all levels of management and employees.
- *Make the tough calls.* It is not always easy to uphold organizational values. Managers must make tough calls like firing an unethical person or dropping an otherwise good supplier for ethical violations such as child labor.
- *Get the right people on the bus and keep them.* Research shows that ethical climate and culture affect the ethical behaviors and commitment of managers and employees. As with organizational culture in general, managers need to create and sustain an ethical culture and climate by selecting people who match the organization's values and by making ethics a condition for retention.
- *Communicate ethical expectations.* Create a code of ethics to reduce ethical ambiguities and lay out the principal dimensions of your ethical climate. This is a formal way of stating the organization's primary values and the ethical rules to follow. Research shows that, when leaders communicate, they are more likely to develop a principled ethical climate.[21]
- *Offer ethics training.* Use seminars, workshops, and external ethical training programs to reinforce and clarify what is in the code and what is in the unwritten normative expectations in the organization.

The above shows the many steps and actions companies can undertake to build the right type of ethical climate. But how can companies maintain an ethical culture when they operate worldwide in countries that may have different norms and cultures? The Global Business Ethics Insight on page 497 shows how GE maintains an ethical culture in the global marketplace.

The Global Business Ethics Insight clearly shows some of the steps that are needed to promote a strong ethical culture. To summarize, Exhibit 11.6 (page 498) shows the key steps of building an ethical culture.

It is important to note that different types of ethical cultures may also exist in companies. Trevino, Weaver, Gibson, and Toffler argue that there are two types of

BUSINESS ETHICS INSIGHT

Ethical Culture at GE

GE is a U.S. company involved across many industries, such as the medical field, aviation, locomotives, and alternative energy. It has operations in over 100 countries and more than half of its sales now coming from outside of the U.S. In the face of such global operations, whereby cultural norms predict different levels of ethical behavior, GE has been able to maintain a fairly uniform culture of ethics and integrity in all of its subsidiaries. How has GE been able to maintain such a uniform culture worldwide?

First, GE demonstrates committed leadership to the ideals of integrity and an ethical culture. Although it seems a cliché to suggest that leaders should show by example, GE overemphasizes this aspect. In fact, GE actually fired a top manager with significant local experience for willingly violating company codes. GE was willing to forgo the extensive experience offered by the manager to show the importance of an ethical culture. However, most surprising was when GE fired some top executives for ethical violations by their subordinates. Although these managers were not aware of these ethical transgressions, GE placed the responsibility on the manager.

Second, GE will always strive to stay ahead of global standards. By regularly assessing its environment, GE is proactive by anticipating potential future regulations and rules. Such actions also show commitment to the ethical culture.

Third, GE understands that it cannot maintain a strong ethical culture unless employees are involved. As such, GE devotes significant resources to educate and train the workers. GE ensures that many aspects of its ethical code and rules are directly applicable to the lowest employee. By making ethics relevant to all workers, GE can ensure that employees are aware of how ethics impact their actions. Furthermore, employees are trained regularly worldwide on the global ethical code. Furthermore, GE acknowledges that the employee often knows best about maintaining ethics. Thus, employees are given voices through many channels. Employees are thus free to voice their ethical concerns but can also contribute to ethics discussions.

Finally, GE strives to develop global standards that transcend the standards in any specific country. GE understands that global ethical standards are necessary even if such standards are in violation of local norms For instance, GE has some of the most rigorous non-discrimination rules in its subsidiaries worldwide.

Based on http://www.ge.com and Heineman, B.W. 2007. "Avoiding integrity landmines." *Harvard Business Review*, April, 100–108.

Key Elements of an Ethical Culture
Formalized policy identifying ethical conduct such as a code of ethics or code of conduct
Demonstrate consistent and committed leadership to ethics issues
Provide employees with training regarding all aspects of ethics
Make information accessible and available
Provide access to advice when employees face ethical dilemmas
Provide employees with the means to report ethical misconduct
Appoint an employee ombudsperson to act on behalf of employees
Have a process to investigate and discipline employees for ethical violations
Make ethics part of the regular employee assessment and performance appraisal
Strive to stay ahead of rules and regulations
Punish employees when necessary but also reward employees for ethical behaviors
Build ethical standards in day-to-day operations—make ethics part of everyday life and relevant for employees
Hold key executives and senior managers as responsible as lower-level employees

EXHIBIT 11.6—Key Elements of an Ethical Culture

ethical cultures: a **compliance-based culture** and a **values-based culture**.[22] A compliance program usually emphasizes the law and prevention, detection, and punishment of violations of the relevant laws. In contrast, a values-based program stresses organizational values that are consistent with ethical ideals. In values-based companies, employees become committed to ethical aspirations.

Research on the two types of ethical culture suggests that the values-based ethical culture is much more effective. A compliance-based culture is much more rooted in respect of the law and its implementation relies on employees focusing on obeying the laws for fear of punishment. However, in contrast, a values-based culture emphasizes self-governance and belief in better ethical ideals. Thus, a values-based culture seems more likely to encourage ethical behavior, as employees believe in the ideals of the culture as opposed to behaving in ways to avoid punishment.

In a study of several corporations, Trevino et al. find support for the effectiveness of the values-based ethical culture.[23] In contrast to compliance cultures, the researchers find that companies with values-based cultures have fewer unethical behaviors and were more aware of ethical issues. Furthermore, employees were more likely to ask for advice in such companies when faced with an ethical dilemma. Finally, values-based cultures are also more likely to encourage report of ethical violations. However, despite these advantages, the researchers also suggest that compliance-based cultures have advantages in that it emphasizes respect of the laws.

WHAT DO WE KNOW ABOUT THE EFFECTS OF DIFFERENT CLIMATE TYPES?

Perhaps the most important research finding is that employees are more ethical in those organizations where the ethical climate and culture encourage ethical behavior.[24] In addition, there are other benefits for organizations with strong ethical values including higher commitment, job satisfaction, and employee performance. Numerous studies[25] link ethical culture and climate to lower rates of observed misconduct, exposure to situations facilitating misconduct, and pressure to compromise standards. Employees in such organizations also show more satisfaction with management's responses to incidents of misconduct and report that they are more prepared to handle potentially unethical situations.

More specifically, affective responses to the organization, such as organizational commitment and job satisfaction, are positively related to the existence of caring climates and negatively related to the existence of instrumental climates. Organizational climates that originate from externally based rules such as professional or religious codes also seem to produce positive relationships with organizational outcomes.

Past research generally indicates that caring, law and code, rules, and independence climates reduce organizational misbehaviors such as stealing and sabotage. This contrasts with the negative effects stemming from perceptions of instrumental ethical climates. Importantly, when rules climates are perceived, these perceptions seem to serve as effective control mechanisms that limit unethical behaviors but do not successfully produce attachment to the organization such as more commitment.[26]

THOUGHTS ON A POSITIVE WORK CLIMATE

A new philosophical approach to the work environment is emerging that represents a type of ethical climate supportive of human flourishing. The **positive work climate** perspective argues that work climates create emotional reactions for employees. If these emotions are predominantly positive, then people will flourish.

Hartel notes that a positive work climate exists when employees perceive "the workplace environment as positive, respectful, inclusive and psychologically safe; leaders and co-workers as trustworthy, fair and diversity open; and policies and decision-making as interactionally, procedurally and distributively just."[27] The research on positive work climates, although recent, is showing that the climate characteristics noted above tend to help people develop an emotional attachment to their organization and, in turn, this results in greater organizational performance.[28] Similar to what we know about caring ethical climates, people are more likely to identify with the organization and relate better with co-workers, ultimately benefiting the company.

DISCOVERING YOUR ETHICAL CLIMATE

As new employees in an organization, it is often a good idea to learn the ethical climate norms and expectations as quickly as possible. This has two benefits. First, you can avoid making mistakes that violate local norms and more quickly fit in with your work environment. Second, and perhaps more important, is that you can assess your fit with the ethical environment. The question pertains to how closely your personal moral beliefs match the expectations from the organization. The famous organizational culture expert Edgar Schein[29] suggests you can understand climate by following the steps below.

1. Observe behavior language, customs, and traditions. Try to understand how these affect ethical decision-making.
2. Understand group norms, standards, and values. Tightly knit groups will often have clear expectations of those who join their team.
3. Observe the published, publicly announced values and formal philosophies such as in the mission statement. These are often in the codes of conduct and mission statements.
4. Learn the informal rules of the game, the unwritten expectations of how things are done around here. Eventually, employees learn the informal organization, which may differ radically from official statements. One way of speeding up this process is seeking a mentor, or someone more experienced in the organization, to give you insider hints.
5. Look for stores or symbols that reinforce organizational norms and values. Most people in organizations can report critical incidents or local folklore that helped define the organizations' values.

CHAPTER SUMMARY

This chapter began with an overview of the ethical climate model and it relationship to the more general concept of work climate. The ethical climate is a type of work climate. The ethical climate represents what organizational members believe are the forms of ethical reasoning or behavior and the expected standards or norms for ethical decision-making within the company.[30] You can determine the ethical climate of your organization or department by looking at such things as what criteria people use to understand and resolve ethical issues.

Ethical climate is not a single component of the organization, but there are several climate types identified by the ethical climate model. Past research has refined these climate types and the important ones are considered in the chapter. Principled climates occur when the organization has norms that encourage people to make ethical decisions based on a set of standards. Some organizations may make ethical decisions based on external codes such as a professional code of conduct. For example, you can see the classic ethical code of physicians, called the Hippocratic Oath. In other organizations, people look to their company's code of conduct to guide their ethical behaviors and decision-making. You saw two examples in the Johnson & Johnson Credo and the Coca-Cola Code, shown in Exhibits 11.2 and 11.3. Organizations can also have a principle ethical climate, called the independent, where each individual is expected to behave in a way that he or she personally considers ethical.

Caring climates occur when the organization has norms that encourage people to make ethical decisions based on looking out for the welfare of others, particularly for team members and those within the company. In most organizations with caring climates, people believe that the right thing to do is to look out for the welfare of friends and co-workers. The Preview Ethics Insight (pages 479–480) showed two companies that are dominated by caring climates. The Business Ethics Insight for Malden Mills (pages 486–7) gave an example of a situation where perhaps caring went too far and the owner lost sight of the need for economic performance to ensure organization survival.

Organizations having an *instrumental* ethical climate see their organizational unit as having norms and expectations that encourage ethical decision-making from an egoistic perspective. Instrumental ethical climates occur when the organization has norms that encourage people to define right and wrong in terms of the consequences to oneself. Thus, when faced with an ethical dilemma, people are expected to make decisions based on what best serves self-interest. Even when considered in a variety of contexts, studies consistently show that instrumental climates are the least preferred.

Organizational culture and climate are closely related ways to view the informal side of an organization. Basically, organizational climates, including ethical climates, are reflections of the basic organizational culture. Because ethical climate is a reflection of the ethical side of the local culture, the chapter reviewed basic principles of how cultures evolve and change, building on the idea of the leading organizational culture expert Edgar Schein.[31] Schein identifies several factors that help leaders build and maintain a culture. These include: what managers pay attention to, measure, and control; manager's reactions to critical incidents and organizational crises; observed resource allocation and criteria for resource allocation; deliberate role modeling, teaching, and coaching; observed criteria for allocation of rewards and status; observed criteria for recruitment, selection; and communicating the desired ethical climate in your organizational culture. The chapter also provided you with a list of practical suggestions for building the type of ethical climate desired by the owners and managers of the organization.

The chapter provided a summary of the basic findings from scientific research regarding the effects of ethical climates on organizations. Importantly, we know that employees are more ethical in those organizations where the ethical climate and culture encourage ethical behavior.[32] Also, affective responses to the organization such as organizational commitment and job satisfaction are positively related to perceptions of caring climates and negatively related with perceptions of instrumental climates. Research indicates that caring, law and code, rules, and independence climates reduce organizational misbehaviors such as stealing and sabotage, whereas instrumental ethical climates may encourage these behaviors.[33]

This chapter introduced a new concept of positive work climates that is based on the philosophy that positive emotions can be created by the climate and that these are beneficial both to individuals and to organizations. Finally, the chapter concluded with some hints to help you identify your own ethical climates when you enter new organizations.

NOTES

1 Reichers, A.E. & Schneider, B. 1990. "Climates and culture: An evolution of constructs." In B. Schneider (Ed.), *Organizational climate and culture*. San Francisco: Jossey-Bass, 5–39; Schneider, B. 1975. "Organizational climate: an essay." *Personnel Psychology*, 36, 447–479.

2 Klein, K.J. & Sorra, S. 1996. "The challenge of innovation management." *Academy of Management Review*, 21, 1055–1080.

3 Mumford, M.D., Scott, G., Gaddis, B. & Strange, J.M. 2002. "Leading creative people: orchestrating expertise and relationships." *Leadership Quarterly*, 13, 705–750.

4 Field, R.H. & Abelson, M.A. 1982. "Climate: A reconceptualization and proposed model." *Human Relations*, 35, 181–201.

5 Cullen, J.B., Parboteeah, K.P. & Victor, B. 2003. "The effects of ethical climates on organizational commitment: A two-study analysis." *Journal of Business Ethics*, 46, 127–141.

6 Cullen, J.B. Victor, B. & Stephens. C. 1989. "An ethical weather report: Assessing the organization's ethical climate." *Organizational Dynamics*, 18, 50–60.

7 Victor, B. & Cullen, J.B. 1987. "The organizational bases of ethical climate." *Administrative Science Quarterly*, 33, 101–125.

8 Dugan-Martin, K. & Cullen, J.B. 2006. "Continuities and extension of ethical climate theory: A meta-analytic review." *Journal of Business Ethics*, 69, 175–194.

9 Kerns, C.D. 2003. "Creating and sustaining an ethical workplace culture: The values → attitude → behavior chain." *Graziadio Business Review*, 6, 3.

10 Ubius, U. & Alas. R. 2009. "Organizational cultural types as predicators of corporate social responsibility." *Inzinerine Ekonomika-Engineering Economics*, 1, 90–99.

11 Wimbush, J.C. & Shepard, J.M. 1994. "Toward an understanding of ethical climate: Its relationship to ethical behavior and supervisory influence." *Journal of Business Ethics*, 13, 637–647.

12 Erondu, E.A., Sharland, A. & Okpara, J.O. 2004. "Corporate ethics in Nigeria: A test of the concept of ethical climate." *Journal of Business Ethics*, 51, 349–357.

13 Friedman, M. 1970. "The social responsibility of business is to increase its profits." *New York Times Magazine*, September 13.

14 Ardichvili, A. & Jondle, D. 2009. "Integrative literature review: Ethical business cultures: A literature review and implications for HRD." *Human Resource Development Review*, 8, 223–244.

15 Ardichvili & Jondle. "Integrative literature review."

16 Ardichvili & Jondle. "Integrative literature review."

17 Schein, Edgar H. 2010. *Organizational Culture*. San Francisco, CA: Wiley.

18 Sims, R.R. & Brinkmann, J. 2003. "Enron ethics (or: Culture matters more than codes)." *Journal of Business Ethics*, 45, 3, 243–256 (at 243).

19 Ethics Resource Center. 2008. *Ethical culture building: A modern business imperative*. Washington, DC: Ethics Resource Center; Robbins, S.P. & Judge, T.A. 2009. *Organizational behavior*. 13th ed. Upper Saddle River, NJ: Pearson Education, Inc.

20 Parboteeah, K., Praveen, Chen, Hsien Chun, Lin, Ying-Tzu, Chen, I-Heng, Y-Plee, Amber & Chung, An Yi. 2010. "Establishing organizational ethical climates: How do managerial practices work?" *Journal of Business Ethics*, 97, 4, 535–541.

21 Parboteeah et al. "Establishing organizational ethical climates."

22 Treviño, L.K., Weaver, G.R., Gibson, D.G. & Toffler, B.L. 1999. "Managing ethics and legal compliance: What works and what hurts." *California Management Review*, 41, 2, 131–151.

23 Treviño et al., "Managing ethics and legal compliance."

24 Ethics Resource Center. *Ethical culture building*; Dugan-Martin & Cullen, "Continuities and extension of ethical climate theory."

25 Ethics Resource Center. 2005. *National business ethics survey*. Washington, DC: ERC; Ethics Resource Center. *Ethical culture building*; Treviño et al., "Managing ethics and legal compliance"; Treviño, L.K., Butterfield, K.D. & McCabe, D.L. 2001. "The ethical context in organizations: Influences on employee attitudes and behaviors." *Research in Ethical Issues in Organizations*, 3, 301–337.

26 Dugan-Martin & Cullen. "Continuities and extension of ethical climate theory."

27 Hartel, C.E.J. 2008. "How to build a healthy emotional culture and avoid a toxic culture." In C.L. Cooper & N.M. Ashkanasy (Eds.), *Research companion to emotion in organizations*. Cheltenham, U.K.: Edwin Elgar, pp. 575–588 (at 584).

28 Wilderom, Celeste P.M. 2011. "Toward positive work climate and cultures." In N.M. Ashkanasy, C.P.M Wilderom & M.F. Peterson (Eds.), *The handbook of organizational culture and climate*. Los Angeles: Sage, pp. 79–84; Hartel, Charmine E.J. & Ashkanasy, Neal M. 2011. "Healthy human cultures as positive work environments." In N.M. Ashkanasy et al., *The handbook of organizational culture and climate*, pp. 85–100.

29 Schein, Edgar H. 2010. *Organizational culture*. San Francisco, CA: Wiley.

30 Cullen et al., "The effects of ethical climates."

31 Schein, *Organizational culture*.

32 Ethics Resource Center. *Ethical culture building*; Dugan-Martin & Cullen, "Continuities and extension of ethical climate theory."

33 Dugan-Martin & Cullen, "Continuities and extension of ethical climate theory."

KEY TERMS

Caring ethical climate: has norms values that encourage people to make ethical decisions based on looking out for the welfare of others.

Compliance-based culture: usually emphasizes the law and prevention, detection, and punishment of violations of the relevant laws.

Educational/learning-oriented codes: suggest general guidelines for decision-making and behavioral reactions when faced with ethically challenging situations.

Ethical climate: represents what organizational members believe are the forms of ethical reasoning or behavior and the expected standards or norms for ethical decision-making within the company.

Ethical codes: documents that identify the ethical principles used to guide the ethical decision-making within an organization.

Ethical culture: refers to the norms and values that guide organizational members when faced with ethical dilemmas.

Independent ethical climate: has norms and values that support ethical decision-making based on personal morality.

Inspirational–idealistic codes: focus on broad virtuous themes such as "Be honest."

Instrumental ethical climate: has norms and values that encourage ethical decision-making that serve the organization's interests or provide personal benefits.

Law and code: a type of principled ethical climate that emphasizes ethical decision-making based on laws or other written codes.

Organizational culture: refers to the general beliefs and views of how things are done in an organization.

Positive work climate: a view that work climates create emotional reactions for employees.

Principled climates: occur when the organization has norms and values that encourage people to make ethical decisions based on a set of standards.

Regulatory codes: specify how to behave in specific situations, typically with a "do and don't" approach.

Values-based culture: stresses organizational values that are consistent with ethical ideals.

Work climates: represent the shared perceptions of procedures, policies, and practices, both formal and informal, of the organization.

DISCUSSION QUESTIONS

1. Ethical climate is one type of work climate. How might other climates such as the climate for safety influence the ethical context of an organization?
2. Consider how organizations communicate their ethical climates to employees. How is this done and what makes it more or less effective?
3. Describe a principle ethical climate.
4. Give examples of a principle ethical climate that has influenced your participation in an organization or group.
5. Describe a caring ethical climate.
6. Give examples of a caring ethical climate that has influenced your participation in an organization or group.
7. Describe an instrumental ethical climate.
8. Give examples of an instrumental ethical climate that has influenced your participation in an organization or group.
9. Discuss the relationship between ethical climate and organization culture.
10. Consider all the ethical climate types and discuss the risks and benefits associated with each type. Risks might include ethical issues as well as general performance issues.

INTERNET ACTIVITY

1. Search the internet for company codes of conduct and find four different codes.
2. Re-examine Professor Kerns type of codes (in this chapter): inspirational/idealistic, regulatory, and educational/learning.
3. Assign each code to a type, or perhaps more than one.
4. Be ready to discuss what type of code seems to have the greater impact.
5. Google your example companies to see how they have handled any ethical dilemma.

For more Internet Activities and resources, visit the Companion Website at www.routledge.com/cw/parboteeah.

WHAT WOULD YOU DO?

My First Company

January 1, 2020 turned out to be one of the best days of your life. After years of savings and sacrifice, as well as some investments that paid off nicely, you purchased a successful BMW car dealership. Prior to making the purchase, you carefully studied the performance of the company over the last five years. Even during tough economic times, they made money selling new and used cars and in providing service. The building was only three years old and the location was great. "I made a great choice," you thought.

A month later you were not so comfortable with your new company. In spite of the economy improving, sales were flat and two of your best sales people quit unexpectedly. What was wrong? Being a "numbers" person, you knew the sales staff did very well, with high commissions on expensive cars. The company also had a great benefits package. You decided to discuss the problem with the sales manager, Frank Whidbey. Frank had been selling cars nearly all of his life and everyone seemed to like him, customers and fellow works alike.

"Frank, what's going on here? This does not seem to be the company I bought." Frank hesitated with your opening question. "Ms. Brooks, things have been changing around here since before you took over," he said.

After a couple of hours of discussion, you began to get a picture of the problem. During a slow period of sales due to general economic conditions and the end of the model year, the previous management had reduced base salaries and increased commissions to motivate more sales. Competition among the sales people soared and the relationships among the sales team began to change. Frank noted, "Previously, the sales people would cover for each other. If you were not on the floor and the customers were looking for you, the person doing the showing would make sure you got your commission. We had a climate where everyone looked out for each other and you knew that you would get your fair share. However, a couple of new sales people really took to the new high commission approach and began taking some of the returning customers away from the old-timers. This did not go over well."

In thinking back to your old business ethics course, you remember the idea of an ethical climate. You now see that changing the compensation scheme was a critical incident that turned a once caring climate into an instrumental climate. You are losing people that fit with the old climate and it seems to be affecting sales. "Maybe I should just hire all extremely competitive people and use that as a motivator to succeed, and everyone will understand how the game is played now," you think. "Maybe I should work to rebuild the caring climate that worked so well in the past."

What are you going to do?

BRIEF CASE: BUSINESS ETHICS INSIGHT

The Zappos Caring Culture and Climate

Zappos was founded in 1999 as an online shoe store. Since then it has expanded its product offerings to clothing and accessories. Zappos' headquarters is in Las Vegas, Nevada and it employs approximately 2,000 people. The company is an example of a caring organizational culture and climate, with core values focusing on the happiness of both its employees and its customers.

CEO Tony Hsieh, a Harvard-educated computer scientist, sees culture as a driving force in his company. He notes, "If you get the culture right, then most of the other stuff, like great customer service or building a brand will just happen naturally." Working with his employees Hsieh developed a list of ten core values that drive the company. Even though he first thought that codifying the core values was too "corporate," he realized that the values could be a rallying point for his employees to deliver superior and ethical customer service. Ultimately, Hsieh believes that core values are more than a vague sense of cultural expectations. To be effective, companies must have "committable" core values. "By committable, you must be willing to hire and fire based on them," he notes.

The ten core values are:

1. Deliver WOW Through Service.
2. Embrace and Drive Change.
3. Create Fun and a Little Weirdness.
4. Be Adventurous, Creative, and Open-Minded.
5. Pursue Growth and Learning.
6. Build Open and Honest Relationships with Communication.
7. Build a Positive Team and Family Spirit.
8. Do More with Less.
9. Be Passionate and Determined.
10. Be Humble.

To reinforce the cultural values, every year, Zappos employees contribute to a "Culture Book." Employees share their thoughts, stories, and photos that identify their personal experiences about what Zappos' culture means to them. Readers of the book note such cultural key words as *fun, family, smile, proud, weird, thank you*, and *I heart Zappos*. The nearly 500-page Culture Book comes out every year and Hsieh provides free copies to anyone who asks.

For Hsieh, the true test of commitment to an organizational culture is whether a company is willing to hire and fire based on cultural fit. As Hsieh notes, "It doesn't so much matter *what* your culture is, so long as you commit to it." As such, all job candidates have an interview with the HR department that focuses only on cultural fit. The HR department uses a series of interview questions to probe an applicant's views regarding the ten core values. To screen for creativity and individuality, the Zappos HR department uses interview questions such as: "How weird are you?" "What's your theme song?" "What two people would you most like to invite to dinner?" According to Hsieh, "We've actually passed on a lot of really talented people that we know would make an impact to our top or bottom line . . . but if you know they're not a culture fit we won't hire them." Even if someone is doing a good job, the company will fire them if they do not fit with the culture. "We do our best to hire positive people and put them in an environment where the positive thinking is reinforced," says Hsieh.

Once through the selection process, all new Zappos employees have five weeks of training. Regardless of level, everyone gets the same training as the call center employees. The curriculum includes company history and customer service training followed by taking real calls from real customers beginning at 7 a.m. Be late or call in sick and you are not Zappos material.

Perhaps the most unusual cultural reinforcing technique is that, when training is complete, all new hires are offered $4,000 to quit! Zappos tells the new employees, "We will pay for the training you've received, and give you an additional $4,000 if you quit right now." Hsieh explains it this way: "We don't want employees that are just there for a pay check. We want employees who are there because the culture is the right fit for them."

For Zappos employees, building a strong caring culture is a daily event. There is the free lunch in the cafeteria, regular happy hours, a nap room, profit sharing, and paid-in full healthcare. There is even a full-time life coach that the employees can consult for confidential advice on just about anything. There is only one requirement to use the coach: employees must sit on a red velvet throne. Zappos managers also spend 10% to 20% of their time with team members outside the office. This builds team commitment to each other and the company. And one does not need to be a boss to pass out rewards—any employee can give a $50 bonus to other employee for good work.

Like most companies, Zappos has faced business events that challenge some of its fundamental cultural values. Two critical incidents show how it responded.

On May 21, 2010 a computer glitch on a Zappos website set the price of every product to $49.95. It took six hours to fix the error and by then Zappos had lost nearly $1.6 million in revenue. Rather than try to cancel these incorrect sales, Zappos made the announcement that they would honor these sales even though the prices were wrong. In spite of such a large loss Zappos remained true to its caring culture that focuses on customers.

A recession economy challenged the caring culture of Zappos when employees are involved: how would they lay people off? Their venture capital backer, Sequoia Capital, demanded that its portfolio companies, including Zappos, cut costs. In 2007, in spite of the economy, Zappos was profitable with a positive cashflow. Still, Hsieh knew he had to act and the top management team identified 124 employees out of 1,500 that they would lay-off.

Zappos' reaction was to make a bad situation as positive as possible. Said Hsieh: "The motivation was, let's take care of our employees who got us this far." Long-term employees who were laid off received four weeks of pay for every year of service. Those with less than two years of service were paid through the end of the year. All laid-off employees received six months of paid health coverage.

Based on Burkus, David. 2011. "A tale of two cultures: Why culture trumps core values in building ethical organizations." *Journal of Values Based Leadership*, 4, Winter/Spring. http://money.cnn.com/2009/01/15/news/companies/Zappos_best_companies_obrien.fortune/index.htm; http://experiencematters.wordpress.com/2008/05/28/discussing-zappos-culture-with-tony-hsieh/; http://www.innovationexcellence.com/blog/2011/06/17/culture-is-king-at-zappos/; http://www.readwriteweb.com/archives/zappos_ceo_talks_culture_fit_a.php

BRIEF CASE QUESTIONS

1. The Zappos culture seems to work well for a small company. How would you transfer such cultural values to a larger organization?
2. A charismatic leader such as Tony Hsieh can be the driver of an organizational culture and climate. Discuss how future managers might continue the cultural traditions of this company.
3. It is difficult to quantify the results of a company that has a caring approach to customers and employees. How would you respond to a critic that notes that Zappos sells good products and good prices and many of the culturally supporting "extras" are just a waste of money?

LONG CASE: BUSINESS ETHICS

CITIGROUP: RESTORING ETHICS AND IMAGE BEFORE GROWTH

Charles Prince, CEO of Citigroup, is facing a daunting challenge as the head of the largest financial services organization in world. He has joined a company that has experienced significant regulatory scrutiny and that has been linked to the biggest scandals in corporate history. Unfortunately for Prince, the problems are pervasive throughout most of Citigroup's diverse service offerings.

In March 2005, Prince announced his strategy to transform the financial giant and to provide a new direction for the future. He called it the "Five Point Ethics Plan" to: improve training, enhance focus on talent and development, balance performance appraisals and compensation, improve communications, and strengthen controls. Due to the size and complexity of the organization, there were significant unresolved questions. How could the plan be effectively revealed? Would the plan be strong enough to change the culture of the entire organization? How should the corporate communications department handle both the initial and long-term communication of this plan to major stakeholders?

About Citigroup

Incorporated in 1998, Citigroup Inc. is a diversified global financial services holding company providing services to consumer and corporate customers. The company has approximately 141,000 full-time and 7,000 part-time employees in the United States and 146,000 full-time employees in more than 100 countries outside the United States. All of Citigroup's services can be grouped in three main areas: Global Consumer, Corporate and Investment Banking, and Global Wealth Management. Citigroup also has two stand-alone businesses: Citigroup Asset Management and Citigroup Alternative Investments. Global Consumer Group was 72% of income in 2004, with Investment Banking coming in second at 13%.[1]

The Citigroup umbrella covers several brands including Citibank, Citifinancial, Citistreet, Citi, Primerica, Banamex, and Salomon Smith Barney (SSB). Citigroup has a 200-year-old legacy of innovation and achievement. The City Bank of New York is Citigroup's earliest ancestor, establishing a credit union for merchant-owners in 1812. Many of the rest of Citigroup's ancestors originated in the late nineteenth century, including Travelers, Smith Barney, Bank Hadlowly, and Banamex. In the twentieth century, acquisitions included IBC, Salomon Brothers, and The Associates. Sandy Weill, former CEO, was recognized as bringing it all together under the one red umbrella of Citigroup in 1998.[2]

Sandy Weill: The Man Who Shattered the Glass-Steagall

"Everything about Weill is big, including his ambition."
(Charles Gasparino, *Blood on the Street*)

Congress passed the Glass-Steagall Act in 1933, which established what was known as the Chinese Wall between commercial banking and investment banking. That same year, the man who would influence the repeal of that act in 1999 was born. Sandy Weill later became one of Wall Street's most influential men as the Citigroup CEO in 1998. He ran the one-stop financial supermarket until 2003.[3]

In the 1960s, Weill grew Shearson Loeb Rhodes brokerage from a mid-sized business into an empire that he sold to American Express Corporation in 1981. After being bounced from Amex, he had one of the most notable comebacks on Wall Street. He merged his insurance company, The Traveler's Group, with the Salomon Smith Barney brokerage and the Citicorp banking empire. This merger made Weill a very rich and powerful man, but the fame also brought a lot of negative publicity. During Weill's era as CEO, Citigroup was associated with numerous corporate scandals, regulatory investigations, and legal settlements.

In an interview with the *New York Times* on September 11, 2005, Weill still defended what he built, saying "I don't think it's too big to manage or govern at all. I'm sure there would have been things that would have been tweaked this way or that way, but when you look at the results of what happened, you have to say it was a great success."

Charles Prince became the next Citigroup CEO after Weill. His advice for Prince: "Don't screw [the legacy] up."[4]

Charles Prince—Maintaining the Legacy

Charles Prince became the chief executive officer with Citigroup in 2003 and has been an employee with the company for 24 years. He began his career in 1975 as an attorney with U.S. Steel Corporation. In 1979 he joined Commercial Credit Company, which Sandy Weill took over in 1986. At that point, Prince became what *Fortune*'s Carol Loomis called "an absolute Weill loyalist, who has promptly accepted whatever assignments Sandy has wanted him to take on."[5] He served as main counsel until 2003, when Weill chose him as CEO. Since 2003, Prince has been a fireman, cleaning up the scandals and improprieties that have been building since the late 1990s. Much of that cleaning has meant removing companies and executives that helped build Weill's legacy, including the sale of Traveler's Insurance.

Prince has been described as "a smart, logical thinker who's big in frame, in laugh, and in capacity for work." One long-time analyst notes, "I believe that non-charismatic Prince is going to be a more positive force at Citigroup than the other three charismatic CEOs going back to the 1960s."[6]

Distributing Biased Research

In 2001, the Office of New York State Attorney General Eliot Spitzer began an investigation into possible conflict-of-interest problems with Citigroup's investment banking practice. This joint investigation between state and federal regulators was resolved and settled in April 2003. In addition to payment of $400 million, Salomon Smith Barney (SSB) was required to adopt a series of reforms and measures. This payment was larger than any other financial institution included in the investigation. The financial impact is even larger due to additional private litigation arising from the settlement. Citigroup took a $1.5 billion charge primarily for litigation reserves in the quarter of the findings.[7]

There were multiple findings from the investigation concerning Citigroup's internal operating practices and communications with clients. The investigation found that the research analysis and correlating ratings were not performed with independence and integrity. SSB business practices encouraged research analysts to provide favorable coverage of companies that were also investment banking clients. A portion of each analyst's compensation was based on revenues from the investment banking unit and investment banking evaluations. The investigation found incidents of fraudulent and misleading research reports. SSB also practiced spinning activities that allocated lucrative shares of IPO stocks to executives at investment banking clients.[8]

One of the most notable reforms required as part of the settlement was to separate the investment banking operations from the research operations of the company. Senior investment banking executives working for a client were forbidden from directly communicating with the research analysts covering the same client. The reforms also required the CEO of SSB's research unit to periodically report to the Citigroup board of directors concerning the quality and independence of the research products.

The Star Telecom Analyst

Jack Grubman was a notorious telecommunications analyst for Salomon Smith Barney. He touted his relationships throughout the industry and earned an estimated $20 million per year. In ten different deals, he helped SSB earn $24 million in fees from investment banking with WinStar Communications.[9]

In January 2001, Grubman assigned a $50 price target and classified WinStar with a "Buy" rating. With the stock subsequently trading at $13, Grubman's assistant e-mailed a large investor, stating, "Buy here and sell in the low $20's." However, Grubman did not change his price target or rating in public. In fact, he maintained the status quo even when WinStar shares were trading at less than $1 and the company was on the eve of bankruptcy. He later noted in e-mail, "we support our banking clients too well and for too long."[10]

The National Association of Securities Dealers alleged that SSB's research was materially misleading after investigating the WinStar incident. SSB agreed to pay $5 million to settle the charges.

Deceptive Lending Practices

Citigroup acquired Associates First Capital Corporation and Associates Corporation of North America in November 2000. They subsequently merged the acquired entity into the Citifinancial Credit Company division. The Associates were one of the nation's largest subprime lenders. Subprime lending serves borrowers who cannot obtain credit in the prime market. The loans carry higher costs due to the additional risk taken by the lender and are frequently held by low-income families.

In March 2001, the Federal Trade Commission filed suit against Associates for deceptively inducing consumers to refinance existing debts into home loans with high interest rates and fees. They also alleged that Associates tricked borrowers into purchasing high-cost credit insurance without their knowledge. In some cases, the fees were included in monthly payments and added thousands of dollars in additional cost. When consumers noticed the fees, the employees of Associates employed various tactics to discourage them from removing the insurance. The FTC described the activities as "systematic and widespread deceptive and abusing lending practices." The result was the largest consumer protection settlement in FTC history and required Citigroup to pay $215 million.[11]

Helping Enron Corporation Commit Fraud

On December 2, 2001, Enron filed for bankruptcy protection from its creditors. Investors later found that the company used highly complex special purpose entities and partnerships to keep $500 million off of the consolidated balance sheet and to mask significant deficiencies in cash flow. Citigroup was one of the financial institutions that helped Enron design these transactions.

The Securities and Exchange Commission initiated enforcement proceedings with Citigroup for assisting Enron in producing misleading financial statements. The Commission alleged that loans to Enron were disguised as commodity trades. The transactions were essentially loans because they eliminated the commodity price risk. Under these transactions, commodity price risk was passed from Enron to Citigroup and back to Enron. Without regard for the change in price of the underlying commodity, Enron was required to make repayments of principal and interest. The commission also alleged that Citigroup helped Enron design transactions that transferred cash flow from financing into cash flow from operations. There was further evidence of similar deceptive transactions with Dynegy. Citigroup agreed to pay $120 million to settle the allegations that it helped Enron and Dynegy commit fraud.[12]

Spinning WorldCom Executives

In May 2004, Citigroup agreed to pay $2.65 billion to settle class action suits related to its role in the collapse of WorldCom. Plaintiffs in the suit alleged that SSB wrongfully provided favorable ratings on the company. Telecom analyst Jack Grubman provided the coverage. WorldCom was not downgraded to "neutral" until WorldCom lost 90% of its value. The U.S. House of Representatives Financial Services Committee additionally found that Grubman warned WorldCom executives, in advance of public disclosure, that Citigroup was dropping the stock from the recommended list.[13]

A former U.S. Attorney General appointed examiner alleged that Bernard Ebbers, WorldCom's chief executive officer, violated his fiduciary duties by passing over $100 million of investment banking business to SSB in exchange for allotments of IPO stock shares. Ebbers was the chief executive during the time when massive accounting fraud and questionable personal loans were discovered. WorldCom subsequently restated earnings by $17.1 billion in 2001 and $53.1 billion in 2000.[14]

512

The End of Japanese Private Banking

Citigroup is the largest and oldest foreign-owned bank in Japan. The history of their operations dates back to 1902. The operations in Japan are some of the largest outside of the U.S. for Citigroup. Bank officials at Japan's Financial Services Agency began investigating Citigroup transactions linked to money laundering, as well as loans that were used to manipulate publicly traded stocks. The FSA warned Citigroup in 2001, but little corrective action was performed.

In December 2004, Citigroup was handed the damaging news that the FSA would terminate all private banking operations in Japan. This included a requirement to close over 5,000 bank accounts. The FSA cited the corporate culture and governance for the infractions. Citigroup executives blamed the problem on the unclear reporting structure for key executives in Japan. Heads of divisions reported to different bosses in New York. In addition to the lost earnings, the closing of the bank accounts represents a challenging blow to Citigroup's image in Japan and threatens the consumer and corporate banking units still operating in the country.[15]

Financial Effects of the Corporate Scandals

By the end of 2002, the effects of the various allegations were weighing heavily on Citigroup. The SEC, FTC, NASD, the New York State Attorney General and other agencies had performed investigations. The reserves set aside for still outstanding legal liability grew by billions because of the costs of regulatory and private litigation.

During 2002, the year that many of these issues were discovered, the company lost over 30% of its market value. In May 2003, Citigroup dropped coverage of 117 firms and fired seven of its top analysts. There were increasing numbers of analyst layoffs up and down Wall Street. J.P. Morgan, Goldman Sachs, and Morgan Stanley cut up to 25% of their research staffs.[16]

In 2005, the Federal Reserve publicly announced that it would not approve any major Citigroup Mergers and Acquisitions until the company resolved these various issues. This unusual warning from the Federal Reserve was especially restrictive to Citigroup because some analysts believed that big acquisitions were the only way to continue the aggressive growth.[17]

Changing Citigroup's Reputation

One of the initial steps Prince took to clean up Citigroup was hiring Sally Krawcheck as Chief Financial Officer and Head of Strategy. Krawcheck was known at Smith Barney as "The Queen of Clean," and Prince hoped that she would continue this trend as Citigroup pushes to clean up its image.[18]

On February 16, 2005, Prince announced his Five Point Ethics Plan in a group memo to his employees as part of his goal to make Citigroup the world's most respected financial institution. While this is the most important goal Prince gave in his public plan, there are other benefits that will, hopefully, come with this ethical improvement. Prince hopes to grow the consumer and international business, and to make the corporate and investment bank the best in its class.

The four-page ethical document listed a series of initiatives that employees would start to see implemented in 12 to 18 months, beginning March 1, 2005.

DETAILS OF THE FIVE POINT PLAN

- *Expanded Training*. This point is designed to instill an appreciation for Citigroup legacy. The ethics program was kicked off with a company-wide broadcast of *The Company We Want to Be* to relate the main three responsibilities within the company: the responsibility to clients, to each other, and to the franchise. Annual training about the history and the culture of the Citigroup franchise will be required for all levels of management. Additionally, all employees will receive Annual Ethics/Code of Conduct training.
- *Enhanced Focus on Talent and Development*. A new initiative will be launched, focusing on flexibility, 360-degree reviews, manager surveys, and business leadership seminars for senior managers. New jobs will be communicated and posted internally to encourage those with outstanding talent to stay within the company.
- *Balanced Performance Appraisals and Compensation*. Standardized performance appraisals and evaluations of all managers will be conducted annually. All compensation for business heads will be based on how Citigroup performs, not just how individual managers perform. Employees will be paid bonuses on the basis of how well they participate in training and the ethics program.
- *Improved Communications*. Charles Prince demonstrated that he takes this initiative very seriously, as he has traveled around, meeting with and visiting managers and employers. Citigroup wants to improve the consistent communication of values and goals. Results of any issues reported to the Ethics Hotline will be discussed, and more conferences will be planned for senior managers.
- *Strengthened Controls*. Such control includes compliance training, risk control self-assessments, and the creation of the Independent Global Compliance function that will be responsible for ensuring Citigroup's compliance with rules and regulations.

Prince Hires Administrative Ethics Officer

Additionally, on September 26, 2005, Lewis B. Kaden joined Citigroup as Vice Chairman and Chief Administrative Officer. Kaden served as a moderator for the PBS's Media and Society seminar, including the *Ethics in America* series, which won a Peabody Award. Kaden was a lawyer from Davis Polk & Wadwell, where he handled issues of corporate governance, mergers and acquisitions, and advised major corporations such as Citigroup on significant issues. Prince said of Kaden, "Lew's deep experience, insight, and integrity will be of great value as we pursue our ambitious agenda to build the most respected global financial services company. We look forward to his contributions."[19]

Reaction to the Plan

"Ethics is something you learn as a child; teaching it doesn't make you an ethical person," said Professor Charles Elson, director of the Weinburg Center for Corporate Governance at the University of Delaware. He did say, however, that "if [Prince's plan] can clarify blurry issues and help instill a culture of compliance to a code, I applaud it. But to teach ethics to make people ethical, that's a bit strained."[20] Elson went on to suggest: "The acid test is going to be sort of a no-tolerance policy for ethical violations, not just legal violations . . . If the company demonstrates to its employees that it will not tolerate violations of its code of ethics . . . then you begin to affect a change in culture." Elson further stated that Prince's efforts were a "good start" but that he would need to distance himself from former administration that did not put compliance first. "Rethinking his board, bringing in new blood would be quite helpful," said Elson. He added that Sandy Weill must go: "I think that Mr. Weill's complete retirement from the company would go a long way to distance Mr. Prince from the earlier regime."[21]

The Departure of Weill's Army

A few months after Prince's plan was announced, Robert B. Willumstad, Citigroup's President, COO, and Director, announced that he was going to leave to become a chief executive of a public company. Willumstad had a key role in creating Citigroup in 1998 with the combination of Traveler's Group and Citicorp. During his tenure as Chairman and CEO of the Global Consumer Group at Citigroup, the company witnessed strong profit growth and several successful acquisitions. Willumstad worked closely with Charles Prince and Sandy Weill for years, and was very disappointed when he was not chosen as CEO. [22]

In the same month, Weill stated that he wanted to end his contract early, and launch a private-equity fund. There are reports that he is frustrated by Prince's Five Point Plan and the Traveler's Group transaction. One bank analyst stated, "Sandy always told me he preferred to fix things as opposed to sell them . . . I'm sure he hated [the Traveler's Group] sale."[23] In spite of these issues, Weill decided to stay on due to conflicts of interest and information access.

A month after the announcements about Willumstad and Weill, Marjorie Magner announced her plans to leave, as well. Marjorie was the chairman and chief executive of the Global Consumer Group segment of Citigroup. Magner plans to pursue a career change outside the financial services industry.[24] She is among the highest-ranking women at Citigroup, and her group contributed more than half of the bank's income over the last several years. Executives at Citigroup knew that Magner disagreed with Prince's plan and major changes. Prince responded to Magner's announcement by saying that she was one of the "legends who built Citigroup," and that he is "most proud" of the people she is developing, including her successors. [25]

On a more positive note, Saudi Prince Alwaleed bin Talal, Citigroup Inc.'s biggest investor, said chief executive Charles Prince would need more time to prove himself as head of the world's largest financial services firm. "This company is a giant," Alwaleed said. "You have to give him time to institute his culture and way of thinking. I'm backing them all the way."[26]

Prince's Response

Charles Prince said of all these initiatives, "The real question is can we execute it in a way that becomes more embedded? The systems are designed to provide sticks. This will all tie to how you pay people. People who don't complete the required training, for example, won't receive bonuses. If we don't pay people the right way, the initiatives risk becoming no more than cynical happy-talk." [27] Prince acknowledged that he has to *own* this program. He said, "If we delegate this to the [human resources] department, it's not going to work".[28]

Chapter 11: Long Case Notes

1   Citigroup, "Annual Report 2004," http://www.citigroup.com.
2   Citigroup, "Annual Report 2004," http://www.citigroup.com.
3   Suellentrop, C., "Sandy Weill, How Citigroup's CEO rewrote the rules so he could live richly." http://www.slate.msn.com, November 20, 2002.
4   "Laughing all the way from the bank/Citigroup's mastermind is still defending his grand design," *New York Times*, September 11, 2005.
5   Wikipedia, the Free Encyclopedia Online, "Charles Prince," http://en.wikipedia.org/wiki/Prince.
6   "For Citi, this Prince is a charm: CEO Chuck Prince is no Sandy Weill when it comes to style, and that has proven to be just what the scandal plagued giant needs," *BusinessWeek Online*, January 28, 2005.
7   "Spitzer settlement to cost Citigroup $1.3 bn," *Financial Times,* December 23, 2002.
8   Office of the New York State Attorney General Eliot Spitzer, "Conflict probes resolved at Citigroup and Morgan Stanley," http://www.oag.state.ny.us, April 28, 2003.
9   "Salomon agrees to NASD fine," *The Asian Wall Street Journal,* September 25, 2002.
10 "Citigroup to pay $5 million fine to NASD to settle charges it issued misleading research to protect an investment ban king client with a focus on Jack Grubman," *CNBC Business Center,* September 23, 2002.
11 Federal Trade Commission, "Citigroup settles FTC charges against the associates record-setting $215 million for subprime lending victims," http://www .ftc.gov, September 19, 2002.
12 "The falls of Enron: Citigroup settles suit over credit insurance," *Houston Chronicle,* September 20, 2002.
13 "World Com files largest bankruptcy ever," *Money,* July 22, 2002.
14 "Citigroup to pay $2.6 billion to settle World Com-related suit," *TR Daily,* May 10, 2004.
15 "Citigroup's misstep in Japan may bruise bank's global image," *The Wall Street Journal,* September 22, 2004.
16 "Citigroup ceases coverage of 117 firms: Seven analysts fired: Research cutbacks mirror rivals' in wake of Spitzer deal," *Financial Post,* May 24, 2003.
17 "US Fed puts check on Citigroup deals," *Financial Times,* March 17, 2005.
18 "Citigroup swaps top jobs," *Guardian*, September 28, 2004.
19 "Lewis B. Kaden to join Citigroup as Chief Administrative Officer," *Business Wire,* June 15, 2005.
20 "Citigroup goes to ethics class," *New York Post,* February 17, 2005.
21 "Films and forums teach value of ethics," *The Times,* March 26, 2005.
22 "Citigroup announces departure of Robert B. Willumstad," *Business Wire,* July 14, 2005; "Citigroup's No. 2 will leave, seek a firm to lead," *Wall Street Journal*, July 15, 2005.
23 "Frustrations of a deal-maker," *New York Times*, July 21, 2005.
24 "Citigroup's Marjorie Magner to leave," *AP,* August 22, 2005.
25 "Citigroup's Prince remakes empire, as Magner leaves," *Business Week,* September 5, 2005.
26 "Citigroup's chief needs time, says Saudi Prince," *Calgary Herald,* September 7, 2005.

27 "Citigroup works on its reputation," *Wall Street Journal*, February 16, 2005.

28 "After scandals, Citigroup moves to beef up ethics," *Wall Street Journal*, February 17, 2005; "Exclusive interview with Citigroup," http://welcome.corpedia.com/index.php?id=236s=news&c= news August 31, 2005.

LONG CASE QUESTIONS

1. Has Citigroup grown too large to enforce corporate governance or internal controls? What effect has the organization's size and complexity had on the continued problems?

2. What effect will the new plans have on Citigroup's investors? What can Citigroup do to mitigate negative responses?

3. How can Citigroup continually communicate the reformed organizational culture to the public?

4. Do you believe it is possible (why or why not) to enforce an ethics program based on changing culture and ethical climate with this or any other organization?

5. As a top manager at Citigroup, what methods would you use to communicate and execute a plan for a Citigroup ethical culture change?

6. Is Prince's plan sufficient, given the magnitude of the problems facing Citigroup?

Corporate Social Responsibility

LEARNING OBJECTIVES

After reading this chapter you should be able to:

- Understand the development of corporate social responsibility during the last few decades
- Understand the arguments that support more social responsive businesses than those that counter this position
- Become aware of the basic models of corporate social responsibility
- Understand the fundamental premises of strategic social responsibility
- Become aware of the social responsibility reporting options

PREVIEW BUSINESS ETHICS INSIGHT

Tata Steel's Company Town: "We also make Steel"

A company town is usually in a remote area where a business needs workers. To attract the needed labor the company builds its own town, giving workers a place to live. The company typically owns the real estate, utilities, hospitals, and small businesses such as grocery stores. In the early 1900s, company towns were common in the West. The U.S. had more than 3,000 and the Cadburys built them in England. For the most part, companies built company towns to solve a practical problem. In the U.S., the vital resources for the mining and lumber industries were in remote places, so it was the only way to get workers.

Some company towns were little better than the gulags, the forced labor camps of the former Soviet Union. The housing was inadequate and often people had to spend most of their earnings at the company-owned store to survive. They were often in debt to the company, making it difficult for them to leave. Basically, this was a mechanism to get labor at the lowest price possible. In contrast, other company towns represented the Utopian spirit of the times. Henry Kaiser, the shipping magnate, and Milton Hershey, of chocolate fame, provided their company towns with decent housing, schools, libraries, and hospitals.

Although company towns have long since faded away in the West, new company towns are being created or making comebacks in the developing world. Jamshedpur, the headquarters location for Tata Steel in India, was built at the turn of the century to solve the same practical problem faced by the U.S. industrialists. The coal and iron ore necessary to make steel were in the middle of an isolated forest. However, Jamsetji Tata, the founder of the town and the Tata Group, had other goals than just the practical need for workers. He wanted a model town with good schools, sports facilities, and modern amenities.

Although Tata Steel is now a global force in the steel industry, it has not broken its ties with the town. Far from that, it has modernized and expanded its relationship. As *The Economist* notes, "The Western doctrine of 'corporate social responsibility' (CSR) has also given the founder's very Victorian vision a new lease of life." Tata provides the town a 900-bed hospital. It owns the local newspaper and the town zoo. Its subsidiary, Jusco, delivers the utilities. Many workers have company houses and company cars. The company also has 250 employees who engage in rural outreach, teaching local tribespeople how to create irrigation systems and grow crops as well as giving health advice. The local sports facility, open to all, is a Tata Steel property. It also serves as a national center for various sports academies.

How central are these CSR activities to the Tata Steel culture? Telling is a phrase in its advertisement: "We also make steel."

Based on *The Economist*. 2011. "Company towns: The universal provider." June 19; *The Economist*. 2010. "Monuments to power: The politics and culture of urban development." October 14.

This chapter considers the broad issue of **corporate social responsibility** (CSR). Up to this point, you have seen how the various stakeholders come into play when managers consider ethical issues. Here we broaden our focus to consider generally the degree to which companies should or perhaps must go beyond the requirements of running an economically viable business within the constraints of the law. We will consider various definitions of CSR below. However, common themes focus on how companies can protect the environment and enhance the well-being of their stakeholders, all while maintaining an economically viable business. The Preview Business Ethics Insight above gives a perspective on how Tata Steel prioritizes its responsibility to the community as a core value. The conditions of some of the gulag-type towns of the U.S. West noted in the Insight is in stark contrast with Tata, yet it illustrates one view of the proper model for companies—let the market drive the price (in this case, for labor).

However, Tata's generosity is not without costs. As *The Economist* commented: "Does Tata Steel know when to say no? Or will it be constantly pulled into new CSR activities that will divert too many resources from its core mission?"[1] Tata has not had a strike since the 1920s so, perhaps, there are benefits not easily measured.

A BRIEF HISTORY OF CORPORATE SOCIAL RESPONSIBILITY

Some scholars trace the "modern" era of corporate social responsibility to the 1960s.[2] However, others see the genesis of CSR, at least as a formal issue, to a debate in the *Harvard Law Review* during the 1930s between Columbia Professor Adolf A. Berle and Harvard Professor E. Merrick Dodd. Berle contended that managers are only responsible to shareholders, while Dodd countered that managers have wider responsibilities and "that the powers of corporate management are held in trust for the entire community." Providing an intellectual basis for what we now know as CSR, Dodd went on to note that the modern firm is "permitted and encouraged by the law primarily because it is of service to the community rather than because it is a source of profit to its owner."[3] Although CSR is on firm grounds throughout the world, this debate has not ended.

One can set the debate for the need for CSR in the context of Adam Smith's classical economic theory. For Smith, the maximum benefits for society are achieved in an unfettered market where people and organizations act in self-interest. The **"invisible hand"** allows the best organizations to flourish because competition favors those who produce the best products at the best prices as consumers also seek their own self-interest in buying those products. As Smith notes in the often quoted statement below:

> It is not from the benevolence of the butcher, the brewer, or the baker, that we expect our dinner, but from their regard to their own interest. We address ourselves, not to their humanity but to their self-love, and never talk to them of our own necessities but of their advantages.[4]

The Industrial Revolution seemed to support Smith's ideas, as many people took jobs in newly created factories, often achieving a better standard of living. However, large organizations now held greater power than ever before and their founders and owners became some of the richest people in the world. The landscape of a laissez-faire economy often encouraged severe and often cutthroat competition among organizations that led to little or no concern for the company's impact on employees, the community, or the larger society.

Paradoxically, many of these same industrialists that ran these companies that exploited workers and local communities were also among the world's greatest philanthropists. Although sometimes referred to as robber barons, the very wealthy of this era gave millions of dollars to charity and educational institutions. Many of the foundations they, and later their families, established are still engaged in philanthropy today. You will recognize some of the names as, for example, John D. Rockefeller, Leland Stanford, Cornelius Vanderbilt, and Andrew Carnegie. However, this was not CSR. If philanthropy occurred, it was done by individuals for their own reasons and not as a representative of a company.

With the start of the twentieth century, criticism of big business increased. More people began to believe that the big corporations were too powerful and used business practices that were anti-social and anti-competitive. As a result, the government responded with laws and regulations that limited the power of large corporations and served to protect employees, consumers, and society at large. Between 1900 and 1960, in response to changes in prevailing cultural values and perhaps the threat of increased regulations, business leaders gradually accepted that corporations have additional responsibilities beyond making a profit and obeying the law.

The 1960s and 1970s continued a cultural shift in the expectations for business in most countries. Movements related to civil rights, consumerism, and environmentalism changed the context for doing business and therefore society's expectations for business responsibilities. Such shifts in expectations resulted in growing legal constraints on business in areas related to equal employment opportunity, product safety, worker safety, and the environment. In the 1970s, social legislation in the United States sent an increasingly strong message to the corporate world that the playing field was changing. Creation of the Environmental Protection Agency (EPA), the Equal Employment Opportunity Commission (EEOC), Occupational Safety and Health Administration (OSHA), and the Consumer Product Safety Commission (CPSC) elevated the influence of many stakeholders in the corporate world. However, going beyond legal compliance and based on the premise that those with greater power have greater responsibilities, most of the developed world called on businesses to become proactive. Increasingly, it became an expectation that it is not sufficient to avoid causing social problems but it is also necessary to help solve social problems.[5] Today this is even more apparent, as you will see later in the chapter when we discuss the rising pressure for CSR performance measurement, reporting, and engagement with stakeholders.

In the U.S., the first legal precedent for the dominance of the stockholder as the prime stakeholder was the influential 1919 case of ***Dodge v. Ford***.[6] Despite its name, the case had nothing to do with competition between automakers. At that time Ford was slowly lowering the price of his cars from $900 to $360. He also decided that he could no longer pay special dividends. He needed to offset the losses from cutting prices and he intended to increase wages and expand production capacity. Ford defended his decision altruistically based on his broader social goals: "to employ still more men, to spread the benefits of this industrial system to the greatest possible number, to help them build up their lives and their homes." He also noted that he had paid out considerable dividends to the shareholders, giving them substantial profits, and they should be content with lower dividends now.

The Dodge brothers (10% owners of Ford and a competitor company) sued, claiming that Ford had no right to use stockholder equity (their money) for his own philanthropic ends. The Michigan Supreme Court sided with the Dodges saying that the corporation exists for the benefit of stockholders. Corporate boards only have flexibility in how they choose to achieve those ends. They left open the idea that a certain amount of philanthropic giving might benefit the company. However, the case largely established the belief in the U.S. that corporations have prime, if not sole, responsibilities to shareholders.[7]

At least in the U.S., the switch from stockholder dominance to corporate philanthropy began with **Smith v. Barlow**,[8] a landmark court decision in 1953. A.P. Smith Manufacturing Company, a manufacturer of valves and fire hydrants, was sued by a stockholder for donating $1,500 to Princeton University under the premise that this was not in the best interest of the stockholders. In *Smith v. Barlow*, the court upheld the contribution as legal ruling against the stockholders. The court ruled that the stockholders, "whose private interests rest entirely upon the well-being of the corporation, ought not to be permitted to close their eyes to present-day realities and thwart the long-visioned corporate action in recognizing and voluntarily discharging its high obligations as a constituent of our modern social structure."

After this case, the dominant model of CSR was corporate philanthropy. Donations to worthy causes such as universities and social services were considered beneficial for the health of society. Associated with this philanthropy was a notion that it should "come from the heart" and not necessarily benefit the company.[9]

Sometimes considered the "father" of CSR, Howard Bowen offered an early definition of CSR that showed movement away from a purely philanthropic position:

> It [CSR] refers to the obligations of businessmen [sic] to pursue those policies, to make those decisions or to follow those lines of action which are desirable in terms of the objectives and values of our society.[10]

During the 1960s and 1970s, the concept of CSR broadened both in practice and in academic thinking.[11] Although over a decade before R. Edward Freeman's classic *Strategic Management: A Stakeholder Approach*, Harold Johnson introduced an array of stakeholders into his 1971 definition of CSR:

> A socially responsible firm is one whose managerial staff balances a multiplicity of interests. Instead of striving only for larger profits for its stockholders, a responsible enterprise also takes into account employees, suppliers, dealers, local communities, and the nation.[12]

The idea of the duties and obligations to stakeholders is now entrenched in both practitioner and academic thinking about CSR.

One way of thinking about CSR, born in the 1970s, but still popular today is the CSR pyramid developed by Archie Carroll.[13] His pyramid is shown in Exhibit 12.1.

For Carroll, there are four essential responsibilities of a business. These include **economic**, **legal**, **ethical**, and **philanthropic**. He accepts that the principal role of a business is to produce goods or services that people need and to make an acceptable profit in the process. Without a surviving and profitable business, all other responsibilities are moot. Businesses must conform to laws and regulations as part of the social contract between business and society that allows them to operate. This is now often called a **license to operate**. Although the legal requirements of business operations may control activities and practices with ethical consequences, such as regulations regarding product safety and consumer protection, businesses must conform to the ethical expectations of society that are not codified into law. These ethical expectations

EXHIBIT 12.1 — Carroll's Pyramid of CSR

reflect what the organizational stakeholders—stockholders, consumers, employees, and the greater community—consider fair, just, and beneficial to society at large. These obligations rest on moral reasoning based principles such as rights and justice and utilitarian logic.

Such ethical expectations often precede formal codification into laws, as changing societal values often drive later legislation. You will see later in this chapter how the formal reporting of CSR performance is gradually moving beyond voluntary and is required in some form in many parts of the world.

At the top of the pyramid is a philanthropic responsibility. This is the responsibility to be good corporate citizens and engage in activities that promote human welfare and goodwill. Contributions to the arts and education fall into this category. What distinguishes philanthropic from ethical responsibility is that philanthropy is not a moral obligation. Stakeholders typically do not see the firm as immoral if it does not engage in philanthropy.

Carroll cautions that the components of the pyramid are not mutually exclusive. In fact, they are in a dynamic tension, with the most critical being between the economic versus the other components. However, it is an oversimplification to view CSR as a concern for profits versus concern for society. The pyramid provides a metaphor to look at the issues and tensions and Carroll's research shows that many companies

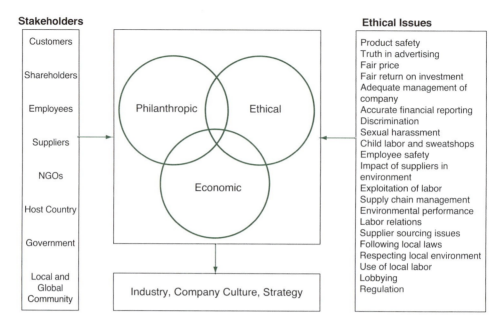

Stakeholders		Ethical Issues
Customers		Product safety
		Truth in advertising
		Fair price
Shareholders		Fair return on investment
		Adequate management of company
Employees	Philanthropic — Ethical	Accurate financial reporting
		Discrimination
		Sexual harassment
Suppliers		Child labor and sweatshops
		Employee safety
		Impact of suppliers in environment
NGOs	Economic	Exploitation of labor
		Supply chain management
Host Country		Environmental performance
		Labor relations
		Supplier sourcing issues
Government		Following local laws
		Respecting local environment
		Use of local labor
Local and Global Community	Industry, Company Culture, Strategy	Lobbying
		Regulation

EXHIBIT 12.2 — Tensions, Stakeholders, and Issues in the CSR Responsibility Mix

organize their CSR efforts around such issues. To emphasize how the core areas of CSR work not necessarily as a pyramid, Carroll has viewed these areas in the perspective of a Venn diagram, with issues and stakeholders pressing for the dominance of one CSR focus over another. A visual representation of this is shown in Exhibit 12.2.

In spite of some CSR advocates such as Carroll giving economic performance and profits a major position in thinking about CSR, during this early rise in CSR interest and activities many academics and business leaders feared that the movement would lead to increased involvement of the government in private decisions.[14] Nobel laureate **Milton Friedman** is probably the most famous critic. His five-page article in the September 13, 1970, issue of the *New York Times Magazine*, "The Social Responsibility of Business is to Increase its Profits," remains to this day the rallying point of those who see CSR as an affront to shareholder rights. For Friedman, there is only one purpose of the corporation: "There is one and only one social responsibility of business —to use its resources and engage in activities designed to increase its profits so long as it stays within the rules of the game, which is to say, engages in open and free competition without deception or fraud." Otherwise, he reasoned, managers are deciding how to spend other people's money. It is better that shareholders get their just share of the profits and decide for themselves as individuals whether to give to charity or support other causes.

Although the increased concern for social responsibility issues is accepted as legitimate in most large multinational corporations around the world, the Global Business Ethics Insight on page 525 suggests that Friedman's position on the role of the corporation still resonates with some people from different areas of the world.

GLOBAL BUSINESS ETHICS INSIGHT

International Reactions to Friedman's Position

Edelman, a U.S. public relations firm that specializes in and measures consumer trust of business, recently conducted a survey of people's reaction to the statement, "The social responsibility of business is to increase its profits." The survey focused on what Edelman calls the "informed public." These are people who are university educated and in the top quarter of the wage earners in their age groups and countries. The survey covered 23 countries. The chart below shows the percentage of people agreeing with the Friedman position from a selection of those countries.

The emerging markets lean in Friedman's direction, with India, Indonesia, Mexico, and Poland nearing the top of the list. The recently emerged markets of Singapore and South Korea are also firmly behind the role of the corporation as being to make profits. However, China and Brazil are closer to the social democracies of Europe, which tend to be pro-CSR. Sweden differs from other social democratic countries, with nearly 60% of the well informed supporting Friedman. *The Economist* speculates that "perhaps people feel little need for CSR when the government cares for them from cradle to grave."

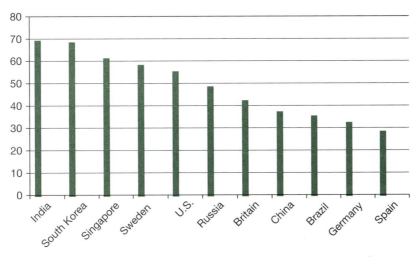

Percent Agreeing: Social Responsibility of Business is to Increase Profits

Based on Edelman. 2011. Trust Barometer; *The Economist*. 2011. "Milton Friedman goes on tour: A survey of attitudes to business turns up some intriguing national differences." January 27.

Much of the contemporary view of CSR supports Carroll's thinking, reflecting a mix of economic and socially responsive actions. Perhaps the major shift in orientation in the recent decade is the specific concern for environmental sustainability and corruption. While sustainability might be subsumed under the general concern for society, it is now a cornerstone of most CSR initiatives in organizations.

A currently popular way of looking at the mix of the components of CSR is called the **triple bottom line (TBL)**, consisting of social, economic, and environmental sustainability. It is also known as "people, planet, and profit." TBL was popularized by John Elkington in his 1998 book *Cannibals with Forks: The Triple Bottom Line of 21st Century Business*. The Global Reporting Initiative, which we consider below, uses a TBL approach to identify CSR issues and measures of performance.

The TBL is a stakeholder approach to CSR that seeks to balance the needs of all. Like Carroll's pyramid and his representation of the areas of CSR from a competition perspective rather than a hierarchy, TBL also contains a concern for philanthropy and going beyond ethical and legal requirements. In the people sector, there is a focus on issues such as fair wages, child labor, occupational health and safety, training, and equal opportunity. There is also a focus on community engagement, such as support for education and the protection of indigenous people.

Planet represents environmental stewardship and sustainable environmental practices. The objective is to reduce the environmental impact in the lifecycle of use. Reduced raw material, energy, and water is combined with lower emissions, waste, and efficient transport of the products to customers. It is often easier to quantify financial returns from environmental savings in waste reduction and energy use.

Profit represents not only standard economic returns to stockholders but also a concern for the benefits of others such as using local suppliers or indirect economic benefits for the local community. Innovation is also part of the economic returns.

The TBL model is summarized in Exhibit 12.3 opposite.

A slightly different way of looking at the relationship between business and society is through the concept of **corporate citizenship**. Although the idea of corporate citizenship is not new, it has gained in use and prominence during the last decade.

What is corporate citizenship? There are three basic views.[15] The "limited view" is similar to Carroll's philanthropic CSR that you read above. A good corporate citizen is a company that gives back to the community as a voluntary action. The focus is on the close environment of the firm, such as supporting local sports teams.

The "equivalent view" of corporate citizenship is very similar to Carroll's view of CSR focusing on legal, ethical, and discretionary responsibilities of business. The "extended view" of corporate citizenship focuses on the role of the corporation as an entity that is independent of the owners and managers and can in many ways be treated like another human being. In this view, the corporation not only has responsibilities to act within the law and within moral expectations, but it also has rights. The corporation has social rights to choose to provide or not to provide individuals with additional social services. The corporation has civil rights to act freely similar to those of other citizens. Finally, the corporation has political rights to participate in the political process and influence its environment, again similar to other citizens.

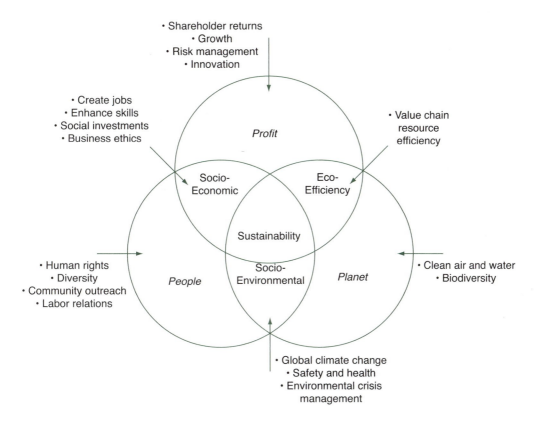

- Shareholder returns
- Growth
- Risk management
- Innovation

- Create jobs
- Enhance skills
- Social investments
- Business ethics

- Value chain resource efficiency

Profit

Socio-Economic

Eco-Efficiency

Sustainability

Socio-Environmental

- Human rights
- Diversity
- Community outreach
- Labor relations

People

Planet

- Clean air and water
- Biodiversity

- Global climate change
- Safety and health
- Environmental crisis management

EXHIBIT 12.3 — The Triple Bottom Model

Why another term for many of the same issues we see in CSR? Professors Matten, Crane, and Chapple argue that much of the language of CSR, particularly the concepts of "ethics" and "responsibility," are not part of the language of business and thus may not be completely accepted.[16] Managers, they argue, can be more comfortable with the idea of "citizenship" where corporations can take their rightful place in society.

Regardless of the approach taken to identify CSR issues, an increasingly popular position is to view CSR as a potential asset. The next section gives an overview of strategic CSR and some ideas of how this can be implemented.

STRATEGIC CSR

Strategic CSR rests on the assumption that "doing good" can be good for a business as well as for society. With strategic CSR, corporations attend to their stakeholders because managers believe it is in the best interest of the company.[17] Is strategic CSR different?

In looking at the evidence of how CSR in general affects company performance, the results are inconclusive.[18] Some research shows that companies engaged in CSR do prosper in the long run, while other studies have found negative or no relationship.[19] Making assessment more difficult, CSR often leads to qualitative outcomes that may help a company but may not be quantifiable, such as employee morale, corporate image, reputation, public relations, goodwill, and popular opinion.[20] Such benefits might not produce immediate financial returns. Although broadly targeted quantitative studies of corporations show no systematic relationships with CSR activities, there is ample anecdotal evidence from individual firms that benefited from CSR. Highly successful corporations that also lead on CSR include the Body Shop, Ben & Jerry's, and Toms of Maine.[21]

Some anecdotal examples of the benefits of strategic CSR include:[22]

- Positive consumer responses and growth in market share. Aravind Eye Hospitals in India charge just $50 a patient for cataract surgeries to target patients that cannot afford a more traditional price. They do over 200,000 surgeries a year, resulting in a $46.5 million profit
- Organizational learning. To help inner-city children learn via technology, Bell Atlantic developed Project Explore in Union City, New Jersey. This led to innovations in networking technology that created Infospeed DSL. This new product more than covered the costs of the project.
- Committed and engaged employees. Research shows that employees who come into direct contact with those who benefit from their efforts work better, harder, and are less likely to turnover.
- Investor relations. Investors are paying attention. Increasing at nearly 20% a year, the amount of money dedicated to socially responsible investing is expected to pass $3 trillion in 2011, just in the U.S.

The examples such as those above suggest that CSR may benefit an array of stakeholders while still contributing to the bottom line. But companies need to find ways to integrate CSR into their business models. Consequently, because of the somewhat uncertain relationship between CSR and organization performance, strategic experts, such as Michael Porter of Harvard University, have begun to develop insights into how CSR could be better linked to competitive advantage and be truly strategic. Professor Porter and his colleague Mark Kramer identified many of these issues in an important article published in the *Harvard Business Review*. Below we will consider some of the highlights of their insights.[23]

CSR is Here and Going to Stay

For business leaders in most every country, CSR either is, or is becoming, a significant priority. Nearly every major stakeholder, including governments, NGO activists, employees, and local communities, demands that corporations consider social responsibility in the business decisions. Consequently, in the current global marketplace, it is an "inescapable priority" that businesses engage in some level of social responsibility in such areas of environmentalism, social accountability to the larger society, and employee health and safety. In a recent McKinsey report,[24] 95% of the CEOs surveyed "believe that society has higher expectations for business to take on public responsibilities than it had five years ago." As a result, the majority of their companies report adding environmental, social, and governance into their core strategies. Although pressures from an array of stakeholders play an important role in these actions, more CEOs see these new demands not only as motivation to address global problems but also as an opportunity to gain competitive advantages.

Although Porter and Kramer recognize that many companies are already improving the environmental and social consequences of their business activities, they see two reasons why many companies have not been as productive as they should be. First, there has been a tendency to pit business against society when it is more productive to realize that the two are interdependent. Businesses need societies with well-educated and healthy workers and a sustainable environment. Society needs businesses to go beyond a self-centered look on profits and participate in making the world better. Second, many businesses think of CSR in a general way, with various check-offs, rather than thinking strategically. So how can businesses overcome these problems?

One of the first suggestions is to find ways to use CSR to do things differently than competitors. Managers need to look at CSR as a strategic tool to lower costs or better serve customers' needs. Porter and Kramer caution against simply throwing money at good causes but, instead, strategically picking areas that align with their expertise. Toyota, for example, is known for innovation in car production and design. Being one of the first to market a hybrid gasoline/electric car, Toyota designed the Prius to meet customer needs for a highly efficient automobile. At the same time, it hybrid engine emits only 10% of the pollutants from a typical internal combustion engine, resulting in environmental benefits to society. Because this is such a differentiated product, Toyota can charge, and customers are willing to pay, a higher price than for a more conventional car.

Porter and Kramer suggest one way to identify potential areas of strategic CSR competitive advantages is to map the impact of the company's value chain. A value chain shows all of the activities a company uses to do business. In looking at these activities, managers can assess positive and negative social impacts from their business operations. The next step is to make plans to mitigate potential negative outcomes and to identify areas upon which to build strategic advantages.

Exhibit 12.4 (page 530) shows the value chain and illustrates potential CSR opportunities and threats linked to each component. The value chain begins with inbound logistics, such as getting parts or raw material into the organization. In an example below, you will see that Starbucks found an economic and socially responsible mechanism to support local farmers while ensuring a supply of high-quality coffee. In the operations component of the value chain, there are often many economically beneficial opportunities to cut costs while also benefiting society such as reducing waste. Consider the example of Hydro in the next section as a company that has made recycling a critical part of their production process a part of their competitive advantage.

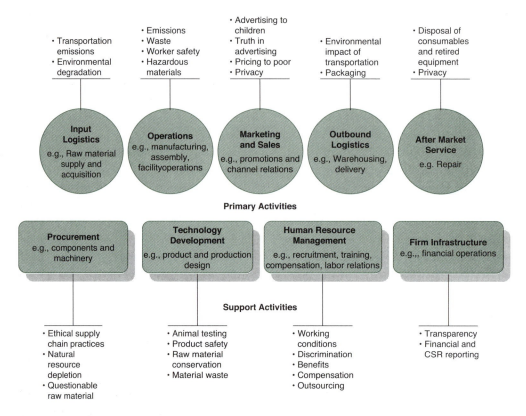

EXHIBIT 12.4—Building CRS Considerations into Porter's Value Chain

In the next section, we expand the view of strategic CSR to identify several guiding principles that managers use to build a competitive advantage.

STRATEGIC CSR PRINCIPLES

Professor Peter Heslin and strategy consultant Jeann Ochoa studied numerous companies to identify seven exemplary strategic CSR principles.[25] They note that not all organizations are excellent at all strategic principles but some excel at some. However, they found many companies that successfully use these strategic CSR principles to build CSR into their value chains. Below, we describe these principles and some organizations that seem to follow them well.

- *Cultivate needed talent*. Marriott International and Microsoft use CSR initiatives to attract and maintain a superior workforce. Marriott's "Pathways to Independence" program focuses on welfare recipients to teach them life skills and job skills. The curriculum includes such job skills as how to search for a job and how to interview. Life skills include developing a household budget. Graduates are offered jobs at Marriott. Marriott benefits by getting a diverse group of eager employees initially at entry-level jobs but also with potential career paths leading to management. Turnover for these employees is 50% less than other employees.

Like Marriott, Microsoft has also used CRS activities to improve the quality of its workforce and those of its suppliers and customers. Microsoft donated $47 million to the American Association of Community Colleges to improve IT curricula and faculty skills at community colleges. To improve diversity in the IT workforce, Microsoft also donated $75 million in software, reference materials, and training materials to the 39 United Negro College Fund member institutions. What is their benefit? In the company's own words, "Microsoft strives to be the leader in attracting minorities and women to careers in technology. We believe that diverse ideas and representation add value to our corporate community and to our products. We are committed to working with colleges and universities to help students achieve the knowledge and necessary skills to thrive in this competitive industry."[26]

- *Develop new markets.* The Dutch multinational Philips is a leading producer of electronic, lighting, and medical products. Philips specializes in finding innovative ways to penetrate markets in the developing world. For example, to deliver high-quality healthcare to rural communities in India, Philips uses traveling medical vans. These vans use satellite technology to link up with high-quality medical facilities in urban areas. This allows patients in isolated villages to get high-quality care.

  Whole Foods Market is the largest natural and organic food supermarket. With a business model that promotes organic farming, Whole Foods not only contributes to sustainable agriculture but also benefits farm workers, who avoid exposure to chemicals that are commonly used in large industrial companies. Whole Foods gives 5% of its total net profits to non-profit organizations and provides time off for employees to perform community service. Traditionally rated as one of the best companies to work for, Whole Foods has an enthusiastic workforce that helps them support a differentiation strategy aimed at a socially conscious consumer who is willing to pay a higher price for its organic products.

- *Protect labor welfare.* Protecting the rights and working conditions of the labor force is a continuing CSR issue. This has been an especially troublesome issue for the companies in the garment industries, particularly with regard to child labor and sweatshops. Levi Strauss found an innovative way to deal with the child labor issue. Their first reaction to dealing the fallout from using children under 15 in some of their factories was to consider firing all underage employees. However, when they considered the labor market in Bangladesh, they discovered that many of the children made significant contributions to the family's income and some were even the sole providers. Their solution: send all underage children back to school with paid wages and, on completion, give them a guaranteed job.

  Starbucks takes an aggressive approach to CSR in its supply chain, noting "we work on-the-ground with farmers to help improve coffee quality and invest in loan programs for coffee-growing communities. It's not just the right thing to do, it's the right thing to do for our business. By helping to sustain coffee farmers and strengthen their communities, we ensure a healthy supply of high-quality coffee for the future."[27] To implement this CSR strategy, Starbucks established Farmer Support

Centers in Costa Rica and Rwanda. These centers provide local farmers with resources and expertise to help lower their costs of production, reduce fungus infections, improve coffee quality, and increase the production of premium coffee. Starbucks also funds organizations that make loans to coffee growers. They have given over $15 million to farmer loan funds. The loans allow the farmers to counter pressures to sell their coffee early at a low price and wait to sell their crops at the best time to get the right price.

- *Reduce your environmental footprint.* Ethel M Chocolates, known nationally for its gourmet chocolates, attracts 700,000 visitors a year. They tour not only the factory but also the Living Machine. Designed and built by Living Technologies of Burlington, Vermont, the Living Machine is a water recycling plant used to purify Ethel M's wastewater. The treatment plant uses no chemicals. Instead, it mimics nature's natural water purification process using artificial wetlands with live bacteria, algae, protozoa, snails, fish, and plants to eliminate pollutants from the water. The treated water ends up in an open pond after a day of travel through the artificial wetlands. The treated wastewater is clean enough for air-conditioning systems, irrigation, and vehicle washing.[28] Not only are there environment benefits but the company also gets positive outcomes by cultivating its reputation and sales as a Las Vegas attraction.

  The Norwegian multinational aluminum company Hydro operates in 40 countries. Hydro has 19 plants for recycling scrap aluminum in Asia, America, and Europe. In 2010 Hydro produced more than a million tons of aluminum, of which 260,000 tons were recycled. By 2020 the company expects to recycle around one million tons. Rather than traditional mining, they call this recycling effort "urban mining." That is, the source of raw materials tends to be in urban centers.[29]

  Recycling requires only 5% of the energy used to produce new aluminum. Roland Scharf-Bergmann, head of Hydro's Recycling unit, notes: "Scrap has become a strategic raw material in regions like Europe, but also across the globe. We know that China views scrap as strategic, so we can expect China to grow their investment in recycling as well as scrap imports significantly." "Hydro's role in the future will be to take our share of the market as a leading integrated producer over the whole value chain. Our position in the market, combined with commercial and technological competence, will provide us with growth opportunities in recycling to help us improving our carbon footprint," Scharf-Bergmann said.[30] Hydro is one example of how an environmentally friendly strategy can become a core strategy of the company.

- *Profit from by-products.* Shaw Industries, a flooring company in Georgia, uses what they call a "cradle-to-cradle" production process so that carpets can be collected and returned to manufacturing, with the raw material used to produce the original product again and again. Shaw invests heavily in technologies that they hope will move all of their products to a cradle-to-cradle future. One innovation is the use Nylon 6 fiber. It is the only residential carpet fiber capable of repeated recycling back into the raw material to make new carpet. Shaw views this manufacturing process as a mimic of natural cycles of renewal, such as occurs with natural products returned to the earth for decomposition to make fertilizers in a cycle of renewal. Shaw recycles carpets of Type 6 nylon at their Evergreen Nylon Recycling facility in Augusta, Georgia. The company believes that cradle-to-cradle is the path to true sustainability.[31] Shaw saves customers money by taking carpets back and giving credit for the use of the raw material.

Manildra is an international producer of grains and starches used for industrial purposes. They have made a business using waste products from grain processing. For example, they make ethanol and agricultural feed from "waste starch." They profit from what otherwise would be discarded and the environment benefits with less waste. Such innovation marries environmental benefits with a sound business model.

- *Involve customers*. Hewlett-Packard's (HP) "Planet Partners Return & Recycling Program" involves customer by allowing them to return and recycle (usually free) products such as computer hardware, batteries, and printing cartridges. HP also gives customers the opportunity to get the fair market value of aging technology. HP Financial Services pays customers for qualified computer equipment they no longer want or need. HP benefits by refurbishing and reselling the products. If customers prefer, HP's donate program makes it easy to donate their used computer equipment to charity. In the U.S., HP coordinates this program with the National Cristina Foundation (NCF).[32] The Cristina Foundation is a non-profit organization that matches donated computer equipment with needy schools and non-profit organizations around the world.

  Patagonia, a privately owned leading manufacturer of outdoor clothing and equipment, engages customers to be environmentally sensitive though its website and catalogue. The catalogue is approximately 45% social message and 55% product content. The message content contains articles related to environment and social issue. Some of the content comes from Patagonia customers. Environmentalism is a prominent tab on its website, positioned next to the product ordering tab. On face value one might think that devoting website and catalogue space to CSR issues might hurt sales. However, Patagonia discovered that reducing message content actually reduced sales.

- *Develop a green supply chain*. A number of companies have shown that there is proof of the link between improved environmental performance and financial gains. Companies have looked to their supply chain and seen areas where improvements in the way they operate can produce profits. In one example, Shanghai General Motors (SGM) recently partnered with the World Environment Center (WEC) for a "Greening the Supply Chain Initiative." This program targeted 125 suppliers of the 50/50 joint venture between General Motors and Shanghai Automotive Industry Corp. This joint venture is one of China's largest vehicle producers. The 125 suppliers invested about $21 million in 498 projects focusing on reducing energy use, water consumption, and waste. The results not only improved the local environment, it generated an expected annual cost saving of approximately $19 million. Some projects were profitable in the first year. The environmental performance included a reduction of 55,400 tons of greenhouse gas emissions, equivalent to the

533

annual emissions produced by more than 35,000 passenger vehicles. Annually, water consumption dropped by more than 282 million gallons. Liquid waste dropped 36 million gallons and solid waste by more than 9,300 tons. "By managing sustainable development initiatives through a business process, SGM has improved the energy and environmental performance across its supply chain, built stronger customer-supplier relationships and increased its ability to adapt to evolving governmental requirements," said WEC President and CEO Terry F. Yosie in a statement.[33]

By automating its supply chain transactions with trading partners, Burton Snowboards, the world's leading snowboard company, significantly reduced its paper usage by substituting electronic transactions. Less postage, paper, and envelopes also reduced costs. In total, Burton saved approximately 4 tons of wood use, 30 million BTUs (British Thermal Units), 5,882 lb CO_2, 22,219 gallons wastewater, and 1,909 lb solid waste in one year of the new automated system's use. Buoyed with the success, Burton plans further reductions in the company's environmental impact through greater use of B2B automation and other paper-reducing initiatives. Goals include saving an additional 40 tons of wood use, 350 million BTUs, 65,000 lb CO_2, 250,000 gallons wastewater, and 20,000 lb solid waste. Burton's success demonstrates that green IT in the supply chain directly impacts both the bottom line and the environment.[34]

In the changing CSR environment for corporations, one issue that more firms address each year is how to report and audit their CSR performance to their stakeholders. The next section gives an overview of CRS reporting and detail on two of the most used systems.

REPORTING CSR

Corporations are required to produce annual reports on their economic performance for their stockholders. As owners, investors can use this information to consider whether to invest more or less in the company. Increasingly, however, corporations are facing growing institutional pressure to also produce **social performance reports**. In some countries, such as the U.K. and Denmark, this pressure is legal. For example, in 2008, the Danish parliament passed a bill that makes it mandatory for 1,100 largest businesses to report on CSR in their annual reports. CSR is not mandatory but the goal is to motivate Danish businesses to take an active position on CSR. Businesses are required to report their CSR practices or state that they do not engage in CSR.

When not required by legal constraints, there are additional pressures on companies to report on their social responsibility activities. One of the more important relates to the trend for socially responsible investing. Increasingly, investors are considering a company's CSR activities as a factor in choosing where to invest their money. According to a recent survey by KPMG the worldwide demand for accountability and transparency is at an all-time high, resulting in the demands for a more complete picture of companies including not only financial information but also information on risk management and value-creation in the social and environmental areas.[35]

After surveying the top 250 companies from Global *Fortune* 500 and the largest 100 companies from 22 countries, KPMG concluded that CSR reporting is becoming entrenched at least among the dominant multinational companies. Nearly 80% of the Global 250 now issue reports. For all companies that issue reports, KPMG identified the following benefits:[36]

- *Differentiation*: allows a company to stand out in the marketplace based on CSR strategies and commitments
- *A license to operate*: gives a company a moral position to operate with the public and specific stakeholders
- *Attracting favorable financing*: as financial markets demand more information on environmental and social performance, those who report CSR activities have an advantage
- *Innovation*: CSR encourage innovation through a better understanding of stakeholder needs and possible risks
- *Attracting and retaining employees*: in a time of high employee expectations, social performance makes a company more competitive for the best talent
- *Enhancing reputation*: reporting shows that a company is truthful in reporting information of tough issues.

Although CSR reporting is on the rise, it is not consistent in form and participation across countries. Exhibit 12.5 shows the percentages of companies reporting stand-alone CSR reports and integrated CSR reports from the KPMG 22-country/largest-100-companies data. **Integrated reports** are those that are built into the annual reports, which traditionally have focused only on financial performance.

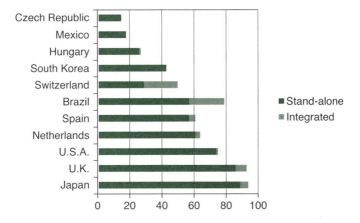

EXHIBIT 12.5—Companies with Stand-Alone and Integrated CSR Reports by Country

What is in a CSR Report?

CSR reporting is still in development and the choice of what is reported, how it is reported, and how the report is verified are still open to debate. A recent 30-country review[37] of mandatory and voluntary CSR reporting standards by the joint efforts of KPMG Advisory N.V., United Nations Environment Program, Global Reporting Initiative, and the Unit for Corporate Governance in Africa found "an increasingly dense network of national and international standards for sustainability reporting." Depending on the country, there is a complex mix of mandatory and voluntary standards. What the study found in the 30 countries included:[38]

- a total of 142 country standards and/or laws with some form of sustainability-related reporting requirement or guidance
- approximately two-thirds (65%) of these standards able to be classified as mandatory and one third (35%) as voluntary
- a total of 16 standards with some form of reporting requirement at the global and regional level
- a total of 14 assurance standards.

We can conclude from the recent trends that CSR measurement and reporting is becoming a requirement driven by both legislative actions and society's expectations. As such, it will be ever more incumbent on future managers to be aware of mandatory and expected standards and how they fit strategically into one's company and industry.

Reporting formats can be general or focus on specific CSR areas such as employee or the environment. Some of the available guides to CSR that provide reporting formats include:

- *AA1000*. AccountAbility's AA1000 series are principles-based standards to help organizations become more accountable, responsible, and sustainable.
- *GRI*. Global Reporting Initiative's Sustainability Reporting Guidelines set out the principles and Performance Indicators that organizations can use to measure and report their economic, environmental, and social performance.
- *Good Corporation's Standard*. Developed in association with the Institute of Business Ethics, this reporting format covers 62 areas of management practice focusing on six stakeholders: employees; customers; suppliers and subcontractors; community and environment; shareholders or other providers of finance; and management commitment.
- *SA8000*. Social Accountability International's standard SA8000 focuses on certifying labor practices for companies and those of their suppliers and vendors. It is based on the principles of international human rights norms as described in International Labor Organization conventions, the United Nations Convention on the Rights of the Child, and the Universal Declaration of Human Rights.
- *ISO 14000*. ISO 14001:2004 gives generic requirements for an environmental management system. When used as a basis for a CSR report, it provides a common

reference for communicating about environmental management issues between organizations and their customers, regulators, the public, and other stakeholders.
- *COP* (*Communication on Progress*). A COP report describes the company's implementation of the United Nations Global Compact's ten universal principles.

Companies may use one or more of the above guides to track and measure their CSR performance and to produce CSR reports. However, the most popular CSR guidelines are based on the **Global Reporting Initiative (GRI)** and the **Communication on Progress (COP)** for the **UN's Global Compact**'s ten principles. We will discuss those CSR monitoring and reporting formats in more detail below, as you will likely use one of them in your organizations.

The UN's Global Compact is based on the following ten principles in the areas of human rights, labor, the environment, and anti-corruption:[39]

Human Rights

- *Principle 1*: Businesses should support and respect the protection of internationally proclaimed human rights; and
- *Principle 2*: make sure that they are not complicit in human rights abuses.

Labor

- *Principle 3*: Businesses should uphold the freedom of association and the effective recognition of the right to collective bargaining;
- *Principle 4*: the elimination of all forms of forced and compulsory labor;
- *Principle 5*: the effective abolition of child labor; and
- *Principle 6*: the elimination of discrimination in respect of employment and occupation.

Environment

- *Principle 7*: Businesses should support a precautionary approach to environmental challenges;
- *Principle 8*: undertake initiatives to promote greater environmental responsibility; and
- *Principle 9*: encourage the development and diffusion of environmentally friendly technologies.

Anti-Corruption

- *Principle 10*: Businesses should work against corruption in all its forms, including extortion and bribery.

Joining the Global Compact initiative is voluntary but, once a company commits to join, it agrees to integrate the principles into its business operations and communicate annually on progress. Business participants are required to submit an annual

STRATEGIC BUSINESS ETHICS INSIGHT

Elements of the COP for the UN's Global Compact

- Example CEO statement of support

> **The Coca Cola Bottling Company of Ghana**   As a company we have shown that we have the character to back our commitments in all the areas of endeavour that we have been committed to: in the marketplace, environment, workplace and our communities. We have by extension displayed our commitment to the principles of the Global Compact and we believe that even as we strive to progress, our drive will be in the direction of reaching out to the entities and people we do business with. We expect to touch them in our own small way to ensure that they also abide by the principles of the Global Compact. Our belief that we cannot be an island all by ourselves and the special meaning we attach to the word "global", as in Global Compact, is what strengthens our resolve. — *2006 COP*

- Example of implementation

> **Talal Abu-Ghazaleh & Co. International (Egypt)**   TAG org shall not discriminate against any employee for any reason such as age, race, gender, sexual orientation, marital status, religious belief, national extraction or disability. TAG org is to guarantee its employees a fair working environment and protection from the loss of their jobs. All employees without any discrimination whatsoever have the right to equal pay for equal work. All candidates seeking to be hired are now required to pass a series of quantitative exams (multiple choice) which ensures objectivity, fairness and equal chances are given to all in our hiring process. We affirm and pledge to uphold the universal human rights of all individuals without limitation. — *2006 COP*

- Example of outcome measurement

> **Martha Tilaar Group (Indonesia)** — *2006 COP*
>
> In our company the minimum age of workers is 18 years old as shown by above data.
>
> | Ages | Management | | | Non-management | | |
> | --- | --- | --- | --- | --- | --- | --- |
> | | 2004 | 2005 | 2006 | 2004 | 2005 | 2006 |
> | Less than 18 years old | 0 | 0 | 0 | 0 | 0 | 0 |
> | 18–20 years old | 0 | 0 | 0 | 8 | 10 | 2 |
> | 21–30 years old | 18 | 13 | 11 | 299 | 238 | 181 |
> | 31–40 years old | 69 | 52 | 62 | 388 | 326 | 330 |
> | 41–50 years old | 41 | 37 | 34 | 107 | 96 | 107 |
> | 51–55 years old | 9 | 12 | 15 | 14 | 16 | 16 |
> | above 55 years old | 2 | 3 | 4 | 6 | 3 | 3 |
> | Total | 139 | 117 | 126 | 822 | 689 | 639 |
>
> Table structure of employee based on age's rank
>
> Note:
> - National age for completion compulsory schooling is 16 years old.
> - Based on company regulation, retirement age is 55 years old.

Source: United Nations Global Compact. 2008. *The practical guide to the United Nations Global Compact communication on progress*, pp. 9–10, 29.

Communication on Progress (COP) and to share the COP widely with their stakeholders. The COP must contain the following elements: a statement by the CEO expressing continued support for the UN Global Compact, a description of practical actions the company has taken to implement the principles, and a demonstration of how outcomes are measured. The Strategic Business Ethics Insight on page 538 shows excerpts from COPs from various companies demonstrating their compliance. By 2011, nearly 5,000 businesses were actively involved in the Global Compact. Other governmental and other non-government organizations also participate. The Strategic Business Ethics Insight shows examples of companies reporting on the three elements of the COP.

The Global Reporting Initiative (GRI) is the most recognized global standard for CSR reporting. The GRI provides principles and indicators that companies can use to identify and measure economic, environmental, and social performance. The third generation of the guidelines was released in 2006 and is available from their website: www.globalreporting.org. An update was launched in March 2011. Exhibit 12.6 provides a copy of the indicators that companies can use as measures.

The GRI also has industry-specific supplements that provide indicators specific to the needs in areas such as Electric Utilities, Financial Services, Mining and Metals, NGOs, Food Processing, Airport Operators, and Construction and Real Estate. Supplements in development include Event Organizers, Media, and Oil and Gas. According to the GRI, using their GRI Framework can demonstrate organizational commitment to CSR, provide measures of organizational performance with respect to laws, norms, standards, and voluntary initiatives, and allow companies to track organizational performance over time.[40] The reasons organizations need such CSR measurement and tracking include:[41]

- Measuring CSR performance allows organizations to identify opportunities to improve operations and avoid risks to the long-term value of their organization.
- Measuring CSR performance indicates an ability to manage CSR impacts that help organizations preserve and increase their value.
- Investors and analysts gain insights into organizational performance and risks beyond that indicated by financial data.
- Transparency increases trust—stakeholders can respond to comparable and standardized information.
- Organizations can mitigate negative impacts in social, environmental, and governance areas.

Recognizing the synergy between the sophisticated measurements and reporting format of the GRI and the Global Compact as the world's largest corporate responsibility platform, the UN's Global Compact and GRI signed an agreement in May 2010 to align their work in advancing corporate responsibility. As part of the agreement, GRI plans to integrate the Global Compact's ten principles into the next version of its Sustainability Reporting Guidelines, due in spring 2013. In turn, the Global Compact will adopt the GRI guidelines as their recommended reporting framework for businesses.[42] This is a natural alliance, as many businesses have adopted the GRI

Environmental

MATERIALS	EN 1	Materials used by weight or volume
	EN 2	Percentage of materials used that are recycled input materials
ENERGY	EN 3	Direct energy consumption by primary energy source
	EN 4	Indirect energy consumption by primary source
	EN 5	Energy saved due to conservation and efficiency improvements
	EN 6	Initiatives to provide energy-efficient or renewable energy-based products and services, and reductions in energy requirements as a result of these initiatives
	EN 7	Initiatives to reduce indirect energy consumption and reductions achieved
WATER	EN 8	Total water withdrawal by source
	EN 9	Water sources significantly affected by withdrawal of water
	EN 10	Percentage and total volume of water recycled and reused
BIODIVERSITY	EN 11	Location and size of land owned, leased, managed in, or adjacent to, protected areas and areas of high biodiversity value outside protected areas
	EN 12	Description of significant impacts of activities, products, and services on biodiversity in protected areas and areas of high biodiversity value outside protected areas
	EN 13	Habitats protected or restored
	EN 14	Strategies, current actions, and future plans for managing impacts on biodiversity
	EN 15	Number of IUCN Red List species and national conservation list species with habitats in areas affected by operations, by level of extinction risk
EMISSIONS, EFFLUENTS, AND WASTE	EN 16	Total direct and indirect greenhouse gas emissions by weight
	EN 17	Other relevant indirect greenhouse gas emissions by weight
	EN 18	Initiatives to reduce greenhouse gas emissions and reductions achieved
	EN 19	Emissions of ozone-depleting substances by weight
	EN 20	NO, SO, and other significant air emissions by type and weight
	EN 21	Total water discharge by quality and destination
	EN 22	Total weight of waste by type and disposal method

EXHIBIT 12.6—The Global Reporting Initiative Performance Indicators

	EN 23	Total number and volume of significant spills
	EN 24	Weight of transported, imported, exported, or treated waste deemed hazardous under the terms of the Basel Convention Annex I, II, III, and VIII, and percentage of transported waste shipped internationally
	EN 25	Identity, size, protected status, and biodiversity value of water bodies and related habitats significantly affected by the reporting organization's discharges of water and runoff
PRODUCTS AND SERVICES	EN 26	Initiatives to mitigate environmental impacts of products and services, and extent of impact mitigation
	EN 27	Percentage of products sold and their packaging materials that are reclaimed by category
COMPLIANCE	EN 28	Monetary value of significant fines and total number of non-monetary sanctions for non-compliance with environmental laws and regulations
TRANSPORT	EN 29	Significant environmental impacts of transporting products and other goods and materials used for the organization's operations, and transporting members of the workforce
OVERALL	EN 30	Total environmental protection expenditures and investments by type

Human Rights

INVESTMENT AND PROCUREMENT PRACTICES	HR 1	Percentage and total number of significant investment agreements and contracts that include clauses incorporating human rights concerns, or that have undergone human rights screening
NON-DISCRIMINATION	HR 2	Percentage of significant suppliers, contractors and other business partners that have undergone human rights screening, and actions taken
	HR 3	Total hours of employee training on policies and procedures concerning aspects of human rights that are relevant to operations, including the percentage of employees trained
	HR 4	Total number of incidents of discrimination, and corrective actions taken
FREEDOM OF ASSOCIATION AND COLLECTIVE BARGAINING	HR 5	Operations and significant suppliers identified in which the right to exercise freedom of association and collective bargaining may be violated or at significant risk, and actions taken to support these rights
CHILD LABOR	HR 6	Operations and significant suppliers identified as having significant risk for incidents of child labor, and measures taken to contribute to the effective abolition of child labor

EXHIBIT 12.6 — *continued*

FORCED AND COMPULSORY LABOR	HR 7	Operations and significant suppliers identified as having significant risk for incidents of forced or compulsory labor, and measures to contribute to the elimination of all forms of forced or compulsory labor
SECURITY PRACTICES	HR 8	Percentage of security personnel trained in the organization's policies or procedures concerning aspects of human rights that are relevant to operations
INDIGENOUS RIGHTS	HR 9	Total number of incidents of violations involving rights of indigenous people, and actions taken
ASSESSMENT	HR 10	Percentage and total number of operations that have been subject to human rights reviews and/or impact assessments
REMEDIATION	HR 11	Number of grievances related to human rights filed, addressed, and resolved through formal grievance mechanisms

Society

LOCAL COMMUNITY	SO 1	Percentage of operations with implemented local community engagement, impact assessments, and development programs
CORRUPTION	SO 2	Percentage and total number of business units analyzed for risks related to corruption
	SO 3	Percentage of employees trained in organization's anti-corruption policies and procedures
	SO 4	Actions taken in response to incidents of corruption
PUBLIC POLICY	SO 5	Public policy positions and participation in public policy development and lobbying
	SO 6	Total value of financial and in-kind contributions to political parties, politicians, and related institutions by country
ANTI-COMPETITIVE BEHAVIOR	SO 7	Total number of legal actions for anti-competitive behavior, anti-trust, and monopoly practices and their outcomes
COMPLIANCE	SO 8	Monetary value of significant fines and total number of non-monetary sanctions for non-compliance with laws and regulations
	SO 9	Operations with significant potential or actual negative impacts on local communities
	SO 10	Prevention and mitigation measures implemented in operations with significant potential or actual negative impacts on local communities

EXHIBIT 12.6—*continued*

Labor Practices and Decent Work

EMPLOYMENT	LA 1	Total workforce by employment type, employment contract, and region, broken down by gender
	LA 2	Total number and rate of new employee hires and employee turnover by age group, gender, and region
	LA 3	Benefits provided to full-time employees that are not provided to temporary or part-time employees, by significant locations of operation
LABOR/ MANAGEMENT RELATIONS	LA 4	Percentage of employees covered by collective bargaining agreements
	LA 5	Minimum notice period(s) regarding operational changes, including whether it is specified in collective agreements
OCCUPATIONAL HEALTH AND SAFETY	LA 6	Percentage of total workforce represented in formal joint management–worker health and safety committees that help monitor and advise on occupational health and safety programs
	LA 7	Rates of injury, occupational diseases, lost days, and absenteeism, and number of work-related fatalities by region and by gender
	LA 8	Education, training, counseling, prevention, and risk-control programs in place to assist workforce members, their families, or community members regarding serious diseases
	LA 9	Health and safety topics covered in formal agreements with trade unions
TRAINING AND EDUCATION	LA 10	Average hours of training per year per employee by gender, and by employee category
	LA 11	Programs for skills management and lifelong learning that support the continued employability of employees and assist them in managing career endings
	LA 12	Percentage of employees receiving regular performance and career development reviews, by gender
DIVERSITY AND EQUAL OPPORTUNITY	LA 13	Composition of governance bodies and breakdown of employees per employee category according to gender, age group, minority group membership, and other indicators of diversity
EQUAL RENUMERATION FOR WOMEN AND MEN	LA 14	Ratio of basic salary and remuneration of women to men by employee category, by significant locations of operations
	LA 15	Return to work and retention rates after parental leave, by gender

EXHIBIT 12.6—*continued*

Product Responsibility

CUSTOMER HEALTH AND SAFETY	PR 1	Lifecycle stages in which health and safety impacts of products and services are assessed for improvement, and percentage of significant products and services categories subject to such procedures
	PR 2	Total number of incidents of non-compliance with regulations and voluntary codes concerning health and safety impacts of products and services during their lifecycle, by type of outcomes
PRODUCT AND SERVICE LABELING	PR 3	Type of product and service information required by procedures and percentage of significant products and services subject to such information requirements
	PR 4	Total number of incidents of non-compliance with regulations and voluntary codes concerning product and service information and labeling, by type of outcomes
	PR 5	Practices related to customer satisfaction, including results of surveys measuring customer satisfaction
MARKETING COMMUNICATIONS	PR 6	Programs for adherence to laws, standards, and voluntary codes related to marketing communications, including advertising, promotion, and sponsorship
	PR 7	Total number of incidents of non-compliance with regulations and voluntary codes concerning marketing communications, including advertising, promotion, and sponsorship by type of outcomes
CUSTOMER PRIVACY	PR 8	Total number of substantiated complaints regarding breaches of customer privacy and losses of customer data
COMPLIANCE	PR 9	Monetary value of significant fines for non-compliance with laws and regulations concerning the provision and use of products and services

Economic

ECONOMIC PERFORMANCE	EC 1	Direct economic value generated and distributed, including revenues, operating costs, employee compensation, donations and other community investments, retained earnings, and payments to capital providers and governments
	EC 2	Financial implications and other risks and opportunities for the organization's activities due to climate change
	EC 3	Coverage of the organization's defined benefit plan obligations
	EC 4	Significant financial assistance received from government
MARKET PRESENCE	EC 5	Range of ratios of standard entry-level wage by gender compared to local minimum wage at significant locations of operation

EXHIBIT 12.6—*continued*

	EC 6	Policy, practices, and proportion of spending on locally based suppliers at significant locations of operation
	EC 7	Procedures for local hiring and proportion of senior management hired from the local community at locations of significant operation
INDIRECT ECONOMIC IMPACTS	EC 8	Development and impact of infrastructure investments and services provided primarily for public benefit through commercial, in-kind, or pro bono engagement
	EC 9	Understanding and describing significant indirect economic impacts, including the extent of impacts

EXHIBIT 12.6 — *continued*

Stakeholder Area Ranks

Rank	Company	Financial	Environment	Climate Change	Human Rights	Employee Relations	Corporate Governance	Philanthropy
1	Johnson Controls Inc.	181	2	2	2	24	248	6
2	Campbell Soup Co.	228	16	3	10	16	1	109
3	IBM	62	1	1	74	77	242	16
4	Bristol-Myers Squibb Co.*	205	28	23	87	23	1	21
5	Mattel, Inc.	60	35	201	10	46	1	24
6	3M Co.	177	25	94	32	36	1	68
7	Accenture plc.	61	97	15	10	65	248	7
8	Kimberly-Clark Corp.	202	8	58	22	32	234	23
9	Hewlett-Packard Co.	464	5	32	25	9	1	8
10	Nike, Inc.	48	102	51	156	25	1	85
11	Gap, Inc.*	354	70	135	3	4	1	27
12	General Mills, Inc.*	121	39	206	41	8	248	33
13	Intel Corp.*	446	4	77	25	2	229	13
14	Coca-Cola Co.	135	75	37	17	42	531	72
15	Pinnacle West Capital Corp.	204	87	67	133	57	1	73
16	Avon Products, Inc.	512	17	24	108	5	248	25
17	Consolidated Edison, Inc.*	161	112	14	236	6	1	127
18	Spectra Energy Corp	182	98	42	122	48	248	1
19	DuPont	169	13	13	17	168	1	385
20	Johnson & Johnson	375	7	5	55	168	1	69

EXHIBIT 12.7 — Top Twenty of *Corporate Responsibility Magazine's* 100 Best Corporate Citizens in the United States

guidelines to report on the performance measurement required by the Compact's Communication on Progress.

One area where reporting CSR performance remains weak is in assurance. **Assurance** is the auditing function to validate that what a company reports in its CSR report is true and accurate. Financial statements require audits but this aspect of social responsibility reporting is still in its infancy, with only a small number of firms using external audits of their CSR reports. However, companies are not out of sight and there are a growing number of CSR rankings that evaluate companies on CSR performance. One popular ranking for U.S. companies is shown in Exhibit 12.7. Similar to ranking of colleges and universities, there is not complete agreement on the methodology or accuracy of these rankings.[43] Nevertheless, they represent a source of information to stakeholders regarding a company's CSR activities.

CHAPTER SUMMARY

The chapter began with a Preview Business Ethics Insight on Tata Steel's company town. Tata illustrated one approach to putting the welfare of workers on a par with, or perhaps even more important than, the actual business of making steel. However, Tata is not without its critics, who fear that a continued emphasis on CSR issues may cause the company to lose sight of its business goals. This case touched on some of the fundamental issues in CSR of finding the right balance among stakeholder interests.

The brief history of CSR traced the intellectual history of the CSR debate from the writings of the classical economist Adam Smith to the current triple bottom line approach to CSR. In the U.S., two landmark court decisions influenced both academic and practitioner thinking about CSR. In the U.S., the first legal precedent for the dominance of the stockholder as the prime stakeholder was the influential 1919 case of *Dodge v. Ford*. Later, the switch from stockholder dominance to corporate philanthropy began with *Smith v. Barlow*, a landmark court decision in 1953 that allowed A.P. Smith Manufacturing Company to donate $1,500 to Princeton University. In *Smith v. Barlow*, the court upheld the contribution as legal ruling against the stockholders. The court ruled that the stockholders, "whose private interests rest entirely upon the well-being of the corporation, ought not to be permitted to close their eyes to present-day realities and thwart the long-visioned corporate action in recognizing and voluntarily discharging its high obligations as a constituent of our modern social structure."

With the start of the twentieth century, criticism of big business increased. More people began to believe that the big corporations were too powerful and used business practices that were anti-social and anti-competitive. As a result, the government responded with laws and regulations that limited the power of large corporations and served to protect employees, consumers, and society at large. The 1960s and 1970s continued a cultural shift in the expectations for business in most countries. Movements related to civil rights, consumerism, and environmentalism changed the context for doing business and therefore society's expectations for business responsibilities.

However, going beyond legal compliance and based on the premise that those with greater power have greater responsibilities, most of the developed world called on businesses to become proactive. Increasingly, it became an expectation that it is not sufficient to avoid causing social problems but it is also necessary to help solve social problems.

During the 1960s and 1970s, the concept of CSR broadened both in practice and in academic thinking. Of particular importance was the clarification of the concept of stakeholders, suggesting that companies have responsibilities to take into account how their actions affect not only stockholders but also employees, suppliers, dealers, local communities, and the nation. The idea of the duties and obligations to stakeholders is now entrenched in both practitioner and academic thinking about CSR.

Archie Carroll introduced the concept of the pyramid of CSR in the 1970s and this is still a popular way that management scholars and practitioners look at CSR. For Carroll, there are four essential responsibilities of a business. These include economic, legal, ethical, and philanthropic. The idea of the pyramid evolved to take into account stakeholders and the tensions among their interests.

Although the acceptance of CSR as a corporate obligation grew considerably in the late twentieth century, there remain critics. The most famous to this day is still Nobel laureate Milton Friedman, who argued that there is only one purpose of the corporation: "There is one and only one social responsibility of business—to use its resources and engage in activities designed to increase its profits so long as it stays within the rules of the game, which is to say, engages in open and free competition without deception or fraud."

The TBL is a stakeholder approach to CSR that seeks to balance the needs of all. It is also known as "people, planet, and profit." Like Carroll's pyramid and his representation of the areas of CSR from a competition perspective rather than a hierarchy, TBL also contains a concern for philanthropy that goes beyond ethical and legal requirements. In the people sector, there is a focus on issues such as fair wages, child labor, occupational health and safety, training, and equal opportunity. There is also a focus on community engagement, such as support for education and the protection of indigenous people. Planet represents environmental stewardship and sustainable environmental practices. Profit represents not only standard economic returns to stockholders but also a concern for the benefits of others, such as using local suppliers or indirect economic benefits for the local community.

Taking a more practitioner point of view, the two concluding sections of this chapter considered strategic CSR and the practicalities of reporting CSR performance. Strategic CSR rests on the assumption that "doing good" can be good for a business as well as for society. With strategic CSR, corporations attend to their stakeholders because managers believe it is in the best interest of the company.

Strategic management experts Michael Porter of Harvard University and his colleague Mark Kramer identified many of these issues related to strategic CSR in an important article published in the *Harvard Business Review*. Although Porter and Kramer recognize that many companies are already improving the environmental and social consequences of their business activities, they see two reasons why many companies have not been as productive as they should be. First, there has been a tendency to pit business against society when it is more productive to realize that the two are interdependent. Businesses need societies with well-educated and healthy workers and a sustainable environment. Society needs businesses to go beyond a self-centered look on profits and participate in making the world better. Second, many businesses think of CSR in a general way with various check-offs rather than thinking strategically.

Porter and Kramer caution against simply throwing money at good causes but, instead, strategically picking areas that align with their expertise. Managers need to look at CSR as a strategic tool to lower costs or better serve customers' needs. Porter and Kramer suggest one way to identify potential areas of strategic CSR competitive advantages is to map the impact of the company's value chain.

All publically owned corporations are required to produce annual reports on their economic performance for their stockholders. Investors can use this information to consider whether to invest more or less in the company. Increasingly, however, corporations are facing increased institutional pressure to also report on their social performance. After surveying the top 250 companies from Global *Fortune* 500 and the largest 100 companies from 22 countries, KPMG concluded that CSR reporting is becoming entrenched at least among the dominant multinational companies. Nearly 80% of the Global 250 now issue reports.

CSR reporting is still in development and the choice of what is reported, how it is reported, and how the report is verified is still open to debate. Depending on the country, there is a complex mix of mandatory and voluntary standards. However, we can conclude from the recent trends that CSR measurement and reporting is becoming a requirement driven by both legislative actions and society's expectations. As such, it will be ever more incumbent on future managers to be aware of mandatory and expected standards and how they fit strategically into one's company and industry.

The UN's Global Compact is based on ten principles in the areas of human rights, labor, the environment, and anti-corruption. Joining the Global Compact initiative is voluntary, but once a company commits to join, it agrees to integrate the principles into its business operations and communicate annually on progress. Business participants are required to submit an annual Communication on Progress (COP) and to share the COP widely with their stakeholders.

The Global Reporting Initiative (GRI) is the most recognized global standard for CSR reporting. The GRI provides principles and indicators that companies can use to identify and measure economic, environmental, and social performance. The third generation of the guidelines was released in 2006.

Recognizing the synergy between the sophisticated measurements and reporting format of the GRI and the Global Compact as the world's largest corporate responsibility platform, the UN Global Compact and GRI signed an agreement in May 2010 to align their work in advancing corporate responsibility. As part of the agreement, GRI plans to integrate the Global Compact's ten principles into the next version of its Sustainability Reporting Guidelines. In turn, the Global Compact will adopt the GRI Guidelines as their recommended reporting framework for businesses.

NOTES

1   *The Economist.* 2011. "Company towns: The universal provider." June 19.

2   Carroll, A.B. 1999. "Corporate social responsibility: Evolution of a definitional construct." *Business & Society*, 38, 268–295.

3   As quoted in Cochran, P.L. 2007. "The evolution of corporate social responsibility." *Business Horizons*, 50, 449–454.

4   Smith, A. 1982. "The theory of moral sentiments," in D.D. Raphael & A.L. Macfie (Eds.), *Glasgow edition of the works and correspondence of Adam Smith*, Vol. I, Indianapolis: Liberty Fund, pp. 26–27. http://oll.libertyfund.org/title/192, accessed June 29, 2011.

5   Barnett, T. 2011. "Corporate responsibility. Reference for business." *Encyclopedia of business*, 2nd edn. www.referenceforbusiness.com.

6   270 Fed. Appx. 200, 2008 U.S. App.

7   Hood, J. 1998. "Do corporations have social responsibilities? Free enterprise creates unique problem-solving opportunities." *Freeman*, 48.

8   13 N.J. 145, 98 A.2d 581, 1953 N.J. 39 A.L.R.2d 1179.

9   Cochran. "The evolution of corporate social responsibility."

10 Bowen, H.R. 1953. *Social responsibilities of the businessman.* New York: Harper & Row, p. 6.

11 Rahman, S. 2011. "Evaluations of definitions: Ten dimensions of corporate social responsibility." *World Review of Business Research*, 1, 166–176.

12 Johnson, H.L. 1971. *Business in contemporary society: framework and issues.* Belmont, CA: Wadsworth, p. 50.

13 Carroll, A.B. 1979. "A three-dimensional model of corporate performance." *Academy of Management Review*, 4, 497–505;. Carroll, A.B. 1991. "The pyramid of corporate social responsibility: Toward the moral management of organizational stakeholders." *Business Horizons*, July.

14 Hood, J. 1998. "Do corporations have social responsibilities?"

15 Matten, D. & Crane, A. 2005. "Corporate citizenship: Towards an extended theoretical conceptualization." *Academy of Management Review*, 30, 166–179.

16 Matten, D., Crane, A. & Chapple, W. 2003. "Behind the mask: Revealing the true face of corporate citizenship." *Journal of Business Ethics*, 45, 1/2, 109–120.

17 Goodpaster, K.E. 1996. "Business ethics and stakeholder analysis." In Rae, S. B. & Wong, K.L. (Eds.), *Beyond integrity: A Judeo-Christian approach,* Grand Rapids, MI: Zondervan Publishing House, pp. 246–254.

18 McWilliams, A. & Siegel, D. 2001. "Corporate social responsibility: A theory of the firm perspective." *Academy of Management Review*, 26, 117–127; Treviño, L.K. & Nelson, K.A. 1999. *Managing business ethics: Straight talk about how to do it right*, 2nd edn, New York: J. Wiley & Sons.

19 Verschoor, C.C. & Murphy, E.A. 2002. "The financial performance of large U.S. firms and those with global prominence: How do the best corporate citizens rate?" *Business and Society Review*, 107, 371–380.

20 Miller, F.D. & Ahrens, J. 1993. "The social responsibility of corporations." In T.I. White (Ed.), *Business ethics: A philosophical reader,* Upper Saddle River, NJ: Prentice-Hall, pp. 187–204.

21 Boatright, J.R. 2000. "Globalization and the ethics of business." *Business Ethics Quarterly*, 10, 1–6: Smith, N.C. 2003. "Corporate social responsibility: Whether or how?" *California Management Review*, 45, 52–76.

22 Heslin, P.A. & Ochoa, J.D. 2008. "Understanding and developing strategic corporate social responsibility." *Organizational Dynamics*, 37, 125–144.

23 Porter, M.E. & Kramer, M.R. 2006. "Strategy and society: The link between competitive advantage and corporate social responsibility." *Harvard Business Review*, December, 76–93.

24 Bielak, D., Nonini, S.M.J. & Oppenheim, J.M. 2007. "CEOs on strategy and social issues." *McKinsey Quarterly*, October, 1–8.

25 Heslin, P.A. & Ochoa, J.D. 2008. "Understanding and developing strategic corporate social responsibility." *Organizational Dynamics*, 37, 125–144.

26 http://www.microsoft.com/about/diversity/en/us/programs/college.aspx# Higher Education Support.

27 http://www.starbucks.com/responsibility/sourcing/farmer-support.

28 http://www.chocolateeuphoria.com/ethelmchocolates/livingmachine.html.
29 http://www.hydro.com/en/Our-future/Technology/Recycling/.
30 http://www.hydro.com/en/Press-room/News/Archive/2010/11/Strong-growth-expected-in-global-aluminium-recycling/.
31 http://www.shawfloors.com/Environmental/RecyclingDetail.
32 http://www.hp.com/hpinfo/globalcitizenship/environment/recycling/unwanted-hardware.html.
33 GreenBiz Staff. 2020. "Shanghai GM green supply chain program saved $19M in 2009." June 16. http://www.greenbiz.com/news/2010/06/16/shanghai-gm-supply-chain-program-saved-19m-2009.
34 http://www.greensupplychain.com/burton-riding_the_green_supply_chain_wave.html.
35 KPMG International Survey of Corporate Responsibility Reporting 2008.
36 KPMG International Survey of Corporate Responsibility Reporting 2008, p. 10.
37 KPMG Advisory N.V., United Nations Environment Program, Global Reporting Initiative, and the Unit for Corporate Governance in Africa. 2010. *Carrots and sticks—Promoting transparency and sustainability: an update on trends in voluntary and mandatory approaches to sustainability reporting.*
38 KPMG Advisory N.V. et al., *Carrots and sticks,* p. 4.
39 http://www.unglobalcompact.org/AboutTheGC/TheTenPrinciples/index.html.
40 https://www.globalreporting.org/information/about-gri/what-is-GRI/Pages/default.aspx.
41 https://www.globalreporting.org/network/report-or-explain/Pages/default.aspx.
42 https://www.globalreporting.org/information/news-and-press-center/newsarchive/Pages/default.aspx.
43 Arena, C. 2010. "Are corporate social responsibility rankings irresponsible?" *Christian Science Monitor,* March 17. http://www.csmonitor.com/Business/Case-in-Point/2010/0317/Are-corporate-social-responsibility-rankings-irresponsible.

KEY TERMS

Assurance: the auditing function to validate the accuracy of a company's CSR report.

Communication on Progress (COP): the reporting procedures for showing compliance to the Global Compact—must contain the following elements: a statement by the CEO expressing continued support for the UN Global Compact, a description of practical actions the company has taken to implement the principles, and a demonstration of how outcomes are measured.

Corporate citizenship: voluntarily giving back to the community with an increased focus on the close environment of the firm; an increased focus on legal, ethical, and discretionary responsibilities of business; a focus on the rights of the firm to be a social actor and participate politically.

Corporate social responsibility: activities when companies go beyond the requirements of running an economically viable business within the constraints of the law to protect the environment and enhance the well-being of their stakeholders.

Dodge v. Ford: the first legal precedent in the U.S. for the dominance of the stockholder as the prime stakeholder.

Economic responsibility: the role of a business to produce goods or services that people need and to make an acceptable profit in the process.

Ethical responsibility: obligation to conform to the ethical expectations of society that are not codified into law.

Global Reporting Initiative (GRI): provides principles and indicators that companies can use to identify and measure economic, environmental, and social performance.

Integrated reports: reports built into annual reports, which traditionally have focused only on financial performance.

Invisible hand: the control by market forces where competition favors those who produce the best products at the best prices as consumers also seek their own self-interest in buying those products or services.

Legal responsibility: obligation to conform to laws and regulations with ethical consequences such as regulations regarding product safety and consumer protection.

License to operate: the social contract between businesses and society that allows them to operate.

Milton Friedman: a critic of CSR who wrote the now famous article in the *New York Times Magazine,* "The Social Responsibility of Business is to Increase its Profits."

Philanthropic responsibility: the responsibility to be good corporate citizens and engage in activities that promote human welfare and goodwill.

Smith v. Barlow: the U.S. court decision that weakened the legal position of stockholder dominance and allowed more corporate philanthropy.

Social performance reports: similar to annual reports on economic performance, they report on CSR performance.

Strategic CSR: corporations attend to their stakeholders because managers believe it is in the best interest of the company; rests on the assumption that "doing good" can be good for a business as well as for society.

Triple bottom line (TBL): the addition of social and environmental sustainability performance to economic performance, also known as "people, planet, and profit."

UN's Global Compact: ten principles in the areas of human rights, labor, the environment, and anti-corruption that guide social performance for signatories.

DISCUSSION QUESTIONS

1. Discuss the legal evolution of CSR.
2. Write two or three definitions of CSR and discuss the underlying assumptions of each.
3. Compare and contrast Friedman's view of the legitimacy of CSR with Carroll's perspective. How to they differ and overlap?
4. Compare and contrast the differences between the two models for looking at Carroll's dimensions of CSR. Which makes most sense? Should economic considerations be a foundation or does a competing values view make more sense?
5. With the continuing move of formally optional CSR actions into the framework of legal requirements, discuss the future of CSR. Will governments mandate what is now optional?

6. Discuss the dimensions of the Triple Bottom Line. How does this perspective relate to Carroll's earlier view?
7. What are the challenges of implementing a TBL strategy?
8. In strategic CSR, companies search for ways to meet the bottom line while being socially responsible in ways that benefit the company. Is this really CSR?
9. Discuss why U.S. firms seem less likely to adopt GRI reporting standards than European firms.
10. What are the major weaknesses of the current reporting practices in CSR?

INTERNET ACTIVITY

1. Go to the internet and find the CSR reports for four companies in two different countries (two from each country). Try to stay in one industry so the companies will face similar CSR challenges.
2. Compare the reports by country. How are they different? How are they similar? Are different issues more important in different countries?
3. Analyze the reports in terms of how well they present the companies' CSR position in a believable manner. Identify aspects of the reports that can be verified.

For more Internet Activities and resources, visit the Companion Website at www.routledge.com/cw/parboteeah.

WHAT WOULD YOU DO?

CSR at Dixie Manufacturing Company

Dixie Manufacturing Company (DMC), located in Tuscaloosa, Alabama is a small manufacturing company of fewer than 50 employees that produces medical instruments such as scalpels, periodontal scalers, and curettes (the tools dentists use to scrape your teeth) for the medical community.

You recently graduated from the University of Alabama and have been working for DMC in the marketing group for six months. Yesterday, George Day, the CEO, called you and asked what you know about CSR. He said, "You're a recent college grad and probably had some courses in business ethics and corporate social responsibility. When most of the senior managers were in college no one worried about these issues. So, I am going to rely on you to help us out."

DMC has no formal code of conduct or CSR policies. They sponsor a local little league team and are pretty generous to the students from the University of Alabama who come by each semester asking for donations. You have noticed that most people think that is pretty good and DMC has little to worry about. However, Day tells you, "I want an outline of a CSR plan in a couple of weeks, as times are changing."

DMC is in a competitive industry and you have heard rumors that some manufacturing might move to Mexico to cut costs. However, some in the plant say that will not work because DMC will not be able to match the quality and reliability of the current plant, where most of the workers have over ten years of experience and on-the-job training is really successful. An alternative is layoffs, yet many of the older workers produce some of the less profitable products, so it would be difficult to take seniority into account.

What will you do first? Who are the stakeholders that you must consider in your plan? If DMC faces a financial crisis now, do you think it is too late to build a viable CSR strategy?

BRIEF CASE: BUSINESS ETHICS INSIGHT

Novo Nordisk, the CSR Superstar

Novo Nordisk is a Danish pharmaceutical firm specializing in diabetes care with over 30,000 employees worldwide. Novo Nordisk has production facilities in 7 countries, offices in 74 countries, and sells its products in 180 countries. In 2010, Fortune ranked Novo Nordisk one of the top 25 best companies to work to work for.

Novo Nordisk is a CSR superstar. Awards for superior CSR around the world abound. Here is just a sampling of their 2011 accolades.

- Sixth Golden Bee International CSR Forum in Beijing—the Harmonious Contributors Award for sustainability commitment and achievements. The Award recognizing companies in areas of customer focus, employee care, and responsible purchasing.
- 2010 TakeAction! award, given to the most impressive employee volunteer activity of the year—employees from Novo Nordisk Pakistan recognized for their rapid response to last year's devastating floods in Pakistan.
- Annual report recognition—two awards for best integrated financial and social reporting, CorporateRegister, a worldwide resource for corporate responsibility reporting, and Justmeans, a corporate social responsibility news service.
- Gold Class in the Sustainability Yearbook 2011, Sustainability Asset Management (SAM) has awarded Novo Nordisk the Gold Class distinction, recognizing the company's strong performance on economic, environmental, and social issues that focus on long-term value creation.
- 2011 Global 100 Most Sustainable Corporations—ranked 16th, up 33 positions.

The company did not become a CSR superstar overnight. They have been working for more than a decade to move from a view of CSR as simply risk management toward what they call "a more opportunity-driven perspective." To achieve their CSR goals Novo Nordisk adopted the triple bottom line approach, striving to conduct all activities "in a financially, environmentally and socially responsible way." Their approach is to integrate TBL into all business activities.

The statement of their commitment to TBL is part of their Articles of Association. More importantly, perhaps, TBL is integrated into their corporate governance structures, management tools, and individual performance assessments. As part of their organizational culture, they note, "the principle of 'preserving the planet while improving the quality of life for its current and future inhabitants' resonates well with Novo Nordisk's business rationale." They are confident, and the external observations seem to confirm, that the TBL allows them to make decisions that balance financial growth with CSR focusing on shareholder returns and stakeholder interests.

In following TBL, Novo Nordisk identifies specific areas that are particularly relevant to the company and the pharmaceutical industry in which they operate. A short overview of the TBL areas shows the degree of integration of TBL into their organizational policies and culture.

Environmental Responsibility

The company has a general concern for environmental sustainability but specific concerns related to issues such as animal experimentation and safety issues regarding the use of genetic engineering.

- *Animal welfare.* Live animal experimentation is necessary for the discovery, development, and production of pharmaceutical and medical products. Also, it is often required by regulatory authorities in different countries. Novo Nordisk is pledged to reduce and or replace live animal experiments and seeks to develop alternative experiments for drug release that regulatory authorities will accept.
- *Environmental management.* The company uses an extremely thorough assessment of its environmental impact with a lifecycle approach monitoring inputs (raw materials, packaging, water, energy) and outputs (emission to the air, liquid and solid waste).
- *Climate change.* Novo Nordisk goes beyond compliance in reducing CO_2 emissions. As a signatory of the Climate Savers agreement, Novo Nordisk has set an ambitious target to achieve a reduction of 10% of its CO_2 emissions by 2014.

Social Responsibility

Novo Nordisk identifies key stakeholders as the people whose healthcare needs they serve and their employees. They also consider the impact of their business on the global society and the local community.

- *Access to health.* Novo Nordisk's strategy for improved access to diabetes care follows the recommendations of the World Health Organization. One of their many strategies is a tiered pricing system for the developed and developing world to allow low-cost access to diabetes drugs in poorer countries.
- *Diversity.* Novo Nordisk has numerous policies and structures to maximize diversity and gender equity. This is not just an HR issue, as they require all senior vice presidents to develop action plans to identify and address diversity issues.
- *Employee volunteering.* The company's TakeAction! program encourages employees to engage in voluntary activities during working hours and integrate the company's triple bottom line approach into their own work lives. Such activities help meet social and/or environmental objectives in the communities in which the company operates.
- *Health and safety.* Historically, the company's health and safety practices were compliance-based, following local standards related to local legislation. As a multinational company, they realized they needed a more globally standardized approach. Novo Nordisk now has the Occupational Health and Safety Management System that identifies the roles and responsibilities for health and safety work, including (but not limited to) safety training of personnel, efforts to identify and document risk factors, and actions to minimize these risks.
- *Human rights.* As a signatory to the United Nations' Global Compact, Novo Nordisk is committed to supporting and respecting human rights throughout its operations and has agreed to report annually how it accomplishes these goals.
- *Workplace quality.* Included in the assessment of workplace quality are the wages and benefits offered to employees, quality of management practices, corporate culture, training and educational opportunities, talent development, appropriate shift lengths, the levels of job stress, and the physical attributes of the workplace.

Economic Viability

To Novo Nordisk, economically viability includes making a profit for the company's shareholders, educating employees, and investing in the growth of the business.

- *Economic footprint.* Broadly, Novo Nordisk's economic footprint includes interactions with stakeholders through the sales of products and services, payments to suppliers, remuneration of employees, dividend and interest to investors and funders, taxes paid to the public sector, and profits generated for future growth of the company. Novo Nordisk also impacts society by using sustainable business practices, providing healthcare knowledge and products. They have several programs that target developing nations that provide jobs and access to healthcare.

- *Financial performance.* Novo Nordisk is a very successful firm. Operating profit growth in 2010 was 27%. Operating profit margin was 31%. From 2006 to 2010, the average operating profit growth was 19% on an average margin of 26%. The main insulin products command nearly 50% of the market.

Conclusion

In summary, for Novo Nordisk, the triple bottom line strategy serves as an integrated CSR management tool. It is not a stagnant system and the company identifies six processes that facilitate organizational learning and innovation in the CSR area:

- monitoring issues and spotting trends that may affect the future business
- engaging with stakeholders to reconcile dilemmas and find common ground for more sustainable solutions
- building relationships with key stakeholders in the global and local communities of which Novo Nordisk is a part
- driving and embedding long-term thinking and the triple bottom line mindset throughout the company
- accounting for the company's performance and conveying Novo Nordisk's positions, objectives, and goals to audiences with an interest in the company
- translating and integrating the triple bottom line approach into all business processes to obtain sustainable competitive advantages in the marketplace.

Source: Adapted from http://www.novonordisk.com/.

BRIEF CASE QUESTIONS

1. Novo Nordisk is a very rich company. Some would argue that this company can heavily engage in CSR activities because of its affluence and this is not what most companies can do. Discuss and assess this position.
2. Novo Nordisk is a model of TBL operations. Benchmark a company you know against this performance.
3. If one looks at the company's website, the CSR philosophy seems strongly driven by the Danish approach to a social democracy. The U.S. subsidiary seems to have more of a legal compliance level of CSR. Investigate and discuss if you perceive this to be true and, if so, why or why not.

LONG CASE: BUSINESS ETHICS

BARRICK GOLD CORPORATION, TANZANIA[1]

By March 2009, Canadian mining company Barrick Gold Corporation (Barrick) had only been operating in the Lake Victoria Zone in Tanzania for a decade. In the same year, Barrick had adopted a new name for its business in Tanzania, African Barrick Gold plc (ABG), which was also listed on the London Stock Exchange. The company was widely considered to be one of the more "responsive" global corporations in the mining industry.[2] Its extensive mining activities in the region employed thousands of local people, and Barrick was engaged in social development projects in various Tanzanian communities.[3] By October 2010, the company operated four main gold-mining sites in the country.[4]

Despite Barrick's efforts to support social development initiatives in the Lake Victoria Zone over the past decade, discontent and resistance at one of its mining sites in North Mara still remained. This area posed challenges. A key question was why the tension and violence had not stopped in certain mining sites in the North Mara mining area, and whether there was much more Barrick could reasonably be expected to do to resolve the problem.

Background on Tanzania

Tanzania was a developing country located in East Africa, with a total land size of 945,087 square kilometres. It had one of the highest levels of unemployment and poverty in Sub-Saharan Africa. Its economy was heavily dependent on agriculture, which accounted for half of the gross domestic product (GDP), provided 85% of the country's exports, and employed 90% of the workforce. Topography and climatic conditions, however, limited cultivated crops to only 4% of the land area. Industry was mainly limited to processing agricultural products and light consumer goods.

Like most developing nations, Tanzania had a very weak national institutional and legal system. It also had a very high rate of corruption.[5] The country needed support from foreign direct investment (FDI) and transnational corporations (TNCs) in order to promote businesses, employment, and other opportunities for its citizens. Tanzania wanted its institutions to be more transparent and accountable, and to regulate the activities of FDI and TNCs in addressing the country's social and ecological issues. Both local and international not-for-profit organizations (NFOs), however, had continued to create a significant impact with respect to promoting responsive behavior in corporate governance practices, positively influencing all involved stakeholders and other social actors to address social issues.

Following independence in 1961, Tanzania opted for a socialist command economic and institutional system, with socialist policies (*Ujamaa* in Swahili) being implemented in 1967. The emphasis of these policies was to promote cooperative institutions and collective villages with the aim of building an egalitarian society, eliminating ethnic and gender barriers, and creating a common language of Swahili for all. Within the practice of Ujamaa, the country had managed to unite its ethnic groups under a common language, with the result that the central government had created strong post-colonial nationalistic ideologies, unity, ethnic harmony and peace among its people. Compared to many post-colonial Sub-Saharan African countries that went through civil and ethnic strife and conflicts after independence in the 1960s and 1970s, Tanzania under Ujamaa appeared to be a successful model.

Towards the end of the 1980s, however, Tanzania began to experience significant economic stagnation and social problems. To combat these issues, in the early 1990s the government sought to privatize its economy and reform its institutions in order to attract foreign investment. The introduction of the famous post-Ujamaa Investment Act of 1997 was intended to encourage free market and trade liberalization in the country. Investment in various private sectors such as mining, tourism, fishing, banking, and agriculture under foreign-owned TNCs served to bolster the country's reforms by creating employment opportunities for the local economy.

As the country continued to privatize and reform its national institutional and legal systems, many foreign companies sought to invest in its economy. The Tanzania Investment Centre (TIC) was created in the early 2000s as a tool for identifying possible investment opportunities and aiding potential investors in navigating any procedural barriers that might exist during the process of investment in the country.[6] The liberalization of the banking industry in 2002, for example, saw the former Ujamaa Cooperative and Rural Development Bank replaced by the Commercial Rural Development Bank (CRDB) and the National Microfinance Bank (NMB), which promoted community investments across the country. In February 2009, the Tanzania Private Sector Foundation (TPSF) was created with the aim of strengthening the entrepreneurial culture among its citizens by providing communities and individuals across the country with entrepreneurial business ideas and grants. In June 2009, the government started an ambitious national resolution under the so-called "*Kilimo Kwanza*" policies (meaning "Agriculture First" in Swahili) to boost the standard of living among the *80%* of citizens who relied on agriculture for their livelihood.[7] It was based on Green Revolution principles aimed at boosting Tanzania's agriculture into the modern and commercial sector, and mobilizing for-profit organizations (FPOs) such as local private businesses and foreign-owned TNCs in the country to increase their investment engagement with the agriculture sector, both at the macro and micro levels (i.e. along with local communities).

In order to ensure that there was sufficient security and peace for private and foreign-owned investors (i.e., TNCs), in 2005 the government introduced a new entity called Tanzania Security Industry Association. The association was based on local, professional private security firms and groups whose main tasks were to safeguard business firms' activities rather than letting the firms rely on local police forces. The largest and best-known local security firm was Moku Security Services Limited, based in Dar Es Salaam, which had over 13,000 employees across the country. Other security groups with over 400 employees were Ultimate Security Company, Dragon Security, Tele-security Company Limited, and Group Four Security Company. Private security employees were mainly retired army and police officers; young people who had lost their previous jobs following the collapse of the Ujamaa policies that provided "jobs for everyone and for life"; and individuals who sought better remuneration in the security sector than in the government public sector. However, due to increased demand for better security across businesses, many foreign-owned TNCs sought the services of security firms from abroad, mainly from South Africa's professional security firms such as the South African Intruder Detection Service Association (SAIDS). Some security personnel had combat experience, which helped them handle sophisticated forms of crime and intrusion.

The Tanzanian economy continued to grow and create job opportunities, training, and innovative development prospects for its people. Earlier, the country had introduced new mining legislation, such as the Mining Act of 1998 and the Mining Regulation Act of 1999, in order to harmonize investment relations between FDI and local interests. However, in April 2010 the government passed another new Mining Act, following consultations with civil society groups such as the Foundation for Civil Society Tanzania (FCST), companies, and other stakeholders. The legislation of a new Mining Act imposed a new form of royalties that required all TNCs and local companies to be listed in the country and gave the state a stake in future projects.[8]

The country possessed vast amounts of natural resources like gold, diamond, copper, platinum, natural gas, and zinc deposits that remained underdeveloped. It was one of the more peaceful countries in Sub-Saharan Africa. In order to attract and protect the interests of FDI and TNCs and, of course, its own people, Tanzania had attempted to harmonize its investment practices and labor legislation. In order to create responsible institutional policies, in February 2010 the National Assembly of Tanzania enlisted a group of local environmental and toxicity experts to investigate environmental and toxic effects on the people and livestock in the North Mara gold mine in Tarime District, Mara Region, by the Tigithe River.[9]

For a number of reasons, Tanzania was a willing host nation for FDI. The country needed the input of TNCs in order to create employment and prosperity. In return, Tanzania could provide TNCs with low-cost labor and a readily available labor force. Low labor costs were an opportunity to support a host nation's development policy in attracting FDI and ultimately in creating a knowledge-based society in the midst of the globalization challenges that were faced by so many developing countries. Furthermore, Tanzania continued to create a local business environment in conjunction with various TNCs' global business interests in order to generate sustainable development policies and practices. It also engaged in market development initiatives that represented innovative learning opportunities and entrepreneurship ventures for its citizens.

Lake Victoria Background

Tanzania's Lake Victoria was surrounded by the three East African countries of Kenya, Tanzania, and Uganda. The lake itself was named after the former Queen of England, Queen Victoria, and stood as the world's largest tropical lake and the second largest freshwater lake after Lake Superior in North America. Covering a total of 69,000 square kilometres, the lake was as large as the Republic of Ireland and lay in the Rift Valley of East Africa, a 3,500-mile system of deep cracks in the earth's crust, running from the Red Sea south to Mozambique. Lake Victoria was the source of the Nile River, which passed through the Sudan and Egypt and finally reached the Mediterranean Sea.

Lake Victoria Zone in Tanzania

The Lake Victoria Zone consisted of the three regions of Mwanza, Mara (formerly called Musoma), and Kagera (formerly called Bukoba), and was one of the most densely populated regions in Africa. Population growth around Lake Victoria was significantly higher than in the rest of Sub-Saharan Africa. During the last five decades, population growth within a 100-kilometre buffer zone around the lake had outpaced the continental average, which had led to growing dependency and pressure on the lake's resources.

Prior to the mining extraction boom in the early 1990s, and following the collapse of Ujamaa, most people living in this region were mainly engaged in rudimentary forms of fishing, agricultural farming, and keeping cattle, as well as other forms of cooperative activities that had been engineered by the country's former Ujamaa policies. Irrigation was limited to a small scale and often used rudimentary technologies to support both individual and cooperative farming activities. Noted for its temperate climate, the area had a mean temperature of between 26° and 30°C in the hot season and 15° and 18°C in the cooler months. The area was rich with tropical vegetation and fruits such as bananas, mangoes, corn, pineapple, and many others. The lake was essential to more than 15 million people, providing potable water, hydroelectric power, and inland water transport, as well as support for tourism and wildlife.

The area remained one of the most fertile for farming activities and continued to attract immigrants from other regions of the country, as well as from Tanzania's neighbors in the war-torn populations of Burundi, Rwanda, and the Democratic Republic of Congo. The presence of hundreds of TNCs engaged in various activities in the area was the main "draw" for these immigrants, who came seeking employment and new sources of livelihood.

The resulting population increase in the Lake Victoria Zone created several problems with respect to the lake and the environment. According to a report by World Watch Institute in Washington, D.C., the once clear, life-abounding lake had become murky, smelly, and choked with algae. It had been reported that:

> The ecological health of Lake Victoria has been affected profoundly as a result of a rapidly growing population, clearance of natural vegetation along the shores, a booming fish-export industry, the disappearance of several fish species native to the lake, prolific growth of algae, and dumping of untreated effluent by several industries. Much of the damage is vast and irreversible. Traditional lifestyles of lakeshore communities have been disrupted and are crumbling.[10]

As a result of the overuse of natural resources in the area, the traditional lifestyles of the lakeshore communities were significantly disrupted, a situation that prompted both social and ecological concerns for the area and its residents.

The fishing industry was badly affected in the region following the introduction of Nile perch (*Lates Niloticus*) and Nile tilapia (*Oreochromis Niloticus*) into the lake. For example, in the 1980s a survey of the lake revealed an abrupt and unexpected increase in numbers among the Nile perch, constituting 80% of all fish in the lake. In spite of working harder, local fishermen caught fewer fish, since the populations of smaller fish, which traditionally had been the fishermen's primary source of livelihood, became decimated. In addition, the big oily Nile perch, generally referred to as *Mbuta*, swam too far out in the open waters for the little local fishing boats and was too big to be caught in the locals' unsophisticated nets.

In response to an increased international demand for the Nile perch, commercial fishing fleets owned by foreign firms displaced local fishermen and many women in lakeside communities who worked as fish processors. The processing of fish, traditionally performed by women, was gradually taken over by large filleting plants. The women resorted to processing fish waste, commonly referred to as *mgongo-wazi*, or "bare-back" in Swahili. The waste, comprising fish heads, backbones, and tails, was sun-dried and then deep-fried and sold to local people who were drawn to its low price and nutritional value. Many fishermen were forced to look for alternative sources of livelihood, mainly seeking employment in extractive mining corporations and other industries as manual laborers.

The water hyacinth posed another threat to the health of Lake Victoria. With the deceptive appearance of a lush, green carpet, the hyacinth was in fact a merciless, free-floating weed, reproducing rapidly and covering any uncovered territory. First noticed in 1989, the weed spread rapidly and covered areas in all three surrounding countries. It formed a dense mat, blocking the sunlight from reaching the organisms below, depleting the already-low concentrations of oxygen and trapping fishing boats and nets of all sizes. The hyacinth was also an ideal habitat for poisonous snakes and disease-carrying snails that caused bilharzia. The government, in partnership with other international agencies, had tried desperately to control the weed. Its most promising approach involved harvesting the hyacinth and using it either for compost or for biogas production.

The health implications associated with the declining state of the lake were extensive. Dumping untreated sewage in the lake and nearby rivers exposed people to waterborne diseases, such as typhoid, cholera, and diarrhea, and chronic forms of malaria. The Lake Victoria Zone was known to have the most dangerous types of malaria in the world. As fish prices soared, protein malnutrition became a significant threat for communities living in the zone. Lack of regular income also meant that many people in the area could not afford to be treated for waterborne typhoid, yellow fever, and various forms of tropical worms such as tapeworms and hookworms.

Mining in Tanzania

Gold-mining activities around the Lake Victoria Zone in Tanzania started during the German colonial period in 1894, when Tanzania was called Tanganyika. World Wars I and II accelerated the demand for gold production in the region and, following the introduction of Ujamaa in 1967, mining became a state-directed activity.

By nationalizing the industry, the government hoped to capture more benefits from mining through the creation of local employment, direct spending on social services for mining communities, and higher budget revenues from having a direct stake in the business. However, despite these high hopes, the mining sector failed to stimulate the industrialization of the country's economy. During Ujamaa, the production of gold declined significantly due to limited government funding and limited technological knowhow within the industry. Mining activities that were performed illegally by small-scale operators contributed to several environmental and social problems.[11]

The collapse of Ujamaa in 1990s, however, resulted in new opportunities for the country to attract mining companies from Canada, the United Kingdom, Australia, and South Africa, all of whom were interested in gold exploration and development activities. Following successful exploration mining activities that began in 1995, Barrick invested in Tanzania in 1999 at the Lake Victoria Zone. It acquired gold reserves in the Bulyanhulu mine, located in northwest Tanzania, East Africa, approximately 55 kilometers south of Lake Victoria and approximately 150 kilometers from the city of Mwanza; Buzwagi near Kahama District; Tulawaka in Biharamulo, Kagera Region; and later at the North Mara gold mine in the northwestern part of Tanzania in Tarime District of Mara Region, approximately 100 kilometers east of Lake Victoria and 20 kilometers south of the Kenyan border.

According to the Tanzanian Mineral Authority and Tanzania Chamber of Minerals and Energy (TCME), since 2000, production of gold had been growing, making the Lake Victoria Zone one of the most attractive areas for employment opportunities as well as for business opportunities in other industries. Tanzania was Africa's third largest producer of gold, after Ghana and South Africa.[12] Tanzania was also richly endowed with other minerals, including cobalt, copper, nickel, platinum group metals, and silver, as well as diamonds and a variety of gemstones. The energy sector was dominated by natural gas. Commercial quantities of oil had yet to be discovered. In 2008, TCME reported that a total of $2 billion in the past decade had been injected into the Tanzanian economy by mining TNCs, and in total mining TNCs had paid the government over $255 million in taxes within the same period.[13]

In 2002, Tanzania joined the African Union's development blueprint, an endeavor that was governed by the New Economic Partnership for African Development (NEPAD), to oversee an African Mining Partnership (AMP) with global mining corporations. The goal of this partnership was to promote sustainable development and best-practice guidelines for African governments as a way to ensure that their mining laws protected ecological and community welfare while maximizing remittances from the mining TNCs to the government budgets in a transparent and accountable way.

The country did, however, develop competitive tax packages and incentives to attract TNCs to invest in high-risk and complex exploration areas such as the Lake Victoria Zone. The government did not devise a practical and engaging strategy to utilize mining resources and revenues paid by TNCs to support the local communities that were situated around mining sites and who had lost their livelihood, homes, health, natural resources, and recreation with little or no compensation.[14] Also, the government did not come up with a concrete strategy to deal with the chronic sewage and environmental issues in the area.

Like any TNC engaged in extractive mining activities in a developing country such as Tanzania, with so many social problems and legal and institutional weaknesses, Barrick had faced conflicting pressures with regard to the way it engaged in locally based community social partnership (see Exhibit 1, page 569). Such partnerships were meant to address the social problems of unemployment, poverty, diseases, and environmental concerns in a sustainable way. Barrick strictly followed Western legal and property approvals to legitimize its mining activities in the country. It also continued to face challenges with respect to its efforts to strike a balance between its global strategies and those of the local subsidiary operations in Tanzania. Mineral wealth continued to fuel and prolong violent behavior by local communities mainly in North Mara, thus failing to diversify economic growth and contribute to the development of communities in the Lake Victoria Zone. Corruption and weak institutional capabilities to enact or enforce the democratic, transparent, and agreed-upon rules and laws that governed the operation and taxation of mining activities were a source of ongoing problems.[15] Also, some local communities did not see the potential benefits of large corporations in their communities.

Barrick Gold Corp. in Tanzania

As a gold producer on the world stage, Barrick used advanced exploration technological systems for its mining development projects.[16] The company owned one of the world's largest gold mineral reserves and a large land position across its subsidiary mining extraction activities. These were located across the five continents of North America, South America, Africa, Australia, and Asia. As one of the largest Canadian mining companies, Barrick shares were traded on the Toronto and New York Stock Exchanges and on other major global stock index centers in London, as well as on the Swiss Stock Exchanges and the Euronext-Paris. It was a shareholder-driven firm. Barrick invested in Tanzania in 1999, following the completion of exploration activities that had started in 1995. The company's initial mining activities were limited to Bulyanhulu in Kahama Dictrict until 2004, when it expanded to other areas surrounding the Lake Victoria Zone.

Socialization was part of the corporate culture used to manage human resources (HRM)[17] in Tanzania. Each mining site had a training department. Barrick recruited university graduates, who worked on administrative activities in corporate offices, and assigned manual laborers to mining sites to work along with expatriates and locals who had experience in mining activities. Also, the company was involved in developing the so-called Integrated Mining Technical Training (IMTT) program, a joint project with the Tanzania Chamber of Minerals and Energy and the Tanzanian government. The goal was to offer locals the skills they needed to participate in the country's burgeoning mining sector and to reduce the industry's reliance on foreign-trained expatriates.[18] Barrick used its Global Succession Planning Program (GSPP), which provided expatriates with a chance to increase their knowledge and expertise by transferring them into assignments at other Barrick sites in Tanzania, and sites in other countries where the company operated.[19] The major role of GSPP was to instill the corporate culture through the training of employees regarding various mining technology skills, and to run the company's daily practices in accordance with the corporate business interests of the company.

Mission, Vision, and Values

Given the questionable reputation of some global mining corporations with respect to sustainable development projects in developing societies, Barrick's core vision and values were to continue finding, acquiring, developing, and producing quality reserves in a safe, profitable, and socially responsible manner. Barrick claimed to promote long-term benefits to the communities in which it operated and to foster a culture of excellence and collaboration with its employees, governments, and local stakeholders.

The company followed global corporate social responsibility standards as part of its larger global business strategies, using the vocabularies of business ethics, human rights, and development. Among these strategies, the company placed significant emphasis on its social relationships with local communities and the right to operate in their land.[20]

Building Social Development Initiatives

Barrick was committed to making a positive difference in the communities where it operated. The company focused on responsible behavior as its duty, as well as creating opportunities to generate greater value for its shareholders, while at the same time fostering sustainable development in the communities and countries where it operated. As a global TNC, Barrick strove to earn the trust of its employees, of the communities where its subsidiary operations were based, of the host nations' governments, and of any other persons or parties with whom the company was engaged in the sustainable development of mineral resources.[21]

In 2008, the corporation established a locally based mining institution in Moshi, Kilimanjaro Region. The aim of the institute was to provide training skills and opportunities for Barrick's mining sites and other mining TNCs in the country.[22] Local individuals involved in the training program included fresh university graduates in engineering and geology, and dedicated individuals from local communities where Barrick operated. Such an initiative supported Barrick's sense of corporate responsibility toward these two groups of people by providing tangible benefits to their communities in the form of employment opportunities and cooperative relationships.

Yet, among community leaders and NFOs, there was clear discontent regarding the various foreign companies:

> The government has not addressed the role of foreign companies in our communities. Some communities have been compensated by the government to clear land for the mining company, but some did not receive any money. Most communities would tell you what was given to them by the government, which is very little. They cannot build a house and send children to school and so on. They feel their livelihood is gone forever.

The mining corporation does not compensate people nor does it explain why it is operating in our communities. Of course, these companies have official binding contracts and the right to operate in our communities from the government. Local communities are in despair . . . the government is nowhere to be seen! The people are angry with the government and the mining company.

People are not happy with the government. They are aware of the extent of corruption among the government officials in the region and districts, but they cannot confront the government the way they are now confronting the mining company. They think that the company might be more sympathetic to them than the government would be with respect to offering them jobs and other opportunities.

The company has initiated several development projects in our communities [North Mara] in education, health and infrastructure. But we do not have jobs to access these better equipped services (education and health) nor essential means to support us to build community enterprises where we could apply our local skills in many activities. Though the company is doing very good projects here, we are still unhappy with the company. Our problems are long-term; they need serious engagement with us.

The company discharges water to the land, which is causing lots of environmental problems on our farms such as land erosion and polluting of the rivers. We have more mosquitoes, snakes and snails at the moment than any time in our lives because of stagnant water caused by the company's water discharge. The exploration and explosive activities conducted at night on mining sites have caused shockwaves, panic and sleepless nights among neighborhood villages, making big cracks on community farms and land.

Two community leaders (representing local stakeholders' interests) commented:

The other night we were all suddenly shaken by the mining blast tremor. Initially, we thought it was the so-called earthquake ("Tetemeko la Ardhi" in Swahili). What is on all the people's minds here in Bulyanhulu is, "When will all this end?"

We need a mutual partnership with foreign companies investing in our communities. There are so many potential benefits we can get from the company with respect to jobs and skill development; also, the company can learn a lot from us when it comes to negotiation strategies with our communities. If the company responds positively to our concerns, we will strive to protect its business interests here and it will operate in harmony in our communities. But the government needs to sit with local communities and tell them why the government has allowed the company to come to practice mining in their land and tell us what potential benefit it will bring in our communities. For the time being, the company is left to itself to address these issues with the local communities.

Amid this climate of discontent among the native Tanzanians, Barrick's mining operations were subject to some hostilities from local stakeholders. In response, the company put into place several CSR initiatives that were aimed at developing sustainable benefits within the communities and around its business operations in the core mining sites of Tulawaka, Bulyanhulu, and Buzigwa. Two NFO officials in Mwanza cut to the nature of the problem:

The company initially attempted to collaborate with local communities and the local government to address the social and ecological issues during its initial stage of entry into the country. But it was not easy to find serious stakeholders right away. Because of the nature of the local institutions, it was also not easy to have things done quickly due to the degree of bureaucracy and the culture of corruption.

The recent protests in North Mara from local communities can be resolved only if the government, company and other social awareness groups sit together to address this situation. Shooting protestors, closing the mining site and sending employees home without pay won't solve the problem in the long run. And the company's legal insistence of its right to operate in the communities isn't enough to convince these angry communities.

The company is not wrong at all . . . it has followed all legal procedures and has the right to be here [in the Lake Victoria Zone], but for local communities, legal papers are NOTHING. The company finds people very unpredictable. The answer is so simple: it is all about deep understanding, integration, and building a trusting relationship.

Mining companies are granted too many tax contracts and subsidies in order to create jobs. During this process, it is very possible for companies to avoid paying taxes that would actually benefit poor countries. There are often "secret contracts" with corrupt government officials. The lack of institutional capacity is also a major problem; the people have not been made to see how these companies can benefit our poor societies. That's why there is still so much poverty, and that's why communities around the mining sites are angry and desperate.

Several local communities felt they were isolated when it came to the social issues that concerned them, e.g., land issues, compensation, employment, and how the presence of the company in their communities would benefit them generally. According to community leaders, few projects were initiated by the company within the various neighborhood communities, and the ones that were enacted showed a lack of any significant sense of local ownership and influence; they did not possess the diverse forms of institutional infrastructure that fostered accountability values in communities and in the management of the company itself. As a consequence, local communities lost interest in pursuing most of the developmental projects that Barrick had initiated.

Following community tensions with Barrick between 2007 and 2009, a different strategy was developed. Implementing a locally based interaction model that promoted mutual partnership with communities seemed like the best strategic legitimacy approach. In early 2009, Barrick encountered discontent from the local communities, as well as from the local media, activist groups, and lobby groups, who felt that the company had not done enough to promote sustainable and inclusive development in the communities where it operated. Barrick's new mining site at North Mara was featured several times in the media.[23] Two local NFOs commented on the dispute:

> The government needs to educate its people as to what benefits TNCs would bring to its citizens; the mining company is extracting our natural resources, causing environmental degradation and pollution, and displacing people, all with a lack of

accountability, and is not doing enough for the host communities to create prosperity, jobs, local innovation and entrepreneurship initiatives.

The source of discontent is from local communities and small-scale miners who
feel neglected by the government. We strongly feel that their livelihoods have been
destroyed with little or no compensation. They also feel that the government and
local authorities have been giving foreign investors much attention at the expense
of local people. Corruption and lack of accountability on the government side is the
source of all these problems. The company is caught in the middle!

Creating a Corporate Responsive Agenda

Barrick developed a responsive initiative to deal with the company's challenges in its
international business activities abroad, including Tanzania. It established a community department in all four mining areas to oversee development initiatives. It also
adopted standardized global CSR strategies as part of its larger international and
localization business strategies, stating that "as a global corporation, we endorse
the definition of Corporate Social Responsibility as proposed by the World Bank—
Corporate Social Responsibility is the commitment of business to contribute to sustainable economic development—working with employees, their families, the local
community and society at large to improve the quality of life, in ways that are both
good for business and good for development."[24]

1 Education in Partnership with Local Communities

Through its newly established community department, Barrick had made a concerted
attempt to identify self-employment opportunities to the communities around the
Bulyanhulu gold mine. In partnership with local governments, NFOs, and communities, the company had used educated locals to promote a broad array of social
entrepreneurship skills in a variety of areas such as finance, accounting, and marketing
(see Exhibit 2, page 570).

The communities surrounding the mine needed a great deal of support in terms of
education in order to be able to exploit the area's potential. By 2008, Barrick had
committed to working closely with eight villages before expanding to another eight
villages along the Bulyanhulu-Kahama road in Bulyanhulu. Seven of the eight villages
were in the Bugarama ward and one was in the Mwingilo ward, but all were located
in the Bulyanhulu mining area.

2 Community-Based Entrepreneurship

In collaboration with local community authorities, Barrick went on to assist several
community groups that already possessed local skills and entrepreneurship initiatives
and which had local resources to generate business activities. Other community
development projects had also been started and were engineered under the same
procedure of governance.

3 Health

Barrick committed itself to upgrading the Sungusungu Health Centre into what became
called the Nyamongo Hospital in the Bulyanhulu area under the so-called Phase I.

Organized by the Evangelical Lutheran Church in the area, several NFOs had entered into an agreement with the local District Office and the Village Councils to provide healthcare that was affordable to the many local residents to treat diseases such as malaria, waterborne diseases, typhoid, yellow fever, and other epidemiology problems. The community trust committed $30,000 towards beds and fittings and for a general upgrade to the hospital. Barrick's overall objective was to make health services available to many disadvantaged communities, and to attempt to curb the number of deaths that occurred among pregnant women when they traveled from the poor communities to the district hospital.

4 Environment

The Lake Victoria Zone was one of the most densely populated areas in Sub-Saharan Africa, but it was also one of the most polluted and environmentally affected places in the world. Barrick, in cooperation with local government authorities, had been working to provide opportunities to the residents of the mining areas to orient themselves with mining operations. The company was creating environmental awareness in order to create local "ambassadors" who could then go out and speak positively about the mining sites to other communities. Adequately addressing the issues of water toxins on rivers and the lake and land degradation had been the major challenge for Barrick.

Protests from so-called "secondary" stakeholders that included local communities, artisanal miners, peasant farmers and their families, and local not-for-profit organizations (NFOs) had occurred to address specific social, environmental, and land heritage and resettlement issues. All these stakeholders had widely varying claims, interests, and rights. In addition, subgroups and individuals with multiple and changing roles and interests existed. They included manual mining workers who felt they had been unfairly dismissed from their jobs with little or no compensation, and felt unjustly treated by either Barrick or the Tanzanian labor court system. Local communities also had expressed anger at the level of noise caused by heavy machines during mining explorations at night and the extent of the company's impact on land in their neighborhoods. There were also individuals, mainly unemployed youths, who were engaged in intrusion, vandalism, and theft at the mining sites.

Barrick had relied on the Tanzanian anti-riot police force, known as "Field Force Unit" (FFU), to quell large-scale mob criminal behavior and demonstrations at the mining sites. Also, Barrick had relied on the Tanzanian legal system and government to protect its business activities in the region. However, the behavior of the FFU, the weak government institutional system, and the loyalty of administrative workers to Barrick had increased anger, frustration, and resentment among communities, small-scale artisan miners and NFOs. The FFU had been regarded by local communities as brutal and uncompromising during confrontations. Responses by the FFU had even led to death,[25] long-term imprisonment of community campaigners' leaders, intimidation, and harassment.[26] The government had been viewed as lacking vision and leadership to reap the benefits of the mining activities in the region and had been criticized for failing to protect the interests of its citizens.

Conclusion

By 2010, a variety of corporate social responsibility (CSR) initiatives were established based on African Barrick Gold's commitment to building a sustainable relationship with local communities. The overall aim was to ensure that the company would build mutual respect, active partnerships, and a long-term commitment with its secondary stakeholders, who tended to have disparate goals, demands, and opinions. Mutual respect, it was argued, was important if such relationships were to be lasting, beneficial, and dynamic. In addition, the company had used its social development department in each of the mining sites to develop practical guidelines in order to facilitate the implementation of its organizational values and mission, including building long-term relationships of mutual benefit between the operations and their host communities, and to avoid costly disputes and hostilities with local stakeholders.[27] Although significant progress and successful collaborations had evolved across local communities at its mining sites, African Barrick Gold still faced serious, unique problems and increased pressure to manage conflicts and reconcile stakeholders' demands in places such as North Mara.

Dimension	Transactional	Transitional	Transformational
Corporate Stance	"Giving Back"	"Building Bridges"	"Changing Society"
Communication	One-Way	Two-Way	Two-Way
Number of Community Partners	Many	Many	Few
Nature of Trust	Limited	Evolutionary	Relational
Frequency of Interaction	Occasional	Repeated	Frequent
Learning	Transferred from Firm	Transferred to Firm	Jointly Generated
Control over Process	Firm	Firm	Shared
Benefit and Outcomes	Distinct	Distinct	Joint

EXHIBIT 1—Three Types of Engagement Behaviors

Source: F. Bowen, A. Newenham-Kahindi, and H. Irene. 2008. "Engaging the community: A synthesis of academic and practitioner knowledge on best practices in community engagement," Canadian Research Network for Business Sustainability, Knowledge Project Series, Ivey School of Business, 1, 1, 1–34.

2006 Environmental, Health & Safety Performance

Bulyanhulu US $1.2 Million	**North Mara** US $0.8 Million	**Tulawaka** US $0.1 Million
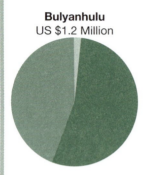	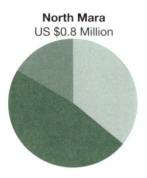	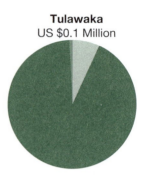

■ Donations in US$

■ Infrastructure Developement in US$

■ Community Initiatives in US$

Value Added in 2006 (USD)

Donations	$ 321,000
Infrastructure Development	$ 1,110,000
Community Initiatives	$ 655,000
Local/Regional Procurement	$104,900,000

2006 Environmental, Health & Safety Performance

EXHIBIT 2—Barrick Spending on Corporate Social Responsibility in Tanzania

Note: Total amount of money in U.S. dollars spent on health and safety training and emergency response training in 2006.

Source: www.barrick.com/Theme/Barrick/files/docs_ehss/2007%20Africa%20Regional%20Rpt.pdf, accessed April 30, 2009.

COMMUNITY	2006	2005	2004	2003
Donations in US$				
Bulyanhulu	20,193	14,000	410,000	485,000
North Mara	294,220	50,000	0	0
Tulawaka	6,778	7,662	5,894	n/a
Infrastructure Development in US$				
Bulyanhulu	631,222	3,570,000	4,374,000	572,000
North Mara	389,384	360,000	350,000	100,000
Tulawaka	89,020	43,697	6,250	n/a
Community Initiatives in US$				
Bulyanhulu	519,793	609,000	0	0
North Mara	135,015	0	not measured	
Tulawaka	304	0	0	n/a
Regional Purchases of Goods and Services in US$				
Bulyanhulu	65,600,000		not measured	
North Mara	37,700,000		not measured	
Tulawaka	1,600,000		not measured	

EXHIBIT 3—Total Amount of Money Spent on Community Development Projects, 2006

Source: www.barrick.com/Theme/Barrick/files/docs_ehss/2007%20Africa%20Regional%20Rpt.pdf, accessed April 30, 2009.

Chapter 12: Long Case Notes

1   This case has been written on the basis of published sources only. Consequently, the interpretation and perspectives presented in this case are not necessarily those of Barrick Gold Corporation or any of its employees.

2   www.barrick.com/CorporateResponsibility/BeyondBorders/default.aspx, accessed March 24, 2009.

3   www.barrick.com/News/PressReleases/PressReleaseDetails/2010/Barrick-Named-to-Dow-Jones-Sustainability-World-Index-for-Third-Consecutive-Year/default.aspx, accessed September 27, 2010.

4   www.tanzaniagold.com/barrick.html, accessed October 1, 2010.

5   See data on Tanzania at www.transparency.org.

6   www.tic.co.tz, accessed April 1, 2009.

7   www.actanzania.org/index.php?option=com_content&task=view&id=121&Itemid=39, accessed February 12, 2010.

8   www.mining-journal.com/finance/new-tanzanian-mining-act, accessed September 27, 2010.

9   www.dailynews.co.tz, accessed February 10, 2010.

10 www.cichlid-forum.com/articles/lake_victoria_sick.php, accessed April 1, 2009.

11 www.douglaslakeminerals.com/mining.html, accessed February 26, 2009.

12 www.mineweb.co.za/mineweb/view/mineweb/en/page67?oid=39782&sn=Detail, accessed May 1, 2009.

13 www.mineweb.co.za/mineweb/view/mineweb/en/page67?oid=39782&sn=Detail, accessed May 1, 2009.

14 "The challenge of mineral wealth in Tanzania: Using resource endowments to foster sustainable development," International Council on Mining and Metals, 2006.

15 www.revenuewatch.org/our-work/countries/tanzania.php, accessed May 1, 2009.

16 www.tanzaniagold.com/barrick.html, accessed, May 1, 2009.

17 www.barrick.com/CorporateResponsibility/Employees/AttractingRetaining/default.aspx, accessed April 24, 2009.

18 www.barrick.com/Theme/Barrick/files/docs_csr/BeyondBorder2008July.pdf#page=4, accessed September 27, 2010.

19 www.barrick.com/CorporateResponsibility/Employees/AttractingRetaining/default.aspx, accessed September 27, 2010.

20 www.barrick.com/CorporateResponsibility/OurCommitment/default.aspx, accessed September 27, 2010.

21 www.barrick.com/CorporateResponsibility/default.aspx, accessed March 25, 2009.

22 www.ippmedia.com/ipp/guardian/2008/04/11/112164.html, accessed February 13, 2009.

23 Several protests by local communities against Barrick's mining activities in Tanzania had been reported. See www.protestbarrick.net/article.php?list=type&type=12, accessed February 17, 2009.

24 www.barrick.com/CorporateResponsibility/Ethics/PoliciesStandards/default.aspx, accessed February 17, 2009.

25 A recent incident at a Barrick mining site in the Mara region had led the Tanzanian FFU to kill an intruder (see www.protestbarrick.net/article.php?list=type&type=12, accessed April 17, 2009).

26 For the behavior of Tanzania's FFU in quelling demonstrations, see www.protestbarrick.net/article.php?id=369, accessed April 17, 2009.

27 Further CSR programs are available at www.barrick.com/CorporateResponsibility/default.aspx, accessed February 24, 2009.

LONG CASE QUESTIONS

1. What are the challenges faced by extractive mining corporations in their attempt to establish subsidiary operations in developing nations?
2. Why and how has Barrick Gold Corporation adopted a global approach to address corporate social responsibility issues in Tanzania?
3. Can tax revenues, rents, and subsidies be effectively utilized by Tanzania (and other developing nations with mining wealth) to generate prosperity in the densely populated area of the Lake Victoria Zone and to break the so-called "resource curse" that occurs in many poor nations? How?
4. Despite Barrick's efforts in the Lake Victoria Zone, protests and tensions had not abated by early 2009. Why have the tensions and violence not stopped? What can the corporation do to eliminate such conditions?

Part IV: Comprehensive Case

COMPREHENSIVE CASE: TATA POWER—CORPORATE SOCIAL RESPONSIBILITY AND SUSTAINABILITY

One Saturday in June 2008, Dr. Gobind Bagasingh, vice president of human resources at Tata Power Company, called a staff meeting after returning from the Bombay Chamber of Commerce and Industry (BCCI) award ceremony. Tata Power Company (TPC) had been awarded the "Civic Award" for social development in recognition of its projects in the Lonavala area, which were developed with a stress on environmental protection. Bagasingh credited retired colonel Prakash Tewari, who had joined TPC as a "DGM-CSR, R&R"[1] in functional excellence in November 2007, as being responsible for this award (see Exhibit 1). He asked Tewari to speak about the role of corporate social responsibility (CSR) at TPC, with an emphasis on how he planned to lead CSR activities. Tewari's speech touched upon the concerns of the present day and listed the challenges faced by TPC in its march towards corporate sustainability:

> Dear colleagues, it gives me great pleasure to be here today! It is an achievement that we have received the Civic Award for social development. Many thanks to you for your involvement in Tata Power's social activities and volunteering your valuable time and effort. As you know, we work on triple bottom line approach for any CSR activity. It means that any activity we take up under social responsibility should add (i) economic value, i.e., income generation scheme, (ii) environmental causes like afforestation, horticulture, etc., and (iii) some social activities like education and health of the people who are staying around the area where power projects are being taken up.

> As one of the most respected organizations in the world, we are responsible to our society. Our responsibility is to take care of the people who are sacrificing their land for our power projects. We are also responsible to take care of the people around that area. At the same time, we need to measure the benefit to the company of our social spending. The awards and accolades we receive for our efforts and community involvement will be dented if we cannot strike a balance between social activity and economic value addition for our shareholders.

(See Exhibit 2 for TPC's vision and mission statement.)

Even in the initial positions that Tewari had occupied during his corporate career, he inspired several people. Despite having achieved a higher position in the company, Tewari himself regarded this as "just the beginning," believing that there was a long way to go, several challenges to face and innumerable opportunities to make the most of. In his office on that June evening, Tewari's thoughts were busy with the course of action that he would have to follow if he hoped to achieve his goal of corporate sustainability through CSR activities.

Over the next three days, Tewari had two important meetings: one with Praveer Sinha, the project director of Eastern Region Projects, and the other with the team of senior managers who worked with him on all CSR initiatives. The purpose of his meeting with Sinha was to discuss the possible CSR activities in the locations where TPC was planning its expansion. The challenge here was the initiation of new activities in the existing set-up. Another concern was whether they would need to seek new channel partners or continue with the existing partners. The purpose of the meeting with the core team of senior managers was to review the impact of CSR activities carried out up to that point in time. In both of these meetings, Tewari had to put forth the long-run strategy and the deliverables for the emerging CSR department that were to take shape under his leadership.

As Tewari was preparing for the meetings, he was primarily concerned with determining whether it was necessary to establish a separate CSR department, or continue with the existing pattern of having CSR as an embedded part of the key result areas for the heads of departments. Tewari wondered: if he went by the scale of expansion of the company and then proposed the establishment of a separate CSR department, then what would the nature of its composition and its deliverables be? Could the CSR activities that had until that point been carried out by project-based organizations (PBOs)[2] or non-governmental organizations (NGOs) provide a possible alternative to the CSR department? The challenge that Tewari faced was the recasting of the CSR department in a way that would ensure that a balance be maintained between the interests of the investors and the interests of the other stakeholders: at the same time, he believed that this should ideally lead to the long-term sustainability of the company and society at large.

TATA GROUP

Tata Group was India's largest privately owned business group, with diverse businesses in seven sectors (see Exhibits 3 and 4). Their revenue was equivalent to 3.2% of India's gross domestic product (GDP). Revenues in 2007–08 were estimated at US$28.8 billion,[3] of which 61% was from business outside of India. The group employed approximately 350,000 people worldwide. The major companies of Tata Group were counted among the significant companies around the world. Tata Steel became the sixth largest steel maker in the world after it acquired Corus. Tata Motors was among the top five commercial vehicle manufacturers in the world and had recently acquired Jaguar and Land Rover. Tata Consultancy Services (TCS) was a leading global software company, with delivery centers in the United States, United Kingdom, Hungary, Brazil, Uruguay, and China, besides India. Tata Tea was the second largest branded tea company in the world, through its U.K.-based subsidiary Tetley. Tata Chemicals was the world's second largest manufacturer of soda ash. Tata Communications was one of the world's largest wholesale voice carriers. In tandem with the increasing international footprint of its companies, the group was also gaining international recognition: Brand Finance, a U.K.-based consultancy firm, valued the Tata brand at US$11.4 billion and ranked it 57th amongst the top 100 brands in the world.

The group was named after its founder, Jamsedji Tata; a member of the Tata family had almost invariably been the chairman of the group. The company was in its fifth generation of family stewardship. The Tata Group helped establish and finance several quality research, educational, and cultural institutes in India. Two-thirds of the equity of Tata Sons, Tata Group's promoter company, was held by philanthropic trusts, which created national institutions in science and technology, medical research, social studies, and the performing arts. The trusts also provided aid and assistance to NGOs in the areas of education, healthcare, and livelihoods. The combined development-related expenditure of the trusts and the companies amounted to approximately 4% of the group's net profits. Tata Sons Ltd., 66% of which was owned by the philanthropic trusts, was the sole proprietor of the Tata brand name and functioned as a group management company.

Tata companies were involved in the welfare of the communities incorporated in the articles of association of major companies. Through its active volunteering program, Tata encouraged more than 11,500 registered volunteers in 20 companies to devote 150,000 man-hours to volunteering. The illustrative initiatives can be seen in terms of Tata Steel's HIV/AIDS Program[4] and Tata Consultancy Services' computer-based Adult Literacy Program.[5] In the 2006-07 financial year, contribution to social welfare was US$60.7 million.

Tata Power Company

TPC was one of twelve companies belonging to the Tata Group (see Exhibit 5). TPC was an India-based company engaged in the business of generation, transmission and distribution of electricity, including thermal, hydro, solar, and wind (see Exhibit 6). TPC started in 1919, with operations in the states of Maharashtra, Jharkhand (at Jojobera), and Karnataka (at Bangalore). Since then, the company grew through expansion as well as product diversification (see Exhibit 7). Following the privatization of the power sector in India, the company became India's largest private player in this sector.

The company was also involved in the manufacturing of electronic equipment and broadband services, as well as project consultancy, terminaling, investments, and oil exploration. Its headquarters was in Mumbai and employed approximately 3,430 people. The company recorded revenues of Rs44.73 billion (US$1.006 billion) during the 2005–06 fiscal year ending March 2006, displaying an increase of 22.1% over 2004–05. The net profit was Rs7121.1 million (US$160.2 million) in the

2005–06 fiscal year, an increase of 20.5% over 2004–05 (see Exhibit 8). The company's operations were divided into two business segments: power and other.

The power segment was engaged in generation, transmission, and distribution of electricity. In the generation business, Tata Power had an installed power generation capacity of 2,300 megawatts (MW) with the Mumbai power business, which had a unique mix of thermal and hydro power. In the transmission business, the company owned and operated 1,200 circuit kilometers (km) of high voltage (220 kilovolt and 110 kilovolt) transmission network.

In the distribution business, Tata Power had a 935 km high tension (HT) and low tension (LT) cable distribution network connecting 17 major receiving stations and more than 85 substations in its Mumbai license area. The company's other segment included electronic equipment, broadband services, oil exploration, and research and development.

Tata Power signed definitive agreements to purchase 30% equity stakes in two major Indonesian thermal coal producers, PT Kaltim Prima Coal and PT Arutmin Indonesia[6] in March 2007, and a related trading company owned by PT Bumi Resources in March 2007. TPC also acquired Coastal Gujarat Power Limited, a special purpose vehicle[7] (SPV) formed for the Mundra ultra mega power project (UMPP) in April 2007. To its credit, TPC had 18 major projects in India and two projects abroad in Dubai and Malaysia (see Exhibit 9).

The company planned to expand its capabilities with 7,500 MW of additional generation capacity by 2012, including the 4,000 MW UMPP in Mundra. This expansion project began in 2006. The major competitors of TPC were Reliance Industries Limited, Torrent Power, Alstom Projects India Limited, Gujarat Industries Power Company Limited, and National Thermal Power Corporation Limited.

Col. Prakash Tewari

Col. Tewari served in the Indian army for almost 25 years. He had worked with Integrated Headquarters, Ministry of Defence as director of Policy Ecology. Tewari won the United Nations Educational, Scientific and Cultural Organization (UNESCO)/Global Alliance for Disaster Reduction (GADR) award in 2005. He was also the vice president and on the board of GADR, which was headquartered in North Carolina, United States. He worked actively in the fields of disaster, conflict, environmental, and natural resource management. Tewari executed projects on biodiversity conservation, wasteland development, groundwater rejuvenation, rainwater harvesting, afforestation, non-conventional energy resources, and environment education.

It was with the intention of serving the community at large that he accepted an offer and began working with TPC, after taking premature retirement from the armed forces. He joined Tata and started work on CSR activities with the purpose of institutionalizing the same. According to Tewari, working with a corporate house is advantageous in terms of the speedy decision-making process and in the delegation of authority: processes in the government were bureaucratic and time-consuming. Corporate houses believed in results, and worked accordingly.

At TPC, Tewari's planned deliverables were the following:

1. Cultivate a sense of ownership among the local communities where TPC functioned.
2. Institutionalize CSR activities and align them for the long-term sustainability of the company.

POWER SECTOR IN INDIA

The availability of reliable and quality power was a prerequisite for the growth of any country. The demand for power in India was enormous, as it was one of the fastest-growing economies. The vast Indian power market offered one of the highest growth opportunities for private players. As per the Indian constitution, the power sector was a concurrent subject and was the joint responsibility of the state and central governments. The power sector in India was dominated by the government: the state and central government sectors accounted for 58% and 32% of the generation capacity respectively, while the private sector accounted for about 10%. The private sector had a small but growing presence in distribution and was making an entry into transmission.

In order to support a desired 7% GDP rate of growth, the power supply's rate of growth needed to be more than 10% annually. The annual per capita consumption, at approximately 580 kilowatt hours (kWh), was among the lowest in the world when compared to the 10,000 kWh per annum consumption of the developed countries. By 2012, India's peak demand would be 157,107 MW, with energy requirements of 975 BTU.[8] India would have a peak electricity demand of 152,746 MW by 2011–12, more than double that of the 75,756 MW it required in 2003. This in itself indicated the growth potential that existed in this sector (see Exhibits 10a and 10b).

Beginning in 2006, TPC was planning to increase its production up to 10,000 MW over the next five years. This massive scale of expansion demanded significant acquisitions of some of the existing players, as well as the acquisition of land and marine resources that were owned by small and marginal populations, such as farmers and fishermen.

Maithon Power Limited was a joint venture between Tata Power and Damodar Valley Corporation, and planned to produce a 1,000 MW power plant. The project was comprised of two generating units: the commissioning of the first unit was scheduled for late 2009, and that of the second unit by mid-2010. The total land required for the project was about 1,200 acres. The majority of these lands belonged to local communities, containing homes and agricultural lands. The government issued most of the land where Tata Power carried out power operations; however, as Tewari observed, "Though the government or legal structure can give us the license to start the production operations, the license to function smoothly can be given only by the local communities." Thus, the cooperation from the local communities had always been an essential factor in the success of the business.

STAKEHOLDERS OF TPC

Farrokh Kavarana, executive director of Corporate Affairs at Tata Engineering, highlighted the importance of CSR activities:

> Community development is a well understood objective and important cornerstone of the Tata business philosophy. Therefore it is incumbent on every Tata company's management to consider it to be an essential component of its strategic plan towards achieving the company's and the group's objectives. The strategy that each company evolves needs to be focused on the real needs of the communities in which the company operates and which it seeks to serve. There needs to be a dovetailing of the skills and strengths of the company and its employees with the immediate and long-term gaps in the overall development of those communities—be they in the field of education, health, environment, civic amenities, infrastructure, family planning, vocational skills, etc. Essentially, one has to ensure that the strategic economic well-being of the community is brought about expeditiously. In Tata companies, we encourage the management to make a declaration of policy, strategy and budgets for environment and community development, and run activities as part of a non-negotiable minimum program aimed at generating the reputation for the Tata brand.

> The stakeholders of the company are its shareholders and customers, as well as the community in which it functions. The identification of the first two is quite simple; however, the problem lies in the identification of the "key community."[9] Thus far, the CSR activities were oriented towards these key communities; "The difficulty was that every location and every key community was distinctly separate from another, and hence their needs differed widely" (see Exhibit 11).

CSR ACTIVITIES AT TPC

The CSR activities of the company were broadly divided into six thrust areas: health, education, infrastructure, energy, environment, and income generation activities for the key communities. The first step when allocating the budget was the need for assessment. The action plan was prepared and the budget was made by the respective heads of departments, such as Hydro or Licensing. The funds were earmarked for the specific locations and particular activities (see Exhibit 12).

Vivek Vishwasrao, executive in charge of the hydro area,[10] described the difficulty of implementing CSR activities in key communities in the hydro area:

> There are 107 villages identified as the "key communities" in the hydro area which are in the vicinity of the hydro electricity power station in Maharashtra. These are the villages which have [been] affected by the construction of dams and hydro-electric production. These villages demonstrate large variety in terms of income levels, standard of living, the state of development and even the level of aspirations among the villagers. Hence it is very difficult to cater to all the villages through

the single uniformed program. We have various activities like training programs (like tailoring classes for women), environmental awareness, conservation of mahseer,[11] pisciculture and eco restoration.

Bharat Nadkarni, senior manager of the hydro area, addressed the issue of assessing CSR activities:

TPC undertakes various activities right from afforestation, bio-diversity conservation study to [the] building of roads, construction of classrooms for the village schools . . . [T]he impact measurement for such activities can be done only in terms of "community satisfaction index" for the target audience. Looking at the diversity of the needs and the wide range of the activities, construction of such [an] index is a major challenge.

Tewari elaborated on the difficulty of impact assessment and implementing CSR activities:

It is difficult to benchmark the activities on a single parameter as the nature and scale of the activities changes, and even the target group. Hence, while doing the impact assessment, the major challenge is going to be institutionalizing the activities across the borders. Especially in the light of the company's expansion plans in Asia and other continents.

Cultivating a sense of ownership among the local communities was a major challenge, as it required a complete transformation in villagers' behavior and attitudes. The villagers were exposed to the world with the help of media and television on the one hand, while their ability to adapt to change was slow: they had a lot of aspirations and expectations from the company. According to Nadkarni, many of the company's efforts to grow were seen by local communities as "tricks," and "[c]ompany representatives are treated as the 'aliens' by the localities. Hence there is a need to plug in the people (either in the form of PBOs or NGOs) who can assimilate with the local communities." He thought it was difficult to create "customers' delight" within these local communities, since there was a gap between the skill sets (in terms of employability) and the level of aspirations. These local communities were one of the major stakeholders for the company.

Vishwasrao stated that "the villagers have the potential to grow and sustain on their own by creating alternative job opportunities," but that it was difficult for them to do so. He highlighted two main challenges: "basic skill sets are missing" and "markets for their products are not readily available." Through discussions with the villagers, these same points were highlighted. Women from rural communities who were trained in the tailoring classes run by TPC said the following:

We wish to undertake these activities on the commercial basis; however, there is no market for the same. The tailoring has made us self-dependent and we earn around Rs800–1,000 per month which is supportive to our family, but we want to move ahead. Beyond this, the road gets blocked because of the limited opportunities.

In order to decide upon the role of employees and "modus operandi" of the CSR activities, a council was established in 1997. This council took into account the feedback of 35 community coordinators from all major Tata companies and came up with a comprehensive draft. The guiding principle according to the draft was to use networking as a solution, a social responsibility that was deeply embedded into the business processes of Tata companies. This was against all temptations of creating a conventional separate "organization" for this purpose. According to the draft, the Tata company would always be the locus of activity, and any efforts it made would only help companies perform better.

In accordance with this principle, TPC was running its CSR activities through the volunteering initiatives of the employees in various projects undertaken in each thrust area. The employees voluntarily participated in various CSR activities in addition to their regular working hours. As of February 2009, there were 259 TPC employees who worked as CSR volunteers: this number had increased from 118 to 259 over six months after the deliberate decision by Tewari to boost employee motivation. In reference to increasing volunteering, Tewari mentioned that the company also developed software and other mechanisms through which they keep track of employee voluntary contributions towards CSR activities. This tracking helped the company evaluate the contribution of each of the employees in terms of the number of man-hours spent by each employee, as well as the areas of contribution.

Tewari described employee motivation for volunteering: "We believe in self-motivated small team[s] who are not participating for the monetary rewards. Of course they get the due recognition as we acknowledge their work, but then that should not be the motivating factor. The real motivation should come from within for such kind[s] of social cause[s]."

TPC ACTIVITIES AND SUSTAINABILITY ISSUES

Power generation activities were one of the major sources of pollution and contributed a quarter of all carbon emissions globally. Issues such as air pollution, waste generation, etc. were highest in coal-based plants. In the year of 2007–08, Tata Power produced 14.71 million MWh of energy, resulting in CO_2 emissions of 11.17 million tonnes, including direct activities of production as well as indirect activities associated with production process, for example, air travel for company work.

India was rich in coal resources and was capable of generating power. However, the huge amount of carbon emission had a direct impact on its ecology. Banmali Agrawala, executive director of strategy and business development of TPC, rationalized this irony: "We as a country have a need for development, hence we can't afford to do anything that may hamper our march. And development needs more energy. Now since coal is the abundant resource it is a challenge figuring out how to balance the carbon footprint with our need for progress."

Climate change was now a significant component of the company's corporate strategy. Agrawala explained, "Our initiative is more out of our concern for balanced development and also to differentiate ourselves from our competitors. Also we are not limited to India in our growth so our efforts in this direction can be implemented and appreciated overseas as well."

The company was working with international agencies like American Electric Power of the United States and European energy major Vattenfall[12] on their 3 Cs (Combat, Climate, Change) global initiative in order to take care of the externalities caused by power generation. Tata Power's power plant emissions were better than the norms laid down by the National Ambient Air Quality Standards (NAAQS)[13].Thus, with respect to sustainability, Tewari identified two key issues: 1) the environmental hazards that were being caused by the increased production activities of power generation; 2) whether or not these environmental hazards could be minimized through the effective CSR activities. If so, how?

In regards to the issue of implementing CSR activities, Deepak Apte, assistant director of the Bombay Natural History Society (BNHS), said the following:

> Ecological balance and environmental concern should be an integral part of any business model for any firm in order to make it "sustainable." Every business activity inevitably takes a toll on the environment. But identifying these threats right in the beginning and working towards harmonizing [them] can result in synergy between the ecology and the business. Unfortunately, in [the] case of many corporat[ions], business comes first and the environmental concern follows later when the actual consequences become very rampant. In reality, both [ecology and business] should go hand in hand.

Apte elaborated specifically on the relationship between BNHS and TPC:

> Our association with TPC is in terms of memorandum of understanding (MOU) for the particular project. Under this project BNHS would create a baseline data and establish a protocol for the project site of TPC in Bhuj (Kucch, Gujrath). The baseline data is in terms of ecology and biodiversity which currently exists at these locations. The laid down protocols will help the company to identify the indicators (like certain species, flora and fauna) which can be monitored in the long run in order to access the impact of the production activities on the environment and ecology.

According to Tewari, NGOs could be involved at every step of CSR, right from the creation of the baseline data to the impact assessment. When undertaking any CSR activity, the first step was the need assessment for which the baseline data[14] was required. In this process, NGOs that were specialized in this function, such as BNHS, could be involved. In the second phase of the actual implementation, the role of NGOs could be minimized. The partnership could be limited to the extent of mutual benefit. In the last phase of impact assessment, the PBO or NGO could be actively involved, whereby the impact assessment could be done by a third party in an unbiased manner.

In the process of incorporating CSR activities, the role of the NGO/PBO varied at every stage. This role variation caused a major challenge: it was difficult to identify the NGOs that would fit at every stage of the process, in terms of the common goals and effective monitoring over their operations. What usually happened with NGOs/PBOs was that they grew over a period of time, and their phenomenal growth gave them a hold over the key communities. This naturally increased the bargaining power of these organizations, making it difficult to carry out checks and controls over them.

TPC's Association with NGOs

In May 2008, TPC signed an MOU with the NGO Population Services International (PSI). According to this MOU, TPC would provide the monetary support as well as manpower through TPC employee volunteering activity. Apart from direct funding, TPC employees participated in PSI's AIDS awareness program. Digambar Gaikwad, field coordinator at PSI, commented on this relationship:

> TPC employees visit to PSI office and participate in the field activities. They are trained for conducting the "crowd-pulling" activities like street-plays, road-shows to spread the AIDS awareness. The skills learnt by this participation are utilized by the TPC employees in conducting similar activities for their "key communities."

Dr. Shekhar, project manager of Connect at PSI, describes relationships between corporations and NGOs:

> In terms of the funds, the NGOs like PSI have to depend on government as well as corporate bodies. While negotiating with the corporat[ions] the major challenge is in terms of providing the framework for the mode of operations and the deliverables. The negotiations become smoother if the target audience for the NGO, as well as for the corporate body, is [the] same. For example, companies like Apollo Tyres, whose major customers are truck drivers, whereas for PSI the same is the audience for spreading AIDS awareness. Hence, the negotiation process became easier. Ultimately for the corporate sector, the CSR is not the core business, whereas for the NGO community service, [it] is the main motive for its very existence.

As of January 2009, the HIV awareness program (under the project name "Connect") had educated 5,800 truck drivers: of this number, approximately 105 visited the voluntary HIV testing centre and 15 were found to be HIV-positive. In terms of the quantitative assessment, the tangible result of the whole activity was the detection of 15 HIV patients: however, the intangible results included those 5,800 community members who became aware of HIV/AIDS. The ideal "impact assessment mechanism" took into account not only the quantitative data, but also the qualitative change in terms of the attitudes and behavioral patterns.

TPC signed an MOU with an NGO called REACHA, which specialized in the field of energy conservation: they made this agreement with the intention of creating awareness about energy conservation. One of the main objectives of this association was to reach out to students and to educate them on conservation and the rational use of energy: it did this through an array of programs, from training teachers, parent-teacher associations, and activities such as online blogging.

COL. TEWARI'S DILEMMA

Tewari was glad that Tata Power had increased its revenue by 45% in the 2007–08 fiscal year. The company had also shown a reasonable stance in CSR activities: however, as the company grew, acquired land, and increased production capacity, the major issue confronting Tewari concerned the composition and structure of the department. Should the company create a separate department with dedicated staff for CSR, or should these activities remain a part of operations? If TPC decided on a separate department for CSR, should such staff be hired externally or should the department evolve from the existing structure? If the CSR department became a separate entity, how would the cost to the company be monitored and how would the costs to the company be assessed?

Taking into account all the strategic as well as functional aspects, Tewari considered another model: the coexistence of a CSR department along with a PBO/NGO. In this model, the crucial task would be to strike a balance between the business and the social cause. Tewari regarded himself as a "social intrapreneur," who acted as a link between the "business" (which worked through traditional CSR) and the "social enterprise" (which consisted of traditional NGOs). Though the end result of both the entities was the same—sustainability through social welfare—their ways and means to achieve the objective were different. While business and growth were the primary areas of concern for the corporate entity, developmental aspects took priority for the NGOs: the concept of sustainable development combined these different priorities into one goal. As the social intrapreneur, Tewari had to resolve the conflicting interests among various stakeholders; thus, he was the one who stayed within the framework of the corporate entity and tried to internalize the social enterprise.

Another challenge that Tewari faced was how to incorporate the interest of various stakeholders while undertaking CSR activities: this might require controlling and limiting the intervention of the PBOs, who over a period of time could begin to pressure and lobby the organization. Finally, the question of how to implement CSR activities within the existing organization still remained. His thoughts were broken when his secretary entered his office to show him the drafts of the agendas for the two meetings. Tewari had a quick look at the drafts and advised her to send the agendas to the members who would be present at the meetings.

Organizational Structure of Tata Power (Top Management)

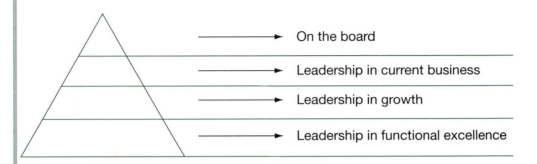

- On the board
- Leadership in current business
- Leadership in growth
- Leadership in functional excellence

EXHIBIT 1—Organizational Chart of Tata Power

Source: Company files.

Vision

To be the most admired integrated power and energy company delivering sustainable value to all stakeholders.

Mission

We will become the most admired company delivering sustainable value by:

- Being a partner of choice and exceeding stakeholder expectations
- Ensuring profitable growth and value to stakeholders
- Innovating and deploying cutting-edge solutions based on eco-friendly technologies
- Relentlessly pursuing opportunities, capitalizing on synergies in the power and energy value chain and expanding our presence in related businesses of interest
- Being an employer of choice and creating a culture of empowerment and high performance
- Caring for the safety, environment and well-being of customers, employees and communities.

EXHIBIT 2—Vision and Mission Statement of Tata Power Company

Source: Company files.

Business sectors	Revenue for the year 2007 (%)	Profit for the year 2007 (%)
Information technology	25.1	11
Engineering	30.1	21.3
Materials	21.4	33.7
Service	7.3	18.5
Energy	5.7	6.4
Consumer product	5.3	4.6
Chemicals	5.1	4.5
Total	100	100

EXHIBIT 3 — Business Sectors of Tata Group

Source: Company files.

Holding Structure of Tata Group

Ownership	Promoter companies	Activities
66% Public trust 3% Families 13% Tata companies 18% Other corporate stakeholders →	TATA Sons	1. Shareholding in main operative companies
	→	2. Investment to facilitate growth of operating companies select
29% Tata Sons 51% Other TATA companies →	TATA Industries	3. Promoters group entry into new businesses
20% Jardine Matheson Group		
Sir Dorabji Tata Trust	Sir Ratan Tata Trust	Other Tata Trusts

66% Shareholding in Tata Sons, the promoter company.

EXHIBIT 4 — Holding Structure of Tata Group

Source: Company files.

Five largest companies	Change from 2007 to 2008 (%)	
TCS	Rs869.49 bn / US$20.3 bn	(30.4)%
Tata Motors	Rs195.63 bn / US$4.6 bn	(24.7)%
Tata Steel	Rs626.19 bn / US$14.6 bn	70.2%
Tata Communications	Rs127.04 bn / US$3.0 bn	(7.7%)
Tata Power	Rs286.21 bn / US$6.7 bn	135.8%

Note: Exchange rate US$1 = Rs42.81

EXHIBIT 5—TPC's Position in Tata Group of Companies

Source: Company data.

There are primarily three processes of power generation: (1) thermal power station, where coal is used to produce electricity; (2) nuclear power station, where nuclear power is used for the generation of electricity; (3) hydro power station, where water is used to produce electricity. Power generated from these stations are of very high voltage (ranging between 275 kilovolts to 500 kilovolts). Power from these stations is then transmitted to extra-high voltage substations, where the voltage is brought down to 154 kilovolts (KV) through one type of power transformer. It is then transmitted to "primary substations," where the power voltage is brought down to 66 KV through another type of power transformer. Power from primary substations is then transmitted to intermediate substations, where power voltage is brought down to 22 KV. High-voltage transmission lines are used to carry power from power generation stations up to intermediate substations. Power is then transmitted from intermediate substations to distribution substations through distribution lines. In the distribution station, the power voltage is brought down to 6.6 KV (6,600 volts). This power is then transmitted to service transformers for domestic and industrial use through distribution lines. The service transformers bring down the power voltage from 6,600 volts to 220 volts/110 volts for domestic use.

EXHIBIT 6—Power Production Process: Power Generation to Distribution

Source: Written by the authors using secondary data sources (i.e., www.tepco.co.jp, authors' own experiences in thermal power industry and onsite discussions with TPC staff).

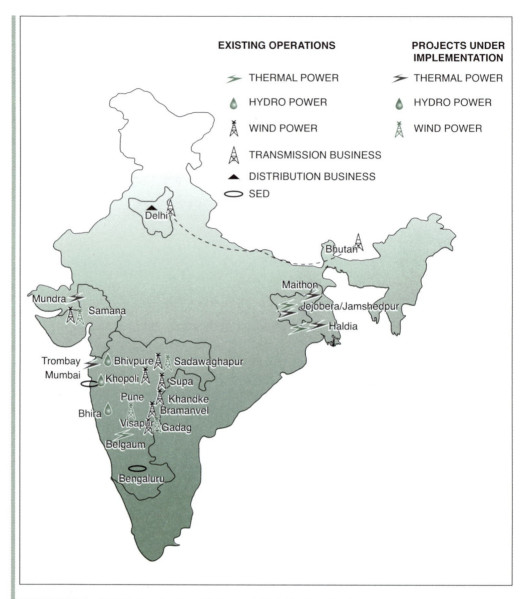

EXHIBIT 7—TPC's Production Units and Distribution Nodes

Source: www.tatapower.com/aboutus/indian-network.aspx, accessed January 2, 2010.

TPC Balance Sheet
(in Rs10 million)

	2008	2007	2006	2005	2004
Capital raised during the year					
Public issue	0	0	0	0	0
Rights issue	0	0	0	0	0
Bonus issue	0	0	0	0	0
Private placement	83.8	0	0	0	0
Preference shares	0	0	0	0	0
Debentures	0	0	0	0	0
Others	0	0	0	0	0
Position of mobilization/deployment of funds					
Sources of funds:					
Paid-up capital	220.72	197.92	197.92	197.92	197.92
Reserves and surplus	7,817.20	5,835.19	5,357.72	4,938.55	4,852.42
Secured loans	2,331.09	1,354.30	946	1,059.07	721.73
Unsecured loans	706.18	2,279.06	1,809.00	1,800.94	999.69
Share application money	0	0	0	0	0
Total liabilities	**11,075.19**	**9,666.47**	**8,310.64**	**7,996.48**	**6,771.76**
Application of funds:					
Net fixed assets	3,005.49	3,030.31	3,003.02	3,246.63	3,476.71
Capital work in progress	1,681.74	781.05	211.81	0	0
Investments	4,430.00	3,570.15	3,412.17	3,502.92	2,728.83
Net current assets	1,956.27	2,278.79	1,668.18	1,224.21	550.59
Misc. expenditure	1.69	6.17	15.46	22.72	15.63
Accumulated loss	0	0	0	0	0
Loans	0	0	0	0	0
Adjustment	0	0	0	0	0
Total assets	**11,075.19**	**9,666.47**	**8,310.64**	**7,996.48**	**6,771.76**
Performance of company:					
Turnover	6,381.75	5,059.32	4,888.40	4,317.58	4,399.07
Total expenditure	5,411.63	4,473.30	4,140.94	3,558.79	3,664.80
Profit/(loss) before tax	970.12	586.02	747.46	758.79	734.27
Profit/(loss) after tax	869.9	696.8	610.54	551.36	509.08
Earning per share (Unit curr.)	41.43	34.02	30.82	27.84	25.72
Dividend rate (%)	105	95	85	75	70

EXHIBIT 8—TPC Balance Sheet (in Rs10 million)

Source: Annual report of the company

TPC Projected Revenue and Expenditure

(in Rs10 million)

**Existing Operations—
Financial Projections**

	2007	2008	2009	2010	2011	2012
Revenue from power supply	3724	3724	3724	3724	3724	3724
Income from operations	681	900	1013	1013	1013	1013
Operating revenue from existing operations	**4404**	**4623**	**4736**	**4736**	**4736**	**4736**
Operating profit	1031	1073	1105	1105	1105	1105
Other income	**110**	**110**	**110**	**110**	**110**	**110**
EBITDA	**1141**	**1183**	**1216**	**1216**	**1216**	**1216**

**Outstanding Principal—
Foreign Currency Debt in
Indian Rupee (INR)**

	2007	2008	2009	2010	2011	2012
ANZ loan	0	0	0	0	0	0
Euro notes 2007	570.6	286.2	0	0	0	0
Euro notes 2017	285.3	286.2	297.66	296.0759	296.0759	296.0759
IFC loan	0	0	0	0	0	0
Kanematsu	0	0	0	0	0	0

**Outstanding Principal
(INR Debt)**

	2007	2008	2009	2010	2011	2012
Total Debt	**1757.7**	**1431.7**	**1085.51**	**997.1759**	**930.0759**	**899.0759**

EXHIBIT 9—TPC Projected Revenue and Expenditure

Source: Annual Report of the company.

Important Ratios in Power Industry

Year	2007	2006	2005	2004	2003
No. of companies	121	52	66	72	89
Key ratios					
Debt-equity ratio	0.75	0.66	0.72	0.79	0.82
Long-term debt-equity ratio	0.73	0.64	0.7	0.77	0.81
Current ratio	1.59	1.62	1.56	1.78	1.88
Turnover ratios					
Fixed assets	0.47	0.43	0.41	0.41	0.52
Inventory	14.2	12.74	13.44	13.52	14.81
Debtors	4.65	5.53	4.46	2.49	2.13
Interest cover ratio	2.96	3.51	3.35	2.63	2.52
PBIDTM (%)	35.38	38.26	39.73	48.07	33.54
PBITM (%)	25.97	29.24	29.82	36.51	23.84
PBDTM (%)	26.61	29.92	30.84	34.19	24.07
CPM (%)	24.73	27.95	28.3	31.4	22.08
APATM (%)	15.32	18.93	18.39	19.84	12.39
ROCE (%)	8.79	8.87	9.44	11.83	9.66
RONW (%)	9.07	9.54	10.01	11.5	9.09

EXHIBIT 10a—Important Ratios in Power Industry

Source: www.capitaline.com, accessed January 30, 2009.

Important Ratios of TPC

Year	2008	2007	2006	2005	2004
Key ratios					
Debt-equity ratio	0.47	0.55	0.53	0.45	0.42
Long-term debt-equity ratio	0.43	0.5	0.52	0.45	0.42
Current ratio	1.81	1.9	2	1.66	1.52
Turnover ratios					
Fixed assets	0.93	0.78	0.8	0.72	0.78
Inventory	13.65	11.27	12.36	12.9	13.15
Debtors	4.11	3.73	5.21	5.56	5.27
Interest cover ratio	4.57	4.06	4.42	3.78	3.59
PBIDTM (%)	18.28	22.62	22.1	27.5	31.9
PBITM (%)	13.39	16.44	16	18.37	24.02
PBDTM (%)	15.35	18.56	18.48	22.64	25.2
CPM (%)	14.51	20.92	16.27	18.67	20.32
APATM (%)	9.62	14.74	10.18	9.53	12.43
ROCE (%)	7.67	8.65	8.99	9.81	14.7
RONW (%)	8.12	12.03	8.7	7.37	10.78

EXHIBIT 10b—Important Ratios of TPC

Source: www.capitaline.com accessed Januray 30, 2009.

Community Support Needs/Expectations

Location	Community	Attributes/Expectations
Trombay, SED, and Broad Band	Urban population in and around plant; operations in the city of Mumbai and Bangalore	Environment protection, health, education and vocational training, particularly for student community
Transmission and distribution	Urban population in and around transmission lines and receiving stations in and around city of Mumbai	Safety and security, health, education, and vocational training, particularly for student community
Hydro	Rural population in and around generating units and headworks and downstream of generating unit	Infrastructure, health, education, environment protection, water supply for drinking and agricultural purposes, as well as for downstream populations
Jojobera, Wadi, and Belgaum	Urban population in the township and rural population in the nearby villages	Health, education, environment protection, additionally for the villages' infrastructural support and vocational training

EXHIBIT 11—Community Support Needs/Expectations

Source: TPC Sustainability Performance Report (2003).

CSR Budget for Hydro Area

It is estimated that approximately Rs30 million are allocated for the various activities listed below.

		% allocation
I	**Infrastructure** (roads, schools, bus stops, wells, etc.)	15.02
II	**Health care** (camps, doctors, vehicles, medicine, surgery, etc.)	7.22
III	**Environment** (aforestration, fisheries, environment education, etc.)	8.23
IV	**Vocational training** (electrician, rural technician, sewing/tailoring, computer education, horticulture training course, handicraft, etc.)	7.22
V	**Income generation** (plantation, distribution of seed, etc.)	2.02
VI	**Drinking water scheme/flood relief/drought relief**	
VII	**Rural electrification**	
VIII	**Awareness programs** (AIDS, etc.)	6.21
IX	**Sports tournaments**	
X	**Misc. and emergencies**	
	Total Budget A	**45.92**
	New special approvals sanctioned	
	Drinking water schemes in seven villages like Mulshi and others; Infrastructure 5 km every year in Mulshi; Learning center at Mulshi; Bhivpuri water scheme special case	
	Total budget B	**54.08**
	Grand total A+B	**100%**

EXHIBIT 12—CSR Budget for Hydro Area

Source: Company documents.

NOTES

1   Deputy General Manager-Corporate Social Responsibility, Rehabilitation and Resettlement.

2   PBOs refer to the project based organizations that are set up to perform a predetermined task. They are independent business entities with a flexible format. From www.pmforum.org/library/papers/2008/PDFs/Thiry-3-08.pdf.

3   One U.S. dollar = 42 Indian rupees.

4   Tata Steel's HIV/AIDS Program was an initiative taken by the company to spread awareness among the employees as well as among the people living in the vicinity of the company. The initiative was a role model for those in the corporate sector who wanted to contribute in the area of STD/HIV prevention. From www.tatasteel.com/corporatesustainability/health.asp.

5   TCS: Computer-based Adult Literacy Program: The program has been developed by Tata Consultancy Services, Asia's largest software enterprise, and it operates under the aegis of the Tata Council for Community Initiatives.

6   Bumi Resources was the first coal-mining company producing quality eco-coal for its international and domestic power generation companies. Bumi Resources acquired Arutmin in 2001 from BHP Mineral Exploration Inc. PT Kaltim Prima Coal, which was the world's largest producer and exporter of thermal coal. From www.bumiresources.com.

7   SPV is a financial agreement between two parties to protect the common interest and secure the interest of individual parties.

8   1 BTU = 0.931×10^{-4} kWh (kilowatt hours).

9   A key community is defined as the local community in the vicinity of the production and transmission areas that has been directly or indirectly affected by the business of TPC.

10 Hydro area was the area in the vicinity of the dams that were constructed for hydro-electric power generation. The area was mainly concentrated at the production sites at Pune, Maharashtra (see map in Exhibit 7).

11 Mahseer was one of the endangered fish species found in the Himalayan regions.

12 American Electric Power is a major power generation company with its presence in 11 states. From www.sourcewatch.org/index.php?title=American_Electric_Power. Vatternfall is an associated member of EEF. It generates and supplies power and energy solutions to millions of customers in Northern Europe and the Nordic region. Its main products are electricity and heat. Industries and energy companies are Vattenfall's biggest customers.

13 http://www.tata.com/company/Articles/inside.aspx?artid=JbLuzxWGihw.

14 Baseline data is similar to that of pre-test and post-test. In the same manner, it is a pre-project assessment of the environment.

DISCUSSION QUESTIONS

1. TPC is undertaking CSR activities in six thrust areas; are the processes and people involved well defined for the six thrust areas? How far will these activities help the company with long-term sustainability?
2. TPC is spending Rs50 to 70 million annually on CSR activities. Are the expenditures sufficient in view of the sustainability? What are the tangible and intangible returns for the company? How would you structure the cost and benefit analysis?
3. CSR was an integrated part of the human resources (HR) department at TPC until now. CSR activities were spread out across the functional departments. Participation in CSR was voluntary and was treated as one of the key result areas (KRAs) for every employee. What are the arguments in favor of having a separate CSR department or having CSR activities integrated with other functional areas?
4. With massive expansions in the company, the existing organizational structure is experiencing change. How should the CSR department position itself in order to synchronize its activities with the company's mainstream functions?

Permissions

21. "Bristol-Myers Squibb: Patents, Profits, and Public Scrutiny." This case was prepared by Research Assistants Meghan Carter, Matt McHale, and Tom Triscari under the direction of James S. O'Rourke, Teaching Professor of Management, as the basis for class discussion rather than to illustrate either effective or ineffective handling of an administrative situation. Information was gathered from corporate as well as public sources. Copyright © 2005 Eugene D. Fanning Center for Business Communication, University of Notre Dame. All rights reserved. No part of this publication may be reproduced, stored in a retrieval system, used in a spreadsheet, or transmitted in any form by any means—electronic, mechanical, photocopying, recording, or otherwise—without permission.

22. "Why Was the Snow Polluted?: A Blind Spot for the Japanese Top Milk Product Company, Snow Brand." Dr. Brenda J. Wrigley, APR, Associate Professor and Chair, Department of Public Relations, S.I. Newhouse School of Public Communications, Syracuse University. Shizuko Ota and Akie Kikuchi, Alumnae, Michigan State University.

Exhibit Sources

Chapter 1

1.1   Based on Transparency International, 2010, Bribe Payers Index, http://www.transparency.org.

1.2   Based on Transparency International, 2010, Bribe Payers Index, http://www.transparency.org.

1.3   Based on Ethics Resource Center, 2010, 2009 National Business Ethics Survey, http://www.ethics.org.

1.4   Based on Association of Certified Fraud Examiners, 2010, 2008 Report to the Nation, http://www.acfe.com.

1.5   Based on Trudel, Remi and Cotte, June, 2009, "Does it pay to be good?" *MIT Sloan Management Review*, 50, 2, 61–68.

Chapter 2

2.4   Adapted from Moodley, K., Smith, N. & Preece, C., 2008, "Stakeholder matrix for ethical relationships in the construction industry," *Construction Management and Economics*, 26, 625–632.

2.5   Adapted from Paloviita, A. & Luoma-aho, V., 2010, "Recognizing definitive stakeholders in corporate environmental management," *Management Research Review*, 33, 4, 306–316.

2.7   Adapted from Moodley, K., Smith, N. & Preece, C., 2008, "Stakeholder matrix for ethical relationships in the construction industry," *Construction Management and Economics*, 26, 625–632.

2.8   Based on Chinyio, E. & Akintoye, A., 2008, "Practical approaches for engaging stakeholders: Findings from the UK," *Construction Management and Economics*, 26, 591–599.

Chapter 3

3.1 Based on Ethics Resource Center, 2010, 2009 National Business Ethics Survey, http://www.ethics.org.

3.2 Based on Kohlberg, L., 1969, "Stage and sequence: The cognitive-development approach to socialization," in D.A. Goslin (Ed.), *Handbook of Socialization Theory and Research*, Chicago, IL: RandMcNally; Rest, J., 1986, *Development in Judging Moral Issues*, Minneapolis, MN: University of Minnesota Press; and Myry, L., Siponen, M., Pahnila, S., Vartiainen, T. & Vance, A., "What levels of moral reasoning and values explain adherence to information security rules? An empirical study," *European Journal of Information System*, 18, 126–139.

3.3 Based on Neubaum, D.O., Pagell, M., Drexler, J.A., Jr., McKee-Ryan, F.M. & Larson, E., 2009, "Business education and its relationship to student personal moral philosophies and attitudes toward profits: An empirical response to critics," *Academy of Management Learning and Education*, 8, 1, 9–24.

3.5 Based on Armenakis, A. & Wigand, J., 2010, "Stakeholder actions and their impact on the organizational culture of two tobacco companies," *Business and Society Review*, 115, 2, 147–171.

3.6 Based on Detert, J.E., Trevino, L.K. & Sweitzer, V.L., 2008, "Moral in ethical decision making: A study of antecedents and outcomes," *Journal of Applied Psychology*, 93, 2, 374–391.

Chapter 4

4.1 Based on Collins, D., 2009, *Essentials of Business Ethics*, Hoboken, NJ: John Wiley and Sons.

4.2 Based on Herring, C., April, 2009, "Does diversity pay? Race, gender, and the business case for diversity," *American Sociology Review*, 74, 2, 208–222.

4.3 Based on Hansen, F., 2010, "Diversity of a different color," *Workforce Management*, 89, 6, 23.

4.4 Based on Smolensky, E. & Kleiner, B.H., 2003, "How to prevent sexual harassment in the workplace," *Equal Opportunities International*, 22, 2, 59–65.

4.5 Based on International Labor Organization Reports, http://www.ilo.org.

4.6 Based on Equal Opportunity Commission Reports, http://eeoc.go/eeoc/statistics/enforcement/sexual_harassment.cfm.

Chapter 5

5.1 Source: http://www.marketingpower.com/AboutAMA/Pages/Statement%20of%20Ethics.aspx.

5.2 Source: http://www.ftc.gov/bp/edu/microsites/redflag/falseclaims.html.

5.3 Based on Committee of Advertising Practice (CAP), 2010, "The UK Code of non-broadcast advertising, sales promotion and direct marketing (CAP Code)," Section 5, Children; iCharter, "Ethical Advertising Standard," http://www.icharter.org/standards/eas405/index.html; International Chamber of

Commerce (ICC), 2006, "Consolidated ICC Code of Advertising and Marketing Communication Practice," Paris.

5.4 Based on Broadcasting Commission of Ireland, 2002, Advertising and Children.

5.5 Cornell Law School Legal Information Institute, 2011, *Greenman v. Yuba Power Products*, 59 Cal.2d 57 (1963).

5.6 Based on US Federal Trade Commission, 1998, Privacy Online: A Report to Congress, http://www.ftc.gov/reports/privacy3/fairinfo.shtm.

Chapter 6

6.1 Based on Johnson, R.A., Schnatterly, K., Johnson, S.G. & Chiu, S., 2010, "Institutional investors and institutional environment: A comparative analysis and review," *Journal of Management Studies*, 47, 8, 1590–1613.

6.2 Based on GlobeWomen, 2010, http://www.globewomen.org.

6.3 Based on DeCarlo, S., 2010, "What the boss makes," Forbes, http://www.forbes.com.

6.4 Based on DeCarlo, S., 2010, "What the boss makes," Forbes, http://www.forbes.com.

6.5 Based on Hofstede, G., 1980, *Culture's Consequences: International differences in work-related values*, Newbury Park, CA: Sage; Li, J. & Harrison, R.J., 2008, "National structure and the composition and leadership structure of boards of directors," *Corporate Governance: An International Review*, 16, 5, 375–385; and Li, J. & Harrison, R.J., 2008, "Corporate governance and national culture: A multi-country study," *Corporate Governance*, 8, 5, 607–621.

6.6 Based on Organization for Economic Development and Cooperation, 2009, "Corporate governance and the financial crisis: Key findings and main messages," http://www.ecd.org.

Chapter 7

7.1 Based on World Bank, 2011, http://www.worldbank.org.

7.2 Based on World Bank, 2011, http://www.worldbank.org.

7.3 Based on World Bank, 2011, http://www.worldbank.org.

7.4 Based on Chambers, D., Hermanson, D.R. & Payne, J.L., 2010, "Did Sarbanes-Oxley lead to better financial reporting?" *The CPA Journal*, September, 24–27; Coville, T.G., 2008, "SOX generated changes in board compositions: Has accounting's academia noticed?" *International Journal of Closure and Governance*, 5, 4, 333–348; and Hazels, B., 2010, "Eight years after the fact: Is SOX working? A look at the Brooke Corporation," *Journal of Business Case Studies*, 6, 6, 19–29.

7.5 Based on Europa, Summary of EU Legislations, http://europa.eu/legilsation_summaries/index_en.htm.

7.6 Based on Anonymous, 2008, "A modern dilemma: How to make ethics = reputation in PR," *PR News*, 64, 22.

Chapter 8

8.1 Based on Edmonds, S., December, 2010, *Transmedia Learning. Technology and Resources*, 36–38.

8.2 Based on Aguilar, M.K., 2009, "How companies are coping with social media," *Compliance Week*, pp. 56, 57, 71.

8.3 Based on World Internet Usage Statistics, 2011, http://www.internetworld stats.com.

8.4 Based on Pollach, I., January, 2011, "Online privacy as a corporate social responsibility: An empirical study," *Business Ethics: A European Review*, 20, 1, 88–102.

8.5 Based on Yayla, A.A. & Hu, Q., 2011, "The impact of information security events on the stock value of firms: The effect of contingency factors," *Journal of Information Technology*, 26, 60–77.

8.6 Adapted from Mortimor, R., June, 2010, "Customer data: Only trust can overcome data privacy fears," *Marketing Week*, p. 26.

8.7 Based on Robison, K.K. & Crenshaw, E.M., February, 2010, "Reevaluating the global digital divide: Socio-demographic and conflict barriers to the internet revolution," *Sociological Inquiry*, 80, 1, 34–62.

Chapter 9

9.1 Based on MIT Sloan Management Review, 2011, "Sustainability: The 'embracers' seize advantage," *The Survey*, Winter, 23–27.

9.2 Based on Environmental Protection Agency, http://epa.gov.

9.3 Based on NSF International, 2011, "Carbon emissions: Measuring the risks," http://www.nsf.org.

9.4 Based on World Business Council for Sustainable Development, 2009, "Water: Facts and trends," http://www.wbcsd.org.

9.5 Based on Gamble, J.E. & Thompson, A.A., Jr., 2011, *Essentials of Strategic Management: The quest for competitive advantage*, McGraw-Hill.

9.6 Based on Global Reporting Initiative, http://www.globareporting.org.

9.7 Based on MIT Sloan Management Review, 2011, "Sustainability: The 'embracers' seize advantage," *The Survey*, Winter, 23–27.

9.8 Based on http://www.sustainable-living.unilever.com.

Chapter 10

10.1 Based on *Fortune* 500 and World Bank.

10.2 Based on World Values Study Group, 2010, *World Values Surveys and European Value Surveys, 1999–2010*, Ann Arbor, MI: Inter-University Consortium for Political and Social Research.

10.4 Based on World Values Study Group, 2010, *World Values Survey and European Value Surveys, 1999–2010*, Ann Arbor, MI: Inter-University Consortium for Political and Social Research.

10.5 Based on World Health Organization, 2010, Regional Report on Status of Road Safety: The South East Asian Nations, http://www.who.org.

10.6 Based on OECD, 2010, Convention on combating bribery of foreign public officials in international business transactions, http://www.oecd.org.

10.7 Based on United Nations, 2010, United Nations Global Compact, http://www.un.org.

10.8 Based on Calderon, R., Alvarez-Arce, J., Rodriguez-Tejedo, I. & Salvatierra, S., 2009, "Ethics hotlines in transnational companies: A comparative study," *Journal of Business Ethics*, 88, 199–210.

Chapter 11

11.3 Source: http://ethics.iit.ed/indexOfCodes-2.php?key=4_234_66 as adapted from The Coca Cola Company Code of Business Conduct, http://www.thecoca colacompany.com/ourcompany/pdf/COBC_English.pdf. Note: Illinois Institute of Technology states that they do not hold the copyright for code information on their site; this exhibit is their adaption of the more elaborate version of the full code on the company website.

11.4 Based on Parboteeah, K.P., Martin, K.D. & Cullen, J.B., 2011, "An international perspective on ethical climates," in N.M. Ashkanasy, C.P.M.Wilderom & M.F. Peterson (Eds.) *The Handbook of Organizational Culture and Climate*, pp. 600–616.

11.5 Based on Ethics Resource Center, 2008, "Ethical cultural building: A modern business imperative," Washington D.C.: Ethics Resource Center.

11.6 Based on Ardichvilli, A. & Jonde, D., 2009, "Integrative literature review: Ethical business cultures: A literature review and implications for HRD," *Human Resource Development Review*, 8, 223–244; and Heineman, B.W., 2007, "Avoiding integrity landmines," *Harvard Business Review*, April, 100–108.

Chapter 12

12.1 Based on Carroll, A.B., "The pyramid of corporate social responsibility: Toward the moral management of organizational stakeholders," *Business Horizons* (July–August): 39–48.

12.3 Adapted from http://www.gcbl.org/economy.

12.4 Based on Porter, M.E., 1985, *Competitive Advantage*, New York: The Free Press, pp. 35, 37; and Porter, M.E. & Kramer, M.R., 2006, "Strategy and society: The link between competitive advantage and corporate social responsibility," *Harvard Business Review*, December, 86.

12.5 Adapted from KPMG International Survey of Corporate Responsibility Reporting, 2008, p.16.

12.6 Source: Global Reporting Initiative—Sustainability Reporting Guidelines, Version 3.0 & 3.1. http://www.globalreporting.org.

12.7 Excerpted from *CR Magazine*'s "100 Best Corporate Citizens," March, 2009.

Index